# EXPLAINING NORTHERN IRELAND

He is quick, thinking in clear images;
I am slow, thinking in broken images.

He becomes dull, trusting to clear images;
I become sharp, mistrusting my broken images.

Trusting his images, he assumes their relevance;
Mistrusting my images, I question their relevance.

Assuming their relevance, he assumes the fact;
Questioning their relevance, I question the fact.

When the fact fails him, he questions his senses;
When the fact fails me, I approve my senses.

He continues quick and dull in his clear images;
I continue slow and sharp in my broken images –

He in a new confusion of his understanding;
I in a new understanding of my confusion.

Robert Graves, 'In Broken Images'

# Explaining Northern Ireland

## Broken Images

*John McGarry*
and
*Brendan O'Leary*

First published 1995
Reprinted 1996

Blackwell Publishers Ltd
108 Cowley Road
Oxford OX4 1JF, UK

Blackwell Publishers Inc.
238 Main Street
Cambridge, Massachusetts 02142
USA

*British Library Cataloguing in Publication Data*
A CIP catalogue record for this book is available from the British Library.

*Library of Congress Cataloging-in-Publication Data*
McGarry, John
    Explaining Northern Ireland : broken images / John McGarry and
Brendan O'Leary.
        p.  cm.
    Includes bibliographical references and index.
    ISBN 0–631–18348–5. – ISBN 0–631–18349–3 (pb)
    1. Northern Ireland–Politics and government–1969–    2. Violence–
Northern Ireland–History. 3. Northern Ireland–History–1969–
4. Irish unification question. I. O'Leary, Brendan. II. Title.
DA990.U46M149    1995                                    94–46969
941.60824—dc20                                             CIP

Copy-edited and typeset in 11 on 13 Baskerville
by Grahame & Grahame Editorial, Brighton
Printed and bound in Great Britain by Hartnolls Ltd, Bodmin, Cornwall
This book is printed on acid-free paper

The extract which appears on page ii is from *Collected Poems 1975* by Robert Graves.
Reprinted by permission of Oxford University Press, Inc. and by permission of
A.P. Watt Ltd on behalf of The Trustees of the Robert Graves Copyright Trust.

# Contents

# Acknowledgements

This book is the last of four we have co-authored and edited in an attempt to understand the conflict in which we grew up.[1] Our activity must be partly blamed on our backgrounds. McGarry was born in Ballymena in Northern Ireland in 1957, O'Leary in Cork, in the Republic of Ireland in 1958, but came to live in Northern Ireland in 1965. We went to the same school between the ages of 11 and 18. Civil rights demonstrations and violent conflict erupted as our secondary education began in 1968–9. We left Northern Ireland in 1975–6, McGarry for the Republic and Canada, O'Leary for England. Since the early 1980s we have returned regularly with what we believe to be the benefits of mental and physical distance. However, whether the distance has been sufficient to improve our scholarship is not for us to decide.

We have unquestionably benefited from the friendship and/or assistance of so many people in Northern Ireland, Britain, the Republic, Canada and the USA that we must distance ourselves from them by not naming them all. We must, however, extend thanks to Graham Archer, Paul Arthur, Peter Bell, Paul Bew, Kevin Boyle, Pat Conway, David Edgerton, Brian Feeney, Chuck Feeney, Desmond Fennell, Barbara Sweetman FitzGerald, Amanda Francis, Steve Greer, Adrian Guelke, Tom Hadden, Joe Hayes, Mary Holland, Michael Keating, Bill Kissane, Tom Lyne, Jim Marshall, Chris McCrudden, Philip McDonagh, David McKittrick, Kevin McNamara, Frank Millar, Margaret Moore, Mo Mowlam, Sid Noel, Fionnula O'Connor, Brendan O'Duffy, Sean O hUiginn, Bob Rowthorn, Clare Short, Clive Soley, Roger Stott, Paul Teague, Jennifer Todd, Lorelei Watson, and Robin Wilson. They have all rendered advice, assistance or critical commentary. Sharon Batkins and Jane Borecky survived being our secretaries, and were exceptionally efficient. Simon Prosser of Basil Blackwell was patient throughout the long birth of this book – which sometimes threatened to be as long as the conflict it attempts to explain.

John McGarry is grateful to the Social Sciences and Humanities Research Council of Canada, the Research Institute for the Study of Man in New York, and King's College Research Grants Committee. He also thanks Paul King, Bob Young, Tozun Bahcheli, Alan Pomfret and Ted Osborne for invaluable assistance. Brendan O'Leary acknowledges the help of the LSE staff research fund for work carried out by John Peterson, Brendan O'Duffy, and Bill Kissane, the aid of the Nuffield Foundation for two travel grants, and of David Hendy and Nicola Meryk of Radio 4's Analysis for interviews conducted with their help. He is especially grateful to the researches of John Ballance, Bill Kissane, Brendan O'Duffy, Michael McGrath and Etain Tannam, from whom he has learned much. He also thanks LSE colleagues, past and present, Brian Barry, Alan Beattie, Patrick Dunleavy, George Jones, Desmond King, Chris Hood, Peter Loizos, James Mayall, Tom Nossiter, George Schöpflin and Anthony Smith, and particularly Jane Pugh, who drew the maps.

The authors acknowledge the permission of Independent Newspapers to reproduce the photograph on the cover; Brian Gable and the *Globe & Mail* for permission to reproduce the cartoon in chapter 5; Martyn Turner and the *Irish Times*, Cartoonists' and Writers' Syndicate, and Steve Bell and *The Guardian*, for the cartoons reproduced in the Afterword.

This book is a joint enterprise. Each of us drafted half the text, but we have rewritten each other's drafts so extensively that it is now no longer clear, even to us, exactly who was originally responsible for what. For this reason we are jointly and individually liable for any remaining deficiencies in evidence, reasoning and judgement.

# Explaining Northern Ireland

# Introduction: Explanations and Images

*Wise up*, explain, make a set of circumstances clear to someone in ignorance of the facts: 'Ach come on. It's time for you to wise up everybody about what happened.'
*John Pepper's Ulster-English Dictionary* [1]

Violence is an issue about which most people have strong opinions, perhaps even violent ones.
*Barrington Moore Junr, American sociologist* [2]

[One key pitfall in the study of nationalism has been] the tendency to discern national strife as predicated principally upon language, religion, customs, economic inequity, or some other tangible element.
*Walker Connor, American political scientist* [3]

We must stress that in the life of peoples external events and conditions exercise a decisive influence upon the internal constitution.
*Otto Hintze, German historian* [4]

The title of this book indicates its purpose. There is conflict in Northern Ireland, and we seek to explain it. This task is complicated because there are multiple disagreements over what kind of conflict it is, and about whether it is 'one' or 'many'; in short there is a 'meta-conflict', a conflict about what the conflict is about. There is little consensus amongst the numerous interpreters and chroniclers of the protracted violence which has scarred Northern Ireland (and Great Britain, the Republic of Ireland and the European continent) for the last twenty-five years. The conflict is variously held to be fundamentally theological, cultural, economic, or ethnic. Some declare it is caused by the Irish Republic, others by the Roman Catholic Church, and yet others by the political culture of Irish nationalism; and various permutations hold all three to be causal agents. Then there are those who blame the British state, or British imperialism in Ireland, or British colonial settlement in Ireland, or the Protestant religion(s), or some permutation of these causal agents. Finally, some argue for a plague on all the houses of Britain, Ireland, and Northern Ireland, holding all the peoples of these islands (or their religions, or economies, or institutions) culpable for failing to manage their differences.

Explaining a conflict is more difficult when some persist in denying that there is one, or instead indulge themselves in a very narrow and military view of what is a conflict. When one of the authors asked Sir Patrick Mayhew, the Secretary of State for Northern Ireland, whether he thought British constitutional and institutional arrangements contributed to the conflict in Northern Ireland he indicated his reluctance to accept that there is a widespread conflict in and over the region.

> First of all, what's the conflict? There's not a conflict between constitutional parties in Northern Ireland. The only 'conflict' is the conflict that is waged by paramilitary forces, whether orange or green, against the forces of law and order, and in practice, against the ordinary people of Northern Ireland – they're the ones who always suffer. So I don't look at this in terms of conflict. I do look at it in terms of what you might call a mismatch.[5]

Not everybody will share this barrister's narrow definition of a 'conflict', or his preference for euphemism. However, Mayhew's contribution to the dissensus about the existence, nature and scale of the conflict may help explain why Northern Ireland needs explaining. Citizens of the British Isles as well as policy-makers need to understand the dissensus about the conflict, even if they insist, as is their right, on maintaining their own understanding of it. The central task of this book is to provide a secondary guide for the perplexed; to examine, critically, the rival explanations of the conflict, the empirical evidence used to support them, and the normative underpinnings of these explanations. Readers need to be warned, however, that this book assumes some familiarity with the general history of Northern Ireland (those without this background are given some recommendations at the end of this introduction).

The subtitle 'Broken Images' is less obvious than our title. It suggests the dilemma illustrated in Robert Graves's poem (printed on p. ii). Ideologues who provide clear images of reality are often accused of dogmatic simplification which increases rather than reduces confusion; and many of the available explanations of Northern Ireland provide 'clear images' which we find wanting. There is however another danger, different from that posed by ideologues, one created by sceptics who produce 'a new understanding of confusion'. Sceptics lead people to conclude, as some wiseacres do, that Northern Ireland 'passes all understanding', exemplified in the proverbial statement that 'anyone who thinks he understands what is going on in Northern Ireland is obviously confused'. The wide range of perspectives, disagreements and confusions does not mean that Northern Ireland is incomprehensible, or at least so we wish to argue. Northern Ireland is complex, but its conflicts, and theories about its conflicts, are structured and explicable. It is, we maintain, like many other divided regions of the world, torn by national and ethnic strife and suffused with rival theories and interpretations of the causes of antagonism. While there are many reasons why the Northern Irish think they are unique, and why the British and Irish governments endorse that view, there is much to be gained by comparing Northern Ireland with other regions of the world.

The subtitle of the book, 'Broken Images', with its iconoclastic suggestions, was also chosen because many of the doctrines through which people have traditionally understood the conflict no longer command the conviction they once evoked. We contribute to the fragmentation of these images. We recognize that 'the worst', as Yeats warned in a now clichéd expression, remain 'full of passionate intensity', but their numbers are somewhat diminished. Images of imminent paramilitary or military victory by one side over the other increasingly lack moral suasion, let alone cognitive compulsion. The local political landscape is increasingly littered with fallen idols, mouldering statues of Edward Carson and faded posters of James Connolly. However, though the persuasive powers of some forms of rhetoric have diminished, leaving the antagonists adrift from the moral high ground and showing signs of moral as well as physical fatigue, that does not guarantee that an end to conflict is necessarily in sight, despite the hopes (and fears) generated by the Joint Declaration for Peace made by the British and Irish Governments on 15 December 1993, the open-ended and unconditional cessation of violence announced by the IRA on 31 August 1994, and the reciprocal but conditional cessation of violence declared by the UVF and the UDA some weeks later.

More than mere exhaustion is necessary to end a war and create a lasting and just peace. It is still possible that the conflict may resume in a violent form, or that instead of a just peace there will simply be a social truce, tranquillity without the resolution of antagonism. To create a constructive peace, rather than the peace of exhaustion, requires intelligent and informed statecraft from all parties in Northern Ireland, the Republic and Great Britain. Building on the works of numerous scholars and researchers, as well as our own previous work, we try to contribute to that statecraft in chapter 9 and our Afterword.

We are not the first to enter this field, and we doubt we will be the last. 'Explaining Northern Ireland' has occupied a considerable army of political commentators, politicians, public officials and social scientists in the last twenty-five years. As well as featuring regularly in the conversations and media of the citizens of the British archipelago, Northern Ireland has prompted considerable government-sponsored research, both in the United Kingdom and in the Republic of Ireland. It is now an extensively interpreted region,[6] and one in which objectivity has been seen to be unusually difficult for academic researchers.[7] The richness and poverty of this enormous outpouring of literature are not, and cannot be, exhaustively surveyed here. Instead we offer a critical guide to the most frequent explanations which address the heart of the conflict, and which have had a political impact on agents within Northern Ireland and on policy-makers outside it.

Explanations should provide compelling answers to questions. They normally provide logical arguments and empirical evidence to support them. They also usually come wrapped in tacit moral and political assumptions. Satisfying explanations of Northern Ireland should answer three frequent and partially overlapping questions:

(i)   *what accounts for the political antagonism in Northern Irish politics?*;
(ii)  *what explains the nature and patterns of violence in Northern Ireland?*; and
(iii) *what explains the protracted and apparently intractable nature of the political stalemate in the region?*

Our analysis examines the logic, evidence and normative assumptions employed in diverse explanations.[8] The major explanations vary in their persuasiveness and in the extent to which they answer all three questions. However, they can be subsumed in a simple classification which distinguishes them by their emphases on exogenous or endogenous causes. This distinction forms the basis for the division between the first two parts of this book.[9]

*External or exogenous explanations* situate Northern Ireland in the context of British–Irish state relations, or in the literature on imperialism and irredentism. They explain the genesis of the conflict, the patterns of violence, and the political stalemate primarily as the outcome, or by-product, of external institutions and agents. They normally include the argument that 'solving' the conflict requires external or international transformations. The best-known of these explanations are surveyed in chapters 1 to 4.

*Internal or endogenous explanations*, by contrast, treat Northern Ireland as a separate unit of analysis, as a distinct political, economic and cultural system which can be examined, in principle, independently of external influences. Such explanations may recognize that 'solving' or resolving the conflict – when that is considered possible – may require exogenous instruments, or external intervention, but their proponents insist that the causes of the conflict, paramilitary violence and political stalemate, are primarily accounted for by Northern Ireland's internal religions, cultures, and economy. These explanations are critically evaluated in chapters 5 through to 7.

External explanations are actively preferred by the key antagonists, namely nationalists and unionists, and are especially preferred by republicans and loyalists, respectively the most militant nationalists and unionists. They are also preferred by their Marxist camp-followers and sympathizers. Psychologists might conclude that blaming the conflict on external institutions and agents is mutually convenient for nationalists and unionists. It enables them to 'scapegoat' outsiders and avoid confronting the importance of their internal relationships with their primary antagonist. However, exogenous explanations are not reducible to their real or alleged psychological bases. They are also proffered by analysts who are not partisan nationalists or unionists. We therefore examine respectively the exogenous explanations of nationalists (chapter 1), green Marxists (chapter 2), unionists (chapter 3), and orange and red Marxists (chapter 4). These schools of exogenous explanation have evident weaknesses, and we use the resources of contemporary scholarship to establish these weaknesses. However, we avoid the academic temptation to prove that men and women of straw have no brains. We present arguments in their strongest possible form before subjecting them to criticism. We also take care to mention when nationalists, unionists and Marxists have gone some way towards abandoning their previously held convictions about the conflict.

Most explanations of Northern Ireland which are not nationalist, unionist or Marxist are overwhelmingly endogenous in their foci for explanation. They articulate 'internal conflict' theories.[10] They may recognize that the conflict 'is also an Irish problem and a British problem' but they insist that 'its roots lie in the social, economic, cultural and geographical structure of Northern Ireland'.[11] These internal or endogenous explanations are actively preferred by British state officials,

British politicians, and British public opinion. They are also increasingly favoured in the Republic by some public opinion-makers, especially by 'revisionists'.[12] Irish public opinion has also shifted towards accepting endogenous explanations, but not on the scale of the British. Psychologists might conclude that blaming the agents within Northern Ireland is very convenient for public policy-makers, media commentators and the mass publics in Great Britain and the Republic, alleviating them of any significant responsibility for the conflict, stalemate and violence. There is insight in this speculation. However, the psychological or political convenience of arguments do not provide sufficient grounds for casting suspicion upon their validity. Since endogenous explanations are endorsed by social scientists who are not partisans or apologists for the British or Irish states they must be taken seriously; and endogenous explanations of the intractability of the Northern Ireland conflict have evident weaknesses which can be probed and exposed without invoking psychological reductionism. At their worst, internal explanations descend into racism – for example the English stereotype of the Irish as a stupid and warlike people. More importantly, and more typically, they lose sight of the importance of British political institutions and the Republic in any rounded account of the conflict. In chapters 5–7 we therefore critically examine religious, cultural, and economic explanations of Northern Ireland respectively.

Chapter 8 provides the beginnings of a synthesis of the explanatory literature on Northern Ireland with the aid of comparative political analysis. External explanation of the conflict – which does not appeal to either the old British or Irish conventional wisdom – must be put centre-stage with endogenous details in any rounded account. Our argument is inspired by the dictum of Otto Hintze, written in 1902, which forms one of the epigraphs to this chapter. We show, in chapters 8 and 9, that external and internal explanations of the conflict can be synthesized. In chapter 9 we summarize our arguments, show the relationships between explanations of the conflict and favoured political prescriptions, and defend proposals for protecting both communities, what we call a 'double protection' or 'double insurance' model, as the most satisfactory way of addressing the exogenous and endogenous sources of antagonism. In an Afterword, in chapter 10, we examine what dynamic changes have been occurring in Northern Ireland, both long-term and short-term, and evaluate the prospects for successful conflict-resolution.

What follows presupposes some knowledge of the history of Northern Ireland, as well as some familiarity with the Republic and Great Britain. There are several suitable guides for readers who lack such knowledge. Political scientist Paul Arthur's *The Government and Politics of Northern Ireland* (1984) and historian Patrick Buckland's *A Short History of Northern Ireland* (1981) remain very useful and readable introductions. Jonathan Bardon's *A History of Ulster* (1992) provides a much much longer historical narrative, covering Ulster from the stone age, which some 'wits' claim it has never left. The earliest in-depth investigation of Northern Ireland by a political scientist, Richard Rose's *Governing without Consensus: An Irish Perspective* (1971), still repays attention, although it will have to be read in a library as it is out of print. The most readable and best-known republican book is Michael Farrell's *The Orange State* (1980), whereas the most articulate of the unionist books are Tom Wilson's *Ulster: Conflict and Consent* (1989) and Arthur Aughey's *Under Siege: Ulster Unionism and the Anglo-Irish Agreement* (1989). In *Ireland: A Positive Proposal* (1985) the legal scholars Kevin Boyle and Tom Hadden provide one of the most lucid short accounts of the key issues at stake. Political scientist Padraig O'Malley's *Ireland: the Uncivil Wars* (1984) and its sequels *Biting at the Grave* and *Northern Ireland: Questions of Nuance* (1990) are consistently insightful; while those who like travelogues will enjoy Dervla Murphy's *Northern Ireland: A Place Apart* (1978). David McKittrick's journalism for the London *Independent* is the most reliable and even-handed source for those who wish to remain up to date on Northern Ireland, and *Despatches from Belfast* (1989) and *Endgame* (1994) contain an anthology of the best of his front-line reportage. Finally, we take the liberty of commending some of our own writings: *The Politics of Antagonism: Understanding Northern Ireland* (1993) provides an introductory analytical history, our edited collection *The Future of Northern Ireland* (1990) allows readers to examine the merits of diverse proposals for resolving the conflict advanced by their proponents, and *Northern Ireland: Sharing Authority* (1993) contains one detailed constitutional model for resolving the problems of Northern Ireland which is consistent with the arguments presented and defended here.[13]

'Happy is the country which has no history' was a nineteenth-century saying. An update might suggest that 'Happy is the region which is not studied by political scientists'. We look forward to when most books about Northern Ireland are travel guides, when the journalism will be about its cuisine, music, and humour; and when the social science articles are written by economists and managerial consultants studying commercial success in bi-cultural lands.

# Part I

---

# External Explanations

# 1

# Nationalist Discourses: British Centrality or British Neutrality?

It is the British presence in Ireland that has created the past Irish problems, and is helping to continue the present problem.

*A. J. P. Taylor, British historian*[1]

Partition is simply the contraction of the area of British power in Ireland. The solution of the partition problem, and of the problems of sectarian strife connected with it, will be found in the further contraction of the United Kingdom's boundaries – until they lie beyond the Irish seas.

*Jack Bennett, Irish Republican*[2]

The essence of the question . . . is that an ancient land, made one by God, was partitioned by a foreign power against the vehement protests of its people.

*Cardinal MacRory, Archbishop of Armagh and Primate of All Ireland*[3]

By its very nature the British presence is not and never has been a just or peaceful presence and because of this relationships between British and Irish people have been poisoned. When the root cause of violence in Ireland is removed then and only then will the violence cease.

*Gerry Adams, President of Sinn Féin*[4]

Nationalism, the most potent modern principle of political legitimacy, is the doctrine that the nation should be collectively and freely institutionally expressed and ruled by its co-nationals.[5] It also stipulates that the nation must choose how it rules itself. Nationalism is therefore a democratic doctrine of political legitimacy. Nationalism should not be conflated with ethnicism, the doctrine that the nation consists of just one ethnic group, or statism, the doctrine that the state defines the nation – though both ethnicism and statism have disfigured Irish and British nationalism, and continue to do so. Nationalism entails identification with a community and the belief that the national community requires political institutions for its defence or expression. Its exponents maintain that nationalism promotes habits of co-operation, mutual trust and fellow-feeling, which in turn facilitate the promotion of social justice and solidarity amongst citizens. Nationalism demands that nations should be free, i.e. not oppressed by other nations, empires or polities; and requires that nations should not oppress other nations or establish empires.[6] It does not require all nations to seek independent statehood, but it does require that members of the nation consent to the form of government under which they live and express themselves, because without such consent they would not be free. This is the meaning of the doctrine of national self-determination. In Northern Ireland rival nations and rival understandings of national self-determination have been locked in combat.

## Varieties of Irish Nationalism

Irish nationalism has aspired to make the Irish nation on the island of Ireland congruent with the boundaries of an Irish state, and to ensure that Irish people exercise self-determination and self-government.[7] There have been and there are many varieties of Irish nationalism, indeed a luxuriant number, though there is nothing uniquely Irish about this. They are representative of the types identified in the scholarly literature,[8] and may be usefully distinguished by whether they define the nation by the people's will or culture, or by some permutation of the two.[9] The purely will-based, voluntarist, elective or civic conception of nationalism implies that a person's national identity is a matter of choice, an outcome of subjective consent to be a citizen of a given nation. In the formulation of the French historian Ernest Renan, 'The nation is a daily plebiscite.' This conception fails to make it plain who conducts the plebiscite, who can vote in it, and where the vote takes place. In extreme contrast the cultural, determinist, or ethnic conception of nationalism implies that a person's national identity is exogenously given, a cultural inheritance at birth, and, in harder-line versions, a biological identity. In this understanding, national identity is not a matter about which there is much choice.

In Irish history both civic and ethnic nationalist definitions and movements have struggled for ascendancy since the late eighteenth century. The first civic nationalist movement was organized by the United Irishmen in the 1790s. Modelling themselves on the French Jacobins, they aimed to establish a republic in which all the residents of the island, 'Catholic, Protestant and Dissenter', would enjoy equal citizenship. Their conception of the nation was thus both civic and territorial. Their successors who have fought British rule in Ireland have ever since claimed to be civic nationalists: Robert Emmett's skirmishers in Dublin in 1803, Young Ireland, the Fenians, the Irish Republican Brotherhood and the current leadership of the IRA and Sinn Féin. Each has declared that theirs is a civic and secular political cause; and that ethnicity and national identity as well as religion and politics can and must be kept separate. They have sought to create a democratic, secular and independent sovereign state; and for that reason republicans often complain that the 'actually existing' Republic of Ireland falls short of their ideals.

The civic nationalism proclaimed by generations of republicans has always been in competition with ethnic Irish nationalism; indeed civic nationalism has always been complemented by and compromised by ethnic nationalism. The first ethnic nationalist movement in the modern sense was a movement of Protestant Irish Volunteers in the 1780s, although this fact is often forgotten. Inspired by the American Revolution, the Volunteers sought greater autonomy for 'the Irish nation'; but their conception of 'the nation' was focused on the exclusively

Protestant parliament. This 'colonial nationalism' was short-lived, partly because any democratic definition of the Irish nation threatened Anglo-Irish Protestant hegemony – though it eased the entry of a minority of radical republicans into the United Irishmen. In nineteenth-century ethnic nationalist movements 'the Irish people' were defined as the descendants of the native Irish – who had preceded the conquering English and their colonial settler stock on the island by at least one millennium. The true Irish, in this construction, were the 'indigenous', who shared historical memories of an ancient Celtic civilization, and were the cultural trustees of the Gaelic language. Ulster Protestants, many of whom are descendants of seventeenth-century Scots settlers, were considered co-nationals since they are genetically and culturally connected to the ancient Gaelic civilization once centred in Ireland. Ethnic conceptions of the Irish nation are not, however, confined to matters of lineage and linguistic ancestry, they also include cultural markers, notably religious identifications. Roman Catholicism has been a critical component of Irish ethnic nationalism because it was and is the clearest badge of native Irish identity, just as Protestantism was and is the clearest badge of the conquering settlers and their offspring. The place of Roman Catholicism in the Irish national identity was secured by its illegalization and brutal repression for the best part of two centuries by English and British conquerors.

Irish ethnic nationalists, like civic nationalists, have varied in their goals and means. A minority of nineteenth-century cultural nationalists promoted the revival of Irish culture – whether defined as the Gaelic language, Gaelic civilization, or the Catholic religion – as an apolitical activity.[10] However, most were not so naive or detached. Ethnic nationalists included those who emphasized the revival of the Gaelic language and culture, restoring the alleged virtues of the island's ancient civilization, and those who emphasized Catholicism and religious renewal and reform. There were those who saw no conflict between these agendas, but ethnic nationalists were divided between those who thought that Anglo-Irish and Ulster Protestants could share the cultural heritage of Gaelic civilization, and those who did not. In the nineteenth century ethnic nationalists mobilized within constitutional organizations, which sought autonomy for Ireland, land reform, and political equality for Catholics, and within militant republican organizations which additionally sought full-scale independence for Ireland.

The contrast between civic and ethnic and between constitutional and militant nationalists suggests four types of Irish nationalist: the civic constitutionalist, the ethnic constitutionalist, the civic militant, and the ethnic militant. Individuals and movements have regularly cut across this fourfold categorization, and Irish nationalists have had other than nationalist political beliefs – they have also been conservatives, liberals, socialists, feminists and adherents of other political doctrines. Nevertheless these four major types of nationalist can be discerned in twentieth-century Ireland, and we can add two further categories: neo-nationalists and those described as 'revisionists'.[11]

*Civic constitutionalists* declare themselves secular and civic nationalists. They hold the British state historically responsible for the cultural and political oppression of Ireland, for its economic underdevelopment, and for the tensions between the rival religious adherents on the island. They blame Britain for the conflict in and over Northern Ireland. They have varied in the degree to which they have held to secular practices, and in their enthusiasm for leftist, centrist and rightist political ideologies. They have numbered Catholics, Protestants, agnostics and atheists amongst their ranks, but the latter three categories have been rarer members of the flock. The element of cultural nationalism which they stress, if pressed, is the Gaelic language rather than the Catholic religion, even though this language is no longer widely spoken in either part of Ireland. Since Gaelic was also the language of many of the seventeenth-century Scots settlers of Ulster, republicans believe that all properly informed Irish people can regard it as part of their heritage. The republican conception of the Irish nation is therefore civic and territorial, especially when formally expressed by political leaders. However, it mostly has an ethnic appeal – Catholic or Gaelic or nativist.

*Constitutional republicans* are committed to the unification of the nation in an all-Ireland republic; for them the national territory is the island of Ireland and its reunification must be achieved by active diplomacy by the Irish state. Constitutional republicanism is officially embedded in Ireland's constitution, *Bunreacht na hÉireann.* Fianna Fáil, the party which usually obtains around 40 per cent of the first-preference vote in the Republic, is the constitutional republican party, indeed it describes itself in the English language as 'The Republican Party'. Its rivals claim that they have an equal right to be called republicans as inheritors of the democratic, egalitarian and inclusive nationalism of the United Irishmen and other heroes of the struggle for Irish national independence. Fine Gael, the Irish Labour Party and the Progressive Democrats often insist that they profess a more genuine civic nationalism, in contrast to what they suggest is the exclusivism of Fianna Fáil. Likewise, within Northern Ireland, the SDLP often challenges Sinn Féin's claim to be an authentic republican party because it has apologized for sectarian paramilitary killings by the IRA.

*Civic militants* share the conception that the Irish nation should be defined inclusively and territorially. However, they also insist that the Irish right to national self-determination can be sought through force of arms, not least because Irish national territory is presently occupied by an imperial power. This is the political posture of supporters of the IRA. For them the choice between armed and unarmed struggle is a matter of strategy rather than of principle – as the IRA's announcement of a complete cessation of its military operations in August 1994 made clear.

*Ethnic constitutionalists* are Catholic in religious origin and belief, generally hard-line on law, order and social policy, and puritanical if not always authoritarian in matters of private morality. They generally endorse economic liberalism, albeit within the limits of Catholic theology. They are usually indifferent or hostile to socialist or social democratic ideas – which are only acceptable in christian democratic language. They hold Britain historically responsible for the cultural and religious oppression of Ireland, and for creating conflict in

Northern Ireland through the partition of the Irish national territory. They were present, some say dominant, in the Irish Parliamentary Party which fought for home rule for Ireland between the 1880s and 1918, and were the backbone of the Nationalist Party in Northern Ireland from the 1920s until the 1960s. People of this disposition were prominent in the Cumann na nGaedheal party which governed the Irish Free State from 1921 until 1932. They can still be found in significant numbers in Fine Gael and Fianna Fáil, and there are some conservative nationalists within the SDLP. They endorse the past struggles of Irish nationalists, but mostly oppose the use of violence to advance the 're-integration' of the national territory – although some are more ambiguous.

*Ethnic militants* defend the right to pursue national self-determination and the liberation of Northern Ireland from British rule through armed revolutionary violence. They see no inconsistency between employing the ballot box and the armalite gun to establish the popular will, because they believe that the will of the nation cannot be democratically expressed as long as Ireland is partitioned. Ethnic militants presently find their political voice primarily through Sinn Féin, 'Ourselves', a party whose title and lineage deliberately echo that of the organization which spearheaded the political and military struggle against British rule between 1917 and 1921. It wins about 10 per cent of the vote in elections in Northern Ireland, and just less than 2 per cent of the vote in the Republic, though this level of support may rise in the wake of the IRA's cessation of violence. Sinn Féin's policy-preferences are laced with socialist language, although this has been toned down in recent years. Although civic republicanism is the official doctrine of the IRA, and other smaller paramilitary organizations which proclaim themselves to be secular, its membership, support-base, symbolism, and political rhetoric make it evident that it has an almost exclusively ethnic appeal to the 'native Irish'.

Those whom we shall call *neo-nationalists* also claim they are authentic republicans, advocates of an inclusive nationalism in which all the peoples of Ireland can be 'cherished equally', in the words of the 1916 Proclamation of the Easter

Rising. They see the conflict as the outcome of exclusivist communalism, and seek the unity of the Irish nation, which they acknowledge is presently divided, through the consent of the relevant people – including 'both traditions' in Northern Ireland. Neo-nationalists claim their ideals embody the spirit of the Irish enlightenment, and are representative of progressive nationalisms elsewhere. They transcend, they claim, the exclusivism of nineteenth-century European nationalisms, and are not as concerned to establish state sovereignty as they are to secure national freedom, equality, and autonomy for the Irish nation within the British Isles and the European Union. They are happiest with liberal or social democratic philosophies. Amongst northern nationalists this perspective has been notably represented by John Hume, the leader of the SDLP, who won 29 per cent of the first-preference vote in the 1994 European election in Northern Ireland. However, similar views are also found within other political parties in the Republic – particularly in the recent speeches of Albert Reynolds, the former leader of Fianna Fáil and Irish prime minister, and Dick Spring, the leader of the Irish Labour Party, and deputy prime minister in the Republic's coalition government. Indeed, since signing the Anglo-Irish Agreement in November 1985 the Republic has been committed to civic nationalism because it implies that the territorial unification of Ireland requires the consent of a majority in Northern Ireland – a position confirmed in the Joint Declaration for Peace in December 1993.[12]

Finally, there are the eponymous *revisionists*, patriots of the present Irish state, who argue that the problems of Northern Ireland are caused by the foregoing species of nationalism, which they claim misrepresent Ireland's past, misdiagnose its present maladies, and misprescribe remedies for its future. They wish to revise the definition of the Irish nation by accepting partition. They are found almost exclusively in the Republic, especially within Fine Gael, the Progressive Democrats and the Workers' Party – though members of Democratic Left in Northern Ireland share their views. They are portrayed by their critics as 'west Britons', even though most of them have a 'native' Irish background.[13] In Democratic Left and the Progressive Democrats, revisionists identify themselves as part of a cosmopolitan and pan-European political community, and condemn the allegedly parochial chauvinisms of their own state. They argue that the Republic should abandon the aspiration to achieve the unification of the island, reject its role as guardian of the northern minority, recognize the legitimacy of Northern Ireland, and devote its public policies towards economic and political 'modernization'. The Progressive Democrats (on the right) and the Democratic Left (on the left) explicitly voice these sentiments and win just less than 10 per cent of the vote in general elections held in the Republic.[14]

Revisionism describes three overlapping currents in political dialogue in the Republic. The first is the widely held view that Irish unification requires the active consent of a majority in Northern Ireland, and is not something to be accomplished as of right, a view which makes neo-nationalists and some civic constitutionalists revisionists. Though it is widely held it is not clear that it is a majority view in the Republic.[15] The second describes the work of recent historians (e.g. Clare O'Halloran), cultural critics (e.g. Conor Cruise O'Brien), and media personalities (e.g. Eamon Dunphy) who are held by their critics to have distorted Ireland's national past, and to have exonerated British rule in Ireland.[16] The third and related version of revisionism blames Irish national and religious culture for the conflict in Northern Ireland – rather than the British government, British institutions, or the beliefs and practices of Ulster unionists – this trend should therefore properly be called 'anti-nationalist' revisionism.[17]

Irish nationalists therefore disagree about four major matters: the present (and future) membership of the Irish nation; the feasibility of unifying the Irish nation within an Irish state; the goals and means for Irish unification; and the fundamental causes of the Northern Ireland conflict.

*Membership of the Irish nation.* The most important disagreement concerns whether Ulster Protestants belong to the Irish nation. Republicans affirm that they do; whatever Ulster Protestants may say, they were born in or of Ireland; are descended largely from peoples of Gaelic/Celtic stock; and even if they cannot feel entirely culturally Irish they are fully entitled to equal citizenship. Neo-nationalists, by contrast, declare that Ulster Protestants can and should become members of the Irish nation and nation-state, but by their own consent. They point out that at least some of them once did so, in the 1780s and the 1790s; that Protestants in the Republic see themselves as Irish nationals; and that there are some Ulster Protestant supporters of Irish unification. Revisionists by contrast declare that Ulster Protestants are not members of the Irish nation, must be free not to become so, and indeed should not seek to become so. Nationalists are agreed, however, that Northern Irish cultural Catholics are members of the Irish nation; their votes for the SDLP or Sinn Féin demonstrate their identification with 'northern nationalism'. The exception to this rule are the revisionists, who tend to be silent on the identity of northern Catholics, suggesting that they are simply a cultural or religious minority in another legitimate state's jurisdiction, and the cause of their own problems.[18]

*The feasibility of unification.* Republicans have generally believed Irish unification is rapidly realizable. Provided that Britain changes its policies and resolves to leave Ireland, as it has left its other colonies, then Northern Ireland can be successfully integrated into all-Ireland political institutions. All that is required is for the British to become 'persuaders' of the unionist recalcitrants. However, the Sinn Féin leadership's commitment to the peace process presently under way probably marks an implicit recognition that Irish unification is not going to be immediate.

Neo-nationalists believe that Irish unification may take a generation, and that it must be dependent upon a protracted process of accommodation and bargaining in the light of the fears of Ulster Unionists. They are willing to embrace mixed or interim resolutions, such as power-sharing and sharing sovereignty, instead of pursuing territorial unification against the express opposition of unionists. Revisionists, by contrast, believe that feasible Irish unification has already been accomplished: the boundaries of the present Irish state are the right ones.[19]

*Goals and strategies.* Irish nationalists have differed over goals and how to interpret the people's will, i.e. over the degree of independence they have sought for the Irish nation and the means to achieve it. From the 1880s many argued that extensive autonomy rather than fully fledged separatism could be a legitimate end-point in establishing national self-determination; and that they needed explicit support to achieve their goals. However, autonomy was also envisaged by many as a first step towards full national sovereignty.[20] Republicans never accepted the legitimacy of British political institutions, however formally democratic, and they were *not* meaningfully democratic before 1918. They have maintained for the last two centuries the right of the Irish people to rebel against British imperial rule. They apply this reasoning to Northern Ireland though, as the IRA's recent cessation of violence suggests, the preference for violence is instrumental.

Since 1937 the constitutional republicanism developed by Fianna Fáil, under de Valera, considers violent insurrection illegitimate, and ineffective – indeed Fianna Fáil has repressed militant republicans in independent Ireland at regular intervals since 1932. Though they frown on armed struggle, constitutional republicans believe that bilateral negotiations between Britain and Ireland can resolve the Northern Ireland question and achieve peaceably Britain's departure – much as de Valera negotiated the withdrawal of British naval bases from Eire during 1937–8. In their eyes Irish unification is a constitutional imperative, not something over which Ulster Unionists can legitimately exercise a veto, since a minority should not be able to veto a nation's right to self-determination. The last leader of the Fianna Fáil party to express these views was Charles Haughey (Taoiseach 1979–81, 1982, 1987–92).

The Irish Constitution codified constitutional republicanism. It contains a territorial claim over Northern Ireland:

*Article 2.* The national territory consists of the whole island of Ireland, its islands and the territorial seas.
*Article 3.* Pending the re-integration of the national territory, and without prejudice to the right of the Parliament and Government established by this Constitution to exercise jurisdiction over the whole of that territory, the laws enacted by that

Parliament shall have the like area and extent of application as the laws of *Saorstát Éireann*[21] and the like extra-territorial effect.[22]

The second article plainly claims Northern Ireland as part of Ireland's national territory. The third claims the legal right of the Irish state to exercise jurisdiction over Northern Ireland, but this right is made dependent on the 're-integration of the national territory', and in the interim Ireland's jurisdiction remains the territory of the twenty-six counties. These articles should, however, be read alongside another which requires the Irish state to pursue diplomatic and peaceful means:

> *Article 29.* Ireland affirms its devotion to the ideals of peace and friendly co-operation amongst nations founded on international justice and morality. Ireland affirms its adherence to the principle of the pacific settlement of international disputes by international arbitration or judicial determination. Ireland accepts the generally recognised principles of international law as its rule of conduct in its relations with other States.[23]

Neo-nationalists do not believe that Irish national unity is a right to be implemented, though many of them are reluctant to see Articles 2 and 3 deleted or modified without cast-iron guarantees that their national identity will be recognized and protected. Neo-nationalists believe that a secular and cultural transformation of the Irish Constitution *and* power-sharing and reform within Northern Ireland are necessary preludes to building support for Irish unity-by-consent.[24] Revisionists, by contrast, think that the Irish state must recognize the legitimacy of Northern Ireland, even without power-sharing or effective reform, and assist in vigorously crushing insurrectionary republican organizations – through abandoning constitutional irredentism, and employing emergency legislation and counter-insurgency techniques.[25]

*Causes of the Northern Ireland conflict.* It should not be surprising therefore that Irish nationalists disagree over the fundamental causes of the conflict in Northern Ireland. The traditional perspective is that it is the product of one exogenous phenomenon: the actions, past and present, of the

British state, especially its partition of the island of Ireland in 1920. This view was widespread in all the Republic's political parties before the late 1960s, and was also held by the Nationalist Party in Northern Ireland. It is central to Sinn Féin's account of the present conflict. The rest of this chapter focuses on this argument. In the last twenty-five years this discourse has been subject to sustained questioning by neo-nationalists, revisionists and others, and we establish which of these arguments are compelling. The chapter concludes with an examination of the arguments of recent neo-nationalists.[26]

## The Case against Britain

Arguments which attributed the key responsibility for conflict in and over Northern Ireland to Britain were extensive and systematic in the diplomatic public relations of the Irish Free State and the Republic until the 1970s. They were also developed by successive generations of political pamphleteers and advocates in Ireland and Great Britain.[27] This classical republican discourse insists that Ireland is the homeland of an ancient European nation: one nation. The antiquity of this nation, according to de Valera, was such that it had been established before Augustine set foot on English soil: Ireland was Irish, so to speak, before England was English. Having been successfully mobilized for its independence in the late nineteenth and early twentieth centuries, after centuries of oppression, this nation should have been granted the entire territory of Ireland for its state boundaries, in accordance with the principle of national self-determination.

Nationalists emphasize one major event in support of the proposition that all the island of Ireland should have been granted its independence. In the Westminster general election held in 1918, the first conducted in the 'United Kingdom' of Great Britain and Ireland under rules approximating universal adult suffrage, the two major parties which supported Irish independence, and opposed partition, won 79 of the 105 Irish seats, i.e. over three-quarters of Ireland's parliamentary

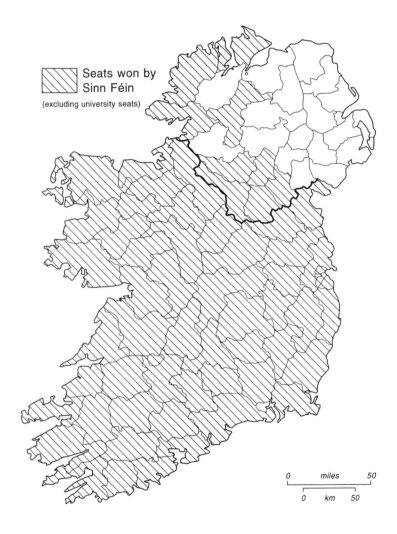

**Figure 1.1** Seats won by Sinn Féin and Unionists in Ireland
in the 1918 Westminster parliamentary elections

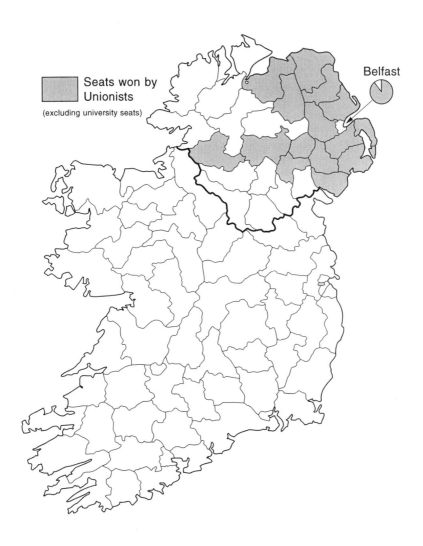

Seats won by Unionists
(excluding university seats)

Belfast

Table 1.1  Party performances in Ireland in the 1918
Westminster parliamentary elections
(includes four university seats)

| Party | Number of seats won | Share of seats (%) | Seats won unopposed | Votes won (%) in contested seats* |
|---|---|---|---|---|
| Sinn Féin | 73 | 69.5 | 25 | 47.6 |
| Irish Parliamentary Party ¶ | 6 | 5.7 | 0 | 21.6 |
| Unionists # | 23 | 21.9 | 0 | 25.7 |
| Labour Unionists | 3 | 2.9 | 0 | 2.9 |
| Labour Representation Committee | 0 | 0 | 0 | 1.2 |
| All Unionists | 26 | 24.8 | 0 | 29.8 |
| All Nationalists | 79 | 75.2 | 25 | 69.2 |

Key:  * The figures on votes won in contested seats exclude the university seats.
    ¶ Nationalists include Independent Nationalists.
    # Unionists include Independent Unionists.
*Source*: B. O'Leary and J. McGarry, *The Politics of Antagonism: Understanding Northern Ireland* (London and New Jersey: Athlone, 1993), 99.

representation (see figure 1.1). In contested constituencies nationalist candidates polled almost 70 per cent of the votes cast; and in nearly one-quarter of the constituencies Sinn Féin candidates, who stood on a republican platform, were returned unopposed (see table 1.1). These results, argue nationalists, demonstrated the will of the overwhelming majority of the Irish people for national independence.[28] This argument has remained an enduring theme in nationalist grievances. In 1984, constitutional nationalist parties from all of Ireland, meeting at the New Ireland Forum, maintained that the Government of Ireland Act of 1920,[29] which partitioned Ireland, had failed 'to accept the democratically expressed wishes of the Irish people', and had created an artificial 'system in the North of supremacy of the unionist tradition over the nationalist tradition'.[30]

The border demarcating 'Northern' Ireland from 'Southern' Ireland, and what later became the Irish Free State, was a denial of the Irish people's right to national self-determination, mediated by the expedient dictates of duplicitous British politicians:

The idea was from the beginning not Irish, but British . . . developed solely as the method by which any grant of any kind of self-government to Ireland might be defeated . . . To say partition was necessary is absurd; to maintain it is in every degree unjust, and to oppose the Irish majority in their effort to bring it to an end is to oppose the very principles upon which stable Government must rest all over the world, if democracy is to endure.[31]

This passage, from Frank Gallagher's *Indivisible Island,* accurately captures republican thought.[32] Éamon de Valera put matters similarly in an interview with the *Evening Standard* in 1938,[33] as did Charles Haughey in his opening address to the New Ireland Forum in 1984: 'The present situation in Northern Ireland is not primarily the fault of anyone living there. It is the cumulative effect of British policy in Ireland over many hundreds of years; a fact which any British Government which wishes to solve the problem must start by recognising.'[34] In 1992, in an interview with one of the authors, Martin McGuinness, a leading figure in Sinn Féin, declared that 'The reason, in our analysis, why the situation is the way it is in this part of Ireland is primarily because of all that the British Government has done in this part of Ireland, and its failure to address its responsibility in all that has happened . . . '[35]

These quotations confirm the nationalist insistence that causal responsibility for the conflict rests with Britain: the border created in 1920 is entirely 'artificial'; it marks no natural geographic frontiers, and no determinate regional, cultural or ethnographic boundaries. It arbitrarily divides Ireland and the historic province of Ulster. It created an entity called 'Northern' Ireland, although the most northerly county of Ireland, Donegal, was excluded from its jurisdiction. The border meanders absurdly through rural Ulster, splitting numerous villages, farms and buildings, with no economic or security rationale, and extends for over three hundred miles, following historic county-government jurisdictions which are now politically irrelevant, and never marked clear cultural boundaries.[36] Most of them refuse to recognize that it has acquired legitimacy. No 'moral statute of limitations' can apply that would sanction robbery and the disadvantaged position of northern nationalists.

The idea that the border approximates, even roughly, a division between 'two nations' is rejected: the Protestants of north-eastern Ireland are ineffably Irish, whatever they may say. When asked Sinn Féin's view of unionists, Martin McGuinness replied:

> We believe they're Irish men and Irish women, just like ourselves, but we also believe they have a particular difficulty about accepting that others who inhabit this part of Ireland are deserving of equal treatment, are people who should not be discriminated against and who deserve to be treated on the same equal basis as themselves.[37]

Unionists are understood to behave as members of a higher caste which refuses to recognize the equality of cultural Protestants and cultural Catholics. They are not members of another nation, 'British' or 'Northern Irish' or 'Scotch Irish', even if some of them think of themselves as British.[38] Ulster may have historical, cultural and regional differences from the rest of the island, but these differences apply to historic, i.e. nine-county, Ulster, are shared by Ulster Catholics and Ulster Protestants, and are considered no different from the regional variations which characterize other nations. The border has one overriding meaning: it is the last outpost of British rule in Ireland. British imperialism, past and present, created an illegitimate political unit in which violent conflict is necessarily endemic, and which prevents the development of a just and rational political settlement, a united Ireland.

Republican accounts vary of the motivations behind Britain's decision to partition Ireland, and its decision(s) to sustain this arrangement. Historically they have argued that an imperialist interest exists amongst the British establishment to dominate the entire British archipelago. Amongst all nationalists partition and political violence are widely blamed on the lack of statesmanship of British politicians,[39] both before and after 1920. The failure of Westminster to grant home rule before 1914, the encouragement and tolerance of revolt by Ulster Unionists against the prospect of home rule, the biased partition of 1920–5, and the humiliating Treaty of 1921 are collectively regarded as the outcome of the machinations of imperialists: Randolph Churchill, Lord Salisbury and Andrew Bonar Law played the 'Orange card'. Resistance to democratization motivated the Conservatives, and their party-interests and opportunism exacerbated Ulster Protestant resistance to home rule.[40] The Liberals advocated home rule for the expedient purpose of generating parliamentary majorities, not because they accepted the right of the Irish to self-determination. Nationalists also complain that the Liberals were spineless in their appeasement of the Conservatives and the Ulster Tories – the Irish policy of the coalition governments led by Lloyd George (1916–22) is seen as having been dictated by his Conservative coalition-partners.[41]

Most nationalists believe three factors account for Britain's Northern Irish policy between 1925 and 1969. First, pure inertia, dictated by an unwillingness to re-open what was falsely perceived as a settled policy-framework for the management of Northern Ireland, partition and Anglo-Irish relations. Secondly, British politicians continued to appease Ulster unionists. The Ulster Unionist Party remained tied to the Conservatives, and the Conservatives governed the UK, alone or in coalition, for all but eleven years between 1925 and 1968. Finally, and most importantly, Britain's strategic interests in maintaining control of Irish territory, ports, and air-corridors, both before and after World War II, reinforced their refusal to budge on Northern Ireland. Most republicans have, however, accepted that the last of these explanations is now redundant. Given the end of the Cold War, there is no longer any geopolitical rationality behind Britain's commitment to Northern Ireland,[42] which may explain the willingness of the British government to pay lip-service to Irish self-determination in the Joint Declaration for Peace made in December 1993.[43] Republicans now attribute Britain's presence in Ireland to inertia, a reluctance to confront unionists, and an expedient unwillingness to be seen to be surrendering to 'terrorism'.[44]

While republicans believe that the British are primarily responsible for the conflict they nevertheless attribute some blame to the governments of the Irish Free State and the Republic. The Free State had British support when it crushed republicanism in the Irish civil war. The Cumann na hGaedheal governments of the 1920s did not press the national question with conviction, made a shameful deal to bury their misman-agement of the Boundary Commission in 1925, and successive Fianna Fáil administrations, although strong on irredentist rhetoric, presided over the marginalization and crushing of militant republicanism in the 1930s, and again in the 1950s. Indeed until 1993 republicans criticized successive Irish gov-ernments for co-operating with the British government in the denial of Irish national self-determination.

*Violence is made in Britain.* Most militant republicans explain political violence in Northern Ireland as the inevitable conse-quence of partition. They are not alone. The New Ireland Forum *Report*, the joint product of constitutional Irish nation-alists, published in 1984, explained political violence as the by-product of British arrangements and actions, especially the British government which gave in to unionist threats after the passage of the third home rule bill in 1912:

> The message – which was not lost on unionists – was that a threat by them to use violence would succeed. To the nation-alists, the conclusion was that the democratic constitutional process was not to be allowed to be effective. This legacy continues to plague British–Irish relations today.[45]

'Endemic violence' flowed from the 1920 arrangements:[46] northern nationalists had their identity denied and had virtu-ally no involvement in democratic decision-making. Unionists presided over a regime of systematic discrimination in which nationalists were deprived of the means of social and economic development and experienced high levels of emigration and unemployment.[47]

Political violence after 1969 is explained by the fact that the peaceful campaigns for civil rights in the 1960s were met with violence and repression,[48] and the burning of the homes of nationalists in West Belfast – a vivid memory amongst the leaders of Sinn Féin who were young people in the late 1960s. In their eyes history had repeated itself: unionists were again the first to resort to violence. The partiality of the local institutions of law and order revived the hitherto dormant IRA as defenders of the nationalist community. After Westminster's intervention and the introduction of troops in 1969, the British army quickly ceased to be impartial and in nationalist eyes bears its share of the blame for occasioning violence.

Nationalists also maintain that British governments' efforts to reform Northern Ireland crumbled too easily in the face of Ulster Protestant intransigence and violence. The collapse of the brief power-sharing executive in 1974, after a loyalist strike, is blamed on the spinelessness of the then British (Labour) government. The events of 1974 repeated the experience of 1914:

> To unionists it reaffirmed the lesson that their threat to use force would cause British Governments to back down; to nationalists it reaffirmed their fears that agreements negotiated in a constitutional framework would not be upheld by British Governments in the face of force or threats of force by unionists.[49]

Constitutional nationalists stress that 'the negative effect of IRA violence on British and unionist attitudes cannot be emphasised enough',[50] but they blame the British-imposed arrangements in 1920, and British 'crisis-management' and 'insensitivity' since 1972, for the social humus which breeds paramilitary warfare. British security policies in the late 1970s and early 1980s deepened the alienation of the northern nationalist community: 'The paramilitary organizations, of both extremes, feed on one another and on the insensitivity of British policy and its failure to provide peace and stability.'[51]

Republican violence has therefore been seen – by neo-nationalists as well as by republicans – as reactive to (unjust and incompetent) British rule. In the words of Gerry Adams, President of Sinn Féin:

> Violence in Ireland has its roots in the conquest of Ireland by Britain. This conquest has lasted . . . for many centuries and, whether economic, political, territorial or cultural, it has used

violence, coercion, sectarianism and terrorism as its methods and has had power as its objective.[52]

Adams explains the onset of the present violence thus:

> The conflict ... began in 1966 with the UVF campaign of assassination of Catholics; it continued in its early stages with attacks by loyalists and RUC on civil rights marchers and graduated to the joint loyalist/RUC attacks on Catholic streets in Derry and Belfast ... The IRA's struggle in this period originated as a defensive response to the combined attacks of the RUC, loyalists and the British army ... The IRA is ordinary people facing up against the monster of imperial power ... [53]

*A stalemate occasioned by Britain.* Republicans insist that the political stalemate since 1972 has flowed from Britain's failure to realize that its presence in Ireland is the fundamental cause of the conflict, its willingness to prop up unionist intransigence, and its granting to unionists of a veto over the Irish people's expression of national self-determination. Until Britain resolves to persuade unionists where their future interests lie Northern Ireland will remain an illegitimate political entity, and continue to be governed through emergency laws as it has been since its inception.[54]

Neo-nationalists concur in blaming Britain for the stalemate between 1972 and 1985:

> Despite the British Government's stated intentions of obtaining political consensus in Northern Ireland, the only policy that is implemented in practice is one of crisis management, that is, the effort to contain violence through emergency measures by the military forces and the police and through extra-ordinary judicial measures and a greatly expanded prison system.[55]

However, neo-nationalists welcomed the Anglo-Irish Agreement of 1985 as the beginning of a proper recognition of the identity of northern nationalists, and they have seen the Joint Declaration for Peace as a prelude to the constitutional construction of an agreed Ireland. By contrast many republicans have contended that in the Anglo-Irish Agreement, and the Joint Declaration for Peace, the British have fooled (some of) the Irish again. In the Anglo-Irish Agreement the Republic was accused of having made a 'contract with the enemy'.[56] Hard-line republicans reacted in the same way to the Joint Declaration for Peace of December 1993,[57] even though it formed the background to the IRA's complete cessation of violence.[58]

## The Chinks in Classical Nationalist Armour

The difficulties with classical nationalist explanations are well-recognized and have been highlighted by neo-nationalists and revisionists. They are also regularly advanced by Ulster unionists. We shall concentrate on five of the most conspicuous problems. First, and foremost, it is not obvious that 'the principle of national self-determination' automatically dictates the unification of Ireland as a natural resolution of the conflict. Secondly, British motivations, behaviour and power are inadequately portrayed. This problem is directly connected to a third, inadequate accounts of unionist motivations, behaviour and power. Fourthly, their explanations of violence are partial and self-serving; and, finally, their accounts of the political stalemate are partisan.

*On self-determination.* Some take issue with any argument predicated upon assumptions about national self-determination on the grounds that nationalist doctrines are incoherent, and that states can only be legitimately appraised by whether they are corrupt and grasping, or just and merciful.[59] More persuasive arguments have been made to the contrary, suggesting that self-government and opposition to 'alien rule' compose a defensible political viewpoint.[60] Defenders of nationalism suggest that there is a strong case for drawing state-boundaries so that 'they correspond with nationality'.[61] We shall take this supposition for granted to probe the merits of republican arguments.

The right to national self-determination automatically creates difficulties when some people want a certain definition of the nation-state and its boundaries, and others want another.

Without further elaboration the right to self-determination is indeterminate. To make it determinate we might stipulate that individuals have the right to participate in a plebiscite in which a majority-vote will determine the boundaries of nation-states – a principle used in many countries in Europe, but not Ireland, after World War I. However, the issue will always be 'decided by the choice of the area of the plebiscite',[62] and the likely minority is always likely to contest that choice. Thus, before 1918, unionists in effect argued that the natural unit of plebiscite was the British Isles, which Irish nationalists rejected as absurd; and, conversely, Irish nationalists argued that the natural unit of plebiscite was the island of Ireland, which Ulster unionists equally rejected. Since 1920 most nationalists have argued that the island of Ireland should be the unit with the right to self-determination, whereas unionists have insisted that Northern Ireland should enjoy this right. As is so often the case a majority-rule interpretation of self-determination seems indeterminate where the unit of self-determination cannot be agreed.[63] These arguments, which may seem abstract, have profound ramifications for evaluating arguments about the partition of Ireland.

There are at least four ways in which majoritarian self-determination might have been exercised after the 1918 election results in Ireland: (i) the entire island could have been treated as the unit of self-determination; (ii) counties and city boroughs could have been the relevant units; alternatively (iii) parliamentary constituencies or (iv) ward boundaries could have been the bases for determining the national fate of peoples and territory.

Take first the island as a whole. The unambiguously pro-independence vote for Sinn Féin in 1918 fell short of 50 per cent of votes cast in contested seats throughout Ireland (see table 1.1),[64] and Sinn Féin's support was territorially concentrated (see figure 1.1). However, the extensive number of uncontested seats won by Sinn Féin (24 per cent of the total) implies that Sinn Féin's underlying level of support was much higher than 48 per cent. What is more important is that 70 per cent of votes cast in all contested seats were for nationalists who sought an autonomous and united Ireland.

**Table 1.2** The 1918 Westminster election results in historic Ulster:
percentage support by county
(excludes Belfast and Londonderry boroughs)

| County | Unionist | Sinn Féin | All Nationalists* |
|--------|----------|-----------|-------------------|
| Antrim | 85.0 | 15.0 | 15.0 |
| Down | 69.4 | 10.0 | 30.6 |
| Londonderry | 63.2 | 23.9 | 36.8 |
| Armagh | 59.0 | 27.3 | 41.0 |
| Fermanagh | 46.4 | 53.1 | 53.6 |
| Tyrone | 45.3 | 28.9 | 54.7 |
| Monaghan | 17.3 | 55.3 | 82.7 |
| Donegal | 10.9 | 44.5 | 89.1 |
| Cavan | – | unopposed | SF unopposed |

Key: see table 1.1.
*Source*: calculated from Walker (1978).

**Table 1.3** The 1918 Westminster election results: in the nine
counties of historic Ulster
(includes Queen's University seat)

| Party | Number of seats won | Share of the seats (%) | Seats won unopposed | Votes won (%) in contested seats* |
|-------|---------------------|------------------------|---------------------|-----------------------------------|
| Sinn Féin | 10 | 26.3 | 2 | 23.5 |
| Irish Parliamentary Party ¶ | 5 | 13.2 | 0 | 15.7 |
| Unionists # | 20 | 52.6 | 0 | 51.6 |
| Labour Unionists | 3 | 7.9 | 0 | 6.5 |
| Labour Representation Committee | 0 | 0 | 0 | 2.6 |
| All Unionists | 23 | 60.5 | 0 | 60.7 |
| All Nationalists ¶ | 15 | 39.5 | 2 | 39.2 |

Key: see table 1.1.
*Source*: O'Leary and McGarry, *Politics of Antagonism*, 99.

Thus the 1918 election outcome supports the claim that an autonomous if not fully sovereign Ireland was supported by a majority on the island as a whole.

Consider now the counties of historic Ulster (excluding the cities of Belfast and Londonderry). Unionists had absolute majorities of the vote in only four counties of the six which became Northern Ireland: Antrim, Armagh, Down and

Londonderry (see table 1.2). All nationalists, by contrast, constituted an absolute majority in the remaining five counties: Cavan (uncontested), Donegal, Fermanagh, Monaghan and Tyrone. Had self-determination been determined on the basis of votes cast in Ulster's counties then Fermanagh and Tyrone should have become part of the Irish Free State, either in 1920, or in 1925 as a result of the Boundary Commission. However, it would not have provided a convincing rationale for why the four counties of Antrim, Down, Armagh and Londonderry should have become part of an independent Irish state. Unionists riposte that they obtained an absolute majority of the vote in contested seats in historic Ulster (see table 1.3), and in the six counties which became Northern Ireland (see table 1.4). They assert that the six counties as a whole were an appropriate plebiscite-zone,[65] and argue that by accepting only six counties they compromised – relinquishing the rights of the majority in the United Kingdom, and their overall majority in the nine counties of historic Ulster. Unionists tend to forget that whereas nationalists took 95 per cent of the votes in what became the Irish Free State, unionists only obtained 70 per cent of the vote in what became Northern Ireland, but their self-determination arguments also have force.[66]

Consider now the votes cast for candidates in Ulster's two major cities in 1918. Self-determination by majority-vote in these jurisdictions would have made the smaller city, Derry/Londonderry, part of the independent Irish state, whereas Belfast would have remained within the United Kingdom (see table 1.5).    Finally, 'majority' self-determination might have been operationalized on the basis of results in parliamentary constituencies – determined according to plurality-rule.[67] In this case the constituencies in Cavan, Donegal, and Monaghan should have become part of the Irish Free State, whereas the constituencies in Antrim and Londonderry County should have remained within the United Kingdom (see table 1.6, p. 42). The 1920–5 settlements respected these requirements, but no others: 22 Ulster constituencies should have become part of Northern Ireland and 15 part of the Free State whereas, in fact, 29 became part of Northern Ireland and 8 part of the

Table 1.4  The 1918 Westminster election results in what became Northern
Ireland (includes Queen's University seat)

| Party | Number of seats won | Share of the seats (%) | Seats won unopposed | Votes won (%) in contested seats* |
|---|---|---|---|---|
| Sinn Féin | 3 | 10 | 0 | 19.1 |
| Irish Parliamentary Party ¶ | 4 | 13.3 | 0 | 11.8 |
| Unionists # | 20 | 66.6 | 0 | 58.3 |
| Labour Unionists | 3 | 10 | 0 | 7.6 |
| Labour Representation Committee | 0 | 0 | 0 | 3.1 |
| All Unionists | 23 | 76.6 | 0 | 69 |
| All Nationalists ¶ | 7 | 23.3 | 0 | 30.9 |

Key: see table 1.1.
*Source*: adapted from O'Leary and McGarry, *Politics of Antagonism*, 99.

Table 1.5  The 1918 election results in Belfast and Derry/Londonderry

| City | Unionists | Labour Unionists | Labour Representation Committee | Sinn Féin | All Nationalists |
|---|---|---|---|---|---|
| Belfast | 47.9 | 25.1 | 10.1 | 7.4 | 16.4 |
| Derry/ Londonderry | 48.5 | | | 50.7 | 51.5 |

*Source*: O'Leary and McGarry, *Politics of Antagonism*, 99.

Free State, i.e. one-third of the seats were inappropriately allocated (see figure 1.2).

The upshot of this lengthy discussion is simple: the majoritarian principle of self-determination cannot unambiguously support the case that all of Ireland should have been granted independence or autonomy by Britain between 1918 and 1925 unless we accept that the entire island was the most reasonable plebiscite-area, an assumption about which unionists beg to differ.

There are two feasible ways nationalists can make the case that all of Ireland should be the unit of national self-determination. One is to maintain, according to present international law, that decolonizing powers should not partition territories to which they are granting (or restoring) self-government. For

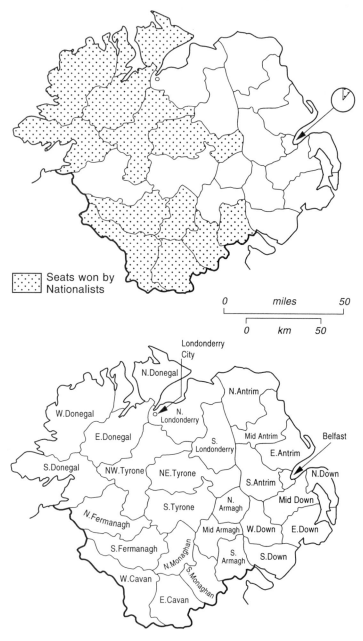

**Figure 1.2** Seats won by Nationalists in Ulster in the
1918 Westminster parliamentary elections

example, a UN Declaration of 1960, on the granting of independence to colonial countries and peoples, declared that any attempt aimed at the partial or total disruption of the national unity and territorial integrity of a country was incompatible with the UN Charter. There are, however, difficulties with this view. Ireland's status before 1920 is contestable: was it a colony or an integral part of the UK, and was what occurred between 1920 and 1925 a partial decolonization, as most republicans insist, or was it a secession, as most unionists insist? These questions take us to the heart of rival historic readings of the causes of conflict. Another difficulty with the view that Britain should not have partitioned a territory in the process of being decolonized has been recognized in a recent speech by the then Irish prime minister: 'That UN Declaration [of 1960] . . . applied to situations that had yet to be settled. It was not intended to reopen territorial settlements that had already been in existence for some considerable time.'[68] It is, of course, a moot point whether there had been a territorial settlement in Ireland given that the Republic's constitution of 1937 clashes directly with the British claim to sovereignty embedded in the Government of Ireland Act of 1920 and repudiates the boundary 'settlement' of 1925. 'International law' provides no easy answer to the question of the appropriate unit for the exercise of self-determination when there is no agreement on the colonial status of a given territory and when the case at hand preceded the development of the law in question.

Another possible argument is to deny that Ulster Protestants should have had any right, either in 1918, or subsequently, to determine the future political status of Ireland – as opposed to having rights as future Irish citizens. The decolonization of all of Ireland on this argument would have been just, because Ireland had been annexed, colonized, and unjustly governed by Anglo-Scots and British rulers, and, so the argument goes, neither the colonists nor their descendants should have had a right to veto any part of Ireland's decolonization given that their presence was a product of conquest, of might rather than right. This case would be similar to that recently advanced by Estonians against giving post-1940 Soviet colonists the

**Table 1.6** Seats won by parties in Ulster constituencies in 1918
(excluding QUB seat)

| Constituency Areas | Unionists | Labour Unionist | Sinn Féin | Nationalists |
|---|---|---|---|---|
| Belfast City | 5 | 3 | – | 1 |
| Antrim | 4 | – | – | – |
| Down | 4 | – | – | 1 |
| Londonderry Co. | 2 | – | – | – |
| Armagh | 2 | – | – | 1 |
| Fermanagh | 1 | – | 1 | – |
| Tyrone | 1 | – | 1 | 1 |
| Donegal | – | – | 3 | 1 |
| Monaghan | – | – | 2 | – |
| Cavan | – | – | 2 | – |
| Derry/Londonderry City | – | – | 1 | – |
| Total | 19 | 3 | 10 | 5 |

*Source*: calculated from Walker (1978).

right to vote on the secession of Estonia from the USSR. However, there is a crucial difference between the cases. Soviet annexation and colonization of the Baltic states were carried out in living memory. Ulster unionists can hardly be held culpable in the same way for the conquests of their ancestors. Surely a 'moral statute of limitations' applies to wrongs enacted in times preceding those of anybody alive today?

Our discussion has highlighted the problems with a majoritarian principle of national self-determination, and has suggested that it does not automatically support republican conclusions.[69] We have also seen that anti-colonial arguments for treating all of Ireland as the unit of self-determination are contestable. Is there any impartial way of evaluating the rival claims to national self-determination? One liberal argument is that every (self-defined) people within a liberal democratic state should be given the right to self-determination, provided that they consent to that prospect, and that the same right is extended by them to every people within any (self-defined) sub-area of the proposed secessionist territory.[70] This iterative argument makes self-determination operational.[71] The principle is that self-determination, to be fair and meaningful, must apply to everybody, majorities as well as minorities. Its practical efficacy, of course, is more debatable, especially when there cannot easily be territorial contiguity and separateness for each successive seceding unit, but the principle provides us with a more impartial normative standard against which to assess claims for self-determination.

The departure of the Irish Free State from the United Kingdom was very fair by this criterion: in the 1918 Westminster elections 95 per cent of the electorate in what became the Irish Free State endorsed parties supporting republican independence or extensive autonomy for Ireland. The same principle justified a very considerable proportion of the population of the north-east of Ireland having the right to opt-out of the departure of the rest of Ireland from the United Kingdom. However, it could not justify the particular border given to Northern Ireland, which left a very significant minority, at least 30 per cent of the electorate, without the ability to exercise its right to self-determination. It is clear from the historical record that the Sinn Féin plenipotentiaries who signed the Anglo-Irish Treaty in 1921, which made provision for a Boundary Commission, accepted the spirit of this liberal doctrine of self-determination. They permitted Northern Ireland to opt out of Irish independence, provided that the Treaty allowed for a readjustment of the border according to local preferences within what became Northern Ireland.[72] However, when the Boundary Commission was convened neither the British nor unionist representatives accepted this principle: areas in which majorities would have opted for unification with the Irish Free State were not granted this right. While unionists insisted on the right of Northern Ireland to secede from an independent Ireland, they acknowledged no such right for peoples or areas within its boundaries.

This argument suggests that the Irish Free State should have been granted jurisdiction over far more people and territory than it actually obtained. It also suggests that while most Ulster unionists had their right to self-determination respected through the establishment of Northern Ireland, most northern nationalists did not – and that this has remained the case.[73] Northern nationalists have the right to resent 'the double standards of British governments which, to avoid imposing on Ireland a system rejected by a quarter of its population, created and defended an artificial Northern Ireland rejected by one third of *its* population'. They have every right to complain that the details of the 1920 settlement 'depended as much on the decisions of a small group of British cabinet ministers as they did on nationalist or unionist opinion',[74],but they have no conclusively compelling argument as to why the entire island of Ireland should have been, and should now be, the sole unit for the exercise of self-determination.

*The motives of Albion.* The second major weakness of republican discourse lies in its account of the motivations of the British state in creating and defending Northern Ireland. British politicians are seen as entirely responsible, through 'the art of creating dissension', for the divisions within the Irish nation,[75] and republicans wishfully attach 'to Britain all the responsibility for unionists' time-honoured preference for rule from London or Belfast over rule from Dublin'.[76]

Imperialist considerations motivated the Government of Ireland Act of 1920 and the Anglo-Irish Treaty of 1921. Many British politicians, especially the Conservatives, believed in a domino-theory: granting Ireland independence would threaten the British Empire. They were worried about the 'demonstration-effect' in Great Britain, where there was a movement for home rule for Scotland.[77] They were motivated to prevent Irish independence, or, if that proved infeasible, to prevent independent Ireland jeopardizing imperial security. The gravity with which British policy-makers held these convictions is demonstrated by their negotiating conditions between 1918 and 1921. They refused to put Ireland on the agenda of the Versailles peace conference, even though it had self-determination and the rights of small nations as part of its remit. They absolutely refused to permit Ireland to become a fully sovereign republic. They were adamant that Ireland could have no more than dominion status under the British Crown and Commonwealth – and imposed this resolution in Articles 1–4 of the 1921 Anglo-Irish Treaty. They required Irish naval ports and dockyards to be available 'in time of peace' and 'in time of war' for British forces – specified in Article 7 of the same

Treaty.[78] These incursions on Irish sovereignty were imperialist and were only accepted by the Irish negotiators under Lloyd George's threat of 'terrible and immediate war'.

These facts are undeniable, but it does not follow that partition was wholly or primarily motivated by imperialist considerations. In both the Government of Ireland Act of 1920 and the Treaty the British government envisaged eventual agreement on Irish unity and self-government – albeit within the 'Empire'. The Cabinet rejected the option of integrating Northern Ireland with Great Britain. The clauses in both texts which facilitated Irish unity, providing that the Northern Ireland Parliament consented, are at odds with a simple British ambition to partition Ireland or to deny it self-government.[79] Moreover, imperialist interests furnish a more unsatisfactory explanation of the role of the British state after 1925. Gerry Adams's thesis is that the British state was directly responsible for all the actions of the Stormont government: 'In instituting the statelet and in imposing partition, the British government also instituted the full apparatus of sectarianism'.[80] This perspective is unsustainable: Britain's role in Northern Ireland between 1920 and 1968 is better understood as that of indirect responsibility through semi-deliberate neglect.[81] The British government originally created safeguards for minorities in both parts of Ireland – instituting proportional representation and illegalizing religious discrimination – and anticipated that Northern Ireland would operate like a miniature version of the British political system. They did not foresee a system of permanent majority dictatorship.[82] The control actually established by the Ulster Unionist Party between 1920 and 1972 was not planned, but rather was sanctioned by the neglect of successive British governments.

Indeed British control over Northern Ireland remained negotiable. Churchill considered offering Irish unification in 1940 if the Irish government was prepared to enter the war on the side of the Allies, or to declare a state of non-belligerency.[83] Even after World War II, during which Eire remained neutral, Northern Ireland remained negotiable because its parliament had the right to secede. This evidence that British governments were prepared to cede Northern Ireland is, of course, open to contested interpretation. Republicans claim these episodes show that Britain does not really regard Northern Ireland as part of its nation. Unionists suggest that Britain's willingness to allow Irish unity to succeed if that prospect could be accomplished with unionist compliance (in the midst of war) or with their consent (in peacetime) shows that the British – unfortunately – are not the imperialists Irish nationalists imagine them to be.

Republicans are partially correct in their diagnoses of the half-heartedness of the commitment of Cumann na nGaedheal and Fianna Fáil governments in the Irish Free State to achieving Irish unity before World War II. In particular the Cosgrave government handled the question of the Boundary Commission of 1925 with spectacular incompetence, pushing for a review in unfavourable circumstances, and then burying its unfair proposals in return for money. Moreover, de Valera and his colleagues' decision to opt for neutrality during World War II, however understandable, had an impact on British policy-makers which is conveniently glossed over by republicans. The contrast with Northern Ireland's participation in the Allied war effort was striking. Despite the large numbers of volunteers from Eire the state's official neutrality made many Conservative, Liberal and Labour politicians regard Northern Ireland as a loyal part of the British nation. The Labour government's passage of the Ireland Act of 1949, in response to the declaration of a Republic by the Irish government, must be seen in this context, as well as in the light of geo-political considerations. (The Ireland Act prevented Irish unification without the consent of the Northern Ireland parliament.)

After the Stormont parliament was terminated in 1972 the then Conservative government created provisions to allow a plebiscite to be conducted on whether Northern Ireland should remain within the UK. A border poll was held in 1973 – 57 per cent supported the continuation of the Union in a poll boycotted by nationalists. The referendum provisions showed that the British state was prepared, in principle, to cede sovereignty over Northern Ireland. In the Anglo-Irish Agreement (Art. 1 (c)) the British government made an agreement with the Irish government declaring that if in the future a majority of the people of Northern Ireland clearly wish for and formally consent to the establishment of a united Ireland, they will introduce and support in the respective Parliaments legislation to give effect to that wish.

The British prime minister, in December 1993, signed a Joint Declaration for Peace which again allowed for the possibility of Irish unification – albeit with the consent of a majority of the electorate in 'the North'.[84] The pattern is consistent. British governments have been willing to permit Irish unification, albeit only with majority-consent in Northern Ireland.

In the late 1960s and early 1970s British governments forced reform upon reluctant unionists and eventually abolished the Stormont parliament, partly because of the successful appeals of the Northern Ireland Civil Rights Association. Since 1972 successive British governments have fitfully endeavoured to reform Northern Ireland and to promote power-sharing.[85] They have recognized, albeit belatedly and grudgingly, the importance of the national identity of the Northern Ireland minority, in attempted political settlements with an 'Irish dimension', and frameworks for a settlement – notably in the Anglo-Irish Agreement of 1985 and in the Downing Street Declaration of 1993.[86] These facts about the historic evolution of British policy on Northern Ireland compel a more nuanced appraisal than the imperialist model in republican discourse.

None of the foregoing considerations deny that the harshest criticisms may be legitimately levelled at British armies, courts, policies, and politicians both before and after 1920, and before and after 1972. None of the foregoing excuses the partiality of the 1920–5 territorial settlement or the British denial of northern nationalists their right to self-determination. However, British power and behaviour are difficult to reconcile with the perpetually malevolent imperialist ogre described by republicanism.[87] In November 1990 the then Secretary of State for Northern Ireland, Peter Brooke, in a major speech, rejected many of Sinn Féin's arguments about the responsibility of 'the British presence' for the continuing conflict. He maintained that there were four distinct aspects to the 'British presence': the British army; the Northern Ireland Office; the British subvention; and its 'heart and core', 'nearly a million people . . . who are, and who certainly regard themselves as British'. He contended that the Army was present to stop violence; that the Northern Ireland Office was willing to have its authority replaced by an agreed devolved assembly in Northern Ireland; that the UK subvention was not dictated by some strategic interest; and that it was the 'Britishness' of unionists which was ignored by Sinn Féin. He also insisted that the British state was not opposed to Irish unity in principle: 'it is not the aspiration to a sovereign, united Ireland, against which we set our face, but its violent expression'.[88] Whether the British state, the Conservative Party, or indeed Peter Brooke, are as neutral on Irish unity as these contentions suggest may reasonably be doubted.[89] However, this speech, and the Downing Street Declaration of 1993, qualifies any simplistic tale of imperialist malevolence.

*Misreading the opponents.* The implausible elements in republican readings of the British state are rooted in their third major explanatory difficulty. They consistently underestimate the intensity of Ulster unionists' preferences. Unionist opposition to Irish home rule or independence before 1920 was grounded in imperial allegiance, national allegiance, political worries, religious anxieties, economic fears, and defence of privilege; it was not the product of mere pawns of manipulative Conservative politicians. Before 1911 Liberals and Irish nationalists foolishly downplayed unionists' hostility to home rule, and their willingness to oppose it by all means at their disposal, including armed struggle.[90] The British state was receptive to the mobilization of Ulster unionists because it was an open parliamentary regime, if not yet a modern democracy. Its Conservative politicians were also receptive to unionism because of widespread anti-Catholicism and pro-imperialist jingoism within their electorate. Although nationalists correctly argue that British politicians were unduly accommodating towards unionist interests, in blocking home rule and in the partition-arrangements, they are wrong to see unionists merely as a 'garrison people', mere agents of British imperialism. Republicans are also correct that unionists disliked partition, not least because it meant the abandonment of Irish unionists and Protestants elsewhere in Ireland, but they forget that Ulster unionists preferred partition to independence or home rule under a Dublin parliament. When given the choice, under the Government of Ireland Act of 1920 and the Treaty of 1921, they opted out of Irish unity *within* the Empire. The constitutional evolution of the Irish Free State confirmed them in their view that they had made the right decision.[91]

Nationalist discourse clearly has profound difficulty in explaining Ulster unionists' political preferences, and in decoding their political identity, both before and after 1920. The difficulties were once well put by an academic: 'What if . . . there are fellows who pass a nationalist examination on race, fail on religion, are passed on geography, but fail on wanting to join in?'[92] Until recently the President of Sinn Féin argued that being 'pro-British', a term he put in quotation marks, was a flexible state of mind for Ulster unionists: the 'pro-British' elements will face up to the reality of the situation only when the British prop and the system which uses them as its tools and stormtroopers is removed.[93] Since the IRA's cessation of military operations the Sinn Féin leader has attempted to reach out to unionists as 'my people', but no reciprocal embrace has been forthcoming.[94] How then do republicans explain the failure of 'pro-British' Ulster unionists to recognize their Irish identity?

Until the 1950s they generally argued that Ulster unionists were duped into mis-specification of their national identity. Alternatively they regarded them as mean-minded materialists, loyal not so much to 'the Crown', but to 'the half-crown' provided by the British subvention. Finally, especially if influenced by Marxism, they drew a distinction between the unionist ruling class and the working-class rank-and-file. The ruling class was regarded as the last of the Anglo-Irish ascendancy, ripe for overthrow and/or expulsion, whereas the rank-and-file were the beneficiaries of institutionalized discrimination. Republicans vary in their accounts of this rank-and-file's consciousness. Sometimes Ulster Protestants are portrayed as the unwitting beneficiaries of discrimination; at other times they are seen as conscious participants in a discriminatory system.

The latter perspective is Sinn Féin's: 'The reactionary nature of Unionism grows from the fact that they have to defend the indefensible.'[95]

The arguments directed at embracing Ulster Protestants as co-nationals are sincerely held by the leaders of Sinn Féin, if not by their rank-and-file, but they usually display a patronizing tone, coupled with a curious inability to see at least some unionists as people with a similar mental make-up to themselves. Consider the following exchange between one of the authors and Martin McGuinness of Sinn Féin in 1992:

> *BO'L* If republicans have a right as a national minority to use armed struggle to resist incorporation into a state that they don't want to be part of, do unionists have a right as a minority to use armed struggle to resist incorporation into a state that they don't wish to be part of?
> *MMcG* I don't believe that there would be any effective armed struggle by unionists once the British government stated clearly to them that their relationship with unionism had changed and declared their intention to leave . . . The vast majority of unionists in my opinion, faced with such a reality, being [the] hard-headed sensible people that many of them are, would sit down and work out along with people like . . . [interrupted]
> *BO'L* Isn't that patronizing to say that they're 'hard-headed and sensible', and therefore they'll come to accept what you say? Couldn't they be hard-headed and sensible and react just like you do to being a minority, by supporting armed struggle against what they regard as unjust?
> *MMcG* I don't think that the same rule applies at all, and I think that all that has happened here, in particular the actions of loyalist paramilitary groups and some of the escapades that they get involved in, I think clearly shows that there is a very important distinction between people who are fighting for national liberation for the freedom of Ireland, and the right of the Irish to self-determination, and a group which wishes to hang onto the coat-tails of another country . . . prepared to cut loose those people from its coat-tails.'[96]

Republicans have frequently denied that the evolution of the Irish state gives any grounds for unionists' anxieties about their prospective absorption into a united Ireland. Alternatively they have declared that they will be generous when unionists are generous in agreeing to redesign a new Ireland – the most recent of the Irish government's promises are contained in the Joint Declaration for Peace of 1993.[97] The fact that Irish governments have not bent over backwards to make the Republic attractive to Ulster Protestants is often forgotten. Republicans in Sinn Féin nevertheless deny that unionists have anything to fear from the new all-Ireland state that will be built after British withdrawal. Indeed they claim that all will benefit from a new pluralist Ireland:

> Catholic church attitudes have to change, the attitudes of political parties in the twenty-six counties and Dublin towards the North have to change; [so do] attitudes amongst many nationalists towards unionists. Protestants also have to change; and they have to accept that the attitude of the Ulster Protestant community and the British government towards ourselves also has to do some changing as well, that unless a change takes place which allows everybody to sit down together and rule this country in the interests of all, rather than the interests of a particular section of the community, unless that happens, there is never going to be peace.[98]

*Violence: Tu quoque?* Republican explanations of violence have been fundamentally self-serving. They correctly point to some of the background conditions which have occasioned violence in Northern Ireland, such as political oppression, discrimination, and unjustifiable inequalities, and correctly complain that unionists often deny these realities. However, they unconvincingly portray all republican violence as reactive, defensive and legitimate; and obdurate facts falsify the claim that all the violence is because of the presence of the British state, or 'England's presence'.[99] Consider the initiation of violence after 1925. In 1939–40 the IRA launched a bombing campaign in England to end partition. It was a fiasco. In 1956 the IRA initiated an armed insurrection in Northern Ireland, which was quickly crushed, but did not end until 1962. In 1969/70 the Provisional IRA shifted from what it described as defensive actions to an offensive against both the Stormont government and the British presence – at a time

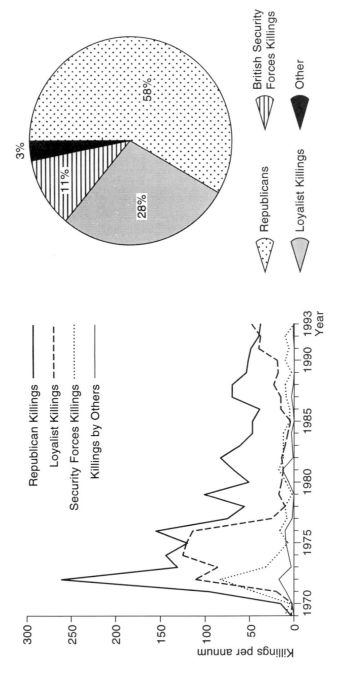

**Figure 1.3** Agents responsible for killings in the conflict, 1969–93
*Source*: M. Sutton, *An Index of Deaths from the Conflict in Ireland* (Belfast: Beyond the Pale Publications, 1994).

when reforms were being promised and implemented after a civil rights campaign. Since 1969 republican paramilitaries have been responsible for nearly 60 per cent of all casualties sustained in the conflict, whereas the British security forces, including the locally recruited security personnel in the RUC and the UDR, have been responsible for about 12 per cent of all deaths.[100] In almost every year for the last twenty-five years republican killings have outnumbered both loyalist killings and killings by British forces (see figure 1.3). Loyalist paramilitaries, 'fellow Irish men and women' in official republican doctrine, have been responsible for over 25 per cent of all deaths. If we count the deaths caused by British security forces, and calculate the proportion caused by locally recruited members of the RUC, the UDR and the RIR, then the percentage of violent deaths caused by the combined actions of 'fellow Irish men and women' rises to over 90 per cent of the total. Republicans should therefore regard the long war which they have just brought to an end as an Irish civil war.

The legitimacy of republican violence has also been questionable, by the criteria established by doctrines of self-determination and by Catholic just-war doctrine. In 1992 the IRA's campaign of violence was supported by at most 10 per cent of the voters in Northern Ireland.[101] In November 1992 1.6 per cent of the electorate of the Republic supported Sinn Féin, compared with 1.2 per cent in the 1989 general election.[102] The level of support for Sinn Féin throughout Ireland suggests that less than 5 per cent of those who vote for nationalist parties electorally endorse republican violence. No other party which supports paramilitary violence attracts any significant electoral support. Therefore the IRA and other republican paramilitaries can claim no mandate of legitimacy for the long war which they have just terminated. In this respect recent IRA violence differs dramatically from the insurgency against British authority between 1919 and 1921. Michael Collins's army had a dramatically superior case for fighting a popularly supported war of national liberation.

The IRA's campaign also failed to meet the recognized criteria for a just war, whether espoused in Catholic theology or in more secular philosophies.[103] Theologically the criteria for a just war are fivefold: the party who wages war must have sufficient authority to do so; there must be a just cause of offence, such as unprovoked aggression; there must be an intention to wage war solely for the sake of peace, or for 'the suppression of the wicked' and 'the sustenance of the good'; there must be a reasonable prospect that the war can be won; and finally, there must be justice in the means employed in the war.[104]

The first criterion – appropriate authority – was originally biased in favour of kings, but the democratic will of the nation is the 'sufficient authority' of our times. The IRA has not possessed such authority for the reasons given above: only a small fraction of the self-defined members of the Irish nation support Sinn Féin electorally, and by implication grant the IRA authority. Even amongst northern nationalists the IRA has enjoyed the support of only one-third of the relevant constituency.

The second criterion is at least debatable. Republicans have not been merely the victims of unionist acts of war, they have also been perpetrators of war. As long as it declared that its violence would continue until its conditions were met, namely the withdrawal of British troops, the IRA made itself a cause of war, not an effect.

The third criterion is almost impossibly vague – even if we tendentiously granted that unionists or Ulster Protestants are 'wicked', which sounds very medieval. It is also not obvious that the primary war-aim of the Provisional IRA was a just peace given that victory would have imposed upon Ulster unionists the same unwanted minority status that its own people have suffered from.

After twenty-five years of conflict it was eminently reasonable to question whether the IRA's war was winnable,[105] and the IRA's decision to announce a complete cessation of military operations in 1994 showed that its leadership had concluded that they had more to gain from peace than from a continuation of war. Even had its campaign eventually led to a British withdrawal it would have been unlikely to generate a united Ireland precisely because republican violence had increased unionist hostility to incorporation within an Irish state, and strengthened revisionist opposition to unification in the Republic, while a precipitate British withdrawal would have been likely to produce the formation of a (smaller) 'Ulster' state, complete with 'ethnic cleansing'.[106] Consider also the economic opportunity costs of political violence. Two separate estimates suggest that between 1971 and 1983, and between 1970 and 1985, over 40,000 manufacturing jobs in Northern Ireland were lost because of political violence.[107] These losses made it more difficult to reform and expand equality of opportunity. It can also be argued that oppression, discrimination and inequality are not sufficient to justify waging war if other methods of political change are available, are efficacious, and have not been exhausted. Indeed if Irish unity can only be accomplished by violence that in itself must lead one to question the merits of the goal, especially if such violence is counter-productive – as the leadership of Sinn Féin has implicitly recognized.

Lastly, republicans did not follow the 'rules of war', and republican violence prevented effective reform and therefore was itself a cause of 'continuing evil'. Concerning the much-abused 'rules of war', the IRA was no better at observing them than the British government, and in this respect it differed radically from the rebels who conducted the 1916 Easter rising – who obeyed the relevant international conventions. The IRA assumed that only one side had the right to 'shoot to kill'; and that its captured volunteers should have been treated as prisoners of war while it considered itself justified in executing captured soldiers.

*It takes at least two to make a stalemate.* The foregoing arguments, or variants on them, have consistently been made by neo-nationalists, constitutional republicans, Irish Catholic bishops, and even by Pope John Paul II in condemning the Provisional IRA.[108] In the end they had an impact upon those republicans who maintained they were fighting a just war of national liberation. Spokespersons for Sinn Féin recognized that violent republicanism had reinforced unionists' intransigent opposition to Irish unification; inhibited reform and inward investment to deprived nationalist areas; provoked the British authorities into further eroding civil liberties through the enactment of emergency-laws; encouraged outrages by the security forces, and injustices in the policing and judicial systems; and facilitated loyalist retaliation. The interpretation of self-determination, and the apparently integral, exclusivist and ethnic definitions of the Irish people and Irish territory espoused in classical republicanism, have been part of the problem rather than part of the resolution.

## Neo-Nationalism: Beyond Boundaries

Classical republicanism still remains an important force in Northern Ireland. It is expressed, albeit in changing form, within Sinn Féin and the IRA, and is sympathetically heard by some within the Republic and in Irish-America. However, since the early 1970s 'traditional republicanism' has been dying out in book-length discussions.[109] There is also some evidence that unreconstructed nationalism enjoys less currency with public opinion in the Republic[110] – though one must always be cautious about decoding national sentiment from public opinion polls. Amongst the political class there are signs that Irish deputies are less likely to blame the traditional exogenous enemy, Britain, or partition, for the causes of the conflict.[111] Revisionism is not triumphant, except perhaps within what is sometimes described as 'Dublin 4', the world of the Republic's political, commercial, academic and media elite, but republicanism no longer enjoys its former hegemony.

Irish nationalism was never monolithic but its exponents' interpretations have become increasingly nuanced. Amongst many northern nationalists in the SDLP, and amongst similarly minded people in the Irish Labour Party, Fine Gael, and Fianna Fáil, four theses are held in opposition to classical republicanism: (i) that Britain is neutral, or at least is not the central obstacle to Irish unity; (ii) that violence is caused at least as much by republicans as by other agents; (iii) that political progress does not necessarily depend upon an immediate or medium-term British governmental withdrawal from Northern Ireland; and (iv) that Irish unification is not the only way in which Irish national self-determination can be realized.

*British 'neutrality' or 'lack of centrality'.* Whereas Sinn Féin insists that British imperialism – or 'the British presence' – is the key cause of conflict, the SDLP's leader John Hume argues that since the Anglo-Irish Agreement the British government has become formally neutral on the national question. Peter Brooke's 1990 speech, discussed above, reinforced Hume's view of British neutrality – which he first advanced in inter-party talks between Sinn Féin and the SDLP during 1988. That Hume could advance such a controversial thesis amongst northern nationalists was proof of the waning compulsion of the classical republican view.

It is not obvious, however, that this thesis about British neutrality is true. Northern Ireland is part of the United Kingdom in British public law, and British governments argue that it is part of the UK in international law. British governments regularly condemn the Irish claim to sovereignty over the island, or, when they are more polite, describe it as 'doubtful' or 'unhelpful' – to use the words of Peter Brooke and Sir Patrick Mayhew.[112] Although the British people may be indifferent about the future of Northern Ireland,[113] and although the British state is a signatory to an agreement which confirms that it will not oppose Irish unification by majority consent of the population of Northern Ireland, that does not necessarily mean that the British government or the British Conservative Party are 'neutral'. The Conservative Party has organized and competed in elections there since 1989, and most of its leading figures, when pressed, say that they positively want Northern Ireland to remain part of the Union. The way in which successive British governments, both Conservative and Labour, conducted security policies targeted primarily at republican and nationalist districts makes it difficult to accept the transparent validity of British 'neutrality'. That these governments usually claimed that the primary cause of conflict was terrorism, usually meaning republican terrorism, did not suggest neutrality. Even Northern Ireland's formal right to join the Republic with the consent of its majority is not proof of neutrality – given that that right in the eyes of most northern nationalists is presently like the right of tramps to dine at the Ritz.

Indeed Hume no longer unequivocally embraces the full British 'neutrality' argument. When asked whether the British sovereignty claim is an integral component of the problem in Northern Ireland he replied 'Yes, the Government of Ireland Act of 1920, together with all other attempts to solve this problem, have failed and failed miserably.'[114] There is no need to belabour the point. Republicans have good grounds for questioning the neutrality of Britain. However, the core of the neo-nationalist viewpoint does not require belief in unequivocal British neutrality. All that it requires is the recognition that British imperialism is not the central obstacle to Irish unification, and that the British government and British political institutions have been merely one set of causal agents in the conflict, violence and stalemate.

*Violence is caused at least as much by republicans.* The second neo-nationalist thesis commands wider assent, at least outside republican circles. Statistical evidence, which we have presented elsewhere, demonstrates that republican paramilitaries have been responsible for the lion's share of the political killing since 1969, and the British security forces have killed far fewer people than either republican or loyalist paramilitaries[115] (see figure 1.3). Hume and the SDLP have advanced this thesis with particular moral power. Until 1994 Hume persistently argued that republican violence was responsible for the British military presence, and during discussions with Gerry Adams after 1988 appears to have shifted the thinking of Sinn Féin on this matter.[116] This thesis directly challenges the republican view that Britain is directly or indirectly the primary cause of political violence. Naturally it does not follow that neo-nationalists unequivocally endorse the British security forces and the administration of justice in Northern Ireland. On the contrary, northern nationalist criticisms of the RUC, the UDR/RIR, and the administration of justice in Northern Ireland persist, have empirical foundations, and are often endorsed by politicians in the Republic.

*Political progress does not require a British withdrawal.* Neo-nationalists maintain that a British institutional withdrawal is not the key step to resolve the political stalemate – at least not at present. The SDLP, established from a combination of civil rights activists of the 1960s, reform-minded members of the old Nationalist Party and National Democratic Party, and socialists within the Belfast and Derry labour movements, marked a genuine change in the character of northern nationalism. Without abandoning nationalist aspirations the SDLP did not say Irish unification was a right, to be implemented through British and Irish diplomacy, but rather a goal to be pursued through political dialogue and participation in constitutional processes. It decisively rejected abstentionism in favour of working the British (and European) political system.

In the SDLP's view agreement is first required amongst all the people 'who share the island of Ireland', to use a favoured phrase of John Hume's, on how to live together, and on shared political institutions which recognize the dual identities of the two primary communities. For them the IRA and Sinn Féin's version of nationalism is territorial, rather than directed at unifying people,[117] and it is counter-productive: Seamus Mallon, the deputy leader of the SDLP, recently warned that republican violence weakened sympathy for Irish unity in the Republic.[118] Neo-nationalists believe that a negotiated political settlement, an agreed Ireland, is more important than seeking a precipitate British withdrawal.

*Irish unification is not necessary for Irish national self-determination.* Finally some neo-nationalists have implied that Irish unification may never happen, and need not happen for Irish national self-determination to be expressed. They insist that Irish unification is worth having if and only if it has the active consent of a majority in Northern Ireland as well as the Republic. Secondly, many of them have argued that they would settle for either a system of British and Irish co-sovereignty over Northern Ireland instead of outright Irish unification, or a system of devolved power-sharing within Northern Ireland supplemented by significant Irish–Northern Irish inter-governmental institutions, and constitutional protection by both the Republic and Britain. Thirdly, many of them maintain that national sovereignty has acquired a different meaning considering European confederation and integration, and that European institutions may provide a better way of increasing co-operation throughout Ireland than traditional models of unification.[119] Finally, Hume, with the backing of many in his party, has argued that any comprehensive settlement should be legitimated by two referendums: in Northern Ireland and in the Republic, an idea which can be implemented under the terms of the Joint Declaration for Peace 1993.[120] This offer implies that no grand settlement, in the immediate future, could produce a united Ireland, because such a settlement would not win majority support in Northern Ireland.

However, despite this evident civic nationalism, and willingness to compromise on the goal of Irish unification, neo-nationalists in the SDLP insist upon three political principles. First, any alternative to Irish unification must have the active consent of northern nationalists so that their opportunity for self-determination is meaningful. Secondly, any grand constitutional settlement must make it legitimate to aspire to the traditional goal of national unification. Thirdly, neo-nationalists maintain that the lack of a fully equal recognition of the Irish identity of northern nationalists, and by contrast the supremacy of the unionists' British identity, has been a key source of antagonism. Britain in their view remains responsible for injustice, but not in the way diagnosed by republicans, and Britain's duty is not to withdraw without consent, but rather to reform Northern Ireland and work with the Irish government to ensure that both communities and identities have fully equal recognition, status, and rights of political participation.

## Conclusion: Towards an Agreed rather than a United Ireland?

In its militant republican form traditional Irish nationalism has a limited electoral constituency – a significant minority amongst northern nationalists, but an insignificant constituency within the Republic. Its central explanatory arguments are partial and problematic, and indeed have helped foster conflict. The persuasive moral power of militant republicanism, both at home and abroad, had been significantly diminished before 1994 – in part by the 'arguments' of assassinations, semtex explosives and knee-cappings. The 'long war' eroded the moral attractiveness of 'heroic resistance' amongst many northern nationalists. However, no one should underestimate the capacity of British policy-makers, unionist politicians and loyalist paramilitaries to give militant republicanism a renewed lease of life: militant nationalism is a dependent variable.

Neo-nationalists are correct that militant republican explanations of the conflict are partisan and dubious. We agree that the aspiration to achieve a united Ireland should be respected, and that self-determination for the northern minority – understood as the consent of northern nationalists to any new constitutional arrangements – is a *sine qua non* of any successful political settlement.

To try to create, by argument, persuasion and consent, a democratic Irish state which encompasses all the peoples of the island of Ireland in a shared national identity can be defended as a legitimate endeavour, whatever one's judgement about its feasibility. Irish unification, if it occurs, will be preceded by an agreed Ireland, which will require not only a continuing British political presence in Northern Ireland, but also appropriate changes in the constitution and public policy of the Republic. This principled posture does not require any Irish nationalist, of whatever hue, to whitewash the nature of British rule in Ireland, past or present.

# 2

# Green Political Economy: British Imperialism as the Prime Mover

Ireland, as distinct from her people, is nothing to me; and the man who is bubbling over with love and enthusiasm for 'Ireland,' and can yet pass unmoved through our streets and witness all the wrong and the suffering, the shame and the degradation wrought upon the people of Ireland – yea, wrought by Irishmen upon Irish men and women, without burning to end it, is, in my opinion, a fraud and a liar in his heart, no matter how he loves that combination of chemical elements he is pleased to call Ireland.

The cause of Labour is the cause of Ireland, the cause of Ireland is the cause of Labour.

*James Connolly (1870–1916), Irish socialist*

The UK state is not 'above' the NI problem, it is an integral part of that problem.

*Liam O'Dowd, Bill Rolston and Mike Tomlinson, left-wing nationalist sympathisers* [1]

Marxism is no longer a vibrant ideology amongst the Western leftist intelligentsia. Nevertheless historical materialism has exercised an important influence on the interpretation of national and ethnic conflicts, which Marxists have often decoded as displaced or camouflaged class conflicts. The Marxist literature on Northern Ireland is typical of socialists faced by national questions. The majority of Marxists are found supporting the rival national camps, critically or uncritically;

while a minority of purists avoid, or appear to avoid, taking an explicit stand.[2] However, Marxist writers have been important, directly or indirectly, in shaping both internal and external commentaries on the region. That is why their explanations merit attention, even though the impact of Marxist revolutionaries on the Irish republican movement used to be routinely exaggerated – especially by the British diplomatic corps in the USA.

'Green' Marxists provide an exogenous explanation of the conflict. Their 'greenness' is not ecological, though it may be naive; it is shown in their bolstering of traditional Irish nationalism. They call political economy in aid, declaring British imperialism and capitalism the primary causes of the conflict. These explanations were prevalent amongst the Irish left in the late 1960s and early 1970s, especially amongst activists in the People's Democracy student-movement, which acted as a self-appointed vanguard of the Northern Ireland Civil Rights Association.[3] Many of the external investigations of Northern Ireland in the early 1970s were significantly affected by green Marxist reasoning,[4] which also had a powerful impact upon the thinking and propaganda of key figures in Sinn Féin, especially in the early and mid-1980s – notably in the writings of Gerry Adams, the President of Sinn Féin.[5] Green Marxist assumptions are also frequently voiced by observers from the academic left, in Britain, Ireland and North America.[6]

Green Marxist thought is of much older vintage than the late 1960s. It has direct historical antecedents in the writings of James Connolly, the socialist leader executed after the Easter Rebellion of 1916.[7] It has even older legitimacy for its perspectives in the Irish writings of Marx and Engels.[8] The founding fathers of historical materialism were sacred authorities in the writings of British and Irish Communists on the Irish question.[9] Green Marxism remains vibrant amongst the last stranded platoons of Irish and British Trotskyists,[10] and watered-down versions of their arguments still have an influential impact upon ultra-left members of the British and Irish Labour Parties, and provide the intellectual underpinning for the 'troops out' movement in Britain. This chapter first summarizes green Marxists' explanations of the genesis of the conflict, the violence, and the protracted constitutional stalemate, and then subjects these arguments to sceptical scrutiny.

Green Marxists locate the genesis of the conflict in British imperialism and capitalist colonialism. Ireland was England's first colony, and North-East Ulster was the site of extensive plantation by English and Scots settlers. The divisions between Catholics and Protestants were divisions between natives and settlers. The Protestant population of Northern Ireland are considered similar to the French *colons* of Algeria[11] and the white settlers of Rhodesia. The Irish nationalist revolution, from its first stirrings in the eighteenth century until the early twentieth century, is seen as a revolution against capitalist underdevelopment. Ireland was exploited by rack-renting landlords. Its industrial growth was inhibited because of the protectionist interests of British capitalists before 1800, and thereafter by the ruthless application of *laissez-faire* doctrines. The most dramatic evidence of underdevelopment, the great famine, led to a drop in the Irish population between 1847 and 1852 of 25 per cent through death and forced emigration.

The Irish nationalist revolution posed a serious threat to the interests of British landlords and capitalists, and consequently throughout the nineteenth century they created and aggravated divisions between Catholic and Protestant peasants and workers. 'Capitalism created sectarianism', as a spokesperson for the British Socialist Workers Party puts it.[12] The unionist coalition, of British and Irish Tories, was a reactionary and counter-revolutionary alliance. Connolly was therefore correct to align his Irish Citizen Army with the nationalist movement in the 1916 rising against British rule: in this stratagem lay the best hopes for a socialist revolution. The partition of Ireland was the response of British imperialism to the Irish nationalist revolution. It separated the resources of the industrially developed north-east from the more agrarian and economically backward south, west, and north-west.

That Protestants in the labour movement were resolutely hostile to home rule and Irish independence in 1913 was an awkward puzzle for James Connolly:

According to all Socialist theories North-East Ulster, being the most developed industrially, ought to be the quarter in which class lines of cleavage, politically and industrially, should be the most pronounced and class rebellion the most common. As a cold matter of fact, it is the happy hunting ground of the slave-driver and the home of the least rebellious slaves in the industrial world.[13]

Connolly 'solved' this paradox by invoking British-orchestrated manipulation: the 'perfectly devilish ingenuity of the master-class', the ceding of privileges to Ulster Protestants, and the power of Orange ideology, which equipped the minds of the people of North-East Ulster 'with conceptions of political activity fit only for the atmosphere of the seventeenth century'.[14]

He warned that partition would be disastrous for Irish socialists because it would sustain sectarian and national battle-cries at the expense of class issues.[15] His followers have taken their cue from their martyred idol. The weakness of Irish socialism is attributed to partition, which benefited the imperialist British state; and the anti-national Orangeism of the Protestant working-class is explained by its status as a 'labour aristocracy' – reaping the benefits of discrimination in the labour market, it has shown no interest in class solidarity. Until this material basis for reactionary politics is removed, Protestant working-class politics will remain retarded. It cannot be removed within existing political structures because Northern Ireland is an unreformable and fundamentally Orange statelet.[16]

The Northern Ireland problem is therefore reduced to one of 'uncompleted national revolution' against British imperialism. The ending of partition is the *sine qua non* for the development of socialism in Ireland. This logic leads many green Marxists to offer their 'critical support' to the Provisional IRA, despite their reservations about aspects of the latter's 'petit bourgeois nationalism'.[17]

In the first rush of blood to the head in the early 1970s some green Marxists attributed all the causes of political violence to capitalism: 'The psychopaths have not taken over. There is a war in Ireland because capitalism, to establish and preserve itself, created conditions which made war inevitable. Essentially there is no other reason. There rarely is for war.'[18]

More frequently green Marxists explain violence in Northern Ireland as the consequence of a war of national liberation, analogous to the wars conducted against imperialism elsewhere in the third world. This perspective is frankly endorsed by the smallest paramilitary organizations, the significantly named Irish National Liberation Army (INLA) and its factional successor the Irish People's Liberation Organization (IPLO). Loyalist violence, by contrast, is the backlash of the Protestant lumpenproletariat. The national liberation war must temporarily divide the Irish working class – pitting the underprivileged against the labour aristocracy. However, this divided working class is considered an artefact of imperialism and the British war of counter-insurgency, and, reassuringly, division will disappear in a post-revolutionary socialist Ireland.

That the Provisional IRA has never claimed to be waging a *Marxist* war of national liberation against British imperialism has been of some concern to green Marxists. The PIRA's opening statement suggested that its legitimacy and goals were derived from the revolutionary nationalist tradition rather than militant socialism:

> We declare our allegiance to the 32 county Irish Republic proclaimed at Easter 1916, established by the First Dail Eireann in 1919, overthrown by force of arms in 1922 and suppressed to this day by the existing British-imposed six county and twenty-six county partition states.[19]

The early leaders of the PIRA did, however, indicate their commitment to socialism, though not of the Marxist vintage,[20] as did the leaders of Provisional Sinn Féin.[21] The leadership of the Official IRA, left over by the formation of PIRA, had become explicitly Marxist–Leninist by the late 1960s, but had largely abandoned the goal of a national liberation war. Its leaders believed in a Stalinist three-stage theory of the Irish Revolution. Stage one would see the establishment of (proper) 'bourgeois democracy' in the North; stage two would see the development of an independent capitalist Ireland; and stage three would culminate in the creation of a socialist Ireland. In this perspective raising the national question before Northern Ireland had been reformed was politically premature,[22] and therefore the Provisional IRA's campaign was roundly condemned from 1969/70 onwards. For these reasons, amongst others of a decidedly non-theoretical nature, the Official IRA eventually became the most vigorous Marxist critics of the Provisionals, transforming themselves in the process into the Workers' Party.[23] Trotskyists were no less critical than the Officials, of the Catholicism and nationalism manifest in the leadership of the Provisional IRA.[24] However, they maintained that the Provisionals' campaign was objectively anti-imperialist and therefore merited the critical support of revolutionary socialists everywhere. Indeed one argued that 'The primary reason why the Provisionals exist is that "socialism" as we presented it was shown to be irrelevant. The Provisionals are the inrush which filled the vacuum left by the *absence* of a socialist option.'[25]

In the absence of evidence from the PIRA that it was fighting a Marxist-inspired national war of liberation, green Marxists have been content to see them as 'objective' revolutionaries, and used to relish British policy-makers' fears about Ireland as the Cuba of the western Atlantic. In the 1980s former British Secretary of State for Northern Ireland James Prior warned of 'the spectre of Marxism' and asserted that 'The Provisional IRA are not simply working for a united Ireland; their objective is a Marxist workers' party state, with all which that would imply not only for the people in the Province and the Republic, but also for the wider security of Britain and Western Europe.'[26] To green Marxists these judgements confirm that the IRA's war is part of a wider anti-capitalist movement. They believe, as Marx did, that the accomplishment of Irish self-determination through revolutionary violence will advance socialism in England and elsewhere.[27]

For green Marxists the political stalemate in Northern Ireland is proof that the 'statelet' is unreformable. Sectarianism will persist as long as Northern Ireland does. The responsibility for the stalemate lies with the British and Irish states which obstruct the full completion of the

Irish revolution. They reject the arguments that the Northern Irish or British labour movements are capable, in principle, of unifying the working class in Northern Ireland, through either trade unionist or electoral mobilization. They point out that the Northern Ireland Labour Party (NILP) failed to generate a significant cross-national appeal during the period of the Stormont parliament because of its eventual decision to support the Union, and that British Labour governments have repressed Irish nationalists as vigorously as have the Conservatives. The correct strategy for the British labour movement therefore is not to press for reform, but for the withdrawal of the British state from Ireland.

The most sophisticated green Marxists search for evidence to support the thesis that Northern Ireland cannot be reformed.[28] Since 1972, they argue, British direct rule has not accomplished the 'social democratization' of Northern Ireland. The British state has proved incapable of reforming Northern Ireland, despite its rhetoric to the contrary. Under direct rule sectarian social relations persist: in employment, trade unionism, regional policy, local government, housing segregation, and policing.

At least in the domain of employment these arguments have been substantially confirmed by subsequent independent research.[29] What is distinctive about these green Marxists is their belief that sectarian issues cannot be detached from class issues: 'To fundamentally reform sectarian division would be to transform class division – an impossibility for a capitalist state.'[30] The inference is that the end of the stalemate and sectarianism lie in a socialist Irish state.

## The Greenness of Green Marxism

Green Marxist discourse, like classical nationalism, faces powerful theoretical, ideological and empirical objections to its core theses. Its diagnosis of the conflict as colonial sits unhappily with the 'one nation' theory of traditional nationalists. Its explanation of the role of the British state in Ireland is implausibly instrumentalist. Its evidence that British imperialism motivates British policy-making is indeterminate about the past and unconvincing in the present. Its accounts of violence are suffused with wishful thinking, and its prescriptions for resolving the stalemate would be comic if it were not for the fact that they have been believed by significant agents in the British Isles.

*Is the conflict colonial by Marxist standards?* There is, as we argued in *The Politics of Antagonism*, considerable merit in understanding the origins of the Northern Ireland conflict in English and Scots colonial settlements of Ireland.[31] Appreciating the consequences of 'settler colonialism' is vital in any rounded account of eighteenth and nineteenth-century Irish politics, the formation of Northern Ireland, and the contemporary 'troubles'.[32] The system of direct rule, by which Northern Ireland has been governed since 1972, has also fuelled the colonial analogy – even amongst unionists.[33]

However, by conventional Marxist criteria understanding the dynamics of the current conflict in Northern Ireland as imperial or colonial is problematic. Consider Trotsky's theory of permanent revolution, which he applied to the entire colonial and ex-colonial world after 1924.[34] The theory asserted that after the Russian Revolution there could be no successful bourgeois revolution in any backward country, and no stable capitalist regime established before the onset of a proletarian revolution. The 'colonial bourgeoisie' could not attain national independence, solve the agrarian question, or establish bourgeois (parliamentary) regimes.

The development of the Irish Free State (and the Republic of Ireland) refutes Trotsky's theory of the colonial world on all three counts – apart from the Republic's failure to obtain jurisdiction over Northern Ireland. Most of Ireland won formal political independence from Britain in 1922, and full effective sovereignty by 1937. The Irish agrarian question, the land-hunger of the semi-feudal peasantry, had been solved by the British state before 1920. Finally, parliamentary institutions were established in both parts of Ireland after 1920, even if the liberal and democratic character of the northern set was questionable.[35]

In short, conflict in Northern Ireland is not focused on what

Marxists have traditionally understood to be classical colonial issues – land ownership rights for peasants and overt political dictatorship by foreigners. These facts create tensions for green Marxist thinking. If the colonial interpretation is wholly correct it is not at all clear why the settlers (Protestants) should be willing to embrace Irish nationalism when British imperialism is defeated. The favoured Algerian analogy would suggest that the settlers' resistance to native nationalism is deep-rooted and not artificially sustained by the metropolis. Green Marxists would have a more coherent – if more morally objectionable – thesis if they argued that decolonization is the best prescription for the conflict, and if they declared that 'Brits out' meant the expropriation – and if necessary the expulsion – of the descendants of those who settled Northern Ireland nearly four centuries ago.[36] However, once one concedes that the conflict is indeed centred on national issues or national identity rather than colonial issues – like 'foreign' and 'foreign aristocratic' land ownership and formal exclusion of natives from citizenship – questions arise as to why Marxists should support one nation rather than another, and why, tactically, they should believe that socialist politics stands a better chance of progress in Ireland than in Britain.

The attempts of green Marxists to explain the political behaviour of Ulster Protestants within a theory of imperialism are economically reductionist and unpersuasive. The undeniable evidence of economic discrimination against Catholics in employment, housing and local government administration, and of Protestants' differentially privileged status in Northern Ireland both before and after 1972, in our judgement do not account for the intensity of loyalist hostility to Irish nationalism. Green Marxists too readily assume that Protestant consciousness is either manipulated or narrowly instrumental. When discussing the formation of Northern Ireland, Michael Farrell asserts that 'The Unionist leaders were not free agents: they had mobilised the Protestant masses to resist Home Rule and inclusion in the Free State, through the policy of discrimination and the ideology of Protestant supremacy. Now their followers were seeking their reward. If a lasting loyalty to the new state was to develop among the Protestant masses, they had to be given a privileged position within it.'[37] As one critic comments, 'This is to claim, not just that these devices strengthened the intensity of Protestant workers' feelings, but that they altered their direction. The implication is that the Protestant working class, if it had not been stirred by "the policy of discrimination and the ideology of Protestant supremacy" would have been instinctively Irish rather than British.'[38] It also suggests that Protestant supremacism was orchestrated 'from above' rather than produced 'from below'. This is a standard defect in Marxist accounts of the formation of ideological beliefs:[39] the fact that certain ideological beliefs may benefit a ruling class is not proof that those beliefs are caused by the ruling class, even though they may take advantage of them. Green Marxists wishfully think that freed from the baneful influence of their ruling class, after the completion of the Irish revolution, the Protestant working class will regard themselves as nationally and politically Irish, a belief which now seems increasingly incredible. Treating national, ethnic and religious discourses as 'superstructural', epiphenomena of economic structures and ruling class interests, is classical historical materialism,[40] but it does not advance understanding of Northern Ireland.

*Why does the British state do what it does?* The mechanisms which lock the British state into a pro-unionist position are not persuasively specified by green Marxists. Instrumental accounts of British interests in Ireland maintain that:

> Britain's interests in Ireland have varied greatly since 1169, when its feudal barons first started to occupy the country.[41] Its rulers today have five reasons for interference: firstly, the historic 'Northern Irish Connection', through which they are influenced by the leading families of the six counties Protestant community; secondly, the military aspect: Northern Ireland is a useful bridgehead on an island that commands Britain's western approaches; thirdly, the fear that social revolution might arise out of any escalated anti-imperialist struggle, as was happening in 1921 and, less effectively, in 1972; fourthly, the classic 'imperialist' reason – economic investment; this, however, has only recently become more important than the fifth reason for British intervention – Irish investment in Britain, its colonies and dominions.[42]

Even if Britain, or its ruling class, has all these interests in Ireland, no account is offered of how and why these interests motivate the British state. It is simply assumed that British capitalist interests motivate the actions of the personnel of the British state. No proof is offered of the continuing pull of key Anglo-Irish families on the British establishment. Little evidence is supplied of the salience of Britain's 'bridgehead' interests, or of the fear of a wider social revolution emanating from Ireland – and while it may have been true once, it cannot be true since the end of the Cold War. Lastly, the idea that the objective, let alone subjective, interests of British capitalists lie in Northern Ireland staying within the United Kingdom is absurd.[43]

The key questions in appraising the merits of green Marxist accounts are whether imperialism explains the role of the British state in Northern Ireland, whether this state is capable of reforming Northern Ireland, and whether a socialist state would do the job any better. We shall examine the reformability of Northern Ireland and the merits of socialist prescriptions later. Here we shall evaluate imperialist interpretations of the conflict, considering in order economic, populist, and geo-political understandings of imperialism.

*Economic imperialism?* At the turn of the twentieth century what became Northern Ireland was a site for the extraction of substantial surplus value, to use Marxist terminology. Belfast and the Lagan valley were the centres of the UK linen trade. Ulster linen companies were major exporters, and Belfast's York Street Flax Spinning Mill was the largest in the world. Major engineering companies grew up to supply the linen industry. While Ulster's distilling and brewing industries were sizeable, Belfast's industries were of world-scale significance. Harland and Wolff's shipyard was the largest in the UK, and its dry dock was the most extensive in the world. Over a quarter of a million shipbuilding tonnage was launched in Belfast in 1914. Ireland was in several respects a highly developed region by the end of the century, but its industrial prosperity was concentrated in Belfast: a city whose population had grown from 20,000 in 1800 to 349,000 in 1901, a growth-rate of 3 per cent per annum during the nineteenth century.[44] The

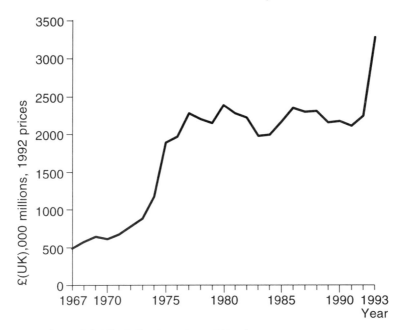

**Figure 2.1** The UK subvention of Northern Ireland, 1969–93
*Source*: Brendan O'Leary, Tom Lyne, Jim Marshall and
Bob Rowthorn, *Northern Ireland: Sharing Authority*
(London: IPPR, 1993), 77.

proportion of industrial output exported from Ireland in
1907 was 'remarkably high', half of the total, 'well in excess
of the corresponding total for Britain or any major country'.
However, 'apart from processed foods and drink, in which the
greater part of exports came from the south, £19.1 million of
the total non-food manufactures of £20.9 were in categories
predominantly produced in the Belfast region'.[45]

In short, there are grounds for supposing that partition
and keeping Northern Ireland, or at least the Belfast region,
within the United Kingdom were in the economic interests
of British imperialists. However, it does not follow that these
interests dictated British policy-making between 1918 and
1925. Historians of partition document British policy-makers'
concern with the integrity of the empire and the territorial
integrity of the United Kingdom rather than a preoccupation
with the economic wealth of the Lagan valley. Historians also
demonstrate that unionists were concerned to ensure that the

largest feasible number of unionists/Protestants, including denizens of undeveloped and agrarian Donegal, could stay within the UK. Unionists certainly argued against home rule and Irish independence on economic grounds,[46] but it does not follow, as Eamonn McCann asserts, that 'The motivation of the Orange leaders *was and is* economic self-interest.'[47] Had economic imperialism motivated the partition arrangements then there would have been no reason for Northern Ireland to include Fermanagh, Tyrone, Londonderry County, South Armagh, and South Down.[48] If economic interests were all that were at stake in the home-rule controversies why were national and religious rhetorics so prevalent amongst both politicians, the press, and the broader public of the British Isles? The classical Marxist answer is that these rhetorics masked economic interests, but this answer begs at least two questions: why were economic interests dressed in national and religious language, and why were the Protestant and Catholic working classes open to such appeals? The mechanisms by which economic imperialist interests allegedly dictated British public policy on the Ulster question before 1920 are not demonstrated, and do not satisfactorily explain the rapport between 'Orangeism' and the 'social imperialism' of the Conservative Unionists.

Whatever one's judgement on the explanatory power of the theory of economic imperialism in motivating British policy before 1920–5, no one can dispute that the objective economic reasons for retaining Northern Ireland within the United Kingdom have declined exponentially over time. Northern Ireland has long ceased to be a good source of surplus value. The Stormont government was extensively subsidized by the British Treasury, especially after the Labour government's extension of the welfare state in 1945. Northern Ireland's major industries experienced rapid falls in output and in their share of world trade in the inter-war years. After World War II nearly all industrial growth was attributable to the operations of large outside firms, rather than local industry: a mere 8.5 per cent of industrial jobs promoted between 1947 and 1967 were created by local companies.[49] The upward trend in the UK subvention of Northern Ireland, i.e. the gap between what is raised in taxation from Northern Ireland and what

**Table 2.1** The UK subvention of Northern Ireland, 1966–93

| Year (i) | Actual Prices £ millions | | | 1992 Prices £ millions (iv) | | |
|---|---|---|---|---|---|---|
| | including security | excluding security | extra army costs | including security | excluding security | extra army costs |
| 1967 (ii) | 52 | – | (iii) | 489 | – | – |
| 1968 (ii) | 63 | – | (iii) | 576 | – | – |
| 1969 (ii) | 74 | – | (iii) | 644 | – | – |
| 1970 (ii) | 74 | – | 2 | 612 | – | 17 |
| 1971 (ii) | 88 | – | 7 | 673 | – | 54 |
| 1972 (ii) | 126 | – | 14 | 883 | – | 98 |
| 1973 (ii) | 181 | – | 29 | 1173 | – | 188 |
| 1974 | 312 | 292 | 33 | 1890 | 1769 | 200 |
| 1975 | 389 | 280 | 45 | 1969 | 1417 | 228 |
| 1976 | 565 | 413 | 60 | 2279 | 1666 | 242 |
| 1977 | 620 | 450 | 65 | 2202 | 1598 | 231 |
| 1978 | 688 | 515 | 69 | 2149 | 1609 | 216 |
| 1979 | 848 | 648 | 81 | 2389 | 1826 | 228 |
| 1980 | 944 | 695 | 96 | 2280 | 1678 | 232 |
| 1981 | 1090 | 781 | 111 | 2224 | 1594 | 226 |
| 1982 | 1064 | 716 | 149 | 1980 | 1332 | 277 |
| 1983 | 1149 | 783 | 143 | 1996 | 1360 | 248 |
| 1984 | 1305 | 921 | 141 | 2167 | 1529 | 234 |
| 1985 | 1489 | 1077 | 121 | 2353 | 1702 | 191 |
| 1986 | 1536 | 1087 | 135 | 2301 | 1629 | 202 |
| 1987 | 1593 | 1099 | 144 | 2312 | 1595 | 209 |
| 1988 | 1570 | 1010 | 166 | 2160 | 1390 | 228 |
| 1989 | 1698 | 1095 | 174 | 2178 | 1404 | 223 |
| 1990 | 1757 | 1095 | 201 | 2115 | 1318 | 242 |
| 1991 | 2018 | 1291 | 218 | 2249 | 1439 | 243 |
| 1992 | 2436 | 1620 | 317 | 2540 | 1689 | 330 |
| 1993 (v) | 3296 | 2365 | (v) | 3296 | 2365 | (vi) |

(i)     Year = Fiscal Year, e.g. 1967 = Fiscal Year 1966/67.
(ii)    Separate figures for security costs within subvention are available only from 1973/74. Until 1978/79 the costs shown were law-and-order costs borne on United Kingdom votes: from 1979/80 the costs are those of the Northern Ireland Office and the Northern Ireland Court Service.
(iii)   Figures for extra army costs are available only from 1969/70.
(iv)    Actual prices have been converted to 1992 prices by applying the appropriate Gross Domestic Product deflator.
(v)     Figures for 1992/93 and 1993/94 are provisional. Revised figure for the total subvention in 1992/93 is £3,156,000,000; the estimate for 1993/94 is £3,394,000,000 (Hansard, 13 July 1994, Written Answer 100).
(vi)    Figures for extra army costs for 1992/93 and 1993/94 not available.
*Source:* House of Commons Parliamentary Question, Hansard, 22 March 1993, col. 498.

is spent by the UK state in the region, shows a picture of increasing dependency (see figure 2.1, p. 73 and table 2.1, p. 75). In 1971/72, at the start of direct rule, the subvention was £126 million. By 1988/9 it had increased to £1.7 billion – or to £1.9 billion if we include the cost of maintaining the British Army and European Community receipts.[50] Since the population of the region is about one and a half million people each inhabitant of Northern Ireland in 1989/90 was therefore subsidized by the British state and the European Community to the tune of nearly £1,500 per annum – and more if we take into consideration the 'one-off' payments to Shorts Brothers PLC in 1988–90. The estimate for the fiscal year 1993/94, when this book went to press, suggested that the annual subvention had risen to £3.4 billion, a per capita subvention of approximately £2,000.[51]

The data in table 2.2 demonstrate that public expenditure per head in Northern Ireland, even excluding military expenditure, was consistently higher than in the rest of the UK in the fifteen years after the introduction of direct rule – which is hardly what one would expect of an exploited territory, especially one without valuable raw materials. In 1990 public expenditure per head for the four territories of the UK was as follows: England, £2,161; Wales, £2,489; Scotland, £2,805; and Northern Ireland, £3,626. The Northern Ireland figure was £1,350, or 60 per cent, higher than the UK average. There are good welfare-state and technical reasons why public expenditure per head should be higher in Northern Ireland than elsewhere in the UK[52] but this subvention does not conform to any Marxist model of economic imperialism known to us.

The region is, in strictly Marxist terms, a site of unproductive labour. The proportion of workers employed in manufacturing has been constantly declining. In 1970 almost 32 per cent of the labour force worked in manufacturing, by 1980 the figure was 22.6 per cent, and by 1990 it had fallen to 18 per cent.[53] Northern Ireland is a lame duck region in which industrial subsidies are much higher than in other depressed areas of the United Kingdom. It is a 'workhouse economy' in which a large part of the population is unemployed, while those

**Table 2.2** Identifiable public expenditure per head in Northern Ireland as a percentage of UK identifiable public expenditure per head, 1973–88

| Year | (a) | (b) | (c) | (d) | (e) | (f) | (g) | (h) | (i) | (j) |
|------|-----|-----|-----|-----|-----|-----|-----|-----|-----|-----|
| 1973/74 | 116.4 | | | | | | | | | |
| 1974/75 | 132.9 | 132.6 | | | | | | | | |
| 1975/76 | 137.8 | 137.5 | 136.5 | | | | | | | |
| 1976/77 | 140.9 | 140.7 | 139.3 | 146.3 | | | | | | |
| 1977/78 | 144.2 | 147.5 | 147.0 | 149.8 | 151.3 | | | | | |
| 1978/79 | | 152.6 | 152.9 | 152.9 | 154.5 | | | | | |
| 1979/80 | | | 147.7 | 147.5 | 148.9 | 149.1 | | | | |
| 1980/81 | | | | 146.5 | 146.9 | 148.7 | 146.6 | | | |
| 1981/82 | | | | | 147.2 | 147.3 | 145.2 | 145.8 | | |
| 1982/83 | | | | | | 146.6 | 144.5 | 145.4 | 141.0 | |
| 1983/84 | | | | | | 149.4 | 145.8 | 146.3 | 141.9 | 142.8 |
| 1984/85 | | | | | | | 148.2 | 146.4 | 141.9 | 142.8 |
| 1985/86 | | | | | | | | 148.1 | 142.8 | 144.0 |
| 1986/87 | | | | | | | | | 142.9 | 143.5 |
| 1987/88 | | | | | | | | | | 143.3 |

Key: Calculations (a)–(j) are based on parliamentary answers in Hansard in the years 1979–88 (David Heald, *Financing a Scottish Parliament: Options for Debate* (Glasgow, 1990), table 6.

*Source*: Adapted from David Heald, *Formula-based Territorial Expenditure in the United Kingdom* (mimeo, 1989); 'Financing an Assembly', in D. McCrone (ed.), *Financing Home Rule* (Edinburgh, 1990); and *Financing a Scottish Parliament: Options for Debate* (Glasgow, 1990).

**Table 2.3** Total public assistance as a percentage of manufacturing GDP factor cost in Britain and Ireland, 1985–6

| | |
|---|---|
| England | 0.5 |
| Scotland | 3.7 |
| Wales | 4.5 |
| Republic of Ireland | 13.0 |
| Northern Ireland | 18.3 |

*Source*: D. M. W. N. Hitchens, J. E. Birnie and K. Wagner, 'Economic Performance in Northern Ireland: A Comparative Perspective', in P. Teague (ed.), *The Economy of Northern Ireland: Perspectives for Structural Change* (London: Lawrence and Wishart, 1993), 44.

who are not 'are chiefly engaged in servicing or controlling each other – through the provision of health education, retail distribution, construction, security and local services . . . Like a typical workhouse, it is supported by taxes levied on the external community, while providing very little in return.'[54] These facts constantly provoke comment in the pro-capitalist press. For instance, in an article subtitled 'Dividends of Death' Britain's most reputable news magazine to espouse economic liberalism, *The Economist*, complains that 'Northern Ireland's economy resembles more closely that of an Eastern European country than Margaret Thatcher's privatising Britain. The ratio of public spending to GDP has been rising inexorably to 78% even while it has been falling for Britain as a whole.'[55] Indeed by some criteria of economic policy-making Northern Ireland is the most socialist region in the United Kingdom. In December 1991, 38 per cent of employed workers were in public-sector occupations. There is very widespread agreement that Northern Ireland suffers from an economic 'dependency culture' amongst both its workers and its capitalists. Public-sector jobs, paid at GB national rates, are the most secure and best paid, and reduce the attractiveness of private-sector work or self-employment. Moreover, the private sector is heavily dependent on public-sector grants and subsidies. The subsidization of inefficiency is more extensive in Northern Ireland than in any other region of the UK, or in the Republic (see table 2.3). These facts falsify any green Marxist supposition that Britain's continuing interest in Northern Ireland is fundamentally economic,[56] unless one supposes that British imperialists are serviced by exceptionally incompetent accountants.

*Populist Imperialism?* Eamonn McCann's *War and an Irish Town*[57] places imperialism and capitalism centre-stage in his account of the conflict. He also regards nationalist republicanism as more progressive than loyalist unionism, a species of populist imperialism: 'the Republican tradition, for all the distortions of history contained within it, stemmed from a genuine, if episodic, anti-imperialist struggle; the Orange tradition, was, objectively, pro-imperialist'.[58] However, McCann differs from his fellow green Marxists. He recognizes, first, that nationalist and Orange ideologies can be relatively autonomous from economic interests: 'ideologies and the political institutions which embody ideologies do not necessarily exist in a constant state of adaptation to the changing needs of the class in whose interests they were originally built. They can resist change. They can have a life of their own and in certain circumstances they can fight for their life.'[59] Secondly, he recognizes that Protestants' fears of Catholicism have played some role in forming their political preferences.[60] Finally, he thinks that Britain's economic interests in Ireland have changed since the nineteenth century; there is no longer an economic basis for partition; and it is now in Britain's interests to balance orange and green, North and South, Protestant and Catholic capitalism in Ireland.[61] But if one accepts the merits of McCann's departures from Connollyite Marxism, and agrees that Orange sentiment and loyalist pro-imperialism have lives of their own, the question necessarily arises: what is the nature of Britain's imperialist interest in maintaining Northern Ireland as part of the United Kingdom?

One answer might be 'populist imperialism'. Following McCann, one might regard populist imperialism as an autonomous ideology, now detached from the economic conditions which originally gave rise to it but still vital in the British political arena. Before 1920 a considerable proportion of the population of Great Britain, of all social classes, supported the Unionist party, as the Conservatives were then known, and embraced an ideology of populist imperialism. These sentiments, and their manipulation, played key roles in UK general elections from the 1880s until the 1920s. However, since then the ability of Ulster Protestants to generate a populist appeal within the rest of the United Kingdom has declined dramatically. Opinion polls consistently show that Britons in Great Britain do not regard Northern Ireland as part of their country.[62] They also show consistent support for a British withdrawal from Northern Ireland, although not necessarily support for a united Ireland. There is therefore little mileage for British politicians in making support for Ulster unionists an issue of national pride or regime-integrity. 'Kith and kin' imperialist ideology amongst the British political class, despite the Falklands/Malvinas war, is not as strong as it was at the turn of the century, and given the British public's attitudes towards Northern Ireland it is difficult to see why populist imperialism should motivate British politicians. Indifference, ignorance, and even idiocy may characterize British policy-making, but not populist imperialism.

*Military or geo-political imperialism?* Another explanation of British imperialism roots it in geo-political rather than populist motivations. By the 1980s Sinn Féin organs, influenced by green Marxist thinking, had abandoned the idea that economic imperialism motivated the British state:

> The British presence, which once made sense in classic imperialist/capitalist terms, can now only be explained in terms of the strategic interest of NATO, and can properly be defined as political imperialism.[63]

What are the merits of this view? Historians agree that Britain's Irish policy in the 1920s, in the 1930s, and during and immediately after World War II, was critically shaped by security considerations.[64] Ireland's neutrality has never been welcome to Britain, whether during World War II or the Falklands/Malvinas war of 1982. Green Marxists therefore have a point, though they overplay their hand.

They, understandably, make much of classified deliberations by British politicians and civil servants after World War II.[65] In 1949 the then Labour cabinet secretly approved a paper which argued that 'as a matter of first-class strategic importance' Northern Ireland 'should continue to form part of His Majesty's Dominions'. It also stated that because of this strategic importance 'it seems unlikely that Britain would ever be able to agree to Northern Ireland leaving His Majesty's jurisdiction . . . *even if the people of Northern Ireland desired it*' (our emphasis). So much for the unity-by-consent option in the Ireland Act then going through the Westminster parliament! The real, but secret, interest of the British state was to maintain Northern Ireland in perpetuity. In 1951 a British Commonwealth Relations Office document, made public in 1982, reiterated Britain's strategic interest:

> Historically, Ireland, which has never been able to protect
> herself against invasion, has been, as she is today, a poten-
> tial base for attack on the United Kingdom. It is the more
> important that a part of the island, and that one strategically
> well-placed, should . . . remain part of the United Kingdom and
> of the United Kingdom defence scheme . . . A United Ireland
> whose willingness and unqualified co-operation could not with
> certainty be relied on, which was neutral, or which was sharply
> divided over neutrality, would be a major problem in the
> defence of the United Kingdom and in the defence and
> support of Western Europe.[66]

Green Marxists also emphasize the widely quoted remarks of
Sir Ian McGough, a former British vice-admiral and NATO
naval commander, that the island of Ireland's strategic significance 'can hardly be exaggerated', and that this fact dictated
a pro-unionist posture by the British government, given the
possible danger of a militant left-wing government in Eire in
time of war with the USSR![67]

When they raise the geo-political dimensions of British
interests in Ireland after 1920 green Marxists are on very
much stronger ground than when they contend that economic
or populist imperialism explains British policy.[68] However,
their case is weakened, but not refuted, by at least four
considerations. First, they operate with a monolithic model
of the British state which assumes that defence/foreign affairs
interests have been paramount over all other considerations
in Anglo-Irish relations. They therefore neglect the evidence
of rival and competing perspectives on Britain's Irish policy
between the 1880s and the 1980s – as well as the autonomous
significance of Ulster unionists in shaping the policies of
the British state and the Conservative Party in particular.
Secondly, they assume that after 1920 – or after 1945 –
Britain's strategic interest dictated maintaining the status quo
in Northern Ireland. This perspective overlooks the possibility
that a united and independent Ireland within NATO would
have met British defence/geo-political interests just as well –
indeed several military commanders considered this solution

the best one from the perspective of British interests. Thirdly, much of the historical evidence furnished by green Marxists comes from the immediate aftermath of World War II, and the beginnings of the most intense phase of the Cold War. Given that Ireland had been neutral during World War II – despite the offer of possible Irish unity in return for support for Britain – the tone of secret British policy-formulation during 1949–51 is unsurprising, if no less reprehensible. Finally, the geo-political salience of Ireland, whether in the eyes of green Marxists or British generals, presently looks anachronistic.

The end of the Cold War has not, yet, led to a British reversal of its commitment to Northern Ireland. It is true that Peter Brooke's 1990 statement, repeated by John Major in the Downing Street Declaration in 1993, which maintains that Britain has no 'selfish, strategic' interest in being in Northern Ireland, was not made until the end of the Cold War was apparent. However, the fact is that the British commitment to the Union remains, at least formally – and it is based on the wishes of the local majority in Northern Ireland. One would have expected, if green Marxists had been right, that the following reasoning should have been widespread in the British policy elite after the end of the Cold War: 'Given that the strategic significance of Northern Ireland has now disappeared, why should we stay?' On and off-the-record statements of this nature abound in Whitehall and Westminster but it is not obvious that they determine policy. The British government is committed to facilitating 'an agreed Ireland' even though it no longer has any obvious strategic interest in Ireland.

*How National Liberationist has the long war been?* Green Marxist descriptions of violence in Northern Ireland as akin to third world national liberation struggles are less compelling than their accusations of past British imperialism. The conflict in Northern Ireland is not agrarian. There are no land-hungry peasants mobilized against the British imperial state. It is not a Maoist war of the countryside against the city. The epicentres of violence are either urban, like Belfast and Derry/Londonderry, or areas contiguous to the border in South Armagh, Fermanagh and Tyrone – though there is also considerable violence in mid-Ulster.[69] In urban areas much of the violence takes place in 'shatter-zones' which demarcate Catholic from Protestant residential areas, or in Catholic areas 'policed' by the security forces. Since the termination of 'no go' areas in the early 1970s there are no regions of Northern Ireland held and administered as 'liberated zones' by the Provisional IRA, even if there are very large tracts where the British Army fear to tread.

Many of the colonial war analogies proffered by green Marxists are unpersuasive. The IRA's war is not analogous to that waged by the Viet Cong because, unlike the latter, they do not enjoy the active military support of the contiguous state which they are fighting to unite with, and they do not enjoy the tacit support of the majority within the conflict-zone itself. Its war is not analogous to that waged by the Zimbabwean liberation movements either in scale or in levels of popular support. The same is true of the most favoured analogy – by any comparison the Algerian FLN enjoyed much greater support in its war against France than the IRA presently enjoys throughout the whole of Ireland. These considerations do not suggest that there is nothing to be said for the colonial analogy. However, they caution against assimilating the Northern Ireland conflict to what green Marxists, *qua* Marxists, should understand as a colonial war of national liberation.

Three types of warfare have been taking place in Northern Ireland since 1969:[70]

- *Classical guerrilla warfare* has been waged between the IRA (and other nationalist paramilitaries) and the security forces. Attacks, mainly by the IRA, have been made on the security forces, on central and local government personnel and installations, and on the infrastructure of the state (public transport, utilities, communication-systems, post offices and so on). There have been corresponding defensive *and* offensive actions by the security forces. They have ranged from peace-keeping operations, through pacification, to counter-insurgency actions. They have also included 'shoot-to-kill' or 'dirty war' practices.[71]
- *Economic guerrilla warfare* has been waged, mainly by the IRA, on commercial and industrial targets. Until 1976–7

the purpose of this warfare was to raise the costs to the British state of staying in Northern Ireland. It was reduced in scale after the mid-1970s because of the desire of the IRA not to antagonize the nationalist community, which reacts adversely to the consequences of the economic activities of the national liberationists. However, in 1988–9 the IRA resumed economic bombing, in both urban Northern Ireland and Great Britain, culminating with massive, spectacular explosions in the City of London in 1992 and 1993.

- *Sectarian or ethnic warfare* has been waged by loyalist paramilitaries against Catholic civilians, and by republican paramilitaries against Protestant civilians. Such attacks have been perpetrated in or on private residences, schools, public halls, clubs, bars, and any other building or location identified with one ethnic or religious group (although churches are very rarely chosen). Retaliatory violence has taken place in the same fora. 'Representative violence' in the form of assassinations has been enacted in revenge: people have been killed solely because of their presumed national or religious identity.[72] Strategies of 'communal deterrence' have also been pursued: paramilitary marching to display ethnic resources and power, and intimidation of homes and workplaces to prevent collaboration across the ethnic or sectarian divide.[73]

Variations of each of the first two types of warfare have been carried on outside Northern Ireland, although outside Northern Ireland *symbolic* warfare has been more important. It has largely been executed by the IRA in England, targeting the key institutions of the British political establishment since the mid-1970s. From the late 1980s the IRA has also sought to conduct classical and economic guerrilla warfare in England, and against British personnel in continental Europe, and with some impact.[74] By contrast loyalist violence against targets in the Republic has been less extensive and sustained – although loyalists were responsible for the biggest single incident of the present conflict when 33 civilian shoppers were killed by bombs left in Dublin and Monaghan streets in May 1974.

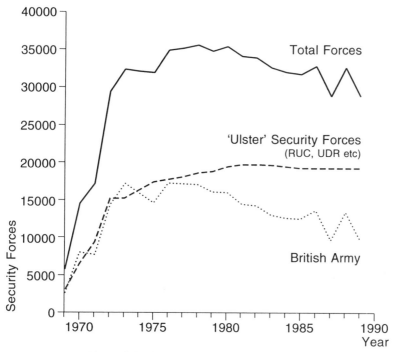

**Figure 2.2** The Ulsterization ratio, 1969–89
*Source*: Adapted from data in Irish Information Partnership,
*Agenda* (1990), 316.

Classical and economic guerrilla warfare characterize all
national liberation conflicts. Much is made by green Marxists of
the scale and nature of British counter-insurgency operations,
black propaganda, and dirty war,[75] although journalists and
other investigators are more sceptical of the degree of official
state-organization of such ventures.[76] Wherever the truth lies
there is a growing literature on British counter-insurgency
scandals in Northern Ireland,[77] and British security forces
have frequently transgressed the rule of law. However, the
'purity' of guerrilla warfare against an imperialist force is
severely compromised by the scale of killing of Protestant
civilians, and by the fact that a very high proportion of the
security forces are members of the locally recruited RUC, the
UDR and the RIR, i.e. 'Ulster Protestants in uniform'. The IRA
may see them all as members of an imperial war-machine, but

in the eyes of Ulster Protestants guerrilla warfare against the local security forces is simply sectarian violence.

Ulsterization, the increasing proportion of the total security forces comprised of local recruits (the RUC and the UDR) as opposed to British soliders, is plotted in figure 2.2 for the years 1969–89. From 1975–6 Ulsterization increased every year until the signing of the Anglo-Irish Agreement in 1985. The deaths suffered by members of the local security forces as a ratio of deaths suffered by members of the British Army consistently rose in the same period.[78] Ulsterization produced a convenient result for the British government. What the British public regarded as Irish people were doing most of the killing or policing of Irish people. British policy-makers were therefore not constrained by large losses of 'real British' lives (i.e. Great British soldiers). Ulsterization and its consequences may also have inhibited potential dissatisfaction within the British Army. Green Marxists claim that 'Ulsterization' hides the real 'anti-imperialist' nature of the war. They see it as analogous to the discredited 'Vietnamization' policy pursued by the American government before it withdrew from South-East Asia.

There is certainly merit in interpreting Ulsterization as a British policy which shifted the costs (and employment-benefits) of security to the local population. However, the scale of ethnic or sectarian warfare within Northern Ireland is a severe embarrassment for the thesis that violence resulted from a war of national liberation focused on the British war machine. According to our analysis 37 per cent of killings caused by republican paramilitaries between 1969 and 1989 were of civilians, i.e. people with no known connection with the security forces or paramilitary organizations. They numbered 597 persons. For loyalist paramilitaries the corresponding figures were 90 per cent, and 634 persons. For the security forces the equivalent figures were 54 per cent, and 136 persons. Republican paramilitaries were killing non-civilians just over 6 times out of 10, not an especially impressive ratio for a national liberation army. Moreover the killings of civilians by paramilitaries (44 per cent of all deaths) outnumbered deaths caused by war between the security forces and republican paramilitaries (35 per cent of all deaths), internecine conflict and self-killings within paramilitary organizations (6.5 per cent of all deaths), and the killings of Catholic civilians by the security forces.[79] Data from a more recent analysis of all republican killings since 1969 is displayed in figure 2.3. It suggests that unintended killings (executing the wrong targets, and other unintended deaths such as IRA activists blowing themselves up by mistake) comprised 21 per cent of all republican killings after 1969, while deliberate sectarian killings comprised 6 per cent of all republican killings. Sectarian killings by loyalist paramilitaries, by contrast, comprised 78 per cent of all deaths caused by loyalist paramilitaries after 1969.[80]

Green Marxists contend that it is not unusual for an imperial power to rely upon 'settlers' to man counter-insurgency armies, or to rely upon 'divide and rule' tactics to divide the 'native population'. However, such arguments must mean that Protestants are, and are seen as, members of another, or a settler, nation. For honest republicans much of the warfare must be seen as conflict between fellow Irish people, including the 'temporarily pro-British', and such intra-national or sectarian

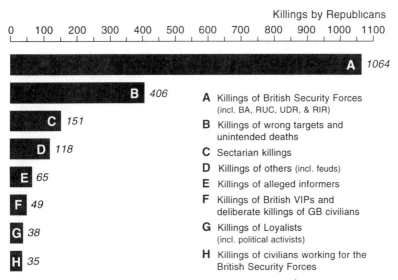

**Figure 2.3** Victims of republican killings, 1969–93
*Source*: Calculated from Malcolm Sutton, *An Index of Deaths from the Conflict in Ireland, 1969–1993* (Belfast: Beyond the Pale Publications, 1994), 196–201.

warfare is not class warfare. Class analysis suggests that war within Northern Ireland has been waged between ethnically or religiously differentiated sections of the working class, small farmers, and the unemployed.[81] The occupations of those killed by the IRA and other paramilitaries in Great Britain between 1969 and March 1993 demonstrate that military or political personnel make up 45 per cent of those killed. The rest have been civilians. Indeed civilian workers, children and the unemployed killed in bombings and other attacks outnumber the service personnel killed in Great Britain (see table 2.4, p. 90). Irish republicans have killed the British working class in Great Britain more often than British service personnel or the elite policy-makers in Great Britain, again evidence of *inter-national* rather than class warfare.

Liberal democracies outside the British Isles have not seen the conflict as a war of national liberation, but rather as an ethnic war or as a holy war. Sympathy for the green Marxist interpretation of the conflict has been found in African national liberation movements, including the ANC, which share an historic animus against British imperialism. British actions in Northern Ireland, including internment without trial, torture, systematic departures from the rule of law, violation of human rights, and repression have caused its policy-makers extensive embarrassment upon the world stage, but Northern Ireland has not become a vibrant international issue, deliberated upon in the United Nations in the normal manner in which colonial questions are treated. There are of course non-intellectual reasons why the definition of the Northern Ireland question as a colonial war of national liberation has not been accepted by the United Nations, such as Britain's status as a Security Council member in possession of a veto, the Anglo-American relationship, Ireland's reluctance to play the colonial card in this forum since the 1950s, and the narrow interpretation of self-determination characteristic of what passes for international law. The pre-*perestroika* Soviet Union made little effort to raise the Northern Ireland question in anti-imperialist discourse. It merely used it for debating points against British Cold War propaganda.[82] Moreover, the United Nations is a club of states not a club of nations, and few states can afford the luxury of supporting the IRA's national liberation struggle, or any other, given that so many of them are vulnerable to secessionist or irredentist claims.[83] Green Marxists have therefore had little success in defining the Northern Ireland conflict on the world-stage as an anti-colonial war of national liberation,[84] although they have influenced the thinking of some European socialists.

The most powerful green Marxist argument suggests that Northern Ireland is unreformable by the British state, and that this fact explains the protracted stalemate.[85] This argument has strong empirical evidence to support it. Northern Ireland after 1920 was characterized by domination and discrimination by Ulster Protestants: in politics, law, employment, public administration, housing, education and culture.[86] Since 1972, under direct rule, successive British governments have failed to eradicate direct and indirect discrimination or to provide effective equality of opportunity for Catholics in employment and in housing.[87] They have also failed to establish a system of policing and an administration of justice which are effectively reformed and widely legitimate and seen to be reformed and widely legitimate. Even the oldest university in the region, Queen's University, Belfast, had not eradicated discriminatory employment practices by the late 1980s, according to the reports of the Fair Employment Commission.[88] We accept and have emphasized in our own work the evidence that the British state has failed to reform Northern Ireland. However, this evidence does not prove that the failure to reform Northern Ireland has been caused by the status of the British state as either capitalist or imperialist – even though there may be good arguments for claiming that the British state is both capitalist and historically imperialist. This evidence also does not prove that a Marxist-led, inspired, or critically supported revolution would eradicate ethnic or sectarian conflict in Northern Ireland, or that a united Irish state would be more successful in reforming communal relations within the region than the British state has been.

The failure of the British state to reform Northern Ireland,

**Table 2.4** Occupations of those killed in Great Britain as a result of
Northern Ireland related violence, 1969–16 March 1993

| Category of victim | Number killed | % of total |
|---|---|---|
| *Political/military personnel* | 52 | 45.2 |
| Members of Parliament | 3 | 2.6 |
| Service personnel (Army, | 44 | 38.2 |
| Navy and Air Force) | | |
| Police Officers | 5 | 4.3 |
| *Civilians* | 63 | 54.7 |
| Professionals/Managers (i) | 15 | 13 |
| Workers (ii) | 34 | 29.5 |
| Housewives | 6 | 5.2 |
| Children | 3 | 2.6 |
| Unemployed | 2 | 1.7 |
| Unknown | 3 | 2.6 |
| Total | 115 | 100 |

*Notes*:
(i)   Professionals/managers killed included a cancer research specialist,
      club manager, company directors, company manager, journalists,
      librarian, management consultant, securities dealer, restaurateur,
      shop manager, stockbroker.
(ii)  Workers killed included car worker, cleaners, courier, door attend-
      ant, electricians, gardener, labourers, maintenance worker, office
      worker, pipe fitters, postman, nurse, plasterers, punch-card operative,
      railway guard, sales clerk, shop assistant, stock controller, store super-
      visor, tube driver, telephonist, typist, wages clerk, waiters/waitresses,
      welders.
*Source*: Hansard, 16 March 1993, cols 166–168. Classification by authors.

we believe, owes more to the fact that it is a *British* state,
than to its capitalist or former imperialist nature. It is the
British national state, and it is British political institutions,
which have failed to reform Northern Ireland. The failure
of the idea of a united Irish state to persuade sufficient
people that it would beneficially reform Northern Ireland
also owes something to the fact that the new state would
be an *Irish* state. If so, it follows that reforming Northern
Ireland requires the development of state-structures which are
neither purely British nor purely Irish, a task which is easier
to accomplish, and certainly more desirable, than a Marxist
revolution.

## Conclusion

The collapse of Marxism in the wider world of ideas and states has been visibly apparent in the early 1990s, and has had its impact upon left-leaning supporters of Irish nationalism. The result is that green Marxism provides another 'broken image' of the conflict in Northern Ireland. New writings in this vein are now only produced and read by small ultra-left sectlets in Britain and Ireland.[89] Insurrectionaries in Sinn Féin, after dallying with 'modernizing' their discourse with Marxist perspectives, are returning to their roots in republican nationalism.[90] This shift is entirely understandable. Whereas green Marxists suffer under the double burden of defending classical Marxism and classical Irish nationalism, Irish republicans have only one cross to bear.

Socialists in Britain and Ireland, and elsewhere, have (too) slowly realized that national, ethnic, and religious conflicts are not mere by-products of capitalism which will disappear in socialist societies. Some have been putting their minds not only to the question of whether socialism can be democratic and efficient, but also to how socialists can claim to manage national, ethnic and religious conflicts better than they are handled in 'actually existing' capitalist democracies. They have, thankfully, ceased to talk in the future perfect tense, which socialists have traditionally preserved for the most awkward questions. The collapse of Marxist–Leninist regimes in eastern Europe and the Soviet Union, accompanied by the vigorous renewal of national, ethnic and religious conflicts, has been educating the educators. Intelligent socialists are aware that, far from being transcended, national, ethnic and religious conflicts were 'solved' east of the Elbe by a different kind of imperialism, hegemonic control by a dictatorial one-party regime. This 'solution' was presumably the one which many green Marxists had in mind for Ireland. If so, they were less than candid. If not, they were more utopian than we have surmised.

# 3

# Unionist Discourses: Irish Irredentism and British Absenteeism

[T]he Catholic minority in the North . . . was encouraged by successive governments of the Republic and the 1937 Constitution to resist its fate and to maintain itself in irredentist disaffection from the United Kingdom.

*Hugh Roberts, left-wing unionist intellectual*[1]

It has been the Republic which has helped to perpetuate divisions within Northern Ireland with a territorial claim it has had little stomach to fulfil.

*Arthur Aughey, conservative unionist intellectual*[2]

I think [the conflict] will end when the British government takes the Dublin government and says: Look, you can no longer claim jurisdiction over Northern Ireland.

*Reverend Dr Ian Paisley, leader of the Democratic Unionist Party*[3]

Unionism is the doctrine that the United Kingdom should be preserved. For 'Ulster' unionists it is the doctrine that Northern Ireland must stay in the Union of Great Britain and Northern Ireland. This objective is keenly shared by some British unionists in the Conservative Party.[4] Unionism is a type of nationalism, a variation of British nationalism, and it has both civic and ethnic dimensions, just like its Irish nationalist counterpart. In the civic versions the Union is conceived as a union of all the equal citizens of the United Kingdom, irrespective of their racial, religious or cultural origins, while in ethnic versions the Union is the expression of British Protestant achievement and Ulster is the home of the descendants of Scots and English settlers who brought civilization to Ireland.[5]

## Varieties of Unionism

Ulster unionists resemble Irish nationalists because they are divided over major matters of value and strategy. They differ over the reasons they advance for maintaining the Union. Some proffer essentially negative ethnic and cultural arguments against Irish nationalism, condemning the Irish state's Gaelicism, Catholicism or its allegedly exclusive nationalism; others emphasize the economic or instrumental benefits of the Union; and yet others advance the positive thesis that the Union makes Northern Ireland part of a modern multi-national state in which all citizens benefit from liberal democracy, pluralism, equal citizenship and the rule of law. They all unite, however, in opposing the idea that they should be coerced or encouraged into the Republic.

Unionists are especially divided over how best to maintain the Union. *Devolutionists* argue that Northern Ireland must have extensive devolved self-government – if only to provide a bulwark against potential British treachery. Their localist or regionalist orientation is not, however, incompatible with national identification with Great Britain and its imperial past. *Integrationists*, by contrast, believe that the Union is best maintained by the legal, political, electoral, and administrative integration of 'the province' with the rest of the United Kingdom.[6] Integration in their view would remove the uncertainty surrounding Northern Ireland's status as part of the Union, and dissolve sectarian particularism through full participation in a pluralist democratic state. However, many integrationists appear to be uninterested in dissolving sectarianism – a very high proportion of the MPs of the Ulster Unionist Party remain steadfast members of Orange lodges, including the leader and deputy leader of the Ulster Unionist Party.

There are multiple sub-divisions within these devolutionist and integrationist camps. Four types of devolutionist can be discerned. First, there are the reactionaries, who would like, if possible, to restore something like the old Stormont parliament. They are supporters of simple majority-rule, the key principle of British democracy. They can be found in Ian Paisley's Democratic Unionist Party (DUP), and also within the Ulster Unionist Party (UUP). Secondly, there are reformist devolutionists, i.e. qualified supporters of local majority-rule. They recognize that there were 'deficiencies' in the old Stormont regime, and are willing to see a Bill of Rights, proportional representation, and a role for minority parties in the committee system of any future devolved assembly. Such people are found both within the UUP and, to a lesser extent, in the DUP. Thirdly, there are power-sharers, who are willing to envisage executive and legislative power-sharing between constitutional nationalists and unionists within a devolved government, and who declare their interest in a politics of accommodation which can embrace the aspirations of unionists for the Union, and Catholics for equality and justice. Such people are found principally in the Alliance Party (APNI), but there is also a small number of such persons in the UUP, and thinkers associated with the UDA have occasionally floated such ideas – most recently in a document called *Common Sense*.[7] Finally, there are pan-British devolutionists, supporters of 'devolution-all-round', who believe that Northern Ireland should share in the wider movement to devolve power to the nations and regions of the United Kingdom,[8] and indeed in the movement to devolve power within the emergent European Union. This semi-federalist theme is supported by some unionist intellectuals and regularly aired in the magazine *Fortnight*. Exponents of these ideas usually favour reformist or power-sharing models of devolution.

There are three different types of integrationist, and to complicate matters, some of these integrationist ideas may be embraced by devolutionists. Legal integrationists, found in the UUP and DUP, want Northern Ireland's status as part of the United Kingdom to be unconditionally confirmed: they want it to be legally part of the Union in exactly the same way as Cornwall, London or Scotland. They want legislation for Northern Ireland to be processed by the Westminster parliament as if it were for any other part of the Kingdom, and not through Orders in Council (under which, laws are in effect made through ministerial decree). Administrative integrationists long wanted Northern Ireland to have its own Westminster select committee,[9] and local government on the Scottish (or is it the English?) model. Their objective is to avoid Northern Ireland being governed in ways which mark it off as 'a place apart'. A minority argue the logic of integration to the point where they see no case for a separate Northern Ireland Office, Civil Service, or government departments: i.e. they want Northern Ireland to be treated as part of England, rather than as a constituent nation of the United Kingdom like Scotland or Wales. Finally, electoral integrationists argue that there is only one central way to give meaning to Northern Ireland's status as part of the Union: all the major British political parties should organize and compete for electoral support in the region. They are less preoccupied with administrative issues, and some even say they could embrace devolution, provided that British parties competed for office in any devolved assembly.

Unionists differ considerably in their perceptions of Catholics and northern nationalists, and in their prescriptions for them. For some, especially loyalist paramilitaries, they are an 'enemy within', with all that that assumption suggests – although such beliefs may be stated *sotto voce* in the company of external visitors. For others they are a minority with unrealistic objectives who must learn to accept their 'fate'; and for another set they are British subjects who must be persuaded to embrace British citizenship through demonstrable proof of the benefits of the Union. Perceptions of Catholics and northern nationalists normally dictate the way in which unionists make their case for the Union, and their prescriptions for making it work. These perceptions in turn are linked to their accounts of the causes of the Northern Ireland conflict. Conventionally unionists argue that the conflict is explicable through one fundamental external cause: the Irish state, and its nationalist irredentism. Although still dominant in unionist discourse, this explanation has been challenged by revisionists who maintain that another fundamental cause is an external 'absence': the absence of a British commitment to make Northern Ireland ineffably British.

All unionists regard themselves as much misunderstood,[10] but, as one of their own suggests, they have not been noted for articulate defences of their philosophy.[11] Unionist writings have been less prolific and sometimes less ably developed than those of Irish nationalists. This judgement does not reflect cultural bias on our part, just the fact that Ulster unionists, by-and-large, have been defenders of the status quo – at least until 1985 – and articulate defences of a political status quo are usually less often required than articulate cases for change. Ulster unionism has often displayed a conservative mentality, unwilling to engage in elaborate rationalist defence of the Union, but one unanticipated consequence of the Anglo-Irish Agreement has been to spur unionists into the field of extended intellectual endeavour.[12]

The first major unionist treatise was not composed by an Ulsterman, but by an Englishman, the constitutional lawyer Dicey, in his now-forgotten polemic *England's Case Against Home Rule* (1886/7).[13] Subsequent unionist literature, following Dicey, has been reactive, produced in moments of crisis, when home rule, Irish nationalism or the IRA are vigorous. The dates of the following significant unionist authors' works tell a story: McNeill (1922), Ervine (1949), Carson (1956), Maginnis (1956), O'Neill (1972), Stewart (1977, 1986), and Faulkner (1978).[14] All were published immediately after republican or constitutional nationalist assaults on the Union. The same pattern is evident in the spate of publications which has followed the Anglo-Irish Agreement. Indeed the current crisis has seen both a quantitative and qualitative shift in the unionist writings. Unionist pamphlets often match the qualities which most reviewers find in the Irish nationalist literature: power, style and wit. Oddly, the best of this literature depends on arguments initially advanced by orange and red Marxists, but it modernizes the unionist case before the bar of British and international public opinion.

# The Conventional Unionist Case against Irish Irredentism

Unionists reject the nationalist argument that Britain's decision to partition Ireland lies at the root of the conflict. In the unionist case irredentist Irish nationalism is responsible for sustaining a conflict which would otherwise disappear.[15] There is not one nation in Ireland – which is a sentimental, irrationalist myth, sustained by fallacious geographical determinism. Unionists insist that they differ decisively from the other people in Ireland in religion, ethnic origin, economic interests, and sense of national identity. They are not Catholics. They are ethnically linked to Scotland and England. Their economic interests are connected with Britain. They regard themselves as either British or Ulsterfolk. *Quod erat demonstrandum.* Although some unionists insist that they are Irish, i.e. culturally Irish, and even ethnically Irish, this identity is, they say, consistent with their British national or political identity and allegiance.[16] They have a dual identity, they are politically British but culturally Irish.

Irredentism, the pursuit of 'unredeemed' Irish nationalist territory, is the exogenous cause of conflict in unionists' eyes. They claim irredentist rhetoric has been propagated by the major Irish political parties for purposes which relate to party-competition in the Republic. Embedded in Articles 2 and 3 of Ireland's Constitution,[17] irredentism inflames northern nationalists' aspirations and, they say, contradicts the commitments of successive Irish governments to obtaining Irish unity by consent of the inhabitants of Northern Ireland. In July 1988 two Ulster Unionist brothers availed of their rights to be Irish citizens[18] to contest the constitutionality of the Anglo-Irish Agreement.[19] Ironically they employed the arguments of republican critics of the Agreement, contending that since Articles 2 and 3 make Northern Ireland part of its national territory it was unconstitutional for the Irish Government to sign the Anglo-Irish Agreement. However, Justice Barrington ruled that the Agreement did not violate the Constitution. The brothers then appealed to the Supreme Court. Its verdict upheld the constitutionality of the Agreement, but on different grounds from those of the High Court.[20] It declared that the reintegration of the national territory of Ireland was a 'constitutional imperative', and that the limitation in Article 3 of the applicability of the laws enacted by the Irish parliament to the twenty-six counties did not derogate 'from the claim as a legal right to the entire national territory'. This ruling confirmed unionists' belief that the Irish Constitution legitimates republican politics, including terrorist republicanism bent on reintegrating the national territory by force; they also maintain that it accounts for the alleged ambivalence of Irish politicians and Irish Courts about the extradition of suspected terrorists.

The gravity with which unionists regard the claims embedded in the Irish Constitution can be seen in the arguments advanced by Dr Christopher McGimpsey and his party leader James Molyneaux at the UUP's annual conference in October 1990.[21] McGimpsey argued that the articles represent 'an irrational and irredentist claim' and are a major source of instability which gives justification to the IRA's campaign of violence. In the Irish Constitution 'the destruction of Northern Ireland and the forced dismemberment of the United Kingdom is a demand that accepts no argument – it is an issue in which our views are deemed to be irrelevant'. He even claimed that 'The South's demand for the destruction of Northern Ireland – Eire's claim to *Lebensraum* – is equivalent to Hitler's claim over Czechoslovakia.'[22] Molyneaux added that the Supreme Court's decision on the meaning of Articles 2 and 3 meant that 'what was once a mere vote-catcher is now a constitutional imperative for all Irish citizens, and every attempt to obey that constitutional imperative hands a sheaf of death warrants to the IRA'.[23] Earlier that summer, Molyneaux had likened the Republic's constitutional claim over Northern Ireland to Iraq's irredentist claim over Kuwait. This viewpoint is not confined to the UUP. The DUP now takes an equally vigorous line on Articles 2 and 3. In an interview with one of the authors in November 1992 the deputy leader of the DUP declared that 'The Government of the Republic of Ireland claims illegally the territory of Northern Ireland, which is a part of the United

Kingdom, and therefore that obstacle must be removed before a new and good relationship can exist with the Irish Republic.'[24] Constitutional euthanasia for Articles 2 and 3 is prescribed as the first step for any political progress.

There is an important inference in the stress unionists put on Irish irredentism. It is that the nationalism of the 'enemy within', especially that of IRA members and Sinn Féin voters, is artificial, capable of an easy and overdue death, but for the external pressure and support of the Republic's political elites, political parties and Constitution. Catholics in Northern Ireland are sustained in 'irredentist disaffection' by exogenous forces, as the statement by Roberts in the epigraph to this chapter suggests.

Unionists maintain that the Government of Ireland, as a party to the Anglo-Irish Treaty of 1921 and the agreement which buried the Boundary Commission in 1925, has no legitimate claims on Northern Ireland. They argue that Irish membership of the United Nations and the European Union obligates the Republic to renounce its territorial claims on the United Kingdom. They claim that the Irish government has never challenged Northern Ireland's status as part of the United Kingdom in any international court or any multilateral organization: only in its relations with the UK does the Irish government refuse to describe the UK as the 'United Kingdom of Great Britain and Northern Ireland'. They charge the Irish state with hypocrisy in its international relations: the Republic's claim to Northern Ireland is, they claim, illegal, which is why it is not tested by Irish governments in international courts; they think it is an unholy mixture of bad-faith and incitement; built into de Valera's constitutional architecture to appease nationalist shibboleths, it now costs lives and prolongs conflict.[25]

Some unionists argue that it is not Ireland, but the British Isles which has suffered from partition since 1921. The central question, according to Molyneaux: 'is not why the Ulster majority – Protestant and Roman Catholic – refuses to cut its links with Great Britain, but rather why the Irish Free State decided to withdraw from the United Kingdom of Great Britain and Ireland in the first place'.[26] Thus the tables are turned: Irish nationalism is responsible for the partition of the UK.

Unionists condemn irredentist 'myths': Irish nationalism is rooted in a literal 'insularism' derived from a simplistic 'map-image', the false dogma that there has been and still is only one nation in Ireland. They draw upon academic political geography to reject the thesis that there are 'natural boundaries' for nation-states, a literature that is often cited by both revisionists in the Republic and unionist politicians.[27] In his address at the UUP's annual conference in October 1990 Molyneaux advanced a countervailing British political geography: geography and history, he declared, point to the interdependencies between the British isles; the North Channel was not a political divide down the ages, but a means of communication: 'It did not divide Ulster from Scotland, but joined them. Political units straddled the North Channel long before the establishment of the United Kingdom.' He cited in evidence several kingdoms which overlay both Scotland and 'Northern Ireland'[28] from the fifth century AD. 'Sea travel' across the North channel 'was easier and safer than hazardous routes to the south of Ireland.'[29]

Unionists reject the republican idea that Northern Ireland is a British colony. Brian Faulkner put his people's complaint ambiguously, and with a touch of racist arrogance, when he declared that Northern Ireland was not a 'coconut colony',[30] but in this respect he spoke for all unionists. Unionists also reject the idea that Ireland was a colony before 1921, claiming that it was an integral part of the United Kingdom, governed by the same legislative procedures as the rest of the state:[31] what happened in 1921 was secession, not decolonization. However, since 1972, and especially since 1985, many unionists have maintained that they are an 'internal colony',[32] because they lack political input into the processes through which they are governed. (The use of the term 'internal colony' is deliberate, because the solution for this condition is integration, whereas 'decolonization' is the remedy for a normal colony.)

Unionists not only reject the supposition that there is just one nation in Ireland,[33] they also maintain that the practice of Irish nationalism has proved them right. Irish independence, they claim, has fulfilled predictions that 'Home Rule meant Rome Rule'. A Republic is not secular in which the preamble to the Constitution vests sovereignty in the Most Holy Trinity;[34] which until 1972 acknowledged the special position of the Roman Catholic Church; and which constitutionally entrenches Catholic morality on divorce and abortion. Unionists are also sceptical of the endeavour of neo-nationalists to make the Republic constitutionally and legally more pluralist – such efforts are decoded as just a different stratagem to achieve Irish unity; or as a Sisyphean task, given the values of most of the electorate in the Republic.

Even if the Irish state fully 'de-theocratized' its Constitution, unionists maintain they would still not regard themselves as possible members of the Irish political nation. They are adamant that they would prefer almost anything to incorporation into the Republic, including independence.[35] They are, however, divided as to the exact nature of their nation. Some maintain that unionists' 'Britishness' pre-dates the formation of Northern Ireland, and, by implication, accounts for its existence,[36] arguments that are contested by others who contend that Ulster Protestants are members of an Ulster nation,[37] or indeed are a compound Ulster–British nation,[38] or an Irish–British nation.[39] Then there are those who maintain that unionists have a complex but consistent multiple set of national and territorial identities.[40] But whatever their disagreements unionists agree that they differ decisively from the other people in the rest of the island in religion, ethnic origin, economic interests, and sense of (political) national identity.

Violence in Northern Ireland, according to unionists, has stemmed from nationalist irredentism, not from discrimination or maltreatment of the minority before 1972 or since. Republican violence in their view is motivated by the cult and culture of Sinn Féin taught in Catholic schools north and south of the border,[41] and sanctioned by the Irish Constitution and the moral ambivalence about the IRA demonstrated by the Republic's politicians. This culture inhibits northern Catholics, by force or persuasion, from giving their allegiance to the British state.[42] The Irish state's founding myth celebrates the actions of the Irish Republican Brotherhood and the Irish Citizens Army in Easter 1916; and the Republic therefore cannot disown the consequence: the glorification of elitist, militaristic, insurrectionary, and Catholic nationalism. The educational dissemination of this culture is the source of Catholics' propensity to irrational violence. The security forces, in contrast, are portrayed as merely deploying legitimate force to prevent the IRA from succeeding in its objectives.

Unionists have simple explanations of why the IRA campaign since 1969 has had such remarkable longevity by comparison with the 1956–62 campaign. First, and foremost, the Irish government is accused of failing to co-operate properly with the authorities in Northern Ireland. The Republic's government did not introduce internment without trial – by contrast with the 1950s. Unionists accuse it of offering a safe haven for terrorists, through non-co-operation on extradition, through failing to provide adequate security on the border, and now through trying to treat Sinn Féin as a normal political party. Unionists also believe that they are victims of a big lie: Irish nationalist propagandists, in Britain, Ireland, America and elsewhere, have successfully persuaded international public opinion that the Catholic minority was and is an oppressed people. The belief that the Northern Ireland Civil Rights Association of the 1960s was the IRA in thin camouflage is not confined to Ian Paisley and his supporters.[43] Nationalist propaganda, according to unionists, has had a negative impact on British policy-makers, stopping them from giving the security forces the necessary powers to crush the IRA's insurrection. They have been denied the use of internment since 1976, and are obliged to operate under the rule of law, for which republican terrorists have no respect. Unionists have called for increased security measures and more powerful counter-insurgency methods, including 'search and destroy' operations, 'hot-pursuit' operations into the Republic, the re-introduction of the death-penalty for terrorist crimes, internment without trial, 'selective detention', media-censorship and the removal of terrorist suspects' common-law right to silence.[44] They contend that 'the liberal bias of the media . . . always operate[s] against the interests of authority',[45] and normally welcome the censorship of those they believe to be terrorist sympathizers. The British Government allegedly has been hampered from the necessary repressive measures to counteract terrorism because it operates in a 'goldfish bowl', i.e. in the full glare of national and international media scrutiny.

Many unionists also embrace the thesis that it is British policy which is ultimately responsible for violence. Following a logic first articulated by Enoch Powell they claim that the root cause of violence is the uncertainty of Britain's commitment to Northern Ireland. The impression Britain gives of 'impending departure' provides succour to the IRA, persuading them that they can win.[46] A liberal establishment myth 'that it is impossible for government to win an urban guerrilla war' has crippled decision-makers; so the key problem is that successive British governments have lacked the necessary 'will to victory'.[47] If British policy-makers really believed Northern Ireland was an integral part of the United Kingdom they would have crushed the rebellion in 'Ulster', just as they would unreservedly crush any challenges to legitimate authority elsewhere in the Kingdom. Finally, unionists believe that British 'reform' policies simply encourage further violence: nationalist appetites grow with feeding. Sustained bouts of IRA violence and Sinn Féin mobilizations bring regular concessions to constitutional nationalists, to the SDLP, and to the Irish government. The latter 'ride on the backs of the IRA', in the words of Ian Paisley. The abolition of Stormont, the attempts to create power-sharing governments, electoral reform, fair employment legislation, and Irish dimensions are the fruits of nationalist 'salami tactics'. The Anglo-Irish Agreement, in this world-view, is an IRA victory, as is the Downing Street Declaration, part and parcel of the 'ratchet-effect' of the 'pan-nationalist' assault on Northern Ireland. The conclusion: as long as Britain fails absolutely to commit itself to Northern Ireland, by law and by military might, the IRA's eventual victory is assured.

The stalemate since 1972 is similarly explained by most unionists. The nationalism of the Catholic minority, supported by the irredentist Irish state, is the fundamental obstacle to political accommodation. The SDLP, by its insistence on an Irish dimension (the Council of Ireland), prevented the power-sharing Executive from being stabilized in 1974, and also blocked subsequent possible rapprochements. The SDLP's demand for an Irish dimension allegedly is sufficient to explain the failure to agree structures for a devolved government in 1975–6, in 1980–1, 1982–6, and during the inter-party talks of 1991–2. The SDLP has not only insisted upon an Irish dimension but also, since 1985, upon a direct role for the Irish government on public policy affecting Northern Ireland, a demand which unionists have so far found completely unacceptable. Thus, for unionists, just as the Nationalist Party was sustained in irredentist disaffection from the state between 1920 and 1972, and encouraged in abstentionist politics by the parties in the Republic, so the SDLP since 1972, egged on by Fianna Fáil in particular, has made a workable political compromise impossible by insisting upon pan-Irish solutions. John Hume's proposals to negotiate an 'agreed Ireland' are decoded as the traditional demand for a united Ireland – a view reinforced in their eyes by Hume's public and private dialogues with Gerry Adams, the leader of Sinn Féin, between 1988 and 1994.

The Anglo-Irish Agreement, according to unionists, merely created a new stalemate in which the core source of conflict was reinforced: the insatiable appetite of Irish nationalists for political control of the whole island. The unionist parties refused to participate in talks under the auspices of the Anglo-Irish Agreement until 1991–2 – and then they only agreed to talks while the Inter-Governmental Conferences were suspended. When their central demand, for the unilateral termination of Articles 2 and 3 of the Irish Constitution, was not met, their leaders rapidly lost interest in the discussions. As with the Anglo-Irish Agreement so with the Downing Street Declaration. The Democratic Unionist Party presently refuses to participate in constitutional talks as long as the Downing Street Declaration remains on the table. As we went to press, the Ulster Unionist Party, which has been more circumspect about the significance of the Declaration and the ensuing cessation of violence by the IRA, is unclear about whether it will engage in inter-party talks with Sinn Féin at some future juncture – in so doing it is responding to the fears of its members that the Declaration marks a further erosion of British sovereignty and that the IRA's cessation of violence is a trap set by a pan-nationalist front.

## The Conventional Unionist Case Dissected

Unionism has been vigorously criticized, and not only by Irish nationalists. We shall concentrate on five crucial defects in conventional unionist discourses. First and foremost, unionism is too often articulated with a noticeable absence: the political minority in Northern Ireland is left unexamined; it figures, if at all, as the fifth column of an exogenous irredentist state. Secondly, exponents of traditional unionism usually reject the existence or deny the scale of discrimination against northern nationalists or Catholics, before or after 1972. Thirdly, unionists have severe difficulties in defending and defining the Britishness of unionists, and in assuming that this Britishness entitles them to the unqualified continuation of the Union on their terms. Fourthly, their accounts of the causes of violence in Northern Ireland are partial and self-serving; and finally, their explanations of the political stalemate after 1972 are highly partisan.

*The missing people.* The absence in conventional unionist literature of any significant treatment of the nationalist minority, one which takes seriously its experiences and preferences, suggests profound political prejudice. Nationalists note how unionists use 'Ulster' as their preferred term for Northern Ireland, and how they employ it in an exclusivist sense.[48] The earliest unionist literature unselfconsciously identified Ulstermen (sic!) with Ulster Protestants.[49] This usage forgets that there is an Ulster outside Northern Ireland (Cavan, Donegal and Monaghan), and that there are a very significant number of people in Northern Ireland who do not primarily identify themselves with Ulster, Northern Ireland or Britain.

Contemporary unionists regularly display tacit exclusivism

and majoritarianism, identifying *the* majority in Northern Ireland with Ulster Protestants, and in turn identifying them with the entire population of Northern Ireland.[50] Anachronisms, oversights, exclusive and narrow definitions of 'the people', and blatant 'majoritarianism' suggest that northern nationalists are the unexamined Other of unionism. Unionists may be correct to consider the Republic's politicians opportunist – like democratic politicians everywhere – but it does not occur to many of them that the virulence of nationalism in the Catholic population may owe more to its experience of Northern Ireland, both before and after 1972, than it does to the manipulation of politicians in the Republic or irredentist indoctrination in Catholic schools.

*The politics of denial.* Unionist literature is suffused with denial of the treatment *the* minority has experienced since 1922. Indeed some DUP politicians go so far as to contend that the direction of discrimination has been substantively in the other direction under direct rule.[51] When they do so they are tapping widespread perceptions amongst Ulster Protestants. In a 1978 poll 60 per cent of Protestants felt that they were being discriminated against more at that time than had been the case ten years earlier.[52] Denial is more subtle amongst academic unionists. One strategy is to gloss over the distinction between nationalists and Catholics: thus the historian A. T. Q. Stewart writes that 'Not only did Stormont not enact discriminatory laws against Catholics; it was expressly forbidden to do so by the 1920 Government of Ireland Act.'[53] This thesis may mislead the innocent reader who mistakenly equates the Catholic and the nationalist, and would sound less impressive if it read: 'Not only did Stormont enact discriminatory laws against nationalists; it was not expressly prohibited from doing so by the Government of Ireland Act.' Stewart is not an isolated example: liberal and highly educated unionists practise denial when discussing northern nationalists. Consider the arguments of Thomas Wilson, a former Oxford don and professor of political economy at Glasgow, who played a key role as an economic adviser to Unionist governments in the 1960s. In 1955 he edited a supremacist book, *Ulster under Home Rule*, in which he suggested that Northern Catholic grievances were more spiritual than 'real'. 'They have less to complain about than the US Negroes, and their lot is a very pleasant one as compared with the nationalists in, say the Ukraine.' He also held that '[Catholics] were made to feel inferior [in the past], and to make matters worse they often *were* inferior, if *only* in those personal qualities that make for success in competitive economic life'.[54] A quarter of a century later the same author displayed greater tact in *Ulster: Conflict and Consent* (1989), but his analysis remained defective in examining the consequences of Unionist public policy before 1972. He contended that discrimination in housing policy was confined to unionist councils west of the Bann,[55] but failed to underline that these were the areas in which Catholics would have been more likely to comprise local electoral majorities had it not been for gerrymandering.[56] Had Wilson written that unionists were efficient political discriminators, who only discriminated where they needed to do so, his readers could not have been misled.[57] Wilson is not isolated[58] – many unionist academics and sympathizers with unionism deny that discrimination in Northern Ireland was or is widespread or systematic.[59]

For Wilson, following a notorious school of American econo-mists, the unfettered operations of the free market are touch-ingly colour-blind and religiously unprejudiced.[60] In this world-view discrimination is economically inefficient – which must set limits on its scale. Discrimination must also be intentional – although Wilson does concede the possibility that the preva-lence of informal employment networks might produce bias of a 'thoughtless' kind.[61] With other unionists he contests the validity of research which shows that Catholic males remain two and a half times as likely to be unemployed as Protestant males and its claims that much of this differential can only be explained by intentional and indirect discrimination.[62] Wilson maintains that such research (and its underlying methodology) is flawed and leads to more 'suspicion and ill-will'.[63] His case, however, is spoiled by curious statements: for example, 'In preferring Protestants to Catholics many employers may well have *believed* that, apart altogether from satisfying any religious or political preferences, they were likely, as a rule, to be employing the more efficient workers.'[64] Wilson has retained

**Table 3.1** Some perceptions of discrimination and equality of opportunity amongst Protestants and Catholics, 1968–89 (in percentages)

|  | Protestants | Catholics | Total |
|---|---|---|---|
| *Q. 1968*<br>People sometimes say that in parts of Northern Ireland Catholics are treated unfairly. Do you think this is true or not? |  |  |  |
| Yes | 18 | 74 | 41 |
| No | 74 | 13 | 48 |
| Don't Know | 8 | 13 | 10 |
| *Q. 1973–4*<br>One of the main causes of the Troubles is the lack of job opportunities for Roman Catholics because Protestants are given preference. |  |  |  |
| Agree # | 17 | 78 |  |
| Disagree | 77 | 17 |  |
| Don't Know | 6 | 5 |  |
| *Q. 1986*<br>Do Catholics and Protestants have the same chance of a job? |  |  |  |
| Same Chance | 68 | 26 | 53 |
| Chances Differ | 27 | 67 | 41 |
| Don't Know | 5 | 7 | 6 |
| *Q. 1989*<br>Some people think that many employers are *more* likely to give jobs to Protestants than to Catholics. Do you think this happens? * |  |  |  |
| A lot | 6 | 26 |  |
| A little | 43 | 54 |  |
| Hardly at all | 42 | 13 |  |
| Don't know | 8 | 8 |  |

# Answers for this question were classed on a Likert scale (i.e. 'agree very much', 'agree a little', 'don't know', 'disagree a little', 'disagree very much'). Respondents who agreed 'very much' included 52.4% of Catholics, but only 5.1% of Protestants, while those who disagreed 'very much' included 62.1% of Protestants, but only 7.9% of Catholics.

* The 1989 survey results produced very similar responses to a question which replicated that in Smith and Chambers' survey, D. Smith and G. Chambers, *Inequality in Northern Ireland* (Oxford: Clarendon Press, 1991).

*Sources*: 1968: R. Rose, *Governing without Consensus: An Irish Perspective* (London: Faber, 1971), 497. 1973–4: R. Miller, *Attitudes to Work in Northern Ireland*, Research Paper No. 2 (Belfast: FEA, 1978), 15. 1986: D. Smith, *Equality and Inequality in Northern Ireland, Part III: Perceptions and Views* (London: Policy Studies Institute, 1987), table 75. 1989: R. D. Osborne, 'Discrimination and Fair Employment', in P. Stringer and G. Robinson (eds), *Social Attitudes in Northern Ireland, 1990–91 Edition* (Belfast: Blackstaff Press, 1991), 33.

two habits from the 1950s. When engaged in apologizing for 'Ulster', meaning the Protestants of Northern Ireland, he is liberal in his use of italics, and deficient in his citation of evidence. Note, however, that Wilson does not completely deny the (past) existence of discrimination, just its scale. This has become the up-to-date liberal unionist response to criticism of the Stormont regime;[65] and given that the critics of any regime always exaggerate its defects such a strategy of defensive denial can always muster some plausible arguments in its defence.[66]

Opinion polls confirm widespread denial of discrimination against the minority by Ulster Protestant unionists. Thus in Richard Rose's 1968 Loyalty Survey, 74 per cent of Protestants denied that Catholics were treated unfairly in any part of Northern Ireland – exactly mirroring the percentage of Catholics who thought otherwise (see table 3. 1). In 1973–4, 77 per cent of Protestants disagreed with the proposition that 'One of the main causes of the Troubles is the lack of job opportunities for Roman Catholics because Protestants are given preference', almost matching the number of Catholics who thought otherwise.[67] In 1986, in response to the Policy Studies Institute Survey two-thirds of Protestants (68 per cent) thought Catholics and Protestants had the same chance of obtaining a job, whereas two-thirds of Catholics (67 per cent) thought they did not. The overwhelming majority of Catholics who believed there was inequality in job-opportunities thought Protestants had better chances than Catholics. In contrast, Protestants who believed there was inequality in opportunity were evenly divided between those who thought Catholics had better chances, those who thought Protestants had a better chance, and those who thought it 'depended on the area'.[68] The objective evidence about Catholics' chances of obtaining jobs as opposed to Protestants is, to put matters mildly, at odds with most Protestants' perceptions,[69] as is the evidence that Catholics, especially Catholic males, are likely to be under-represented in high-status occupations and over-represented in low-status occupations and among the long-term unemployed (see table 3.2). This persistent pattern of denial of past or present maltreatment of the minority, whether articulated in response to public opinion polls, in the speeches or pamphlets

**Table 3.2** Male social class (by occupation) and religious
background, 1991 census

|  |  | Protestant (%) | Catholic (%) | Others (%) | All |
|---|---|---|---|---|---|
| i. | Professional | 4.7 | 3.4 | 5.8 | 4.4 |
| ii. | Managerial / technical | 23.3 | 18.6 | 22.6 | 21.6 |
| iii (N). | Skilled Non-manual | 11.9 | 7.6 | 12.3 | 10.4 |
| iii (M). | Skilled Manual | 29.5 | 31.7 | 28.0 | 30.1 |
| iv. | Partly Skilled | 14.4 | 12.8 | 12.6 | 13.6 |
| v. | Unskilled | 5.0 | 6.2 | 4.6 | 5.4 |
| Armed Forces, inadequately described and not stated | | 4.7 | 2.4 | 3.2 | 3.7 |
| Government Training or Employment Scheme | | 1.6 | 3.1 | 1.8 | 2.1 |
| No paid job in last ten years | | 4.8 | 14.2 | 9.2 | 8.7 |

*Source*: A. M. Gallagher, R. D. Osborne, and R. J. Cormack, *Fair Shares?
Employment, Unemployment and Economic Status. Religion and the 1991
Population Census* (Belfast: Fair Employment Commission, 1994), 15.


**Table 3.3** Self-descriptions of their national identity by Northern
Ireland Protestants, 1968–90

|  | 1968 | 1978 | 1984 | 1990 |
|---|---|---|---|---|
| British | 39 | 66 | 77 | 66 |
| Ulster | 32 | 22 | 11 | 10 |
| Irish | 20 | 7 | 4 | 4 |
| Other | 9 # | 5 | 8 | 19 ## |

*Notes*:
# In Rose's Loyalty Survey this 'Other' category was made up as follows:
6% said they were 'sometimes British; sometimes Irish', 2% said they were
'Anglo-Irish', and 1% 'didn't know'.
## The British Social Attitudes Survey asked: 'Which of these best describes
the way you usually think of yourself: British, Irish, Ulster or Northern Irish?'
Protestants who answered 'Northern Irish' numbered 16% and those who
said they were 'sometimes British/sometimes Irish' numbered 3%.
*Sources*: 1968: Rose, *Governing without Consensus*, 208. 1978: E. Moxon-
Browne, *Nation, Class and Creed in Northern Ireland* (Aldershot: Gower,
1983), 69. 1984: M. Gallagher, 'How Many Nations Are There in Ireland?',
paper presented to the Political Studies Association of Ireland Conference,
Cork, October 1990, 16. 1990: J. Curtice and T. Gallagher, 'The Northern
Irish Dimension', in R. Jowell, S. Witherspoon, and L. Brook (eds), *British
Social Attitudes: the 7th Report* (Aldershot: Gower, 1990), 198.

of unionist politicians, or in academic articles by unionist dons, is a major public-relations defect in unionist discourse. *What are Britons and what are their rights?* Unionists' battery of sincere arguments often focus on their proclaimed 'British-ness'. Most of them now think of themselves as British – at least that is what survey evidence suggests. However, this Britishness faces three related difficulties: first, there are some problems in establishing that Ulster, even meaning just Protestant Ulster, genuinely regards itself as British; secondly, the majority of 'the indisputably British', i.e. the Great British of England, Scotland and Wales, generally do not think that the citizens of Northern Ireland are British; and finally, even if one accepts, as we do, the authenticity of unionists' British identity that fact alone does not automatically entitle them to the unqualified continuation of the Union.

Consider first Ulster unionists' self-descriptions of their national identity. The data in table 3.3, though based on different surveys with slightly different question-wordings, con-firm that the 'Britishness' of Northern Ireland Protestants is a variable rather than a constant. The 'Britishness' of Ulster Protestants has increased in the crisis-conditions prevailing after 1969, much as it may have done between the 1880s and 1921. Thus Northern Irish Protestants specifying their national identity as 'British' nearly doubled between 1968 and 1984, from 39 per cent to 77 per cent, while those defining their national identity as 'Irish' fell by 80 per cent, from 20 per cent to 4 per cent, in the same period. It is tempting, but methodologically improper, to conclude that the fall in the percentage of Protestants identifying themselves as British between 1984 and 1990 (from 77 per cent to 66 per cent) reflects reaction against the Anglo-Irish Agreement, but the figures suggest volatility in Protestants' perception of their national identity.[70]

This volatility obscures the fact that some Ulster unionists have always regarded themselves as British, consistently have Greater Britain as their 'imagined community' of identity and belonging, and defend the Union according to criteria of what is properly British in culture and custom.[71] Equally the volatility obscures the fact that there has been a persistent

Ulster 'loyalist' tradition, which despite its self-description, is much less loyal to Britain than the British unionists, and more equivocal about the national identity of Ulster Protestants. They display 'settler insecurity', and their primary imagined community is themselves.[72] Their loyalty is to the Crown, rather than Parliament, provided the Crown defends Protestant liberties in Ulster.[73] Loyalism can also be interpreted as an older form of British nationalism because it is not based upon cultural identification with the present peoples of Great Britain. It is also worth observing that a small minority of unionists define themselves as of Irish nationality, while proudly valueing their British citizenship; they identify culturally and even ethnically with Ireland but politically with Britain.

To summarize: a very significant fraction of Ulster Protestants, according to both poll-data and the research of well-respected academics, either do not have a British national identification, or have a variable national identification. More exactly Ulster Protestants are divided between those who identify themselves as British (now the preponderant, but perhaps temporary, majority), those who have no precise national identity whether British or Irish, those who combine both, and a large fraction whose sense of national identity is subject to very volatile changes. This variation is not necessarily evidence of an 'identity crisis', either collective or individual, but it does put in perspective the slogan that 'Ulster is British', as indeed do the attitudes of the Great British.

Ulster Protestants are not usually regarded as British by people living in Great Britain. If we can be forgiven the mixed metaphor, they are not widely thought of as *kosher* British. When they migrate to Great Britain Ulster Protestants frequently find themselves classified as Irish, sometimes to their chagrin. They have to protest their Britishness to a very sceptical audience, like the fabled Orangewoman of Sandy Row who complained to a British reporter 'Hey mister, we're British, and that's something you British had better remember!' The 'real' British response is Shakespearian: 'Methinks the lady doth protest too much!' The English and Welsh, if not the Scots, believe that Northern Irish Protestants are Irish people who by some twist of imperial history happen to be entitled to British passports. A more nuanced British view of their cultural and geographical identity is held by former Secretary of State Merlyn Rees, who explains that 'I felt in Northern Ireland that the moment you left Belfast you were in Ireland.'[74]

The correct title of the state is 'The United Kingdom of Great Britain and Northern Ireland', which minimally indicates that Northern Ireland is not part of *Great* Britain, and may suggest to the international observer that it is also not part of Britain, full stop. However, that inference depends on whether or not Britain is treated as a synonym for the United Kingdom – which would mean that Britain is 'greater' than Great Britain – and Unionists have not entirely failed in vying for the title of *little Britain* for 'their province'. 'The British mainland', their preferred designation of Great Britain, implies that Northern Ireland is part of Britain, albeit 'off the mainland'; and is used by much of the British media, especially when they report IRA actions in Great Britain. However, as unionists complain, in the more substantive arena of constitutional and legal description Northern Ireland's position as part of the United Kingdom has never been recognized as fully British.

Since its inception, unlike any other part of the Kingdom, its status in the Union has been conditional. England, Scotland and Wales are not declared in law or in international agreements to be part of the United Kingdom 'as long as their local parliaments or peoples so desire'.[75] They are not subject to international agreements which specify how they might become part of another state, as is the case with Northern Ireland under Article 1 of the Anglo-Irish Agreement. Indeed Northern Ireland's anomalous constitutional position has led one unionist sympathizer to pose the question 'Is Britain part of the United Kingdom?'[76] 'The people of Northern Ireland' arguably received separate identification from the rest of the United Kingdom in Northern Ireland Constitution Acts of 1973–4 and in the Anglo-Irish Agreement, and the system of 'apartness' has been taken a step further by the Downing Street Declaration, in which they are defined as part of the people of Ireland. In the view of one unionist academic 'the Declaration officially and for the first time has translated the British people of Ulster into an opposing category of Irishness'.[77]

The arguments for British withdrawal from Northern Ireland, proffered regularly in the editorial columns of papers like the *Daily Mirror* in the 1970s and 1980s, and occasionally in the *Sunday Times* during the same years, are evidence that sections of the British elite contemplate with equanimity withdrawing from what unionists insist is an integral part of Britain. Since 1981 the Labour Party has officially been committed to seek the unification of Ireland by consent, and the Conservative governments of Margaret Thatcher and John Major have signed agreements in which Irish unification can occur with the consent of a majority in Northern Ireland but which do not allow 'the people of Northern Ireland' to secede and create an independent state.

As with the policy-making elite so with the mass. There is now a twenty-year history of public opinion polling which shows that a preponderant plurality, and usually a majority, of the (Great) British public favours troop withdrawal from Northern Ireland *and* the departure of Northern Ireland from the United Kingdom. In a recent Gallup poll conducted for the *Daily Telegraph* nearly half of the Great British, 44 per cent, regarded events in Northern Ireland as occurring mainly 'in some other country', and a mere 12 per cent could be described as being in any sense 'strong Unionists'.[78] For the future of Northern Ireland the most favoured option of the (Great) British in opinion polls is most often an all-Ireland state. A selection of the results of these polls is displayed in table 3.4. Such polls dramatically confirm that Northern Ireland is not regarded as properly British by most of the British electorate. Even the response to a question posed in 1978 in which those favouring Irish unity (21 per cent) were outnumbered by those favouring Northern Ireland's retention by the United Kingdom (25 per cent) can have brought little comfort to unionists, because the same poll showed that 58 per cent favoured solutions in which British sovereignty over Northern Ireland came to an end (i.e. Irish unity or independence for Northern Ireland) or was shared by the Republic. Perhaps most suggestively of all, in a survey published in the *Sunday Times* in December 1981, 63 per cent said that if a referendum was held on whether Northern Ireland should remain part of the UK they would vote for its expulsion.[79] These surveys do not mean that (Great) British public opinion is necessarily pro-Irish nationalist, but rather that many British people resent being burdened by 'the Irish question'. The polls have also been less graciously interpreted as suggesting that the British public think that 'the best thing Britain can do is leave and let the mad Paddies fight it out'.[80]

Whatever polls suggest about what the indisputably British think of Northern Ireland, a major normative question remains. Since Ulster unionists regard themselves as British, what follows for their political rights? Do Ulster unionists have the right to full institutional expression and protection of their British identity? The New Ireland Forum Report argued that they have the right 'to effective political, symbolic, and administrative expression of their identity'.[81] However, as one academic of Ulster Protestant background has suggested, this right cannot be unqualified. Not all aspects of unionists' British identity should be guaranteed institutional expression.[82]

**Table 3.4** A selection of British public attitudes towards Northern Ireland and public policy

(a) British public attitudes towards Irish unification

*Q.* Would you approve or disapprove if our Government encouraged Northern to join up with Southern Ireland?

| Date | (1) Approve (%) | (2) Disapprove (%) | Don't know (%) | (1) minus (2) |
|---|---|---|---|---|
| May 1969 | 43 | 24 | 33 | 19 |
| Sept. 1969 | 47 | 23 | 30 | 24 |
| Aug. 1971 | 41 | 29 | 30 | 12 |
| Sept. 1971 | 46 | 29 | 25 | 17 |
| Jan. 1976 | 36 | 29 | 35 | 7 |
| Feb. 1976 | 40 | 29 | 31 | 11 |
| June 1976 | 38 | 24 | 38 | 14 |

*Source:* Gallup Political Index; and R. Rose, I. McAllister and P. Mair, 'Is there a concurring majority about Northern Ireland?', *Studies in Public Policy* (Glasgow: University of Strathclyde, Paper 22, 1978), 29.

*Q.* Do you think that the long-term policy for Northern Ireland should be for it to remain part of the United Kingdom or to unify with the Republic of Ireland?

| Date | (1) remain part of the UK (%) | (2) unify with the Republic of Ireland (%) | (3) up to the Irish (%) | (4) other responses (including don't know) | (1) minus (2) |
|------|------|------|------|------|------|
| 1989 | 30 | 55 | 4 | 11 | 25 |
| 1990 | 29 | 56 | 4 | 11 | 27 |
| 1993 | 28 | 54 | 3 | 11 | 26 |

*Source:* British Social Attitudes Survey 7th Report, 8th Report and 9th Report. Thanks to Alison Parker of SCPR.

(b) British attitudes towards troop withdrawal and withdrawal in general

*Q.* Which of the following statements comes closest to the way you yourself feel about the number of British troops in Northern Ireland?

| Date | We should withdraw our troops (%) | We should carry on with the same number of troops (%) | We should increase the number of troops (%) | Don't know (%) |
|------|------|------|------|------|
| Oct. 1971 | 39 | 24 | 20 | 17 |
| Nov. 1971 | 46 | 22 | 17 | 15 |
| Feb. 1972 | 43 | 27 | 17 | 12 |
| July 1972 | 46 | 19 | 24 | 11 |
| Aug. 1972 | 34 | 29 | 28 | 9 |
| June 1974 | 59 | 21 | 11 | 9 |
| Dec. 1974 | 55 | 22 | 10 | 13 |
| Dec. 1975 | 64 | 13 | 11 | 11 |
| Jan. 1976 | 54 | 15 | 20 | 11 |
| Feb. 1976 | 57 | 17 | 14 | 11 |
| June 1976 | 60 | 16 | 12 | 11 |
| Feb. 1977 | 53 | 26 | 10 | 12 |
| March 1978 | 53 | —30— | | 17 |

*Source:* Gallup Political Index; and Rose, McAllister and Mair ('Concurring majority', 28).

*Q.* Apart from the question of the number of troops, some people have suggested that the British Government should declare an intention of withdrawing entirely from Northern Ireland whether the majority in Northern Ireland agrees or not. Other people disagree with this suggestion. Which of the following statements on this card comes closest to your view?

|  | % agreeing |
|------|------|
| The British Govt. should declare an intention of withdrawing | 56 |
| The British Govt. should not declare an intention of withdrawing | 33 |
| Don't know | 11 |

# Unionist Discourses

*Source:* E. E. Davis and R. Sinnott, *Attitudes in the Republic of Ireland Relevant to the Northern Ireland Problem: Vol. 1 Descriptive Analysis and some Comparisons with Attitudes in Northern Ireland and Great Britain* (Dublin: Economic and Social Research Institute, 1979), 86.

---

*Q.* Which of these statements comes closes to the way you yourself feel about the presence of British troops in Northern Ireland?

| Date | withdraw immediately (%) | withdraw within five years (%) | remain in NI until settlement reached (%) | should not withdraw (%) |
|---|---|---|---|---|
| Sept. 1978 | 32 | 23 | 28 | 10 |
| Jan. 1979 | 40 | 18 | 25 | 7 |
| Sept. 1979 | 44 | 15 | 27 | 7 |
| Aug. 1981 | 37 | 17 | 33 | 7 |
| Jan. 1988 | 24 | 20 | 42 | 7 |

*Source:* Gallup Political and Economic Index.

---

*Q.* Some people think that government policy towards Northern Ireland should include a complete withdrawal of British troops. Would you personally *oppose* or *support* such a policy?

| Date | Support (%) | Oppose (%) | Neither/Don't Know/Other (%) | (1) minus (2) |
|---|---|---|---|---|
| 1989 | 59 (38) | 34 (19) | 7 | 25 |
| 1990 | 60 (37) | 34 (18) | 6 | 26 |
| 1993 | 54 (34) | 36 (21) | 10 | 18 |

*Source:* British Social Attitudes Survey 7th Report, 8th and 9th Report.
*Note*: The numbers in brackets represent the percentage strongly supporting or strongly opposing the policy option. Thanks to Alison Parker of SCPR.

---

(c) British attitudes towards constitutional solutions for Northern Ireland

---

*Q.* The Convention which was set up to decide a constitution for Northern Ireland has come to an end and the Northern Ireland politicians have not reached full agreement on a form of self-government. In the next few months the British Government has to decide its policy on what form of Government there should be for Northern Ireland. Would you look at each policy and tell me whether you personally would find it acceptable or not? Of those policies you said are acceptable which would you prefer the British Government to adopt?

**118**                    *External Explanations*

Personally acceptable (%)

| | |
|---|---|
| Plan to withdraw the troops from NI and leave the Protestants and Catholics to their own fate | 32 |
| Encourage the North and South of Ireland to unite into one country | 25 |
| Impose some form of power-sharing in Northern Ireland which means that the majority Protestants would have to form a coalition government with the minority Catholics – as tried in 1973 | 14 |
| Continue with direct rule from Westminster – as at present | 13 |
| Allow majority rule by the Protestants despite the Catholics' wishes – as at the time when the present troubles started in 1969 | 3 |
| None of these / don't know | 13 |

*Source:* NOP Market Research (1976).

*Q.* There has been a lot of talk about the present problem in Northern Ireland. Which of these is the most preferable to you as a solution?

| Date | NI to remain part of the UK | NI and Republic of Ireland to unite | NI to be independent | NI to be jointly controlled by Britain and the Republic of Ireland |
|---|---|---|---|---|
| Sept. 1978 | 25 | 21 | 24 | 13 |
| Aug. 1981 | 24 | 21 | 37 | n/a |
| May 1986 | 26 | 24 | 35 | n/a |
| Jan. 1988 | 26 | 21 | 36 | n/a |

*Source:* Davis and Sinnott (1979), 61; and Gallup Political Index.

*Q.* What would you prefer to happen?

| Date | NI to remain part of UK | NI to become part of the Republic of Ireland | NI to become independent from both the UK and the Republic | Don't know, Don't care |
|---|---|---|---|---|
| Nov. 1981 | 24 | 21 | 37 | 18 |
| June 1986 | 26 | 24 | 35 | 15 |
| Jan. 1988 | 26 | 21 | 36 | 16 |
| July 1992 | 28 | 20 | 36 | 16 |
| Apr. 1993 | 27 | 15 | 41 | 17 |

*Source:* Gallup Political and Economic Index, 1981–93; and F. Cochrane, 'Any Takers? The Isolation of Northern Ireland', *Political Studies*, 42, 3, (1994), 387.

*Q.* Various solutions have been suggested for the future of Northern Ireland. Which of these proposed solutions would you personally favour?

| Proposal | (%) |
|---|---|
| Full integration of NI with the Republic of Ireland | 21 |
| A NI State independent of both the UK and the Republic of Ireland | 20 |
| Full integration of NI into the UK | 13 |
| NI with a devolved government jointly guaranteed by and responsible to the British and Irish Governments | 10 |
| Devolved government for NI in the UK with power-sharing | 8 |
| Continuation of direct rule through a Secretary of State and the Anglo-Irish Agreement | 7 |
| Re-partition of the island of Ireland, with a smaller NI fully integrated into the UK | 5 |
| Don't know | 16 |

*Source:* B. O'Leary, 'Public Opinion and Northern Irish Futures', *Political Quarterly*, 63, 2 (1992), 147.

### (d) British attitudes towards an Irish dimension

| | |
|---|---|
| *Q. 1992* | If constitutional talks do finally lead to a new consitutional settlement for Northern Ireland, what role, in your opinion, if any, in the affairs of Northern Ireland should that settlement give to . . . ? |

| To the . . . | | (%) |
|---|---|---|
| British Government | a major role | 32 |
| | a minor role | 38 |
| | no role at all | 16 |
| Irish Government | a major role | 49 |
| | a minor role | 25 |
| | no role at all | 11 |

*Source:* O'Leary, 'Northern Irish Futures', 159.

Jennifer Todd contends that there are three distinct aspects of unionists' British identity.[83] The first is cultural. It includes characteristics shared in common with the rest of the peoples of Ireland: the English language, parts of the English common law, and the traditions of parliamentary government. However, others traits are distinctive to Ulster: its profound historical connections with Scotland, including the near-Scottish accents of Antrim and Down, its nineteenth-century participation in industrialization, and a separate Protestant sense of the differentiation of the public and private spheres.[84] With the exception of the latter, which is often exaggerated, these cultural traits are none the less held in common with Ulster

Catholics. But whatever its precise content there are no liberal reasons why this culture should not have institutional expression and protection.

The second aspect of British identity is state-centred, focused upon the benefits and claims unionists enjoy as citizens within British political institutions. It includes identification with the Crown, Westminster, the NHS, British media, the British legal system, British labour relations, the British economy, and educational and examination systems which define British-focused career-paths. It also includes modern British material culture – for instance its road-systems and sports centres. This sense of British identity can only find *full* institutional expression and protection through the unqualified continuation of the Union. However, Todd argues that unionists should not have an *unqualified* right to the Union. They can only do so if Northern Ireland is regarded as part of Britain by all the British. After all, British citizens abroad do not have the right to British rule. They do have the right to retain their citizenship, including the right to vote, but no more. Other arguments have to be advanced by unionists if they wish to be entitled to the *unqualified* Union. The arguments unionists use to reject the nationalist case that all of Ireland should be part of one Irish nation-state can be deployed just as effectively to reject the unionist case that all of Northern Ireland should be exclusively part of the British nation-state.[85]

Many of the benefits and claims which unionists see as components of their political identity are not dependent on the unqualified Union. Irish migrants to Britain enjoy unqualified rights (including electoral rights) as citizens of the United Kingdom. The Irish in Britain and the British in Ireland are formally equal citizens within each state's jurisdiction, a status which will be enhanced by deepening European integration. The Republic has also inherited, although it has altered, many British political institutions, including its parliamentary system, its legal system and its system of labour relations. British media are also widely disseminated in Ireland. Thus not all aspects of unionists' political identity require full incorporation within the UK state for their institutional expression and protection. By implication all of unionists' legitimate British identities might be fairly protected within an institutional structure where both the British and Irish states share sovereignty over Northern Ireland, and where unionists are protected from being forced into a united Ireland against their consent.

Finally, there is the supremacist aspect of some unionists' British identity, which is based on a profound contempt for Irish nationalism and Catholicism. It includes such attributes as proclaiming the merits of being part of a great imperial power as opposed to a small independent neutral nation; assuming British culture to be the acme of civilization and Irish culture to be the converse; asserting Protestantism to be incontestably superior to Catholicism; regarding Britain as the epicentre of genuine liberty, democracy, and justice by contrast with benighted Ireland; and taking opposition to British institutions as a sign of ineffable backwardness, amorality, immorality, or cultural immaturity.[86] We agree with Todd that there are no good reasons why this supremacist British identity deserves institutional expression and protection. Indeed 'one should call on those unionists who still hold such attitudes to rid themselves of this restrictive aspect of their identity which impedes progress and reconciliation'.[87]

We would add the following addendum to Todd's case: even if unionists' claim to be British was more widely accepted, by the Great British and by Ulster Protestants themselves, and even if the indisputably British wanted Northern Ireland to remain within the Union, it would not follow, on the liberal principle of self-determination which we outlined in chapter 1, that unionists are automatically entitled to demand an unqualified Union for Northern Ireland with Great Britain. The present normative position of many unionists is partial and unreasonable. They are committed to an illiberal theory of self-determination. In their philosophy only a majority, or as they usually say 'the majority', has the right to self-determination.[88] 'The majority' for most unionists is not the majority within the United Kingdom as a whole, but rather the majority within Northern Ireland. However, most people, on reflection, agree that what is sauce for the goose should also be sauce for the gander. If unionists maintain that the majority within the United Kingdom should not be able to over-rule the preferences of the majority within Northern Ireland then they must also concede that the majority within Northern Ireland has no right to over-rule the preferences of the minority within Northern Ireland. Majoritarian thinking cannot find a fair resolution for Northern Ireland.[89]

Unlike militant republicans, unionists have their illiberal version of self-determination presently enforced by state power, in British public law. Most unionists are implicitly committed either to the doctrine of 'one nation, one state', or to that of 'one people, one state'.[90] Even if one was to concede Arthur Aughey's claim and regard unionists as non-nationalist 'statists' then most of them are presently 'one and indivisible sovereigntists' – committed to the doctrine of unified and monopolistic sovereignty expressed in one state's authority. Proof of this trait can be found in the widespread hostility to European integration within the unionist community, which mirrors that found in republican arguments against European integration.[91] In short, the same arguments we used in chapter 1 to reject republican claims to a united Ireland as of right are equally compelling in rejecting the claim of Ulster unionists that all of Northern Ireland should be exclusively subject to British sovereignty.[92] A liberal theory of self-determination excludes not only the republican case for a unified Ireland but also the unionist case for unqualified British sovereignty over Northern Ireland.

*There are motes in their eyes.* Unionist accounts of violence in Northern Ireland, like those of republicans, are frequently partisan and self-serving. Consider first their arguments about the Republic's constitutional succour for republicanism. They fail to recognize that Britain's constitutional claim to Ireland, entrenched in Section 75 of the Government of Ireland Act of 1920, and to Northern Ireland in the Ireland Act (after 1949), is seen by northern nationalists to be just as contentious and provocative as the Republic's constitutional claim in Articles 2 and 3. Northern Ireland is a site of contested sovereignty claims, and to the outsider neither the British nor the Irish sovereignty claim has automatic moral credibility. When berating Articles 2 and 3 of the Irish Constitution unionists usually fail to mention that Article 29 of the same Constitution binds the Irish state in the three significant sub-clauses cited in chapter 1:[93] Ireland 'affirms its adherence to the principle of the pacific settlement of international disputes by international arbitration or judicial determination' and 'accepts the generally recognised principles of international law as its rule of conduct in its relations with other States'. These sentences, together with Ireland's membership of the Conference on Security and Co-operation in Europe, refute the idea that Articles 2 and 3 support the violent irredentism of the IRA. One key element of public international law is that border changes should take place peacefully rather than through war – and the Republic is committed to Irish unification by peaceful means.

Unionists are also tendentious when they describe the Irish constitutional claim as 'illegal'. In so far as international law is considered valid, meaningful and operational, it has normally been construed as offering support for the republican position because it prohibits the partition of territories due for decolonization – i.e. it prohibits what occurred in Ireland during 1920–1. It is for this reason, amongst others, that Northern Ireland is internationally considered illegitimate.[94] Unionists claim, in contrast, that neither Ireland nor Northern Ireland were colonies, that the Irish Free State recognized Northern Ireland in 1921 and 1925, and that therefore the international law of self-determination legitimizes Northern Ireland's present status as part of the United Kingdom. Republicans reply that these so-called 'recognitions' were coerced – the Treaty by Lloyd George's threat of war, and the Boundary Commission by a biased and improperly conducted review. These conflicting interpretations of international law show how unhelpful is its present reading of self-determination, and demonstrate its lack of utility in resolving the problems of Northern Ireland, and, in this context, that it does not offer unequivocal support for unionists' arguments.

The validity of some unionist claims about the historic origins of violence is even more questionable. Unionists' defiance of the laws passed by the Westminster parliament in 1912, through legal, quasi-legal and paramilitary mobilizations before 1914, is treated triumphally by most unionists, and their historians.[95] Intellectuals who acknowledge that the UVF damaged the political, law-abiding and democratic reputation of unionists still maintain that it is 'a highly question-begging description' to refer to their armed defiance of parliament.[96] They fail to recognize that the paramilitary resistance of the UVF to home rule persuaded some Irish nationalists, including Padraig Pearse, that only militaristic separatism would accomplish political autonomy for Ireland. They do not remember the unionist movement as an illegal and unconstitutional rejection of the sovereignty of parliament, but rather as an affirmation of Ulster loyalism or British nationalism against the illegitimate governing authorities.

Similarly the actions of the RUC and the B Specials in assaulting civil-rights demonstrators in the late 1960s are apologetically treated as over-reactions to provocation, or worse, retrospectively justified as attempts to crush IRA-inspired actions. The sectarian Malvern Street murder carried out by the UVF in 1966, and the subsequent bombing of the Silent Valley Reservoir in 1968/9 at a moment of extreme communal tension, tend to be forgotten in unionist accounts of the onset of the current 'troubles'. The latter action was intended to be attributed to the IRA. It was for a while, and helped bring down Terence O'Neill. The role of Ian Paisley in organizing counter-demonstrations against the civil-rights movement of the 1960s also tends to be forgotten, and unionist accounts of the loyalist strike to bring down the power-sharing executive and the Council of Ireland in 1974 are similarly soft-focused. The massive intimidation that characterized that strike is often ignored.

That the introduction of internment without trial in August 1971 increased rather than dampened down the scale of violence is usually rationalized away by unionist 'law-and-order' zealots.[97] The evidence of large-scale loyalist paramilitary assassinations of Catholics, responsible for at least a quarter of all those killed since 1969 – and of collusion by members of the security forces in such actions – is also underplayed in many articulations of traditional unionism. Evidence of collaboration with loyalist paramilitaries in the locally recruited Ulster Defence Regiment, and its successor the Royal Irish Regiment, are denounced as IRA propaganda. However, in the five years

1985–9 members of the UDR were one and a half times more likely to be convicted of scheduled (i.e. terrorist) offences than the civilians they were supposed to be protecting.[98] The UDR, whose Catholic membership was less than 3 per cent before it was wound up in 1992, was accused of 'deficient' vetting procedures by an English Deputy Chief Constable, John Stevens, appointed in 1989 to investigate collusion between the security forces and loyalist paramilitaries. However, this collusion is seen by some unionists as necessary communal deterrence in the absence of appropriate powers and resources being granted to the security forces.

A standard unionist canard is that constitutional nationalists, like the SDLP, do not back the police.[99] The evidence: the fact that the SDLP does not endorse everything the police do and its insistence that the RUC acts impartially in upholding the law. Nothing less than a blank-cheque endorsement of the actions of the RUC, the British Army and the Northern Irish courts appears to be satisfactory for such unionists. That unconditional support for all the actions of the security authorities is the hallmark of anti-democratic philosophies does not seem to occur to such unionists. Their condemnations of the SDLP, which consistently criticized the IRA and sought to ensure that it abandoned violence, are also exceptionally one-eyed: spokesmen for unionist parties, especially Bill Craig in the 1970s, and Ian Paisley throughout his career, have regularly issued inflammatory statements that have been seen by many as giving the 'orange light' to loyalist paramilitary assassins.[100]

*It takes at least two to stalemate.* Conventional unionist accounts of the constitutional stalemate since 1972 are coloured by partisan and self-serving arguments. The preponderant majority of unionists not only opposed the creation of an 'Irish dimension' in any new constitutional designs drafted after the fall of Stormont, but also opposed any kind of internal power-sharing on principle. After 1974 unionists mostly debated amongst themselves as to which hard-line political strategy would best ensure the Union. For over a decade this issue was centre-stage in political competition between the unionist parties – and in the internal debate within the two largest unionist parties.[101] Rather than seek dialogue with the nationalist minority, address the question of an Irish dimension or internal power-sharing, or consider how public policy might be managed so as to encourage Catholics to be citizens who might accept the legitimacy of Northern Ireland's political institutions, they berated the British government for not being sufficiently firm in stamping out terrorism. Indeed it was only after the Anglo-Irish Agreement that a considerable number of Ulster unionists altered their analyses of the causes of the conflict, and their perceptions of the best strategies for addressing them.[102] There was little recognition amongst the unionist political elite that their insistence on a full-scale British dimension – with no Irish dimension – had played its part in establishing a stalemate. In this respect unionists are no different from other 'integral nationalists': they have refused, in principle, to recognize the existence of another national community within Northern Ireland, and will recognize it, if at all, solely as a minority community, rather than as one entitled to equal institutional recognition.

## Revisionist Unionism: the Fault Lies with British Absentees

Revisionist unionists add an additional exogenous cause of the conflict, an 'absent cause': the lack of a British commitment to the Union which would find its full expression in the electoral integration of the region with the rest of the British party system.[103] They maintain that 'to reduce unionism to evangelicalism, or an identity crisis or to conditional loyalty does not adequately capture its character'.[104] Ulster unionists are not, they insist, *colons*, or settlers – indeed this misperception accounts for the defects in British public policy.[105] Properly construed and articulated, unionism is a philosophy of the modern state which seeks to maintain rights of equal citizenship for all in a liberal democratic state.

Arthur Aughey's eloquent book describing the Unionist reaction to the Anglo-Irish Agreement is the exemplary statement of liberal unionist revisionism.[106] He tries to develop a political philosophy of unionism – which he suggests has always been implicitly based upon a commitment to the modern state rather than the nation as its central organizing concept. The cornerstone of unionism, when properly stated, is the idea of the British state as the embodiment of pluralism and liberal individualism.[107] Unionism, unlike Irish nationalism, is deemed a genuinely modern philosophy because it is not predicated upon an ethnically, culturally or religiously defined nation-state. Aughey recognizes the embarrassing fact that 'Unionist politics, [with] all its parochial stupidities, [has] identified itself with the inherited if not always the current values of the British state'[108] but would have us believe that underneath the provincial backwardness and secondary prejudices of his co-unionists has consistently lurked the philosophy of modernity – the idea of the liberal state.

In this perspective the fault-line in Northern Ireland's political structure is not caused by the conditional loyalty of unionists to the British state, but by 'the consistent policy of London to be conditional in its loyalty to the United Kingdom'.[109] The case for electoral integration is advanced: British political parties must organize in Northern Ireland as proof of their commitment to the Union and as the one sure way of building a politics which transcends ethnic conflict and religious sectarianism.[110] The alleged failure of British political parties to make this commitment in the past condemned Northern Ireland to sectarian squalor. Revisionist unionists think that devolutionists, in the DUP and elsewhere, are victims of 'the Stormont virus' which led them away from a correct understanding of the Union. Devolution was a by-product of British absenteeism and Britain's lack of understanding of the Union. Those committed to power-sharing devolved government are put in the same dock: they will institutionalize sectarianism, and thus corrode the liberal freedoms that have characterized the British state. The idea of the state as the sphere of what Hegel called 'objective right' would be 'completely transgressed' by power-sharing or consociational solutions, and the 'two sectarian political camps [would] lose all need to reform themselves'.[111] The Anglo-Irish Agreement is condemned as a 'constitutional monstrosity' which 'resembles more than anything else a land deal between two feudal dynasties'.[112]

## The Revisionist Unionist Case Dissected

There are fundamental difficulties with revisionist unionist explanations and prescriptions. We shall state most of them briefly, in order to concentrate on their core proposition that electoral integration is the best way to resolve conflict in and over Northern Ireland. However, before we state these criticisms we must remark that the revisionist unionist case marks intellectual progress, even if it lacks realism. It is after all a form of civic nationalism – founded on a commitment to equality and liberal democratic principles – a philosophical gulf separates it from the more ethnically and religiously prejudiced forms of traditional unionism and loyalism. Our normative objection to revisionist unionism is not that it is a form of liberalism, but that it does not recognize that it is antithetical to the genuine pluralism which a richer version of liberalism would underpin.

*A very liberal reading of history.* The historical bases of revisionist unionist arguments are open to challenge on at least five grounds. First, the denial of *any* colonial dimension to the conflict is misleading.[113] Secondly, defending the Union for liberal reasons was not uppermost in the mobilization of the Orange Order against home rule. There is no persuasive evidence that the bulk of unionists defended the Union in the 1880s in the manner in which Aughey and Roberts might have us believe. Indeed one unionist reviewer of a detailed study of the early history of Ulster Unionism declares: 'Jackson shows us clearly that just as it is simplistic to reduce Unionism to a form of racial supremacism, it is equally misleading to play up its British and liberal-democratic character to the exclusion of its seamier side.'[114] Thirdly, Ulster Unionists may have had devolved government imposed upon them in 1920, but they accepted it in 1921, worked it with enthusiasm, and showed few regrets about it until after 1972. In 1936 the Ulster Unionist

Council declared that 'Had we refused to accept a parliament for Northern Ireland and remained at Westminster there can be little doubt but that now we would be either inside the Free State or fighting desperately against incorporation.'[115] The frequency with which integrationists quote Edward Carson's anxieties about the formation of a devolved government in Northern Ireland begs the question of how representative were the opinions of the Dublin-born and British-resident lawyer. Fourthly, revisionist unionists tend to assume that all Irish nationalists, past and present, have been and are Gaelic romantics or Catholic reactionaries with no commitment to the philosophy of the modern liberal state, while Ulster unionists have allegedly mostly been devotees of a purely instrumental and rational philosophy of statehood. Such views, sadly, are cultural stereotypes rather than arguments. There is in fact an Irish Enlightenment tradition which is not sectarian in either the Gaelic or Catholic modes.[116] It may be true that the Irish Enlightenment tradition has been less potent than the Catholic and Gaelic romantic one, but then liberal unionism has been less potent than the unionism of the Orange Order, the B Specials, and discriminatory employment practices. Finally, sceptics correctly question the claim that British parties were never organized in Northern Ireland after 1920. The Conservative Party and the Ulster Unionist Party were institutionally tied together, in both their names and their origins, with Unionist MPs taking the Conservative whip – and in some cases sitting in the Cabinet or acting as junior ministers – until the Heath government of 1970–4. Membership of the Young Unionists and the Young Conservatives overlapped right up until 1986, just after the signing of the Anglo-Irish Agreement. The Northern Ireland Labour Party, by contrast, was not so closely connected to the British Labour Party, but it did proclaim its commitment to that party and competed in the region's elections on that commitment after 1949 with the help of a subsidy from the British party. Thus fair facsimiles of the British political parties were present in Northern Ireland after 1920, and their presence did not dissolve the region's sectarian politics. The argument that only the originals would have done, rather than the photocopies, is for the reader's judgement.

*How civic are states and the British one in particular?* The claims which revisionist unionists make about modern states, and the British state in comparison with the Irish state, can be challenged on both empirical and philosophical grounds. First, the claim that the modern state *should* be ethnically neutral is different from the thesis that it *is* so in fact. All states, without exception since the ending of apartheid, now grant citizenship, in principle, to all the resident descendants of their indigenous populations. However, most states, modern and non-modern, place considerable constraints on access to citizenship by those who have no ancestral or ethnic ties to the state in question. Citizenship may be a civic ideal, but almost all modern liberal democracies provide it with an ethnic base – spelling out what kinds of immigrants are acceptable and what cultural qualifications are required of them, before or after they apply for citizenship. Moreover, the proposition that the UK state is a model of civic citizenship, devoid of national or ethnic cultural content, or that the UK's institutions are ethnically neutral, would produce a hollow laugh amongst 'visible minorities' in Britain, as well as audiences of potential immigrants from India, Pakistan, Bangladesh and the West Indies.[117] The idea that the United Kingdom is superior to the Republic as a liberal democracy which protects secular rights, individual human rights and minority-rights is also not as obvious as it might seem to a reader of secular disposition.[118]

To begin with one should not forget that the British state's management of Northern Ireland, before and after 1972, is a withering refutation of this claim. The United Kingdom lacks proportional representation. Unless one counts the aristocracy there is no minority or territorial representation in the second chamber of its parliament, and no written constitution or legal vetoes for minorities. Consider also the fact that the Irish Republic is a republic. It has no hereditary monarchy or aristocracy with political privileges, which constitute a considerable blemish on equal citizenship in the UK. It is a republic with no endowed church.[119] Indeed in 1972 its population voted to remove the legally meaningless but contentious provisions which appeared to grant a special place to the Roman Catholic Church.[120] By contrast, the United

Kingdom's political institutions are a zone of feudal and theological particularism rather than of liberal modernity. In both England and Scotland there are established state-churches. The head of state must be an Anglican in England and a Presbyterian in Scotland (making the monarch a theological schizophrenic); and the head of the government, the First Lord of the Treasury, and the Lord Chancellor must not be Roman Catholics. There has been no Catholic head of state in England or Scotland since 1688, and by law there cannot be. By contrast the Republic's first head of state was a Protestant and its present head of state is married to a Protestant. The latter is not a matter of public note in the Republic. A prospective Catholic marriage partner for a senior member of the House of Windsor remains taboo in the United Kingdom.

The Irish Supreme Court and the Irish state has a good record, especially since the 1960s, in defending the human rights of individuals – other than gypsies or 'travellers' as they are called in Ireland – against the state. This record includes its decision in the world-famous child-rape and abortion case of X in the spring of 1992.[121] In its provisions for constitutional review of legislation affecting fundamental rights, the Irish Constitution is more liberal than its British counterpart – whatever that might be. There is, of course, no gainsaying the illiberal provisions of the Irish Constitution which illegalize divorce (added in 1937, the subject of an attempted repeal in 1986, and proposed for repeal in another promised referendum by the present Irish government), and which outlaw abortion (added to the Constitution in 1983 but effectively rendered ambiguous by a Supreme Court decision in 1992). However, though the Republic has lagged behind Britain in liberalizing these domains of private life it does not look as if it will remain this way for much longer.[122] It is also worth observing that the British government has not extended liberal abortion legislation to Northern Ireland because of the opposition of both religious communities there, not just Catholics; and that the legalization of homosexuality in both parts of Ireland required external legal interventions in European courts. In short, most Ulster Protestants were

Table 3.5  Social change in the Republic of Ireland, 1961–93

|  | 1961 | 1993 | Change (%) |
|---|---|---|---|
| Population | 2,818,000 | 3,563,000 | + 26 |
| GNP | £(IR) 7.2 bn | £(IR) 27.7 bn | + 284 |
| GNP per capita | £(IR) 2,555 | £(IR) 7,774 | + 204 |
| GNP per worker | £(IR) 6,407 | £(IR) 24,171 | + 277 |
| % employed in agriculture | 34 | 12.6 | – 63 |
| % employed in manufacturing | 24.5 | 27.2 | + 11 |
| % employed in services | 41.5 | 60.2 | + 45 |

not hungering for moral liberalism before the 1920s, and it is not clear that most of them do now. Indeed the Republic's treatment of its Protestant minority, outside of the constitutional ban on divorce and abortion – which were opposed by some rather than all Protestants – stands up remarkably well in comparison with the treatment of the Catholic minority in Northern Ireland, and favourably with the treatment of minorities in some other states.[123] The portrait of the Republic in revisionist unionist literature is therefore overdrawn, and just not credible.[124] To argue that the Republic is committed to 'the construction of a homogeneous, confessional political order'[125] is to conflate an entire political system with some actors within that system, to assume that only one illiberal reading of the Irish Constitution is valid; and to ignore the claim that an Irish nation-state which contained Ulster Protestants would necessarily have been more heterogeneous, and at least bi-confessional, if not much more secular.

Finally, revisionist unionist writing does not acknowledge the extent to which the Republic has changed significantly in the last thirty years. It is now socially, economically and politically unrecognizable from the bucolic Ireland of de Valera and his critics. Its social and economic transformation is demonstrated in table 3.5, which draws on research by Cyril White.[126] The data show significant alterations in the demography of the Republic, its extensive urbanization, and the growth, at the expense of agriculture, of its service and manufacturing sectors. This socio-economic 'modernization' of the Republic has also been reflected in changes in its politics, where moral liberalism is advanced by a range of political parties, and where the influence of traditional nationalists is less than that of neo-nationalists who seek the unification of a pluralist Ireland with the consent of a majority in Northern Ireland.[127]

*Northern Ireland really is different.* The key argument that electoral integrationists make, 'Northern Ireland is different because it is treated differently by the British political parties', is unpersuasive. The converse is truer. Nicholas Scott, then deputy Secretary of State for Northern Ireland, outraged integrationists when he wrote in 1986 that 'Northern Ireland is Different and must be Governed Differently' but his argument is correct.[128] Northern Ireland differs from the rest of the UK in that it is the site of a former colonial settlement which has given rise to competing national allegiances, and to suggest that it needs different political institutions from those elsewhere in the United Kingdom is *prima facie* reasonable.

The importance which electoral integrationists attach to the consequences of British party-organization in the region, and to a firmer British commitment to the Union, can be debated on strictly empirical grounds. Experience elsewhere in Europe and North America does not suggest that the presence of state-wide parties is an especially important method for assuaging ethnic conflict. Canada and the United States have had severe ethnic conflicts, and much of Eastern Europe will continue to have ethnic and national conflicts, despite the existence of state-wide parties competing for electoral support. The artificial formation of state-wide pan-ethnic parties has not had a great record of success in post-colonial countries. The electoral integrationist argument also simply forgets that pan-British party organization existed in Ireland until the 1880s, i.e. until the onset of democratization. Far from inhibiting national and sectarian conflict the existing British party organizations were simply wiped out by the emergence of local ethnic parties or by local capture of British parties in the case of the Conservative and Unionist Party.

Survey data suggest that the impact of formal British political party organization in Northern Ireland would not substantively erode national allegiances or sectarianism. The electoral integrationists cite polls which show that a significant proportion of the local electorate want British parties to contest elections, and would be prepared to vote for them, as proof that the population is not irredeemably wedded to local sectarian parties. However, the claim that the organization of the British parties would break down bloc politics is valid only if those prepared to vote for the British parties have non-national, non-ethnic or non-religious motives. A poll of October 1988 which broke down party preference and religious affiliation in Northern Ireland was very revealing on this issue.[129] It showed that 21 per cent of Catholics would, hypothetically, support Labour but that only 6 per cent of Protestants would do so. Moreover, hypothetically 24 per cent of Protestants would vote Conservative but only 6 per cent of Catholics would do so. This striking differential in hypothetical support cannot be explained adequately by class differences between the two communities, although that may account for some of it. According to these polls, in the event of British parties organizing in Northern Ireland, 70 per cent of Catholics would vote for parties advocating a united Ireland (the SDLP, Sinn Féin, and the British Labour Party) while 81 per cent of Protestants would continue to vote for parties which are broadly supportive of the union (UUP, DUP, Alliance, and the British Conservative Party). It is therefore wishful thinking to claim that the organization of British parties in Northern Ireland will result in the Northern Irish adopting the political culture of the (Great) British. While there may be (contestable) arguments for the major British parties to seek a mandate in the region, given the existence of direct rule, it is doubtful that this step will lead to the disappearance of deeply-rooted national and ethnic cleavages or sectarianism.[130] The poor showing of the Conservatives in their first electoral outings in Northern Ireland between 1989 and 1994 has not dampened enthusiasm for electoral integration amongst revisionist unionists, who are now campaigning for the British Labour Party to follow the Conservatives.[131] The 'triumph' of hope over experience is not unusual in politics – so even if the

Labour Party decided to organize in Northern Ireland it could look forward to losing its deposits.

Electoral integration offers no panacea. Consider the following thought-experiment: would it satisfy the political aspirations of Irish nationalists? The answer is obvious. Irish nationalists, including neo-nationalists, reject British integrationism by definition. British electoral integration is hardly likely to encourage the Provisional IRA to maintain its cessation of military operations, or bring Sinn Féin and SDLP activists and voters into the embrace of British political parties. The belief that electoral integration is the route to progress is therefore either naive,[132] or simply a new way of seeking British hegemony in Northern Ireland.

*Consociationalism is not racism.* The argument made by most revisionists and integrationists that power-sharing – or consociation – necessarily institutionalizes ethnic hierarchies or sectarianism is fallacious. It rests on the erroneous premise that the sole alternative to liberal individualism is some form of racist apartheid. Power-sharing, properly understood, aims to achieve equality and proportionality between divided communities, i.e. to erode discrimination and untrammelled majority control, and to permit cultural autonomy. These principles are meant to inhibit ethnic or sectarian domination, or forced integration. They are not meant to, and need not, institutionalize hatred for other communities, or indeed hierarchical relations between them. They are intended to foster tolerance, mutual recognition, and respect for differences. Moreover, the institutionalization of power-sharing is a route through which communal identifications can (eventually) be eroded peacefully, as has arguably occurred in the Netherlands.[133] There are difficulties attached to promoting consociational ideas in Northern Ireland, but the arguments of unionist integrationists do not provide convincing normative grounds for rejecting them.[134]

*On British romanticism.* The admiration electoral integrationists display for the Westminster model of two-party competition as a means of regulating national, ethnic and religious conflict is bewildering. This British romanticism matches that of Gaelic romantics in its worship of a mythical past.

It is sufficient to make two points. First, the British two-party model of competition worked in Great Britain after 1920, to the extent that it did, only after the bulk of Ireland had seceded from the Union – and electoral competition could therefore focus on socio-economic cleavages within a largely British, and largely pan-Protestant or secular political culture. Thus the two-party model of electoral integration worked effectively only when the United Kingdom was made more culturally homogeneous by the secession of the Irish Free State. This causality is entirely different from that suggested by electoral integrationists: electoral integration in Great Britain followed the resolution of (a lot of) the national question in part of the UK. Perhaps even this point is too generous: the re-emergence of Scottish and to a lesser extent Welsh nationalism in the 1970s raises the question whether the electoral integration of the peoples of Great Britain has been anything more than a brief interlude. Our second point can be made more briefly. The idea that the British model of government is the one best way to solve national or ethnic quarrels is not one that withstands comparative political analysis – indeed the Westminster model is widely and correctly criticized by analysts of ethnic-conflict regulation.[135]

The recent conversion of some unionists to electoral integrationist philosophies suggests a new-found British romanticism, or an Anglo-Irish Agreement-induced conversion, rather than a pluralist and principled liberalism. The character of some support for electoral integration suggests a widespread desire on the part of some unionists to follow any course which enables them to insist on British nationalism, while denying that that is what they are doing, and to avoid having to accommodate the minority in Northern Ireland – other than in respect for its members' individual human rights. In short only one community's collective rights are to be protected. However, that said, revisionist unionists have broken decisively with the shibboleths of traditional unionism, and have thereby played a partly constructive role in breaking the hold of traditional images of politics in Northern Ireland.

# Conclusion

The defects in unionist discourses do not mean that principled cases for the Union are not made, or cannot be made. However, unionists' arguments and actions must change if they are to persuade audiences in Northern Ireland and elsewhere in the British Isles of their sincere commitment to equal citizenship for northern nationalists as well as Catholics.

Conventional unionist discourses mirror those of traditional Irish nationalists. Each blames exogenous agents for the conflict. Unionists blame the Republic, republicans Britain; both unionists and nationalists also blame their own patron-state for being insufficiently committed to their national cause. Each, additionally, deliberately misreads the other's national identification. Just as nationalists argue that unionists are really Irish and are manipulated into thinking of themselves as British, so unionists argue that northern Catholics are really capable of being British, and are externally or educationally manipulated into thinking of themselves as the lost tribe of Erin. If authentic recognition of one's opponents is a necessary part of conflict-resolution then conventional unionist discourses, like those of traditional nationalism, must be criticized and transcended. Unionist electoral integrationists need to recognize that they are British nationalists, and that their versions of British nationalism and British integrationism, like similar versions of Irish nationalism and Irish integrationism, have played their parts in causing conflict, provoking violence, and sustaining a protracted stalemate.

# 4

# Oranges and Reds: Revisionist Marxism

There is nothing inherently reactionary about the Protestant working class or, for that matter, a national frontier which puts Protestants in a numerical majority.
*Paul Bew, Peter Gibbon and Henry Patterson, left-wing unionists*[1]

Just as the extreme Shi'ite Muslims hold that Archangel Gabriel made a mistake, delivering the message to Mohammed when it was intended for Ali, so Marxists . . . like to think that the spirit of history or human consciousness made a terrible boob . . . [the] message intended for classes . . . by some terrible postal error was delivered to nations.
*Ernest Gellner, anthropologist, philosopher, and sociologist*[2]

This chapter surveys the writings of Marxists who reject green Marxism. We do them this honour because their influence has extended beyond the small political sects in which they flourished. Thus the 'orange Marxist' literature, initially developed by the British and Irish Communist Organization (BICO) in the early 1970s, shaped the development of revisionist unionist arguments in the 1980s, and the personnel involved in the BICO in the early 1970s reappeared as enthusiasts for electoral integration in the 1980s.[3] The red Marxist literature has been influential in less obvious ways, but shaped the evolution of the political stance of the Workers' Party before it disintegrated in 1992.[4]

After 1969 it became increasingly difficult to argue that Protestant workers were closet Irish nationalists, who had their national preferences manipulated by capitalists and landlords.

The loyalist backlash against the civil-rights movement, the paramilitary campaigns of the UVF and the UDA, and new unionist and loyalist political organizations were grassroots phenomena. Protestant marchers, paramilitaries, and strikers protested against the unionist establishment as well as the treacherous Westminster government. Some left-wingers reacted by rejecting green Marxist analysis and the belief that a united Ireland was the best means to socialism, maintaining that Protestant working-class resistance to a united Ireland was and is autonomous of ruling class suasion. These Marxists can be located on an orange–red continuum, from sectarian to non-sectarian dispositions.[5] At the orange end was the British and Irish Communist Organization (BICO) and a number of authors intellectually associated with it.[6] The BICO is now defunct, although some of its former members still publish.[7] It regarded the Union as more important than working-class union, believed uncritically in the benefits of British rule in Ireland and elsewhere; justified, or denied discrimination against Catholics in Northern Ireland; and called for hard-line measures against the IRA, but not against loyalist paramilitaries. Its Orangeism was evident in its retrospective support for the Williamite settlement in Ireland, which it regarded as unqualifiedly progressive.[8] We include the BICO's writings in the Marxist revisionist camp, despite their often visible sectarianism, because they used Marxist language and described themselves as Marxists. Conor Lynch, who was a member of the BICO, and Hugh Roberts, who was not a member of the BICO but was a member of the Communist Party, have subsequently developed arguments similar to that of the BICO.[9] They are the unionist counterparts of green Marxists who 'critically' support Irish nationalism. In their eyes reactionary Catholicism and irredentist Irish nationalism are the primary exogenous causes of conflict – though they also believe that these forces are artificially sustained by the folly of British policy-makers and parties.

Other Marxists are closer to the red end of our continuum, though their hues of crimson and orange vary.[10] The Workers' Party, before it collapsed in 1992, was inspired by red Marxism, and by a virulent rejection of traditional nationalism. Red

Marxists claim to be internationalists, and more interested in working-class unity than in particular national or constitutional arrangements.[11] They do not accept that certain constitutional structures are *a priori* regressive or progressive. They may prefer, for tactical purposes, one arrangement of state boundaries over another, or they may accept the status quo by default, much as Lenin did in the former Czarist empire. The red Marxist authors discussed here just happen to have supported either independence for Northern Ireland or its continued membership of the United Kingdom – pending, of course, the creation of global socialism. What distinguishes them from their orange brethren is their attitude towards the minority community. They acknowledge and usually condemn discrimination against Catholics, and oppose repressive measures directed against them.

## Red Marxist Accounts

Red Marxists agree that partition can be attributed to the uneven development of capitalism in Ireland: the 'stark reality' of the contrast between 'bustling progressive industrial Ulster' and 'backward', 'stagnant', 'peasant southern Ireland'.[12] Uneven capitalist development is attributed not to imperialist divide-and-rule policies but to different settlement-patterns and ensuing modes of production,[13] different forms of land tenure,[14] or the tendency of capitalism to develop unevenly across space.[15] The divergence between the north and south of Ireland, and the different political interests to which it gave rise, account for the conversion of eighteenth-century Protestant nationalists into nineteenth-century Protestant unionists and, ultimately, the establishment of two 'states' in Ireland in 1921.[16] Uneven economic development was a 'much more significant' explanatory variable than economic differentials between Catholics and Protestants within Northern Ireland.[17]

Divergent economic interests were reinforced by religious sectarianism, but this phenomenon, understandably for Marxists, is of secondary importance.[18] Sectarianism developed independently of manipulation, even if the Unionist bourgeoisie and elements of the British ruling class cheerfully exploited it. Orangeism was rooted in the 'conditions of existence' of the Protestant masses including the centuries of conflict which followed their plantation in Ulster, and their persistent fears of being dispossessed by the Catholic majority.[19] Rather than being induced to be sectarians by the bourgeoisie, working-class Protestants were capable of abandoning the bourgeoisie and landlords when their interests were threatened.[20]

Red Marxists maintain that Britain's attitude towards partition was more flexible than green Marxists assert.[21] The interests of colonialists and imperialists diverged. The former wanted partition, not the latter.[22] Leading members of the British ruling class were prepared to concede Home Rule to Ireland in 1886, 1893 and 1912; and during 1919–21 they were more interested in ensuring a moderate government in Dublin than in partitioning Ireland.[23] In 1940 Churchill considered abandoning Northern Ireland in return for de Valera's participation in the Allied war effort.[24] While de Valera's insistence on neutrality and Northern Ireland's war-time loyalty temporarily strengthened the unionist position and led to a limited appreciation of Northern Ireland's strategic importance, these events are held to have had no lasting effect.[25] After 1949, the geo-political importance of Northern Ireland declined, and it became clear that Irish governments would happily join NATO in return for the termination of partition.[26] The British government's direct intervention in 1969 was reluctant, and did not indicate a robust commitment to the Union.[27]

Ruling-class flexibility about the Union is explained by Ireland's economic marginality in the British calculus, as early as 1921,[28] and by the argument that British imperialist exploitation did not require formal political control of the island.[29] When the present crisis broke out, Northern Ireland was even more economically peripheral – dependent on subventions from Westminster, paid for by British industry without any compensating benefits.[30] Red Marxists therefore reject 'imperialism' as an explanation of Britain's role in Ireland, and even more vehemently the idea that the nationalist struggle is 'anti-imperialist'. Following their master Lenin, they see imperialism as a specific stage in the development of capitalism, its reorganization as an international system, which reached its apogee at the beginning of the twentieth century – when Irish politics had already taken recognizable shape. 'Imperialism' in the Leninist sense helps explain why the north, a part of the imperial metropolis, prospered.[31] In this world-view a group can legitimately describe itself as anti-imperialist only if it aims at undermining the international basis of capitalism.[32] Irish nationalist 'anti-imperialism' was limited to extricating Ireland from British control and therefore was not anti-capitalist.

Red Marxists argue that it is incredible to regard Britain as the obstacle to Irish unity; indeed for some of them the British government is regarded as a party to the 'plot' to reunite Ireland, and has long 'devoutly desired' to get out of Northern Ireland.[33] *The* obstacle to Irish unification is the resolute support for the Union by 'one million Protestants', a neat but inaccurate figure. Loyalists are at their most belligerent when the Union is under threat (1912, 1920–5 and 1974).[34] The militant republicanism of the late 1960s and the early 1970s unleashed sectarian pogroms, played into the hands of loyalist reactionaries, and ruled out more fruitful socialist strategies.[35] Red Marxists concur that unifying Ireland would produce a more intense war, rather than advance socialism.[36]

They do not accept that the Stormont parliament was doomed to be reactionary, or the thesis that Northern Ireland's future is confined to the 'devastatingly simple' choice 'between . . . a semi-fascist Orange statelet in the North matched by a pro-imperialist police state in the South, and . . . an anti-imperialist and socialist revolution'.[37] They also reject the thesis that the Stormont regime was progressive, and that British rule is inherently beneficial. Instead, they argue that partition was, in principle, compatible with progressive politics, even if the Stormont regime was in fact reactionary: 'the problem of the involvement of the British state in Northern Ireland lies not in its existence but in its specific forms'.[38]

So how do red Marxists explain why Northern Ireland developed a reactionary political form before 1972, and how do they account for the outbreak of the current crisis and the protracted stalemate? The underlying claim, predictably, is that discrimination in Northern Ireland was a by-product of capitalism, and that the solution lies in non-discriminatory socialism. Some of them explain sectarianism by the immaturity of the region's economic development. Dominated by small-scale businesses and without large-scale state intervention, Northern Ireland was governed after 1921 by an Orange clientelist system, which distributed public and private favours on a discriminatory basis.[39] This economy contrasted negatively with the more impersonal and religion-blind labour markets found in more advanced capitalist economies, and explains why sectarianism and religious extremism prevailed over trade unionism, reformism, and secularism, and why Northern Ireland is incomprehensible to the denizens of more advanced capitalist formations.[40] While this social formation existed, there could be no question of a transition to a liberal- or social-democratic society on the Great British model. However, in the 1950s and 1960s the development of the welfare state led to a recasting of this archaic structure. The decline of local and traditional capital and its replacement by the modern 'monopoly' capital had a similarly corrosive effect. The contradiction in Northern Ireland was not between British imperialism and national liberation forces, but between 'the Orange paternalist or "clientelist" version of capitalism, and twentieth-century managerial capitalism'.[41] Multi-nationals had no ties to the local community, no interest in maintaining an Orange alliance, favoured less personalized relationships with their employees, and were less prone to discriminate.[42] Conflict in the 1960s was therefore between modern impersonal capital, sponsored by Terence O'Neill and later Brian Faulkner, and the representatives of traditional capital, like Bill Craig, allied with Protestant workers who benefited from the clientelist system. O'Neill's reforms won the support of Catholics who embraced the notion of a new capitalist democracy, but provoked a furious Protestant backlash. In this story another episode in a long saga of ethnic conflict is decoded as a crisis of modernization, a clash between two radically different kinds of capital: 'the manifestation at the political level of the transition from one variant of a capitalist social formation to another'.[43]

Prescriptions followed. Rather than regarding capitalism, imperialism and Orangeism as coincident, Anders Boserup urged Irish socialists to make a tactical alliance with the new progressive forces against the representatives of traditional capital. However, not all reds shared his faith in the progressive potential of monopoly capital; they pointed out that monopoly and international capital were only weakly represented in Ireland, and that multinational investment in Ireland had been halted by the economic crisis of the 1970s and by the repercussions of sectarian violence.[44] Rather than striking up 'fatalistic' alliances with monopoly capital, Belinda Probert reasoned that the politically correct socialist strategy was to unite the working class against both local *and* monopoly capital. Encouraged by class-consciousness among Protestant workers and in loyalist organizations she highlighted the ability of the Protestant proletariat to overthrow the Sunningdale settlement, which 'had little to offer the workers', and its alleged willingness to compromise with the Catholic working class. She even saw radical potential in Paisleyism and in the deliberations of the 1975 constitutional Convention.[45] Showing a true catholicity and protestantism in her paramilitary tastes she urged socialists to support progressives within working-class organizations, even those of the IRA and UDA.[46]

Tom Nairn agreed that the conflict in the 1960s was brought about by economic modernization,[47] but differed in his explanation of the Stormont regime. He attributed its peculiarity to Protestants' physical, political and cultural isolation from Great Britain, combined with their self-conscious frontier status. As a result, they had not been able to develop the normal response of threatened societies, nationalism: 'Instead what one observes historically is a lunatic, compensatory emphasis of the two ideologies already strongly present in its community: militant Protestantism and imperialism. It is as aberrant substitutes for nationalism that these idea-systems have to be understood.'[48] Consequently, he supported an independent Northern Ireland as the desirable and probable outcome of economic and political changes. Economic modernization had destroyed the Orange order and unionist unity, and produced a Protestant working-class movement capable of defeating 'three bourgeois governments' during the 1974 strike and of asserting its national independence.[49] Nairn predicted an independent Northern Ireland by the end of the 1970s.[50] It would allow Protestants to develop a modern national identity, superseding their support for 'the Orange Order, Calvinist bigotry and Kiplingesque empire'.[51] What remained of the minority problem in Nairn's blasé view could be overcome by 'the tried and mundane techniques of border-manipulation, minority-guarantees, appeals to UNO and other international tribunals, occasional troop-manoeuvres etc.'.[52]

The works of Paul Bew, Peter Gibbon, and Henry Patterson differ from these other red Marxist accounts. Following the French and Greek Marxists Louis Althusser, Etienne Balibar, and Nicos Poulantzas they take as their central organizing concept the capitalist state, and at times they write in a similar style to these masters of the dialectic.[53] They define the state functionally: its task is to disorganize the working class and maintain the social conditions for the exploitation of the proletariat.[54] State strategies adopted to this end reflect the strength of different social forces within a particular society. The Stormont regime resulted from an alliance between a dominant populist faction of the ruling class and the sectarians amongst the Protestant working class – facilitated by the unreliability of the British state as an ally of the unionists, and fostered by the successes of Sinn Féin during 1919–20.[55] Sectarianism emerged as the logical and appropriate means of dividing the proletariat.

Stressing the heterogeneity of Protestants, Bew, Gibbon, and Patterson argue that significant sections of the Protestant working class were not wedded to the Protestant cross-class alliance – though they were committed to the Union.[56] In certain circumstances, such as the outdoor relief riots in Belfast in 1932, some Protestants displayed class-militancy in alliance with Catholic workers. The state then reacted by visibly and ritually excluding Catholics. However, discrimination was not, as green Marxists and nationalists allege, an instrument used to delude proletarian dupes; nor, as Orange Marxists and unionists argue, a justifiable reaction to republicanism; nor, as Boserup and Probert claimed, a result of archaic economic development; nor, as Nairn argued, the result of Protestants being doubly isolated from Britain. Instead discrimination was a logical response by the capitalist state, given sectarian conditions, to the possibility of class conflict.[57] The logicality of the capitalist state, often elusive to capitalists, can always be detected by determined Marxists!

While 'sectarian exclusivism' was an important element in the repertoire of state strategies, it was not the only or even the most dominant one. The state had to manage changes in the material conditions of the masses which might promote class conflict. Thus it adopted Keynesian policies in the 1930s, and welfare reforms in the 1940s, even though the latter benefited Catholics.[58] The crisis of the 1960s was not caused by economic modernization.[59] 'O'Neillism' was no liberal assault on sectarianism, but a strategic response to significant electoral victories by the Northern Ireland Labour Party in 1958 and 1962.[60] The 'determinant social force' causing O'Neillism was 'the working class, in particular that section of the Protestant working class which voted NILP . . . [and which] seemed to presage large-scale working-class defection [from the Unionists] if drastic action was postponed'.[61] Bew, Gibbon, and Patterson, by contrast with Boserup, Probert, and Nairn, insist that secular and progressive forces were dominant within the Protestant working class in the 1960s.[62] Class conflict was prompted by a severe economic recession in Belfast between 1958 and 1962, persistently high unemployment in Northern Ireland (by contrast with full employment in Great Britain), and a bipartisan commitment in Great Britain to the elimination of regional disparities. A large proportion of the Protestant working class were 'not the dupes of Orangeism . . . but were influenced by a secular ideology of opposition to regional deprivation, articulated by the NILP'.[63] O'Neill attempted to steal the NILP's clothes by supporting regional planning, and promoting new inward investment.[64]

Bew and his colleagues also have different interpretations of Catholic politics during the late 1960s from those of Boserup, Probert, and Nairn. They reject the argument that the civil-rights movement was based on a new Catholic middle class created by the welfare state and multinational investment.[65] They think that it cannot explain the broad base of the campaign, the Catholic working class's 'indifference to moderation', or the emergence of republicanism in the economically marginalized areas of the region.[66] The civil-rights campaign received broad support not because of past improvements for working-class Catholics, but because they continued to suffer under the Stormont regime.[67] The British government (like Boserup, Probert, and Nairn), exaggerated the degree to which O'Neill could or was willing to reform sectarianism, and mistakenly supported him rather than the real progressive force in Northern Irish politics, the NILP.[68]

Bew and Patterson, like other red Marxists, prescribe socialism. Given the resilience of Protestant working-class opposition to a united Ireland, progressive forces can only do well when the Union is safe[69] – so the Union should be supported. Reforms aimed at improving the position of the Catholic working class should not be linked to the national question[70] – so there should be no Irish dimension.[71] Reactionaries in the minority community, i.e. nationalists and republicans, can be undermined by reforms aimed at removing sectarian inequalities and the repressive regime that governs life in the ghettos.[72] Such reforms would create the basis for progressive politics and the erosion of sectarianism. 'Primacy, therefore, should be given not to advocating an 'independent Ulster' or 'complete integration' solutions but rather to *reducing the extent of divisions within the masses themselves* [through] the construction of a progressive alliance to reform the state and create the best possible conditions for the development of class struggle'.[73] Bew and his colleagues are sceptical that their favoured route forward will come to pass. The IRA's campaign has reinforced working-class divisions, and constitutional nationalists and republican socialists continue to reject the autonomous nature of unionism.[74] The British state lacks the commitment to removing structural inequalities in Northern Ireland, and is engaged in mere crisis-management, promoting the cheap options of repression and 'institutionalism', while occasionally musing about withdrawal.[75] The result is the mutually-reinforcing ascendancy of reactionary groups in both communities.[76]

## Revisionist Marxism: Orange Accounts

Orange Marxism strikingly affirms that Marxism can be used as a weapon of ethnic conflict. If the BICO had not brought it into existence we would be tempted to invent it, to demonstrate symmetry in our arguments. Orange Marxists argue that the exogenous cause of conflict lies in the reactionary irredentism of the Irish state. They maintain that there are two nations, not one, on the island of Ireland, and that the evolution of these nations, and partition, are explicable through the uneven development of capitalism.[77] Uneven development is allegedly rooted in the 'Ulster custom' which gave tenants greater security on the land and therefore a sounder basis for capital accumulation. Industrialized, urbanized and developed Ulster had objective economic reasons for sustaining the Union. By contrast the agricultural and petit bourgeois sectors of Irish society were the epicentres of a religiously-inspired communal nationalism, unprogressive by historical materialist criteria.

Orthodox historical materialism judges social systems by their capacity to develop the productive forces and their degree of proximity to the social preconditions for advanced socialism. The nineteenth and twentieth-century Protestant working class, according to Orange Marxists, rightly assumed that its class interests and progressive politics were best served by the Union. Responsibility for the current conflict rests not with British imperialism but with the aggressive irredentist Catholic bourgeoisie of the Irish Republic, who inhabit a backward and reactionary theocracy. It is not the denial of the Irish people's right to self-determination but rather the denial of the Protestant nation's right to self-determination which is at the heart of conflict in Northern Ireland.[78]

The Orange Marxist explanation of uneven economic development in Irish history has an unsubtle sectarian flavour, providing a paean to Protestantism and British imperialism,

and an unremittingly hostile commentary on Catholicism and
Irish nationalism. Much of this praise and criticism is couched
in cultural rather than class discourse. It may be said of the
BICO that it composed *The Protestant Workers' Ethic and the
Spirit of Sectarian Socialism.* The industrialization of the north-
east of Ireland is attributed to the 'superior industrial character' of the Protestant settlers;[79] Protestants out-produced
and out-performed their less industrious and more benighted
Catholic neighbours;[80] and Catholics were 'the cannon-fodder
of feudalism',[81] not disposed to challenge their landlords
(sic!), and constantly threatened Protestants by offering a
supply of tenants to landlords who accepted rack-renting.[82]
Industrialization, according to the BICO, was not caused by
capital investment from England or subsidies from the British state. On the contrary, most external capital investment
went into a southern 'sinkhole', a Catholic feudal society with
anti-utilitarian and Luddite characteristics.[83] Protestant settlers
who arrived in Ireland in the seventeenth century are portrayed
as the democratic vanguard of an enlightened Scottish peasantry who succeeded in throwing off the authoritarian shackles
of the Catholic church.[84] They led the democratic charge
against the absolutism of Charles I and James II.[85] They were
on the right side in the American war of independence, the
French Revolution, and over the issue of Catholic emancipation.[86] They swung behind the Union after 1800 because of its
progressive potential, including its capacity to redress Catholic
grievances.[87] Far from being reactionary, the Protestants of
Ulster were in the vanguard of the struggle against feudalism.
Democratic commitments determined Protestant responses to
the Home Rule movement of the 1880s; unionist pan-class
opposition was dedicated to defending the 'most democratic
state on earth' (sic!) against reactionary ultramontane Catholic
nationalism.[88]

Orange explanations of Northern Irish politics after 1921
differ significantly from those of red revisionists. The central
'contradiction' was not between fractions of the ruling class, or
between the bourgeoisie and proletariat, but between unionist progressives and nationalist reactionaries. The existence
of unjustifiable discrimination against Catholics is denied.

Unionists had not wanted a Protestant state; they wanted Catholics and Protestants to be treated equally under the United Kingdom.[89] Abandoned by the British in 1921 and forced to withstand unrelenting aggression from Irish nationalists within and without,[90] they were forced to overlook their class divisions and establish an exclusivist state capable of protecting their position.[91] What 'discrimination' occurred resulted from the persistent refusal of Catholics to recognize the state.[92]

In this world-view the collapse of the Stormont regime in the 1960s was not the result of a conflict between different forms of capital, but rather the work of a nationalist plot. The civil-rights movement was a republican front, without the slightest interest in securing British rights within the Union, and which went out of its way to provoke Protestant resistance.[93] 'The Catholic minority . . . *never supported* . . . a policy of positive reforms within the Union.'[94] Militant republicanism was orchestrated by the southern ruling class and aided by British disarmament of Protestants.[95] The granting of the civil-rights movement's demands by 1970 did nothing to prevent the escalation of the republican campaign. Concessions to nationalists just whetted their appetites and increased their expectations.[96]

The BICO's prescription for resolving Northern Ireland was its full-scale integration into the British 'multi-national' state: 'the policy which would immediately command the greatest cross-section of support, create the best political conditions for ending terrorism, [and] enable normal political development to take over most quickly'.[97] Britain, a liberal-democratic, prosperous and pluralist state, was far more progressive than the Republic. Integration would suit those Catholics 'who reconcile themselves to the continuance of the union', although the fate of the rest is left ambiguous.[98] The BICO recognized no major obstacles to integration, such as the Irish national identity of the minority community.[99] Their solution required only an act of British political will.[100]

Since the BICO stopped publishing, a number of intellectually related groups and individuals have put forward variants on its analysis, sometimes in less overtly prejudicial terms.[101] These intellectuals focus on the absence of British class-based parties in the region after 1921: Northern Ireland allegedly escaped the therapeutic effects of British party competition. The failure of British parties to organize contributed to sterile sectarian politics and left large numbers of class-conscious individuals with only sectarian parties to choose from.[102] British 'electoral integration' is the way forward. This policy is said to be not only a pre-requisite for normal class-based politics but also an essential democratic right – they believe that every political party aiming to win governmental power is obligated to compete in every constituency in a state's territory.

Electoral integrationists claim that the British Labour Party overcame sectarianism in Clydeside and Merseyside, and could perform similar feats in Northern Ireland.[103] They produce polls which show that a significant proportion (53 per cent) of the Northern Ireland electorate want the British parties to contest elections in Northern Ireland and would be prepared to vote for these parties,[104] and argue that 'support for sectarian parties in Northern Ireland is anything but immutable . . . '.[105] One pamphlet confidently proclaims that British party organization in Northern Ireland would be followed by class voting within a decade.[106] Hugh Roberts is more precise: electoral integration would 'practically wipe out the APNI's support and deprive the [UUP] of nearly 60 per cent of its vote, while virtually halving the current support of the DUP and the SDLP'.[107]

## Eating the Reds

Some red Marxists offer better explanations of Northern Ireland politics after 1921 than their green rivals. Moreover, their analyses of the public-policy trajectory of the British state, and of Protestant resistance to a united Ireland, are often adept and empirically supported. Their appreciation of the nature of the Stormont polity is in keeping with the recorded historical evidence, unlike many traditional unionist or Orange analyses.[108] Most of them also recognize the difficulties that Marxists have always faced with national questions. However, these merits in their analyses do not require Marxist intellectual underpinnings. Similar arguments have been forwarded by authors who do not subscribe to Marxism and carry no Marxist burdens.

*The autonomy of nationalism and ethnicity.* Northern Ireland is a difficult case for all Marxists, for whom a capitalist polity is fundamentally divided along class lines. Other bases of collective identity, such as nationality, ethnicity, religion, or language, are considered superficial, impermanent, superstructural and ultimately the result of false consciousness. Red Marxists believe that both Protestants and Catholics are deluded about their real interests (green Marxists argue that only Protestants are deluded, and Orange Marxists argue only Catholics are deluded). The relevant delusions are attributed to artificial obstacles raised by capitalist development, which can be surmounted, with varying degrees of difficulty, through class analysis and struggle.

Ethnic or national solidarities, however, are no less meaningful and no less fundamental than solidarities based on people's position in a matrix of productive forces and relations of production.[109] These solidarities may arise from a common culture, religion, language, shared historical experience, and multiple permutations of these variables; and they may be reinforced if they coincide with class divisions in production relations. National or ethnic solidarities need not be rooted in objective economic conditions, and can be built upon by intellectuals and political entrepreneurs who recycle or invent myths and promulgate conflict. But such 'manipulation' has no necessary relationship with capitalism, although it may be connected with industrialization.[110] The history of former communist states demonstrates that national or ethnic solidarities do not necessarily 'wither away' under non-capitalist conditions, and the post-communist fragmentation of some of these states along their ethnic fault-lines suggests that under many conditions nationality and ethnicity are more binding and explosive forms of solidarity than class.[111]

*The trouble with class struggle is that there's not very much about.* The credibility of red Marxist beliefs – that capitalism and class struggle are fundamental in explaining Northern

Oranges and Reds 153

**Table 4.1** Strong social identifications in Northern Ireland in 1968 (percentage 'strong' identifiers)

|  | Protestant | Catholic | Total |
|---|---|---|---|
| Religion | 45 | 38 | 42 |
| Nationality | 45 | 28 | 38 |
| Party | 28 | 16 | 23 |
| Class | 13 | 10 | 12 |

*Source*: R. Rose, *Governing without Consensus: An Irish Perspective* (London: Faber, 1971), 389.

**Table 4.2** Social identifications in Northern Ireland and Great Britain in 1989

| Percentage saying they feel very or fairly close to: | Northern Ireland | Great Britain | Difference |
|---|---|---|---|
| People who have the same class background | 65 | 59 | 6 |
| People who have the same religious background | 64 | 36 | 28 |
| People of the same race | 64 | 56 | 8 |
| People born in the same area | 58 | 49 | 9 |
| People who live in the same area now | 58 | 46 | 12 |
| People who have the same political beliefs | 50 | 34 | 16 |

*Source*: J. Curtice and T. Gallacher, 'The Northern Irish Dimension', in R. Jowell, S. Witherspoon and L. Brook (eds), *British Social Attitudes: the 7th Report* (Aldershot: Gower, 1990), 197.

Ireland and that socialist working-class mobilization is a practical possibility – depend on significant evidence of class solidarity and cross-ethnic class action. Thus Bew and Patterson play up the electoral fortunes of the NILP in the 1950s and early 1960s; Boserup, Probert and Nairn saw potential for class politics in the wake of industrial changes in the 1960s; Probert and Nairn believed in the progressive potential of the Protestant working-class organizations which emerged in the early 1970s; and others argue that the high levels of support for unionist and nationalist parties reflect the absence of the British Labour Party, rather than inherent sectarianism.

None of these claims, however, withstand sceptical scrutiny. Political attitudes and voting behaviour in Northern Ireland have always correlated more closely with ethnicity (or religion) than with class – and this is discussed further elsewhere in this book.[112] It was evident in Ulster from the 1880s, and was equally apparent in the run-up to the present crisis. One comparative historical study of the relative influence of religious background (or ethnicity) and class on party support in Belfast in the 1960s found that religious background exerted six times the influence of class.[113] Richard Rose's Loyalty Survey, conducted in 1967–8, showed that while the difference between middle-class and working-class Protestants' support for the constitution of Northern Ireland was 4 per cent, and the difference between the Catholic classes was 2 per cent, middle-class Catholics and Protestants differed by 36 per cent, and working-class Protestants and Catholics by 30 per cent.[114] Table 4.1 reproduces Rose's findings on the percentage of Protestants and Catholics in Northern Ireland who strongly identified themselves with 'their' nationality, religion, party and class. In the period immediately preceding the outbreak of the current crisis, ethnicity (religiously defined) was more important in shaping people's identifications than their class-locations. In 1989, two decades after the present protracted conflict began, the British Social Attitudes Survey found cross-religious voting in Northern Ireland virtually non-existent outside of the small Alliance Party. Indeed cross-class voting in Great Britain is far more frequent than cross-sectarian voting in Northern Ireland.[115] The survey also found that people in Northern Ireland are more likely to say that they 'feel very or fairly close to' people of the same background as themselves than are their counterparts in Great Britain (see table 4.2).[116] Although class identity in 1989 appeared to be stronger in comparison with religious (or ethnic) identity than it was in Rose's Loyalty Survey, class remained of far less political salience than religious or ethnic identification, and this increasing class identification had clearly accompanied increasing ethnic or national division rather than cut across it.

Support for the NILP existed in the late 1950s and early 1960s. However, multiple cautions are in order about its electoral performance. Figure 4.1 displays the NILP's share of the total votes cast and of the total electorate in elections held for Stormont and the Northern Ireland Assembly between 1920 and 1976. Its share of votes cast reached an apparently impressive 26 per cent in 1962, but the party never

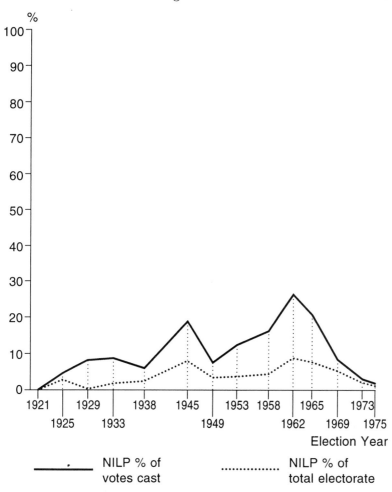

Figure 4.1 The performance of the NILP in Parliamentary, Assembly
and Convention elections, 1921–75
*Sources*: calculated from S. Elliott, *Northern Ireland Parliamentary
Election Results* (London: Chichester, 1973); and W. D. Flackes and
S. Elliott, *Northern Ireland: A Political Directory, 1968–1988
(Belfast: Blackstaff Press, 1990).*

managed to attract the support of more than 8.5 per cent of
the total electorate. Its occasional moderately high overall
share of the vote owed much to nationalist and republican
abstentionism and to the large number of uncontested seats
between 1921 and 1969 – in 1958, for instance, a staggering
46.2 per cent of seats were uncontested.[117] An average of just

13.7 Nationalist or Republican candidates stood for the 52 seats at Stormont during the elections held between 1921 and 1969, and in the post-war period (1945–69) more NILP candidates (88) stood for Stormont than Nationalist and Republican candidates (78).[118] Abstentionism amongst republicans and nationalists inflated perceptions of the NILP's performance – additionally boosted by tactical anti-UUP voting by Catholics who did not have a nationalist or republican candidate to support.[119]

The NILP's core support in Belfast came predominantly from Catholics (approx. two-thirds), superficially suggesting, *pace* red and Orange Marxists, that working-class Catholics were more socialist than working-class Protestants. However, Catholic support for the NILP owed more to its role as a parliamentary opponent of the UUP than to its timid and tepid socialism. When offered a choice between nationalists and the NILP, Catholics preferred the former.[120] The reason: Catholics were never likely to transfer their loyalties *en masse* to the NILP because the party, while less prejudiced than the UUP, was, after all, unionist. In 1971, the NILP's leader, David Bleakley, was co-opted into the Unionist government with the 'overwhelming support' of his party.[121] From 1949 the NILP had been solidly pro-partition. It had little to say about Catholic grievances about discrimination, favoured strong measures against the IRA, and was pervaded with a strong Protestant cultural ethos.[122]

Two of its four Stormont MPs elected in 1958 were Protestant lay preachers 'ever proclaiming their loyalty'.[123] The party also split over the (Protestant) issue of Sunday closing in 1965.

The Protestants who supported the NILP were never dominant in unionist politics. In Rose's Loyalty Survey, seven times as many Protestants preferred unionist parties to the NILP.[124] The weakness of Protestant working-class support for the NILP is telling, because after 1949 their support for the NILP involved no stark conflict between their national and their class interests. It is revealing that Bew and Patterson acknowledge that the NILP and other allegedly 'progressive forces' – from the Walkerites at the turn of the century, through the Midgelyites in the 1930s, to the Workers' Party in the present day – could only do (modestly) well among Protestant workers when the national question was not on the agenda. This historical trend suggests that a minority of Protestant workers sought to reconcile their (putative) class interests with their (British) national identifications, but even for this minority their (putative) class interests were less important than their national preferences.

Far from being united on class lines, the NILP was an unstable coalition of Protestants and Catholics connected to trade unions, who disagreed on nationality issues (and in the trade unions these issues were not discussed because they were obviously 'divisive'). Rose's Loyalty Survey remarkably suggested that 35 per cent of the NILP's Protestant supporters were loyalist 'ultras' while 43 per cent of its Catholic supporters endorsed illegal republican demonstrations.[125] In short, support for the NILP did not affect Catholic opposition to the Stormont regime or Protestant support for it.[126] Not surprisingly the party disintegrated in the deeply polarized climate that developed after 1969, just as the Irish labour movement had split over home rule and partition in the first two decades of the twentieth century. The NILP's support fragmented between the SDLP, the APNI, the UUP and loyalist organizations, with Catholics and Protestants heading for their respective national camps.[127] The most telling historic view of the NILP is that the party's line on any issue depended on who answered the telephone.[128]

What of the claim that class-conscious people vote for sectarian parties, or abstain because of the absence of class-based alternatives, and that this problem could be resolved by electoral integration with a Great British socialist party? It is difficult to square the arguments with survey evidence. Polls and votes indicate that both blocs regard their national identity as much more politically important than class – regardless of which parties participate in electoral contests in the region. Even though there is plenty of evidence of class consciousness the fact is that it is subordinated to national identifications. In 1974 industrial action by Protestant electricity workers – Protestant because of historic anti-Catholic discrimination in the sector – brought down the local devolved government, in which Catholics were serving for the first time, a power-sharing devolved government supported by both the British and Irish governments. In the 1990s workers in the same service did not consider strike action when the privatization of Northern Ireland Electricity threatened their employment prospects. The claim that the strength of ethnic/national identity is the (superficial and mutable) outcome of the absence of class parties endows political parties with powers historical materialists usually attribute only to economic forces. The intensity of the ethno-national preferences indicated in tables 4.1 and 4.2, suggests that the British Labour Party – to the extent that it remains a class-based party – would face a more difficult task succeeding in Northern Ireland than electoral integrationists assume. The truth is mundane: Northern Ireland has no significant class parties because class divisions are not as serious as its other divisions. The class divisions which are politically salient occur within rather than across national communities.

The claim that Labour Party organization in Northern Ireland would erode sectarian politics is also only valid if those who would vote Labour had non-sectarian motives for doing so, and, as we have argued, there is evidence to the contrary.[129] Moreover, since the movement for electoral integration established itself in the mid-1980s it has been tested in two ways: in public opinion polls and in election contests. The polls suggest that Northern Ireland people say they would vote for British political parties but also that such support breaks down on ethno-national lines, with Protestants being disposed towards the Conservative Party, and Catholics towards the Labour Party.[130] However, the tests of election contests are more empirically decisive and interesting. Since 1989 Conservative candidates have contested region-wide elections for local government districts (in 1989), for the European parliament (in 1989), and for the Westminster parliament (in 1992). They have obtained about 5 per cent of the vote, well behind their showing in the polls, and their support has been narrowly concentrated in highly Protestant territories, like North Down. The Conservatives' decision to mobilize in Northern Ireland has produced what might have been expected: a fragmentation in the way Protestants vote for the Union without increasing 'pan-bourgeois' class solidarity on the part of middle-class Catholics. The impact of the Conservatives' decision to organize in Northern Ireland separately from the Ulster Unionist Party is consistent with that from other ethnically-divided regions of the world where state-wide parties compete throughout the relevant territories. They either fail to attract much pan-ethnic support or they significantly fail to reduce ethnic tensions – as in Canada, Belgium, Spain, or the Bernese Jura region of Switzerland. The only odd feature of the Conservatives' decision to organize in Northern Ireland is that it should have been welcomed by Marxists. In no other part of the world have self-confessed Marxists argued for the mobilization of a bourgeois political party!

All Marxists, red, orange and green, were wrong about the prospects for class politics in Northern Ireland in the early 1970s. Boserup, Probert and Nairn exaggerated the backward or 'feudal' nature of Northern Ireland before the 1960s, and the changes which had occurred since. They also exaggerated the transformative powers of economic change. Northern Ireland was a highly industrialized society in the late nineteenth century. Trade union membership, class awareness and other indicators of modernization were as high there as in many other 'modern' industrial societies,[131] but they did not determine political attitudes in the ways expected by liberal sociologists and Marxists. For example trade union membership had no effect on either community's political views – members held the same views as non-members.[132] Sectarianism, and ethno-nationalist divisions, have persisted alongside industrialization and modernization in Northern Ireland, as elsewhere in the world. Indeed there are as good grounds for believing that modernization escalates ethnic conflict as there are for believing that it facilitates its termination. In any case the argument that multinational investment was transforming sectarianism and clientelism must be dismissed on empirical grounds. Multinational employers had no significant impact upon eradicating religious discrimination or inequalities in employment.[133]

The thesis that there was progressive socialist potential

**Table 4.3** Loyalist killings, 1969–93

| Nature of killings | Numbers killed |
|---|---|
| Deliberate killing of Catholics in Northern Ireland (i) | 670 |
| Deliberate killing of Catholics in Republic of Ireland (i) | 43 |
| Killings of other loyalists in feuds | 46 |
| Unintentional killings (unintended targets and deaths) | 32 |
| Killing of political activists (republicans and others) | 32 |
| Republican military activists | 32 |
| Killing of others including alleged criminals | 32 |
| Killings of alleged informers | 16 |
| British Security Forces (RUC, UDR, British Army) | 3 |

*Note*: (i) These figures include Protestant civilians killed because they were mistaken for Catholics or associated with Catholic civilians.
*Source*: M. Sutton, *An Index of Deaths from the Conflict in Ireland*, 1969–1993 (Belfast: Beyond the Pale Publications, 1994), 202–3.

in Protestant working-class militancy also relied on a rose-tinted view of loyalist paramilitaries. The growth of the UDA, the Loyalist Association of Workers, and the Ulster Workers Council, and the continuing influence of the UDA, had much less to do with increasing class consciousness than with ethnic insecurities – arising from the perception of British unreliability, and the IRA's campaign. The 1974 UWC strike was not a display of non-sectarian class consciousness, but a reaction against the Council of Ireland set up under the Sunningdale agreement, and the failure of the unionist establishment to resist it.[134] These loyalist organizations were exclusively Protestant and, while they displayed a lack of deference to their 'social superiors', they were much more antagonistic towards Catholics of their own class: twopence halfpenny looked down on twopence. Without appreciating the irony, Probert described the fact that two of the three socialist-inclined leaders of the UDA (to whom she pointed as proof of its progressive potential) were executed by their own comrades, while the third gave the *Sunday Times* a story on 'the extent to which the development of non-sectarian, working class ideology had gone within the UDA' from a hideaway in England where he had fled from his 'friends' in the UDA![135] When not executing their socialist-inclined leaders Probert's working-class heroes were killing Catholics, 713 sectarian killings were executed by loyalist paramilitaries between 1969 and 1993 (78 per cent of all the killings carried out by them in this period – see table 4.3).[136] The socialism of the loyalist paramilitaries has clearly been of the 'national' rather than the international variety.[137]

The weakness of class politics and the strength of nationality are perhaps best demonstrated by the polarization of Northern Irish Marxists along national and ethnic lines. There are rare Protestant green Marxists, and rare Catholic red and Orange Marxists, but religious origin reliably predicts a person's brand of Marxism or socialism. Orange Marxists are to unionism what green Marxists are to nationalism. Each band of intellectuals aimed to become the vanguard of their respective communities rather than of the working class. The BICO explained the Catholic minority's politics in cultural rather than historical materialist discourse; portraying them as the feckless dupes of an archaic and reactionary religion, mirroring the green Marxist view of Protestants as short-sighted and economically opportunistic dupes of British imperialism.

## Squeezing the Oranges

Catholics are blamed for their own fate by Orange Marxists. 'Blaming the native' is not unusual in settler-societies like Israel, South Africa or North America,[138] and the BICO's description of the plantation of Ulster is similar to Israeli, Afrikaner and white North American accounts of their respective settlements. In each case, economic development, historical progress, manners and civilization are tied to the plantation-settlement – only the settlers could have made the valleys (plains or *velt* or desert) bloom. Not surprisingly Orange – and red – Marxists are very touchy about any classification of Northern Ireland as a 'settler society'. Indeed, Hugh Roberts has devoted an entire book to rejecting the 'Algerian analogy'.[139] His target, Oxford political scientist Bill Johnson, had argued that the Britishness of Northern Ireland is as much a myth as the Frenchness of Algeria, and that Ulster Protestants are analogous to the European *colons* of Algeria.[140]

However, while there are many differences between Northern Ireland after 1921 and Algeria in the 1950s and 1960s, there are also multiple similarities between British state-building failure in Ireland and French state-building failure in Algeria.[141] The outlying territory (Ireland, Algeria) failed to be assimilated into the political culture of the dominant political community; the native populations (Catholics and Muslims) were subjected to massive land-expropriations, to the benefit of (Protestant and European) settlers; the relevant settler community formed the core of anti-democratic challenges to the political system when it appeared to be willing to make concessions to the natives (in 1911–14 in Ireland, and during 1955–61 in Algeria). In one case the descendants of the settler community were powerful enough to ensure that part of the outlying region remained within the metropolitan political system (the six counties of historic Ulster), whereas in the other they were not able to do so (none of Algeria was kept for those who believed it was French). These parallels escape Roberts's attention.

Orange Marxists make serious historical errors of fact and interpretation when they portray Ulster Protestants as politically progressive on the question of political reforms for Irish Catholics from the eighteenth century to the end of the nineteenth century. They ignore the important role that Orange sentiment, especially amongst lower-status Ulster Protestants, played in Irish Protestant opposition to Catholic emancipation and to the disestablishment of the Church of Ireland. Hereward Senior's historical investigation of *Orangeism in Ireland and Britain 1795–1836* should be prescribed reading for anyone disposed to swallow the BICO's interpretation of history.[142] Many Ulster Protestants rallied behind the reactionary preachers, Henry Cook and Roaring Hugh Hanna, in the nineteenth century. The exclusivist, sectarian and triumphalist nature of Ulster Protestantism from the 1880s onwards cannot be convincingly portrayed as a mere reaction to the exclusivism, sectarianism, and triumphalism of nineteenth-century Irish nationalism. Yes, there have been progressives in the history of Ulster Protestantism, but they have been atypical rather than typical. The Ulster Protestants who backed the United Irishmen in the 1790s were unusual.

The bulk of their co-ethnics did not favour land, liberty, and equality for Catholics or Irish nationalists. Edward Carson, a revered figure in liberal unionist and Orange Marxist history, was a Dubliner, an Irish rather than an Ulster Unionist, and his rhetorical espousal of 'equal citizenship' was not typical of those whom he led. And lest it be forgotten, the Ulster Protestants who are alleged to have brought democratic values to North America felt obliged to leave Ulster.

The BICO's assertion that there are two nations on the island of Ireland is more sensible than the assertion that there is just one, but in their writings it is an ambiguous and exclusive claim: ambiguous because they did not clarify to which nation Ulster Protestants belong, and exclusive because it signally failed to treat adequately the position of the minority within Northern Ireland. The BICO's front-organization, the 'Workers' Association for the Democratic Settlement of the National Conflict in Ireland', admittedly adopted two key demands in the early 1970s: '(i) full recognition of the right of the Ulster Protestant nation to remain within the UK state; and (ii) full recognition and accordance of the democratic rights of the Catholic minority in the Northern Ireland/UK state, and of the Protestant minority in the Southern Ireland state.' However, we must underline that the second demand was for the rights of religious minorities, not for the rights of national minorities. If there are two nations on the island of Ireland, and the principle of democratic self-determination is of such import, then the border across Ireland was drawn badly in 1920, and the political institutions of Northern Ireland do not adequately reflect its dual national character. These conclusions do not leap from the pages of the BICO.

*Orangewashing history.* The BICO's post-1920 history of Northern Ireland whitewashes the unsavoury features of Stormont government. Discrimination against Catholics and nationalists in political representation, employment, and the provision of public services between 1922 and 1972, let alone the present, is ignored in this perverse conception of progressive politics. Alternatively it is lamely attributed to the impact of Irish irredentism, or the system of devolved government imposed on Northern Ireland by the British government. The BICO's history also offers a far-fetched account of a theocratic Irish state which is contrasted with a much more liberal Northern Ireland or an ultra-modern, pluralist and democratic United Kingdom. The thesis that the Republic is a theocratic state is not supported by any reputable historian or political scientist,[143] and the BICO's exceptionally generous description of Northern Ireland and the British state would be regarded as 'Whiggish' if not 'Toryish', were readers not alerted to its provenance. Finally, while the BICO may be correct to argue that there is or was no labour aristocracy in the strict Leninist sense in Northern Ireland, there was extensive discrimination in the local labour markets – in which trade unions often colluded. These are matters which one would normally assume to be of intense interest to those genuinely ambitious to unify the working class for political struggle, but they do not figure in the writings of Orange Marxists.

*The sins of materialism.* Red and Orange Marxists fail to appreciate the importance and durability of ethnicity, and thus ignore or downplay national or ethnic demands and fears, or worse, acknowledge the importance of just one community's ethnic demands and fears. They either regard constitutional questions, especially partition, as unimportant, or consider them divisive, which leads them to accept the status quo by default. For example, implicit in the writings of Bew, Patterson and Roberts is the assumption that Irish nationalism amongst cultural Catholics in Northern Ireland, but not British union-ism, can and should be conjured out of political existence, largely through economic reforms and policies. This assump-tion is similar to that held by some in the now defunct NILP, and that held by some members of the now disintegrated Workers' Party. From a northern nationalist perspective the thinking of such red Marxists is no different from that of the Orange Order: their political allegiance is read as a sign of their impoverishment.

Bew and Patterson's currently espoused prescription, often articulated by other socialists or ex-communists in the maga-zine *Fortnight,* is that class solidarity or a progressive politics of equal citizenship can be achieved by the removal of structural inequalities between Catholics and Protestants. This thinking is progressive, but wishful. While social equality, equality of opportunity and affirmative action are desirable and worthy goals, and though they will go some way towards redressing minority grievances, it requires a considerable leap of faith to envisage most Sinn Féin and SDLP voters, or several thousand IRA militants and ex-prisoners, surrendering their nationalist aspirations just for jobs, or better jobs. National identification or assimilation cannot be so easily bought or sold. The tendency of peoples to resent and resist being ruled by those deemed aliens appears to operate quite independently of economic variables,[144] and all Marxists, like many liberals, are guilty of 'an unwarranted exaggeration of the influence of materialism upon human affairs'.[145] Northern nationalists are no more likely to give up their national aspirations for economic gains than unionists are to accept a united Ireland if they could be persuaded of its economic advantages.

Exaggerated materialism also lies at the heart of the uneven-development explanation of partition. If uneven development was the primary or 'crucial' force behind partition, then only the industrial areas of Antrim and Down should have remained in the UK, and Catholics living within these areas should have been (or have become) as unionist as their Protestant neighbours. Conversely, Protestants from outside the industrial pale should have been (or have become) as fiercely nationalist as their Catholic neighbours. Instead, national conflict in Northern Ireland (as elsewhere) has taken place without respect for economic developmental boundaries. In any case the BICO's economic 'history' is highly stylized and shrouded in myth. The thesis that the Ulster custom lies behind the economic development of north-eastern Ireland, by contrast with the rest of the island, which lacked this custom, has been challenged by economic historians;[146] and the argument that Ulster was economically more developed than the rest of Ireland needs to be carefully qualified. The argument applies at best to Ulster east of the Bann (three counties), and even then it is relevant primarily for the Lagan valley, north of the Mountains of Mourne and south of the Glens of Antrim (i.e. Belfast and its environs). Secondly, the degree of economic unevenness between the two parts of Ireland has varied since the beginning of the century, with no obvious effect on political attitudes or differences.[147] Finally, Marxists cannot explain, without deviating from economic determinism,[148] why uneven economic development produced a political and cultural response in Ireland markedly different from that in more ethnically homogeneous societies, such as those of England, Germany and France.[149]

The impoverished materialism of Marxist political theory continually misleads its devotees. Thus Nairn, who advocates independence for Northern Ireland, gets the axis of conflict profoundly wrong and ignores the national preferences of both groups.[150] Protestants are unionists. They are not (unconscious) Ulster nationalists fighting the British, and do not want independence – no matter how much the British public and politicians might want them to do so.[151] They consider independence an option of last resort. Many Catholics, whom Nairn scarcely mentions, want a united Ireland, and have no wish to be subjected to Protestant majority-rule without the possibility of British arbitration. This is why independence, contrary to Nairn's prediction, has not materialized. If independence was ever realized, it would also be unlikely to result in the modernized society Nairn anticipates – where the Protestant Jekylls confront the Hydes. Entrapping two antagonistic communities within its frontiers, an independent Northern Ireland would experience ethno-national conflict over the organization of political institutions and the allocation of scarce resources, and civil war – as occurred in Croatia, Bosnia and Serbia following the break-up of Yugoslavia. Such a war would be followed by a second partition of Ulster, and the formation of a small 'Ulster' 'Protestant' state with little progressive pedigree or potential.

# Conclusion

The national nature of the Northern Ireland conflict appears better able to explain its intractability than class conflict – however disguised. If the conflict was significantly about class, it would, despite what Marxists imply, be less violently revolutionary and counter-revolutionary because class conflict is much more manageable than national conflict. The history of industrialized democracies in the twentieth century has shown that class conflict is more bargainable, and conducive to negotiated settlements, than ethnic conflicts centred on rival national identities.

Feasible prescriptions for Northern Ireland require that the national question be tackled directly, rather than wished out of existence. Any democratic socialist politics in Ireland must suggest sensible ways of protecting as well as transcending the rival national identities on the island. Marxists may react to this argument by labelling us 'bourgeois' social scientists.[152] So be it. We would simply remind them that calls for class unity do not amount to what Lenin called the concrete analysis of concrete situations. The concrete in this case is composed of national, ethnic and religious identities. Any post-Marxist analysis must start from this reality.

# Part II

---

# Internal Explanations

# 5

# Warring Gods?
# Theological Tales

Foreign journalist: Who is King Billy?
Ulster Protestant: Ach away man, and read your Bible!'
*Apocryphal Belfast story*
'Religion' one student said 'is a red herring'. I said if so it was
a red herring about the size of a whale.
*Conor Cruise O'Brien, Irish agnostic, literary critic,
politician, and journalist* [1]
Northern Ireland is best-considered a bi-confessional society.
*Richard Rose, American political scientist* [2]
The trouble with Christianity [in Northern Ireland] is not that
it has been tried and found wanting, but that it has been wanted
yet never tried.
*Simon Lee, English Catholic and law professor* [3]
In [Ulster] . . . the scriptures have been the single most compel-
ling determinant of the way people have thought about their
world.
*Donald Akenson, American historian* [4]

Modernization is supposed to mean secularization, declining
religiosity, and preoccupation with 'this-worldly' or material
matters. Northern Ireland is located in the UK, the birthplace
of modernity according to the ancestors of social science.
Yet significant numbers of journalists, historians and social
scientists place religion at the heart of the conflict: and Brian
Gable's cartoon captures their feelings (see figure 5.1). Much of
the British public shares this verdict. If they are right important
implications follow. Socio-economic inequalities, cultural or

**Figure 5.1** Brian Gable's view of theological sentiments in
Northern Ireland (*Globe & Mail*, 2 November 1993)

national differences, inter-state relations, and political institutions must be of secondary or no importance. The conflict
must be pre-modern, with essentially endogenous roots.[5]
Policy-implications also follow: 'religious' solutions have to
be canvassed such as secularization, ecumenism, or integrated
education. Alternatively despair may be encouraged, because
the devout are not famous for tolerance.

We will argue that those who think the conflict is fundamentally or primarily based on religion are wrong. Conflict
is indeed waged between two communities whose members
are religiously differentiated, but they are also divided by
broader cultural differences, national allegiances, histories of
antagonistic encounters, and marked differences in economic
and political power.

Their sense of different and shared kinship, although marked
by religion, is not reducible to religion. These divisions are
multiple and reinforcing, and, to the extent that they can be
separated, of varying importance to different individuals. With
some exceptions those who are strongly religiously motivated
are not the major causes of antagonism, stalemate, or political
violence. Nevertheless the views of those with whom we
disagree must be fairly considered, so we first present the

available religious explanations in their clearest and most persuasive articulations.

Four generic types of religious explanation of Northern Ireland can be found, and shall be considered in turn:

- religion matters equally to Protestants and Catholics,[6] and is the cause of antagonism;
- religion matters most to Protestants, and Protestantism is at the root of the conflict;
- religion matters most to Catholics, and Catholicism is at the source of the conflict; and
- religion matters in maintaining and reinforcing social boundaries between Catholics and Protestants, i.e. it matters socially rather than theologically.

## Northern Ireland as a Conflict between Catholics and Protestants

Religious devotion is extremely high in Northern Ireland: 1,280 of 1,291 respondents to Rose's Loyalty Survey, conducted in 1968, gave a denominational identification when asked their religion; 95 per cent of Catholics reported going to mass at least once a week, a rate about three times as high as nominal Catholics in France or Austria; 46 per cent of Protestants attended church at least once a week, a rate over twice as high as that of Protestants in Great Britain; and Northern Ireland rated second among Western polities in church attendance, beaten only by the Republic of Ireland.[7] The Policy Studies Institute's Survey revealed that in the 1980s 70 per cent of adults in Northern Ireland went to church at least once a month, compared with 21 per cent in Great Britain.[8] Other indicators of religiosity establish a similar picture of formally devout peoples, as do recent surveys.[9] Although table 5.1 suggests declining religiosity, in so far as church attendance measures religiosity, the region still 'deserves its reputation as a religious society'.[10] The proportion of the population which professes no religion (12 per cent) is considerably less

**Table 5.1** Church attendance in Northern Ireland, 1968–89

| Year of Survey (high and low attendance rates) | All | Roman Catholics | Protestants |
|---|---|---|---|
| 1968 | | | |
| Once a week or more | 66 | 95 | 46 |
| Never | 4 | 1 | 5 |
| 1978 | | | |
| Once a week or more | 53 | 90 | 39 |
| Never | 10 | 3 | 10 |
| 1989 | | | |
| Once a week or more | 54 | 86 | 44 |
| Never | 16 | 3 | 15 |

*Sources*: R. Rose, *Governing without Consensus: An Irish Perspective* (London: Faber, 1971); E. Moxon-Browne, *Nation, Class and Creed in Northern Ireland* (Aldershot: Gower, 1983); and J. Curtice and T. Gallagher, 'The Northern Irish Dimension', in R. Jowell, S. Witherspoon, and L. Brook (eds), *British Social Attitudes: the 7th Report* (Aldershot: Gower, 1990).

than that in Great Britain (34 per cent) and we can testify to the pressures to conform to religious norms encountered by young non-believers.

Observers describe the groups in conflict as Catholics and Protestants, or use Catholic/Protestant and nationalist/unionist as interchangeable sets of antonyms.[11] This careless terminology derives from undeniable facts: nationalist parties and republican paramilitaries derive their support almost exclusively from Catholics, while unionist parties and loyalist paramilitaries are overwhelmingly supported by Protestants. The correlation between political partisanship and religion is very high. In one 'index of religious voting' Northern Ireland's score was 81 – in a possible range from 0 to 100.[12] Compared with other countries with Protestants and Catholics, Northern Ireland registered an 'unprecedented magnitude': Great Britain measured 7, the USA 16, Australia 14, and Canada 14. Even West Germany and the Netherlands, which have had major historical confrontations between Catholics and Protestants, had scores of 29 and 50 respectively.[13] In a more recent comparative evaluation of the association between religious affiliation and party political support Northern Ireland had the strongest association – way ahead of the Netherlands, Norway,

Italy, West Germany, the USA, Hungary, East Germany, Great Britain and New Zealand.[14] The 'index of dissimilarity' between 'regular' Protestants and Catholics, i.e., regular church-goers, was 77 points – 77 per cent of the sample would have had to change political preferences for the two distributions to become identical. The index of dissimilarity between 'irregular' Protestants and Catholics was not much lower, at 67 points.

Such evidence produces an understandable but superficial reaction: the conflict must be religious if the groups engaged in electoral competition and paramilitary struggle are religiously defined.[15] This reading is strengthened by the highly visible political role of Protestant clergy. Three of the thirteen unionist members of the Westminster parliament elected in 1992 are Protestant ministers: the Reverend Dr Ian Paisley of the DUP, who is also one of Northern Ireland's three members of the European Parliament, the Reverend Martin Smyth of the UUP, who is also the head of the explicitly anti-Catholic Orange Order, and the Reverend William McCrea, whose profitable country-and-western singing mimics the Protestant fundamentalism of the deep South of the USA. Paisley, a graduate of Bob Jones University, also located in the deep South of the USA, is probably Northern Ireland's best known and most (locally) popular politician. He began his public life as an incessant scourge of ecumenism, and by encouraging a celebrant of black masses. His protests against the Catholic Archbishop of Westminster's invitation to a Royal wedding,[16] the Pope's visit to Britain, diplomatic relations between the UK and the Vatican, and the Pope's address to the European Parliament, reinforce the perception of Northern Ireland as a site of theological war.

Secular people find it difficult to understand how a religious conflict could be fought in Western Europe in the late twentieth century; so, having persuaded themselves that they have found one, they attribute it to the peculiar, atavistic and anachronistic devoutness of Irish Catholics and Protestants. The condescension with which the English often regard the Irish is reinforced by their perception that the latter are culturally retarded, still engaged in struggles which modern nations (like England) have resolved. As one English journalist comments: 'The passions which are shared by Mass-going Gael and Calvinist planter, which sustain them indeed in the fashion of two drunks tilted out of the horizontal into a triumphal arch, are nothing to us.'[17]

Local atheists share these prejudices, blaming the conflict on their superstitious neighbours. Thus the Ulster Humanist Association attributes Northern Irish politics to the dogmatic and uncompromising nature of the religious beliefs which 'provide meaning to the lives of most people'.[18]

The secular view that *the* problem is one of conflicting religions is shared by the ecumenical movement, inside and outside Northern Ireland. Ecumenists attribute the conflict to Christian churches stressing their differences, rather than their similarities: it is no 'Holy War'[19] in their eyes; it is profane. The rival churches are condemned as sectarian apologists for the political movements in their communities.[20] This perspective was illustrated by one of McGarry's colleagues. Seeing him with Gallagher and Worrall's ecumenical *Christians in Ulster* under his arm, she looked quizzically at the title before remarking that she didn't think there were any Christians in Ulster.

Catholicism and Protestantism are widely blamed for violence, for replaying the clash between reformation and counter-reformation forces in the seventeenth century,[21] and for conducting a religious war otherwise allegedly confined to the Middle East.[22] Some hold the churches responsible for violence because they create a sectarian environment and selectively condemn atrocities:[23] Protestant churches are criticized for condemning republican violence and condoning the excesses of the security forces, while the Catholic church is criticized for alleged ambivalence towards republicanism and for condemning the 'security' forces.

There is a widespread assumption amongst liberals that religious beliefs make people more rather than less disposed to engage in violence; 'sacred violence' absolutizes politics. The corollary, that a more secular Northern Ireland would be less violent, is rarely openly argued – although it is assumed. A direct connection between religion and political violence has been advanced forcefully by the political scientist David Rapoport,[24] who maintains that religions have both violence-reducing and violence-producing dimensions. They inspire total loyalties; are used to justify wars; and wars of religion are amongst the most ferocious of all. No major religion 'eschews violence under all conditions'.[25] Christianity is the most warlike of the world-religions. 'The foremost authority on genocide, Leo Kuper, has concluded that in virtually every case of genocide religious differences were an element.'[26] The discourses of religions are ambiguous, suffused with violence as well as critiques of violence.[27] Religion may be used to tame violence, especially domestic violence, but it can also be marshalled negatively, to sanction violence against outside communities. Northern Ireland is tailor-made for this perspective, which makes it comprehensible why people fight and kill one another. Brian Walker, Chairman of the New Ulster Movement, holds this view.[28] Richard Rose writes:

> Religion, by contrast [with class], often raises issues based upon a non-bargainable absolute value . . . The history of the Roman Catholic Church and of various Protestant denominations illustrates the impossibility of compromise when transcendental and worldly values are in conflict.[29]

Another commentator attributes some of the violence of Catholic and Protestant paramilitaries to the social doctrines of both theologies – the Catholic doctrine of a 'just war' and the Protestant 'Covenant theology'.[30]

Ecumenists and secular humanists differ in their prognoses and prescriptions. Ecumenists see salvation in common Christian values.[31] They commend Dietrich Bonhoeffer's suggestion for peace through a 'religionless Christianity' which transcends sectarianism.[32] Humanists, by contrast, regard secularization as the best hope for peace. A 'critical mass' of unbelievers will lead to normal politics – negotiable disputes over the allocation of economic resources and manageable ideological conflict between conservatives, liberals and socialists.

## Protestantism is at the Root of the Conflict

Some claim the Protestant religion is central to understanding Northern Ireland, even though, as table 5.1. suggests, Protestants display, statistically, less overt religiosity than Catholics. The idea is that the intractability of the conflict stems from the distinctive Protestantism found in Northern Ireland. This perception partly accounts for the unpopularity of the unionist cause in international circles. Protestants are portrayed as 'a bitter and bigoted clan of power-hungry, religious fanatics'.[33] The *Oxford Children's History* describes Ulster Protestants as extremists who are not 'like our Church of England people . . . They just hate Catholics in a way that we find difficult to understand'.[34] And many Irish Catholics agree that the religious zealotry of Protestants is more culpable than any failings in their own religion.

Numerous analysts claim that Protestantism is central to unionism while maintaining that Irish nationalism, by comparison, is a largely secular phenomenon. An historian of the home rule controversies writes that 'For Catholics the problem was largely political; for Protestants largely religious';[35] a psychologist maintains that 'For Protestants, their differences with Catholics are primarily religious . . . Catholics' objection to Protestants concern not their religion, but their political outlook . . . ';[36] a political scientist believes that 'The Protestant perspective, is . . . essentially religious';[37] and an agnostic literary critic argues that whereas 'Ulster Protestants do fear Catholicism, Ulster Catholics do not fear Protestantism'. The typical Catholic 'may fear the material power of Protestants, but he has no fear whatever of Protestantism. He knows little and thinks little about it; there is simply no equivalent on his side to the Protestant brooding on the Pope of Rome.'[38] This verdict is shared by Richard Rose:

> Protestants tend to see their regime as a bulwark of religious faith against Catholics within the six counties, against the mere Catholic Irish outside their provincial pale, and against the forces of error and darkness everywhere growing stronger in a threatening and increasingly ecumenical world.[39]

**Table 5.2** Religious denominations in Northern Ireland, 1961–91

| Denomination | 1961 | 1971 | 1981 | 1991 |
|---|---|---|---|---|
| Roman Catholic | 35 | 31 | 29 | 38 |
| Presbyterian | 29 | 28 | 24 | 21 |
| Church of Ireland (Anglican) | 24 | 23 | 20 | 18 |
| Methodist | 5 | 5 | 4 | 4 |
| Baptist | 1 | 1 | 1 | 1 |
| Brethren | 1 | 1 | 1 | 1 |
| Congregationalist | 1 | 1 | 1 | 1 |
| Free Presbyterian | 0 | 0 | 1 | 1 |
| Other Protestant denominations | 1 | 2 | 3 | 4 |
| Not stated | 2 | 9 | 20 | 8 |
| Atheists/Agnostics/None | n/a | n/a | 0 | 4 |

*Notes*:
1. The figures are expressed as a (rounded) percentage of the total respondents to the census.
2. In 1971, 142,511 people refused to answer the religious question. In 1981, 274,584 people refused, and many thousands refused to be enumerated. In 1991, 114,827 people did not state an answer to the question on religion.
*Sources*: Northern Ireland Census of Population (1961, 1971, 1981, 1991).

This school of interpretation believes that Catholics are confident about their religion and have no fear of Protestant proselytism.[40] Roman Catholics are the largest single denomination in Northern Ireland, part of a large majority on the island, and members of a church with a highly visible international organization. Moreover, the disrupted censuses of 1971 and 1981 masked the fact that Catholics make up a growing percentage of Northern Ireland's population, as table 5.2 suggests.[41] Therefore, it is said, Catholic fears about Protestant evangelicalism cannot have rational foundations and cannot explain the conflict; Catholics separate their faith from their politics; Catholics see the conflict as one over political power, national identity and economic inequality; moderates seek economic and political equality whereas militants want a secular united Ireland; northern nationalism is liberal or socialist; and Catholics have no difficulty supporting nationalist Protestants, whether they be Wolfe Tone, Charles Stewart Parnell, or Ivan Cooper, the civil rights leader elected to Stormont in 1969.[42]

However, so the argument goes, Protestants fear the resourcefulness and power of the Roman Catholic church,[43] though they despise the Catholic community's lack of material power. Unlike Catholics, Protestants are uncertain about their national identity, and fall back upon their religion for symbolic solace.[44] There is no Protestant equivalent to the Catholic tradition of following leaders from the other community. Catholics did not stand as unionist candidates during the Stormont regime, and the Orange Order opposed Catholic participation in the UUP. Even today the explicitly sectarian Orange Order remains integrally linked to the Ulster Unionist Party.

The most complete statement of the view that Protestantism is central to the conflict has been advanced by the sociologist of religion Steve Bruce:[45] 'The Northern Ireland conflict is a religious conflict. Economic and social differences are also crucial, but it was the fact that the competing populations in Ireland adhered and still adhere to competing religious traditions which has given the conflict its enduring and intractable quality.'[46] The Ulster plantation introduced a devoutly Protestant people into counter-reformation territory. The Calvinist doctrine of predestination and the Westminster Confession of Faith encouraged exclusivist attitudes towards Catholics. Communal conflict was religiously based and eventually organized by the Orange Order, which insisted on pan-Protestant religious supremacy and apartheid. Partition and devolution after 1920 gave rise to a 'Protestant parliament for a Protestant people', in which Protestant privileges were protected. The collapse of Stormont was precipitated because Terence O'Neill adopted secular liberalism, compounding Protestant insecurities flowing from the ecumenical movement prompted by the second Vatican Council (1962–5).

Ulster Protestants, according to Bruce, are an ethnic group defined by their religion. Non-religious collective identifications have been rejected because secular socialism and liberalism do not erect barriers between Protestants and Catholics. The fact that many Protestants do not practise their religion is very conveniently explained: 'Protestantism' is a form of ethnic identity with crucial religious content – secular Protestants 'are not far removed from an evangelical religious commitment' and 'find something appealing about evangelicalism'.[47] They have been raised by practising Protestants, attended Sunday schools, and retain sufficient commitment to persuade their wives (sic!) and children to attend Church![48] According to Bruce four features of unionist politics have religious roots:

(i)   *their unwillingness to accommodate Catholics.* No unionist politician can accommodate Catholics and retain substantial trust amongst Protestants.[49]

(ii)  *their unwillingness to entertain a united Ireland.* Fears about the power of the Catholic church in a united Ireland provide the 'main' reason why Protestants object to a united Ireland.[50]

(iii) *their desire to maintain the Union.* The Union protects their Protestant way of life, including their civil and religious liberties, which are far more important than their national identity. Protestant loyalty to the Union is conditional on Britain upholding the Protestant Constitution of 1688 and protecting them from a Catholic Republic. Opinion polls, in Bruce's view, record a significant reluctance amongst Ulster Protestants to embrace Britishness,[51] because Great Britain is secular and offends the 'religious and ethical sensibilities' of Ulster Protestants, who believe it is progressively abandoning the Protestant Constitution.[52] These considerations allegedly explain the lack of support for integration among Protestants.[53]

(iv)  *Unionists' support for Paisley and the DUP.* The huge electoral support for Paisley, who wears his religion on his sleeve, and for the DUP, a party distinguished by its evangelicalism, confirms the salience of religion.[54] In elections to the European parliament Ian Paisley easily out-polls competition from non-evangelical unionists.

In a comparative study, Don Akenson pursues a similar argument to Bruce, but an historically more precise one. He argues that Ulster Protestants, Afrikaners and Israeli Jews all saw themselves as 'chosen people', people with an Old Testament biblical covenant with God.[55] The Ulster Protestants' belief that they were a chosen people explains their sense of superiority to Catholics, their willingness to discriminate, their

endorsement of endogamy, their cohesiveness, their unwillingness to compromise, their rejection of religious pluralism, the
strangeness of their political language to outside observers,
and their attachment to Ulster, which they saw as a promised
land.[56]

Catholics, by contrast, are politically motivated by secular
nationalism: republicans adopt political positions hostile to
the Catholic hierarchy of Ireland and of Rome, who can do
nothing to stop IRA violence.[57] Bruce's argument, written
from a perspective which claims to be empathetic – if not
sympathetic – to evangelical Protestants, in fact reproduces
that of many nationalists who agree that Protestants lack a
real British identity, and that they would fully embrace an
Irish national identity and be content in a united Ireland if
it respected their religious sensibilities and freedoms.[58]

## Catholicism is at the Root of the Conflict

By contrast, many believe that the Roman Catholic church
plays a greater role in promoting conflict than Protestantism.
A minority of Protestants, mainly evangelicals and fundamentalists, think that the Irish nationalist movement is under the
control of the Vatican, pursuing the extirpation of Protestantism. Rome is held responsible for 'religious genocide' in the
Republic, where the Protestant minority declined from 10 per
cent of the population in 1911 to 4.1 per cent in 1971 (see table
5.3).[59] The decline is attributed to Papal laws on intermarriage,
which once obliged the Catholic *and* the Protestant partner to
bring up their offspring as Catholics. The Catholic church's policy towards the offspring of mixed marriages is held responsible
for the 'genocide',[60] and for tipping the increasingly delicate
demographic balance in Northern Ireland. More generally,
the atmosphere created by the hierarchy's insistence that
Catholic morality be enforced in public policy is held to have
prompted Protestant emigration from the Republic,[61] though
no systematic evidence is cited in support of this thesis. Liberal
unionists accuse the Catholic hierarchy of teaching nationalist
doctrines in school; of refusing to accept the legitimacy of

**Table 5.3** Religious denominations in independent Ireland

| Religious denomination | 1926 | 1936 | 1946 | 1961 | 1971 | 1981 | 1991 |
|---|---|---|---|---|---|---|---|
| Roman Catholic | 92.6 | 93.4 | 94.3 | 94.9 | 93.9 | 93 | 91.6 |
| Church of Ireland | 5.5 | 4.9 | 4.2 | 3.7 | 3.3 | 2.7 | 2.5 |
| Presbyterian | 1.1 | 0.9 | 0.8 | 0.7 | 0.5 | 0.4 | 0.4 |
| Methodist | 0.4 | 0.3 | 0.3 | 0.2 | 0.2 | 0.2 | |
| Jewish | 0.1 | 0.1 | 0.1 | 0.1 | 0.1 | 0.1 | 0.04 |
| Other religion | 0.3 | 0.2 | 0.3 | 0.4 | 0.2 | 0.3 | 1 |
| No religion | – | – | – | – | 0.3 | 1.2 | 1.9 |
| Not stated | – | – | – | – | 1.6 | 2.1 | 2.4 |

*Notes*:
(i) Figures expressed as a percentage, and rounded to one decimal place.
(ii) The 1951, 1956, 1966 and 1979 censuses did not include religious questions.
(iii) From 1911 until 1961 'No religion' and 'Not stated' were included in 'Other'.
(iv) Until 1991 'Protestants' without specific denomination were classed as Church of Ireland, so we have treated this as one category.
*Sources*: Census of Ireland (1926, 1936, 1946, 1961, 1971, 1981, 1991).

the Union, the Stormont parliament, and the security forces; and of conspicuously refusing to excommunicate members of the IRA – as it did during the Irish civil war of 1922–3.[62] Their sympathizers, like Conor Cruise O'Brien, maintain that 'Irish nationalist ideology, Irish Republicanism . . . beneath an increasingly perfunctory pseudo secular cover, is Irish Catholic holy nationalist.'[63]

For some unionists the 'unfinished business' of Irish nationalism is Catholicization and the eradication of the Protestant religion:[64] the 'Roman Catholic IRA', the full title given to the IRA by Paisleyites, is the Vatican's storm-troopers, and its killing of Protestants is merely a more direct form of genocide than that practised by its co-religionists across the border.[65] In a submission to the inter-party talks held at Stormont in June 1991, Ian Paisley declared 'These talks cannot and will not stop the Roman Catholic IRA nor will it stop acts of terror by those who claim the name Protestant.'[66] In this perspective republican paramilitaries *are* Catholics, loyalist paramilitaries are not *real* Protestants. Since Catholics are bent on eradicating Protestantism, accommodation must be resisted. Paisley and his supporters point to the explicit support for a united Ireland expressed by the former Catholic Primate of all Ireland, Cardinal O'Fiaich, and other members of the hierarchy. They highlight the refusal of the Catholic church to condemn the 1981 hunger-strikers,[67] the willingness of the church to bury hunger-strikers and IRA dead in consecrated ground, and the finding of IRA arms on Catholic church grounds.[68] The alleged participation of priests like Father Ryan in the IRA's activities, and the massacre of Protestant evangelicals at prayer by republican militants in 1983, are presented as proof of the indissoluble alliance of Irish nationalism and Catholicism. As Jim Allister of the DUP declared:

> It is this insoluble (sic!) marriage of Roman Catholicism to militant Irish republicanism, where the latter is seen as the 'political' expression and promoter of the former, which makes [impossible] what should otherwise be possible, namely the co-existence of the political expressions of Protestantism and Roman Catholicism in Ireland.[69]

Liberal and socialist unionists also emphasize the link between Roman Catholicism and Irish nationalism.[70] They agree with the fundamentalist Protestant critique of the Republic, but attack the Roman Catholic church's influence from a perspective formally critical of fundamentalism. They reject the view that Protestantism defines unionism, and maintain that the false juxtaposition of secular Irish nationalism with a religiously exclusive unionism alienates the British on whom the unionists depend, and plays into the hands of republican intellectuals.[71] The international unpopularity of unionism and the external sympathy for Irish nationalism, even in Britain, are attributed to the high profile of Protestant fundamentalists with Cathophobic views.[72] Liberal unionists therefore stress a competing tradition in Ulster unionism.[73] Religious exclusivism, they claim, triumphed over liberalism, not because Protestantism was fundamental to unionism but in reaction to strident Catholic nationalism. Only when Catholicism and nationalism became 'indissolubly linked' did the divisions between fundamentalist and liberal unionism disappear.[74]. Exclusivist unionism became ascendant after 1920 because Britain foisted devolution on the unionists, cutting them from the British liberal mainstream.[75] In this perspective, unionists have no intrinsic desire to dominate or exclude Catholics. In fact, some Catholics are unionists, which Bruce's analysis cannot explain. The UK is defended as a pluralist, tolerant and diverse state, not because of the sectarian Williamite settlement and the desire to lord it over Catholics; and the Republic is seen as its Manichean opposite, a sectarian, intolerant and homogenizing state. They think that recent constitutional travails over divorce, contraception and abortion have shown how distinctive the Republic wants to remain – at a time when there was every incentive to prove its liberality and when this appeared to be the official strategy of successive governments.[76] Thus the tables are turned. Unionists are not anachronistic religious fanatics; and the real axis of conflict is between unionists who want a tolerant UK, and nationalists who want to follow principles of 'national homogeneity and religious authority'.[77]

## Religion Maintains and Reinforces the Social Boundary

Social scientists, especially anthropologists, agree that Northern Ireland is a segmented society with a clear social boundary between two major communities,[78] cemented by endogamy and educational and residential segregation. These boundaries make social interaction difficult and, especially in working-class districts, facilitate communal ghettos which promote group solidarity, myths, mutual ignorance, intolerance, prejudice, and stereotyping. Many social scientists and secular intellectuals (overlapping categories) hold the churches directly and indirectly responsible for maintaining this social frontier.

Churches provide a meeting place for members of their flock. Attendance at religious services spills over into other religiously driven activities. The Catholic church organizes associations like the St Vincent de Paul Society, the Pioneer Association of the Sacred Heart, and the Legion of Mary, as well as various youth organizations. Protestant churches have Sunday schools, Bible study groups, Boys Brigades and

Girl Guides.[79] In addition, the Orange Order preaches and practises religious apartheid and condemnation of Romanist 'idolatry'. Most adverse commentary centres, however, on the churches' role in maintaining and reinforcing social division through their attitudes to endogamy and segregated education. This 'is the most significant aspect of the role of religion in the divisions and conflicts in Ireland and goes to the heart of the matter'.[80]

*Endogamy.* In 1968 96 per cent of respondents to Rose's Loyalty Survey had parents of the same religion.[81] Research suggests that mixed marriages formed 6 per cent of the total in Northern Ireland during the four decades 1943–82, which compares strikingly with marriage patterns in England and Wales, where 67 per cent of marriages involving Roman Catholics are mixed.[82] Given the importance of parents in transmitting values to children, this high level of endogamy, even though it may have fallen in recent years, is extremely important in maintaining group boundaries.[83] Blame has often been pinned on the Catholic church's animosity towards intermarriage and on its insistence in the papal *Ne Temere* decree of 1908 that *both* partners in a mixed marriage had to agree to raise their children as Catholics. This decree has been relaxed since the apostolic letter *Matrimonia Mixta* of 1970 – only the Catholic partner is now required to give this undertaking. Though the Protestant churches do not have the same explicit barriers to intermarriage, they do not encourage it.[84] The Orange Order prohibits members participating in any Roman Catholic religious ceremony, including marriages and funerals.

*Segregated education.* Northern Ireland's education system is almost totally segregated into Catholic and state schools at the primary and secondary levels – less than 2 per cent attend integrated schools. The two universities are formally integrated, although one study of Queen's University Belfast showed that it is no haven of liberal integration in a sectarian sea,[85] while third-level teacher-training colleges are explicitly segregated.[86] The Catholic hierarchy promotes separate Catholic education because it believes it is the best way to reproduce Catholic values.[87] Less kindly, the Roman Catholic church's motives are defined as ethnocentric and reactionary, based on its historic campaign against proselytism and its contemporary battle against secularism.[88] However, the segregated system is broadly supported by the Protestant churches because the state schools are in effect Protestant – biblical readings are normal in such schools. Despite the idea prevalent amongst academic foreigners that segregated education is a product of the Catholic church,[89] Protestant churches helped build the present system and vigorously opposed past attempts at integration.[90] The scale of educational segregation is such that less than 2 per cent of children attend integrated schools.

Numerous commentators believe segregated education fosters conflict; it promotes bloc solidarity; strengthens sectarianism; and encourages ignorance of the other community. The two school systems teach a culturally biased curriculum, not just in religious instruction, but in potentially divisive subjects like history and language. They encourage different games: Catholic schools promote Gaelic sports, like hurling, camogie and handball; state/Protestant schools encourage sports associated with the British Empire, like rugby or cricket.[91] The divided schools exacerbate socio-economic differences between Catholics and Protestants: Catholic schools allegedly encourage the arts while Protestant schools put greater emphasis on science and mathematics, which some claim differentially affects pupils' prospects in the labour market.[92] Similarly, one observer claims that Catholic under-representation in public service can be explained by a self-fulfilling prophecy – Catholic teachers tell their students they will not be hired in governmental institutions, so they do not apply![93] Less controversially, segregated education has undoubtedly contributed to religiously based teaching unions, erecting obstacles to cross-cutting cleavages based on employee solidarity.[94] The location of schools also reinforces residential segregation.

For many it follows that integrated education would be a positive development, promoting understanding and reconciliation.[95] Some claim it would be 'the single potentially most helpful step'.[96] Supporters of integrated education have included lobby movements like *All Children Together*; Lord Londonderry (Northern Ireland's first minister of education);

**Table 5.4** Public opinion on what the government should do
on mixed schooling

|  | Protestants | Catholics |
|---|---|---|
| Encourage it | 57 | 67 |
| Discourage it | 9 | 5 |
| Leave things as they are | 33 | 28 |

*Source*: A. M. Gallagher and S. Dunn, 'Community Relations in Northern Ireland: Attitudes to Contact and Integration', in Peter Stringer and Gillian Robinson (eds), *Social Attitudes in Northern Ireland, 1990–91 Edition* (Belfast: Blackstaff Press, 1991), 16.

Sir James Craig, *before* he became Northern Ireland's first prime minister; Terence O'Neill;[97] as well as several academics.[98] More surprisingly, perhaps, the harmful effects of segregated education have been noted by a leading Catholic journal;[99] by Jesuits and professors at Maynooth, the Republic's leading seminary; and by at least one Catholic bishop.[100] A 1986 survey of Northern Irish Catholic priests found that 33 per cent agreed that 'integrated education would reduce some of the problems in Northern Ireland' while 41 per cent did not oppose it 'in principle'.[101] Integrated education received some support from the education minister in the brief power-sharing executive which sat during early 1974, from the Labour government during 1974–9 and, most recently, from the Conservative government which in 1990 made more funds available for integrated education. The Education Reform (Northern Ireland) Order 1989, which became law on 19 February 1990, temporarily created a privileged new category of school, 'grant-maintained integrated' (GMI) schools, which had all of their recurrent and capital expenditure met by the Department of Education – unlike Catholic schools before 1992. Indeed from 1988 until 1992 it appeared that the government intended to support integrated schools at the expense of mono-religious state schools.

Opponents of segregated education muster survey evidence in support of their cause. A 1968 survey, for example, showed that 64 per cent of adults favoured integrated education.[102] A survey in 1978 found that 81 per cent of Protestants and 84 per cent of Catholics disagreed with the statement 'It is a bad idea to mix Protestant and Catholic children in the same schools.'[103] The 1989 Social Attitudes Survey produced the responses displayed in table 5.4. These figures suggest that a 'positive climate' exists for integrated schools – even though significant minorities of Protestants (42 per cent) and Catholics (33 per cent) do not want the government to encourage mixed schooling.[104] They also suggest that segregated education is something which majorities in both communities regard as amenable to change.

## The Limits to Religious Explanations: Two Religions in Conflict?

The foregoing accounts attach fundamental or primary importance to religion in explaining political antagonism, political violence and political stalemate. However, as the following arguments suggest, there are major flaws in these analyses.

Measurable levels of religiosity, such as church attendance, are remarkably high in Northern Ireland when compared with elsewhere in western Europe,[105] but the fact is that conflict started, escalated, and has continued while these levels have been declining. Other measures of religious irregularity – of divorces or of children born outside marriage – indicate that Northern Ireland is becoming more secular. Since 1981, the divorce rate, while lower absolutely, has been increasing at about the same rate as in Great Britain. Between 1981 and 1987 the rate of births outside marriage more than doubled, compared with an increase of 83 per cent in the whole of the UK. By 1987 the illegitimate birth-rate level had reached the UK rate for 1981, so on this 'index' Northern Ireland is a mere six years behind the UK.[106] Such 'secularization' has not affected the continuing high levels of support for nationalist and unionist political parties, so it is at least questionable whether more of the same will make a significant difference.

Significantly, there is no noticeable correlation between those areas most affected by the conflict and the intensity of the religious convictions of the inhabitants. Rural areas around Ballymena, heartlands of support for Paisley, are tranquil and generally free of political violence. Nationalist towns like Crossmaglen may be devoutly religious but it is more difficult to make this argument about West Belfast, where there have been noticeable declines in church attendance in both blocs.[107] John Darby reported in 1986 that church attendance was estimated by local clergy in one Catholic area of Belfast at 33 per cent.[108] One study of the Shankill, where Protestant paramilitaries and the DUP have significant support, indicated that Protestant church attendance had dropped to about 15 per cent in the late 1970s.[109] Another detailed analysis of the Protestant working class in Belfast depicts them as distinctly secular, like the working class in industrial cities elsewhere:[110] the Reverend Martin Smyth's pious observation that Shankill working-class Protestants 'are bible-lovers if not bible-readers' is scarcely compelling evidence of religious consciousness.[111] The spatial and per capita distribution of violence is highly concentrated in urban sites, which are, as elsewhere in the world, less religious than rural zones.[112] Indeed one can go further and suggest that urban paramilitaries become religious, or more religious, *after* they have been incarcerated!

Relations between the churches were improving when conflict erupted in the late 1960s. The second Vatican Council had formally abandoned the Roman Catholic claim that 'outside the Church there is no salvation', paving the way for ecumenism. Even if we concede, for the sake of argument, the Paisleyite claim that this step marked religious imperialism in a new tactical guise, it is difficult to understand why ecumenism should have been more successful in promoting Catholic violence, or Protestant counter-violence, than Rome's previous and blunter claim that all Protestants were heretics. Since the conflict erupted in the late 1960s there has been a fair amount of ecumenical activity and inter-church co-operation,[113] and the present co-operation of the churches is very different from what occurred in earlier crises: for example, during the home rule controversies the Protestant churches played leading roles in promoting the Ulster Covenant. The churches have not always taken a united position on excesses by the security forces, paramilitary violence, or political proposals, but this behaviour often indicates that they are following their flocks, rather than leading them. To expect a consensus from pastoral churches in divided communities is wishful thinking. In any case, claims that partisan statements by church leaders are responsible for the violence are exaggerated, and no more plausible than the view that religious statements against violence have kept it at lower rates than would otherwise have been the case.

Significantly, political activists in Northern Ireland seek to avoid religious labels. The organizations of the minority embrace secular political values in their titles: 'nationalism' or 'republicanism', 'social democracy', and 'socialism' provide their vocabularies. No minority party or paramilitary group describes itself religiously – only Paisleyites describe the IRA as the 'Roman Catholic IRA'. Politically they refer to 'their community' as 'the northern nationalist community'. Nationalists boast proudly of a famous tradition of Protestant nationalists – though as one revisionist historian has observed, they are important as 'deviants, not as representatives of a latent syndrome'.[114]

Politicians who are Catholics have been and are lay people with differing religious commitments – by contrast with Latin America, no Catholic clergy have stood for political office. The old Nationalist Party had close links with the Catholic church, but the civil-rights movement of the late 1960s was led by lay Catholics, and at present neither of the two major northern nationalist parties enjoys a particularly close relationship with the church, although the SDLP has much greater standing and respectability with the hierarchy than Sinn Féin. Republican paramilitaries include practising and non-practising Catholics, and there is little or no correlation between the intensity of Catholic (or Protestant) religious views and fighting-commitment.[115] Catholic voters have shown willingness on many occasions to support individuals who enjoyed a closer relationship with Trotsky and Marx than with the Pope, returning one 'cradle Catholic', Bernadette Devlin, to the Westminster parliament in 1969. One of her opinions was that[116] 'Among the best traitors Ireland has ever had, Mother Church ranks at the very top, a massive obstacle in the path to equality and freedom.'[117] In 1981 Catholic voters in Fermanagh and South Tyrone elected another MP, Bobby Sands, a convicted IRA man, whose distinctly untheological qualification was that he was starving himself to death in British custody.

Nationalist politicians propose secular not theological policies. Their micro-proposals are for economic reforms or changes to the policing and judicial systems. Campaigning on religious issues, like full-funding for segregated education, was left to the Catholic church by the SDLP to an extent unimaginable during the era of the Nationalist Party – although the SDLP has been equivocal and divided on public policy on contraception and Brook clinics, and its members generally oppose legalizing abortion, whereas Sinn Féin supporters are more liberal on these matters. The key macro-policy of nationalist politicians and militants is an agreed or united Ireland which would transcend sectarianism, rather than the construction of a Catholic state. The formal targets of republican paramilitaries between 1969 and 1994 were those who defended the Union, not those who defend Protestantism. Republican paramilitaries generally avoided targeting Protestant religious personnel and institutions. Only one Protestant cleric was killed by republicans between 1969 and 1994, the Reverend Robert Bradford, and he was a hard-line UUP MP with outspoken views on how to deal with the IRA hunger-strikers. The isolated incident at Darkley in 1983 when republican gunmen – probably from the INLA – killed three Protestant evangelicals during a religious service, may provide proof enough of republicans' religious agenda for Free Presbyterians, but it will not do for social scientists.

IRA violence cannot be convincingly explained, as Fulton believes,[118] by the argument that its activists have been motivated by the Catholic doctrine of a 'just war'. The Catholic hierarchy pronounced that the situation in Northern Ireland did not meet the criteria necessary for a just war,[119] and what, in any case, is intrinsically 'religious', never mind 'Catholic', about taking up arms against a perceived aggressor or oppressor?[120] Few religions, or for that matter value-systems, reject armed retaliation against tyranny. Franz Fanon, no theist, thought that violence was the only way to cleanse a people of oppression, and his French admirer, atheist Jean-Paul Sartre, declared that violence was like Achilles' lance – it healed the wounds it made.[121] These masculine and romantic justifications of violence resemble those articulated by many republicans; they did not need, and did not receive Papal endorsement. And even if Catholic 'just war' doctrine had justified IRA violence, it would not have followed that religion had been 'causing' the violence. Its root causes are better undertood against the background of institutions which provoked people into declaring a just war in the first place and in the opportunities and perceived benefits from violent collective action. It is possible to explain – though not justify – republican violence strictly through reference to nationalist ideology, the suppression of economic, cultural and political rights, and the historically widely dispersed lesson that 'force can work'. When interviewed, these arguments pour naturally from the lips of former IRA activists and supporters of Sinn Féin. There is no need to invent ingenious religious agendas to account for militant republican paramilitarism.

On the unionist side, political organizations define themselves as 'loyalist' or 'unionist'. There is one interesting example since 1969 of a unionist party describing itself religiously, Paisley's Protestant Unionist Party. However, it changed its name to the Democratic Unionist Party in 1971 because of the limited attractiveness of the explicitly religious label – and it was some time before the party attracted significant support. Loyalist paramilitaries also generally shun religious appellations – with the exception of the Protestant Action Force. The absence of denominational titles in political and paramilitary organizations is all the more remarkable given their existence in other countries which are not racked by conflict, religious or otherwise. The Ulster Unionist Party, the Democratic Unionist Party, the Social Democratic and Labour Party of Northern Ireland, and Sinn Féin are not religiously labelled, even if their support-bases are religiously differentiated. The objectives of these parties, with the possible exception of the DUP, are secular. The IRA, the INLA, the IPLO, the UDA, and the UVF are not religious bodies. Finally, we can make our point counterfactually. Imagine that

Northern Ireland's two major political parties, the UUP and the SDLP, had denominational titles – say the Protestant Popular Party of Ulster and the National Catholic Democratic Action Party. These labels would not necessarily signify a religious conflict, since they might just serve as markers for two ethnic blocs, defined by religion, but whose members did not practise their ancestral beliefs. As we have seen, the political language of both protagonists appeals to the discourses of nationalism, the principles of self-determination and democratic majoritarianism, ideas which are, in principle, and in practice, detached from religious world-views. Moreover, the sectarian interest-associations, like the Orange Order and the Ancient Order of Hibernians (AOH), are far less significant than they were seven decades ago. The AOH is now better supported on St Patrick's Day in the USA than in any part of Ireland. The Orange Order was by-passed as a vehicle of ethnic organization, both in 1974, when the Ulster Workers Council organized a loyalist strike against the power-sharing Executive, and after the Anglo-Irish Agreement of 1985, when the newly formed Ulster Clubs organized pan-unionist opposition.

The principal unionist parties and the loyalist paramilitaries are exclusively Protestant, but many of their supporters do not practise any faith. The high profile of Protestant clerics notwithstanding, the overwhelming majority of unionist politicians are lay people. They address themselves to secular issues, calling for a strengthening of the Union and for stronger security policies. They do not call for a Protestant theocracy – although one could read the 1688 British Constitution in that light! Of course, national preferences might be dictated partly by religious motivations – a united Ireland, after all, would be overwhelmingly Catholic while the UK is overwhelmingly Protestant or secular – but if these political agents are primarily interested in these religious agendas, they have done a good job of concealing it, from their followers as well as others. Loyalist paramilitaries generally shun overtly religious targets. Catholic churches have remained relatively inviolate, and not one Catholic priest has been killed by loyalist gunmen – though one, Father Fitzpatrick, was killed by an army sniper as he was administering the last rites.[122] It must be perplexing for those

**Table 5.5** Perceived causes of 'The Troubles', by religion

|  | Protestants | Catholics |
|---|---|---|
| 1 Political, constitutional | 35 | 32 |
| 2 Discrimination, rights | 21 | 27 |
| 3 Violence, terrorism | 16 | 7 |
| 4 Attitudes | 15 | 15 |
| 5 Religion | 13 | 12 |
| 6 Social, economic | 11 | 15 |
| 7 Segregation | 5 | 4 |
| 8 Others | 18 | 15 |

*Source*: D. Smith and G. Chambers, *Inequality in Northern Ireland* (Oxford: Clarendon Press, 1991), 68.

who believe that the paramilitaries are involved in a *jihad* that 'Protestant' gunmen assiduously avoid clearly marked, accessible and unarmed priests and nuns when searching for targets. Individuals engaged in authentic religious wars – during the Inquisition, the Reformation and the Counter-reformation – had no difficulty in despatching heretics to hell.

Religious motivations undoubtedly underlie much of what the Catholic and Protestant clergy do. Many Catholic priests support a united Ireland, and most Protestant clergy support the Union. However, these national preferences are autonomous of religious beliefs. Clerics on both sides, after all, have been socialized in their respective communities. They live, have families and perform pastoral functions within them. It is not surprising, therefore, that they share their flock's political aspirations. As Ian Paisley complained of Cardinal O'Fiaich, 'You can take him out of Crossmaglen but you cannot take Crossmaglen out of him.'[123]

It is important to realize that the external perception that the conflict is religious does not square with local perceptions.[124] The Policy Studies Institute's Survey in 1986 asked respondents: 'What, in your opinion, are the main causes of the current Troubles in Northern Ireland, which began in the late 1960s?' The question was designed to make the respondents think about factors that were still relevant in 1986, and they were able to list more than one cause. The results were classified and are reported in table 5.5. They are complex, but only 13 per cent of Protestants and 12 per cent of Catholics thought religion was one of the main causes of the troubles, and some of these respondents thought the problem was 'a lack of religion' rather than religious bigotry. Catholics are more likely to hold discrimination, civil rights or socio-economic issues responsible for the conflict, whereas Protestants are more likely to blame violence or terrorism. The classifications listed in table 5.5 overlap, and if categories 1 and 2 and 6 are combined – linking civil rights, discrimination and socio-economic inequalities – then non-religious factors unequivocally emerge as the most important perceived causes of conflict.[125] The overwhelming majority of Northern Irish agree that they are not engaged in a *jihad*. We have heard the response that such evidence should be discounted as collective 'denial', but we find that thesis neither plausible nor testable.

## Is Protestantism at the Core of the Conflict?

Protestants believe that the conflict has multiple causes, as table 5.5 demonstrates. We believe, like most of them, that their opposition to a united Ireland, their support for the Union, their unwillingness to accommodate the nationalist minority, and their support for Ian Paisley and the DUP cannot be fundamentally or primarily reduced to their religious values and beliefs.

While cultural differences between Protestant and Catholic may be indiscernible to outsiders, and their historical linguistic differences have long since been eroded, the two blocs have different practices in a range of cultural activities, including music, sport and literature.[126] The Gaelic revival of the late nineteenth century made Irish nationalism more unattractive to Protestants, and this was reinforced by the implementation of a Gaelicizing agenda in independent Ireland – including compulsory knowledge of the Irish language for the educational leaving certificate and certain careers in public service. The anti-British atmosphere in independent Ireland, which led to its departure from the Commonwealth and the declaration

**Table 5.6** Structured sources of Protestant opposition to a united
Ireland in 1978

|                                                          | % agreeing |
| -------------------------------------------------------- | ---------- |
| 'would lose British national identity'                   | 89.6       |
| 'standard of living would go down'                       | 77.5       |
| 'fear of the power of the Roman Catholic Church'         | 74.5       |
| 'would be in a minority in the Republic'                 | 70.9       |
| 'want to keep privileged position in Northern Ireland'   | 66.1       |

*Source*: Moxon-Browne, *Nation, Class and Creed.*

of a Republic, made a united Ireland an additionally uninviting
prospect for people who felt themselves British monarchists.[127]
   There have always been economic as well as cultural reasons
why Ulster Protestants resist incorporation in a united Ireland.
The Protestant bourgeoisie and proletariat thought that Irish
home rule would mean submergence in a polity whose leaders
promised protectionism and import-substitution. Today, Protestants – and some Catholics – continue to believe that their
economic position would rapidly deteriorate if they joined
a state whose major export seems to be its own citizens.
A unified Ireland would turn the present British, unionist,
and Protestant majority in Northern Ireland into a political
minority and would also denote a victory for their enemy, the
Provisional IRA. These fears are sufficient to explain – though
they do not justify – why so many Protestants are unwilling to
accommodate nationalists.
   Professor Bruce's argument that Protestants resist a united
Ireland primarily for religious reasons depends on an un-
professional use of data. His apparently powerful claim that
74.5 per cent of unionists give 'fear of the power of the
Roman Catholic Church' as their reason for being unionist
is misleading.[128] The same data is used elsewhere to argue
that fear of the Roman Catholic church's power is the 'main'
reason for Protestant opposition to a united Ireland.[129] The
impression conveyed is that Protestants have been asked to
choose one reason for their opposition to a united Ireland and
three-quarters have selected this religious reason as their main
reason. However, the survey to which Bruce refers allowed
Protestants to select a number of reasons for opposing Irish

unification (see table 5.6). The responses show that Protestants clearly agree on multiple reasons for opposing a united Ireland. Had they been asked whether they opposed a united Ireland because that is what the IRA was fighting for, we can be sure that they would have concurred. The question-wording in table 5.6 does not allow us to infer which fears are of most intense importance to Protestants, but more were concerned that they would 'lose their British identity' and that their 'standard of living would go down' than were worried about the power of the Roman Catholic church. Moreover, 70.9 per cent of Protestants feared 'they would be a minority' in the Republic and an honest 66.1 per cent 'wanted to keep their privileged position in Northern Ireland'. Fear of the Catholic church, therefore, is not the 'main' reason Protestants resist incorporation into an all-Ireland republic – just one of a number which have different weights for each individual Protestant. When Ian Paisley implied, during a radio interview in 1971, that the conflict could be resolved if the political influence of the hierarchy in the Republic was removed, he was forced to make a quick retraction by his confused followers – who had plenty of non-religious reasons for opposing a united Ireland.[130]

Richard Rose's Loyalty Survey is often used to confirm the view that fear of the Roman Catholic church is at the forefront of Protestant minds. Indeed Rose includes the following quotation at the top of his chapter on religion:

*Interviewer*: What do you have against Roman Catholics?
*Belfast Protestant*: Are you daft? Why, their religion of course.[131]

When readers recover from the joke they must realize that the question is hardly neutral. Would the same response have been given if the Belfast Protestant had been asked what s/he had against 'republicans' or 'nationalists'? More significantly when asked about the position of the Catholic church in the Republic, 69 per cent of Protestants thought it was 'politically important', 'powerful' or 'too powerful', but when asked what they disliked about the Republic's government only 7.6 per cent of them mentioned interference or dominance by the Roman Catholic church.[132] In any case fear of the position of the Catholic church in the Republic does not necessarily indicate that the Protestant religion is central to unionism. Rejection of 'Romanism' may be a rationalization of a whole complex of attitudes and interests, ranging from cultural contempt to ardent secular liberalism. Secular unionists, or Protestant atheists as they are colloquially known, vigorously oppose a united Ireland, and have more reason to do so than the bulk of Ulster Protestant believers who share the moral conservatism which historically has been entrenched in the Republic's constitution and public policies.

Protestants' desire to maintain the Union also cannot be reduced to their religion, especially as Great Britain is increasingly less Protestant. Great Britain is now largely secular – only 13 per cent of the English claim any church membership.[133] While Protestants are divided over their national identity, many, indeed most, now regard themselves as British[134] – the same Professor Bruce who argues that 'Ulster Protestants have not developed a clear sense of nationality' provides details of a 1978 survey which indicates that 67 per cent of Protestants consider themselves to be 'British'.[135] Unionists like being part of a large, still relatively powerful, 'Great' British state, and older unionists remain proud of their collective sacrifices during two world wars and of their service to the Empire. Economic self-interest buttresses national identity. Northern Ireland enjoys measurable subsidies and it does not make sense to argue that these have no bearing on Protestant motivations. Determined to stress the salience of religion, Bruce points out that marginalized Protestants remain solid unionists despite the fact that they gain least economically from the Union.[136] However, this argument is economically mistaken: marginalized Protestants may gain least from the Union, but they still gain, so their cost–benefit calculus favours the Union. There is also nothing surprising about marginalized groups acting vehemently to protect what others may regard as meagre economic rewards – consider the behaviour of 'white trash' in the deep South of the USA or poor Afrikaners in South Africa. We are not, however, advancing the counter-error of reducing unionism to economics. In short we agree with those who question whether unionism must have a fundamental attribute, a dimension more important than any other,[137] but if it has to be given a fundamental attribute then it must be seen as the political expression of an ethno-national community which is religiously demarcated – and not the political expression of *a* religious community.

Unionists' reasons for resisting accommodation with Catholics obviously include religious motivations, but apart from fundamentalists, these reasons are not paramount or widespread. There is a simpler reason: for unionists accommodating Catholics means accommodating nationalists. They were far more perturbed by Terence O'Neill's meeting with Sean Lemass than by his visits to Catholic convents. Their opposition to power-sharing focuses on its linkage to an Irish (nationalist) dimension, not a Vatican dimension. Even loyalist paramilitaries say they are happy to accommodate Catholics if and when they accept the Union.[138] They are far more worried about public policy concessions to nationalists – which may restrain 'their' security forces – than they are about concessions to Catholics *qua* Catholics. When the British government announced in 1992 that Catholic schools would receive 100 per cent capital funding there was no major discontent in the unionist press.[139]

The claim that 'the Northern Ireland conflict is a religious conflict' because 'that is the only conclusion that makes sense of Ian Paisley's career', his electoral success in particular, is also misleading.[140] For a start it proves nothing about what motivates those Protestants who vote for the APNI (approximately 10–12 per cent) and the UUP (between 40 and 60 per cent). To sustain his thesis Professor Bruce seems intent on exaggerating the DUP's support.[141] He acknowledged that only 'half of Ulster's unionist voters' support the DUP, but did not observe that this figure relied on a selective concentration on untypical election results and neglected the Protestant electorate who vote for the APNI.[142] Bruce's favoured electoral illustration is the untypical European parliamentary election,[143] in which Paisley's personal charisma, the nature of the campaign, the electoral system, and the dullness of his UUP opponents, help Paisley receive a proportion of the poll which dwarfs what his party obtains in other regional elections.[144] If instead

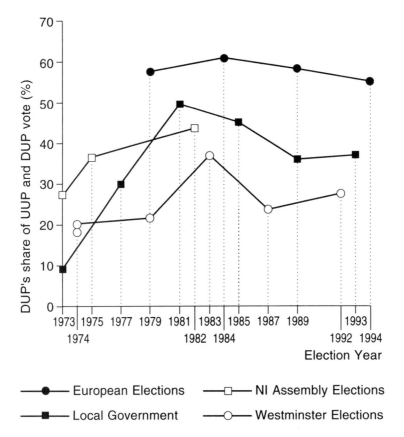

**Figure 5.2** The competition for votes between the DUP
and the UUP, 1973–94

we highlighted the DUP's share of the poll at Westminster
elections – which ranged from 8 to 10 per cent during the 1970s
and from 13 to 20 per cent during the 1980s – we could present
a misleading impression of the weakness of the DUP. To do so
would be no worse than the argument adopted by Bruce.

The lesson is simple: sociologists of religion, over-ambitious
to apply their insights, should be more cautious with electoral
data. There are after all political rather than religious reasons
for the variability of the DUP's electoral performance. Figure 5.2 shows the DUP's share of the DUP and UUP vote
in elections held between 1973 and 1994. We have distinguished the DUP's performance in European elections from its

**Table 5.7** Members of the Free Presbyterian Church in Northern
Ireland, 1961–91

|                        | 1961 | 1971  | 1981  | 1991   |
|------------------------|------|-------|-------|--------|
| Absolute Numbers       |      | 7,337 | 9,621 | 12,363 |
| Percentage of respondents | 0.07 | 0.4 | 0.7 | 0.8 |

*Source*: Census of Northern Ireland (1961, 1971, 1981, 1991).

**Table 5.8** Electoral support for major unionist parties in the 1975
Convention and the 1982 Assembly

|                                 | 1975 (%) | 1982 (%) |
|---------------------------------|----------|----------|
| Ulster Unionist Party (UUP)     | 25.8     | 29.7     |
| Democratic Unionist Party (DUP) | 14.8     | 23       |
| Vanguard Unionist Party (VUP)   | 12.7     | (–)      |

*Source*: B. O'Leary, 'Appendix 4. Party Support in Northern Ireland,
1969–89', in J. McGarry and B. O'Leary (eds), *The Future of Northern
Ireland* (Oxford: Clarendon Press, 1990), 343.

performance in other region-wide elections (Westminster elections, local government elections and assembly elections). The graphs demonstrate that the DUP's level of support is more variable, and more heavily dependent upon the nature of the election, the electoral formula and the electoral districts, than Bruce's arguments would suggest. These variations cannot be explained by changes in people's religious commitments. The UUP usually has a higher vote-share than the DUP – except in European elections – though the DUP's weaker performance in Westminster elections results from its decision not to compete in certain constituencies for fear of letting nationalists win them.[145]

The DUP nevertheless enjoys significant electoral support, so *prima facie* evidence for the salience of religion in politics remains. The key question can therefore be put: do Protestants support Ian Paisley and the DUP for religious reasons?[146] Table 5.7 shows the numbers of persons identifying as followers of the Free Presbyterian Church, the church founded by Paisley, in the four censuses held since 1960. The tenfold growth in membership of the Free Presbyterians may be significant, but the Free Presbyterians still make up a tiny fraction of Northern Ireland's population (less than 1 per cent), and there has been a far higher rise in the absolute numbers of those declaring that they have no religion.

It is important to realize that the DUP is not only a party with large numbers of Free Presbyterians in its membership, it is also a hard-line unionist party. It consistently opposes compromise with nationalists, and calls for the 'smashing' of Sinn Féin and the IRA. In the DUP 1982 Assembly manifesto, for example, the party supported majority rule, offered 'the firmest stand against all attempts to force Ulster down the Dublin road', and called for all-out war against the IRA, and the return of the death penalty. Only in the last paragraph was there a reference to the party's support for evangelicalism.[147] The DUP also spearheaded loyalist assaults on the Anglo-Irish Agreement of 1985, and the Joint Peace Declaration of 1993. The message? Unionists can be confident that the DUP will not sell them out. They cannot feel so confident about the UUP, home to such notorious 'Lundies' as Terence O'Neill, James Chichester-Clark, and Brian Faulkner, and individuals like Harry West, Ken Maginnis, and Chris McGimpsey, who have proposed power-sharing with nationalists.

The DUP was not anywhere near as popular in the mid-1970s as it became in the early 1980s (see figure 5.2 and table 5.8). The reason was that in the 1970s the DUP had to compete with the Vanguard Unionist Party (VUP), which was a hard-line loyalist party, and secular. Its leader, William Craig, had even welcomed ecumenism when it emerged in the early 1960s.[148] Until 1976 Craig was far more militant than Paisley, and feared by nationalists as a fascist exponent of independence for 'Ulster'. The VUP collapsed, however, when Craig appeared to compromise in discussions with the SDLP during the Constitutional Convention, opening the field of uncompromising extremism for exclusive occupation by Paisley's party. The DUP became the home of most former VUP supporters after that party disintegrated in the wake of its leader's national, rather than religious, 'treachery', as table 5.8 suggests.

The DUP wins a significant share of the Protestant working-class vote. The party's evangelicalism cannot be the basis of this electoral success as the urban Protestant working class is not particularly religious.[149] It fears losing the benefits of the Union, dislikes nationalists or Catholics, and distrusts the 'furcoat brigade' in the establishment UUP. The DUP attracts this working-class vote, not by wearing evangelicalism on its sleeve, but by downplaying it. To increase its appeal to non-evangelical Protestants the party changed its name from Protestant Unionist to Democratic Unionist, compromised its commitment to temperance and sabbatarianism, and pushed interventionist rather than free-market economic policies.[150] That Protestants' vote for DUP candidates because 'they like them and what they stand for'[151] has obvious and non-religious explanations.[152]

What of Akenson's thesis that Ulster Protestants are, like Afrikaners and Israeli Jews, a 'covenant people'?[153] First of all Akenson makes a largely historical rather than contemporary argument, maintaining that religion is now much less important for Ulster Protestants than it was. They are no longer a covenant people: the popularity of ecumenism, the increasing moderation of sects other than the Free Presbyterians, doubts about the correctness of discrimination, and the fragmentation of Protestant political unity are increasingly putting the notion of a covenant people into their cultural past. Secondly, and crucially, Akenson's own evidence from South Africa, Israel, and Ulster suggests how neatly the selective use and interpretation of the Old Testament coincided with the ethnic interests of these three settler peoples. In South Africa and Ulster the Protestant settlers, intentionally or otherwise, forgot that Christ's sacrifice was supposed to have transformed God's covenant with the Jews into a universal faith to be preached to Jew and Gentile alike – a covenant between Christ and humanity. The 'chosen people' theme in the history of Ulster Protestantism is therefore capable of being interpreted in a much more hard-headed manner than that customary amongst historians and sociologists of religion. The theological 'covenant' which Protestants invoked to justify their privileged status and discriminatory behaviour was a conveniently group-interested misinterpretation of Christianity, in which ethnic politics shaped religious world-views more than vice versa, and in which religion was selectively used as an ideological power-resource rather than propagated as an authentic and universal belief system.

## Is Catholicism at the Core of the Conflict?

The Catholic church has considerable influence and power in the Republic, even if its role has been exaggerated by unsympathetic commentators.[154] This power and influence, even though it is waning,[155] undoubtedly buttresses unionist opposition to a united Ireland. However, it cannot be validly inferred that successive revolts by northern nationalists have had religious causes, or that the aims of Irish nationalists are synonymous with those of the Catholic church.

Discrimination against their religion *qua* religion played little part in motivating Catholics to boycott the Northern Ireland parliament after 1921. Almost all explicitly religious discrimination in the UK had been legally abolished before partition in 1920. While nationalists and Catholics were on the receiving end of substantial discrimination,[156] Catholics were relatively well treated *qua* Catholics. Catholics were discriminated against because they were perceived as disloyal nationalists/republicans, not because they said the rosary or believed in the doctrine of transubstantiation. Even Michael Farrell, who has documented exhaustively the maltreatment of the northern minority, believes – oddly – that Catholics did rather well in educational provision.[157] Schools were segregated, with the approval, or even the insistence, of the Catholic hierarchy. Catholic schools and hospitals did not receive the same level of funding as state institutions – and this was an issue in northern nationalist politics during the Stormont era and after[158] – but full state support for voluntary or religious schools was infrequent in English-speaking democracies and dominions, and non-existent in the USA.[159]

It is redundant to seek religious explanations for Catholics' political hostility to the Stormont regime. They had more than enough non-religious reasons to consider revolt or protest.

It is sufficient to refer to the disadvantages they suffered, politically, legally, economically, and culturally, to explain their political attitudes.[160] Moreover, the disparities between Catholics and Protestants in recruitment and positions in employment cannot be significantly attributed to differing religious values and methods of education, as some Protestants and unionist commentators believe.[161] These disparities were (and are) mostly because of direct and indirect discrimination, as we shall subsequently discuss.[162]

Conspiracy theories which held the Catholic church responsible for critically supporting republican violence are just incredible. The Catholic church, world-wide, has been noticeably (and notoriously) willing to accept and work with all types of regimes, at least before World War II. The Catholic church did not enthusiastically endorse the partition of Ireland, and could not have done so without alienating most of its constituency. However, in practice the Catholic hierarchy reached various accommodations with the unionist regime, including appointing a chaplain to the Stormont parliament in 1963.[163] The Irish hierarchy has exacerbated communal divisions by its continuing insistence that the Constitution and public policy in the Republic should enforce Catholic doctrine as far as possible, and by its position on mixed marriages. However, Catholic churches have advocated these public policies everywhere in the world. They can scarcely, on their own, account for conflict, violence and stalemate in Northern Ireland.

The argument that the Church is, however indirectly, responsible for republican violence is difficult to substantiate, and scoffed at by republican paramilitaries.[164] The Church's lack of control over the IRA was demonstrated most spectacularly by the failure of Pope John Paul II's plea for peace made in September 1979, made on bended knees as he said mass in Drogheda.[165] The Catholic clergy condemn unjustified state violence, but they have also consistently condemned the IRA.[166] It is difficult to see how this dual condemnation legitimized the violence of the IRA, as several critics have argued, any more than it justifies the excesses of the security forces. Such criticism, directed against the Catholic church by

Paisleyites and others, is substantially the same as that levelled against the SDLP by unionists. The only way for the Catholic church (and the SDLP) to avoid these criticisms, it appears, is for them to become uncritical supporters of British state authority.

## Is Religion Responsible for the Social Boundary in Northern Ireland?

It is difficult to imagine, despite one political scientist's argument to the contrary, that the two communities that have co-existed in Ulster since the seventeenth century would have been able to maintain their separateness so successfully in the absence of religious differences.[167] There are, despite Belfast folk wisdom, no phenotypical differences distinguishing the two communities; and linguistic differences were eroded relatively quickly after the plantation, even though some claim to detect differences in accents and dialects between Protestants and Catholics from the same areas, and it is a local shibboleth that Protestants and Catholics pronounce the letter 'H' differently. However, though we accept the salience of religion as an ethnic marker it cannot be over-emphasized that ethnic divisions cannot be reduced to religion, or church policy on education, or mixed marriages.

The high rates of endogamy in Northern Ireland, at least in urban areas, owe as much to residential segregation and the resulting lack of social interaction, as to church policy;[168] and residential segregation in rural areas extends back in time to the colonial plantations. If Catholics do not meet Protestants, and vice versa, they are unlikely to want to marry them. In a zone of ethnic conflict where people emphasize solidarity and maintaining numbers, and display distrust if not hatred of the 'other side', endogamous practices prevail even among those who do not practise their religion.[169] Endogamy makes it more likely that the offspring will not only be of the same religion, but of the same political views. Marriage across religious lines carries more than dangers of religious censure – it can mean social ostracism, accusations of treachery and, in the most extreme cases, assassination.[170]

The conflict, in our judgement, cannot be attributed to the segregated education system. To begin with, research on whether the segregated education system has exacerbated community divisions is inconclusive.[171] Children attending different school systems have opposing political attitudes but it has not been proved that this difference follows from their school experiences.[172] Integrated education elsewhere in the world does not necessarily lead to the diminution of ethnic conflict. The curricular differences between the two dominant schooling systems, including the controversial area of history, have been exaggerated. The most important factor affecting curricular procedures are external examinations, and these are common to both school systems.[173] While Gaelic games are exclusive to Catholic schools, many sports, such as field athletics, basketball, and soccer, are played in common. The Catholic church's argument that a Catholic education promotes pacifism[174] may be hard to swallow given the activity of some of its alumni, but it does not follow that a Catholic or a separate education causes or increases violence. For one thing, the conflict between the ethnic communities, which were defined over three centuries ago, predates the modern education system by two centuries. Both communities maintained segregation and animosities without formally segregated education – and could do so in the future. Contrary cross-national evidence on the alleged link between denominational education and communal conflict also exists. The cases of the Netherlands and Canada demonstrate that denominational educational systems may be characterized by peaceful co-existence. The worst that can be said about the segregated education system, though a serious enough charge, is that it makes no significant contribution to breaking down ethnic stereotypes produced by other forms of socialization, and may reinforce them.[175]

Sophisticated critics of segregated education recognize these arguments but maintain that the need to promote inter-communal understanding makes a denominational system less justified than it may be in more placid societies. However, even they recognize that a deliberate move towards integrated education, through coercion or through severely biasing the public funding of educational finance, might not produce any positive consequences, and would probably be counterproductive. The minority community apparently enjoyed better relations with the Northern Ireland Department of Education than with other government departments during the Stormont period. For all their understandable complaints about facing the 'double burden' they paid – supporting their own schools and paying taxes for schools their children did not attend – education was the one policy sector in which minority self-government was permitted. It remains this way today. This cultural autonomy is often considered essential by minorities – as it is by Protestants in the Republic. Similar arrangements have formed essential parts of political settlements in Canada and the Netherlands.[176] The segregated education system has also provided stable, relatively prestigious jobs for Catholics when many other sectors have been relatively closed – and a disproportionate number of the Catholic middle class is employed here.[177] When the civil-rights campaign emerged in the 1960s, it was led by the products of the Catholic education system. Their complaint was not that they had received a bad education, or had been denied access to state schools and universities, but that they were not receiving the jobs for which their qualifications entitled them.

Though surveys show that both communities would accept integrated education,[178] this support is exceptionally soft. Previous attempts to form an integrated education system, in Ireland in 1831 and Northern Ireland in 1923, foundered on the rock of serious opposition within both communities.[179] When one member of the power-sharing executive floated a trial balloon on integrated education in 1974, there was no significant interest,[180] and there was no noticeable response to legislation in 1978 which provided funding for integrated schools where sufficient demand existed.[181] Few parents have sought changes to the present system,[182] and it has not been a burning issue for political elites. Moreover, mixing the children of Catholics and nationalists, and Protestants and unionists, would not necessarily have positive consequences. Research points in several directions. The 1968 Loyalty Survey revealed that those who experienced integrated education were not significantly more tolerant than those who did not – a conclusion consistent with studies in other countries.[183] This judgement has been supported by subsequent research.[184]

The interaction of blacks and whites in the United States is said by a psychologist to have increased prejudice there – although he does not believe the same would happen in societies where differences are not ascriptive.[185] One recent study claims that children develop more moderate attitudes as they progress through integrated schools.[186] However, integrated schools can also provide additional 'interfaces' for conflict to those which already exist. Contact can confirm or even increase prejudice rather than reduce it. 'A Catholic in a mixed school may learn that when Protestants say "Not an Inch" they mean it, just as a Protestant may learn that his Catholic schoolmates refuse to regard the Union Jack as the flag to which they give allegiance.'[187] It is worth remembering that those who suffered most in 1969 were the Catholics and Protestants housed outside their respective ghettos. Sometimes 'good fences make good neighbours'.

Policy-makers have three feasible options in the education field. They can:

- impose integrated education, by abolishing the segregated system, or by depriving it of the funds to operate;
- bias funding towards the integrated sector, to which parents could send their children on a voluntary basis; or
- support all three sectors, the integrated, and the two denominational systems, equally, while preserving a common educational curriculum.

The first option risks explosive consequences. It could only work if integration was sought by overwhelming and determined majorities on both sides, i.e. if there were already a consensus. There is not. Coercive integration would be regarded by sizeable groups as prejudicial to their culture and/or religion. It would be opposed by Catholics in a political system with a Protestant majority; but also by Protestants, because in many areas of Northern Ireland their children are now a minority in all age-cohorts.[188] Increased funding for voluntary integration poses fewer problems, but it is no panacea. It appeared to be the policy on which the Conservative government embarked in 1988. The problem is that those who use integrated education may be those who least need it. The more intransigent parents hold back. Even if they do not, a significant integrated system has to overcome the consequences of widespread residential segregation. Parents balk when faced with the prospect of bussing or chauffering their children into 'enemy territory'; and without this, secondary education would remain segregated.

Equality of funding for all educational systems – integrated and denominational – is the best foundation of cultural security for all, and we therefore welcome the agreement reached in late 1992 between the Catholic church and the British government which will, for the first time, enable equality of funding for all schools in the region.[189] A recent study by the Standing Advisory Commission on Human Rights has shown that the failure of Catholic schools to prepare students for certain scientific courses and occupations owed more to capital underfunding than to any intrinsic Catholic propensity to avoid teaching science.[190] Equality of funding for the Catholic sector – with funding to make up for past inequalities in resources – will go further to resolving conflict than more heroic changes to the schools. There are other modest steps which can be developed in the education system. There is room for more inter-cultural activity in arts, games, athletics, and debates, and for joint fieldwork in relevant subjects. History and religion can be taught with less sectarian and more cross-cultural content. The Education Reform (Northern Ireland) Order, passed in February 1990, sensibly insists on a cross-curricular approach which encourages mutual understanding of both cultures.

## Conclusion: Putting the Gods in their Place

Interpretations of Northern Ireland which emphasize the primacy of religion err by ignoring the multiple nature of the

*Internal Explanations*

divisions between the two communities, and by understating the evidence which shows the national conflict to have greater salience. Protestants and Catholics are divided by religion, by definition, but they are also divided by differences in economic and political power, by historical experience, and, most intensely, by national political identity.

The thesis that religious motivations are not primary for either nationalists or unionists, or for republican or loyalist paramilitaries, is in our judgement convincing. Religion is the key ethnic marker, facilitating the residential, marital and educational segregation which helps reproduce the two eth-nic/national communities. Because religion is the key marker its importance is exaggerated. It is an analytical mistake to endow the boundary-marker with more significance than the fact that there is a boundary. People belong to 'religious communities' irrespective of their actual religious or non-religious convictions, because the religious label is an ethnic label, whence the well-known, and only half-joking references to Protestant and Catholic atheists.

No social scientist has satisfactorily demonstrated that theo-logical beliefs are particularly important either individually or in aggregate in explaining political violence in the region. Although we share the liberal prejudice that religious fanati-cism and dogma are likely to be productive of violence, we are not persuaded that they are the keys to understanding violence in Northern Ireland. If one wants to argue that there is an important religious dimension to the conflict it is more prudent to argue that there exists a conflict between 'civil religions' or 'secular religions', i.e. to maintain that each community worships its own nation and does so in an exclusivist manner. Whether the disposition to sacralize the nation is greater in more religious communities is not something which has been properly investigated.[191] Never-theless it is an argument which states that religion reinforces nationalism, not the other way around. We would be happy to accept this formula if it is demonstrated – because we deny the primacy of religion this does not mean that we think religion is irrelevant, unimportant, epiphenomenal or a red herring.

If it is incorrect to believe that the two communities are only or essentially fighting over religion, that Protestantism is at the core of unionism, that Catholicism is at the heart of nationalism, and that the churches are responsible for social divisions in Northern Ireland, what follows? Increasing secularization or ecumenism will not bring a sustained peace, as neither deal with the material concerns of both communities or the political question of national identity and the national character of the state. Secularization and/or ecumenism should be welcomed for their own sake, not for their presumed by-products.[192] The consolidation of a pluralist Republic should be developed for its own sake, not because it will attract Protestants into a united Ireland. Depicting nationalists as zealous Catholics will solve nothing, and will not address their subordinate political and economic position or their aspiration for a united Ireland. Finally, even if the churches can be persuaded to change their policies on intermarriage and education, these changes alone will not significantly improve relations between the antagonistic communities.

Explanations which accord primacy to religion create blind-alleys for policy-makers and inhibit understanding. They absolve important political agents of responsibility. If the antagonisms are religious, then they cannot have been caused by the historic legacies of colonial conquest, plantation and oppression, by the Stormont regime's practice of political and economic discrimination against nationalists, by successive British governments' mismanagement in Ireland before and after 1972, or by British political institutions. If the conflict is religious then the historic nature of the Republic's nationalism, as opposed to its Catholicism, receives less attention than it should. Explanations which emphasize the primacy of religion therefore need to be exposed to strong light. When that happens, they evaporate, leaving little residue.

# 6

# Fiery Values:
# Cultural Interpretations

When I hear anyone use the word 'culture' I reach for my gun.
> *attributed to Herman Goering, Nazi Minister for the Luftwaffe*[1]

When I hear the word gun, I reach for my culture.
> *Alexander Gerschenkron, economic historian*[2]

The most penetrating commentaries on Northern Ireland's troubles are to be found in the artistic and emotional intricacies of work which often does not even mention the place . . . The nuances of tribal and religious animosities from which the violence springs are so subtle and complex that an oblique approach seems the only one possible.
> *John Banville, novelist and literary critic*[3]

. . . . . . . Of the 'wee six' I sing
Where to be saved you must only save face
And whatever you say you say nothing

. . . . O land of password, handgrip, wink and nod,
Of minds as open as a trap

Where tongues lie coiled, as under flames lie wicks,
Where half of us, as in a wooden horse
Were cabin'd and confined like wily Greeks,
Besieged within the siege, whispering morse
> *Seamus Heaney, Irish poet*[4]

All signs which we shew to one another of hatred and contempt, provoke in the highest degree to quarrel and battle (inasmuch as life itself, with the conditions of enduring scorn, is not esteemed worth the enjoying . . . ).
> *Thomas Hobbes, English philosopher*[5]

Wherever there is a conflict in which values, identities, and aspirations are at stake, analysts and poets naturally assume that clashing cultures lie at the heart of the antagonism. Two centuries ago Immanuel Kant claimed that nature had two means to separate peoples, differences of language and of religion, both of which tended to lead to mutual hatred and pretexts for war.[6] And it seems straightforward to emphasize the importance of cultural differences in accounting for political conflict, violence and constitutional stalemate in Northern Ireland, so straightforward that much commentary rarely goes further. There is a widespread supposition that the locals are culturally intolerant, and lack the civic skills that elsewhere have produced philosophies of 'live and let live'. Two favoured terms are invoked in this reading, atavism and tribalism.

*Atavism* is the tendency for people to resemble their distant ancestors more than their parents; describing those who have returned to a previous and older state of being it implies both regression and retardation. Popular atavistic explanations are reflected in the British perception of the Northern Irish as engaged in an ancestral rather than a contemporary conflict. 'The Irish are at it again' is a common refrain – as if they have some distinctive genetic propensity to war amongst themselves every second generation, if not every second of the day,[7] and always over issues which are dated, or, as it is usually put, 'irrelevant'. *Just what are they fighting for?* is a question we regularly encounter. The Northern Irish, in this view, are trapped in a time-warp, their quarrels available to twentieth-century televisual audiences as instructive commentaries on the merits of modernity.[8] Each community, as we have seen, is regarded as possessed by archaic and fundamentalist versions of their faiths; each is classed as reactionary in its nationalism, whether British or Irish; and each provides embarrassing reminders to the British and Irish of what their great-grandparents were like.[9] Whether described as Catholic or nationalist, or Protestant or unionist, the two communities are portrayed as encased in ancestral myths: Protestants in the myth of a besieged people, obsessively remembering 1690 as the date of their partial deliverance; Catholics in the myth of an oppressed people, obsessively recalling their conquest and subordination by British Protestants, recycling their grievances rather than looking forwards – 'besieged within the siege, whispering morse'.

*Tribalism* is an even more popular term for the conflict, especially amongst journalists. Here the idea of a regression to ancestral conditions is clear – as is the erroneous assumption that 'tribal warfare' or 'barbarism' is worse than 'modern warfare'. Whenever civilians, especially children, are killed or maimed as a result of political violence the terms 'tribal', 'frenzied tribalism', or 'barbarism' are sure to follow. The belief is widespread that tribal nationalism or loyalism distorts, narrows and regresses the psyches of those enveloped within these mind-sets. By implication, tribalism has been abandoned by modern or 'post-modern' persons, the citizens of Great Britain, the Republic, and denizens of elsewhere (i.e. Western Europe and North America), but not in the benighted hearts of darkness of Northern Ireland, in the ghettos and farmlands never reached by the Enlightenment.

Popular atavistic explanations are reinforced by academic versions. Northern Ireland has been cited in socio-biological explanations of ethnic conflicts[10] – even Richard Rose felt obliged to observe that blood group A is dominant in England, blood group O in Ireland, and that the population of the other parts of the British Isles has a mixture of blood groups.[11] Northern Ireland might also have been designed as a happy hunting ground for physical anthropologists who decode communal conflicts as by-products of the 'territorial imperative' alleged to structure ethnic relations.[12] Atavistic explanations are also favoured by some historians who fall victim to their professional pathology: past precedents and analogues to current political behaviour are invoked without telling us why they have explanatory power in accounting for the current antagonisms. Indeed some become the custodians of their community's myths, interpret the past as the present (and vice versa), and portray the present conflict as a mere repetition of a perennial antagonism. Historians, of course, are not alone in this respect.

In the social sciences cultural explanations fit with much received wisdom in anthropology, social psychology, sociology and political science. In these disciplines 'cultures' rather than 'institutions' are frequently invoked to explain social phenomena.[13] This thinking is present in political science in which 'political culture theory imputes some importance to political attitudes, beliefs, values and emotions in the explanation of political, structural, and behavioural phenomena'. Its proponents deny that political culture theory has ever 'been advanced as the unidirectional "cause" of political structure and behaviour',[14] maintain that the relationships between cultures and structures or institutions are interactive, and accept that cultural dispositions cannot be explained without reference to historical experience and contemporary structural constraints and opportunities. Nevertheless they insist that cultural dispositions, once developed, persist for a significant time despite institutional efforts to transform them.

This reasoning is regularly used to explain Northern Ireland. Its proponents specify the nature of the cultures in conflict and let these descriptions stand as explanations for why they have such polarizing consequences. If this approach is right, or even half right, important implications follow: instead of overtly focusing on constitutional or institutional design, policy-makers should focus on addressing cultural antagonisms, through the promotion of cross-cultural education, reconciling the 'two traditions', and encouraging and exhorting mutual appreciation and tolerance. Education, in schools and post-school, and interactive learning in community-encounter groups – or in the form of collective therapy known as 'conferences' or 'problem-solving workshops' – must be necessary to break down the fateful embrace of literally murderous cultural myths.[15] Mutual misunderstanding is the cause of conflict, understanding will resolve it. This thinking has been common within the New Ulster Movement, the Two Traditions Group, the Irish Association, the British–Irish Association, Education for Mutual Understanding, the Fortnight Educational Trust, and the Cultural Traditions conferences hosted by the Institute for Irish Studies at Queen's University Belfast.[16] The inference is that the peoples of Northern Ireland are locked in rigid and negative cultural identities which they need to recognize, confront and transcend.

This chapter critically surveys cultural interpretations of Northern Ireland's antagonisms, political violence, and constitutional stalemate. We then highlight the deficiencies of these interpretations, which, in our judgement, fail to account for the dynamics of conflict, diminish the rationality of the agents involved, and underplay the importance of political institutions and the scope for institutional change. We suggest that other explanations of violence, in particular, are more compelling than broad and imprecise cultural accounts. However, that said, we recognize the central importance of one cultural clash: the clash of rival nationalisms. This cultural clash, however, is not purely endogenous to Northern Ireland, is part of the wider historic conflict between British and Irish nationalism, is largely political in character, and is explicable much more by its institutional setting than by the parochial local cultures of the region, or the content of the cultural differences between the communities.

## Which Cultures and which Divisions?

To begin with, the questions arise: which cultures are in conflict and what is the nature of the divisions between them? In the previous chapter we reviewed and noted the problems with the argument that the conflict is one between Catholics and Protestants. However, many understand the religious labels to include cultural Catholics and Protestants, i.e. non-believers who are identified with belonging to, or originating from, one community or the other – even if they are not theologically disposed. In this case the religious labels designate ethnic descent groups, in which membership is defined by religious background (and not belief). This is the way the labels are used by most people in Northern Ireland, and this use corresponds to Anthony Smith's definition of an *ethnie* or an ethnic community, that is 'a named human population, with a myth of common ancestry, shared memories, and cultural elements; a link with a historic territory or homeland; and a measure of solidarity'.[17] The 'cultural elements' defining an ethnic group may be incredibly variable (including dress, food, music, crafts, and architecture, as well as moral customs and social institutions) but the most important shared cultural elements are usually language and religion.

Some distinguish the communities in Northern Ireland regionally and territorially. Thus the Dutch geographer Heslinga distinguishes 'Ulstermen' from 'Irishmen'.[18] This classification forgets that there are Ulster 'men' outside Northern Ireland, and people within Northern Ireland who do not identify with Ulster, and besides, its unconscious sexism is now unacceptable. However, it has the virtue of indicating that the two communities have differing conceptions of their 'historic territory'. A fourth possibility is to designate the communities by a mixture of regional and national identifications. Thus T. J. Pickvance distinguishes the Ulster British from the Ulster Irish,[19] but these terms have found, so far, little popular or academic favour. A fifth possibility is to describe the communities by their overarching political identifications, i.e. to distinguish nationalists from unionists, as we have done throughout this book. One can of course add regional identifications to the political, for example, by differentiating northern nationalists from Ulster unionists, or Irish nationalists from British nationalists.

This variation in the naming and classification of the two communities – and the different emphases given by different people to religious, ethnic, territorial and political dimensions – suggests a difficulty with the 'two cultures' or 'two traditions' understanding of Northern Ireland, namely imprecision. Naturally it is open to people to insist that all the dimensions matter, or that it is their specific combination or accumulation which matter. However, it does make the specification of the salience of cultural variables problematic. We favour either the ethnic or the political classification of the communities because neither presumes extensive cultural integration within each community or major cultural divisions between them. The ethnic differentiation of the communities (proven by very high levels of endogamy) and the political classification of the communities (proven by their very different voting behaviour) are established by empirical fact. So is the religious classification, but whereas one community shares a common religious and cultural heritage in Catholicism, the other is internally fragmented into various types of Protestant and non-Protestant, i.e. it is culturally unified only by its anti-Catholicism.

Culturalists vary in the emphases they give to the central element which divides or partitions the rival communities. Religion, predictably, is usually emphasized. Thus the geographer Heslinga sees the British Isles at one level as a cultural entity, a 'unity',[20] but maintains that the major internal cultural division in its geography does not run between east and west, between Britain and Ireland, but rather between north and south.

The Irish border is a political expression of 'a cultural divide' which demarcates the northern Protestant peoples of the British Isles from the southern, Catholic and Anglican peoples. Though the border established in 1920 is 'arbitrary' it expresses this 'important spiritual divide',[21] and both the secession of Ireland from the UK and the partition of Ireland originate

> in the desire to preserve, or to accentuate, regional contrasts which are, fundamentally, religious contrasts – and, therefore, are not older than the Reformation (and Counter-Reformation) period. Viewed in this light, both sections of the Irish Border, the sea and the land boundary, are in the last resort religious frontiers.[22]

However, Heslinga also defines Ulster as 'a broad transition zone'[23] between the rival cultures, an idea put more positively by a literary critic who sees it as 'a cultural corridor' in which the cross-fertilization of traditions is blighted by benighted bigots: 'Unionists want to block the corridor at one end, republicans at the other. Culture, like common sense, insists it can't be done. Ulster Irishness and Ulster Britishness are bound to each other and to Ireland and to Britain.'[24]

Other than religion and its spiritual offshoots the divisions identified by culturalists signify that the different communities are 'parallel societies', that is they are separately schooled and marry endogamously, have different linguistic heritages, consume different media, and participate in different sports and other forms of leisure and entertainment. In an investigation of the factors responsible for demarcating the communities, John Whyte identified endogamy and educational segregation as more powerful than residential segregation, economic differentiation, membership of the Orange Order, or party-political affiliation.[25] The dividing lines between the two communities in schooling and marriage have already been discussed in chapter 5, and therefore are not considered in detail below. Instead we shall concentrate on 'cultural elements' such as language, media and sports, because they appear to differentiate the communities significantly – unlike their cuisine, dress, food, music, crafts, and architecture.

Formally *language* is not a major demarcation between the communities. Both speak and write English as their first language – with a heavy Scottish overlay in eastern Northern Ireland – but the accents of Protestants and Catholics are not distinguishable, though a minority claim otherwise. Aside from the pronunciation of a few words, and, allegedly, the letter 'H', communal identification is not phonetically apparent. The percentage of speakers of Gaelic (as a second language) is small, though it has been rising in areas where Sinn Féin is politically strong. Catholic schools have taught Irish since 1920 but not with the same vigour (or coercion) as their counterparts in independent Ireland.[26] Historically Gaelic has been treated by most Ulster unionists, including liberals, with contempt: it was a dead and useless language, its resurrection a quixotic and romantic indulgence, a hopeless enterprise.[27] Nevertheless unionist education ministers did their best to obstruct any danger of a Gaelic revival in Catholic schools during the period of devolved government.[28] Moreover, the naming of streets in Irish, and the use of Irish names in official documentation or in public institutions, were activities that were either prohibited or discouraged.

The cultural contempt of the dominant community for the linguistic heritage of the minority community is well documented, and is plainly a source of antagonism. This contempt is not, however, purely cultural or ethnic – after all some of the Scottish Protestant settlers in Ireland had been Gaelic speakers, and some Ulster Protestants' surnames suggest a Gaelic past.

Moreover, cultural contempt for Irish is not exclusive to unionists – lack of pride in their native language, and a preference for modern languages, has also been common amongst middle-class Irish Catholics.[29] The contempt for the Irish language amongst Ulster unionists mostly hails from political insecurity – the fear that in a united Ireland compulsory Gaelicization would be public policy, enforced by the Irish political majority on the minority. Independent Ireland did much to encourage this fear, although at no stage did Irish governments implement anything other than a bi-lingual educational policy.

This said, in our judgement the Irish language is largely a symbolic rather than a major substantive issue in the conflict between the rival national communities. No serious northern nationalist seeks a uni-lingual Gaelic education system; very few seek a genuinely bi-lingual Ireland; it is a small minority which seeks to have the choice of having Irish language schools. Moreover, no serious Ulster Protestant fears acculturation and assimilation into a Gaelic culture. Irish language issues did not figure in the civil-rights protests of the 1960s, nor have they been central elements in the campaigning of the SDLP. Sinn Féin has become enthusiastic about the language, but partly, it is plain, as a badge of difference. Northern nationalists seek the recognition of, respect for, and protection of their linguistic heritage, but they do not seek Gaelicization as a programme of government, either for themselves or for most of their children. Just as the citizens of independent Ireland feel secure in their national identity without the benefit of being fluent in Gaelic, so do their northern cousins, who are more aggravated about their ancestral language when it is attacked by Ulster unionists than they are about the visible reluctance of their co-nationals to embrace it in everyday life.

The Standing Advisory Commission on Human Rights recently declared that the way in which the Irish language is treated is a 'touchstone' of the extent to which the existence of two traditions is taken seriously by the government, and recommended legislation to facilitate its use by individuals or bodies in public administration.[30] The government responded by observing that it funds the cultural and educational development of the Irish language, and by drawing a distinction between cultural (and educational) support and the establishment of political language rights. It maintains that 'the levels of usage and the demands for services in Irish' mean that its current policy is appropriate and does not require legislation.[31] Irish therefore remains a subject of controversy and disagreement between nationalists and the British government, and between liberal pluralists and their opponents. However, these controversies should not be understood to be primarily about language rights *per se*; for most they express, symbolically, the clash between Irish and British nationalism, and the demands for the protection and expression of Irish, and the rejection of such demands, are explicable within this wider clash.

The partial existence of separate societies – despite some residential, workplace and tertiary educational intermingling – is visibly demonstrable in the existence of separate media and in sporting segregation. The two communities tend to read different newspapers, although not in a monolithic way. The northern nationalist and pro-SDLP daily, the *Irish News*, has a circulation of 44,000 and an estimated readership of 140,000 people. By contrast, the unionist and pro-UUP daily *NewsLetter* has a circulation of 33,000, and an estimated readership of 133,000.[32] Together the readership of these papers is about 270,000, a very high proportion of Northern Ireland's population. The much less overtly partisan *Belfast Telegraph* generally projects a moderate and accommodationist unionist line, has a circulation of about 135,000, and manages to attract a more bi-communal readership – partly because it has a virtual monopoly of the afternoon and evening regional press. The British qualities (the *Daily Telegraph*, *The Times*, *The Independent*, *Guardian* and *Financial Times*) have a circulation of nearly 17,000, and an estimated readership of 57,000, but the most wide-selling of these, the *Daily Telegraph*, is mostly read by Conservative or UUP-supporting Protestants. The Irish daily quality, the *Irish Times*, has an estimated Northern Irish readership of 18,000, mostly of liberal Catholics, but it includes some liberal (Alliance-supporting) Protestants. There is less evidence about the consumption of the much more widely read tabloid newspapers. However, it is common knowledge that British tabloids are read and purchased more than Irish tabloids, such as the *Irish Press* (estimated readership 8,000), and that amongst tabloid readers there are clear divisions – with working-class Protestants more likely to purchase the *Sun* and working-class Catholics the *Daily Mirror* (both of which adapt their papers slightly for the local market).[33] To a much lesser extent the two communities differentially consume broadcasting media, with northern nationalists being much more likely to tune in to RTE programmes than Ulster unionists.

Participation in and consumption of sport and leisure also divide the communities more than they integrate them, especially their respective working classes.[34] Gaelic games – especially hurling (camogie for women), handball, and football – are organized by the Gaelic Athletic Association (GAA), and exclusively taught in Catholic schools. Of these, hurling has the oldest pedigree on the island, but all were revived as part and parcel of the Irish-Ireland movement of the nineteenth century – when athleticism and cultural nationalism were linked throughout much of Europe. Founded in 1884, the GAA was and remains constitutionally committed to strengthening Irish national identity, and to that end historically organized three 'bans'. Members of the British security forces were banned from membership; British sporting events were boycotted; and members of the GAA were banned from participating in (and in some cases watching) 'foreign games'. These bans have subsequently been revoked – apart from the significant ban on members of the British security forces. The GAA has been the most successful cultural nationalist organization in Ireland, and has undoubtedly revived and strengthened traditional 'native' sports – and on a wholly amateur basis. However, its success has been at a price. Ulster Protestants and the security forces have viewed the GAA with suspicion, as a nursery school for republicans – Padraig Pearse was one of its most famous graduates, and numerous convicted IRA prisoners have followed in his footsteps. It is therefore not surprising that GAA games and members have been subject to harassment. The occupation by the security forces of the GAA's headquarters in Casement Park, West Belfast, and the construction of security-installations on GAA lands in Crossmaglen, are perhaps the most provocative examples of such cultural warfare.

'British sports', especially cricket, hockey, and rugby union, were not transmitted to Ireland as extensively or as successfully as elsewhere in the British Empire.[35] In part this was because of the efforts of the GAA, which stigmatized these activities as English and 'foreign'. In what would become independent Ireland cricket was the sport of the garrison and the Anglo-Irish gentry. However, cricket, rugby, and hockey are unusual because they have continued to be organized on an all-Ireland basis, despite the political partition of the island in 1920, and a unified all-island Irish national team continues to be fielded in these sports. The explanation is relatively simple. These sports were not partitioned for two reasons: *either* they were games largely played by Protestants across all of Ireland, such as cricket and hockey, and therefore weaker secessionist or partitionist pressures were brought to bear on them; *or* they were games played by the Ulster Protestant middle class and the privately schooled middle class of independent Ireland, such as rugby football. Precisely because northern Catholics, or their schools, do not play rugby, all-Ireland integration has remained feasible – though it has not been without its tensions. In short, and crudely speaking, all-Ireland integration in sports has been easiest to achieve where it does not involve integrating Ulster Protestants with northern Catholics, especially working-class male Catholics and Protestants.

World sports like cycling, sailing and golf, have also been subject to national and communal divisions in and across Ireland, but much the most important and telling divisions have occurred within *the* world sport, association football, or soccer. This sport is played by both Protestants and Catholics. Though originally more extensively and keenly played by urban working-class Ulster Protestants it is now played and watched throughout urban Ireland. The sport's organization was partitioned in 1920 when the Football Association of Ireland (in the Irish Free State) seceded from the Irish Football Association (headquartered in Belfast). Remarkably however, until 1950 the latter selected teams on an all-Ireland basis, and, until the 1960s, insisted that its 'national team' should be described as Ireland – further proof that the switch to a British rather than an Irish national identification is a recent development amongst Ulster Protestants.

Within Northern Ireland ethno-national divisions have affected soccer considerably. Infamously, a long-running and intense rivalry between Protestant Linfield and Catholic Belfast Celtic culminated in 1948, when incensed Linfield fans assaulted and broke the leg of a Celtic player, Jimmy Jones, after which Belfast Celtic was wound up by its directors in disgust. In urban Belfast these animosities have continued, with Catholics likely to back teams rivalling Linfield (such as Distillery or Cliftonville); while in Derry/Londonderry the local football club, Derry City, has seceded from the IFA to join the League of Ireland. Although both Catholics and Protestants play for Northern Ireland, the following the team enjoys at home matches is disproportionately Protestant, in part because the matches are played at Linfield's ground in Windsor Park and the regalia on display are British or loyalist in character. Soccer also audibly expresses the region's divisions, as any listener to the choral and abusive skills of local football fans soon discovers.

One illuminating survey shows the extent to which sporting preferences express the wider national divisions.[36] A hundred Catholic and a hundred Protestant football supporters were asked to rank how they would like to see the following soccer teams finish in an international tournament: England, Northern Ireland, the Republic of Ireland, Scotland, and Wales. Of Protestants surveyed 88 per cent wanted Northern Ireland to come first, which compared with 91 per cent of Catholics who preferred the Republic. Amongst Protestants second preferences were divided evenly between Scotland (41 per cent) and England (39 per cent), while 62 per cent of Catholics gave their second preference to Northern Ireland (and 8 per cent their first preference). In contrast, 60 per cent of Protestants wanted the Republic to finish fourth or last, while 64 per cent of Catholics wanted England to finish last. This evidence suggests that a world-sport like football does not transcend national divisions but rather reveals their depth, especially within the working class. It also provides telling proof of a divided society, or of parallel societies. In the summer of 1994 the machine-gunning of Catholics in a pub in Loughinisland as they watched the Republic of Ireland team playing in the World Cup, demonstrated, among other things, that loyalist paramilitaries had no sense of kinship with the other Irish soccer team.

## Cultural Antagonisms and Historians

Historians are especially prone to cultural explanations of the conflict. The pervasiveness of this form of thought is evident in the relevant writings of widely respected students of Ireland and Ulster: F. S. L. Lyons, David Miller, Roy Foster, Marianne Elliott, Ruth Dudley Edwards, A. T. Q. Stewart, and Oliver MacDonagh.[37] These authors, except Miller, think that both communities are obsessed with a view of the past which they, as professional historians, believe to be mythical. They also portray both as highly localized and parochial illustrations of Irish and British religious and nationalistic belief-systems, and some of them consider Irish Gaelic and Catholic cultures especially guilty of providing romantic sanctions for political violence.

*Too many cultures in such a small place.* Invoking Matthew Arnold's famous book, Leland Lyons's *Anarchy and Culture* is the most determinist work of these historians: 'the essence of the Irish situation [is] . . . the collision of a variety of cultures within an island whose very smallness makes their juxtaposition potentially, and often actually, lethal . . . ' These are 'seemingly irreconcilable cultures, unable to live together or to live apart, caught inextricably in the web of their tragic history'.[38] Ireland at the turn of the century was at the centre of a war of two civilizations: a resurgent Gaelic, Catholic and separatist culture ranged against an Anglo-Irish pluralist culture. In this perspective four cultures played their parts in nurturing anarchic antagonism: those of the native Irish, the English, the Anglo-Irish, and the Ulster Protestants (composed of Episcopalians and Presbyterians). In Ulster, the site of English conquest and Scots settlement, there were further complications: 'three creeds ... collided – a triumphant and arrogant Anglicanism, a rigid post-Tridentine Catholicism, and [strict] Calvinist orthodoxy'.[39] These cultures feel mutually insecure: 'In that small and beautiful region different cultures have collided because each has a view of life which it deems to be threatened by its opponents and power is the means by which a particular view of life can be maintained against all rivals.'[40]

*The antiquated and the absent culture.* The most influential cultural interpretation of Ulster unionism[41] is David Miller's account of the political doctrinal history of Ulster Protestants and, by implication, of their present political beliefs and behaviour, which he portrays as a fundamental obstacle to conflict-resolution. His key argument is that Ulster Protestants have a pre-nationalist 'contractarian' political philosophy. They are a people without a conception of the nation; and for this reason they are culturally bizarre,

> The central peculiarity in Ulster's political culture is that no community – not Britain, not the United Kingdom, not 'Ulster', and certainly not Ireland – has attained for Ulster protestants all the characteristics which a nation commonly possesses in the modern world.[42]

This absence of a national identity explains an otherwise allegedly inexplicable phenomenon, the conditionality of their loyalty to British political institutions. Its historical antecedent is 'a venerable theory of political obligation – that of the social contract thinkers', and the distinctive Scottish variant of contractarian thought and practice, 'covenanting', which the settlers brought with them to Ireland.[43]

The title of Miller's book, *Queen's Rebels*, encapsulates the allegedly pre-modern philosophy of Ulster loyalists. They are loyal to the Crown, and not, despite green Marxism, the half-crown. They are certainly not loyal to particular British governments or parliaments, against whom they take to the streets at the slightest hint that their position is about to be weakened. Their loyalty, or conditional loyalty, depends upon the Protestant way of life being upheld by British political institutions, that is the nature of their contract with the United Kingdom. This account dovetails neatly with Louis Hartz's notion of 'fragment societies', i.e. societies in which ideas and practices in the colonial world survive long after their abandonment in the mother (or father) country.[44] Ulster Protestants are living fossils, mummified representatives of Scottish covenanters and contractual relations between Crown and people which have elsewhere passed into oblivion.[45] It is precisely because they lack a nationalist political philosophy that the apparently rational solutions to the Ulster question – two Irish nation-states or an Irish federation – lack significant support amongst Protestants.[46]

*Gaelic romanticism and Anglophobia.* In different ways, and with different degrees of sophistication, Irish revisionist historians and biographers have emphasized features of the Gaelic revival and the social consequences of resurgent nineteenth-century Catholicism which they believe generates a culture of political antagonism, violence and impasse in Northern Ireland. Roy Foster, Ruth Dudley Edwards and Marianne Elliott share the belief that Northern Ireland is the repository for the most dated and dysfunctional aspects of militant Irish republicanism – its autarkic economic vision, its Gaelicist exclusivism, its Irish-Irelandism, and above all its cult of violent redemption. Thus Foster's *Modern Ireland: 1600–1972* treats Irish republicanism, romanticism and Anglophobia as a package of interrelated traits;[47] Ruth Dudley Edwards's biography of Padraig Pearse assaults the militaristic, sectarian, sacrificial and romanticist traits in the life and work of the leader of the Easter Rising of 1916;[48] while Marianne Elliott attempts to suggest that Wolfe Tone is not correctly regarded as the forefather of revolutionary republican nationalism.[49] The more or less explicit implication is that the Provisional IRA is the current bearer of an irrational, romantic, religiously enthused communal hatred, which takes its 'cultural' polish from the Gaelic and Catholic revivals of the nineteenth century.[50] Religious and romantic spiritualism are identified as key traits of Irish political culture, and culpable for its lack of modernization.

*Precedents, patterns and analogues.* Two of the most elegant historians of Ulster and Ireland, both of whom are witty, learned and intelligent, A. T. Q. Stewart and Oliver MacDonagh, are respectively sympathetic to the unionist and nationalist traditions – though these mild biases do not generally mar their writings. Their evocative texts are not entirely reducible to cultural readings but they provide much to feed such views. *The Narrow Ground: Patterns of Ulster History* seeks to identify, as its title suggests, recurrent patterns in the history of Ulster since 1609. Stewart places special emphasis on the historically rooted siege mentality of the Protestant settlers, and maintains that 'recurrent siege is part of the cycle of the Ulster conflict . . . it is precisely because the most cruel and treacherous warfare has broken out over and over again, and usually after a period of relative security, as in 1641 or 1798 or 1920 or 1969, that the besieged suffer such chronic insecurity'.[51] They fear insurrection by the natives/Catholics; they fear betrayal from within their own ranks – the archetypal figure here being Governor Robert Lundy, the traitorous Governor at the Siege of Derry in 1690; and they fear betrayal by Britain. As he sums up this view, 'The factor which distinguishes the siege of Derry from all other historic sieges in the British Isles is that it is still going on.'[52]

Enduring features of the Ulster landscape generate recurrent patterns, according to Stewart. Topography, he maintains, is the key to the conflict.[53] The small towns of rural Ulster still have English Street, Irish Street, and Scotch Street; villages still show the impact of the seventeenth-century plantations; the uplands are Catholic, the lowlands are Protestant. Even urban Belfast displays territorial stability in the distribution of the rival populations, linking local territories to collective identities, and explaining the delicate territorial equilibriums which can be disturbed by marches, processions and incursions from 'the other side'. Ulster in this perspective is 'a landscape with bandits',[54] and he perceives 'endemic' regularities in Irish culture, such as the 'capacity for very reckless violence, allied to a distorted moral sense which magnifies small sins and yet regards murder as trivial'.[55] These traits are not, in his judgement, modern consequences of 'the troubles' of the

1920s or of the present day. He maintains that historical sources – such as evangelists and novelists like John Wesley and Sir Walter Scott – testify that distorted mentalities of this nature have been around on the island for a very long time.

Oliver MacDonagh is equally preoccupied with the repetition of mentalities in the course of two centuries of British–Irish conflict since 1780.[56] For him distorted geographical images of Ulster, and of Ireland, on the part of unionists and nationalists, are partly culpable for the creation of a bad frontier in 1920,[57] and, just like Stewart, he maintains that both communities use history as ammunition, and have a timeless sense of justice and injustice when reading the island's past: 'no statute of limitations softens the judgement to be made on past events, however distant'.[58] Where MacDonagh is most original, however, is in his decision to turn Oscar Wilde's dictum that 'Irish history is something which Irishmen should never remember, and Englishmen should never forget' into a sober cultural observation: the Irish never forget and the English never remember. For instance, the nationalist Irish never forget that their history is one of treacherous treaties: the Treaty of Limerick of 1691, which promised religious toleration of Catholics, but was succeeded by the Penal Laws; the Act of Union of 1801, which, it was promised, would be accompanied by Catholic emancipation, but was not; the Government of Ireland Act of 1920, which promised protections for minorities, but was ineffective; the Anglo-Irish Treaty of 1921, which was accompanied by promises of cross-border institutions and a major boundary revision which were not delivered; and, some would add, the Anglo-Irish Agreement of 1985, which was to be accompanied by judicial and security reforms which have not (yet?) been implemented. These treaties are cumulatively seen as illustrations of the treatment of the Irish at the hands of English and British rulers. The nationalist Irish also never forget 'the constant relationship between the oscillation of coercion and conciliation on the part of the overlord, and the oscillation of negotiation and the threat of violence upon the part of the subjected.[59] MacDonagh observes that in only sixteen years of the first

hundred years of the Union was Ireland 'normal'; otherwise
it was governed under coercive emergency legislation.[60] He
might have added, Northern Ireland has *always* been governed under such legislation. Seeing their history as one
of subjection, betrayal and defeat, MacDonagh suggests that
it is not surprising that Irish nationals developed a culture
which displayed a 'distrust in achievement', and prized the
moral against the actual, and the bearing of witness as against
success.[61]

He interprets Ulster Protestant besieged political culture
in much the same manner as Stewart, before declaring that
Ulster unionists share much with northern nationalists: 'Their
ultimate world-views are extraordinarily similar. This being
so, such a phrase as "the solution" or "a solution" to the
Northern Ireland question has little meaning or promise for
either. They are committed too deeply to ancient roles and
modes of interpreting the historical flow, and the patterns
they perceive in – or, if you will, impose upon – the past,
are at once a cause of the present crisis, and a force making
for its continuance.'[62]

More distinctively, MacDonagh suggests that British political
culture has been as important as the local Irish varieties in
sustaining conflict and antagonism. In particular in England's
persistent opportunism, and forgetfulness, lie Ireland's difficulties. Absorbed in the immediate, regarding Ireland as a
distraction and an irrelevance, successive English and British
rulers have failed to follow through on settlements, deals
and understandings – displaying a recurring 'fundamental
irresponsibility'[63] which obstructs conflict-resolution. Just as
English amnesia exacerbated conflict in the 1780s so it does
in the 1980s and 1990s.

# Violent Cultures

Many authors detect the development of two political cultures
predisposed towards 'communal deterrence', 'intimidation',
and 'defenderism', and argue that both display widespread

tolerance of their own paramilitaries, who are seen as 'defenders' of their community against the predations of the opposing side.[64] Below we discuss and in some places construct the elements of a political culture theory of violence in Northern Ireland, first by highlighting the dispositions which both ethnic communities are held to have in common which drive them towards conflict; and then by considering cultural explanations which are specific to each community. These cultural dispositions are understood as being socially embedded in ways which are more profound than mere attitudes or stereotypes,[65] and region-wide, rather than geographically specific.[66]

Five motifs are regularly put forward to account for dispositions towards violence in both communities:

- 'the fighting Irish' stereotype entrenched in English culture;
- a distrust of the modern state, which leads to an intimidatory political culture, and a willingness to support non-state militancy;
- a localist and egalitarian culture within each community which inhibits disciplined pan-ethnic organization and facilitates quasi-anarchic violence;
- a popular wisdom which entrenches pessimism about the prospects for peace, anticipates cyclical bouts of conflict, and achieves through social learning the regulation of protracted violence; and
- a traditionalist patriarchal socialization which sustains 'soldierly' conceptions of the appropriate roles of males.

The first 'culturalist' theory of Irish violence does not merit any serious analytical attention, though its popular resonance in Great Britain should not be underestimated. It is the dogma of 'the fighting Irish'.[67] In this folklore, throughout the world, from the bar-rooms of Chicago to the bar-rooms of Melbourne, the Irish male can be found displaying the alleged traits of his people: aggressive and unreasoning violence, facilitated by excessive alcohol consumption. It is a very old stereotype – indeed a colonial stereotype. The English maintained that the Irish were murderous savages in the course of murdering and savaging the natives – this indeed was how they welcomed Ireland into 'peaceful civilization'. Such stereotypes – and their counter-stereotypes – should not be taken seriously. Northern Irish paramilitaries are more likely to be recruited for their disciplined, ascetic and puritanical characters than for their prowess with the beer glass. English holders of this view of the Irish are best directed to the mirror of world-history – in which they will find that they (and their cousins) have a much more widespread reputation for being an aggressive, warlike, piratical and imperial people. They are also advised to ask themselves which nation's soccer fans are most welcome outside the British Isles, the Irish or the English?

In a more serious vein many authors suggest that both communities have a profound distrust of the state and a predisposition to support non-state militancy. The Gaelic Irish never developed a modern state. Natives/Catholics/nationalists, in the nearly four centuries since the conquest and plantation of Ulster, have never been governed by a state they have regarded as legitimate.[68] Their ethnic history, their collective memory of their fate at the hands of English, British and devolved governmental institutions is one of dispossession in their own homeland, the outlawing of their religion, cultural erosion of their language, and political subjugation and economic discrimination at the hands of their ethnic enemy. In this perspective militant republicans can be seen as the latest wave in a long line of secret native Irish banditti, the successors to peasant violence against illegitimate state institutions. A long tradition links native woodkerne of the sixteenth century, peasant 'Defenders' of the eighteenth century, nineteenth-century agrarian combatants, and the Provisional IRA.[69] Each of these secret armies have portrayed themselves as defenders, preventing encroachment upon their traditional lands, customs and mores by settlers, Protestants and the British state. They have all been rooted in a strong rejection or distrust of the state.

An extreme if elusively written version of the assumption of an anti-statist (and by implication anarchic and non-modern) animus amongst Irish nationalists can be found in Charles Townshend's *Political Violence in Ireland: Government and Resistance since 1848.*[70] The subtitle conveys the suggestion that the history of Irish political violence is that of a dialectic between state authority and resistance to that authority by organized groups and other 'inchoate forms of communal struggle'. So deeply entrenched is the culture of resistance that Townshend feels free to deliver the verdict, presumably of the modern IRA, that 'The commitment of the "physical force party" to armed struggle, amounting at times to obsession, cannot be construed as a rational response to British domination, physical or cultural. The persistence of Fenian reasoning in face of a great deadweight of reality cannot be explained by the intellectual or even the emotional power of republican ideology, but only by an inheritance of communal assumptions validating its methods as much as its ends.'[71] In this perspective the Provisional IRA is considered a throwback to eighteenth-century 'Defenderism', and its campaigning is 'episodic and Protean, marked rather by resilience than by clarity of intention or effect'.[72]

The ethnic history of Ulster Protestants in the four centuries since the conquest and plantation is one of dual insecurity, which leads them also to distrust the state. On the one hand they fear that they will be overrun by native, Catholic or republican insurrections, as happened in 1641 and 1689/90, and almost occurred in 1798 and between 1916 and 1922. On the other hand they fear that they will be abandoned by metropolitan Britain, retreating from its last colonial outposts, as was foreshadowed in the Home Rule debates between the 1880s and the 1920s, again during World War II, and has been thinkable since 1969. This culture of settler-insecurity amongst Ulster Protestants makes them unwilling to trust either the British state or Irish natives. Doctrines and practices of self-reliance, public banding and public marches to deter native/Catholic/rebel areas from supporting insurrection and paramilitary mobilization are repercussions of this insecurity.[73] This is what explains Orange marches through Catholic districts, and what explains their willingness to take the law into their own hands to repress Catholics/rebels/republicans. In short each community is culturally disposed to regard itself as oppressed or besieged, and distrusts (British) state institutions, and therefore tolerates or supports unofficial violence from its own side.[74] It is a viewpoint lucidly expressed in Churchill's prejudiced dictum that the Irish have a genius for conspiracy but none for government.[75]

Each community is regularly portrayed as having developed, at least in more recent times, an egalitarian political culture which precludes the development of a strong hegemonic party to represent it, and inhibits the creation of authoritative political leaders who might lead and discipline their communities. Ulster Protestantism, heavily influenced by Presbyterianism, has, in this view, always had a strongly anti-hierarchical thrust: religious factionalism and egalitarian sectarianism, in the strict sense, have always been rife amongst them and these traits have spilled over into their political culture. In consequence there is no one overarching hierarchy of organizations upon which their political leadership can draw. Considerable effort was put into constructing the unity and hegemony of the Ulster Unionist Party after 1920, which was only possible because of particular external conditions,[76] but since the late 1960s the natural factionalism of Ulster Protestants has re-asserted itself. The results manifest themselves in parties which compete for the allegiance of Ulster Protestants, and in paramilitary organizations which distrust constitutional Unionist politicians. Fear of their own internal divisions and factionalism in turn increases their insecurity. Egalitarian cultures are well known for their almost paranoid fear of the enemy within,[77] and Ulster Protestant political culture, it is said, is always on the lookout for the 'Lundy', the traitor within, who is willing to open the gates to the rebel/papist forces. Negativity, suspicion and a deep distrust of the British state are the features of what Steve Bruce has chosen to dignify as 'the Ulster loyalist political vision'.[78] Those who would build bridges towards Catholics are treated with the utmost suspicion: Ian Paisley famously commented on Terence O'Neill 'A traitor and a bridge are very much alike, for they both go over to the other side.'[79]

Irish Catholics were, at least until the 1960s, hierarchically organized through the Catholic Church. Indeed their very religious unity has been seen as a threat to the more religiously disorganized Protestants. However, although Catholics may have taken their religion hierarchically from Rome, Catholic politics was much more likely to be taken from domestic circumstances, in which the peasant/native Irish had long been divested of 'their own' aristocracy. The civil war divisions in the Irish Free State, between the pro-Treaty and anti-Treaty forces, and between pragmatists and idealists, were mirrored in Northern Ireland, albeit without extensive fratricide. Irish Catholics/nationalists were divided between supporters of constitutional nationalism, in the tradition of the Irish Parliamentary Party of Parnell, and supporters of militant republicanism who argued that if violence had accomplished the liberation of twenty-six counties it could accomplish the same task for the remaining six counties. Moreover, as the Catholic middle class began to expand in the 1960s, and the influence of Catholic clergy over nationalist politicians began to wane, internal Northern Irish Catholic politics fragmented dramatically, before returning to a conflict between constitutional nationalism (the SDLP) and militant republicanism (Sinn Féin), a conflict with a definite class coloration. In short each ethnic community has a history of internal division and competition, in which their 'ultras' are not controlled by one overarching organization or party. These intracommunal divisions and competitions make conflict-resolution extremely difficult, and facilitate those willing to employ violence.

A fourth cultural element in the antagonism between the rival communities has been the development of a local logic of violence.[80] A history of communal struggles, continually reproduced and passed on in oral tradition, leads to predictable responses when new cycles of violence recur. The two patterns of intimidation identified by Darby are pressures placed on people to leave their workplaces, which has been a subordinate theme 'to the extensive and recurrent intimidation of people from their homes'.[81] Each community is aware of a history of precedents for each stage in a new round of conflict. Indeed, some are tempted to argue that each phase of violent conflict has become more intense, since cultural learning and mimesis mean that the participants progress from initial skirmishing to full-scale war much more rapidly in each new cycle of violence.

One can, fifthly, find culturalist explanations which suggest that Northern Irish males are socialized in a traditionalist and patriarchal fashion which sustains 'macho' or 'soldierly' conceptions of their appropriate roles as defenders of their families ('their' women and children) and their nation. This thinking can be found amongst Irish feminists, but it is not confined to feminists or females. Stewart observes that in the local vernacular 'the boys' is a phrase generally, and sympathetically, taken to refer to the (favoured) local paramilitaries. The Irish meaning of 'boy' thus retains 'something of its Elizabethan connotation as a swaggerer, a warrior, an armed man'.[82]

The preceding explanations of dispositions towards violence point to features which the nationalist and unionist communities are held to have in common. However, there are also theses which emphasize the distinctive cultural sources of violence within each community. Irish republicanism, both before 1920 and since, is standardly portrayed as imbued with a culture of elitist, romantic and militant revolutionary nationalism – allegedly sustained since 1920 by the constitutional ethos of the Republic and the pedagogy of Catholic schools. Albert Reynolds, the former Irish prime minister who until very recently led Fianna Fáil, has given credence to this perspective: 'one has to appreciate that the IRA are in a cocooned world of their own, of idealistic violence'.[83] An absurd extension of this argument is offered by Paul Wilkinson, who claims that under terrorist brutalization 'a cult of bombs and guns' can be created in which 'headstrong youths can become so hooked on the life of terrorist murder that they perform their tasks in a kind of sacrificial ecstasy'.[84]

Five stages in the ideology of nationalist violence, which together constitute a 'syndrome', have been traced by Oliver MacDonagh: from the secret agrarian societies came the habituation to force and conspiracy, and the alternative to the state's law; from the United Irishmen, came the beliefs that Britain was the cause of Ireland's ills, that religion was used by the imperial power to divide the Irish nation, and that a virtuous republic was the proper goal of Irish nationalism; from the Young Irelanders came cultural nationalism and militarist romanticism; from Fenianism came the assertion that Ireland was at war with Britain, that the Irish army 'in the field' had governmental rights to prosecute that war irrespective of Irish opinion, and the development of a repertoire of political techniques, such as mass demonstrations at the funerals of dead heroes, the creation of front-organizations, and the infiltration of others' organizations; and finally, from Padraig Pearse, came the religion of violence, the cults of blood, youth, and sacrifice, generational witness, historic roles, and the supremacy of the gesture.[85]

*Biting at the Grave: the Politics of Despair* is a specimen of just such an understanding of the cultural 'syndrome' of republican violence. It is Padraig O'Malley's account of the hunger strikes of 1980–1 in which ten IRA and INLA prisoners, led by Bobby Sands, starved themselves to death to achieve the status of political prisoners. They failed to do so, but won massive sympathy throughout nationalist Ireland, and elected Sands to the House of Commons and two other prisoners to Dáil Éireann before their deaths. They also 'broadened the battlefields' in Sands's words, and helped establish Sinn Féin as an electoral force.[86] O'Malley explains the hunger-strikers' behaviour mainly through references to the motifs, traditions and dispositions in Irish Gaelic, Irish Catholic and Irish nationalist cultures – which he plainly regards as less than modern and less than praiseworthy. He provides a lengthy discussion of fasting as a form of protest in Gaelic and Brehon cultures,[87] the sacrificial themes in Christian thought, and the tradition of republican protests and hunger striking stretching back to the Fenian movement founded in the 1850s. He then suggests in his core explanation of the 1981 hunger strikes that

the prisoners did what they were supposed to do. *Their actions, ultimately, were not the actions of autonomous individuals,* but rather a reflexive embrace of the way in which political prisoners throughout Irish history were presumed to have behaved. Their self-images, reinforced by the chronicles of oppression on which they had been raised and the experiences of their young lives, impaired their ability to act independently and diminished their capacity to act on their own behalf. *In the end they were the victims of our myths.*[88]

The homily for Irish nationalists is clear: abandon the culture which caused these suicides and which still fuels mayhem and antagonism – a message well received by British reviewers, comforted to learn that Irish cultures, rather than British institutions, are at fault for Irish deaths in Ireland.

Loyalist violence is also seen by many analysts as flowing from a political culture of despair – but one less richly endowed with literary and poetic accomplishments than Irish republicanism. Indeed Ulster loyalism is regularly portrayed as the reactionary violence of the slightly privileged; dressed up in its Sunday best in the garb of seventeenth-century theological ideology it in fact displays the standard resentments of a lumpenproletariat, the culture of 'Protestant trash'.[89] In a tough-minded vein the eloquent Irish historian Joe Lee maintains that unionism is an inherently supremacist ideology, one deeply imbued with racist assumptions. Early twentieth-century unionist discourses, he observes, were 'embedded in a clearly hierarchical concept of race relations', a *Herrenvolk* mentality in which Catholics were inferior or non-persons. In a much more empathetic treatment, Steve Bruce portrays the loyalist political vision as negative and bleak, but not as racist. He entitles his chapter on the subject 'The Dismal Vision'.[90]

## Deadlocked Cultures lead to Dead Politics

Two distinct cultural diagnoses explain why constitutional stalemate persists. The first suggests that local political elites succeed in being elected, and in maintaining their status as leaders, through displaying their credentials as intransigents, or as tribunes, rather than as exponents of statecraft or diplomacy. In consequence they have no electoral incentives to engage in compromise. The second suggests that 'the two traditions' share a debilitatingly primitive conception of democracy, one which understands it purely and simply as majoritarian rule, and which sanctions coercion to sustain it, or the use of violence to establish it.

In the pre-democratic UK – i.e. before the widening of the male suffrage in 1884 – neither community had developed a tradition of political accommodation at elite level. After the extension of the suffrage, party mobilization in Ulster therefore took place around existing ethno-religious cleavages. Politicians who now had to compete – rather than pay – for votes quickly found that communal exclusivism reaped the greatest electoral rewards. The Liberal Party withered before the success of the Unionists and the Irish Parliamentary Party in the 1880s. Similarly, after the formation of Northern Ireland the politicians and political parties which sought to obtain bi-national or bi-confessional support failed consistently.[91] As a result, ambitious politicians know that the price of accommodation is repudiation by one's party colleagues and electoral humiliation, a fate encountered by those foolish enough to believe that there were votes in compromise, such as Brian Faulkner, Bill Craig, and Gerry Fitt in the 1970s. Some suggest that the lesson has been overlearnt. Politicians may have more room for compromise than they imagine – indeed the Opsahl commissioners imply that local politicians are simply ignorant, poorly socialized in democratic political skills, and would benefit from appropriate training programmes in Germany, Sweden and the USA 'tailored both to present and prospective politicians'.[92]

It is also widely agreed that each community has acquired one feature of British political culture: *majoritarianism*.[93] The belief that the majority should have the right to self-determination, control of the government, and the making and implementing of law and public policy, became widely established in nineteenth-century Europe, especially in Westminster's House of Commons. Where majoritarianism developed in nationally

# 242 *Internal Explanations*

divided regions, as in historic Ulster, it had explosive implications. Each community claimed to be part of the relevant majority, either in the 'British Isles' or in 'Ireland'. Each thinks of itself as part of a (rightful) majority, but also considers itself to be an insecure and maltreated minority; indeed the conflict has been defined as a 'double minority' problem because each simultaneously behaves with the arrogance of a majority and the grievances of a minority.[94] Perhaps it is better to say it is one of both 'double minorities and double majorities'. Northern nationalists are a minority in Northern Ireland, Ulster unionists are a minority within the United Kingdom, and would be a minority in a united Ireland; Irish nationalists would be a majority in a united Ireland, and Ulster unionists are a majority in Northern Ireland. In addition, across Northern Ireland there are variations in the extent to which the two communities consider themselves local minorities or majorities.

These perceptions generate negative repercussions. The weakness or absence of non-majoritarian political philosophies, of a federal or consociational kind, have been insufficiently noted by historians of British and Irish political culture,[95] and arguably help account for the unwillingness of the parties to the conflict to split their differences in the form of power-sharing arrangements.

## Cultural Explanations: Illusory Illuminations or Descriptions?

Culturalist explanations of political phenomena, let alone Northern Ireland's antagonisms, political violence and constitutional stalemate, are open to multiple objections. This fact, and what follows, does not mean that they are never worth attempting. However, many culturalist explanations are either imprecise or redundant. We shall look at some general difficulties with culturalist arguments before paying especial attention to their explanations of political violence. Let us begin, however, with an elementary but frequently forgotten observation: all societies and communities have myths about their past, all engage in celebrations and commemorations of their histories, and all have cultures which are historically informed. 'Atavistic' cultural expressions are, in this sense, universal. There is, however, in our view no well-established evidence of a special Irish or Ulster Protestant obsession with the past, or of obsession with those historical events which are held to have shaped key political institutions, or particular patterns of social domination. Knowledge, albeit selective knowledge, and assertions about the past are normal components of most political cultures; so is the stress on decisive, significant historic events. The fact that Northern Irish myths stress historical antagonisms between the communities is also not surprising; they reflect current realities rather than a peculiar atavistic celebration of the past.

A similar argument applies to many of the cultural traits that we have discussed above. They cannot be seen as purely internal to Northern Ireland, and they exist elsewhere without generating such antagonism, violence or stalemate. Thus patriarchy and traditionalist relations between the sexes exist in many cultures without generating the types of violence which exist in Northern Ireland. Equally majoritarianism and ethnocentrism can be found in both Great Britain and the Republic, yet they are not wracked by ethno-national conflict. Indeed both Northern Irish communities see themselves as branches of these external political cultures – even if metropolitan representatives of these external cultures are less willing to champion them than they once were. Despite the present academic temptation to focus on 'the invention of tradition',[96] and by implication to subvert the collective histories of nations, there has been an underlying history of national conflict in Ulster which has underpinned the clash of communities, and these clashes, naturally, have been expressed in cultural forms. The real question is whether these cultural forms are causes or symptoms.

*Are cultures more caused than causal?* There is a long-running debate in the social sciences between rationalists, who focus on interests in explaining political and social phenomena, and culturalists, who focus on values and social norms. Rationalists favour economic explanations, and see agents as 'pulled' by incentives, while culturalists see agents as 'pushed' by quasi-inertial forces; and whereas rationalists see humans as strategists, culturalists portray them as creatures of habit.[97] Rationalists maintain that people undertake actions, not as cultural automata, but because it is in their interests; culturalists, that people's perceptions of their interests and their normative codes governing pursuit of their interests are culturally determined. Each school attempts to reduce the insight of the other, but plainly each has its merits. Our methodological preference is to seek rational explanations before resorting to cultural ones. This preference is defensible because we prefer not to assume that people are mindless executors of historic cultures, and because we believe that many cultural norms can be seen as rational when the context in which they flourish is properly specified.[98]

To consider the Northern Irish culturally strange or distinctive because they are passionately and bitterly divided over their national allegiances is indefensible. Debates, conflicts, and wars over national political identity, national territory, and national sovereignty have dominated European history for over a century. The Northern Irish are only exceptional in that their debates, conflicts and wars have not been resolved, an irresolution which owes little to local atavism, tribalism, or lack of modernity or intelligence. It is merely the outcome of the stalemate itself. The determination of the boundaries of the state and sovereignty matter because they decisively affect key political and economic (and, yes, religious and cultural) powers, rights and opportunities. The politics of antagonism, we submit, stem less from the peculiarity of the local cultures than from perceived, and rationally perceived, constitutional and political insecurity in both communities. Neither feels it belongs politically, that it has a political home, whether in Britain or Ireland, though each is sure where it does not wish to belong. Belonging to a community, in the last instance, is belonging to a group which will protect you from domination and violence, it requires no deeper cultural identification than that; conversely, hostility to a group requires no more than the belief that they are a danger to your security, it requires no more profound cultural antagonism.

The culturalist school which sees the IRA as an offshoot of Gaelic, romantic, Catholic culture can be usefully contrasted with that which sees republican paramilitaries as rational agents pursuing strategic objectives, namely a united Ireland.[99] The recent announcement of a complete cessation of violence by the IRA does not represent the abandonment of Gaelic, romantic, or Catholic culture, but rather the calculation that unarmed struggle is more likely to be successful, in the long run, than continuing the long war. Whether that calculation proves to be correct is less important than the fact that culturalists have no easy way of interpreting it. Even the apparently difficult case of the republican hunger strikes of 1981 can be used to demonstrate the merits of rationalist as opposed to culturalist interpretations.[100] We suggest that it is feasible, and better, to read these strikes in a very different manner from that suggested by Padraig O'Malley. Far from being the prisoners of their culture the prisoners were autonomous agents – albeit within the republican organizations which operated inside and outside the Maze prison. They had a goal – to have their organizations recognized as political, and themselves as prisoners of war – and they experimented with a range of tactics. Eventually a minority of them hammered out a policy to go on hunger strike, and to wage a battle of endurance in which they were prepared to risk their lives to strike back at their enemies. Having participated in the 'dirty protest' for four years they opted for a hunger strike partly because so many prisoners were losing heart and dropping out of the 'dirty protest'. Hunger strikes would raise the stakes and, if successful, would serve a double purpose: to increase solidarity amongst the prisoners, and to assist the political struggle outside the prison gates. A minority decided to risk death, although they were prepared to consider compromises, providing that the essential elements of their demands were met. They then framed five demands for the British government which would be difficult but not impossible for them to concede. Far from acting as automatons, the hunger-strikers were playing a risky strategy, a form of what theorists call the chicken game – in which an agent seeks to persuade the rival antagonist that he will not 'flinch' from self-destruction in order to encourage the other to back down.[101]

The prisoners knew what they were doing. In some cases they seem to have literally weighed the benefits of political martyrdom (damage to the enemy and personal posthumous reputation) against the costs of serving out a life sentence. Each of the ten who died miscalculated the prospects for a British surrender, and they plainly miscalculated the 'pay-offs' the British authorities, especially Mrs Thatcher, were willing to consider. However, that does not mean they were irrational, or victims of Gaelic, Catholic and nationalist culture, and for at least five reasons. First, starving oneself, and killing oneself, in political protest are not unique to Brehon, Gaelic or Irish cultures. Secondly, Catholic religious culture explicitly prohibits suicide.[102] Thirdly, since the hunger-strikers were nationalists, invoking nationalist culture as an explanation of their behaviour is close to trivial tautology. Had they not been nationalists they would not have been republican paramilitaries, and had they not been paramilitaries they would have been much less likely to be in prison, and so on. It is also problematic. The key question is why were some nationalists more disposed than others to behave in the manner of the hunger-strikers? Was it because they had imbibed more of the relevant cultures? If so, why had they done so? An easy explanation exists. The evidence is in O'Malley's own book. The hunger-strikers had experienced oppression at the hands of Protestants or the state authorities.

Fourthly, consider the following thought-experiment. Imagine that just as Sands (or any of his subsequent colleagues) was about to die the British government decided to make the concessions which it did, as a matter of fact, make just after the last of the hunger-strikers died. This speculation is not an absurd counterfactual. This scenario had been foreshadowed when a previous set of hunger-strikers had called off their fast, several months before Sands and his colleagues began theirs, after having been led to believe that the government was about to make concessions.[103] The interesting question is how Sands and his colleagues would have reacted to such a scenario.

Logically they could have accepted the concessions, or rejected them, or negotiated over the details. They could even have accepted them, and subsequently another set of strikes could have been launched by different prisoners. The point is this: knowledge of Brehon, Catholic, or Gaelic cultures does not enable anybody to predict how Sands and his colleagues would have reacted.

Finally, there is a lack of reciprocity in O'Malley's and other culturalist explanations of the hunger-strikers. The behaviour of the British authorities, especially Mrs Thatcher's government, is not explained through knowledge of Anglican/Methodist, English or imperialist cultures. Mrs Thatcher's behaviour during the hunger strikes is explicable through knowledge of one political strategy she had learned – never compromise unless you absolutely must – but it is not one distinctively associated with British politicians. Thatcher miscalculated the consequences of her obstinacy during the hunger strikes: Sinn Féin was able to enter the electoral arena with considerable success, and her government was pushed into a set of negotiations with the Irish government which eventually led to major concessions being made in the Anglo-Irish Agreement. However, this set of events, and their unintended consequences, are not easily decoded through culturalist readings of her Methodism, her Englishness, or of British imperialism.

The whole saga of the hunger strikes can be seen as a rational short-term game or manoeuvre in a long-term political war of position; and as more rational and political, and less shrouded in culture and psychology, than O'Malley, and others, suggest.[104] Sands and his colleagues successfully 'broadened the battlefields'. In fact O'Malley's text shows that the hunger-strikers were self-consciously using the cultures they had very recently mastered within the prison walls. They did so to wage a struggle to humiliate their enemies, and to win support for their cause in the nationalist community and the Irish diaspora. Far from being victims of Ireland's cultural legacies they were exploiting them. Indeed, O'Malley's book and David Beresford's *Ten Men Dead* make plain that many of the prisoners arrived in jail with very little culture of any kind, and that they learned Gaelic, republicanism, and in some cases even their Catholicism, in prison. Moreover, learning Gaelic served instrumental purposes – such as facilitating communications which could not be understood by predominantly Protestant wardens – as well as sharpening the prisoners' differentiation from the enemy.[105] Synthesis between rationalist and culturalist interpretations of the hunger-strikers is, of course, possible: culture may be invoked to explain the preferences of paramilitaries, whereas rationality may be used to explain the means chosen to achieve the cultural preferences. However, our parsimonious methodological principle suggests that unique cultural explanations should only be resorted to in the last instance, rather than in the first instance.

Consider, now, Miller's culturalist interpretation of Ulster unionism as imbued with a pre-modern contractarian and conditional philosophy. This thesis is objectionable on at least two grounds. In the first place contractarianism is not pre-modern, but characteristic of a range of modern political philosophies, including nationalist philosophies; and secondly, conditional political obligation is characteristic of rational individuals and communities, especially communities which do not trust the state to look after them – in this case the British state.[106] Miller's fixation on the contractarian tradition occludes his more important point, the claim that unionists are not nationalists, an argument which we believe to be mistaken. The range of identities within unionism has not prevented a national allegiance to the British nation-state – even though most of the British do not recognize unionists as co-nationals. Moreover, unionists' British nationalism expresses their present political, economic and religious self-images and interests; it is no fossilized product of seventeenth-century Scottish theology. Though the latter may be invoked by loyalist politicians, and indeed by preachers, one should not mistake form for substance.

One must also be sceptical that unionists have drunk so deep in Britain's majoritarian political culture that it inhibits them from displaying greater constitutional flexibility. It is true that unionist elites point to the 'democratic weaknesses' of power-sharing – its apparent denial of majority-rule principles, its lack of an effective opposition and an alternative government – or its contraventions of the Westminster model.[107]

However, these claims are transparently based on strategic interest, rather than cultural norms, and are put forward for propaganda purposes. Politicians can draw on whichever elements of a cultural history best suit their interests. When Vanguard leader Bill Craig pointed out in 1976 that a voluntary power-sharing coalition to cope with an emergency was consistent with British constitutional practice in wartime and during the depression, he invoked a cultural precedent but it didn't sway many of his followers.[108] In fact most of his party deserted him, and he was relegated to political oblivion, losing his Westminster seat to a unionist hard-liner in 1979. His was not a cultural failing. He erred in thinking that he could persuade his followers that their best interests lay in a coalition government with nationalists from the SDLP. One can expect unionists' cultural concerns about power-sharing to fade rapidly if they ever find themselves a minority in a united Ireland or indeed a minority in Northern Ireland.[109] Unionists' cultural 'democratic principles' are extremely flexible. They rejected the claims of the UK majority in 1892–3 and 1911–14, the Irish majority in 1918, the right of local nationalist majorities to govern various areas of Northern Ireland after 1921, and the right of the British majority to make policy for Northern Ireland after 1972. The Reverend Ian Paisley has displayed no cultural inhibition about accepting STV (PR) rather than the plurality rule method characteristic of Westminster elections – he has thanked Providence for the rewards STV (PR) has brought his party.[110]

*Circular and static tales?* The circularity in culturalist interpretations of Northern Ireland is obvious. When told that republican and loyalist cultural values are explanatory we often find that the evidence for these values simply amounts to descriptions of the behaviour which these values are supposed to 'explain'. This criticism of circularity is true of Leland Lyons's *Culture and Anarchy in Ireland* – 'proof' of cultural determinism is established by defining conflict as an expression of cultural antagonism. Culturalist explanations are also regularly accused of having a static character, of being incapable of accounting for political change. In Northern Ireland they define each community in essentialist ways; each is said to express continuously, almost timelessly, a given set of cultural traits, even though such assumptions do not withstand momentary inspection.

The essence which has persisted in each case is an ethnic one, a sense of shared descent. After all, Northern Irish Catholics are not Catholics in the ways their seventeenth-century ancestors were; they are not even Catholics in the ways in which their parents were. They are no longer linguistic Gaels who speak Irish as their mother-tongue. Politically northern nationalists have acknowledged and adapted to their wider political environment; the predominantly socially and economically conservative politics of the Nationalist Party has been displaced by the languages of social democracy (the SDLP) and of radical socialism (Sinn Féin). Sinn Féin's pamphlets, newspapers and discussion documents of today are almost unrecognizable successors of the republican writings of the early 1970s. Similarly very few Ulster Protestants are Protestants in the manner of their seventeenth-century ancestors; and, as we have seen, very many of them are thoroughly secularized. Unionist politics too has refracted its international political environment, containing liberals, conservatives, and socialists who share much in common with contemporary Europeans.

*What really matters, institutions or cultures?* Critics of theories of political culture maintain that political institutions explain political cultures much more than vice versa.[111] They argue, first of all, that there is considerable evidence that political cultures are much more malleable than sociologists suggest, and that they respond to relatively short-run institutional treatment. For example, in the 1940s Germans were alleged to be politically authoritarian and incapable of sustaining a democratic political culture. However, by the 1950s West German political institutions had put down roots, changed people's political behaviour, and they, in the main, expressed a democratic civic culture. In Northern Ireland it can, similarly, be argued that political antagonism and stalemate are best explained by specific political institutions (and violence by the breakdown of specific institutions) rather than by vague appeals to historic cultures.

The devolved parliament of 1920–72 was modelled on Westminster lines; designed to create strong governments, it facilitated a dictatorship of the majority. The cultures which emanated from Stormont's institutional nexus can be understood as caused rather than causal; that is to say the hegemonic and exclusive character of Ulster unionism and the disorganized and disloyal nature of Northern nationalism were, in part, the consequences of inappropriate institutional design. The political insecurity of Ulster Protestants, by their own declarations, is also partly caused by the Republic's institutions, especially its Constitution; whereas the grievances of northern nationalists, by their own declarations, owe much to their experience of British political institutions, before 1920, before 1972, and after 1972. Moreover, loyalist paramilitarism can be understood as a response to the collapse of Unionist control, and its associated institutions in the late 1960s, rather than as the response of cultural automata to republican discontent. Conversely, republican paramilitarism can be understood as a response to the political opportunity occasioned by the breakdown of unionist control between 1969 and 1972.

A cruder way of making the same point is to declare that cultures don't just happen, and don't just persist of their own accord. They persist because they are institutionally supported or because they serve people's interests. As historical sociologist, Barrington Moore, put the issue polemically:

> To maintain and transmit a value system, human beings are punched, bullied, sent to jail, thrown into concentration camps, cajoled, bribed, made into heroes, encouraged to read newspapers, stood up against a wall and shot, and sometimes even taught sociology. To speak of cultural inertia is to overlook the concrete interests and privileges that are served by indoctrination, education and the entire complicated process of transmitting culture from one generation to the next.[112]

This hard-line organizational materialism does not have to be embraced entirely but it helps to qualify the merits of culturalist readings of Northern Ireland. It also asks us to consider exactly how much cultural differences matter.

*How much do cultural differences matter?* The underlying premise of culturalist explanations is that 'difference' is the source of antagonism, violence, and stalemate. It seems an obvious idea, but it can and must be questioned. An ethnic group can share very many cultural traits with its rivals and yet these similarities may not diminish their enmities. Consider two contrasting cases. Some claim that the Hutu and Tutsi of Burundi and Rwanda have no very significant cultural differences – they have the same religion, the same language, and are now so phenotypically mixed that identity cards are required to distinguish the groups reliably.[113] By contrast the Quebecois are territorially, religiously and linguistically distinguishable from the other inhabitants of Canada. A believer in the salience of differences has to explain why in the former case ethnic conflict has taken a genocidal form, whereas in Canada the relevant groups have remained relatively peaceful. It is also the case that an ethnic group may be deeply culturally divided and yet unified against its enemies. Consider Israeli Jews: Sephardic Jews are much closer to Arabs in culture yet are much more hostile towards them than Askenazi Jews. In the extreme case antagonistic ethnic groups may not be culturally distinguishable – their only boundary difference might be the fact (or belief) that they are descended from different ancestors.[114] Richard Rose's findings in his survey of the 1960s demonstrated how small the differences between Northern Irish Catholics and Protestants were on almost all issues, *except* those relating to specifically political and constitutional questions (and to ecumenical matters).[115] The point is that if there are political and ethno-national disagreements between groups the specific cultural content of the differences between them may not matter very much in explaining antagonism or violence. After all, in many places acculturation, and what is loosely called modernization, erodes cultural differences between ethnic groups without necessarily diminishing their political animosities or their political identities. This is certainly the truth about the peoples of Ulster since the seventeenth century. It is also not exceptional. The 'native' Irish were becoming more culturally like the English – in language, material culture, and public and private morality – when they mobilized behind nationalist movements in the nineteenth century. Today the Irish of the Republic speak English, and consume British media; but this shared culture does not induce them to consider political reunification with Great Britain. Outsiders find the communities within Northern Ireland almost impossible 'to tell' apart:[116] only gradually do they learn how to decode the signs of difference – first names, surnames, addresses, schools attended. Attitudinal differences between the communities on social issues are, as Rose first demonstrated, not major, except in so far as they pertain directly to political and constitutional conflict.[117] In short, if cultural differences lie at the heart of ethnic antagonisms in Northern Ireland then they may be exemplifications of what Michael Ignatieff, following Freud, calls the 'narcissism of minor differences':[118] the smaller the real differences between two peoples the larger they are bound to loom in their imagination. We would prefer to express this insight in the following way: the more cultural differences there are, and the deeper they are, then the greater the likelihood that collective identities will be secure rather than threatened.

## On Violent Disagreements

Culturalist understandings of violence are open to comparative, normative and empirical challenges. If Irish Catholic culture is such an important catalyst of political violence, it is difficult to explain why Irish Catholics in the Republic – and, for that matter, in Great Britain, the USA, Australia, and Canada – do not significantly engage in politically violent organizations. Given that the Republic has been subject to massive developmental pressures, urban deprivation, mass unemployment, and extensive inequalities in income and wealth, it should be surprising that the culture of militant republicanism has not spawned significant insurrectionary violence since the 1920s.[119] The obvious explanation is that the political institutions of the Republic – and for that matter of Great Britain, the USA, Australia, and Canada – are regarded as legitimate by Irish Catholics and their descendants, whereas those of Northern Ireland are not. The same argument applies, *mutatis mutandis*, to Ulster Protestants. Their diaspora has not significantly engaged in paramilitary violence in Great Britain, the USA, Australia, Canada or New Zealand. Though there have been communal tensions with the Irish Catholic diaspora in these countries, these Orange and Green disputes outside of Ireland have never led to protracted armed warfare. The obvious explanation is that migrant Irish Catholics and Protestants are less prone to engage in protracted violent ethnic conflict with one another. True, but this differing behaviour cannot be because of different cultural dispositions – since several generations of migrants arrived in new lands with the cultures of their places of origin. Interests matter more than culture in explaining the differences: in Northern Ireland the homeland is at stake (irrelevant for the respective diasporas), one community regards itself as native (by contrast both diasporas are migrants or settlers), and the institutional setting is very different. It seems reasonable to suggest that structural context is more important than the nature of the rival cultures in accounting for protracted and violent conflict.

There are also no parochial oddities in the discourses about violence of either republican or loyalist paramilitaries. Adrian Guelke notes that they use the same justifications found in other societies, and that they are much more amenable to rational interpretation than Paul Wilkinson, for example, suggests. Precisely because paramilitary violence is instrumental rather than expressive, the IRA and the UDA/UVF were regularly obliged to justify it – as defensive, as a military attack on the enemy, as the pursuit of national self-determination, as the killing of legitimate targets, as the mistaken killing of civilians in pursuit of an otherwise legitimate military objective, as 'pre-emptive retaliation', as 'reactive' and so on.[120]

Culturalist explanations of republican violence are especially facile. Few analysts seek to explain the behaviour of 'normal' political parties by reference to their poems and ballads, or their organizational myths of heroes and saviours, villains and enemies, or their tales of militant self-sacrifice in the collective cause. Normally analysts focus on the goals of organizations, assess which cleavages they express, why they can mobilize interests and create 'a community of belonging' which identifies with the relevant party. We see no reason why Sinn Féin (or the DUP) should not be understood in this way, or for that matter, the UDA and the IRA. They are the political and paramilitary expressions of their respective ethnic communities, rather than the by-products of cultural pathologies. We agree with the objection that

> The notion that a glorification of 1916 in poems or ballads leads to recruits for the IRA is insulting to the general intelligence of the general public and of the IRA. What created the modern IRA was not any cultural force, but the bleak . . . realities of life in the corrupt statelet of Northern Ireland. During *Operation Motorman* in Derry in 1972, an *Observer* journalist interviewed a dying volunteer, who assured her that 'Mother Ireland' or 'Cathleen ni Houlihan' meant nothing to him; he was dying simply to defend his neighbours in the street on which he had grown up. The idea that IRA violence is rooted in the Christian Brothers' teaching of history is far too simple . . . [121]

There is another major empirical problem with culturalist explanations of violence: the present conflict has dwarfed in duration all previous armed political conflicts in Ireland, and in intensity it has exceeded all conflicts since the beginning of the nineteenth century, with the possible exception of the civil war in the Irish Free State in 1922/3 (see table 6.1). The number killed since 1969 is proportionately greater than that in each episode of extended political violence in the first six decades of the twentieth century. The number killed in the past two decades is absolutely and proportionately higher than the death-tolls in the Irish war of independence (1919–21) and the fighting which accompanied the formation of Northern Ireland (1920–25). It exceeds the combined toll during the Irish war of independence and the formation of Northern Ireland. On one estimate the present death-toll in Northern Ireland is absolutely and proportionately higher than the numbers killed in the Irish civil war of 1922–3;[122] while on another, the present death-toll is proportionately (but not absolutely) higher than the death-toll in the Irish civil war.[123] The worst

Table 6.1 Numbers killed in political violence in Ireland, 1886–1993

| Duration and location of political violence | | Numbers killed |
|---|---|---|
| (a) 1813–1907 Communal riots (Belfast) | | 60 |
| (b) 1886 Home rule riots ('six counties') | | 86 |
| (c) Easter 1916 (Ireland) | (i) | 514 |
| | (ii) | 450 |
| (d) 1919–21 War of independence (Ireland) | | 1,468 |
| (e) 1922–3 Irish Civil War (Irish Free State) | (i) | 600–700 |
| | (ii) | 4,000 |
| (f) 1920–2 Formation of Northern Ireland (Northern Ireland | (i) | 544 |
| | (ii) | 428 |
| | (iii) | 232 |
| (g) 1939–40 IRA bombing campaign (Great Britain) | | 7 |
| (h) 1956–62 IRA campaign (Northern Ireland) | (i) | 18 |
| | (ii) | 19 |
| (i) 1969–93 Conflict (Northern Ireland, GB, Republic) | | 3,285 |

*Sources*: (a) I. Budge and C. O'Leary, *Belfast: Approach to Crisis. A Study of Belfast Politics, 1613–1970* (London: Macmillan, 1973), 143. (b) C. Townshend, *Political Violence in Ireland: Government and Resistance since 1848* (Oxford: Clarendon Press, 1983/1984), 342. (c) (i) B. Fitzpatrick 'Ireland since 1870', in R. F. Foster (ed.), *The Oxford Illustrated History of Ireland* (Oxford: Oxford University Press, 1989), 213–74, 514; (ii) F. S. L. Lyons, *Ireland since the Famine* (London: Collins, 1973), 375. (d) B. Fitzpatrick, 'Ireland since 1870', in R. F. Foster (ed.), *The Oxford Illustrated History of Ireland* (Oxford: Oxford University Press, 1989), 249. (e) (i) D. J. Hickey and J. E. Doherty, *A Dictionary of Irish History* (Dublin: Gill and Macmillan, 1980), 73; (ii) Lyons, *Ireland since the Famine*, 467–8. (f) (i) Budge and O'Leary, *Approach to Crisis*, 143; E. Aunger, *In Search of Political Stability: A Comparative Study of New Brunswick and Northern Ireland* (Montreal: McGill–Queen's, 1981), 157; (ii) C. Townshend, *Political Violence in Ireland: Government and Resistance since 1848* (Oxford: Clarendon Press, 1983/1984), 342; (iii) R. Rose, *Governing without Consensus: An Irish Perspective* (London: Faber, 1971), 89. (g) Hickey and Doherty, *Dictionary of Irish History*, 256. (h) (i) Bowyer Bell, *The Secret Army: The IRA, 1916–79* (Dublin: Academic Press, 1979), 334; (ii) Aunger, *In Search of Political Stability*, 157. (i) M. Sutton, *An Index of Deaths from the Conflict in Ireland, 1969–93* (Belfast: Beyond the Pale Publications, 1994), 195.

five years of the present crisis (1971–6) led to over 1,650 deaths, proportionally very close (.10) to the higher estimate of the per capita death-toll in the Irish civil war (.13).

The scale of the present conflict is potentially an embarrassment for culturalist explanations. If culture is long-term, persistent, and durable why then have the last twenty-five years been so violent, compared with the preceding four decades? The number of deaths since 1969 may owe something to contemporary technologies which make it cheaper and easier to conduct successful paramilitary campaigns. It may be that 'cultural learning' has led to the current escalation of the conflict to previously unparalleled levels – violence may have increased through mimesis. However, such responses seem *ad hoc*, and unpersuasive. The most straightforward observation is that what is distinctive about the present conflict, and the earlier phase of high levels of violence (1919–21), is the large-scale presence of Great British security forces in a directly coercive, albeit 'peacekeeping' capacity. When local Protestants were allowed to control historic Ulster and Northern Ireland (from 1920 until the late 1960s) they were able to do so, and for reasons which were anything but cultural. In this period organized domination effectively inhibited the possibilities of extensive republican violence.[124]

The timing of the present conflict can also be explained without direct reference to cultural factors. Alexis de Tocqueville's 'adaptive expectations' account of why people are prepared to engage in mass protest and collective insurrection suggests that violence against an old regime occurs in two circumstances: when a bad government seeks to reform itself, and when expectations of the remedying of grievances have been raised.[125] The British welfare state was extended to Northern Ireland after World War II. One long-term consequence was an absolute expansion of the Catholic middle class. Expectations of social mobility after past exclusion sharpened Catholics' sense of social injustice precisely because improvement was now regarded as feasible. This is another Tocquevillian hypothesis: it is as conditions improve that people's expectations that injustice can be rectified become sufficient to mobilize them. These hypotheses suggest that violence occurred in the late 1960s after a period of rising economic expectations within the Catholic community, and rising political expectations generated by the choice of a new unionist prime minister, Terence O'Neill, in 1963, and the election of a Labour government in 1964, led by a sympathetic prime minister, Harold Wilson.

Evidence of expectations of improvements amongst Catholics can be found in Rose's survey, conducted on the eve of the outbreak of protracted conflict[126] – though it cannot be used to infer *rising* expectations as there is no preceding poll for comparison. Rising expectations of reforms were soon dashed by the failure of O'Neill's government to deliver, which helped spark a civil-rights movement that further radicalized Catholic expectations. In turn these developments prompted a loyalist backlash which facilitated the creation of a new IRA.

*Violence as rational collective action.* The collective action approach, made famous by Charles Tilly and his co-researchers, consolidates the reasons for rejecting culturalist readings of political violence.[127] It emphasizes that militant behaviour is purposeful and rationally oriented towards a collective objective, and based on collectively shared interests, and identities. Political violence is seen as highly continuous with other forms of political action, especially protest action, rather than as something which is especially qualitatively distinct. It arises out of deep differences of interest, but its timing, rate and intensity depend fundamentally upon 'the political opportunity structure'. Political violence will be employed sometimes as an alternative to institutionalized channels in liberal democracies, and sometimes as a supplement. Perhaps most fundamentally of all, *organizations* are the key agents in political violence: and these organizations (and their leaders) continuously weigh expected costs and expected benefits in deciding whether or not to employ violence. They stress that violence occurs in conditions of strategic interaction – state agencies and many other organizations are continuously adjusting their tactics to one another. The hypotheses derived from this tradition of theory about collective political violence have been neatly summarized:[128]

- expect participants in political violence to be roughly typical of the groups whose interests are represented in such actions, i.e. one should not expect them to be deviants or marginals;
- expect most episodes of political violence to be outgrowths of non-violent forms of collective action;

- expect higher rates of violence from groups who experience a sense of rightful claim to the contested resources
  or prerogatives;
- expect high levels of militant collective action when the
  stakes (for collective interests) are especially high;
- expect no militant collective action except where participants are endowed with a modicum of resources and a
  minimal degree of mobilization; and
- expect violent collective action, or threats of violent collective action, to be used or tacitly threatened by constitutional politicians.

The collective action perspective is not without flaws. In
particular it too easily assumes that there are shared interests and goals between activists and their constituencies; that
*all* militant collective action serves instrumental rather than
expressive or symbolic purposes; and that all political violence
is strategically aimed at the state and its agencies, rather
than being local, opportunist or particularistic in its focus.
However, its hard-headed flavour has many merits and is
of considerable value when applied to Northern Ireland. It
makes better sense of paramilitary activities than the cultural
explanations which we have read. These organizations have
goals, the creation of an all-Ireland sovereign state in the case
of republicans, the preservation of the Union in the case of
loyalists. Other empirical evidence can be considered in the
light of the above hypotheses.

*The social characteristics of IRA and UVF/UDA members suggest
that they are very typical of the Northern Ireland working-class
and small farmer population.*[129] They are not psychopaths, or
sociopaths.[130]

*Republican paramilitarism mushroomed out of the civil-rights pro-
tests of 1967–9.* Although it could draw on established cultural
tradition, the fact is that as a military organization the IRA was
practically extinct by 1969, and the Official IRA was by-passed
by the militants, who participated in demonstrations and went
on to form and join the Provisional IRA. Conversely, loyalist paramilitarism mushroomed out of counter-mobilizations
against the civil-rights movement. The UDA and UVF could

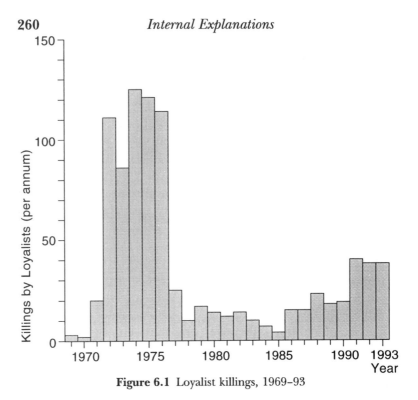

**Figure 6.1** Loyalist killings, 1969–93

draw upon established repertoires of mobilization, but the UVF, like the IRA, was minuscule in the late 1960s.

*The civil-rights movement of the late 1960s was highly motivated by grievances about collective discrimination, and its demonstrations often led to aggressive interactions with the police and loyalists.* The higher degree of violence emanating from the smaller ethnic community fits the assumption that those who are most normatively motivated engage in the highest levels of militancy.[131]

*The peak years of political violence occurred between 1971 and 1976* (see figure 1.3, p. 52). These years saw the breakdown, suspension and abolition of the Stormont parliament. Loyalists feared a British withdrawal and republicans hoped to accomplish just that, and quickly. After failing to get political results from a ceasefire in 1975–6, i.e. a British withdrawal, republicans settled down to conduct what they called the long war. What was at stake had profound and obviously understood repercussions for the political power and status of both communities. The territorial boundaries and statehood of the region were perceived to be at issue between 1971 and 1976, which is why loyalist violence was so high. From 1977 loyalist paramilitaries relaxed, assured that their actions and the British state could contain the threat from the IRA (see figure 6.1). The upsurge of violence after the Anglo-Irish Agreement of 1985 and in the early 1990s is also consistent with Tilly's theses. Loyalist violence was extensively re-activated by renewed fears of a prospective British disengagement, or concessions to the IRA and 'the pan-nationalist front'. In other words the peaks in violence have occurred when the highest interests, i.e. national interests, have been at stake; just as the collective-action model suggests.[132]

*Mobilization for mass collective action, and the use of political violence by republicans, were quite rare in Northern Ireland between 1922 and 1969 – which is not what one would expect if culturalist theories were correct.* Such actions did not occur before the 1960s because the Ulster Unionist Party ran a regime which could exercise control over the minority. Territorial, electoral, coercive, legal, and administrative domination disorganized the opposition very effectively before the 1960s, making revolt and effective dissent appear unworkable to most.[133] This system of control broke down first because the Irish state appeared to cease to have the same interest in unification, leaving northern nationalists with no option but to pursue their interests internally, and secondly, because the Westminster government began to intervene in ways which raised Catholic expectations that their grievances could be remedied. The post-war welfare state increased Catholics' resources, their material welfare, their hope of social mobility, and their desire for equal citizenship. The brilliant strategic choice of a civil-rights movement, one which imitated that which had appeared to be so successful in the USA, undermined the Stormont regime in British and international public opinion. Therefore unionists could not exercise repression effectively, as they had in the 1930s and 1950s. Once the system of control broke down, Catholics developed the resources to engage in protracted ethnic conflict. (Protracted conflict appears to be the normal consequence of the breakdown of regimes of control in ethnically divided territories (see contemporary Bosnia), so Northern Ireland is not unusual or culturally unique in this respect).

*Finally, many politicians in Northern Ireland, who describe themselves as constitutionalist, whether they be in the UUP, the DUP, or the SDLP, have used the political violence issuing from their own ethnic constituencies, either directly or indirectly, as a threat to advance their political goals.* UUP politicians have regularly warned of the dangers of bombs in the streets of Dublin to deter the Republic from advancing Irish unity; SDLP politicians regularly warned in the early 1980s that the alienation of the nationalist community threatened instability and required an Irish dimension to remove it; since the Anglo-Irish Agreement, DUP politicians have made the same 'warnings' about loyalist alienation. Even when the politicians concerned are not strategically using the violence of others, or deliberately encouraging it, that is nevertheless how they are perceived.

This was especially evident in the period preceding and succeeding the IRA's announcement of a complete cessation of violence.[134] If one's constitutional rivals are seen to facilitate, threaten or engage in violence, it makes sense to reciprocate with actual violence. Historically there have been four modes of Irish resistance to British rule – parliamentary oppositionism, civil disobedience and passive resistance, the construction of rival forms of government, and the direct challenge of armed insurrection.[135] These means have been very effective when they have been fused, as they were beween 1918 and 1921. Similarly, there have been four modes of unionist resistance to Irish nationalism – parliamentary control or alliances, civil disobedience against a treacherous British government, the construction of parallel forms of government, and the direct challenge of communal violence. These means have also been most effective when fused, as they were between 1911 and 1914, in the early 1920s, and again in 1974. These lessons have not been lost on rationalist readers of the past.

Rationalist interpretations of political violence in Northern Ireland are more compelling than culturalist accounts. That is because we believe that the fundamental political disposition of individuals (or groups) is to maximize their influence, or power, over decisions, and that they do this especially when they feel insecure. For these reasons most individuals (or groups) will consider violence if they believe it will advance their security and power.[136] To the extent that cultural patterns play a role in explaining violence, they may inhibit violence as much as promote it – because cultures also contain many lessons about the costs of violence as a political instrument, both for individuals and for groups.[137] Political violence, in our judgement, has been both the consequence and the cause of conflict. Its self-perpetuating dynamics were not simply cultural reflexes, but intrinsic to 'the sovereignty trap' in which both communities are locked. Violence is partially motivated by the belief that only one side can win; it is also motivated by the belief that threatening and using violence is the best way of preventing the other side from winning; and, not least, it is motivated by the belief that the other side benefits from using violence so it must pay to make it costly for them.

These arguments may appear to be too cool and detached, symptoms of the academic failure to illuminate the ferocity of ethnic violence. They may appear to leave insufficient role for the emotions, for frustration, aggression and hatred, or for the propensities of angry young men – all of which may be culturally channelled. We do not deny any evidence of virulent emotional hatred, prejudice and ferocious hostility towards their ethnic enemies displayed by people within Northern Ireland – not least within paramilitary organizations.[138] What we deny is that these emotions, culturally channelled or otherwise, are fundamentally explanatory. These psychological possibilities are latent in all societies. What is distinctive about ethnic conflict, all other things being equal, is that these emotions are easily provoked and channelled by organizations into collective violence.

# Conclusion: Culture, Nationalism and the Sovereignty Trap

The stereotypical reading of the Irish as 'wild men and women', imbued with fiery values, will not do as a general explanation.[139] The emphasis some scholars give to the local cultures

in Northern Ireland also seems misplaced; their local coloration is less important than the fact they are sub-cultures of two
national cultures, one British, the other Irish. Moreover, both
communities, at least according to their own protestations,
are happy to tolerate the other's culture, meaning its religion
and national culture. What they find problematic is that the
state of the other community claims national sovereignty over
the territory, and that the other community seeks different
political institutions. There is also no fundamental problem
of cultural misunderstanding in Northern Ireland. Each community knows what the other wants. They appreciate – and
sometimes over-appreciate – the rational stratagems adopted
by the other community. There is a fear of extinction or
subordination in each community, and it is these fears which
make it politically important for many to commit themselves
to their community's cultural manifestations.

That said, Northern Ireland is the site of one fundamental
cultural clash: the clash of rival political nationalisms. In the
national sovereignty trap, which is not unique to Northern
Ireland, there is a deadly belief that each national culture
must have one, and only one, political roof for its protection
and expression. The central problem which must be addressed
in the peace process potentially underway in Northern Ireland
is how to transcend this national sovereignty trap so that
each national community is equally secure, recognized and
expressed.

# 7

# Mammon and Utility:
# Liberal Economic Reasoning

If you give Roman Catholics a good job and a good house, they
will live like Protestants, because they will see neighbours with
cars and television sets.
        *Northern Ireland Prime Minister Terence O'Neill, 1969* [1]

If work can be found for 10,000 unemployed boys in west
Belfast, . . . that in itself will do more to impact on the political
and security areas than anything else.
        *Northern Ireland Office Minister Richard Needham, 1989* [2]

Assigning [Northern Ireland's] violence to religious hatreds or
skewed nationalism or mere senselessness is too easy. In fact,
the hardmen have a very good reason for wanting to sabotage
any prospect of peace, one that has less to do with flags or
gods and more to do with money.
        *Scott Anderson, American journalist, 1994* [3]

If over a period of time the identity of interest between the
two parts of Ireland on vital issues within the [European]
Community became evident, and the divergence of interest
between Britain and both parts of Ireland became equally
clear, then this . . . could encourage the North to contemplate
what would then be a more logical and valid arrangement –
viz. the representation of Irish interests within the Community
by ministers and parliamentarians of a united Ireland.
        *Garret FitzGerald, former Irish prime minister, 1972* [4]

Liberal social scientists share the Marxist temptation to explain
conflicts materially. However, while Marxist materialism has
been widely, and rightly, criticized, liberal economic materi-

alism has been less extensively scrutinized in orthodox social science. True, the differences between Marxist and liberal materialism are fundamental. Liberals define the rational, self-interested individual as the key agency in society,[5] rather than social classes or class struggle; and they also express support for a free-market system, while often disagreeing on the range of intervention needed to ensure its efficiency and fairness. Nevertheless, red Marxists and liberals share some assumptions in their interpretations of nationalism, not least their conviction that it is generally reactionary. Thus the massive upsurge in ethnic violence which has occurred in the 1990s is dismissed as a hangover from a 'precontractual age'.[6] The liberal and red Marxist conviction that nationalism is almost invariably reactionary explains why they often find common cause in condemning national chauvinism and xenophobia.

Political stability in democratic states is also understood by many liberals in materialist ways. Thus the relative lack of class and ethnic conflict in Western industrial societies is sometimes ascribed to prosperity and the ability of Western regimes to provide increasing economic benefits to their citizens.[7] Ethnic conflict is seen as a reflection of economic deprivation – thus world-wide waves of national and economic violence in the early 1990s have been widely and confidently attributed to the deep world-wide recession.[8] It is also explained by liberals as a consequence of impediments to free markets within states. Conflict between states is also ascribed to economic rivalries and protectionism, while equality of opportunity, free trade, and economic interdependence are credited with the potential to dissolve even bitter national and ethnic animosities. We might dub this liberalism's benign theory of national and ethnic conflict, and 'neo-functionalism' its method of conflict-resolution. Its malign theory associates national and ethnic conflict with economic opportunism, or 'rent-seeking', on the part of certain rational agents: in this view conflict must always profit somebody.

Observers of Northern Ireland, including journalists, politicians and academics, are influenced by the liberal materialism which we have only slightly caricatured. Few analysts are resolutely and crudely reductionist, but many assign a central role to economic forces and usually give these more weight than, say, religion, national identity, or culture. In this chapter we divide their explanations into two broad categories.

(1) *Direct economic explanations which focus on the concepts of inequality, deprivation and opportunism.* The relevant groups are portrayed as fighting to remove (or maintain) inequality, to escape (or impose) deprivation, or to take advantage of opportunities for private gain. Some groups are also seen as having a vested interest in perpetuating antagonism, violence and constitutional stalemate.

(2) *Indirect economic explanations which recognize that the rival groups are divided by their national identities, but maintain that these are crucially embedded in and underpinned by different material interests.* Exponents of these views often credit functional cross-border economic co-operation, and especially European integration, with great conflict-terminating potential. They believe that economic change will erode the material foundations of national differences.

These related explanations suggest precise public-policy measures. Prescriptions must deal with the underlying material causes of the conflict rather than its superstructural manifestations. For materialist liberals, ethnic attachments are best diluted through the expansion of prosperity, measures that make conflict non-profitable, the provision of equality of opportunity, and the promotion of free trade and economic co-operation across state boundaries. That is what 'really' matters, rather than changing constitutions to pander to group interests or reforming the administration of justice and policing.

Materialist interpretations also suggest benign prognoses about the prospects for conflict-resolution, since it is commonly accepted that disputes over market opportunities, production, profits, investment, jobs and wages are negotiable and soluble.

## Direct Economic Explanations

*Inequality: the salience of differentials.* Materialist liberals often explain political instability as the result of irrational discrimination or inequality of opportunity, and invariably prescribe the outlawing of discrimination and effective provision of equality of opportunity. They waste no time pandering to cultural or ethnic pluralism. They recognize that protest against injustice may be expressed in ethnic mobilization and demands for cultural separatism, as with Malcolm X in the USA, the Pan Africanist Congress in South Africa, or the Provisional IRA, but such liberals argue that the cultural froth surrounding such movements should be decoded and paid less attention than its causes. In what Nathan Glazer calls the liberal expectancy thesis, the provision of civil equality and equality of opportunity will stabilize multi-ethnic societies and ensure societal integration.[9]

This philosophy is dominant in the American civil-rights movement, in the formerly exiled leadership of the African National Congress, and in several readings of Northern Ireland. Many have contended that the conflict derived from inequalities in socio-economic and civil rights rather than from national differences. They have included the Northern Ireland Civil Rights Association in the 1960s, the Cameron Commission, appointed to examine the origins of the conflict in 1969, many supporters of the Alliance Party, and a significant minority of the SDLP's supporters.[10]

On a number of occasions, especially in 1968–72, 1976, and 1989, the British government has expressed sympathy for this view and has supported legislative and other measures to address inequality. Various American organizations and politicians have demanded that inequalities between Catholics and Protestants be addressed as a crucial step towards peace. Numerous US states have passed the MacBride principles, which link American investment in Northern Ireland to equality of opportunity in the workplace. American aid for the International Fund for Ireland, approximately $120 million between 1985 and 1993, is largely based on the view that directed growth in Catholic areas will promote stability. According to the former Speaker of the US House of Representatives, Tom Foley, 'there is one overriding reason for US support . . . The fund's emphasis on economic development and employment as a means to peace and reconciliation in Ireland is a powerful alternative to the death and destruction offered by the men of violence who oppose it.'[11]

This school of thought has even received backing from some unionist integrationists who accept that Catholics were treated unequally by the Stormont regime (although they pin ultimate responsibility on the British government for foisting devolution on Protestants against their will). They believe that fair economic treatment of Catholics will terminate their nationalism. The case for inequality as the key cause of the conflict has also received academic and professional social-scientific support. In a 1972 article, Derek Birrell attributed the outbreak of the conflict to Catholic 'relative deprivation'.[12] The most exhaustive academic statement of the argument, however, is put forward in a major book by David Smith and Gerald Chambers, entitled *Inequality in Northern Ireland*, based on research commissioned by the Standing Advisory Commission on Human Rights.[13]

For Smith and Chambers, the conflict's roots were forged in the initial plantation of Ulster, which extracted the best land for Protestants and relegated the Catholics to less fertile hilly land or to jobs as farm-labourers. This disparity was reinforced by penal legislation which prevented Catholics from owning land and acquiring wealth needed for industrialization.[14] The gap has been maintained into the present by discriminatory practices, the result of informal social norms and networks, and overt exhortations by successive unionist leaders after 1921. The result has been persistent and significant differences between Catholics and Protestants in unemployment rates, quality of employment, and overall living standards.[15] The most striking difference can be found in rates of unemployment, with Catholic men being about two and a half times more likely to be unemployed than Protestant men (see table 7.1). Among those who are in work, Protestant men tend to be over-represented in non-manual occupations, especially in the higher-paying professional and managerial categories; Catholic

**Table 7.1** Male unemployment rates by religion, 1971–91

|  | Catholics | Protestants | Difference | Ratio |
|---|---|---|---|---|
| 1971 Census | 17.3 | 6.6 | 10.7 | 2 : 6 |
| 1981 Census | 30.2 | 12.4 | 17.8 | 2 : 4 |
| 1991 Census | 28.4 | 12.7 | 15.7 | 2 : 2 |
| 1983–4 CHS | 35.8 | 14.9 | 20.9 | 2 : 4 |
| 1985–6 CHS | 35.5 | 14.2 | 21.3 | 2 : 5 |
| 1988–90/91 CHS | 27.2 | 12.2 | 15.0 | 2 : 2 |
| 1985–6 LFS | 29.1 | 11.5 | 17.6 | 2 : 5 |
| 1990–1 LFS | 21.3 | 9.6 | 11.7 | 2 : 2 |

*Note*: CHS = Continuous Household Survey; LFS = Labour force Survey.
*Sources*: Census of Population (1971, 1981, 1991); and A. Murphy and D. Armstrong, *A Picture of the Catholic and Protestant Male Unemployed, Employment Equality Review, Research Report*, No. 2 (Belfast: Central Community Relations Unit, 1994), 1.

men are over-represented in manual occupations, especially in the low-paying unskilled-manual category.[16] Higher unemployment and poorer quality of employment, added to the tendency of Catholics to have larger families and work less overtime, result in a lower standard of living for Catholics. In the Continuous Household Surveys of 1983–5, 34 per cent of Protestant households enjoyed incomes of over £10,000 per annum compared with 21 per cent of Catholic households; while 47 per cent of Protestant households had incomes of less than £6,000 per annum by comparison with 59 per cent of Catholic households.

The current violence, according to Smith and Chambers, erupted because of inequality rather than nationalism or religiosity.[17] The civil-rights campaign began over a dispute over public housing at Caledon in 1964, and, as the Cameron Commission concluded, the minority's protests were based on grievances which had little to do with the national question. A survey conducted by Smith and Chambers apparently confirmed that inequality is at the heart of the conflict. Asked to pick from a number of options, a plurality of Catholics selected 'unemployment' as the biggest problem in Northern Ireland and 'equality of opportunity' as the change most likely to end the troubles.[18] Additionally Smith and Chambers persuasively argue that the existence of inequality can be primarily explained by the presence of direct and indirect discrimination in the private and public sectors. They call for strong equal-opportunity policies, including vigorous affirmative action to combat entrenched discrimination.

Related to this view, that Catholics are fighting to achieve economic equality, is the claim that Protestants are struggling to protect their economic privileges: Smith and Chambers, for example, note Protestant resistance to anti-discrimination policies,[19] while Birrell put forth the concept of 'reverse relative deprivation' to explain Protestant resistance to Catholic protests in the late 1960s (Protestants began to feel relatively deprived as the gap between them and Catholics closed).[20] Other authors, who focus almost exclusively on Protestant motivations, support somewhat similar arguments.[21] In hearings held by the Opsahl Commission in the Shankill area in early 1993, several speakers attributed recent violence from loyalist paramilitaries to their perception that Catholics were doing better than they were – a reversal of roles from the late 1960s. Shankill residents complained of 'reverse discrimination' and claimed that government redevelopment and expenditure-allocation decisions discriminated in favour of Catholics.[22]

*Deprivation: the war of the impoverished.* Many stress the role of deprivation in explaining the conflict, especially its violent manifestations. They point to the fact that Northern Ireland is the most economically deprived region of the United Kingdom on a wide range of indices,[23] and that a considerable proportion of violence emanates from deprived Catholic *and* Protestant ghettos, and suggest that the most militant political parties, Sinn Féin and the DUP, and republican and loyalist paramilitaries, draw disproportionate support from the less well-off within their respective communities.

Deprivation-based arguments focus on absolute levels of income or welfare rather than relative inequalities. Their exponents are normally more closely associated with support for general economic growth than with support for affirmative action or directed growth policies.[24] This perspective has adherents in both the Northern Irish and British labour movements.[25] Their prescription is vigorous governmental intervention to revive the economy and generate investment. Roy Mason, as Labour Secretary of State for Northern Ireland between 1976 and 1979, emphasized economic growth, at least rhetorically, as the most fruitful peacemaking strategy. Some Thatcherite Conservatives, on the other hand, regard the Northern Ireland conflict as a particularly virulent strain of the 'British disease', exacerbated by the very forms of interventionism advocated by Labour. They call for the creation, instead, of an 'enterprise culture' to solve the region's problems and/or for cuts in public expenditure.[26] In turn, some on the political left attribute the continuation of the conflict after many years of Tory government to the latter's excessive 'new right' ideological zeal.[27] Academics also support deprivation-based arguments. John Whyte argues that deprivation helps to explain the conflict and that prosperity would improve community relations;[28] Paidraig O'Malley noted a close correlation between deprived areas and paramilitary activity and called for a significant investment of resources to combat the problem,[29] and the authors of the Opsahl Report repeated this argument while acknowledging that 'the relationship between Northern Ireland's socio-economic problems and any political and constitutional settlement is a complex one'.[30]

Relative deprivation explanations of political violence were popular with social scientists in the earliest stages of the present cycle of conflict,[31] and, as we have seen, they have enjoyed some direct support amongst Catholic respondents to social surveys. Relative deprivation theories come in various forms:[32] in some, emphasis is placed upon *perceived* deprivation by a group in relation to another group, whereas in others it is focused on the psychic states of individuals. The latter give rise to the notion that violence is caused by an aggressive response to frustration. The former, by contrast, are based on attitudes, expectations, and conceptions of justice and entitlement. However, all these theories view the probability of collective violence as the summation of individual levels of undeserved frustration, indignation or perceived injustice,[33] and little attention is paid to organizational or resource-differences between groups in their capacities for violence. Relative deprivation theories generate hypotheses which are capable of being tested: one should expect levels of violent behaviour to vary directly with levels of objective social conditions believed to be frustrating; one should expect participants in violent events to be high in self-reported or otherwise individually demonstrated relative deprivation, and one should expect those low in relative deprivation not to participate in such events.[34]

*Economic opportunism: who benefits?* Sometimes, however, conflict is directly attributed to economic opportunism, rather than inequality or deprivation. Exponents of rational choice explain participation in the production of political violence as one might explain participation in any activity dedicated towards the achievement of a 'public good'.[35] The supposition is that people participate in collective action if and only if the individual net benefit exceeds net costs, and if each individual judges that their participation is critical to the accomplishment of the deed. In other words collective action is likely to be chronically under-supplied because of the free-rider problem.[36] This approach to paramilitary political violence generates some insights. It suggests that without 'selective incentives' there are likely to be few participants in paramilitary organizations (as is the case). Positive selective incentives might take the form of benefits which only members of the paramilitary organization would receive (such as present status as a local hero or defender, or the prospect of future jobs in a post-revolutionary government/society), whereas negative selective incentives might take the form of severe threats and coercion being exercised on non-members, or members who wish to exit after joining the organization (as has also been the case).

Opportunistic explanations suggest that political violence is rational if and only if it gratifies the narrow interests of individual actors. In Northern Ireland such explanations have taken different forms depending on whether the interpreters are seeking to explain the violence or the persistence of the political stalemate. Some Protestants have believed that Catholics have engaged in conflict because 'it pays' – republican violence has prompted an infusion of government money into Catholic areas. Recent loyalist violence has been attributed by one Protestant Pastor to the desire to get access to such governmental largesse.[37] Another commentator notes that the Protestant-dominated security forces, among the best paid workers in Northern Ireland, have no obvious vested interest in peace.[38] A similar perspective is offered by those who maintain that the British subvention of Northern Ireland, together with Britain's willingness to pay the bills for the costs of violence, helps perpetuate the stalemate because the economic costs of conflict are not borne by the Northern Irish, but rather by British and European tax-payers: 'a perverse incentive is at work: security expenditure by the British government brings a great deal of income and employment to the region, mainly, but not exclusively to the Protestant community [and] in the short-run, at least, much of the region actually benefits from security expenditure and has no economic incentive to see it reduced'.[39]

There are other more blatant 'rent-seeking' explanations of the political stalemate. The failure of Unionist leaders to consider power-sharing devolved government is sometimes attributed to the fact that they have secure jobs at Westminster, and do not wish to share political patronage with other unionist politicians, let alone nationalists. (Conversely, the potential of a local assembly to offer paid political positions has been held to explain the moderation of some second-ranking nationalists and unionists.) However, by far the most frequent opportunistic explanation ascribes narrow rent-seeking behaviour to the paramilitaries. Government officials from Britain and the Republic have freely used emotive expressions like 'mafias', 'gangsters', 'racketeers', 'criminals', 'Godfathers', and 'mobsters' to describe the paramilitaries, implying that the pursuit of personal profit has been a more important motive than ideology in explaining violence.[40] An RUC detective informed one author that both sets of paramilitaries had more criminals than patriots.[41] While one might expect such statements from the authorities or pro-establishment journalists, this interpretation of paramilitary conduct has some popular resonance throughout Northern Ireland, and amongst non-establishment figures.[42] The salience of racketeering among paramilitaries has been 'exposed' by a number of academics, authors and journalists.[43] The importance of acquisitiveness has been highlighted by, among others, a former leading Catholic politician[44] and a former high-ranking paramilitary.[45] The prescription implied by this perspective is tougher anti-racketeering measures and a clampdown by the security forces.

## Indirect Economic Explanations of the Conflict

The foregoing explanations of the politics of antagonism, violence and political stalemate directly invoke economic interests. By contrast, indirect materialist explanations argue that a number of aspects of national allegiance relevant to the conflict, including the nationalism of northern Catholics, the unionism of Ulster Protestants, and the ambivalence about union with Northern Ireland expressed by the citizens of Great Britain and the Republic, are crucially connected to material considerations. It is also often argued, by the same interpreters, that economic co-operation, perhaps in the form of deepening European integration, will create a transcendent identity which will overcome the current national divisions. National and ethnic conflict will dissolve through functional co-operation and the balm of shared economic interests and threats. The implication is that the indirect causes of conflict can be tackled directly through appropriate economic policy.

*The material roots of Irish Nationalism.* Like their Marxist counterparts, some liberals attribute a dominant role to material interests in explaining the Irish desire to govern themselves. This thinking has venerable antecedents. From the 1880s, while the Liberal government was committed to a political solution to the Irish crisis, the Conservatives came to believe that the Irish ambition for home rule could be killed by material 'kindness'. They eventually passed what were then revolutionary measures, transferring land ownership in Ireland from landlords to their tenants. The suppositions behind this thinking were plain – Irish nationalism had material causes which could be treated through direct economic interventions. More recently, two academics have argued that the unwillingness of Sinn Féin's supporters to accept the Union with Great Britain must be partly explained by their lack of a stake in the British economy.[46] Liberal unionists, from former premier of Northern Ireland Terence O'Neill through to the APNI and contemporary integrationists, have persistently tried to undermine Catholic support for separatism by stressing the economic merits of the Union. They leap eagerly upon opinion poll evidence when it suggests that the Catholic middle class who support the Alliance Party or the SDLP are more willing to accept the Union than their deprived co-religionists within Sinn Féin, and jump to the conclusion that material deprivation explains not only nationalist extremism but also nationalism itself.

*The material roots of Ulster unionism.* Many Irish Catholics believe that Protestants, just like their Scottish forebears, are grasping and that their unionism is based on economic calculations: Protestants are said to be more loyal to the half-crown than to the Crown. This view is shared by some liberal nationalist politicians, historians and intellectuals. Irish unionism was undoubtedly the political expression of the Anglo-Irish aristocracy and the Protestant professional classes in what later became the Irish Free State. Ulster unionism is often understood similarly, as a politics of economic privilege, in which British national identification is decoded as a rationalization of economic interests. Garret FitzGerald, in explaining Protestant opposition to Irish independence in 1921, once argued that it was not certain that religious and political motives would have sufficed to make Ulster Protestants hostile to Irish nationalism had they not been reinforced by economic dependence on the British market.[47] When attempting to win unionist support for a united Ireland he pointed to the reduction of trade barriers between Ireland and the United Kingdom in the post-war period, implying that unionists should be able to see a good deal when offered one.[48]

Nationalists and their sympathizers have also focused on the economic subvention from Britain as the linchpin of loyalism and unionism.[49] The subvention certainly matters materially: it is rising steadily towards £(UK)3.5 billion; and it accounted for 23 per cent of Northern Ireland's GDP in 1992.[50] In one survey a majority of respondents in the Republic expressed the belief that subsidies were the main reason that loyalists were loyal.[51] Eamon de Valera thought that the British government simply had to abandon the subvention to persuade Protestants of the merits of a united Ireland.[52] Garret FitzGerald once believed that if London could be persuaded to continue paying the subvention – to a united Ireland and for a lengthy transitional period – it would help to undermine unionist opposition to Irish unity.[53] More recently Bob Rowthorn and Naomi Wayne argued that the subvention could (and should) be used to compel Protestants into a united Ireland. The key to a successful withdrawal would be for Britain to make continuation of the subvention, for a transitional period of 15–20 years, contingent on Protestants joining a united Ireland, and remaining on their best behaviour. Those who would refuse and insist on establishing an independent state could be brought to their knees quickly by 'a concerted programme of economic sanctions'.[54] The belief that Protestants are rational economic agents allowed Rowthorn and Wayne to explain both why loyalists threaten massive bloodshed if Britain withdraws and why this possibility can be avoided if Britain leaves in an appropriate manner.[55]

Nationalists have long tried to persuade Protestants of the economic merits of a united Ireland, on the supposition that economic anxieties or interests must lie at the heart of unionism. Sean Lemass developed an ambitious plan for economic growth in the late 1950s partly because he believed it would facilitate unification. He was an exponent of what Tom Lyne has called 'technocratic anti-partitionism'.[56] In the late 1970s, after a period of spirited economic growth in the Republic, Garret FitzGerald's Fine Gael party released a policy pamphlet most of which was dedicated to demonstrating the economic benefits which Protestants could expect from Irish unification, or at least confederation. Similar arguments have re-surfaced in both parts of Ireland in the light of the opportunities and threats posed by deepening European economic integration.[57]

*The material roots of ambivalence among the citizens of Great Britain and the Republic.* While a minority of nationalists and green Marxists may continue to believe that Britain remains in Northern Ireland to extract profit, or to protect British investments in Ireland, few take these arguments seriously anymore. A more prevalent, and diametrically opposed, view is that Britain is ambivalent about the Union, or wants out, because Northern Ireland costs too much. Irish nationalists and their sympathizers have often played on this ambivalence by stressing the savings which Britain can expect if it leaves Ireland.[58] Much IRA activity against economic targets, in Northern Ireland and Great Britain, especially spectacularly expensive attacks on the City of London in 1992–3, assumed that increasing the costs of governing Northern Ireland would sap Britain's will to stay. Unionists are equally concerned that Britain's ties to them may cut no deeper than narrow economic calculations. Their spokespersons go out of their way to counter the 'extravagant rhetoric' that 'Ulster . . . is bleeding the British taxpayer dry.'[59] Many of them are fearful that the British prime minister's statement in the Downing Street Declaration that the British government has no selfish, economic or strategic reasons for staying in Northern Ireland may spell the end of the Union. If Britain has no selfish economic 'interests' in Northern Ireland and does not recognize Ulster Unionists as fundamentally British then the full-scale betrayal of unionists is merely a matter of time.

Other commentators argue that the cost of governing Northern Ireland or of economically integrating it at current living standards and expectations must explain why the Republic has only a rhetorical interest in Irish unification. In the words of Conor Cruise O'Brien, the Republic's posture towards Britain is 'Please go, but for God's sake stay.' The Republic's unwillingness to take concrete steps to achieve a united Ireland is said to be indirectly linked to material considerations. Many authors draw attention to opinion polls which show support for Irish unification declining when respondents are asked to link national unification to higher taxes.[60] Unionist academics relish pointing out that the Republic could not afford unification, at least without massive tax-hikes or major reductions in the standard of living of the peoples of Northern Ireland.[61] A recent report by a Dublin-based economic consultancy quietly points out that 'In the context of any hypothetical change in the constitutional status of Northern Ireland, it is apposite to note that the UK subvention is roughly equal to the annual revenue from income tax in the Republic.'[62]

*European economic integration and the alleged erosion of national antagonisms.* Some observers claim that European integration will affect the conflict and stalemate in a variety of salutary ways. They can broadly be classified as nationalist, unionist, and Europeanist in perspective.

*Nationalist perspectives on Europe: unity will sprout through Brussels.* Since the 1950s, liberal nationalists have portrayed the breakdown of economic barriers between Northern Ireland and the Republic as conducive to securing Protestant support for a united Ireland. Future Taoiseach Liam Cosgrave out-lined this thinking in a speech to Dáil Éireann in 1954, and it played an important part in convincing Sean Lemass to abandon attempts at autarky, to sign a free-trade treaty with the United Kingdom, and to go north to meet Terence O'Neill to improve economic co-operation.[63] In the referendum on entry to the European Community, many northern nation-alists voted 'yes' (while unionists voted 'no'), not because of the strictly economic merits of free trade, nor because they were fervent Europeanists, but because they thought it would bring a united Ireland closer. Nationalist backers of European integration hope that exposure to the European nations which have buried their antagonisms – after two vicious wars this century – will provide a model for reconciliation in Ireland. In what is sometimes called John Hume's 'single transferrable speech' the leader of the SDLP regularly invokes Franco-German reconciliation within the European Union as a model for the two communities in Ireland. At the level of the two governments, it has been argued that regular contact in the council of ministers eases British–Irish relations in ways which further the nationalist cause.[64] Nationalists currently refer to examples of co-operation between Northern Ireland's Euro-MPs to support this argument.[65]

Nationalist intellectuals and politicians regularly point to numerous ways in which the EC and the EU have made a united Ireland more attractive from an economic perspective. The entry of the UK and the Republic into the EC, and the preceding signing of the Anglo-Irish Free Trade Treaty in 1965, mean that Protestants can now accept a united Ireland without losing access to British markets, a luxury they could not be assured of in 1921. The economic interests of Northern Ireland and the Republic are now more similar – in agriculture and regional policy in particular – than those of Northern Ireland and Great Britain, and so it has been argued that an all-Ireland government would represent Northern Ireland's interests in the EC or the EU better than Whitehall.[66] In addition, the disproportional representation of small states in EC and EU institutions means that the north as a relatively large part of Ireland would fare much better in its political capacities than it can as a small and insignificant part of the United Kingdom.[67] Moreover, it is hoped by many that the EU will expand to take over social expenditures in its constituent states, thus making the British subvention less important to Protestants, while the cession of several powers from Westminster to Brussels will take some of the 'emotional impact' out of the transfer of powers from Westminster to an Irish government.[68] Finally, it is sometimes more fancifully claimed that the EU may be willing to finance Irish unity, offsetting Protestant fears about losing the British subvention.

Despite the failure of this analysis to bear fruit, it remains intact and has been given a boost by the Single European Act and by the Maastricht Treaty. It is believed, or hoped, that increased peripheralization will force both parts of Ireland, the only parts of the EC without a land link after 1994,[69] to co-operate for reasons of economic self-interest, and that this shared functional interest will enhance the prospects for Irish unity or at least a strong 'Irish dimension'. Charles Haughey, visiting Belfast in April 1990 in his capacity as President of the European Council, outlined the same advantages of North–South co-operation that FitzGerald had referred to earlier.[70] When the Chair of the Ulster Bank and of the Northern Ireland Institute of Directors recently proposed an integrated 'island economy' in the context of the single market, the *Irish News* lauded the plan as 'paving the way for unity and peace'.[71] Northern nationalists and their sympathizers can currently be heard calling for the democratization, i.e. the strengthening, of central European institutions,[72] and for the EU to treat Ireland as one unit when disbursing its financial largesse. During 1991–2 the leader of the SDLP, John Hume, tabled proposals for the creation of an executive to govern Northern Ireland, modelled on the European Commission. The proposed executive would have included three elected representatives from Northern Ireland and three appointees from the British and Irish governments and the European Commission respectively.

*Liberal unionist perspectives on Europe: the road to ruin need not go through Rome.* Despite their pivotal role in passing the Maastricht Treaty at Westminster in 1993, Unionists have traditionally been Europhobes. Fearing European sympathies for Irish nationalism,[73] and the erosion of the sovereignty of the Westminster parliament, they have regarded European integration negatively. Recently, however, liberal and socialist intellectuals with unionist sympathies have begun to challenge the nationalist analysis that European integration should result in political or constitutional links between both parts of Ireland. Robin Wilson, a liberal unionist with a Marxist past, and the editor of *Fortnight* magazine, has asserted that the decline of the 'nation-state' in modern Europe provides the 'key' to unlocking the problem of Northern Ireland. He proposes a regional assembly that establishes a 'stable framework for the governance of Northern Ireland as, for the foreseeable future, a constituent part of the United Kingdom', and thus rejects any link between Europeanization and Irish national integration.[74] Similarly, in a booklet, *Northern Limits*, published in late 1992, the Cadogan Group claim that European integration has not removed barriers to Irish unification but rather, by developing the concept of a common European citizenship, and ensuring freedom of movement, has eased the plight of national minorities in existing states. In their view the minority in Northern Ireland should be content to accept its position in a sovereign UK within European institutions, a UK which is pluralistic and accommodates 'various nationalities, cultures and identities'.[75]

*Europeanist perspectives: We are the future*. The concepts of sovereign Irish or British nation-states retain a pivotal place in nationalist and unionist analyses of European integration. However, enthusiastic Euro-federalists maintain that European integration has already involved the erosion of absolutist conceptions of national sovereignty, and will do so to an increasing degree as European institutions are democratized and the principle of 'subsidiarity' begins to bite. They also maintain that European integration will facilitate the development of transcendent Euro-wide alliances and identities, and complex and plural notions of citizenship.[76] Exponents of these ideas include Professors Tom Hadden, Kevin Boyle and Elizabeth Meehan. They are British and Irish illustrations of the wider movement amongst the European intelligentsia which claims, despite evidence to the contrary, that the European Union is a new, post-national and transcendent political system, capable of resolving the traditional national and religious antagonisms of European peoples.[77]

## Putting Materialism in its Place

Economic factors can hardly be dismissed when explaining Northern Ireland. It is clear, for example, that paramilitarism and political extremism have been far more abundant among the deprived than among the affluent. However, this evidence does not mean that the conflict is essentially economic or material, or that economic factors are more important than (or as important as) ethno-national factors. We shall highlight the problems with some of the arguments presented above and put materialist readings of Northern Ireland in perspective. However, it is as well to state, first, the position from which we make our arguments. We share Walker Connor's judgement that analysts of national and ethnic conflicts 'have been beguiled by the fact that observable economic discrepancies are near universal concomitants of ethnic strife'.[78] This judgement does not suggest that economic discrepancies should be ignored in explaining the depth or weakness of hostility between ethnic communities, nor does it imply that public policy should ignore unjustified economic discrepancies. As Connor suggests, 'economic arguments can act as a catalyst or exacerbator of national tensions but this is something quite different than acknowledging economic deprivation as a necessary precondition of ethnonational conflict'.[79]

*The difficulties with inequality-based arguments: individual versus national recognition.* Most commentators acknowledge the existence of significant inequality between Catholics and Protestants. That most Catholics believe this gap exists because of discrimination is also widely accepted.[80] However, it is usually conceded that opposition to discrimination is not exclusively materialist but rather is also rooted in norms about justice and fair play – which is why well-to-do Catholics are as incensed about discrimination as those without jobs, and why it is difficult to separate complaints about economic discrimination from those about political or cultural oppression.

Informed controversies about economic inequalities focus on two issues: first, what causes inequality and how should it be dealt with?; and secondly, to what extent is the conflict based on inequality? With regard to the first issue a number of explanations have been put forward by academics and unionists which *apparently* do not rely on discrimination as a key cause of the employment and unemployment disparities between Catholics and Protestants:[81]

(i) More jobs are available in Protestant than in Catholic areas;

(ii) Catholics are concentrated in depressed industries to a greater extent than Protestants;

(iii) A higher proportion of Catholics than of Protestants belong to the lower socio-economic groups, which are far more likely to experience unemployment than the higher ones;

(iv) Protestants are more likely to have the skills and qualifications required for available jobs;

(v) People with low earning potential and a large number of dependent children (disproportionately Catholic) are likely to choose not to work because they derive more from welfare benefits than from employment;

(vi) The number of economically active Catholics is growing while the number of Protestants is stable;

(vii) A higher proportion of Catholics than of Protestants belong to the younger age-cohorts, which are subject to higher levels of unemployment;

(viii) A growing population (Catholics) will have a higher rate of unemployment than a static one, even if members of the two groups have the same chance of getting a job;[82] and

(ix) Differences in unemployment-rates are a result of differential employment in security-related occupations and are a result of choice rather than discrimination.

However, as Smith and Chambers point out, many of these 'explanations' take the historic background of institutionalized discrimination for granted.[83] Thus explanations (i) and (ii) accept the existence of separate labour markets without explaining why they exist; while explanations (ii), (iii), (iv), and (v), if true, establish that Catholics are disproportionately concentrated amongst the poor and the educationally disadvantaged, without providing us with any reasons why this is so. In other words, even if many of these explanations were correct, which is questionable, they are still compatible with explanations which suggest that direct and indirect discrimination are at the root of Catholics' economic disadvantages.

Some of the explanations, moreover, are simply wrong. Thus explanation (vii) faces the double difficulty that the differential in unemployment rates amongst Catholic and Protestant males remains constant across age-cohorts, *except* among the youngest cohort (aged 16–24).[84] Explanation (iv) faces the problem that the differences between Catholics and Protestants in educational qualifications cannot account for the scale of the variation in employment opportunities, and that when educational and practical qualifications are held constant, very large differences remain between Protestant and Catholic unemployment rates.[85] Locational explanations of differential employment opportunities are also effectively refuted by

Smith and Chambers:[86] throughout Northern Ireland there is a fairly uniform tendency for Catholics to have a higher chance of being unemployed than comparable Protestants. In Smith and Chambers's regression model, after socio-economic status, number of children, age, travel-to-work area, and academic or practical qualifications are taken into consideration, the difference in the rate of unemployment amongst Catholics and Protestants is reduced, compared with the actual rates, but 'for the typical group selected, the rate of unemployment predicted for Catholics is almost double the rate for Protestants in most travel-to-work areas'.[87] Smith and Chambers also calculate that if we falsely assume that all of the 26,000 security-related jobs in 1984 were held by Protestant males, and work out what would have happened if all these jobs were re-allocated on a proportional basis, then the Protestant male unemployment rate would be 18.8 per cent and the Catholic one would be 29.7 per cent, compared with the actual position in 1983–5 of 35.1 per cent for Catholics and 14.9 per cent for Protestants. Given the empirical and analytical weakness of the alternative explanations for the unemployment gap and the resulting inequalities in standards of living, Smith and Chambers's emphasis on the existence of inequality of opportunity and discrimination is entirely warranted.[88]

So far, we agree with Smith and Chambers. We also share their belief that an end to discrimination is needed to reduce minority alienation and that British efforts in this regard have not been far-reaching enough.[89] The Fair Employment Act of 1989 is a step in the right direction but it is limited in various ways: affirmative action is restricted by the duty not to discriminate, directly or indirectly. Affirmative action training programmes targeted at the minority are, therefore, effectively prohibited – even though they are permitted under comparable legislation in Great Britain. Small employers (those with under 250 employees) are not required to register with the newly created Fair Employment Commission. The monitoring provisions do not cover part-time work of less than 16 hours a week, i.e., frequently female employment. There are no targets or timetables for reducing the gap in male unemployment rates. Moreover, an explicit exemption on 'national security grounds' available for some employers may prove an extensive loophole. Finally, there are legal criticisms of the Act and of the way it is administered.[90]

We take issue, however, with Smith and Chambers's tacit argument that the conflict centres on individual inequality, and the implication that treatment of this alone will lead to a settlement. Their arguments implicitly represent a brand of liberalism based on the notion that people exist primarily as individuals with a fundamental (and moral) desire to be treated equally to others. This view is appropriate for societies where there is a consensus on national identity, such as in ethnically homogeneous states or multi-ethnic immigrant societies. In these instances, citizens usually see their relationship with the state primarily through individualist lenses and seek equality of treatment as individuals. However, in bi- or multi-national political systems, where there is no agreement on a common national political identity, matters are rather different. When the national nature of the state is at issue, many see themselves not just as bearers of individual rights but also as members of distinct national communities. Unable to grasp the importance of national identity or argue for the equal validity of rival versions of it, conventional liberalism not only fails to grasp what is at stake, it ends up accepting the nationalism, and its associated institutions, of the dominant community by default.[91] In the case of Northern Ireland, Smith and Chambers's implicit prescription requires the nationalist minority to enjoy equality as individuals within the United Kingdom. In fact, by failing to cater to or recognize what most Catholics consider integral to their conception of the good life, i.e. the appreciation, recognition and institutional equality of their national identity, this prescription would fall short of prescribing authentic equality, including equality of individual self-esteem.[92] In Northern Ireland authentic equality requires that both groups' (national) identities be accepted as equally valid and legitimate.

It is not difficult to see that it is the denial of the national identity of the minority community and the denial of its institutional recognition and equality, and not just the denial of individual rights, which fuels conflict. Minority alienation from the political process has remained intact despite the creation of institutions designed to combat discrimination and despite the provision of greater equality in the allocation of public housing and education rights. Nor has it shown much sign of dissipating in the wake of Westminster's latest anti-discrimination measures.[93] As for Smith and Chambers's reliance on a survey which shows that individual grievances are highly salient, it is not unusual for national protests to be cloaked in the language of 'personal' grievances over issues like discrimination. In the crucial act of voting, as opposed to responding to surveys, the vast majority of Catholics overwhelmingly support parties whose *raison d'être* is nationalism, rather than individual equality within the United Kingdom. Parties which espouse the latter goal, such as the APNI or the Conservative Party, receive only derisory minority support. Non-party integrationist organizations, such as the Campaign for Equal Citizenship, are overwhelmingly Protestant, and what Catholic membership they have is not representative. As for republican paramilitaries, their campaign of violence clearly has been waged over the issue of the border and Irish national self-determination rather than fair employment. Sinn Féin simply links economic inequalities to the existence of the border and the denial of Irish national self-determination. It is very unlikely that nationalist political parties will lose significant support merely if the UK government passes and implements more effective fair employment legislation – and the IRA cessation of military operations in 1994 had nothing to do with the Fair Employment Act of 1989. While we have no survey data on the relative importance which paramilitaries attribute to unemployment compared with constitutional matters, their statements rarely refer to the need for jobs as a key goal. Smith and Chambers's survey does, however, measure the attitudes of the supporters of Sinn Féin, the political wing of the IRA. Their data show that 23 per cent of SF voters felt unemployment to be the biggest 'problem' in Northern Ireland, but also reveal that 68 per cent of them chose straightforwardly nationalist responses: 'British rule' (44 per cent), 'the presence of British troops' (13 per cent), or 'the existence of the border' (11 per cent). In the table which reports responses from party supporters as to which change is needed to end the troubles, the option of a united Ireland has been accidentally omitted.[94] Elsewhere we are told, however, that nearly one half of Sinn Féin supporters thought creating a united Ireland was the change most needed.[95] It is nowhere made clear why 'equality of opportunity' within the United Kingdom will satisfy this group, especially given the fact, which Smith and Chambers recognize, that their survey, like all surveys of opinion in Northern Ireland, underestimates support for Sinn Féin.[96] It makes sense, therefore, to conclude that a comprehensive settlement of the Northern Ireland conflict, one which can incorporate the bulk of Sinn Féin's supporters, needs to address the rights and aspirations of both national communities as well as the rights and aspirations of individuals.

Unionists, for their part, are indeed firmly opposed to anti-discrimination legislation, but it would be wrong to attribute their opposition just to a vulgar materialist desire to protect privileges. They are, just as importantly, unwilling to accept that their group is guilty of unjustifiable discrimination, and very likely to believe also that Catholics' disadvantages are their own fault, rather than the consequences of discrimination. Moreover, they display a general hostility towards Catholics as Irish nationalists, the enemy within, which is as likely to motivate collective discrimination as a purely instrumental desire to protect individual jobs.

*Problems with deprivation-based arguments: the poor are not always revolting.* It is clear that paramilitary activity in Northern Ireland has been concentrated in deprived areas.[97] It is also apparent that the two most militant parties – Sinn Féin and the DUP – get disproportionate support from the underprivileged.[98] It makes sense, then, to argue that decisive steps to reverse the economic malaise which exists in Northern Ireland will help the position of moderates. This reasoning does not mean, however, that deprivation is the key or even a key cause of the politics of antagonism, conflict, or stalemate, or that a single-minded attack on it will produce a peaceful and consensual settlement. Leon Trotsky once argued that if mere deprivation explained revolutionary conduct then the masses would always be in revolt. Likewise if deprivation

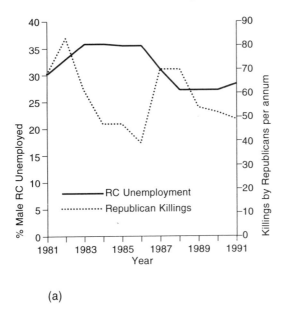

(a)

(b)

**Figure 7.1** (a) Catholic unemployment and Republican violence, 1981–94; (b) Protestant unemployment and Loyalist violence, 1981–91

alone produced paramilitary violence we would expect to see analogous activities in similarly deprived areas of English and Scottish cities. Parts of Dublin, being more deprived than parts of Belfast, would be more politically explosive. We might also expect conflict to be waged by the deprived against the privileged. Instead republican paramilitaries have more frequently attacked members of the security forces than privileged members of the 'ruling class', while loyalist paramilitaries more frequently kill members of the Catholic working class than Catholic members of the salariat.

Long-wave theory predicts that conflict and violence should be more intense in bad economic times than in good. On this reasoning British–Irish conflict would have been at its most intense during the Great Famine rather than in 1798 or 1916–21. In Northern Ireland the current conflict broke out during a period of relative economic growth, falling unemployment, and increasing prosperity, suggesting a political trigger rather than a directly economic one. Fluctuations in intensity in political violence have been more closely related to political events, internment, the deliberations of the Northern Ireland Convention, or the Anglo-Irish Agreement, for example, than to changes in the business cycle.[99] Figure 7.1 charts paramilitary killings against the male unemployment rate amongst Catholics and Protestants between 1981 and 1991, on the supposition that males are more likely than females to engage in paramilitary violence. The data suggest no clear relationship between unemployment and either republican or loyalist violence – if anything they suggest that increasing unemployment is an effective way of reducing violence![100]

Even if fluctuations in ethnic conflict and political violence were to be causally linked to changes in the economic climate, liberal economists do not pay enough attention to explaining why the fissures erupt along ethnic lines. After all, deprivation without the mobilizing glue provided by ethnic identity is more likely to be associated with apathy, self-abuse, and criminal violence rather than the organized and goal-oriented paramilitary organizations which exist in Northern Ireland. Richard Needham's view that finding work for '10,000 unemployed boys in West Belfast' is the best way to reduce the conflict, is too facile. A policy package which addresses deprivation but which does not address the national conflict is unlikely to resolve the stalemate.[101]

Relative deprivation theory is of some heuristic value in explaining the onset of violence in Northern Ireland in the late 1960s. However, it has obvious deficiencies. It is difficult to establish its empirical validity because we cannot infer psychic states of mind from objective indicators of deprivation. Moreover, at least one analyst, Christopher Hewitt, has argued that the areas in which riots and early republican paramilitary action occurred correlate better with indices measuring the degree of nationalism of the areas than they do with measures of economic deprivation.[102] That said, Hewitt's data show a very high degree of correlation between economic deprivation and measures of political violence: thus objective measures of economic deprivation and of nationalist identity are both correlated with the initial outbreaks of violence.

Secondly, while it is clear that relative deprivation theory, like Tocqueville's ideas about adaptive expectations,[103] may be useful in explaining the initial outbreaks of republican violence in 1968–70, it is less credible in explaining its persistence thereafter, and cannot successfully account for loyalist paramilitary violence. Persistent paramilitary violence requires planning and strategic foresight; it cannot merely be explained as an aggressive response to frustration. Though it is a crude but valid characterization to maintain that it is the working class who have participated in paramilitary activity,[104] British Army reports do not portray the IRA as an army of unskilled and unemployed people, and data on arrested republicans in the early 1970s also showed that they tended to be without criminal records.[105] Interviews with paramilitants, on both sides, appear to show that the sense of being collectively threatened was more important than the repercussions of individual deprivation in explaining their recruitment.[106] There is also evidence that experience of repression (internment, arrest, harrassment of self or friends) is a better explanation of the decision to join paramilitary organizations, especially republican ones, than objective deprivation.[107] By contrast, reactive violence by loyalist paramilitaries is generally carried out by people who are from objectively deprived backgrounds, but at least until recently they have regarded themselves as better off than their reference group (Catholics).

The dramatic take-off in levels of political violence in 1971–2 is better explained as the direct response to repression on the part of republican paramilitaries (reacting against internment), and to the collapse of the Stormont regime on the part of loyalists (responding to a political threat). In the former case mobilization took place against a background of increased repression, whereas in the latter it took place against the (perceived) weakness of state repression of republicans. In short, relative deprivation theory, as elsewhere, is of limited utility in explaining political violence. The work of the best known exponent of relative deprivation theories,[108] shows that his multi-variate causal models of political violence held up quite well, but that the specific role of deprivation in inducing conflict (turmoil, conspiracy or internal war) was much less important than predicted, and variables measuring past salience of conflict and the balance of forces between dissidents and the state frequently have greater explanatory power. This argument fits well with the evidence from Northern Ireland.

*Problems with some opportunism-based explanations: it little profits a paramilitary . . .* Opportunistic explanations, that the pursuit of profit underlies the conflict, or that vested interests sustain the stalemate, are also problematic. The view held by some Protestants that Catholics have engaged in conflict because it 'pays', overlooks the destruction which violence has wrought in Catholic areas and the economic plight of the Catholic community in West Belfast and border regions. Even the claim that it is individually rational for particular Catholics to engage in violence, even if it is not in the collective interest of poor Catholics, is suspect.

Rational-choice theory might suggest that paramilitary organizations are primarily rent-seeking organizations (in it for profits from protection), or offering rival services to state monopolies (such as their versions of law and order). It might, more sensibly, suggest that the outbreak of large-scale violence in 1968/9 occurred because the benefit/cost ratio suddenly rose for large numbers of people as it became clear that the security-resources of the Stormont regime were either exhausted or incapable of being mobilized with full rigour. Moreover, rational-choice theory would appear to be capable, in principle, of resolving an apparent paradox in the empirical literature on political violence.[109] The paradox is that deterrence appears to work in some circumstances, and yet appears not to work in others, i.e. repression by regimes may either reduce or escalate dissent by opposition groups – as happened after the introduction of internment in August 1971. The rational-choice resolution of this paradox is that because of rational cost–benefit calculations an increase in a government's repression of non-violence results in an increase in the violent activities of an opposition group – as happened amongst nationalists after 1969–71. In other words, dissident groups are seen as 'price-takers'; their budgetary constraint is the amount of repression they are willing to incur to obtain the government output they desire. The balance of effects, that is, whether an increase in repression increases or decreases the opposition group's total dissident activities, depends upon the government's accommodative policy to the group. Government accommodative and repressive policies which are consistent work, whereas inconsistent policies produce dissent.[110]

Although aesthetically appealing, this model rests on a set of assumptions which clearly do not apply in Northern Ireland. It assumes that the opposition is a unitary actor which is easily capable of choosing between non-violent and violent activities – and that the regime is a unitary actor. Moreover, republican paramilitaries primarily have sought one governmental output: the termination of British government in the region, rather than a series of particular public policies – though the IRA's recent cessation of military operations suggests that they may settle for less in the short to medium term. While correctly emphasizing the instrumental rationality of paramilitary violence, that is, treating it as goal-oriented rather than as merely reactive to frustration, the rational-choice approach to individual participation in paramilitary organizations is very implausible. The IRA, the INLA, the UDA, and the UVF have required recruits willing to risk their lives or very long prison sentences for a very short career as a terrorist, and therefore non-egoistic motivations appear to be essential to sustain recruitment and retention of activists. On the pure rational-choice model nobody should have joined the IRA or the UDA because no single participant could rationally expect his or her participation significantly to affect the output of the organization's actions. It appears that, as with voters, such participants are mission-committed rather than driven by narrow personal interests.

The claim that the pursuit of personal profit has been an important motive for paramilitaries downplays their national motivations. It is mistaken to imagine that becoming a para-military represented a good 'career move'. Paramilitaries have faced a high probability of incarceration, a life on the run, surveillance by their own organization, which will kill them if it suspects them of being informers, and constant sur-veillance of themselves and their families by the state.[111] As Bishop and Mallie show, life as an IRA volunteer was hardly designed to appeal to those interested in maximizing profits.[112] Paramilitaries engaged in the 'pursuit of happiness' were likely to incur the wrath of their colleagues in addition to that of the security forces. Unlike mobsters, they have had political goals and react to political stimuli. They receive more support from their respective communities than those significantly engaged in criminal activities, and both sets have been famously resistant to prison management techniques that criminals normally accept without rancour: it is often forgotten that loyalist paramilitaries also went 'on the blanket' to win recognition as political prisoners.[113] Suggesting that significant elements among the paramilitaries are opportunistic criminals overlooks the 'contribution' of the security forces to the popu-larity of paramilitarism, and encourages the delusion that the conflict can be contained by anti-criminal or anti-racketeering measures. Even the government itself, between 1972 and 1976, recognized explicitly the inadequacy of treating the paramilitaries as mere criminals, and abandoned this policy only for reasons of expediency. We would put forward a very different thesis: a constitutional resolution of the conflict may actually lead to an increase in criminality or racketeering as unemployable paramilitary soldiers opt for a life of crime after the termination of their military campaign. This viewpoint also appears to be held by the RUC, fighting for its budget since the cessation of paramilitary violence.[114]

Protection rackets, of course, have been organized by both sets of paramilitaries, as well as construction rackets in which 'ghost employees' are paid for work. But the proceeds have mostly been directed towards political goals, and are even regarded as 'legitimate taxation' by some within their respective communities.[115] Personal criminal racketeering has been relatively rare among paramilitaries, especially on the republican side – and may have been no more pervasive than white collar crime amongst the middle classes. When the small-scale INLA started to peddle drugs to raise funds they were 'closed down' by the Provisional IRA. While the loyalist side has had its notorious gangsters, like James Craig and Artie McFee, they are less prevalent now than in the past. Since McFee's incarceration and Craig's murder (by his own side) in the late 1980s, the UDA/UFF has been taken over by young Turks eager to restore the organization's political integrity. The change of guard resulted in a significant increase in loyalist violence in the early 1990s (see figure 6.1, p. 260), which suggests that political motivations have been more lethal than criminal ones.[116] Finally, it is worth observing that Northern Ireland has had the lowest per capita levels of criminal violence but the highest levels of political or ethnic violence in the UK, and that the conflict over the last twenty-five years has not produced the 'societal disintegration' associated with the triumph of anarchic and anomic criminality in some of the world's cities, evidence which further underlines the national and political nature of the conflict.[117]

We accept, by contrast, a less widespread view, and one which made us no friends amongst the professional middle classes or the security forces in Northern Ireland, namely that the structure of British public policy from 1974 onwards offered perverse incentives for conflict-resolution. The costs of the conflict have been borne by the British tax-payer; the Northern Irish economy has been cushioned by the subvention; and social spending undertaken by the British government to dampen down conflict has accrued, in part, to public-sector professionals, who have enjoyed the combination of British salary levels (or better than British rates of pay in the case of the police and social workers) and the relatively low cost of Northern Irish housing. This pattern of economic incentives diminished the interest of the middle class in conflict-regulation. They have been quarantined from the costs of conflict, and in some cases, unintentionally, benefited from it. Without suggesting exact analogies, it is interesting to observe that because Afrikaners bore at least some of the costs of conflict in South Africa they had economic incentives to come to a comprehensive deal with black South Africans, while Israeli Jews, cushioned by massive American aid, have had less economic incentives to come to a comprehensive settlement with Palestinians. The prescriptive implication of this argument is not that Northern Ireland should be subjected to trade sanctions – although external investment should be withheld from unfair employers – but rather that policy-making should ensure that the locally more privileged sections of the community bear some of the cost of security in the region, which would at least give them some positive economic incentives to reach a comprehensive political settlement. One way to achieve this objective, whatever constitutional design is adopted for Northern Ireland, is to have a local 'security tax'.[118]

*Does nationalism have a material basis?* Nationalism has a social psychological basis rather than a purely or largely materialist foundation. National identity is rooted in a sense of community with one's co-nationals and a sense of distinctiveness from others. Such an identity may be formed through shared historical and geographical experiences. It is facilitated by a common culture, or language, or religion. It is strongest amongst those who are or imagine themselves to be a kinship group. Shared material experiences, such as deprivation or discrepancies in income accruing to different communities, may be used by ethnic mobilizers and entrepreneurs to strengthen national identity and to heighten secessionist sentiments, or indeed to provoke animosity towards non-national outgroups. However, the relevant identity must already exist, if only in prototype, if these arguments are to have meaning and to be persuasive. Moreover, understandings of material experiences are likely to be ethno-national, and for this reason may be rooted in perception as much as they are rooted in fact.

Considering Northern Ireland in comparative perspective is important here. National separatists elsewhere in the world often put forward an economic case for secession, just as political unionists offer contrary economic arguments. These claims are not irrelevant. When the economic advantages of union are clear-cut, and ethnic animosities low-key, they may strengthen unionist sentiment among ethnic minorities – as in Newfoundland's decision to join Canada in 1949, or in the eventual decision of the Danes to support the Maastricht Treaty on European Union. But even here the decisions to join were very close-run things. In numerous other instances, national minorities have campaigned or fought for secession when its economic consequences have been unpredictable, and even when it has been clear that it would entail significant costs: most secessionist movements in Africa and Asia have involved regions which, in Horowitz's words, 'stood to lose economically from autonomy or independence'.[119] Secessionist movements are no respector of Mammon, and nationalist movements plainly offer much non-economic utility to their supporters.

It also seems unlikely that material factors decisively determine the strength of unionist resistance to secession-ist movements. More important factors include the ethnic make-up of the seceding area and whether it forms an integral part of the national territory. Thus the secession of Slovenia was tolerated by 'Yugoslavia', despite the economic losses involved, because it was almost devoid of Serbs. The violently contested secessions of Croatia and Bosnia owed most to the existence of large Serbian minorities in both entities, rather than to any obvious economic calculus – both regions were poorer than Slovenia. Any vigorous bid in Kosovo to secede from the rump Yugolsav state will also be vehemently resisted, despite the clear economic arguments for ditching it, precisely because it is 'nationally sacred', the reputed ancestral heartland of Serbs. Finally, many irredentist claims exist over areas with few resources to contribute to national well-being. Enthusiasm for 're-union' with a sundered national territory may be tempered if huge costs are involved, but ethnic groups are usually prepared to make considerable material sacrifices to reunite a 'national territory' and its people. While West Germans may have been unaware of the full cost of German unity, few can have thought that the costs would be trivial. Moreover, it was the political feasibility of German unification rather than its economic feasibility which determined shifts in public opinion on the subject between the 1950s and the 1980s; and once it became politically feasible it was overwhelmingly supported in both prosperous and poor parts of Germany. We might expect the same to occur if Korean reunification becomes feasible.

*Immaterialism in Irish Nationalism.* The comparative evidence that ethnic groups are often prepared to put self-determination before materialism can be readily applied to Ireland. It seems unlikely that Irish nationalists sought independence before 1921 for primarily economic reasons. Separatist sentiment increased after the British government had settled the fundamental economic grievances of the Irish peasantry in the Wyndham Land Act of 1903.[120] While Sinn Féin, like nationalists everywhere then and now, mounted an economic case for independence, separatist sentiment soared during the First World War, even though the Irish economy benefited from the first years of the war. 'Blocked social mobility' is important in accounting for the rise of Sinn Féin, but these blockages were political and cultural as well as economic.[121] In any case Sinn Féin's argument for protectionism could hardly directly motivate many when Catholic Ireland had no significant industry to protect. It was, rather, overwhelmingly agricultural, and its markets were integrally linked to Great Britain. In Ireland, as in Slovakia, a better economic case existed for maintaining the existing union than for separating. And, after the rapid development of the British welfare state, with its commitment to redistribution of wealth from rich to poor regions, economically motivated nationalists should have been suing for re-union with the UK rather than continuing to take pride in their independence.

As for contemporary northern nationalists, their support for Irish national unification or for a direct role for the Republic in the affairs of Northern Ireland exists in spite of the advantages of the British welfare state and the relative poverty of the Republic. In Richard Rose's loyalty survey of 1967, 66 per cent of Catholics indicated that they wished to abolish the border but only 13 per cent thought it would make economic conditions better – 68 per cent thought it would make no difference or would make matters worse.[122] There is little reason to believe that contemporary republicans or SDLP voters are under any illusions that Irish national unification will make them more prosperous, immediately or in the medium term, but knowledge of where their 'true economic interests' allegedly lie does not appear to affect their voting behaviour.

*Immaterialism amongst Unionists.* Unionist enthusiasm for the Union is reinforced by sound economic arguments, but is hardly determined by an economic rationale. Historic prosperity based on close economic links with Britain helps explain why Protestants became vehement unionists during the nineteenth century, but other reasons were also important. Support for unionism was also related, for example, to the threat posed by Catholic emancipation and the ensuing link of home rule with native or Catholic domination in an autonomous Ireland. While the present massive British subvention may seem reason enough for the existence of unionism, it should not be crudely deconstructed to explain why the Protestants are unionists (most Catholics are not, even though they share in some of the benefits of the subvention). For one thing the subvention was not always as big as at present. In fact, when Northern Ireland was created, no subvention was envisaged, and it was expected to contribute to 'imperial' activities such as defence as well as to pay exclusively for devolved functions.[123]

Opinion polls continue to indicate that Protestants have diverse reasons for opposing a united Ireland.[124] While 43 per cent of Protestant respondents to Rose's survey claimed that the economic effect of abolishing the border would be to 'make conditions worse', a more surprising (given the economic evidence) 32 per cent thought it 'would make no difference', while a remarkable 3 per cent thought it would 'make conditions better'.[125] Given that practically all Protestants (then as now) opposed a united Ireland, their opposition clearly went beyond a preoccupation with living standards. An ethnic group which seeks to maintain its right to self-determination may not be swayed by the pocket-book. The survival of the Protestant people of Ulster and their culture, which has both religious and secular elements, and shades of both national Britishness and regional parochialism, is not seen to be possible in a united Ireland. Economic arguments against a united Ireland merely reinforce unionists' pre-existing national preferences. It is unlikely, therefore, that even a very significant improvement in the Republic's economic performance will persuade a critical mass of unionists to convert to nationalism. It is also doubtful that they could be compelled to accept a united Ireland through the application of rigid British sanctions.[126] Far from being quick to sue for peace, in these circumstances Protestants would be more likely to tighten their belts and fight, as their cultural and political survival would be perceived to be at stake. In this scenario sanctions would be no more liable to bring Protestants scurrying to the negotiating table than they have been in convincing Bosnian Serbs to sue for peace in the Balkans.

*Immaterialism amongst the Great British and in the Republic.* The British government and public's ambivalent attitude towards the Union cannot be attributed mainly to the subsidization of Northern Ireland. British ambivalence preceded the present massive growth in the subvention; even Winston Churchill, albeit ambiguously, offered Northern Ireland to de Valera in 1940.[127] If large subsidies determined the attachment of the British core to peripheral regions, there should be a similar level of ambivalence about links with parts of Scotland, Wales and northern England. There is not. These examples suggest that it is the fact that the Great British do not consider Northern Ireland to be fully British – an integral part of the British nation – which explains why they lack the sense of obligation necessary for redistributive policies to be sustained without complaint. In any case while the British public's ambivalence may be partly related to the 'costs' of staying in Northern Ireland it also has other sources, such as doubts about the legitimacy of Britain's presence in Ireland, and perceptions of costs of a non-economic nature, such as the threat to life and convenience posed by Irish terrorism in Britain, deaths of British soldiers in a war without end, and so on.

As for the Republic, the most politically relevant aspect of public irredentism is not that it weakens when the costs are considered, but rather that it still has widespread popular and elite support *despite* the acknowledged costs of running a united Ireland. Harvey Cox found, for example, that 45 per cent of the Republic's electorate were 'ultra unificationists, people prepared to opt for Irish unity come what may, despite costs and regardless of alternatives'. The same survey found 68 per cent support for a united Ireland as 'the most acceptable and workable solution' and that 78 per cent favoured an 'agreed' British withdrawal.[128] Regardless of the regularly pronounced hopes of unionist-inclined commentators, these figures and subsequent polls conducted in the late 1980s and early 1990s, and the position of every major party in the Republic (with the possible exception of the Progressive Democrats), suggest that the Republic's political leaders are no more free to abandon their ethnic compatriots, northern nationalists, than are Serbian or Turkish leaders free to abandon their co-ethnics in Bosnia and Cyprus, respectively. Even a dilution of the Republic's constitutional claim over Northern Ireland, the transformation of Articles 2 and 3 into aspirational rather than imperative forms, will require an overall political settlement which has the support of northern nationalists. The reason is that the Republic's leaders calculate, correctly, that their citizens are not as revisionist or as materialist as the Dublin intelligentsia. Moreover, to the extent that the Republic's citizenry is anxious to distance itself from Northern Ireland this distancing has significant non-economic dimensions; it requires little imagination to foresee the institutional disruption and potential instability which would be occasioned by the incorporation of a recalcitrant national minority into the Irish state. The intensity of irredentist feeling in the Republic has undoubtedly been reduced by the twenty-five years of armed conflict in the North, but we think that economic considerations are of secondary significance in explaining this shift. In any case, we believe that if perceptions of the political rather than the economic feasibility of Irish national unification were to increase, through some combination of a growth in the population of northern nationalists, a significant shift in the attitudes of Ulster Protestants, and a British willingness to depart without occasioning instability, then the emotional enthusiasm for re-unification in the Republic would swamp more pragmatic economic calculations.

*Will Euro-manna provide a way out of the stalemate?* There is little substantive comparative proof that increased economic transactions or increasing economic interdependence between warring national or ethnic factions dramatically softens their rivalries. If matters were otherwise, it would be difficult to explain the existence of bitter ethnic animosities within states – many of which are long established and are tightly integrated economic zones. The experience of the EC since 1958 shows as much that groups which have overcome their rivalry can then proceed to increase trade, as it proves that increased trade removes animosity between warring groups. Conversely, strong ethnic rivalries and insecurities can prevent increased economic integration or reverse it, as the European Union may yet discover.

Nor is there much evidence that the discovery of even substantial common economic interests and a decision to co-operate in advancing them need affect the *political* preferences of rival ethnic groups. Common economic interests are no more likely to produce a common political identity among antagonistic ethnic groups than common class interests, common workplace interests, or common residence in a particular economic region. While some ethnic groups may be willing to integrate both politically and economically with others, the more ethnically defensive can support economic co-operation while resisting political integration. The support of Danes for the Maastricht Treaty, for example, depended heavily on its backers convincing Danish voters that they could have the benefits of the former without the risks of the latter. In Canada, even the most vociferous government backer of North American economic integration would not dare associate it with political integration with the USA. The

nationally insecure often block economic co-operation altogether, even while acknowledging that this is against their
economic interests, if it poses risks to their political identity.
Many of these comparative points apply with particular force
to Northern Ireland. It should be noted, first, that the already
significant reduction in economic barriers which has taken
place between Northern Ireland and the Republic since the
1960s, and especially since both the UK and Republic joined
the EC in 1973, has done nothing to overcome unionist–
nationalist rivalries. In fact, while protectionist policies were
pursued by the Fianna Fáil government between the 1930s
and 1950s Northern Ireland was characterized by relative
stability, and in contrast the current episode of protracted
violent conflict has occurred simultaneously with a reduction
in trade barriers. It is therefore fair to say that there has been
a closer correlation between peace and economic segregation
between the North and the South than between peace and
increasing economic integration.

In Northern Ireland, unionist leaders have varied between
rejecting economic co-operation with the Republic because
of the associated political risks and animosities, and supporting economic co-operation to further common economic
interests, while insisting strenuously on the maintenance of
the Union in an unadulterated form. The former position
is associated with militant loyalists: for example, those who
reject Kinsale gas just because it comes from the Republic.
The latter position is associated with moderates, and formed
the basis of O'Neill's co-operation with Lemass and more
recent discussions about a Dublin–Belfast economic corridor.
Unionists who presently concede the potential economic benefits of north–south co-operation are careful to stipulate that
this can only be negotiated by a Northern Ireland executive
which is exclusively unionist or in which unionists clearly
predominate. In response to nationalist calls for north–south
joint economic ventures, the unionist economist Tom Wilson
stipulates that these can and should take place without changes
in the border.[129] Similarly, when 'Euro-optimists' refer to the
co-operation which takes place among Northern Ireland's
MEPs as evidence of the integrating effect of the EU, they

often fail to note that the co-operation is on economic matters only and occurs alongside undiluted political intransigence on the national question.[130] In fact, it is as easy to point to how the rival camps have used the EC as a platform for their rival and irreconcilable political aspirations as it is to refer to their co-operative endeavours in the economic field.[131] The current support from the unionist business community for co-operative ventures and economic integration in the context of the Single Economic Market is not, as the *Irish News* contends, implicit support for Irish unity. Rather, as Anderson and Shuttleworth argue, it is clearly support which is expressed for economic integration as an end in itself.[132]

There is also no evidence that European integration has significantly diluted the ethnic identities of the respective camps or given rise to a transcendent European identity. To the extent that a Euro-identity has emerged it is confined to the intelligentsia, but even here ethnic backgrounds are often telling: with those from Protestant backgrounds, like Robin Wilson, seeing European Union as a means of avoiding tampering with the border, while those from Catholic backgrounds, like Mark Durkan, Chairman of the SDLP, see European Union as a way of abolishing the border.[133] Both communities, as indicated earlier in this chapter, still regard the EC almost exclusively through ethnically partisan lenses. Rather than promoting accommodation, European integration has increased unionist insecurities and reinforced their intransigence. Religious fundamentalists in the DUP regard the EU as a popish-inspired plot to extirpate Protestantism and could never give their support to an institution whose founding document was entitled the 'Treaty of Rome'.[134] They and more secular unionists fear that support by the British government for increased economic co-operation with the Republic is an attempt to create their 'voluntary' consent to a united Ireland as foreseen in the Anglo-Irish Agreement.[135] Rather than learning accommodative practices or mentalities from the European countries which have overcome their animosities, as the SDLP hopes, the unionists so far see themselves as captive participants in an integration project over which they have no control. The Ulster Unionist Party backed the Maastricht

Treaty in the Westminster parliament not through conviction but because they thought the alternatives would be worse – a collapse of the government and the election of a Labour government seeking the unification of Ireland by consent – and because they believed they could thereby have a British prime minister in their debt for the lifetime of a parliament. However, unionists are very aware that the EC – which offered support for the Haagerup Report and the Anglo-Irish Agreement and treats Ireland as one unit for the purposes of disbursing certain EC funds – has member states which are more sympathetic to Irish nationalism than Ulster unionism. They feel increasingly besieged as British sovereignty is whittled away to Brussels and as the border becomes less important. Some are coming to advocate not closer relations with the Republic within the context of the SEM but an independent Northern Ireland within a 'Europe of the Regions', in which Ulster Protestants could protect their identity.[136]

Nor is there much evidence that northern nationalists are becoming 'new Europeans' who have transferred their loyalties to Brussels, or that European integration has increased the acceptability of the Union with Great Britain. The concept of a sovereign Irish nation-state remains alive and well in the nationalist vision of an integrated Europe. In this sense, they are like minority nationalists in other parts of the European Union, like the Scots, or the Basques, supporting European integration for politically instrumental purposes.[137] Hume in particular has played the European card well – and realizes that, as in America, there is more sympathy for the nationalist than the unionist cause in Europe.[138]

These considerations do not mean that the EU will have no effect on Northern Ireland. Where the EU has made a difference is not in reconciling the warring factions within Northern Ireland but in facilitating better working relations between the Republic and the United Kingdom. Ireland's membership of the EC and the EU, including the European Commission, and its veto powers over community policy, have made it a political force which the UK is less likely to ignore, and the two states have often shared similar perspectives on the high politics of European economic policy. Numerous meetings in Euro-institutions have given both governments additional opportunities to discuss their joint interests, including Northern Ireland. These factors, combined with pressures from the European Parliament, and the precedent of sovereignty-dilution involved in EC membership, played some role in disposing Westminster civil servants and Conservative politicians to sign the Anglo-Irish Agreement. This logic may continue. Evolving British–Irish relations, and the pooling of sovereignty within the context of the EU may well lead to even closer co-operation, including pooling sovereignty over Northern Ireland. Unionists will not like this, especially if it is portrayed as a prelude towards a united Ireland, but it is doubtful that they will be able to stop it. There remains the possibility that they will make concessions from a position of weakness – agreeing to some all-Ireland institutions in return for safeguards of one sort or another – but this form of 'bargained agreement' should not be confused with the voluntary variety at the centre of economic integrationist thinking, or of the wishful form of neo-functionalism espoused by Euro-enthusiasts.

## Conclusion

The Northern Ireland conflict has been waged paramilitarily and politically between two communities with different national identities, not between two aggregates of individuals mainly interested in promoting their economic well-being. Economic factors have impinged upon the conflict, but they do not determine it. Recognizing the importance of national identity rather than materialist deconstructions of people's identities requires analysts to listen to what the political representatives of both communities say about themselves rather than what they (and outsiders) say about each other. The biases and pitfalls of the latter approaches need to be underlined. While some Irish nationalists allege that Protestants are unionists for economic reasons, they would never concede that they themselves should fully integrate with the United Kingdom if this was in their economic interests. Unionist integrationists, by contrast, argue that Catholics should be happy with equality of opportunity and prosperity in the UK, but they themselves would never accept the same offer within a united Ireland. What people say about themselves matters. When a conflict is really over economic matters, as with employee–employer conflicts, for example, the contestants have no difficulty in admitting that their concerns are economic.

Resolving the Northern Ireland conflict, therefore, must involve steps to tackle the conflict of rival nationalisms and rival political identities as well as addressing the region's economic problems. Affirmative action, economic growth, anti-racketeering offensives, cross-border economic co-operation, the promotion of more competitive enterprises, and European economic integration, while welcome for a host of plausible reasons, must be welcomed for their own sake, but it must always be remembered that at best they will fall short of what is required to resolve the conflict, and at worst they may even deflect attention and energy from the crucial political measures necessary to change the logic of the cruel game in which the participants are presently trapped.

# Part III

---

# Synthesis and Futures

# 8

# No Place Apart: Comparative Political Analysis

Why was Ireland so sensitive an issue in English politics? It was, of course, our postern gate through which foreign enemies – first the Spaniards, then the French sought to attack us. It was to us what Poland was to Prussia once Prussia was strong and Poland weak; and through fear we treated it similarly: colonisation, expropriation, discrimination, partition. The response too was similar: exasperated nationalism inflamed by religious difference, religious difference inflamed in turn by awakened nationalism.

*Hugh Trevor Roper, British historian*[1]

Because Northern Ireland politics differs so much from the Anglo-American ideal, it may provide better insights into world-wide problems of authority than a study of England, America or New Zealand.

*Richard Rose, American political scientist*[2]

We tried to answer, spoke of Arab, Jew,
of Turk and Greek in Cyprus, Pakistan
and India; but no sense flickered through
that offered reason to a modern man
why Europeans, Christians, working-class
should thresh and struggle in that old morass.

*John Hewitt, Ulster poet*[3]

Practically all the explanations we have discussed consider Northern Ireland in isolation, even though they may emphasize exogenous sources of conflict, and even though their exponents may work with implicit comparative explanations in mind. However, only 'fundamentalist historians' would insist on the uniqueness and the incomparability of Northern Ireland. Such historians are no longer as numerous as they once were, and as the above quotation from Hugh Trevor Roper suggests, historians are more than capable of drawing insightfully upon comparative analysis. It should be transparent that national, ethnic and religious conflict, economic inequality, political instability and political violence are not unique to Northern Ireland, a point which is not lost on nationalists and unionists, who frequently provide comparative interpretations designed to win sympathy for their position.

*Nationalist comparisons: Britain's first colony and Britain's first blacks.* Republicans depict Northern Ireland as a colony, like other British colonies, and argue that it has never been a candidate for integration into the British nation, like Scotland and Wales. This comparison dovetails with the view that the conflict is unfinished business left over from the imperial era, and would be resolved by a British withdrawal. According to Adrian Guelke, the international community accepts the analogy, which is why republicans are winning the international propaganda struggle.[4] There is some evidence that the British accept the view that Northern Ireland is a colony, despite the occasional protestations by British prime ministers like Margaret Thatcher that it is 'as British as Finchley'. Otherwise it would be difficult to explain British public opinion, the peculiar constitutional status of Northern Ireland, the exclusion clauses in the Prevention of Terrorism Act, the unwillingness of the Labour and Liberal Democratic parties to organize and compete in elections in Northern Ireland, or, in the case of the Conservatives, to organize enthusiastically.[5] Regular slips by British political elites indicate that many of them think of Northern Ireland in a colonial context, and certainly contexts in which it is not British and is seen as 'foreign': Reginald Maudling warned when considering Northern Ireland that the constitution of Britain is not 'easily exportable';[6] Peter Brooke later declared that the British experience in Cyprus had taught him that one should 'never say never' about political possibilities; Jim Callaghan suggested in 1969, again comparing Northern Ireland with Cyprus, that it was much easier to get involved in these conflicts than to get out of them,[7] an argument apparently repeated by Douglas Hurd nearly twenty-five years later, when he counselled European Union foreign ministers that they should avoid military intervention in Bosnia for fear of having a protracted commitment like Northern Ireland on their hands. The last piece of advice was most instructive, suggesting that *external* intervention in Bosnia was comparable with Britain's allegedly *internal* intervention in Northern Ireland.

More radical republicans drew analogies between Northern Ireland and Vietnam at the end of the 1960s and the beginning of the 1970s:[8] 'Britain's Vietnam' was a refrain also popular with the British ultra-left. Republicans also drew analogies between Northern Ireland and South Africa.[9] Expressions of solidarity with the ANC (in wall murals, for example) have been commonplace in republican districts.[10] The analogy is accurate to a limited extent – in both cases ethnically exclusive governments have oppressed their ethnic rivals. It also makes sense from a propaganda perspective, as South Africa has until recently been *the* international pariah. And there is evidence that the analogy is accepted by others, including Nelson Mandela. The MacBride principles, adopted to promote regulation of American investment in Northern Ireland, were modelled on the Sullivan principles established to govern trade between the USA and South Africa. The analogy is inexact in so far as Northern Ireland was a site for majoritarian oppression of a minority, rather than 'minoritarian' oppression of a majority, and because the minority was not formally excluded from citizenship. It also poses problems for republicans, as the South African conflict has been in part a conflict between natives and settlers, rather than between a nation and foreign imperialists. There are some black nationalists in South Africa (particularly in the Pan African Congress) and some republicans in Northern Ireland who regard their ethnic enemies as aliens ripe for 'repatriation' on the nearest available boats or aeroplanes, but these 'arguments' are incompatible with the formally dominant ideology in Sinn Féin (and the ANC) which is civic and inclusive.

Moderate nationalists are more likely to compare Northern Ireland with the deep South of the USA between the 1880s and the 1950s. Here the key comparison is the extent to which the local majority (whites or Ulster Protestants) abused their political position to control the local minority (blacks or northern Catholics) through systematic gerrymandering, manipulations of the franchise, economic discrimination, cultural oppression, and ethnically partisan policing and administration of 'justice'. In both case the central authorities (the Westminster government, the federal institutions in Washington) turned a blind eye to their political backyards until civil-rights movements developed in the 1960s. This comparison, popular amongst reformist northern nationalists, was not merely abstract: the Northern Ireland Civil Rights Association modelled its campaign in the 1960s on its American counterpart, demanding reforms of the voting system, public administration, policing, and justice; and used the same methods of protest – non-violent marches through previously 'no go' areas (dominated by whites or Protestants) – to expose the ethnic partisanship of local state institutions. The major difference between these cases is that most blacks were not nationalists, of either the militant or the constitutional variety, whereas most northern Catholics were.[11]

*Unionist comparisons: victims of irredentism.* Unionists reject the colonial comparisons favoured by nationalists. They depict Northern Ireland as a victim of irredentism and external aggression. James Molyneaux has compared Northern Ireland with Kuwait, casting the former Irish prime minister Charles Haughey in the role of Saddam Hussein, while his colleague Chris McGimpsey has compared Northern Ireland with the Sudetenland, and compared the Anglo-Irish Agreement with Munich – casting Irish nationalists as irredentist Germans and Ulster Protestants as doughty liberal Czechs.[12] Unionist academics are more sophisticated. Anthony Alcock, in an exemplary re-statement of traditional unionism, uses the comparative method to justify unionists' intransigence, their unwillingness to extend rights and benefits to the minority, and their refusal to share power. He argues that Finnish, Italian, Swiss, Spanish, and French majorities only granted autonomy to the Aland islands, the South Tyrol, the Bernese Jura, Euskadi, Catalonia, and Corsica because 'state boundaries were mutually recognized and thus minorities generally ceased to be seen [as] threats to the territorial integrity of states.'[13] In Cyprus and Northern Ireland, by contrast, no reconciliation has been possible because there has been no consensus on territorial boundaries:[14] it is therefore the Republic's irredentism and British ambivalence about Northern Ireland which prevents effective conflict-resolution.

*The case for comparison.* Neither nationalists nor unionists are wrong to put Northern Ireland in comparative perspective. Their specific comparisons, however, tend to be partisan. One splendid illustration occurred when the Berlin Wall came down. John Taylor of the UUP maintained that it showed that an agreement could not be imposed on a people (he had the Anglo-Irish Agreement in mind), Mitchell McLaughlin of Sinn Féin said that it showed the need to end an externally imposed partition, John Hume of the SDLP declared that it showed that progress (presumably towards national unification) could be made without violence, while the editor of *Fortnight* magazine, Robin Wilson, called for 'people power' to overthrow the established frameworks of authority (presumably in favour of civic integration and civic democracy?).[15]

Comparison is a key way of overcoming ethnocentricity, and even where comparisons are discovered to be inappropriate they may be as revealing as those in which directly persuasive analogies can be advanced. Case-studies can also falsify general propositions, or lead to their refinement. We have already argued, in chapters 2, 4 and 7, that the general bias amongst liberals and Marxists towards economic or materialist explanations of conflict fails to illuminate key features of Northern Ireland. Moreover we possess the bias of our profession – we seek, *where possible*, to establish explanations which do not assume the uniqueness, particularity or incomparability of social phenomena. The variations in the scale of national and ethnic antagonisms, political instability, and political violence have led many scholars to develop political explanations of these phenomena, which are then tested – or left open to testing – through comparative political analysis.

This chapter explores the merits of some of these theories for understanding Northern Ireland. Among the most prominent explanations of political instability are classical pluralist theory, consociational theory, linkage theory, and state-building theory. There is also a number of 'middle range' or regionally delimited comparative explanations of political instability and violence pertinent to Northern Ireland – particularly modernization theory, nation-building theory, and settler colonial theory, which we shall incorporate in our discussion of the more prominent approaches.

Classical pluralist theory was developed by a number of political scientists and political sociologists. Sometimes known as 'cross-pressure theory', it explains political instability by the absence of a balanced distribution of conflicting interests. Such instability is likely to occur when social divisions, whether they be racial, linguistic, religious or economic, reinforce rather than cross-cut one another, when for instance memberships in different voluntary associations are cumulative rather than overlapping. Cross-pressure theory is rooted in the pluralist view that political stability is facilitated by the dispersal or fragmentation of interests.[16] 'Consociational' or power-sharing theorists put greater emphasis on political institutions and the statecraft of politicians in explaining political stability or instability. For them, political instability results from the unwillingness or the inability of political elites to negotiate and maintain political compromise, and they have specific theories to explain power-sharing failures and successes. Linkage theory, developed at the interface of comparative politics and international relations, seeks to explain the domestic stability (or instability) of states by focusing on the external or inter-state arena, or to explain inter-state stability (or instability) through focusing on the domestic arena of the states in question. In our language, it relates exogenous and endogenous causes. The linkage approach to explaining internal conflicts is critical of the tendency of many comparative political analysts to downplay or ignore exogenous factors. Finally, state-building theory definitionally attributes political stability to state-building success, and instability to state-building failure. State-building success may be the result of social, technological, political or economic factors, or some combination of these, depending on the perspective taken. Those who stress economic factors attribute successful state-building to the diffusion of economic forces and markets throughout the regime which break down parochial boundaries, create transcendent social formations, and force economic interdependence. State-building failure results conversely from the absence of such dynamic economic penetration.

Developers of these four bodies of theory include the cream of political scientists and specialists in international relations, and not surprisingly scholars have turned to their ideas to help explain instability in Northern Ireland. Thus cross-pressure theory has been applied to Northern Ireland by Richard Rose, Edmund Aunger, and by Ian Budge and Cornelius O'Leary; consociational theory by Arend Lijphart and ourselves; linkage theory, at least implicitly, by Claire Sterling, Dervla Murphy, Jack Holland, Frank Wright, Adrian Guelke, Jennifer Todd, Joe Ruane, Tom Hadden, and Kevin Boyle; while state-building theory has been developed by Ian Lustick for pre-1920 Ireland (and adapted by us to account for certain developments in Northern Ireland), and comparative studies of settler colonialism have also been made by Michael MacDonald, Ronald Weitzer, Barry Schutz, Douglas Scott, and Donald Akenson.[17] In this chapter we summarize how these theories have been used and then scrutinize them.

## Classical Pluralist Explanations

A number of political scientists explain political instability in democracies by reference to the absence of cross-cutting social cleavages or overlapping memberships in voluntary associations. The intuitive idea is that stability is reinforced when social divisions are cross-cutting, such as when an individual is divided from another by language but linked by class, or when associational memberships are overlapping, for example when a political party is drawn from more than one group. In these circumstances individuals are subjected to constant cross-pressures which are supposed to moderate political attitudes and facilitate compromise. Whenever conflicts occur they are seldom explosive, as they develop along different axes and involve changing coalitions. On the other hand, when social divisions are reinforcing or when voluntary associations are drawn from just one group, democratic instability is likely. In this situation, there are no shifting coalitions, and conflicts always range the same group against the other.[18]

Pluralist theory has been endorsed by a number of prominent American political scientists, including Robert Dahl and Seymour Martin Lipset. In 1972, Eric Nordlinger described the cross-pressures account of the causes of stability and instability as 'probably the explanatory hypothesis most widely accepted among American political scientists'.[19] The intuitions behind cross-pressures theory are driven by the contrasting American experience of the white immigrant 'melting pot' and the more explosive black and white racial conflict historically rooted in slavery. It is not surprising that cross-pressure theory shaped the first political science research on instability in Northern Ireland. It provides the main intellectual thrust behind Richard Rose's major text *Governing without Consensus: An Irish Perspective* – although his book is also associated with the thesis of the special 'non-bargainability' of religiously rooted conflict. Rose classifies Northern Ireland as 'a divided regime', having distinguished regimes by their degree of support – by which he means 'a diffuse feeling that the institutions of a regime merit positive endorsement'[20] – and by the degree to which they secure compliance, or the obedience of their subjects to basic political laws. He argues that there are four extreme ideal-typical regimes: the fully legitimate, the coercive, the isolated, and the repudiated (see table 8.1). Most political systems are arguably moving towards one or other of these extremes, although movement into the repudiated form is irreversible. Regimes like that which prevailed in Northern Ireland before 1972 are best understood as 'divided': they secure medium levels of support and compliance. Northern Ireland is 'agitated' at some point between full legitimacy and

**Table 8.1** Richard Rose's placement of Northern Ireland in a
typology of regimes

| | | degree of compliance | | |
| --- | --- | --- | --- | --- |
| | | HIGH | MEDIUM | LOW |
| | HIGH | legitimate regime | (–) | isolated regime |
| degree of support | MEDIUM | (–) | *divided regime* | (–) |
| | LOW | coercive regime | (–) regime | repudiated |

*Source*: Adapted from R. Rose, *Governing without Consensus: An Irish Perspective* (London: Faber, 1971), 32.

full repudiation[21] – although his typology also suggests it is at some point between full coercion and complete isolation (which he fails to elaborate). This typology generates five ideal-typical outlooks: the fully allegiant person, the repressed (who gives full compliance but not support), the rebel, the ultra (who provides high support but low compliance), who match the four corners, while the ambivalent person matches the divided regime. Rose's case is that Northern Ireland lacks sufficient cross-pressures to generate enough allegiants and ambivalents, and that its reinforcing cleavages produce too many republican 'rebels' and loyalist 'ultras', and consequently its political system lacks the consensus essential for legitimate democratic government.

Rose made some rapid comparisons with other cases of religious and ethnic conflict, but these discussions did not provide the major focus of his work, which expounded the results of a social survey showing the extent to which Northern Ireland was divided. Subsequently cross-pressure theory was more extensively investigated, both for Northern Ireland as a whole, and for Belfast in particular. In a tightly focused comparison Edmund Aunger, a Canadian political scientist, compared unstable Northern Ireland with the stable Canadian province of New Brunswick to test 'the value of pluralist theory which relates social fragmentation to political stability'.[22] He concluded that New Brunswick is stable because its Franco-British ethnic cleavage is cross-cut by religious and class cleavages, and because the rival elites engage in co-operative practices. Northern Ireland, by contrast, is unstable because its class, religious and ethnic cleavages are strongly reinforcing, and because its rival elites engage in confronta-tion.[23] In New Brunswick, conflicts become dissociated from each other, are single-issue rather than multi-issue, and are thus less severe than in Northern Ireland, where all con-flicts pit Catholics against Protestants.[24] Aunger maintains that cross-cutting cleavages are essential to political stability,[25] and that his findings are 'consistent with the theory of crosscutting cleavages'.[26]

A comparative study of the politics of Belfast and Glasgow, carried out by Ian Budge and Cornelius O'Leary, also buttresses cross-pressure theory.[27] To explain why Belfast is violent and unstable compared with Glasgow, they demonstrated, using 1960s survey evidence, that there was significantly lower cross-cutting between party and religion in Belfast than between party and any background characteristic in Glasgow. Political parties in Glasgow, having more heterogeneous rep-resentation, were subject to more cross-pressures than political parties in Belfast. This contention follows Lipset's argument that 'a stable democracy requires a situation in which all the major parties include supporters from many segments of the population. A system in which the support of different parties corresponds too closely to basic divisions cannot continue on a democratic basis, for it reflects a state of conflict so intense and clear-cut as to rule out compromise.'[28] The authors concluded that their evidence offered 'powerful support to cross-cutting explanations of Belfast's instability'.[29]

## Consociational Theory

As developed by Arend Lijphart,[30] consociational theory focuses on political elites. While it accepts that cross-cutting pressures can facilitate political accommodation, it maintains that divided (or plural, or segmented) societies can attain democratic stability *despite* the absence of cross-cutting social cleavages. Democratic stabilization can occur provided rival elites reach, and maintain, agreement on how to run the political system. Such 'consociational democracies' emerge from historic compromises which entail four institutional features: first, an over-sized coalition government in which political parties representing the main segments of the divided society share governmental power; secondly, proportionality rules that apply throughout the public sector; that is, each cultural community is proportionally represented in the legislature(s), in the executive, the judiciary, the civil service and the police, i.e. the core institutions of the liberal democratic state;[31] thirdly, autonomous norms operate which leave each cultural community a degree of reciprocally recognized self-government over those matters of most profound concern to them, for example their education, their language or their historic territorial unit of government; and fourthly, entrenched vetoes for minorities, which may take various forms, and can include constitutional as well as informal blocking powers.

For consociational settlements it is essential that political elites are willing and free to seek compromise without alienating their followers. The question for consociational analysts is straightforward: if agreements can be reached in divided societies, why hasn't one been forthcoming in Northern Ireland – apart from a brief five-month period in 1974? It is certainly not for want of trying. British governments have been trying to develop a power-sharing or consociational settlement in Northern Ireland since 1972.[32] Analysing Northern Ireland, Lijphart argued that Protestants do not want to share power, and also pointed to the lack of a number of factors conducive to power-sharing.[33] Later, in a general theoretical formulation, he identified eight background conditions 'conducive to the establishment and maintenance of consociational democracy':[34]

(i)   a multiple balance of power among the segments of the divided society, i.e. no segment must have a majority and the segments must be of approximately equal size;
(ii)  a multi-party system with segmental parties;
(iii) a relatively small population, which facilitates co-operation;

(iv)   external threats perceived as a common danger by the different communities;

(v)    some society-wide loyalties, such as a sense of common national identity;

(vi)   the absence of extreme socio-economic inequalities between the communities;

(vii)  the relative spatial isolation of the communities; and

(viii) pre-democratic traditions of political accommodation which predisposed the communities to power-sharing.[35]

Most of these favourable conditions have been absent in Northern Ireland.[36] Between 1920 and 1972 there was no stable multiple balance of power. The Ulster Unionist Party enjoyed electoral hegemony, commanding the loyalties of just less than two-thirds of the electorate. Northern Ireland had the hallmarks of a 'majority dictatorship'. Lijphart's intuition is that if no group enjoyed unrivalled majority status, consociational democracy would be facilitated. Political elites who are unable to govern alone (democratically) have incentives to share power. A 'dual balance of power' is less favourable for consociation, because where there are two groups of roughly equal size each may realistically aspire to domination rather than co-operation. The worst scenario occurs when, as in Northern Ireland, one group is in a permanent or seemingly permanent majority, and is capable of exercising hegemonic power.[37] This imbalance is underlined by other political scientists.[38] Unfortunately, so it is implied, both communities are majoritarian: one is and one seeks to be a hegemonic majority. Lijphart notes that Protestants, schooled in British political culture, are unwilling to embrace 'continental' forms of government based on power-sharing: 'The Protestant majority is passionately attached to its tie with Great Britain, and Britain also provides them with the normative standards of governmental organisation.'[39] He might have added that this majoritarian political culture is also present in the Republic, and among Irish nationalists, who insist that they are the real majority on the island.[40]

The creation of a multi-party system since 1972 has not been conducive to power-sharing. The fragmentation of unionists into the UUP, the Democratic Unionist Party, the APNI, and more recently the Conservative Party, and the splintering of nationalists between the SDLP and Sinn Féin, have created a 'dual party system' – in which competition occurs within rather than across each bloc, and cuts against the prospects of accommodation.[41] This party system is not based on strictly communal lines (given the cross-denominational support for the APNI), but it is clearly a dual system, and more importantly, a multiple balance of power does not exist because the bulk of the unionist bloc, although divided, has generally been united in its hostility to compromises with nationalists, and has continued to command a majority of the electorate.[42]

The communities do not perceive a common external threat worth uniting against. For unionists, as we have seen in chapter 3, the key external threat is posed by the Irish Republic, variously aided and abetted by the Vatican, Moscow, Libya, the American State Department, the European Union, and the British Foreign Office; whereas for nationalists, as we saw in chapter 1, the external threat is already manifest in the British presence in Ireland. The rival communities therefore differ fundamentally on the nature of the most important external threat.

The few society-wide loyalties do not serve to lessen ethno-national differences, as we have argued in chapters 5 and 6. The two communities share Christianity but this faith also divides them. They also share anti-cosmopolitan and anti-metropolitan values, but these common allegiances do not significantly cross-cut what separates them politically. The most important society-wide loyalty, some sense of shared (political) national identity, is absent.[43] Lijphart argues that some national solidarity aids consociational democracy because 'the centrifugal tendencies of subcultural cleavages are counterbalanced to at least a certain degree by an overarching consensus'. However, in Northern Ireland, national solidarities deepen the other cleavages.[44]

Athough there are not *extreme* socio-economic differences between the rival communities, there has been, and there is, as we have discussed in chapter 7, sufficiently extensive discrimination – and belief in discrimination – to sow immense distrust.[45] The persistence of considerable socio-economic inequalities, despite British governments' commitment to ensuring equality of opportunity, has been documented by objective research.[46] These inequalities are rooted in the relations of domination and exploitation established during the plantation of Ulster and the wars of conquest and rebellion in the seventeenth century, which helps explain why Northern Ireland had no strong pre-democratic traditions of political accommodation before the advent of mass democracy or the creation of the regime. The partition of Ulster which accompanied the foundation of Northern Ireland took place against a background of armed communal mobilization and civil war.

The conducive background conditions which Northern Ireland apparently possesses – small size, and the relative isolation of the segments – are unfortunately causal factors, which critics have argued are based on implausible premises.[47] The implications are bleak: Lijphart's checklist suggests that voluntary power-sharing experiments in Northern Ireland are bound to fail; and all such experiments have so far failed. The successive attempts to establish a devolved settlement commanding widespread cross-community agreement have been unsuccessful: the Sunningdale settlement of 1973–4; the Constitutional Convention of 1975; the Atkins all-party talks of 1979–80; the Northern Ireland Assembly (1982–6) established by James Prior's 'rolling devolution' scheme; and the promotion of power-sharing under the auspices of the Anglo-Irish Agreement.[48] Many predict the same fate awaits the political parties if and when they sit down to constitutional negotiations after the British and Irish governments have agreed the 'framework document' which they have promised to issue in early 1995. Policy-makers persuaded by Lijphart's theory seem to face two options: to promote partition or to engineer the conducive background conditions. The latter option, consociational engineering, must entail trying to create the following favourable conditions:

- a multiple balance of power,
- a commonly perceived external threat or the removal of the rival threats,

- overarching society-wide loyalties, and
- socio-economic equality between the communities.

There are three feasible ways in which a multiple balance of power can be realized. The first is through a deep split between the UUP and the DUP, deep enough to make the UUP favour power-sharing with the APNI and SDLP. However, this prospect would at best create a cross-communal majority, and not a grand coalition – since both the DUP and Sinn Féin would be excluded from such a coalition. The second way to create a multiple balance of power is through a significant growth in the SDLP and Sinn Féin electorate, fostered by a higher Catholic population growth and (at least) proportional rates of emigration amongst Catholics and Protestants.[49] The third way to create a multiple balance of power is deliberately to design institutions which ensure such a scenario, and we shall return to this possibility in our penultimate chapter.[50]

The only easily imaginable way to create a common and strong external threat is to threaten a second partition of Ulster – in the hope that this external threat to Protestants in western and southern Northern Ireland and to Catholics in West Belfast might generate appropriate motivations for a consociational settlement. However, threatening another partition of Ireland is unlikely to be contemplated by either government. The only positive way to remove the rival threats experienced by both communities, in our judgement, is to create a system of shared sovereignty, a point to which we shall return in our conclusion.

Working on removing socio-economic inequalities is diffi-cult. It produces animosity amongst the majority, who deny that discrimination exists, or claim that they are the victims of 'reverse discrimination'. Reforming Northern Ireland, at least in the short-run, increases unionist hostility to power-sharing, and even when the reforms are successful they do not guarantee a more accommodating attitude on the part of the minority.

The creation of 'overarching society-wide loyalties' is a feat beyond consociational engineers. Manufacturing a shared national or Christian or political identity is beyond the immediate grasp of policy-makers. The promotion of consociation therefore seems unlikely to succeed, and for these reasons, amongst others, power-sharing has been widely dismissed as an unworkable solution to the conflict,[51] although consociational theory illuminates why the conflict is so intractable. However, as we shall argue later, there are ways to deploy Lijphart's thinking to devise a more feasible consociational arrangement than he has envisaged.

Lijphart advocates consociation when the background conditions are not at all favourable, and did so for South Africa long before its recent and as yet unproven consociational experiment.[52] Should policy-makers follow Lijphart's normative advice, despite the pessimism which his own comparative analysis induces? On the one hand political-science determinism tells us that the conditions for consociation are absent, therefore power-sharing does not appear viable; on the other hand Lijphart suggests that idealist voluntarism, sufficient good will and social learning on the part of well-motivated elites, can do the trick, and create consociational settlements even in very unfavourable conditions.

## Linkage Explanations

Pluralist and consociational theories stress endogenous factors when explaining the conflict.[53] Such an approach is so common that the late John Whyte described the 'internal conflict' approach as the dominant paradigm in the literature.[54] However, a number of writers, including ourselves, have questioned this concentration on endogenous factors, whether they be reinforcing social cleavages, the lack of a multiple balance of power, majority abuse of the minority, minority failure to recognize the regime, internal economic inequalities, or parochial cultural aberrations. Instead, these authors stress the interdependence between domestic and external factors, following, if often only implicitly, political scientists who have developed the concept of 'linkage politics'.[55]

These accounts can be divided into three categories, in

ascending order of analytical merit: first, those who believe
the conflict is significantly influenced by international funding
for paramilitaries;[56] secondly, those who believe the conflict
is underpinned by Northern Ireland's lack of international
legitimacy;[57] and thirdly, those who think that the Republic and
United Kingdom have importantly shaped the conflict.[58] These
'linkage' approaches are significantly different from those put
forth by unionist, nationalist and Marxist schools of thought.

*External support for paramilitaries.* A number of commentators have stressed the importance of external support for
the paramilitary groups. Jack Holland claims that the IRA
gets 'many if not most of its weapons from Irish-American
supporters'.[59] For Claire Sterling, the aid channelled from
Gaddafi's Libya to the IRA is an integral part of an alleged
international 'terror network'.[60] She claims that Gaddafi was
supplying the IRA with around $5 million a year in the late
1970s, which made Libya a significant supplier of arms. Some
'experts' on 'international terrorism' have also implicated the
Soviets as IRA sponsors.[61] One former British army officer,
now an academic specializing in terrorism – if that is not a
contradiction in terms – draws attention to alleged KGB–IRA
links, and manages to imply that the Soviets were 'responsible'
for Bloody Sunday.[62] Unionist leader James Molyneaux once
claimed that Soviet submarines were supplying arms to the
INLA,[63] and a Catholic priest has stated that the Provisionals
in the Creggan area of Derry/Londonderry had North Koreans
among their personnel.[64] A number of writers have drawn
attention to connections between loyalist paramilitaries and
the South African Defence Force,[65] and one has discovered
close links between the UDA and a wide 'network of right-wing
Euro-terror groups'.[66] The exposure of links between the IRA
and a number of other terrorist groups has been going on
for much longer.[67] Finally, as we mentioned in chapter 5,
some DUP members suspect that the Vatican runs guns to
the IRA.

*The international illegitimacy of Northern Ireland.* In an important book, Adrian Guelke argues that the international perception that Northern Ireland is illegitimate has had a 'very
considerable effect upon the course of events'.[68] Guelke argues

that the region runs afoul of accepted international norms of self-determination, according to which political units governed as colonies should be decolonized intact rather than partitioned.[69] As a result, the 'overwhelming weight of world opinion' favours a united Ireland.[70] This influences important aspects of the conflict.[71] It helps to explain the constitutional stalemate because it increases unionists' insecurities and encourages nationalists to hold out, and reduces their incentive to compromise. It also helps to explain the violence. It promotes a siege mentality among unionists that provides a justification for the actions of loyalist paramilitaries. The external credibility of the Provisional IRA's claim that it is engaged in an anti-colonial struggle against British imperialism encourages it to believe that it can be successful without wooing the Protestants, and facilitates fund-raising activities among the American-Irish.

*The external impact of the British and Irish states.* Travel-writer Dervla Murphy explains the stalemate and violence as by-products of actions taken by the British and Irish states. Murphy argues that the conflict can be explained by both Irish irredentism and the British constitutional guarantee. 'The British "guarantee" allows free rein to unionist irrationality, while the Republic's oft-proclaimed wish for unity encourages the gunmen to fight on.'[72] The solution is the joint withdrawal of the exogenous actors, leaving an independent Northern Ireland, in which the internal actors would be forced to work out their differences without their respective external crutches.[73]

Two lawyers, Kevin Boyle and Tom Hadden, and an anthropologist and a political scientist, Joseph Ruane and Jennifer Todd, also attribute considerable responsibility for the conflict to the Irish and British states. Boyle and Hadden specify the Republic's overwhelmingly Catholic and nationalist ethos, and its relative poverty, as impediments to conflict-resolution.[74] 'The substance of the criticism that the Republic carries its own responsibility . . . for the state of majority–minority relations within Northern Ireland is amply demonstrated.'[75] They recognize the need for 'an Irish dimension' – if not a say for the Irish government in the affairs of Northern Ireland – and for a while put their faith in a European dimension, and European citizenship, as ways of transcending British–Irish antagonisms: 'the Europeanization of both islands . . . will force a reassessment of all relationships on these islands and in particular of the two principal influences on the present tragedy of Northern Ireland, "Britishness" as an historical integrating force and the reactive tradition of Irish separatism'.[76] Ruane and Todd observe that Britain, for its part, has been unable or unwilling to devote the necessary resources to address seriously the economic inequality between the two communities. The achievement of cultural equality is made difficult by Northern Ireland's inclusion in a political system which ranks British culture ahead of Irish. British security measures have also antagonized the minority community. There is a clear connection between the conflict and exogenous factors: nationalists have a fundamental interest in equality which is blocked not just by unionist resistance, but by British unwillingness to act, while unionists have a fundamental interest in security which is threatened not only by northern nationalists, but by the proximity of an unreconstructed Republic. While Ruane and Todd, and Boyle and Hadden, hold Britain and Ireland partly responsible for the conflict, they do not accept Murphy's prescription of independence. Instead they call for increased British–Irish co-operation to address the problems of both communities.[77]

The late Frank Wright's work was the most ambitious comparative analysis to employ the themes of 'linkage politics'. In his view Northern Ireland is more than a mere segmented or plural society; it is best understood as 'an ethnic frontier', a site of contested sovereignty between two broader national communities, Irish and British. In an ethnic frontier, conflict is crucially affected by the actions of external powers beyond the frontier. If one external power intervenes to side with an internal protagonist then the other will also seek external help, compelling a dramatic escalation in conflict; and once external agents have intervened the task of displacing them may be all but impossible. Thus he holds an unstable external environment responsible for the ferocity of past and present conflicts in the Balkans, Cyprus, and the Lebanon.[78] The relative stability of Belgium and Switzerland, by contrast, can be explained by a tradition of non-interference and restraint by larger neighbours who have avoided intervention on behalf of their co-ethnics,[79] leaving the relevant communities free to act largely as cultural rather than as national entities, and to develop appropriate consociational and federal ways of living together.[80] When ethnic communities in a frontier zone are already mobilized around different national visions then the best that can be hoped for is that the interested external powers should co-operate with each other to contain the conflict rather than siding purely with their co-nationals. In this respect, Wright argued that the most positive feature of Northern Ireland is that the British and Irish governments enjoy reasonably good relations, and it is in the deepening of their collaboration that hope for the future lies. Understandably, therefore, he was a strong supporter of the Anglo-Irish Agreement and argued in favour of a fully blown form of joint British–Irish authority over the region: 'without some kind of authority that depends upon both the British and Irish governments, there will be no authority in Northern Ireland at all – and therefore a total chaos . . . like Cyprus or Lebanon . . .'.[81]

# State-building and the Repercussions of Settler Colonialism

Successful state-expansion has two ingredients: first, the acquisition, violent or otherwise, of new territory by a state-building core region, and secondly, the elicitation of loyalty from the newly-acquired area. Considerable historical and comparative work has been done on the circumstances and policies which encourage such transfers of loyalty.[82] Non-political factors include the diffusion of language, education, technological change and integrated and expanding economic markets, all of which are presumed to break down cultural parochialism and build new alliances. Political factors include the establishment of efficient government, a fair system of law and order, the sharing of economic benefits, the co-optation of local elites, and, eventually, the ceding of participation rights to the local masses.

In much of this historical and social science literature, the United Kingdom, at least until the 1960s, was considered one of the success-stories of European state-building. However, that is now less obvious, especially in Northern Ireland. From our perspective the key point about British state-building is that it failed in Ireland before 1921, and has continued to fail in Northern Ireland. The British state has never elicited widespread loyalties in Northern Ireland in the manner of successful state-builders. For this reason one solid approach to explaining the conflict is to analyse it as a state-building failure.[83]

Many of the partisan explanations discussed in this book also do this, implicitly or explicitly. Irish nationalists claim that Ireland is Irish, too different from Britain to have been integrated successfully into the *British* state. They declare geography to be an insurmountable obstacles to British state-building – it was feasible for the English to integrate Scotland and Wales but not Ireland. Nationalists claim that Britain was more interested in exploiting Ireland than integrating it; that the British state was never interested in sharing its markets with Ireland or in establishing a fair legal system there; and that it resisted Catholic participation until forced to relent under mass pressure. Unionists, on the other hand, charge the British elite with being indifferent to the Union and unwilling to take on republican militants in the manner required. The British political parties are also blamed for not wanting to organize (or organize sufficiently) in the region. According to Marxists, British state-building was unsuccessful because the economic diffusion essential to the construction of new social formations and the breakdown of parochial boundaries did not take place. For green Marxists, uneven economic development between Ireland and Britain killed the prospects for the political integration of Ireland; and for Orange Marxists, the uneven economic development between northern and southern Ireland explains why the latter was not integrated.

A different account of British state-building failure, and the only one apart from our own to employ explicitly the literature on state-building theory, is provided by Ian Lustick.[84] The large-scale introduction of settlers into sixteenth- and seventeenth-century Ireland, according to Lustick, fundamentally disrupted a pre-requisite for successful state-building, the elicitation of loyalties from the newly-acquired area: 'settlement . . . was a sufficient . . . condition for interruption of the processes of loyalty transformation and legitimation of central administrative authority identified by state-building theorists as necessary for successful state formation'.[85] The plantation settlement frustrated the co-optation of local elites and the eventual extension of rights of political participation to natives. Providing the recruits for the Irish bureaucracy and being the bearers of information to the metropolis, settlers and their descendants were well placed to ensure that natives remained in subordinate economic and political positions. Conciliatory positions taken towards natives by the Crown, ranging from Henry VIII's 'surrender and regrant' programme to William III's original Treaty of Limerick, were converted, at settler insistence, into policies designed to keep the yoke on native shoulders. The refusal to accompany the Act of Union of 1801 with Catholic emancipation blocked central governmental efforts to integrate the native Irish. In the wake of the 1798 uprising and the continuing threat of French invasion, it was the Westminster government's intention that Ireland be permanently and stably integrated into the British state. Essential to the planned impact of Union was the emancipation of Catholics so that they could sit in Parliament. However, the Union was not accompanied by emancipation because of the opposition of the Irish Protestant ascendancy, its manipulation of anti-Catholic sentiments in Britain, and the distraction of Pitt by weightier events: 'Thus was the union of Ireland and Great Britain prevented from solving the Irish problem by legitimising British rule among the Catholic majority.'[86] As a result, when Catholic mass mobilization developed it took a separatist direction. Even when emancipation was granted, in 1829, it was quickly followed by the Repeal (of the Union) movement, and by a sequence of nationalist mobilizations which led to the break-up of the United Kingdom.

For Lustick, the colonial settlement of Ireland distinguished it from Scotland and Wales, and indeed from those English areas outside the original state-building core of Wessex. In these other areas, protection of local rights and co-optation of local elites made it more likely that when social mobilization at the mass level occurred, the political consequences for Great Britain would be centripetal in effect. In France, a state-building core which, like its British counterpart, had successfully legitimized its rule in several heterogeneous, peripheral areas, similarly failed to integrate Algeria – and for the same reasons. States, for Lustick, are 'political configurations' built by political processes and struggles. They are not 'expressions of transcendent geographical, historical or religious principles'.[87] Settlers are also not construed as dupes, but rather as rational actors protecting their interests, who often resisted key metropolitan elites.[88] Nor does Lustick accept the arguments of 'troops out' advocates who use the Algerian analogy to argue for a British withdrawal.[89] In Lustick's view, it is not nationalists or their British bedfellows who are responsible for the failure of Britain to integrate Ireland, as unionists allege, but rather the settlers' descendants themselves.[90] 'The settlers . . . by preventing stable incorporation of Ireland and Algeria, helped create conditions that eventually broke the ideological consensus which included Ireland within the United Kingdom and Algeria within the indivisible French republic.'[91] This approach adds an original perspective to the state-building literature which largely failed to discuss British (or French) state-building *failures*, and has also neglected the effect of settlers on the state-building process elsewhere.[92]

Settler colonialism is also the central theme in other comparative analyses of Northern Ireland.[93] Settler–native antagonisms provide the occasions for particularly bitter ethnic conflicts: 'settler societies are *extreme* examples of "plural" or "communally divided" societies'.[94] The initial interaction between the rival communities normally involves dispossession of the natives, and leaves a lasting legacy of bitterness: settlers' claims that the land was vacant or under-utilized can usually be disregarded as mythical.[95] If the settlers are not assimilated or the natives are not wiped out the relations between the rival communities normally develop into hierarchical and hostile forms. Settlers justify their dominant position with myths of cultural superiority,[96] while natives regard the settlers as alien interlopers and talk nostalgically of a golden age before the settlers came. In these situations caste-based divisions of labour and endogamy are prevalent and political accommodation becomes extremely difficult when democratization changes political norms. This story fits historic Ulster. Its atmosphere helps explain the prevalence of segregation, endogamy and segmented labour markets. The initial act of dispossession bequeathed a legacy of inequality which continues to poison inter-group relations.[97]

Settler colonial societies are threefold in type. The first is the economic colony, controlled and exploited by the metropolis with a skeletal military and administrative apparatus, 'administrative colonialism'. When this type of colony ceased to be useful, or when native mobilization made control impossible, decolonization could proceed relatively smoothly, as was the case in many British and French imperial territories. The second is the exclusively settler society, like those which developed in Australia, Canada, New Zealand, the USA, and many Latin American countries. Through genocide, intended or unintended, and dynamic settlement policies, 'the native problem' in these territories ceased to be a major political problem. 'Democratization' posed no difficulties in these settings. Rid of a significant native population such societies were free to develop as liberal democracies and to become self-proclaimed bastions of individual rights. The third is one in which large numbers of settlers and natives, or their descendants, have co-existed. For this reason historic Ireland, and historic Ulster in particular, has been compared with South Africa[98] and Rhodesia.[99] Before 1921 Ireland was controlled by its settler minority in ways comparable to these other British colonies, though reforms of the position of the 'natives', both as citizens and as holders of landed property, went much further in

Ireland. The settler minority remained strong enough to resist decolonization in Ulster, and, within the formal institutions of liberal democracy, was able to create an exclusionary system of control similar to those which operated in South Africa, Rhodesia, and French Algeria.

Interpreting Northern Ireland as an example of settler colonialism differs from the conventional republican and green Marxist story – in which British imperialism is the source of conflict. In this interpretation the settlers and their descendants rapidly became autonomous from the metropolis – as occurred in Algeria, and may be occurring on the West Bank of the Jordan river.[100] This perspective emphasizes the caste structures created by colonialism, and the associated privileges, not merely of an economic nature, which flowed to the descendants of settlers;[101] it insists that the settlers fomented native violence through repression and discrimination and exaggerated native disloyalty for their own interests;[102] and it implies that, far from being irrational, or the product of some Irish cultural pathology, violence is embedded in a settler colonial structure which has resisted full-scale democratic transformation.[103] It also helps explain why the pre-democratic traditions of accommodation which helped established consociational settlements in other divided societies, like Canada and the Netherlands, were absent from historic Ulster. Consociations are usually agreed between different sets of settlers (as with British and French settlers in Canada) or between different sets of natives resident on their homelands (as with Dutch Catholics and Protestants, and Belgian Flemings and Walloons). They are less often agreed by settlers and natives.

In a number of other accounts, Northern Irish Protestants are portrayed not simply as a settler society but as a 'fragment' or 'offshoot' society. A fragment society has been geographically separated from its host for a sufficient period for it to develop separate interests and an identity: examples include the Spanish in Latin America, the English in North America, the Quebecois, Afrikaners and Rhodesian whites.[104] Richard Rose adds a twist to this theme by suggesting that Northern Ireland is a double fragment society – because both communities are offshoots from their mainstream societies.[105]

## A Critical Evaluation of Comparative Explanations

All of the foregoing approaches to understanding Northern Ireland are illuminating. They transcend ethnocentricity, and in different ways seek to establish what specifically makes Northern Ireland so antagonistic, violent, and locked in protracted stalemate. However, they are not without deficiencies.

*Pluralist theory.* It is often accepted that conflicts between groups separated by a number of reinforcing social divisions will be more problematic than uni-dimensional conflicts. Thus conflict in South Africa is difficult to resolve because its racial divisions are reinforced by massive socio-economic inequalities. Similarly a just settlement in Northern Ireland requires a resolution of the national question and the weaker economic position of Catholics. This does not mean, however, that the conflict is a result of cumulative social divisions.

Contrary to what is suggested by cross-pressure theory, some social solidarities are more politically salient than others. National and ethnic attachments tend to be much more binding and explosive in historically established and stable communities than alternative solidarities like gender or class.[106] This may explain why the removal of less serious social divisions may leave national or ethnic quarrels intact. In Northern Ireland, for example, the removal of the linguistic division between Protestants and Catholics in the seventeenth century had no noticeable effect in forging integration or assimilation, and, as we have observed, the current reduction in religious commitments – the result of secularization – has been occurring during the current crisis.[107]

The key problem in Northern Ireland is not that social divisions are reinforcing. Protestants and Catholics may constitute disproportionate shares of the middle and working class respectively, but there is also a significant Protestant working class and Catholic middle class. The reality is that class-based pressures have not been strong enough to challenge the primacy of national or ethnic loyalties – notably in the electoral arena. Politicians have consistently demonstrated their inability to develop cross-national or cross-ethnic class alliances, not because there is no basis for them, but because their potential followers are more susceptible to ethnic or national appeals, so that class-based parties are normally limited in their appeal to one ethno-national community. The main difference between New Brunswick and Northern Ireland is therefore not, as Aunger suggests, that one territory has cross-cutting social divisions and the other has not, but rather that one has a more serious ethno-national division than the other. As for Budge and O'Leary's well-documented argument that political parties in seriously divided cities like Belfast are more socially homogeneous and less subject to cross-pressures than in less seriously divided cities like Glasgow, we are tempted to ask 'so what?' This is surely what one would expect to find. Their findings can be more plausibly interpreted as a reflection of the conflict, rather than an explanation of it.

There are two further serious difficulties with cross-pressure theory. First, it completely ignores exogenous factors. New Brunswick and Glasgow exist in a dramatically different context from Northern Ireland and Belfast. New Brunswick is not bordered by an irredentist state with legitimate historic grievances, or attached to a political centre which has settled it and subsequently demonstrated profound ambivalence about retaining it. Glasgow contains a large Catholic minority descended from Irish Catholic migrants. They do not seek the unification of Glasgow with Ireland. To the extent that they are interested in Catholic politics they are interested in ensuring equal treatment for Catholics within Scotland and Great Britain. Belfast, by contrast, contains a large Catholic minority, which considers itself part of the native population of Ireland, and wishes to see Belfast become a city within a politically unified Ireland. Even if New Brunswick and Northern Ireland, and Glasgow and Belfast, had exactly the same degree of cross-cutting religious and class cleavages, they would still be affected by these radically different exogenous contexts.

Secondly, the cross-pressure thesis rules out the prospect of accommodation in areas of congruent divisions.[108] There have, however, been several instances of political accommodation in parliamentary regimes where divisions are as reinforcing as in Northern Ireland – for example in Canada between 1841 and 1867, Lebanon between 1943 and 1975, Fiji in the years preceding 1987, and Malaysia from 1955 until at least 1969.[109] Elites can reach accommodation or depoliticize ethnic differences, despite the absence of significant cross-pressures.[110] These examples of relatively durable ethnic conflict management suggest that the intractability of the Northern Ireland conflict must be sought in factors beyond those of reinforcing social divisions.

*The limitations of consociational explanations.* A consociational settlement would be normatively attractive, both because it would be consistent with liberal democratic norms, and because it would mean that the conflict would be regulated by the peoples of Northern Ireland, or their representatives, parties, and social organizations, rather than by outsiders. Consociationalists insist on accommodation and wish to prevent power being monopolized by a unionist majority in Northern Ireland, a nationalist majority in Ireland, or a British majority in the UK. Consociationalists also realize that communal or ethnic divisions are resilient rather than rapidly biodegradable, and that they must be recognized rather than wished away. In this respect consociationalists lack the naïveté of assimilationists.

The problem with consociationalism is not its normative orientation, but rather that it has not worked – and the difficulties with Lijphart's explanations of why it has failed. Lijphart's observation which suggests that it is unionists' majority status, and their potential ability to govern alone, which prevents them from sharing power, makes sense; but in comparative terms its significance is less obvious. There are countries where majorities in linguistically divided societies have been willing to share power with large minorities – for instance the English-speaking majority in Canada has mostly been willing to share power with Francophones since 1867[111] – and there have also been cases where ideological majorities have been willing to share power with minorities – as in Austria after World War

II. There are also many cases of 'over-sized' coalition governments in homogeneous societies. More importantly, between
the imposition of direct rule by Westminster in 1972, and
1985 when the Anglo-Irish Agreement was signed, the choice
for unionist politicians was not between governing alone or
power-sharing, but rather between accepting direct rule (and
not governing) or power-sharing. After 1985, their choice was
restricted further: either they accepted power-sharing or they
faced the prospect of British direct rule with overt influence
by the Republic's government. The Anglo-Irish Agreement
deliberately altered the 'balance of power' to induce unionists
to agree to power-sharing,[112] but, so far, to no avail. In short
there may be something other than their structural majority
status which inhibits unionists from accepting consociational
arrangements.[113]

The general validity of Lijphart's set of 'conducive background conditions', which he thinks explain the success of
consociations, has been widely disputed – and we cannot
review these arguments here.[114] The outcome of the debate
is that three theses remain highly plausible. First, consociation
can be achieved only by elites sufficiently motivated to engage
in conflict-regulation: 'the independent actions of political
elites, often taken in opposition to their followers' demands,
rather than societal variables, . . . best account for conflict
regulation successes and failures in democratic regimes'.[115]
Secondly, consociation is favoured where political elites enjoy
predominance over a deferential and organizationally encap-
sulated following.[116] Finally, consociation is promoted not so
much by a multiple balance of power, but rather by the stability
of the communal cultures in a divided society.[117] The logic
is straightforward. Conflict-regulation can take place when
elites are motivated to engage in it. However, goodwill is not
enough. The elites must be confident that they can drag their
followers behind them, in other words the conditions specified
in the second hypothesis must be met. Finally, well-motivated
elites, enjoying some autonomy from their followers, must
be sure both of their social bases and of the intentions of
their rivals. Any movement which weakens the stability of the
relations within the communities will reduce the attractiveness

of power-sharing. These theses explain the failure of successive British governments' attempts to promote power-sharing.

*The absence of the required elite motivations.* Elites might consider power-sharing to fend off a common external threat, to maintain the economic welfare of their community, to avoid violence, or to obtain governmental office. These motivations have evidently not been present in a 'critical mass' amongst Northern Ireland's politicians. There is no agreed major external threat. Radical economic decline has not concentrated enough minds on the merits of accommodation, and indeed, as we have seen in chapter 7 there have been perverse incentives at work because the economic costs of the conflict are not borne by the local population, let alone the local elites.[118] The desire to avoid war has also not been sufficiently intense. The rhetoric of even the most 'responsible' leaders has continued to foment conflict, confirming their followers in the belief that politics is a zero-sum game. The desire to obtain office has also been insufficiently strong. The APNI's leaders alone have remained consistently interested in sharing power and governmental office. The leaders of Sinn Féin, until recently, have said they want a united Ireland or nothing. The SDLP's leaders, by contrast, desired local office, especially between 1972 and 1976, not only as proof of unionist willingness to share power but also to demonstrate that reform, pending a united Ireland, was possible. However, after the rise of Sinn Féin in the early 1980s the SDLP's leaders have been prepared to play abstentionist politics. They boycotted the Northern Ireland Assembly between 1982 and 1986, and sought a guaranteed 'Irish dimension' ahead of local power-sharing; since 1986 its leaders have displayed no special enthusiasm for any kind of devolved government. On the unionist side, the DUP have generally been seen to be the most consistent local office-seekers; eager to build the party to win hegemony over the UUP; but until recently they have wanted devolution, with simple majority rule, and 'the return of a Stormont-style parliament precisely as a veto on Britain's untrustworthy intentions'.[119] Since 1974 the UUP has been as firm as the DUP in its intransigence on an Irish dimension, but the party's leaders have had strong integrationist sympathies.[120]

These sympathies dampen their enthusiasm for local office, an attitude strengthened by the relative over-representation of the UUP at Westminster (in 1992 the party won 9 of Northern Ireland's 17 seats, i.e. 53 per cent, on 34.5 per cent of the vote). Britain's position as direct ruler has also been fundamentally important in preventing either side from having the motivation to share power. Direct rule, after all, is a form of unionist rule, even if it is not any unionist's most-preferred option. It gives them insufficient reason to accommodate the minority.

*The Absence of Sufficient Elite Predominance.* An old story from the French revolutionary era applies, *mutatis mutandis*, to Northern Ireland. Ledru-Rollin, the red republican, was asked what he was going to do about a crowd on its way to protest the violation of the constitution. He replied 'I am their leader, I really ought to follow them . . . '. The leaders of Northern Ireland's political parties have frequently resembled Ledru-Rollin in their willingness to put themselves in front of their crowd, as opposed to leading them. There are good reasons for this behaviour. The key political leaders do not enjoy 'structured elite predominance', i.e. the ability to lead their followers in directions which the followers would initially oppose.[121]

Structured elite predominance can exist in four circumstances: the masses have to be apolitical; or deferential; or integrated into patron–client relations pyramided from the local to the national level; or integrated into modern mass political parties with extensive organizational capabilities.[122] The first two sets of circumstances are absent from Northern Ireland. The third, the existence of patron–client networks, is latent. However, the unionist network of patronage surrounding Stormont was destroyed in 1972; and, in the absence of a share in political power, nationalist political elites have found it very difficult to build powerful clientelist relations. What of the fourth condition? One of the obstacles to consociation in Northern Ireland is the cultural feature we discussed in chapter 6, egalitarianism. Rather than an 'iron law of oligarchy', a high degree of 'democracy from below' exists, leaving political leaders constantly looking over their shoulders, both to their electorate and to potential rival elites in their party.[123] The major political parties *either* do not display structured elite predominance, *or*, if they do, either the party is too small to matter or, worse still, the autonomy of its elites has been counter-productive for power-sharing – as with the DUP and Sinn Féin.[124]

*The absence of intra-segmental stability.* Political elites need to feel secure before embarking upon the hazardous enterprise of compromise. Northern Ireland's political elites have not felt this way since the late 1960s. The political crisis, and the changes in the electoral system for local, regional and European elections, have encouraged the fragmentation of the rival communities. The unionist monolith collapsed first, breaking into five fractions (the UUP, DUP, Vanguard, UPNI and the Alliance), then into three (the UUP, the DUP and Alliance), and then four (the UUP, the DUP, the APNI and the Conservatives). Competition within the unionist bloc weakened any impetus for power-sharing and accommodation. The DUP, and Vanguard before it, have forced the UUP to be as bellicosely anti-nationalist and loyalist as themselves. The nationalist bloc first consolidated behind the SDLP (as the civil-rights activists and traditional nationalists made their peace) but then threatened to fragment under the lack of political progress. Competitive pressure, first from the Irish Independence Party and then from Sinn Féin, when it decided to participate in elections in 1981, left the SDLP also looking over its shoulder when considering compromise. The pattern of fragmentation within the majority and minority has also not been conducive to compromise. The fraction of the nationalist bloc prepared to consider power-sharing has been consistently relatively larger than the fraction so disposed amongst the unionist bloc. These arguments suggest that Northern Ireland has lacked not only Lijphart's conditions conducive for power-sharing, but also those specified in the reconstructed theory of consociation based on a synthesis of Lijphart's critics.

A comprehensive explanation of the failure of consociation also requires a substantive account of what divides the protagonists. The conflict is protracted, intense and violent,[125] and that is related to the fact that the conflict is national or ethno-national. In this respect Northern Ireland differs from Lijphart's success stories, like Belgium, and the Netherlands, and is much more like countries where consociational experiments have failed, such as Cyprus and Lebanon, or where they have not yet been tried or tested to destruction, like South Africa or Sri Lanka.[126] Actual inter-communal violence and memories or myths of past atrocities pose difficult challenges for elites willing to contemplate compromise.[127] National and/or ethnic conflicts, even in advanced industrial states, seem to be more intractable or prone to violence than those based on confessional disputes, like those of the Netherlands, or those based on ideological disputes, such as the conflict between conservatives and socialists in Austria. 'It simply does seem to be the case that acts of gross inhumanity are more readily engaged in or supported when the victims are members of an ethnically defined out-group than when the basis of differentiation is class or religion.'[128] As we argued in chapter 6, national and ethnic groups are perceived as kinship groups, as imagined extended families. The ties among such groups generally appear to be closer, more intimate, and less instrumental, and the relations with out-groups more distant, exclusive and potentially adversarial than is the case with the other types of collectivities grouped by Lijphart under the rubric 'plural societies'.[129] Northern Ireland represents a particularly serious sub-set of ethnic conflict, because the relevant communities are sub-sets of 'national communities', that is they are committed to different nation-states rather than to living together. Such conflicts have a zero-sum quality if they are ultimately focused on the legitimacy of the existing territorial boundaries of conflict, rather than on how the given territory should be governed.

Consociational arrangements are not impossible in ethnically divided societies.[130] Consociation can serve to obstruct the emergence of ethnic separatism and secessionism, or to inhibit such propensities, but it is much more difficult to put together a voluntary consociational arrangement *after* one of the communities is committed to secession, or long-term integration with another state. Northern Ireland's conflict has been particularly intractable because the secessionist community not only wants to leave, it wants to take its unwilling neighbours with it, and to use consociation as an interim step in that direction; and, because the non-secessionist community wants to keep the secessionists under its control, it refuses consociation as a Trojan horse for Irish unification, and it wants to integrate those of its neighbours it can control into the British nation-state.

This perspective enables us to understand better unionists' refusal to share power. It owes more to their fear that Northern Irish Catholics are committed to Irish nation-statism than it does to their belief they can govern alone, or to their cultural commitment to British models of governance. Unionist protests against the 1973 Sunningdale Agreement, the Anglo-Irish Agreement of 1985, and the Downing Street Declaration of 1993, focused on their 'Irish dimensions', specifically the Council of Ireland promised in 1974, the Inter-Governmental Conference established in 1985, and the definition of the people of Northern Ireland as part of the people of Ireland rather than the people of Britain, in 1993. Unionists reject power-sharing on the grounds that they are being asked to share power with nationalists who do not recognize Northern Ireland.[131] Some unionists are prepared to offer power-sharing – providing that the minority surrenders nationalist aspirations.[132] The failure of voluntary consociation therefore cannot be simply attributed to *unionists'* unwillingness to embrace it – as Lijphart implies. The minority is also unwilling to accept variants of consociation which have an exclusively United Kingdom context. The SDLP has insisted since 1972 that power-sharing must be accompanied by a significant institutionalized Irish dimension, and that the latter is not tradable for the former, while Sinn Féin presently refuses to consider any form of power-sharing within the United Kingdom. In short, consociational theory, at least as Lijphart articulates it, understates the exogenous sources of conflict, and focuses too heavily on purely internal prescriptions.

*Exaggerated and implausible linkages.* Explanations which consider both exogenous and endogenous sources of conflict, and how they interact, are superior to those which consider endogenous factors alone. None the less, the approaches surveyed in this chapter have some shortcomings. Direct international support for republican and loyalist paramilitaries is more conspicuous by its absence than by its presence,[133] especially in historical perspective. In the past, foreign powers were willing to arm the native or Catholic Irish against the English, as in the sixteenth century, 1798, and during 1914–18, but foreign interference of this sort has been absent during the present conflict. Britain has been criticized by the USSR, the USA, various western European and other states for the way in which it has mismanaged Northern Ireland, but there is no convincing proof that these powers have directly aided either paramilitary faction.[134] While the Libyan government has directly armed and funded the IRA (and the UDA), its role, or that of the Irish American public, in provoking the violence should not be exaggerated.

The warring paramilitary factions have not been dependent on aid from abroad. They have considerable legitimacy within their own communities. They have their own supporters who donate money, and they are also adept at raising funds through a variety of activities, including racketeering and bank robberies. Some of the guns, and other materiel, used by the paramilitaries come from inside Northern Ireland (e.g. thefts from or raids on the security forces), including legitimate weapons held by, or supplied by, renegade elements of the security forces. It should also be remembered that all the 'legal' deaths and injuries caused by the security forces can hardly be blamed on external suppliers.

Even if the supplies of guns and semtex, from wherever they are funded, could be kept out, it is highly unlikely that this would end the violence. Warring parties, in South Africa or Bosnia for example, have consistently demonstrated a remarkable ability to fashion weapons of war from whatever materials are at hand. Thus, while the most efficient explosive might have come from Czechoslovakia, through Libya, the paramilitaries can, and do, manufacture their own explosives and incendiary devices – from fertilizer and petrol. They also routinely press a range of other 'household tools' into serving the cause – electric drills, blowtorches, nails, and tar and feathers. Rocks, paving stones, hurling sticks, and knives have also come in handy on occasion.[135]

Apart from the inaccuracy of the charge, a serious problem with pinning the blame on external agents for channelling the violence is that it leads to neglect of other more fundamental causes. Our explanations of these misleading accounts vary with those who do the misleading. Many 'terrorism experts' are sympathetic to the state against whom the terrorism is directed and are unwilling to accept that terrorism may be the result of state mismanagement or genuine national or ethnic grievances, and they are also unwilling to accept that the state in question can behave terroristically. One of the academic experts we have discussed is a former British army information officer, who had the job of countering IRA propaganda.[136] Journalists have different motivations. They routinely exaggerate external links between paramilitaries and outside powers because these stories make good copy. Partisans also blame external sources to divert attention from their own responsibility. Thus loyalists focus more on Irish Americans, foreign Marxists, and the Vatican than on their own shortcomings.[137] Similarly, the establishment of links between South African whites and loyalists confirms the worst nationalist prejudices.

Adrian Guelke rightly regards external funding for Northern Ireland's paramilitary factions as relatively unimportant.[138] However, he exaggerates the influence of world opinion – an unmeasurable phenomenon – on the course of the conflict. Even if the Republic's claim to Northern Ireland is backed by international opinion, we do not think that means that Irish irredentism is dependent on international public opinion, nor would Guelke think so if pushed. Other national and ethnic groups have maintained territorial claims in the face of a hostile international consensus – consider Israel's claim over the West Bank, or Serbia's claim over parts of Bosnia and Croatia, and all of Kosovo. Nor can Britain's ambivalence about the Union be explained solely with reference to international public opinion, because Britain has violently resisted territorial claims sanctioned by international norms – consider the resistance to Argentina's claim to the Falkland Islands.[139] The British governing elite also has concrete reasons for resisting the integration of Northern Ireland which are independent of world opinion: it is after all an ethnic conflict zone, it is not rich, and its elected politicians are not reliable parliamentary allies.

Even if international norms did explain Irish irredentism and British ambivalence about the Union it is doubtful if the violence could be meaningfully explained by these particular exogenous causes. If international public opinion reversed itself, the Republic abandoned its constitutional claim, and Britain strengthened its commitment to the Union, it would still be the case that Northern Ireland consisted of two communities with an antagonistic relationship, and different views on the destiny of the territory and its rightful statehood. The only significant change would be that nationalists would be confronting international opinion and unionists would be benefiting from it, the reverse of what is happening now.[140]

The other authors who emphasize linkage politics sensibly attribute significant responsibility for the conflict to Britain and the Republic. However, the problem with Dervla Murphy's argument – that the conflict is due to London and Dublin's intervention and that peace could be secured simply by their withdrawal – is that it overstates the exogenous and understates the endogenous causes of the conflict. A reader of Murphy could be forgiven for believing there is no internal basis for conflict. While Britain and Ireland are not blameless, it can still be argued that the British presence since 1972, and Anglo-Irish co-operation, have prevented the violence from escalating beyond present levels.[141] There are also good grounds for believing that an independent Northern Ireland would be disastrous, leading to a Bosnian scenario complete with civil war, ethnic cleansing and partition.[142]

Conceding that Britain and the Republic have played some positive role, however, does not mean that their interventions have been uniformly positive. The perspective put forward by Boyle and Hadden and by Ruane and Todd, that the Republic has exacerbated unionist fears, and that the British government must share considerable responsibility for minority alienation within Northern Ireland, is accurate. In our own work, we have also attributed considerable responsibility to the British and Irish states for the evolution of the conflict.[143] Northern Ireland is properly understood as the site of twin nation-building failures, an area with two peoples which the British have been unable to integrate successfully into the British nation and which Irish nationalists have been unable to integrate into the Irish nation. It is also the territorial and popular miniaturization of the historic conflict between British and Irish nationalism. It is a site of two competing sovereignty claims, each of which is morally problematic and legally contestable. The political elites and institutions of Great Britain and the Republic, their governments and their constitutional arrangements, have both intentionally and unintentionally fostered conflict between their co-nationals. Their constitutions and institutions have, at least historically, been unwelcoming to their respective minorities.[144] Historically, elites in Great Britain and the Republic have mobilized national, ethnic and religious sentiments amongst their co-nationals, adding fuel to the flames of national passions. Today, these processes no longer have their past vibrancy. Instead both Great Britain and the Republic display similar emotional ambiguities about Northern Ireland. The British commitment to the Union is significantly qualified by Northern Ireland's express right to become part of the Republic if a majority within the region so wish, and most British politicians, like the British public, have made it clear that that possibility is one which they can foresee with equanimity, and even enthusiasm. This ambiguity about their unionist co-nationals worsens the latter's insecurities, and persuades them that they cannot rely on their patron-state. In contrast, the Republic's overt constitutional commitment to integrating Northern Ireland, specified in Articles 2 and 3 of its Constitution, has been politically qualified by the Republic's implicit assent to the idea that Irish unification should only come about through the consent of a majority in Northern Ireland. This practical revision of the Republic's irredentism is not enough to satisfy Ulster unionists but nevertheless worries some northern nationalists who are afraid that the Republic will effectively abandon them, as they believe occurred between 1925 and

1969. They note the development of 'revisionism' amongst the Dublin media and the intelligentsia of 'Dublin 4' with trepidation, believing that the Republic's opinion-formers have already frozen out the North from their conception of the nation.[145] Moreover, both northern nationalists and Ulster unionists observe that the Republic has not exactly been accelerating its constitutional and legal changes to make itself more attractive to those with whom it aspires to share a state. The Republic's citizens, in two referendums in the 1980s, voted to make abortion unconstitutional and not to lift the constitutional prohibition on divorce. Had the majority voted otherwise it would have signalled a public readiness to embrace a more accommodating, secular and liberal set of institutions, but the majority chose to vote without regard to the possible implications for national unification.

It is clear therefore that any adequate explanation of the conflict requires an understanding of the subtle connections between endogenous and exogenous sources of antagonism, violence and stalemate. The endogenous and exogenous are linked because the two ethnic communities have been partially but not fully mobilized into the British and Irish nations. Within Northern Ireland there is a nationalist–unionist conflict which has important internal and external roots. This conflict can be traced to the colonial interaction between planters and natives in the seventeenth century, to unionist treatment of the northern nationalist minority since 1921, and to the unwillingness of this minority to recognize the legitimacy of Northern Ireland. The planters were introduced from Britain for Britain's, or rather England's, defence. Their descendants now look to Britain for their defence. They see themselves, understandably, as a besieged people, an attitude reinforced by Britain's ambivalence and the Republic's irredentist claims. The Great British and the citizens of the Republic are in turn exasperated by unionists' political intransigence, which in turn persuaded the IRA to sustain its campaign, and invited loyalist backlashes. Northern nationalists refuse to accord anything more than partial legitimacy to Northern Ireland not only because they receive exogenous succour from the Republic, but also because the existing entity has so far given a permanent majority to their traditional ethnic enemies, and because of the way they have been treated, both under unionist control before 1972, and afterwards under British direct rule. British reforms have never been effectively harmonized with the impartial enforcement of law. The minority's alienation and the violence issuing from it produce sporadic British repression, which inflames traditional grievances and perceptions without producing order, while reinforcing Britain's reluctance to integrate Northern Ireland, and making it more difficult for the Republic to modify its territorial claim to sovereignty for fear of being accused of betraying its co-nationals. These linkages explain why any settlement of the conflict must address both the endogenous and exogenous sources of antagonism, violence and stalemate. They also suggest the importance of understanding the conflict through the lenses of the comparative literature on state-building and settler colonial societies.

*State-building.* We are persuaded by Ian Lustick's account of the role of settler colonialism in explaining British state-building failure in Ireland. One problem with this approach, however, is that by considering settlers the exclusive obstacle to successful state-building, it glosses over the responsibilities of the British state. The metropolis had considerable clout over the settler population, just as it has had such clout over their descendants, and it might have been more forceful in imposing its will on it, or more resourceful in offering inducements to it to be more accommodating towards the natives. British state-building failure has owed something to a British lack of will, as well as to settler intransigence. Historically the idea of making any Catholics, let alone Irish Catholics, co-equals in the British nation has proved extremely difficult for British political elites, and indeed the British public.[146]

Notwithstanding this criticism, Lustick's perspective helps explain the failure of Britain to integrate Ireland before 1921, and can also be used to help understand the failure of British state-building after 1921, and especially since 1969–72. It is widely accepted outside of loyalist and traditional unionist circles, for example, that unionist treatment of nationalists under the Stormont regime played an important role in preventing

the integration of Catholics.[147] Unionist opposition to civil-
rights demands in the late 1960s also helped to block the
possible integration of the minority. Since 1972, unionist opposition has often frustrated, or prevented altogether, reforming
efforts from London. The Anglo-Irish Agreement's failure to
deliver the reforms sought by its supporters has also been due
in part to loyalist opposition, and the British government's
unwillingness to antagonize unionists.[148]

Interpreting Northern Ireland as a settler–native zone has
distinct advantages – it is more precise than the generic
descriptions preferred by many political scientists, e.g. plural,
or segmented, or divided society. Settler–native zones tend
to be especially polarized, replete with antagonistic cultures
and socio-economic inequalities. In these respects Northern
Ireland has had more in common with Palestine and South
Africa than with Belgium, Switzerland and the Netherlands.
However, there are different types of settler–native conflicts.
They may be mono-national, in which the competing communities accept the state's territorial integrity, and the central
axis of conflict is over internal political power, in which case
consociational and integrationist techniques can be adopted
and can work – as in Zimbabwe, South Africa, Malaysia and
Fiji. Secondly, they may be bi-national or multi-national, with
at least one community demanding its own nation-state, in
which case internal solutions cannot work, while secessionist
or partitionist solutions can – for example, a two-state solution
in historic Palestine now seems inevitable. In the third, what
Frank Wright calls an ethnic frontier, the conflict zone is
inhabited by two or more communities which belong to nations
outside the conflict-zone. In these cases there are both internal
and external dimensions to the conflict. Northern Ireland is an
exemplary specimen. It is for this reason that we think that the
idea that Northern Ireland is a fragment (or a double fragment)
society is misplaced. The geographical and psychological distance between the communities in Northern Ireland and Great
Britain or the Republic is much less than that between the
former white settlers of the European empires in America and
Africa and their societies of origin – after all, both communities
regard themselves as part of the British and Irish nations, and

neither supports independence for Northern Ireland. They are better seen as communities on the frontiers of their respective national communities, with different conditions of existence from their co-nationals, but still attached to them.

## Conclusion

The comparative explanations discussed here contribute to our understanding of the Northern Ireland conflict, and offer insights that are missing from the previous chapters. However, they also suffer from varying defects. One way to evaluate their rival merits is to determine how they cope respectively with two fundamental facts, namely that Northern Ireland is a conflict zone, shared by two antagonistic communities; and secondly, that the conflict has been influenced in a number of ways by exogenous agents, particularly, Great Britain and the Republic.

In this perspective, the weakness of both cross-pressure and consociational theories is that neither does enough to distinguish ethno-national divisions (and conflict) from a range of other less explosive antagonisms. Instead of concentrating on the substantively ethnic and national nature of the conflict, and explaining its intensity, both cross-pressure and consociational theories over-emphasize relatively insignificant structural facts, such as whether a range of social divisions overlap or cross-cut, or the number and size of groups that are party to the conflict. These theories also fail to devote adequate weight to the role of exogenous agents in promoting antagonism, stalemate or conflict. Several of the 'linkage'-based accounts, on the other hand, devote too much weight to exogenous factors and occasionally blur over the elementary fact that Northern Ireland houses two antagonistic communities. The perspective of state-building theory, especially that articulated by Ian Lustick, and the comparative linkage accounts of Frank Wright, take into account the ethnic quarrel within historic Ireland, and explain its subsequent trajectory within a fateful settler–native–metro-politan triangle. Lustick and Wright also deal successfully with the exogenous context: the settlers were created as an act of English imperial policy, and Britain's role as the sovereign power in all of Ireland until 1921, and in Northern Ireland since 1921, is appropriately acknowledged. Lustick's historic account would have been improved if, instead of focusing on settler intransigence, he had also more vigorously examined the responsibility of the British state and its institutions for the pattern of conflict and the breakdown of British rule in Ireland. Frank Wright's work, while stylistically confusing, correctly homed in on the metropolitan responsibility for the break-up of the UK in 1921, and the development of Northern Ireland after 1920. Finally, it must be acknowledged that while the settler colonial literature illuminates British state-building failure it is less insightful in accounting for Irish nation-building failure. Though post-colonial independent Ireland succeeded, against British expectations, in establishing a mature democratic state, it failed to make itself attractive to the descendants of the former settlers in Northern Ireland, something which cannot be blamed on the settlers' descendants or on the British government.

# 9
# Pain-killers, Panaceas and Solvents: Explanations and Prescriptions

In the foreseeable future, no solution is immediately practical.
*Richard Rose, American political scientist, 1971*[1]

Violence . . . is killing the desire for unity.
*Liam Cosgrave, Irish prime minister, 1974*[2]

Termination of the conflict by either accommodation or a struggle to the finish seems improbable. The word that most aptly describes Northern Ireland's political condition is intractable.
*Adrian Guelke, South African political scientist, 1994*[3]

We want 'to counter one facile, thought-stopping, and pessimistic article of faith which has come to dominate academic, administrative and intelligent journalistic commentary on Northern Ireland . . . the notion that there is *no* solution to the conflict'.
*John McGarry and Brendan O'Leary, 1990*[4]

Throughout this book we have argued that the conflict in Northern Ireland is ethno-national, a systematic quarrel between the political organizations of two communities who want their state to be ruled by their nation, or who want what they perceive as 'their' state to protect their nation. Ethnic communities are perceived kinship groups. Their members share a subjective belief in their common ancestry, shared history and common culture,[5] and in specific situations such communities are prone to competition and antagonistic conflict, especially when such conflict has a national character. The sense which such communities have of real or imagined kinship may explain the ubiquity of ethno-nationalism – it satisfies the human need to belong, to feel 'at home', in an otherwise atomistic world.[6] Since an ethno-national group regards itself as a large extended family,[7] its members regard an attack on one as an attack on all, and they are often prepared to undertake significant sacrifices or engage in violent conflict for the well-being of the whole. Explosive national conflicts arise between politically mobilized ethnic communities. Territory, sovereignty and national esteem are their media. Land, power, and recognition are their bloody issues. Northern Ireland has been the site of such ethno-national conflict.

Not everybody, of course, falls into the ethno-national camps, or falls exclusively into them. A minority espouse cosmopolitan and secular values. The residents of Northern Ireland have a range of non-national political opinions and values. And not everybody is an uncompromising ethno-national partisan. Cultural Catholics as a whole may be less wholeheartedly committed to separatist nationalism than Protestants, as a whole, are to unionist integrationism – though this apparent difference may merely reflect the historic political weakness of Catholics in the region. However, despite these necessary qualifications, the national conflict has been the primary source of antagonism, violence and constitutional stalemate. This verdict nevertheless remains controversial, at least in some quarters.

## The Conflict about the Conflict

As we noted in our Introduction, there is a conflict about the conflict, a meta-conflict, and the bulk of this text has been a critical appraisal of this meta-conflict. Some schools of thought have emphasized endogenous causes, others exogenous causes. In this chapter we briefly present our views on the endogenous and exogenous causation of the conflict and compare our position with those discussed in previous chapters. We have also observed that just as there has been a conflict about the nature of the conflict, there has also been a conflict over political prescription(s); and illuminating the linkages between explanations and prescriptions is the second purpose of this chapter. Finally, we attempt to construct the elements of an intellectual consensus which we believe should underpin the present efforts of policy-makers and politicians in Northern Ireland, Great Britain and the Republic.

*Internal Explanations.* The crucial endogenous cause of conflict has been the presence of two competitive ethno-national communities within the same territory. Armed and unarmed struggle has been waged by organizations from two communities who want their state to be ruled by their nation, or 'their' state to protect their nation. They have both sought national self-determination, and their self-determination claims have been regarded by them, as well as by outsiders, as contradictory and antagonistic.

Ethno-national groups seek self-determination for self-protection and for self-expression. They may seek to exercise this right through demanding autonomy within a multinational state or by seeking independence; or if it suits their collective interests better, through maintaining the status quo. Ireland's ethno-national conflict has its origins in the colonial settlement of historic Ulster. Since the nineteenth century, both populations in Ireland, and what became Northern Ireland, have been mobilized within competing nationalisms: cultural Catholics have consistently voted, organized, struggled, and fought for a united autonomous or independent Ireland, while cultural Protestants have consistently voted, organized, struggled, and fought for the retention of the Union with Great Britain. The national question has motivated and distinguished republican and loyalist paramilitaries; it has accounted for the major cleavage separating the dominant political party blocs since 1921; and it has severely polarized the communities from 1969 until the present day. It follows that the national question must be addressed squarely by politicians and peace-makers intent on successful conflict-resolution.

The nature of the ethno-national conflict has been much

misunderstood. Many commentators have mistaken the ethno-national basis of the conflict for something else, or have believed that the ethno-national division is relatively mutable and capable of being transcended sooner rather than later. A common intellectual failing has been the conversion of the 'markers' which distinguish the two groups with distinct national identities into factors that are claimed to have crucial explanatory content in their own right. Typically religion (see chapter 5) and/or a range of other cultural differences (see chapter 6) are said to explain the conflict, violence and stalemate. Alternatively, in the manner of classical pluralists, the severity of the ethno-national conflict has been linked to the number and extent of divisions between the communities – other things being equal it is assumed that groups divided by multiple cleavages, such as religion, language and economic welfare, are more polarized than those divided by one national cleavage (see chapter 8).

The fundamental failing of this perspective is that it forgets that ethnic groups can maintain themselves and continue to fight with each other even in the face of significant accultura-tion – whether that acculturation is occasioned by secularism, linguistic homogenization, or other cultural dilution. Accul-turation, the sharing of culture, does not necessarily lead to assimilation, a sharing of identity, either in Northern Ireland or elsewhere. Indeed, as Walker Connor has pointed out, the communications revolution, and the acculturation which has accompanied it, may have exacerbated ethnic conflict by bringing groups with separate identities into closer contact with each other. The point is simple, but often refused: as long as groups have *any* way of telling each other apart – names or clothes can be substituted for religion or language – ethno-national divisions can be maintained. The vital feature of ethnic markers is not their particular religious, linguistic, or cultural signs, but rather that they provide evidence of common origin and shared experiences, a basis for recognizing members and non-members, and therefore potential friends and potential 'strangers'.[8]

It is also a mistake to believe the conflict can be explained primarily by economic variables – even though there are significant and unjustified economic inequalities between the two communities, and even though significant sections of both are relatively deprived in relation to others outside the conflict zone (see chapter 7). Ethno-national conflicts exist between groups which enjoy similar standards of living as well as between communities differentiated by clear inequalities, and ethno-national antagonisms mark reasonably affluent people as well as the deprived. It is true that unequal living standards facilitate ethnic mobilization, and claims and counter-claims about discrimination play an important part in ethno-national rhetoric. The evidence suggests that one community has been significantly discriminated against by the other, and that the other fears it will be discriminated against in any new political order. However, there is also significant evidence that the central goals of the ethno-national communities have been political rather than economic, and that they have been, and are, willing to promote the former at the expense of the individual material interests of their members. Those who emphasize the economic basis of the conflict are guilty, in Walker Connor's words, of 'an unwarranted exaggeration of the influence of materialism upon human affairs'.[9]

Finally, the endogenous explanations discussed in chapters 5 to 7 fail to devote adequate attention to the role of external agents and the external environment in shaping the conflict.

*External explanations.* Despite the dominance of endogenous explanations in the literature,[10] ethno-national conflicts do not occur in a quarantined geographical space or in sealed policy isolation-units, uninfluenced by external agents and the external environment. This does not mean that the exogenous explanations put forward by the ethno-national partisans in the first four chapters of this book are accurate, nor do we seek to deny that certain external agents, notably British governments, have sought to quarantine Northern Ireland and treat it as a policy isolation-unit.

In most cases the exogenous accounts discussed in chapters 1–4 should be seen as self-serving disinformation rather than as scrupulously honest intellectual endeavours to illuminate the conflict. The nationalist emphasis upon British imperialism, while historically convincing, lacks credibility as an account of the present. The Crown and the Westminster parliament and government may have been responsible for settling Protestants in historic Ulster but these settlers have long since become autonomous political agents. In fact, nationalists mostly appreciate that the British government, far from being responsible for Ulster unionism, often wishes it did not exist. Britain's preparedness to create a united Ireland if a majority in Northern Ireland want it, displays a remarkable willingness to cede part of its territory, rather than a chauvinist or an imperialist urge to maintain a unionist veto over the region's destiny. Indeed these arguments were, it seems, successfully presented by John Hume to Gerry Adams between 1988 and 1994 and contributed to the Provisional IRA's complete cessation of its military operations in August 1994. The traditional unionist emphasis on Irish irredentism is equally far-fetched. The Republic of Ireland is not primarily responsible for the existence of nationalism amongst the minority in Northern Ireland. Nationalism existed amongst Ulster Catholics before 1921, especially in rural Ulster, and its appeal was strengthened by the treatment of Catholics in Northern Ireland after 1920, by both the Stormont and London governments.

Nor can the conflict be explained adequately by the workings of British imperialism or the machinations of international capital as the dwindling community of Marxists believe (chapters 2 and 4). Imperialism shaped British policy towards Ireland, especially in the past. At the turn of the century imperialists feared that home rule for Ireland would be followed by the break-up of the Empire. The important point, however, is that this concern was not decisive – home rule, and then greater autonomy, were granted to the Irish Free State even though the British state's coercive capacity had not been exhausted. The retention of Northern Ireland was not a policy driven by simple imperialism – green Marxists gloss over the fact that the British government wanted to grant autonomy to all of Ireland and that the most sustained opposition to this idea came from within what was to become Northern Ireland. British colonial policy and its legacy are more relevant for explaining the Northern Ireland conflict than imperialism in any strictly Marxist sense. Given the contraction of Britain's empire, the growth of the European Union, and the development of the world market economy since World War II, it makes increasingly less sense to attribute 'the British presence' in Ireland to imperialism. The red Marxist thesis that capitalism (or the capitalist state) divides the working class through sectarian or ethno-national appeals does not satisfactorily explain why capitalists or 'capitalism' should want to create such unpropitious circumstances for 'exploitation', or why similar conflicts abound in non-capitalist societies. The ex-Soviet Union, ex-Yugoslavia, and ex-Czechoslovakia suggest that ethno-national conflict has no necessary connection with capitalism. The glaring weaknesses of Marxist exogenous accounts explains why few take them seriously anymore – though they survive in attenuated form in the arguments of electoral integrationists. Nationalist, unionist and Marxist partisans are not alone in putting too much emphasis on certain exogenous factors. There is, as we have insisted, no compelling reason to believe that the conflict intrinsically depends (or depended) on links between paramilitary or political groups in Northern Ireland and external agencies such as Libya, Irish America or South Africa (see chapter 8).

The foregoing external explanations ignore or underrate the internal sources of conflict, but this is not to concede that there are no important exogenous factors. Four external influences have crucially shaped the development of conflict, violence and political stalemate:

*First, ethno-national divisions can be exploited by an external state interested in destabilizing a competitor, and in turn this possibility may make that state less accommodating towards its minorities than it might otherwise be. Conversely, where such divisions are unlikely to be exploited by external powers a state finds it easier to be tolerant in its treatment of its minorities.* Thus the fact that Ireland was a weak link in the British defence system, exploitable by Spain, France and other continental powers, helped influence the colonization of what became Northern Ireland at the beginning of the seventeenth century, and helped drive the Union of Ireland and Britain in 1801. England's danger was

Ireland's opportunity, but it was also the cause of Ireland's subordination. England's dangers, and its sense of possible dangers, threatened settlers as well as natives. The prospect of defeat in World War II led Britain to consider offering Irish unification (reinforcing unionist insecurity), whereas subsequent victory led British policy-makers to re-emphasize their strategic interests in Northern Ireland (reinforcing republican arguments). Britain's interests, which have shaped the conflict, violence and stalemate in a variety of ways, were related to its declining imperial commitments, as well as to the international balance of power. Its withdrawal from its colonies and the termination of the Cold War in 1990 help explain recent ministerial statements that Britain has no 'strategic interest' in Northern Ireland, and the relaxation of British geopolitical insecurity has undoubtedly aided the reconstruction of British public policy in the 1990s.

*Secondly, when ethno-national combatants have co-nationals living in adjacent territories, it makes sense to claim that the actions of the external group(s) affect the internal conflict.* In comparative perspective, minority secessionist sentiment is usually strengthened by irredentism amongst neighbouring co-nationals. The same pattern reinforces unionist insecurity, which in turn influences the majority's treatment of the minority within the conflict zone. Northern Ireland is such a conflict zone – an ethnic frontier where the British and Irish nations meet. It is a site of conflicting sovereignty-claims, by Great Britain on the one hand, and by the Republic on the other.

*Thirdly, ethno-national combatants' behaviour, both conflictual and antagonistic, may be decisively influenced in both intended and unintended ways by the behaviour of the key states in question.* We have argued in *The Politics of Antagonism* that Northern Ireland's internal political development since 1920 has been crucially affected by British and Irish state-building and nation-building failures, both intended and unintended. The British failed to incorporate Irish Catholics in the emergent British nation-state, while the Irish Free State's political development minimized its attractiveness to Ulster Protestants. British constitutional arrangements and British policy-inertia enabled the Ulster Unionist Party to establish a system of domination over the minority between 1920 and 1972, while the constitutional architecture of the Irish Republic was inimical to a politics of accommodation in Northern Ireland. Moreover, political accommodation within Northern Ireland has been negatively affected by unintended developments in Great Britain and the Republic: in February 1974 a switch in government at Westminster contributed to the destruction of the Sunningdale agreement, and in November 1994 the fall-out between the Fianna Fáil and Labour coalition partners in the Dublin government led many to fear that the peace-process could falter.[11]

*Fourthly, in addition to being decisively influenced by developments in Great Britain or the Republic, and by competition between Britain and its external enemies, the conflict in Northern Ireland (and Ireland pre-1921) has been shaped by wider global developments, which have impacted on the region.* Contrary to what one may read in tourist brochures or war-journalism, Ireland and Northern Ireland have not been places where time has stood still. The international normative power of democratic majoritarianism and doctrines of national self-determination have decisively shaped the contours of conflict and argument in the region. The political mobilization of the Catholic and Protestant communities in the nineteenth century was partly a consequence of the spread of the doctrine of nationalism. In Northern Ireland northern nationalism received oxygen from what Walker Connor describes as the 'demonstration effect' – the success of other nationalist movements, the appeals to 'self-determination' which followed the First World War, the decolonizations which occurred after World War II, and the collapse of communist multinational states in the early 1990s. The outbreak of armed conflict in the late 1960s was crucially connected to the distributive repercussions of the expansion of the welfare state, a world-wide development in advanced industrialized countries, and it was also linked, by deliberate imitation, to the tactics and strategies used by other groups pursuing minority rights, particularly blacks in the United States. Since 1969, agents within the conflict have presented and understood their cases within a wider canvass, within Europe, North America, and beyond, which has in turn influenced their conduct. The effect should not be exaggerated, but the willingness of the ANC and the PLO to suspend their armed struggles to secure constitutional change made it easier for the IRA to declare a cessation of violence in August 1994 and to sell its merits to their supporters.

Adequate explanation of Northern Ireland requires, in short, the synthesis of the key endogenous and exogenous causes. The major endogenous cause at play has been the presence of two ethno-national communities within one territory whose boundaries were ill-chosen and have been perpetually contested. However, the relationships between these two communities have been consistently affected by a variety of exogenous causes, the most important of which have been the constitutional evolution and public policies of the British and Irish states.

## The Conflict over Prescriptions

Explanations of the conflict can be classified according to the importance they attribute to ethno-nationalism. We have identified three broad patterns:

- cosmopolitan perspectives, which declare that the conflict is not primarily about rival nationalisms, or maintain that national divisions are relatively mutable and capable of being transcended sooner rather than later;
- ethno-national partisan arguments, which accept that the conflict is indeed about nationalism but believe that it flows directly from a unilateral assault on their community's right to self-determination; and finally
- neo-pluralist arguments, which maintain that the conflict is focused on two competing and equally legitimate demands for self-determination.

Each of these analyses offers implicit or explicit prescriptions. The prescription associated with the cosmopolitan perspective is that the conflict can be settled or ameliorated without directly addressing the national (constitutional) question. The prescription associated with partisans is that the conflict can be resolved if the right to self-determination of one of the two competing communities is properly respected, i.e. either the protection of the Union or the creation of a united Ireland. Neo-pluralist analysis suggests that both nationalisms must be taken seriously and accommodated. We are exponents of this position.

*Cosmopolitanism, or anti-national integrationism.* Numerous commentators on Northern Ireland and other ethno-national conflicts have prided themselves on being cosmopolitans, or 'neutral integrationists': neutral because of their desire to accommodate the warring factions; integrationist because they believe that the relevant national divisions are not fundamental, and are capable of being transcended through the appropriate integration of people as individual citizens of a modern political system.

Red Marxists, while acknowledging that the conflict seems to be about nationalism, have treated it as epiphenomenal – believing that beneath superficial ethnic solidarities lie more fundamental class divisions. Like their Yugoslav and Soviet forebears they have prescribed class-conscious socialism as the route to modernity. Such views are now widely and justly regarded as utopian, if not bizarre. There is little evidence from Northern Ireland, or from other deeply divided ethno-nationally mixed territories, that transcendent class-consciousness can be easily or successfully promoted as an alternative to nationalist mobilization.

Red Marxists are not alone in being naive. Liberal Christians and secular liberals, both of whom proclaim universal or cosmopolitan faiths, frequently maintain that the political conflict, violence and stalemate are fundamentally religious in their genesis, and argue for the secular or ecumenical integration of Northern Ireland's citizens into wider and less benighted values. We have argued that this perspective is wrong-headed (see chapters 5 and 6). Politically speaking, being 'Catholic' or 'Protestant' denotes membership of rival ethno-national groups and describes both those who devoutly practise their faith and those for whom religion is of little or no importance (cultural Catholics and cultural Protestants). Their political demands, with the important exception of the members of the DUP, have little religious content, and the most religious – rural evangelicals – are usually the least politically violent. The political demands of the relevant communities have focused on their respective appeals for self-determination. To see the conflict as religious may be part of either an ecumenical or a secularizing agenda, with which we have no quarrel, but religiosity or secularization has no important role in understanding the conflict or in fostering its resolution.

The above examples of cosmopolitan 'anti-national' integrationism are matched by the perspectives of those civic integrationists who explain the conflict by reference to civil and socio-economic inequalities, and who suggest that an end to discrimination should be the goal of peacemakers. The view that economic investment in deprived areas will produce political benefits continues to have considerable support. So does the belief that the rival national, religious and cultural divisions can be significantly attributed to the segregated education system, and that integrated education is the progressive way forward (see chapters 5 and 6). Many also maintain that European integration is a very helpful development.

These cosmopolitans do not sufficiently recognize that the Northern Ireland conflict is being waged by nationally-mobilized groups, or that Northern Ireland has been more like Cyprus or Bosnia than the United States or South Africa. Northern Ireland's Catholics have not simply sought individual equality and respect within the confines of the existing state; instead many of them seek to join with the state which is governed by their ethnic compatriots, or at least to be fully protected by it. Giving them individual rights or integrated schools in a state dominated by their ethno-national antagonists will be as unlikely to satisfy them as equivalent packages would content Turkish Cypriots or Bosnian Serbs. Even 'minority rights' will not satisfy them. The SDLP declared in response to recent constitutional proposals, which would have given northern Catholics collective and individual rights, and which were tabled by the unionist political parties at the Brooke–Mayhew talks, 'While in general terms, such proposals might be both acceptable and sufficient in a society in which equality of treatment for minorities was the only issue, they are not sufficient in a society in which allegiance is a central problem.' Pan-European integrationists downplay the fact that both groups are predominantly nationalist rather than supranationalist. And it is wishful to think that they will soon be otherwise. They want their nation-state, or its protection, not a multi-national super-state, and they support (or oppose) the European Union only in so far as it will help them to obtain their primary goal.

The arguments of other anti-national integrationists discussed in chapter 8 are broadly pluralist in character but in our judgement they imply, wrongly, that Northern Ireland can be stabilized without the national question being frontally addressed – their hope is that just as long as some common interest(s) or cross-cutting cleavage(s) can be successfully promoted conflict-resolution can work. The popularity of this sentiment, and the prescriptions attached to it, are related to the assumption that there is little point in dealing with constitutional questions because the national aims of the rival groups are believed to be irreconcilable. It should be pointed out, however, that the proclaimed 'neutrality' of all anti-national integrationist authors is subject to an important qualification: they generally accept the Union, i.e. the preferred option of British nationalists, by default.[12]

*Partisan nationalism.* Partisan nationalism and integrationism have predominated within Northern Ireland. Its exponents call upon their opponents to embrace their nation-state, or to acquiesce in it as a minority. Even here, however, many of the extreme exponents in the respective partisan camps have given way to positions which are less radical in nature. Irish nationalists have traditionally believed that only their nationalism should be taken seriously (see chapter 1); that unionism is an artificial construct, maintained in existence by the partition of Ireland, British constitutional guarantees, the British subvention, political, economic and cultural privileges for Protestants, and, less often, by the failure of the Irish state to embrace Protestants in its constitution and public policy. Green Marxists supported this position, dressing the same message in the language of historical materialism (see chapter 2). In their judgement the split in the 'Irish' working class was a result of British imperialism. The British ruling class and their allies artificially divided the Irish proletariat by playing the 'Orange card', stoking sectarianism and creating a reactionary, bigoted and fundamentally anti-democratic ideology amongst Protestant workers. For this camp, the prescription is a united Ireland, to be achieved by removing unionism's external props, and organizing British, Irish, and American public opinion behind a democratic resolution of Britain's last colonial question.

These verities are now less strongly held. A quarter-century of protracted warfare has convinced many nationalists that unionism is autonomous and relatively resilient. Few seriously believe anymore that the British government is determined to hold on to Northern Ireland, or that it derives any strategic or economic advantage from the Union. There is growing support in nationalist ranks for the principle that a united Ireland cannot (and should not) be imposed without the consent of a majority in Northern Ireland – and some go further, advocating super-majority consent within Northern Ireland before Irish unification can be accomplished. Irish governments have recognized the need for majority consent in Northern Ireland for Irish unification in several documents, most recently in the Joint Declaration for Peace of 1993. Before and since the IRA's cessation of violence, republicans and nationalists had switched to talking about 'persuading' rather than forcing unionists to join a united Ireland. While they are by no means adverse to reinforcing this 'persuasion' by asking various external parties to bring appropriate pressures to bear, this shift must still be seen as progress.

Movement by unionists is also detectable. However, there are still significant numbers who believe that the nationalism of the northern minority is maintained in existence by the irredentism of the Irish government and reinforced by the unwillingness of Britain to make a commitment to Northern Ireland (see chapter 3). Electoral integrationists continue to suggest that it is the failure of the British parties to organize in Northern Ireland which is ultimately responsible for the conflict, despite the manifestly poor performance of the Conservative Party in all electoral contests in the region since 1989. Their Orange Marxist brethren reinforce this message by blaming partition on 'reactionary' Catholic nationalism, and by arguing that progressives have no alternative but to support the Union between Britain and Northern Ireland (see chapter 4). For this brand of unionism (as with Orange Marxism and Irish revisionism), political prescription still remains primitively partisan: they demand the end of Irish irredentism, a permanent commitment by the British to the Union, the firm suppression of republican terrorist organizations, and the organization of the major British parties in Northern Ireland.

However, not all unionists are such ethno-national partisans. There are those within the Alliance Party, for example, who have long been prepared to make concessions to the nationalist minority, including Irish dimensions. There are also moderate unionists in the ranks of the Ulster Unionist Party willing to accommodate the minority with committee chairs and even cabinet positions within a new devolved government. Some unionist intellectuals have suggested that the nationalist minority can be accommodated in a pluralist 'multi-national' United Kingdom, just like Scottish and Welsh nationalists. Others have demanded that the Ulster Unionist Party should sunder its links with the explicitly sectarian Orange Order. The development of these liberal tendencies has been stunted both by suspicions about the British government's long-term intentions, and, of course, by IRA violence, but they may blossom if the peace process can be maintained.

*Neo-pluralism: the politics of reconciliation versus the politics of antagonism.* Throughout this volume our intention has been to make clear that the dominant brands of integrationist thinking, both cosmopolitan and partisan, both nationalist and unionist, are problematic. There is little evidence to suggest the conflict can be resolved without the national question being addressed, or without it being addressed in a fair and even-handed manner.

We are led, therefore, to commend prescriptions which are built on the belief that both sides' nationalisms are durable and should be accommodated in an even-handed fashion. From this standpoint, three potential options stand out: partition, shared sovereignty, and a settlement package which, while falling short of shared authority, would seek to establish equality and parity of esteem for the two ethno-national groups and the same substantive safeguards as a system of shared authority.

*Another partition?* Some have suggested that a partition of Northern Ireland may have some merit, and that a plausible threat of a new partition of Ireland might have some effect in motivating rival leaders to seek a settlement. However, there are considerable arguments against pursuing this option. These include the fact that almost no-one wants partition. The JRRT/Gallup polls of July 1991 showed that this option attracted a mere 1 per cent level of first-preference support within Northern Ireland: 2 per cent of Protestants favoured it, 0 per cent of Catholics concurred. Repartition of Ireland also had low levels of first-preference support in the Republic (5 per cent) and in Great Britain (4 per cent). Partition proposals, moreover, are not publicly favoured by any British, Irish, or Northern Irish political party.

In addition, there is no easy way to partition Northern Ireland along ethnic lines. Any plausible boundary (or set of boundaries) would leave Belfast, which contains around a third of Northern Ireland's nationalist population, within unionist boundaries, or create a nationalist enclave within unionist boundaries. Given that many of the newly partitioned areas would remain ethnically heterogeneous, there would be question-marks surrounding the durability of the new frontiers, the kind of uncertainty which encourages 'ethnic-cleansing'. Nor do previous British-administered partitions (in Ireland, Palestine, or India) inspire confidence in this option. The sole purpose of considering partition is to consider it as the option of last resort. As Tom Hadden and Kevin Boyle have suggested in a recent book, the choice facing Northern Ireland is between separation and sharing.[13] They make clear that they prefer sharing to separation – which would be the ultimate goal of any new partition. However, if radical separation must be ruled out, and if, as we have suggested, radical integration cannot work, of either a nationalist or unionist kind, what options remain?

*Shared authority?* We have argued elsewhere that because of the dangers associated with partition the most attractive option for Northern Ireland is a model of 'shared authority'.[14] In this perspective both national traditions would be protected and accommodated through shared sovereignty. A democratic and autonomous condominium would be established in which power and responsibility would be shared between the British and Irish governments, the peoples of Northern Ireland, and their political institutions. Within Northern Ireland, the democratic structures of the condominium could include a collective executive, a separation of executive, legislative, and judicial powers, and a system of checks and balances. These institutions would provide a capacity for self-government in certain policies which could be extended as broad agreement and co-operation emerged amongst the political parties. The model also provides for the United Kingdom and the Republic to be external co-sovereigns, and guarantors of the internal settlement. Its detailed constitutional architecture is described elsewhere, but its logic is a combination of shared sovereignty and consociational principles.[15] Each community would enjoy self-government in the religious, cultural, and educational domains; proportionality rules would operate throughout government and the public sector; consensus would be required in policy domains such as security; and each community would have effective *de jure* and *de facto* veto powers to protect its national identity.

Underpinning shared sovereignty is the idea of splitting the differences, satisfying each community's claim to national self-determination to the extent that it does not conflict with the other's. Each community would obtain the protection of its nation-state at the expense of having to share the territory, sovereignty and political power with the other community and its nation-state. Any workable system of shared authority would, of course, have to be durable. Unionists would have to be convinced that it was not a short-term transitional arrangement leading to the establishment of a united Ireland. Durability could be achieved by entrenching the new status of Northern Ireland in the constitutional law of the United Kingdom and Republic of Ireland, and by making any changes to the system contingent on overwhelming support (say two-thirds) expressed in a referendum in Northern Ireland. This latter amending formula would protect equally the current minority and a possible future minority from being exclusively incorporated into one state's jurisdiction against its will.

The idea of shared authority would provide fair arrangements which balance the conflicting nationality claims. It is normatively superior to an independent united Ireland since the latter is inconsistent with the self-determination of the unionist people, and it is superior to the existing United Kingdom because this is inconsistent with the self-determination of the nationalist people. Shared authority could also take advantage of one of Northern Ireland's few advantages, at least when compared with some other sites of ethnic conflict, the fact that the external patrons of the respective groups enjoy friendly relations and a desire to work together to resolve the conflict.

However, despite the significant merits of shared authority, it is unlikely that it would be accepted by a majority of the Northern Ireland electorate in present circumstances. In the past we have been sympathetic to the argument that such opposition should be by-passed. The two governments, we believed, could have imposed a compromise on the parties, adopting the same path they embraced when they signed the Anglo-Irish Agreement. They could have argued that imposition was necessary to break the constitutional deadlock, and that what would have been imposed respected the vital interests and equality of both communities. The hope would have been that the nationalist community would be content with such arrangements, and that the unionist community, realizing they would be more strongly protected against an independent united Ireland under a system of shared authority than they are under the Anglo-Irish Agreement (or before it), would subsequently participate in the new institutions of government.

However, we recognize that imposing a model of shared authority against significant unionist opposition would be problematic. Moreover, given the growing support for the principle of 'consent', it has become increasingly evident that neither the British nor the Irish governments are willing to impose changes in the constitutional status of Northern Ireland. Originally, as expressed in the Anglo-Irish Agreement and in the Joint Declaration for Peace, 'consent' involved the right of a majority of the Northern Ireland electorate to stay within the United Kingdom on the one hand or to join a united Ireland on the other. Since September 1994, however, with John Major's announcement that there will be a referendum in Northern Ireland on any final constitutional package freely negotiated between political parties in Northern Ireland, it is evident that active rather than tacit 'consent' is now necessary for any widespread constitutional settlement.

As any explicit model of shared authority is unlikely to pass a referendum requirement in Northern Ireland (as opposed to the Republic), it is necessary to look at functionally equivalent ways in which equality and parity of esteem for the two national groups can be protected and expressed. Any such scheme will have to be consistent with the Anglo-Irish Agreement and the Joint Declaration for Peace. It will also have to be acceptable, given the referendum requirement, to a majority of the Northern Ireland electorate, and also to a majority in the Republic of Ireland. The details of one such scheme, which we have entitled 'Double Protection', are provided below.

*Double protection: a neo-pluralist framework for Northern Ireland.* Any effective settlement must address three related issues: the constitutional status of Northern Ireland; the internal arrangements for governing Northern Ireland; and effective external arrangements, including the protection of the settlement by the two governments.

*The constitutional status of Northern Ireland.* In the Anglo-Irish Agreement of 1985, and again in the Joint Declaration for Peace in 1993, the Irish and British governments recognized that Northern Ireland should remain within the United Kingdom for as long as a majority of its population so wishes. They have also agreed that the creation of a unified Ireland should occur if and when a majority in Northern Ireland so desires. These principles offer unionists their present guarantee while assuring nationalists that they can achieve their long-term goal constitutionally. They are accepted by most parties to the conflict. The most evident exception is Sinn Féin, but its leaders now appear to be prepared to accept a settlement of this nature provided that it is an integral component of the exercise of Irish national self-determination, and provided it is accompanied by a substantive erosion of British sovereignty and powerful cross-border institutions.[16]

The principle of majority consent is expressed in an international treaty, but to be fully consistent both governments must entrench this commitment in their domestic constitutional law so that no one can dispute the integrity of their respective commitments. The Westminster government can achieve this objective by deleting or modifying Section 75 of the Government of Ireland Act of 1920 (as amended), which presently expresses unqualified Westminster sovereignty over Northern Ireland. In this way the exercise of Westminster's sovereignty would be made clearly conditional upon the consent of a majority of the people of Northern Ireland to remain within the United Kingdom – at present British public law is ambiguous on this matter. In the event of agreement on a balanced constitutional settlement, the Irish Government has agreed that it will organize a referendum proposing that Articles 2 and 3 of its Constitution be modified so that Irish unity is made conditional upon the consent of a majority of people in Northern Ireland. Naturally the ability of the Irish government to carry its people in such a referendum, and to reassure northern nationalists that Dublin is not about to forsake its responsibilities, will be dependent on the rest of the settlement package.[17]

*The internal settlement* The cornerstone of the internal dimension of a settlement must be a new regional assembly and executive, elected for a fixed period of office. Proportionality rules must be used to elect the assembly – STV is the obvious voting system, given that it has been in use in local government, European, and Assembly elections in Northern Ireland since 1973.[18] Proportionality principles will also have to be used by the assembly to establish its committee structures and chairs; and they must be used to elect the executive. The executive could be determined on the basis of parties' share of the first-preference vote, or on the basis of parties' share of seats in the assembly. There are a range of proportionality rules which could be used to determine the composition of the executive, but we believe that the technical Sainte-Laguë rule is the fairest one for small parties, and in our judgement it should be used in preference to the d'Hondt rule, which benefits larger parties – and which, understandably, has been supported by the Ulster Unionist Party and the Democratic Unionists in previous negotiations. A rule like Sainte-Laguë, which is fair to small parties, will give both the Alliance Party and Sinn Féin a stake in any new executive or committee-structure for a new assembly, as we illustrate below.

To establish party-shares of seats from party-shares of votes, the d'Hondt rule uses divisors of 1, 2, 3, . . . n, whereas the Sainte-Laguë rule uses divisors of 1, 3, 5, . . . n. The effect of the Sainte-Laguë divisors is to help the relatively smaller parties.

The procedure is demonstrated below on the supposition that Northern Irish parties would be allocated seats in a 7-person executive on the basis of their first-preference vote in the region as a whole. Imagine that the percentage distribution of the first-preference vote for each party in an Assembly election is as follows:

UUP 34, SDLP 25, DUP 18, SF 12, APNI 8, and Others 3.

The numbers in parentheses, below, indicate seats on the executive in the order in which they would be allocated. Under the Sainte-Laguë rule the largest party, the UUP, gets the first seat, then its seat share is divided by three. Now the second largest party, the SDLP, has the highest number and thus wins the second seat, and has its vote total divided by three. The process then continues until all 7 seats have been filled.

| divisors | UUP | SDLP | DUP | SF | APNI | Others |
|---|---|---|---|---|---|---|
| 1 | 34 (1) | 25 (2) | 18 (3) | 12 (4) | 8 (7) | |
| 3 | 11.3 (5) | 8.3 (6) | 6 | 4 | | |
| 5 | 6.8 | | | | | |

In this example the Sainte-Laguë rule would generate an executive of 2 members of the UUP, 2 of the SDLP, 1 from the DUP, 1 from Sinn Féin, and 1 from the Alliance Party. By contrast, under the d'Hondt rule the executive would be constructed as follows.

| divisors | UUP | SDLP | DUP | SF | APNI | Others |
|---|---|---|---|---|---|---|
| 1 | 34 (1) | 25 (2) | 18 (3) | 12 (6) | 8 | |
| 2 | 17 (4) | 12.5 (5) | 9 | 4 | | |
| 3 | 11.3 (7) | | | | | |

In this example the d'Hondt rule would generate an executive of 3 UUP members, 2 SDLP members, 1 DUP member and 1 SF member. The use of these different rules on the same first-preference voting figures shows how d'Hondt would benefit the largest party, the UUP, and how it would hurt the smallest party, the Alliance. On a pure proportionality rule, parties should have the following share of seats on a 7-person executive: UUP 2.38, SDLP 1.75, DUP 1.26, SF .84, Alliance .56 and Others .21.

 Given that pure proportionality is impossible, rules of approximation, like d'Hondt or Sainte-Laguë, are necessary to allocate seats. It is easy to see that deviation from proportionality, however measured, is less extensive under Sainte-Laguë than under d'Hondt – which is why we commend it.

Proportionality rules of whatever kind, and however equitable, will not be enough to ensure the consent of northern nationalists to any new constitutional order. While fairer than the Westminster model,[19] where plurality rule operates and the legislative majority wins all executive seats, proportionality is still consistent with simple majority-rule by unionists – one of the major political causes of conflict in the Stormont years. For this reason, some type of 'power-sharing' will also be required, though it need not apply to every policy function. The executive should be required to proceed by consensus in specified areas of policy, such as security and policing; and committee chairs, who would come form different parties, could have limited policy-initiating autonomy. The legislature could also be prevented from bringing down the executive – except by a weighted voting procedure requiring more than a two-thirds majority.

In our judgement the more power that is devolved to Northern Ireland the better. If significant control over finances and security is devolved, it will ensure greater incentives for politicians to participate in and work any new system. Ideally, the Northern Ireland Office and the Secretaryship of State for Northern Ireland should be abolished and their functions transferred to the new executive and committee chairs. The Foreign Secretary, the Home Secretary and the Attorney General could carry out British responsibilities for those functions which had not been devolved in the British Cabinet and in the inter-governmental conference established by the Anglo-Irish Agreement.

A new constitutional settlement could also include a reordering of the local government system. One option would be to increase local government powers to roughly what they were before the Macrory reforms of the early 1970s – though fears of local clientelism will inhibit the SDLP from supporting this option. If local government boundaries remain as they are now, or if new boundaries create heterogeneous jurisdictions, it will be necessary to ensure that proportionality and power-sharing principles are applied at the local government level. There have been some attempts to work local power-sharing arrangements already, and it is likely that the will to operate these would be greater in the absence of violence and in the context of an overall settlement. The overall settlement could therefore provide incentives to share power at the local government level, with a proportion of the block grant, or control over certain powers, being made conditional on such arrangements. It could also be decided to make the very existence of any particular local government dependent on consociational practices. If a council was not prepared to operate these, it would not be permitted to function, and its powers would be taken over by the Northern Ireland executive.[20]

Apart from the reorganization of local government, it will be necessary to implement a variety of other changes aimed at ensuring that the two major national communities enjoy full parity of esteem and treatment. To this end a Bill of Rights will be necessary, which will protect collective cultural rights as well as individual human rights, and which will allow for the promotion of disadvantaged groups. Bills of Rights are useful in divided societies because they help to restrain the majority's abuse of executive and legislative power. By allowing individuals from the minority to bring the executive, legislature, local governments or police to task, Bills of Rights reduce the risks which minorities face in entering consociational arrangements. The Bill of Rights should be interpreted by a Northern Ireland Supreme Court, and its decisions in turn should be capable of being appealed to the European Court in Strasbourg – by-passing the British House of Lords. It would be helpful in this regard if, as in Canada, public funds were to be made available to allow citizens to challenge government decisions.

A number of other changes will be necessary if there is to be equality and parity of esteem for the two major traditions. These must entail the creation of a Northern Ireland Police Service (NIPS) to replace the Royal Ulster Constabulary, and a Northern Ireland Judicial Commission rather than Crown Courts. There must also be substantive changes in the recruitment and composition of the police and senior judiciary, and in the oaths presently required by jurors, judges, barristers, and police, which are at present far more royalist in Northern Ireland than in Great Britain. It might be thought appropriate to invite experienced officers from the Garda Siochana to join the NIPS. This measure would help to offset the current unavailability of experienced personnel from the northern nationalist community. Another possibility would be, as in North America, to organize the police on a local basis under the control of local police boards made up of local councillors as well as appointees from the Northern Ireland executive. Such a step might help to encourage northern nationalists to join and, as well as rendering the police more locally accountable, might help to win minority support for the institution. Even if the police are not locally organized, it would make sense if officers were operationally deployed to take into account the composition of the communities they police. Any inflexibility or internal rivalries within the service which might result from the implementation of this principle would be outweighed by the consequent gains in legitimacy and public co-operation.

The construction of bonds between the police and the

community they service will also be facilitated by their rapid disarmament and by their use of regular police vehicles rather than armour-plated Land-Rovers. This, of course, will only be possible in the event of peace being sustained. The personnel of the Northern Ireland Police Authority should be proportionately selected by an appropriate committee of the new assembly, operating along lines of consensus. The new body should replace the present one, which consists of NIO appointees, has never called for an inquiry into any policing controversy, and does not command the support of the minority community.

The promotion of equality and parity of esteem between the two groups will also require a strengthened commitment to fair employment. This will involve promoting affirmative action, restricted at the moment by the duty not to discriminate included in the Fair Employment Act of 1989. Small employers should no longer be exempted from the Act's provisions, monitoring of the workforce should be extended to include part-time work, and targets or timetables should be adopted for reducing the gap in unemployment rates between the communities. An overall settlement will produce some significant funds from the United States and European Union, which can be targeted to develop the economic infrastructure of border-regions and the deindustrialized areas of Northern Ireland.

Equality and parity of esteem will require a continuing commitment to equal provision for all kinds of primary and secondary education (including both denominational and integrated schools). The cultural insignia of both national traditions must also be equally protected or equally unused – so, where it is fitting, both or no national anthems should be played, and both or no national flags displayed. Where appropriate, both the British Monarch and the Irish President should be invited to ceremonial functions. In areas where there are significant Irish nationalist populations, they should be free to give Irish names to streets, and to use Irish in schools and other public institutions.

*The external dimensions.* A proposed settlement which incorporated the above dimensions would nevertheless be insufficient. The external dimensions of the conflict necessitate a number of additional measures if they are to be addressed effectively.

Institutional British and Irish dimensions are required, and it will be best if it is made plain that these will survive any future transformation in the status of Northern Ireland, i.e. that they will continue to exist whether Northern Ireland remains within the United Kingdom or if it comes under the sovereignty of the Republic at some future juncture. The inter-governmental conference established by the Anglo-Irish Agreement must remain, though its scope and functions must be refined. The inter-parliamentary tier of the Agreement must be expanded to include members from the new Northern Ireland Assembly as well as representatives from Westminster and Dáil Eireann.

The most urgent priority here is to establish all-Ireland cross-border co-operation and British–Irish co-operation, especially in policy functions affected by the European Union. It is the former which will be the most problematic. It is crucial for the nationalist minority that there be some institutional link between Northern Ireland and the Republic. Indeed it is considered a litmus test of any successful settlement by many Irish nationalists and will therefore be critical to the passage of amendments to Articles 2 and 3 in a referendum in the Republic. It is unlikely that any settlement could endure without cross-border institutions of some kind – if it could get off the ground at all. There are a number of formats such an all-Ireland institution could take, and it would be best if these are not seen as guaranteeing any creeping political unification of Ireland.

The most comprehensive form of all-Ireland cross-border co-operation would be a directly elected body, with jurisdiction over a limited number of areas of common concern. The representatives from each jurisdiction could be required to proceed by consensus, though they could, by consensus, delegate powers to subordinate agencies. This model would not mean a united independent Ireland was being constructed, because Northern Ireland would continue to be part of the United Kingdom. It would represent an imaginative attempt to address the problems of an ethnic frontier region, which would co-operate with the rest of Ireland for certain

limited purposes while remaining a devolved region of the
United Kingdom for the rest. Alternatively, the all-Ireland
institution could be indirectly elected, being comprised of representatives from Dáil Eireann and the new Northern Ireland
legislature, or even from local jurisdictions in both parts of
Ireland.

It is possible that it might be judged that such institutions
could not achieve majority support in a Northern Ireland
referendum. In this eventuality there are several alternatives.
One is to create an institutionalized Irish dimension consisting
of appointed cross-border agencies, in some cases modelled
on the European experience, such as the European Steel
and Coal Community. Commissioners could be appointed
by their respective jurisdictions for fixed periods to carry out
certain technocratic tasks, with executive powers to harmonize
functions and policy in specifically delimited areas. In some
cases, these commissions would be UK–Republic bodies, but
in other cases they would be Northern Irish–Republic agencies.
Another possibility would be to establish British–Irish bodies
mandated by the sovereign governments which would not be
in the constitutional package submitted to the electorate in
Northern Ireland.

It will be an essential task of political leadership to persuade the unionist population that the establishment of these
agencies will not imply any direct erosion of either state's sovereignty; that there are straightforward economic and functional
benefits to be derived from them, and that such delimited
bodies will represent a considerable compromise on the part of
the nationalist population. If these arguments can be successfully made, sufficient support may be forthcoming amongst
the unionist population. Consideration may, however, need to
be given to a default mechanism, to ensure that cross-border
bodies will survive any malfunctioning of Northern Ireland's
internal arrangements. Without such a mechanism the population of the Republic may find that it has transformed its
Constitution without any guarantees that its goals and wishes,
or those of northern nationalists, have been durably protected.

*Double protection.* A crucial aspect of the external dimension
to a settlement will therefore be mechanisms which empower

the two governments to protect any agreed constitutional set-tlement of the above kind. The most obvious step to take here is to allocate the inter-governmental conference the role of safeguarding and guaranteeing the constitutional settlement. In this way each community will be reassured that it has the background protection of its respective nation-state. The most powerful way of achieving this goal would be to empower each government in the inter-governmental conference, after legal remedies have been exhausted, with the right to veto any law or measure of public policy in Northern Ireland which it deems fundamentally to threaten national, religious or human rights. A weaker version of this approach would empower the two governments, acting in agreement, with such a veto capacity.

Such mechanisms would ensure that northern nationalists could be confident that there would be no return to the Stormont nightmare, and that cross-border institutions would survive any malfunctioning in Northern Ireland's internal gov-ernment. It would be objected by some that unionists would see any such mechanisms as an intrusion by the Irish government in the affairs of Northern Ireland, and therefore tantamount to joint authority or joint sovereignty. The answer to this objec-tion is fourfold: first, such double protection mechanisms must apply to both communities (for example, protecting unionists against a perverse legal verdict); secondly, these mechanisms do not positively involve either the British or Irish states in governing Northern Ireland, but rather provide a check against a possible internal abuse of power within Northern Ireland itself; thirdly, to be effective such mechanisms must be used very sparingly and must exist largely as deterrents; and finally, to be balanced such double protection mechanisms must be institutionalized so that they would survive any change in the sovereignty of Northern Ireland. In short, the British government must have the same role in protecting the British community if and when Northern Ireland became part of a federal Ireland as that which the Irish government should have now as long as Northern Ireland remains part of the United Kingdom.

Double protection or double insurance might be further entrenched in the following way. It could be constitutionally established that whatever arrangements were now agreed for the governance of Northern Ireland would continue to apply if and when Northern Ireland voted to join a federal Ireland. The entire constitutional package would be transferable, apart from the fact that the two governmental protectors of the constitutional arrangements would change places (one would now be sovereign whereas the other would be a background protector of its national community).

This model settlement would be consistent with the thinking which delivered the Anglo-Irish Agreement and the Joint Declaration for Peace. It offers a constructive way forward. While not representing shared sovereignty it achieves the same practical consequences – permanent institutional protections for both national communities – and it does so without violating the principle of majority-consent for any change in the sovereign status of Northern Ireland. It would improve upon the status quo for northern nationalists while reassuring unionists that if and when they become a minority they will receive the same protections to which northern nationalists should now be entitled. It is also a prescription consistent with our explanations of what has driven conflict in Northern Ireland, and of what has to be done to remove the prime motors of antagonism.

# 10

# Afterword: The Sound of Breaking Ice?

Peace hath her victories
No less renowned than War.
*John Milton, English poet, 'To the Lord General Cromwell', 1652*

You may track Ireland through the statute-book of England, as a wounded man in a crowd is tracked by his blood.
*Thomas Moore, Irish poet, 1824*[1]

Changes are occurring underneath the frozen surface.
*John Whyte, Irish political scientist, 1990*[2]

I am satisfied that Irish nationalism, if properly mobilized and focused, at home and internationally, now has sufficient political confidence, weight and support to bring about the changes which are essential for a just and lasting peace.
*Gerry Adams, President of Sinn Féin, August 1994*[3]

We have a lifeboat here that could capsize at any moment, so we have to be very careful how fast we move it in any direction. For the moment we are just happy to have so many people on board.
*Senior British Official, 1994*[4]

Peace cannot be erected upon a 'peace process' which does not exist.
*Dr Ian Paisley, leader of the DUP, New Year Message for 1995*[5]

## When the Shooting Stopped

At midnight on 31 August 1994 the IRA unilaterally implemented a complete cessation of its military operations. It did so because of the 'potential of the current situation and in order to enhance the democratic peace process'. It noted that the Downing Street Declaration was not a solution,[6] and saluted its comrades. Six weeks later, on 13 October 1994, a reciprocal cessation of violence was announced by the Combined Loyalist Military Command acting on behalf of the UVF and the UDA. Its cessation was dependent upon the continuation of that of the IRA. Both announcements were fronted by the political parties of republicanism and loyalism, Sinn Féin, and the much smaller Ulster Democratic and Progressive Unionist parties.

In the interval between the two cessations of violence[7] the airwaves and newspapers in Britain and Ireland focused on the absence of the word 'permanent' from the IRA's statement. Though the President of Sinn Féin described the Irish prime minister's interpretation of the ceasefire as permanent as being 'correct', most British politicians, taken by surprise, remained publicly uncertain, as did many unionist politicians – though the DUP warned it was a ruse. Nevertheless, small but significant transformations in the British military presence and the operations of the RUC were soon visible – spoiled by the deployment of the Parachute Regiment in West Belfast, a step later reversed. A week after the IRA's announcement Gerry Adams and John Hume publicly shook hands with the Taoiseach in Dublin. On the same day, 6 September, the British prime minister, John Major, effectively ejected Ian Paisley from 10 Downing Street. The following day the American Vice President, Al Gore, indicated that Washington accepted that the IRA's ceasefire was permanent. Two weeks later the British government lifted its broadcasting ban on Sinn Féin, promised the population of Northern Ireland a referendum on any constitutional settlement, and announced the opening of border roads previously sealed for years by the military. Meanwhile, the Irish justice minister, Maire Geoghegan-Quinn, announced that she was considering the early release of some republican prisoners held in Irish jails. The Irish prime minister stated on 17 September that a united Ireland was at least twenty years away – just before Adams embarked upon a tour of the USA, during which he warned that a new generation of republicans could resume 'armed struggle' if the peace process faltered.

Having received reassurances that neither the British nor Irish governments had agreed a secret deal to terminate the Union, the loyalist paramilitaries eventually announced their own ceasefire. Their small political parties, the PUP and the UDP, emerged from obscurity, indicating remorse for the killings of innocent civilians carried out by their comrades, and displaying more political sophistication than they had been previously accredited. Just over a week later John Major went to Belfast to announce that he was making the 'working assumption' that the IRA's ceasefire was permanent, that exploratory talks between government officials and Sinn Féin would start before Christmas, that all cross-border roads would be re-opened, and that the exclusions orders preventing Adams and Martin McGuinness from travelling to Great Britain would be lifted.

Thus far the peace process had developed relatively smoothly, though tensions had arisen between the Irish government's desire to bring republicans in from the cold as quickly as possible, and the British government's wish to reassure unionists that they were not being sold out. However, two serious hiccoughs threatened to derail developments. First, on 10 November a postal worker was shot dead by IRA personnel during an armed robbery in Newry – prompting the Irish government to delay its planned release of prisoners until later in the year. The incident minimally suggested dissident or undisciplined activity within the IRA, but reassurances from republicans eventually satisfied both governments. Then a week later the Irish prime minister was forced to resign for misleading Dáil Éireann in a complex affair involving his choice of candidate for Attorney General, and the latter's role in an extradition case involving a paedophile Catholic priest. The coalition government of Fianna Fáil and Labour broke up in acrimony and a month ensued before the formation of a new three-party government composed of Fine Gael, Labour and Democratic Left. This crisis endangered the peace process because the Fine Gael leader John Bruton had previously displayed little sympathy for republicans or northern nationalists, while both Sinn Féin and the SDLP had been happy with the role played by Reynolds, a tough negotiator with the British government. Nevertheless, when elected Taoiseach on 15 December, Bruton made plain his determination to continue the work of his predecessor; the Labour Foreign Minister Dick Spring pledged continuity; and spokespersons from Sinn Féin, after wavering, indicated their willingness to work with whoever was in charge of the two governments.

The crisis in Dublin delayed the planned release of a framework document for discussion and negotiation by political parties in Northern Ireland, but compelled the British government to sustain the momentum. On 9 December a Sinn Féin delegation, led by Martin McGuinness, opened discussions with Northern Irish officials at Stormont, followed within a week by representatives from the UDP and the PUP. The first meetings went well; the second were less successful.[8] As the year ended Northern Ireland was experiencing its longest period of calm since the late 1960s. Though the talks with republicans and loyalists were just beginning – and looking as if they might stall over the decommissioning of weapons, demilitarization and the early release of prisoners – a negotiated end to conflict appeared feasible. As the new year began, the publication of the framework document by the two governments was eagerly and fearfully anticipated – the deposed Irish premier had made clear in a radio interview that it included an all-Ireland body with executive powers.

# How the Shooting Stopped

The roots of this drama lie in four immediate sources: political and military developments within both the republican and the loyalist movements; the 'second track' diplomatic activities of the leader of the SDLP John Hume, and third-parties, including an Irish-American peace delegation; clandestine discussions or negotiations between the British government and the IRA; and the (eventual) co-operative diplomacy of the British and Irish governments following the Anglo-Irish Agreement.[9]

After the Anglo-Irish Agreement republicans were forced to

take stock of their position. Sinn Féin's growth as an electoral force, north and south, had been thwarted. Though not beaten, republicanism was not winning, militarily or politically. The Republic was hostile to the long war. Sinn Féin's participation in electoral politics had, moreover, obliged it to develop greater political sophistication. Republicans started to reconsider their explanations of the conflict, and the place of Protestants in a new Ireland. More sensitive political language began to creep into their documents – as evidenced in *Towards a Lasting Peace in Ireland* (1992) and its predecessor *Scenario for Peace* (1987). British and Irish ministers, and Hume, took notice. In a speech in 1990 Secretary of State Peter Brooke directly addressed republican explanations of the conflict in an attempt to portray the British identity of Ulster unionists, rather than the British state, as the major obstacle to a united Ireland;[10] and a secret meeting took place between Martin McGuinness and a representative of the British government in October 1990 – followed by continuous exchanges/negotiations between the government and the IRA until the winter of 1993. In 1988 the leaders of the SDLP and Sinn Féin had discussed rival interpretations of the conflict, and though the talks broke up, they had shifted the thinking of some key republicans, and had put down a marker.

However, the potential thaw in the republican position was not very visible. The early 1990s were marked by the revival of loyalist paramilitarism, prompted by the unionist reaction to the Anglo-Irish Agreement and by the clearing out of informers from their ranks. They also saw the initiation and collapse of inter-party talks sponsored by the two governments in 1991–2.[11] No one at the time appeared interested in any type of negotiation – a position satirized in Martyn Turner's cartoon (see figure 10.1). The IRA renewed extensive urban bombing in Northern Ireland and in Great Britain, while loyalists increased their attacks on real and alleged republicans. Having lost Adams's Westminster seat in West Belfast in the 1992 British general election Sinn Féin's political morale was at a low ebb. The stalemate may have been hurting.[12] Sinn Féin and the IRA considered a change in strategy. In April 1993 a journalist reported that Hume and

Figure 10.1 Martyn Turner's perspective on negotiation
*Irish Times*, Cartoonists' and Writers' Syndicate

Adams had resumed discussions. They subsequently issued a joint statement in which the concept of 'self-determination' was prominent, and in September 1993 announced an agreement which they refused to publish (it remains unpublished). Critics of Hume *either* thought he was trying to avoid the resumption of the talks technically lying in suspended animation between the two governments and the constitutional parties, *or* suggested that he was deliberately constructing a 'pan-nationalist' front.[13] (The latter explanation, believed by loyalist paramilitaries, led them to target SDLP members.) Hume insisted that the agreement threatened 'no section of the people of Ireland' and that it held out the prospects of peace. But when he announced he was presenting the agreement to Dublin the Irish government at first reacted coldly – apparently thinking it might upset work on the resumption of inter-party and inter-governmental talks – while the British prime minister, whose government was then engaged in secret dialogue with the IRA, declared that talking to Adams would turn his stomach.

In October 1993 the IRA sent Thomas Begley on a mission to kill the leadership of loyalist paramilitaries who were known to meet above a fish shop in the Shankill Road. Ten Protestant civilians, as well as Begley, but no loyalist paramilitaries, died in the carnage. Loyalists responded by killing thirteen Catholics within a short period – machine-gunning six to death in a bar in Greysteel in the 'trick or treat' massacre. Most thought that the Hume–Adams initiative was dead, and that Hume, ill and isolated, was politically finished. However, nationalist public opinion, north and south, obliged the Irish government to take the Hume–Adams initiative seriously, and Reynolds dedicated himself to the task, slowly winning the agreement of Major that a statement, incorporating a commitment to Irish national self-determination and recognizing that Sinn Féin's electoral mandate entitled them to a place at the negotiating table, would produce a republican termination of violence. The result, after much bargaining of texts, was the Joint Declaration for Peace, also known as the Downing Street Declaration, of 15 December 1993.[14]

Republicans did not reject the Declaration outright, but called for its 'clarification' (see figure 10.2). The Irish government obliged, the British government refused. The Irish government lifted its broadcasting ban on Sinn Féin. The latter initiated 'peace commissions' to consider the Declaration at the end of January 1994; and the American administration, lobbied by influential Irish-Americans, and with the goodwill of the Irish government, granted Adams a visa to go to New York to address a peace conference.[15] Further steps towards a cessation of violence were slow in coming – indeed the IRA mortar-bombed Heathrow airport in March and in the summer killed a leading figure in the UDP. A brief three-day ceasefire by the IRA in April did, however, suggest a willingness to move. In April Secretary of State Sir Patrick Mayhew said that a republican termination of violence would not be judged a surrender, and in the following month the British government clarified the Declaration by responding to questions sent by Sinn Féin – a reply described by Ian Paisley as 'a twenty-one page love letter to Gerry Adams'. In June the Irish prime minister reciprocated by clarifying the Declaration

PLEASE CLARIFY OR I WILL HAVE NO OPTION BUT TO CONTINUE WITH THE RITUAL EXPLOSIONS

THIS IS NOT A REPEAT NOT A CLARIFICATION I AM SIMPLY WAVING UNION JACKS AT YOU

**Figure 10.2** Steve Bell's perspective on clarification,
*The Guardian*, 18 May 1994

for the Ulster Democratic Party; but in July, when Sinn Féin rejected the Declaration at a special conference in Letterkenny, renewed gloom was widespread. The republicans' intention had been to indicate that they did not accept the Declaration, but that it was something that could be worked on; but this subtlety was not immediately apparent. At the end of August, after another visit from the Irish-American peace delegation, and another meeting between Hume and Adams, the IRA made its announcement, opening an historic opportunity for peace.

## Passivity, Prophecies and Predictions

Political scientists share with politicians the propensity to open their mouths and subtract from the sum of human knowledge, and with prophets the capacity to be memorably wrong about the future. These health warnings are advanced so that readers know that we do not claim knowledge of the future – about which it has sensibly been said that all that we know about it is that we do not know it. However, explanation and prediction are closely linked; and prediction, unlike prophecy, is falsifiable and therefore consistent with one conception of social science. Moreover, having critically reviewed so many explanations, readers will rightly think it incumbent upon us to provide if not a 'history of the future', at least some falsifiable predictions about the prospects for conflict-resolution. Before we provide that we must have a few more words about Northern Ireland's past, and its interpretation.

*The treasons of reasonable intellectuals.* Intellectual conservatism has been a terrible failing of many analysts of Northern Ireland. With honourable exceptions many intellectuals in Ireland and Britain allowed their minds to be imprisoned by the conflict – while others acted as *aides-de-camp* to the respective national causes. Attempts to explain Northern Ireland often sought to show that matters could not have been otherwise. It became a commonplace to insist that the conflict was insoluble – incapable of constructive resolution through negotiation, dialogue and constitutional innovation. The assumption was that one side or another must first lose.[16] This bleak reasoning at least recognized the ethno-national traits of the antagonism, unlike the many liberals and Marxists who interpreted them as epiphenomena (of a transient nature). A more vulgar failing, also commonplace, was to insist that the conflict was not political, but rooted in criminal terrorism – which meant that vigorous repression of paramilitaries was the most appropriate policy-response.[17] This passivity, quietism and occasional outright cynicism within the intellectual world aided and abetted the long-term maintenance of a policy framework in which politicians refused to imagine the unimaginable.

The mainstream consensus was that it was unthinkable for governments to talk with paramilitaries, let alone negotiate with them. The task of government was to build the moderate centre rather than to address the concerns of the respective extremists. It was unrealistic to consider all-inclusive dialogues across the political spectrum from republicanism to loyalism, and it was considered irrelevant to suggest major constitutional changes in British public law and in the Irish Constitution, i.e. significant modifications of the structures of the two states, as ways of resolving the conflict. Northern Ireland had to be either British or Irish; the choice was dichotomous. Analysts who suggested otherwise were considered idealistic fools, stooges or fellow-travellers of the paramilitaries. Thankfully this consensus, to which not all subscribed, has passed away.

The task of responsible intellectuals is to speak truth to power.[18] The first lesson Harold Nicolson drew from the failure of the Versailles Peace Treaty was that 'those who desire to make peace must first understand the causes of war'.[19] The lesson in this case is that the causes of conflict lie in ethno-national antagonism, waged between two societies and their political organizations, as well as by their respective paramilitaries, in conditions exacerbated by British and Irish political institutions, and by the national sovereignty trap. It follows that no internal settlement, confined to the UK's jurisdiction, can work. Equally no policy of obliging unionists to accept a united Ireland without their consent can work. The national question cannot be by-passed. It motivates republican and loyalist paramilitaries. It accounts for the major cleavage between the political parties. The secondary cleavage in the party system is also ethno-national – between the moderates (SDLP and UUP) and the ultras (Sinn Féin and DUP) in the respective traditions. It follows that the ethno-national antagonisms must be addressed.

If renewed conflict is to be avoided, let alone resolved, then each community must identify with whatever new political institutions are devised. Each community must have *security*, constitutional, legal, and policing arrangements which protect them; *recognition*, respect for national identity, culture and allegiances; *autonomy*, community self-government and protection in education, civil association and languages; and *equality*, equal civil, individual, and collective rights. In chapter 9 we outlined two constitutional settlements in which these goals can be met: (i) a formal system of shared sovereignty and (ii) a set of constitutional 'double protection' mechanisms. To be successful, negotiations must move towards one of these settlements. Initially the double protection model is the more feasible. We accept the logical corollary. If negotiations do not move towards one of these settlements then conflict will re-erupt. That is the first of our predictions, but before we make any more, we must discuss three prophecies about the future of Northern Ireland.

## The Nostradami: Two Angry Old Men's Visions

Consider two negative and conservative prophecies, fittingly expressed by one Englishman and one Irishman. One is pressed by Enoch Powell, former Professor of Greek, former Conservative Health Minister, former UUP MP, and a man not noted for his constructive contributions to ethnic relations. Powell has insisted that unionists and the British government should not give anything at the negotiating table, but should treat the IRA's cessation of violence as tantamount to surrender, and seize this moment to be resolute integrationists.

It would appear to be Powell's dream-scenario that across the negotiating tables James Molyneaux of the UUP addresses Hume and Adams in the following vein, 'Mr Adams and Mr Hume, thank you for arranging the surrender of the IRA . . . However, as you know, we've never really cared for a power-sharing devolved parliament or for "high-wire negotiations". A bit of calm is now called for, after all this excitement . . . What we need is a period of good administration by Her Majesty's Government, an increase in the competencies of local government along English lines, or perhaps Scottish lines . . . ' This negotiating (or rather non-negotiating) posture is conceivable. After being fearful that the British government had sacrificed them some unionists may suffer from hubris, and think that victory should be consolidated after the lifting of the nationalist siege – a familiar response in their ethnic memory.

However, Powell's dream need not materialize. Neither the British nor the Irish Governments intend to permit it. At the Conservative Party Conference in October 1994 Sir Patrick

Mayhew insisted that Northern Ireland is different and needs to be governed differently. The Anglo-Irish Agreement and the Downing Street Declaration point towards the construction of a power-sharing devolved government *and* an agreed, but not (at any rate, not yet) unified, Ireland, in which there will be extensive all-Ireland cross-border institutions. Moreover, if the UUP follows the DUP in reacting to the cessation of republican violence with constitutional negativism even its dullest members realize they will be recreating the conditions for armed conflict. That this fact is appreciated is plain from the measured tones of some key people in the UUP, and their reiteration of the party's previous commitments to proportionality, if not power-sharing, in a new Northern Ireland Assembly, and to good neighbourly relations with the Republic. The UUP's leaders know that if they refuse to engage in constitutional accommodation, they will face, albeit at some later date, the danger of being by-passed by the two governments, who might negotiate something akin to shared sovereignty over their heads. In the absence of a constructively negotiated constitutional resolution the two governments would feel obliged to deepen their co-operation, if only to stem renewed conflict. Even if formal shared sovereignty was not established then British direct rule would continue, but with a greater Irish governmental input, and with a place for a reformed Sinn Féin as well as the SDLP in governmental patronage and policy-formulation.

Nevertheless, Powell's scenario may develop if the UUP is tempted to rely upon the short-term parliamentary weakness of the Conservative Party, and its present leader John Major, to prevent any significant re-inventing of Northern Ireland. At least two variants of this scenario can be foreseen. In one there is a return to the status quo ante, paramilitary combat and political stalemate. The IRA resumes its long war. Sinn Féin splits or the organization distances itself from active support for the IRA. The UDA and the UVF also resume their campaigns. The two governments reconsider internment without trial and ferocious repression as well as deeper inter-governmental co-operation. In the other variant there is no immediate resumption of active paramilitary combat. Aside from desultory actions by dissidents there is a state of armed truce between the two antagonistic peoples, what the late Frank Wright called a condition of tranquillity as opposed to peace, a condition in which a return to conflict is latent.[20] These vistas should be kept in mind as 'long negotiations' begin to replace the 'long war'.

The second negative conservative prophecy has been sketched by an Irishman, Conor Cruise O'Brien, former diplomat, former academic, former Irish governmental minister, former Fleet Street editor, and a former radical turned reactionary. In this prophet's writings observers and supporters of the unfolding peace process have been condemned as fools, some as unwitting fools, others as the 'useful fools' of the IRA. Dr O'Brien greeted the IRA's cessation of violence with dire predictions in British newspapers, culminating in a saga of catastrophe that included 500,000 refugees, 10,000 dead in a civil war which terminates with the construction of a smaller but ethnically homogenized Northern Ireland, a military coup in Dublin, and extensive explosions in British cities. This prophecy seems to flow from one of two simple premises: either the IRA is seeking to dupe the British government into demilitarizing Northern Ireland, in the expectation that if the British Army is withdrawn it will not be sent back to deal with renewed conflict; or the republican movement plans to destabilize Northern Ireland through provocative demonstrations which eventually lead the British Army into a war on two fronts which then prompts a British withdrawal.[21]

All conspiracy theories, and this is conspiracy theory about a conspiratorial organization, are impossible to disprove. However, we are sceptical about this prophecy, and not just because O'Brien's other prognoses have been wildly wrong. Neither the British nor the Irish governments are eager for a complete British military withdrawal – as opposed to demilitarization and the return of the Army to barracks – before the achievement of a widely agreed settlement. Moreover, there is a more straightforward explanation of the current posture of the IRA and Sinn Féin. Recent developments suggest that leading republicans no longer believe that the IRA can win a united Ireland through war, with or without the presence of the

British Army. The metaphor we have heard is that republicans believe that they have 'won a draw' on the field of battle.

If so, they can only expect to win a draw at the negotiating table. It is true that the republican cessation of violence is pragmatic, not a principled renunciation of its past use. The republican movement, or at least its leadership, has persuaded itself that it can do better, eventually, from the negotiating table and democratic processes than it can do from continuing paramilitary conflict. For this belief to be sustained it is essential that negotiations produce a momentum which at least establishes 'parity of esteem' for the two national communities. If they result in deadlock, then the IRA, or sections of it, may go back to war, and Adams and McGuinness may be pushed to one side. However, such developments would not be the deliberate result of the conspiracies imagined by O'Brien.

## A Benign Prophecy: From Antagonism to a Cold Peace

The foregoing prophecies should be treated as useful for concentrating minds. There are numerous dangers and difficulties ahead, and within each community there are those so fearful that they have lost that small sparks might send them back to war. There are traditions of political violence in Ireland, not to be confused with the argument that the Irish are politically violent, and there is a tradition of 'outflanking' in both communities, in which leaders who make compromises are condemned by rivals in the leadership stakes. Therefore no one can sensibly be starry-eyed about the peace process. In the next two years expect a world of negotiating musical chairs, in which some parties walk in and out of conference chambers threatening either never to come, or never to return; expect disagreements about the pace and content of negotiations between the two governments; expect sabotage by disgruntled republicans and loyalists; and anticipate attempts to disrupt progress by those in the security sector who must expect to lose their jobs if there is peace.[22]

It is always possible that mismanagement by either the British or the Irish governments (especially British dilatoriness or Irish overkill), or intransigence on the part of unionist or nationalist parties, will mean that the best that occurs is drift, tranquillity without peace, order without legitimacy, an unresolved stalemate without war.

However, a relatively benign future *is* possible. Aside from the vital, thorny, but relatively mundane questions of the long-term decommissioning and safe disposal of the arms of paramilitary organizations, the return of troops to barracks, the early release (if not general amnesty) of those convicted of paramilitary offences, the termination of emergency legislation and the establishment of normal and reformed civilian policing, successful negotiations must culminate in agreed institution-building. We outlined in chapter 9 five elements of a settlement which would provide protection and security for both communities, which would be consistent with the Joint Declaration for Peace, and address directly the sources of ethno-national antagonism. They bear repeating:

(i)    Agreement to establish *consent on sovereignty* and over how sovereignty over Northern Ireland might change, which will require amendments to the 1937 Irish Constitution and to the British Government of Ireland Act of 1920;

(ii)   Agreement to establish *power-sharing and proportional representation* arrangements for the government of Northern Ireland and its representation in Westminster, the European Union, and in cross-border institutions;

(iii)  Agreement to establish *full parity of esteem* for both national communities, through a Bill of Rights which protects collective (religious, cultural and linguistic) rights, and through fair employment and a reconstructed police service and judiciary;

(iv)   Agreement to establish democratic and accountable *cross-border institutions* within Irish, British and European frameworks, institutions which can have consultative, harmonizing and executive functions; and which *may, but need not*, lead to deeper confederal or federal arrangements within an all-Ireland framework, or an all-British

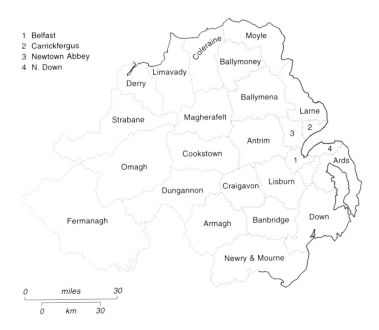

1 Belfast
2 Carrickfergus
3 Newtown Abbey
4 N. Down

Coleraine
Moyle
Ballymoney
Limavady
Derry
Ballymena
Larne
Strabane          Magherafelt
3   2
Antrim
Cookstown          4
1   Ards
Omagh
Lisburn
Dungannon    Craigavon
Fermanagh          Armagh   Banbridge   Down
Newry & Mourne

0        miles        30

0        km        30

**Figure 10.3** The changing demography of Northern Ireland: (a) Northern
Ireland's local government's district councils, 1991; (b) increases
and decreases of the percentage of Catholics, 1971–91

Isles framework, or within the European Union, or within
permutations of all these possibilities; and

(v)    Agreement to establish *double protection mechanisms* which
guarantee the overall constitutional settlement, through
empowering the British–Irish inter-governmental conference with this task, and through the design of a 'swing
constitution' which provides effective protection of collective and individual rights, whether Northern Ireland
remains within the Union or becomes, later, part of the
Republic.

A settlement built on these elements would mark an
improvement upon the status quo for northern nationalists;
and it would reassure unionists that if and when they become
a minority they will receive the same protections to which
northern nationalists should now be entitled. The construction
of a just and lasting peace will be possible to the extent that

Catholics

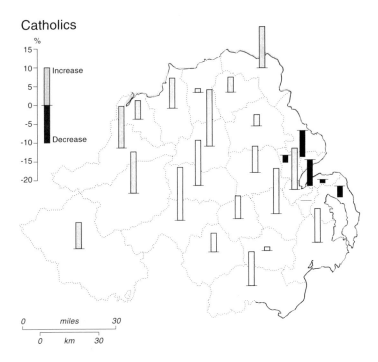

these elements are present in the framework document to be published by the two governments, and to the extent that they can command assent at the negotiating tables and subsequent referendums. The framework document may not materialize in exactly this form, but expect variations on these elements to be at the heart of its design and subsequent negotiations.

There are other grounds for believing that a settlement may be possible. First, there is continuing constructive third-party intervention in Northern Ireland, by the British and Irish governments, and by the administrations of the USA and the European Union. Secondly, all-inclusive negotiations, involving all with potential veto-power over the implementation of any settlement, are promised to follow the publication of the framework document and the successful termination of exploratory dialogue with the republican and loyalist parties. Thirdly, the public statements of most major political agents, excepting the DUP, suggest that the images with which they have interpreted the conflict are breaking down, and that

Protestants

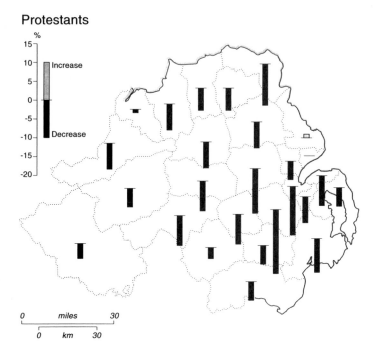

**Figure 10.3 (contd.)** (c) the increase and decrease of the percentage of
Protestants, 1971–91; (d) the increase and the decrease of the percentage
of those who have no (or who do not state a) religious identity, 1971–91

prospects exist for multi-lateral concessions, and the invention
of new institutions.

If this is the benign scenario it is not difficult to imagine
the stumbling blocks. In the first instance unionists may vehemently reject a double veto or double protection mechanism
being built into a settlement, or letting the inter-governmental
conference act as its ultimate guarantor. They may also refuse
to be involved in the design of a 'swing constitution'. However,
if so, they will weaken their own long-term collective insurance
at the price of not satisfying nationalists. It is likely that some
unionists will reject any significant all-Ireland cross-border
agencies, and to the extent that they are successful in
preventing their construction northern nationalists (and the
Irish government) are less likely to consent to a re-invented
Northern Ireland. It is possible that many unionists will reject

Not stated / none

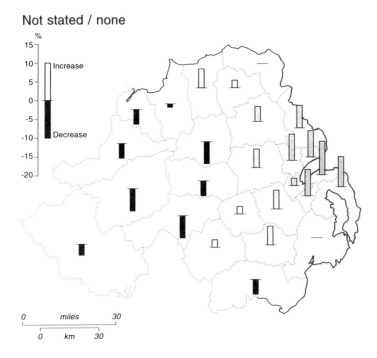

the radical public policy implications of 'parity of esteem' – so far the debate on the nature of policing since the dual ceasefires has not been marked by a spirit of imaginative reconciliation or the imagination and generosity promised by Sir Patrick Mayhew. Without parity of esteem the re-ignition of conflict becomes more likely: Northern Ireland cannot be democratically stable if it is purely British or purely Irish, and its policing and legal institutions must adapt to this dual reality. Some unionists may hold out against any power-sharing (or government by consensus) beyond the concept of simple proportionality – in which case unionists will be following closely to the path advocated by Enoch Powell. Some unionists and some nationalists may also reject any agreement based on majority consent within Northern Ireland for any change in sovereignty. Some loyalists may insist that Northern Ireland should never be allowed to become part of an Irish Republic; while some republicans may insist that requiring majority consent for changing the constitutional status of Northern

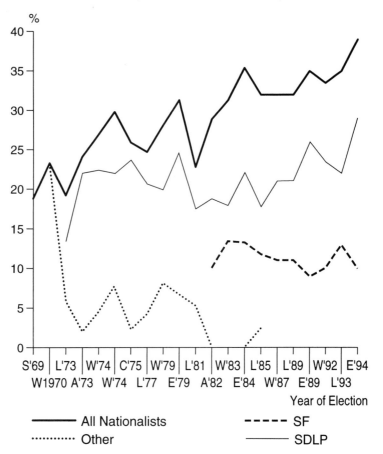

**Figure 10.4** The rising Northern Nationalist vote, 1969–94
Key: S = Stormont, LG = Local Government Districts, A = Assembly,
W = Westminster Parliament, C = Constitutional Convention
and E = European Parliament.

Ireland is tantamount to granting unionists a veto, and a denial of the Irish people's right to self-determination. Provided such objections take the form of constitutional anti-constitutionalism there need not be disaster here. Pluralist democracies can and should flourish despite the presence of anti-system parties. Nevertheless crunch issues lie buried here.

Lastly, any settlement must pass the hurdle of two referendums, in the Republic and in Northern Ireland. These hurdles are significant – and policy-makers need to be especially aware of the fallacies that electorates are necessarily more moderate than their leaders, and that whatever the negotiators agree will be acceptable.[23] A referendum in the Republic to amend the Constitution will need the support of northern nationalists and Fianna Fáil – no amendment of the Irish Constitution has occurred without the latter's active support. A referendum in Northern Ireland will have to pass by more than a mere majority; what is required is majority-consent in both the unionist and nationalist communities if the referendum is to legitimate an agreed settlement. This means that any settlement must be balanced, and have something in it for everybody, which in turn suggests that no referendum should be risked before a sufficient consensus across all major parties exists, and before both governments have agreed a co-ordinated and sustained public-relations campaign.

*Final Forecasts*. We conclude with some long-term forecasts, some less controversial than others, which are related to the prospects of a successful constitutional settlement. First, expect a continuing growth in the cultural Catholic population, as evident in the inter-censal shift between 1971 and 1991 (see figure 10.3).[24] This growth in the cultural Catholic population may be enhanced by protracted peace. Stability and possible prospects of prosperity at home may staunch the relative rate of Catholic out-migration, while fair employment, delivered by law and parity of esteem, will give Catholics stronger reasons to stay. The growth in the number of cultural Catholics, which has now reached just less than 43 per cent of the population of Northern Ireland, has geographic and political implications. Western, southern and rural Northern Ireland will increasingly have Catholic demographic majorities, and also Catholic electoral majorities. Belfast is likely to be a city with a cultural Catholic (and possibly a nationalist) majority in the first decade of the next millennium.

The political implications are not entirely straightforward, but we think that they may, on balance, be beneficial. The growth of the cultural Catholic population may beckon a united (presumably confederal or federal) Ireland within three decades – which may generate corresponding unionist anxieties. However, that is neither demographically nor politically certain, and three decades is a long time. What is important in the short to medium term is that the demographic shift presages equality between the two communities, and therefore, creates incentives for bargained co-operation. In moderately democratic conditions when two communities are relatively matched in size and political and economic resources, one community cannot politically dominate the other, and one cannot police the other, at least very easily. Though it will be some time before reform feeds through to economic equality, political equality will follow from a weightier cultural Catholic population and provide a demographic impetus for power-sharing, proportionality and parity of esteem. In the long run this shift presages the completion of a century-long shift from 'stratified' to 'segmentary' relations between cultural Protestants and cultural Catholics.[25] Correspondingly, any return to the hegemonic control unionists exercised between 1920 and 1972 is increasingly unlikely. The chances of the two major unionist parties winning over 50 per cent of the regional vote are progressively receding, and the prospects of small inter-ethnic parties holding the balance of power in a Northern Ireland Assembly must correspondingly increase.

Our second forecast, which relies on the first, is that the nationalist vote is likely to continue to grow, at least for the rest of the century. More precisely, the combined Sinn Féin and SDLP vote should rise – though there will be variations depending on the election and the electoral formula. Such growth would be consistent with electoral trajectories since 1969 (see figure 10.4).[26] In the 1994 European parliamentary elections the combined SDLP and Sinn Féin vote was the highest nationalist share of the regional vote since the inception of Northern Ireland. Growth in the nationalist bloc will affect any future Northern Ireland Assembly elections – where vote-transfers by nationalist voters under the STV system would consolidate a strong nationalist presence without a formal coalition arrangement between Sinn Féin and the SDLP. The full electoral unification of the nationalist bloc is unlikely but unionists and British policy-makers intent on preserving competition between nationalists should consider the merits of introducing proportional representation for

Westminster elections – since the present system of plurality rule will increase demands for co-operation between the SDLP and Sinn Féin in constituencies where nationalists outnumber unionists. Growth in the aggregate northern nationalist vote will occur on the demographic Catholic tide and both Sinn Fein and the SDLP can make electoral gains. An expanding and confident nationalist electorate should see great merit in the ballot box rather than the armalite. Sinn Féin can grow if a vote for the party is no longer a vote for war. Furnished with American money and greater democratic experience, it is capable of party-building beyond its present 10 per cent core-vote in Northern Ireland.[27]

Our third forecast concerns the electoral destiny of the unionist bloc. For the time being the unionist bloc will probably continue to shrink, albeit slowly; but, more importantly, we believe it may eventually fragment in peacetime conditions – especially if the sense of being besieged is reduced by a settlement and the constitutional reconstruction of the Republic. The degree to which the unionist bloc fragments will, naturally, be dependent upon the degree of competition between the SDLP and Sinn Féin, and unionists' fears about the likelihood of a united Ireland. It will not fragment because of electoral integration through the organization of British political parties in the region. The Conservative Party will probably remain in the region, but is unlikely to prosper; while the British Labour Party is most unlikely to organize. The UUP may experience pressure from those who would like to modernize the party – for example by breaking its links with the Orange Order – but it should survive, and for the time being remain the largest party in Northern Ireland, and the major player in unionist politics. Its leaders and members may also find it more congenial to work with the Alliance Party and the SDLP in a Northern Ireland Assembly than with the DUP.

The party most threatened by long-term peace is therefore the DUP. Its electoral base, crudely speaking, consists of rural evangelical Protestants and urban secular working-class Protestants – while its leadership derives almost exclusively from evangelical Protestants who have thrived on a politics of fear. In conditions of peace, and if proportional representation applies in all elections, there is no compelling reason why the DUP's electoral bloc should hold together.[28] It will require very skilled fear-mongering about the prospects of a nationalist victory at the ballot box and an imminent shift to a united Ireland to hold the DUP's base together. There is electoral space for a populist secular unionist party which can articulate the interests of poor working-class cultural Protestants. The cadres of the demobilized loyalist paramilitaries, and their political representatives in the PUP and the UDP, may be capable of filling this space, at least in Belfast, but here we enter the realm of speculation rather than of prediction.

The speculation is, however, rooted in the comparative analysis of national and ethnic conflicts. To the degree that ethnicity is politicized, the more it dominates other expressions of identity, be they rooted in class, religion, gender or ideological affiliation. Conversely, when ethnic communities feel secure the pressure to sustain ethnic solidarity is reduced, and the greater the likelihood that a more pluralist politics can emerge within them. This pattern may occur within Northern Ireland, within both communities, rather than across them – especially if it is accompanied by the constitutional reconstruction of both the UK and the Republic within a wider European federation. But one must not exaggerate these possibilities. Communal tensions, territorial segregation, and endogamous social and sexual relations will remain dominant features of social and political life in Northern Ireland, with or without a definitive constitutional settlement. Ethno-national cleavages and politics can be managed; and they can be managed equitably; but they cannot be wished away.

# Conclusion

One wise observer of ethnic politics has concluded that although some ethno-national conflicts 'are definitively settled, the great majority rise, subside, and recur'.[29] As the third millennium beckons, Northern Ireland has reasonable prospects of being settled for our lifetimes with peace and justice. We are much more hesitant to conclude that its conflict will be definitively resolved. Evidence from the study of national and ethnic conflict-resolution inspires unremitting bleakness: 'genocide, military defeat, exile or enforced separation of contending parties are more likely to mark the end of violent ethnic conflicts than negotiated peace accords'.[30]

However, we have presented some grounds for hope, and in contradistinction to the poet Byron we believe that hope is more than the paint on the face of human existence, and that a brush with truth does not, and should not, erase it.

# Appendix A: The Joint Declaration for Peace,
## statement made at Downing Street, 15 December 1993

1. The Taoiseach, Mr Albert Reynolds TD, and the Prime Minister, the Rt Hon John Major MP, acknowledge that the most urgent and important issue facing the people of Ireland, North and South, and the British and Irish Governments together, is to remove the causes of conflict, to overcome the legacy of history and to heal the divisions which have resulted, recognising that the absence of a lasting and satisfactory settlement of relationships between the peoples of both islands has contributed to continuing tragedy and suffering. They believe that the development of an agreed framework for peace, which has been discussed between them since early last year, and which is based on a number of key principles, provides the starting point of a peace process to culminate in a political settlement.

2. The Taoiseach and Prime Minister are convinced of the inestimable value to both their peoples, and particularly for the next generation, of healing divisions in Ireland and of ending a conflict which has been so manifestly to the detriment of all. Both recognise that the ending of divisions can come about only through the agreement and co-operation of the people, North and South, representing both traditions in Ireland. They therefore make a solemn commitment to promote co-operation at all levels on the basis of the fundamental principles, undertakings, obligations under international agreements, to which they have jointly committed themselves, and the guarantees which each Government has given and now reaffirms, including Northern Ireland's statutory

constitutional guarantee. It is their aim to foster agreement and reconciliation, leading to a new political framework founded on consent and encompassing arrangements within Northern Ireland, for the whole island, and between these islands.

3. They also consider that the development of Europe will, of itself, require new approaches to serve interests common to both parts of the island of Ireland, and to Ireland and the United Kingdom as partners in the European Union.

4. The Prime Minister, on behalf of the British Government, reaffirms that they will uphold the democratic wish of a greater number of the people of Northern Ireland on the issue of whether they prefer to support the Union or a sovereign united Ireland. On this basis, he reiterates, on behalf of the British Government, that they have no selfish strategic or economic interest in Northern Ireland. Their primary interest is to see peace, stability and reconciliation established by agreement among all the people who inhabit the island, and they will work together with the Irish Government to achieve such an agreement, which will embrace the totality of relationships. The role of the British Government will be to encourage, facilitate and enable the achievement of such an agreement over a period through a process of dialogue and co-operation based on full respect for the rights and identities of both traditions in Ireland. They accept that such agreement may, as of right, take the form of agreed structures for the island as a whole, including a united Ireland achieved by peaceful means on the following basis. The British Government agree that it is for the people of the island of Ireland alone, by agreement between the two parts respectively, to exercise their right of self-determination on the basis of consent, freely and concurrently given, North and South, to bring about a united Ireland, if that is their wish. They reaffirm as a binding obligation that they will, for their part, introduce the necessary legislation to give effect to this, or equally to any measure of agreement on future relationships in Ireland which the people living in Ireland may themselves freely so determine without external impediment. They believe that the people of Britain would wish, in friendship to all sides, to enable the people of Ireland to reach agreement on how they may live together in harmony and in partnership, with respect for their diverse traditions, and with full recognition of the special links and the unique relationship which exist between the peoples of Britain and Ireland.

5.  The Taoiseach, on behalf of the Irish Government, considers that the lessons of Irish history, and especially of Northern Ireland, show that stability and well-being will not be found under any political system which is refused allegiance or rejected on grounds of identity by a significant minority of those governed by it. For this reason, it would be wrong to attempt to impose a united Ireland, in the absence of the freely given consent of a majority of the people of Northern Ireland. He accepts, on behalf of the Irish Government, that the democratic right of self-determination by the people of Ireland as a whole must be achieved and exercised with and subject to the agreement and consent of a majority of the people of Northern Ireland and must, consistent with justice and equity, respect the democratic dignity and the civil rights and religious liberties of both communities, including:

*   the right of free political thought;
*   the right of freedom and expression of religion;
*   the right to pursue democratically national and political aspirations;
*   the right to seek constitutional change by peaceful and legitimate means;
*   the right to live wherever one chooses without hindrance;
*   the right to equal opportunity in all social and economic activity, regardless of class, creed, sex or colour.

These would be reflected in any future political and constitutional arrangements emerging from a new and more broadly based agreement.

6.  The Taoiseach however recognises the genuine difficulties and barriers to building relationships of trust either within or beyond Northern Ireland, from which both traditions suffer. He will work to create a new era of trust, in which suspicion of the motives or actions of others is removed on the part of either community. He considers that the future of the island depends on the nature of the relationship between the two main traditions that inhabit it. Every effort must be made to build a new sense of trust between those communities. In recognition of the fears of the Unionist community and as a token of his willingness to make a personal contribution to the building up of that necessary trust, the Taoiseach will examine with his colleagues any elements in the democratic life and organisation of the Irish State that can be represented to the Irish Government in the course of political dialogue as a real and substantial threat to

their way of life and ethos, or that can be represented as not being fully consistent with a modern democratic and pluralist society, and undertakes to examine any possible ways of removing such obstacles. Such an examination would of course have due regard to the desire to preserve those inherited values that are largely shared throughout the island or that belong to the cultural and historical roots of the people of this island in all their diversity. The Taoiseach hopes that over time a meeting of hearts and minds will develop, which will bring all people of Ireland together, and will work towards that objective, but he pledges in the meantime that as a result of the efforts that will be made to build mutual confidence no Northern Unionist should ever have to fear in future that this ideal will be pursued either by threat or coercion.

7. Both Governments accept that Irish unity would be achieved only by those who favour this outcome persuading those who do not, peacefully and without coercion or violence, and that, if in the future a majority of the people of Northern Ireland are so persuaded, both Governments will support and give legislative effect to their wish. But, notwithstanding the solemn affirmation by both Governments in the Anglo-Irish Agreement that any change in the status of Northern Ireland would only come about with the consent of a majority of the people of Northern Ireland, the Taoiseach also recognises the continuing uncertainties and misgivings which dominate so much of Northern Unionist attitudes towards the rest of Ireland. He believes that we stand at a stage of our history when the genuine feelings of all traditions in the North must be recognised and acknowledged. He appeals to both traditions at this time to grasp the opportunity for a fresh start and a new beginning, which could hold such promise for all our lives and the generations to come. He asks the people of Northern Ireland to look on the people of the Republic as friends, who share their grief and shame over all the suffering of the last quarter of a century, and who want to develop the best possible relationship with them, a relationship in which trust and new understanding can flourish and grow. The Taoiseach also acknowledges the presence in the Constitution of the Republic of elements which are deeply resented by Northern Unionists, but which at the same time reflect hopes and ideals which lie deep in the hearts of many Irish men and women, North and South. But as we move towards a new era of understanding in which new relationships of trust may grow and bring peace to the island of Ireland, the Taoiseach believes that the time has come to consider

together how best the hopes and identities of all can be expressed in more balanced ways, which no longer engender division and the lack of trust to which he has referred. He confirms that, in the event of an overall settlement, the Irish Government will, as part of a balanced constitutional accommodation, put forward and support proposals for change in the Irish Constitution which would fully reflect the principle of consent in Northern Ireland.

8.   The Taoiseach recognises the need to engage in dialogue which would address with honesty and integrity the fears of all traditions. But that dialogue, both within the North and between the people and their respresentatives of both parts of Ireland, must be entered into with an acknowledgement that the future security and welfare of the people of the island will depend on an open, frank and balanced approach to all the problems which for too long have caused division.

9.   The British and Irish Governments will seek, along with the Northern Ireland constitutional parties, through a process of political dialogue, to create institutions and structures which, while respecting the diversity of the people of Ireland, would enable them to work together in all areas of common interest. This will help over a period to build the trust necessary to end past divisions, leading to an agreed and peaceful future. Such structures would, of course, include institutional recognition of the special links that exist between the people of Britain and Ireland as part of the totality of relationships, while taking account of newly forged links with the rest of Europe.

10.   The British and Irish Governments reiterate that the achievement of peace must involve a permanent end to the use of, or support for, paramilitary violence. They confirm that, in these circumstances, democratically mandated parties which establish a commitment to exclusively peaceful methods and which have shown that they abide by the democratic process, are free to participate fully in democratic politics and to join in dialogue in due course between the Governments and the political parties on the way ahead.

11.   The Irish Government would make their own arrangements within their jurisdiction to enable democratic parties to consult together and share in dialogue about the political future. The Taoiseach's intention is that these arrangements could include the establishment, in consultation with other parties, of a Forum for

Peace and Reconciliation to make recommendations on ways in which agreement and trust between both traditions in Ireland can be promoted and established.

12. The Taoiseach and the Prime Minister are determined to build on the fervent wish of both their peoples to see old fears and animosities replaced by a climate of peace. They believe the framework they have set out offers the people of Ireland, North and South, whatever their tradition, the basis to agree that from now on their differences can be negotiated and resolved exclusively by peaceful political means. They appeal to all concerned to grasp the opportunity for a new departure. That step would compromise no position or principle, nor prejudice the future for either community. On the contrary, it would be an incomparable gain for all. It would break decisively the cycle of violence and the intolerable suffering it entails for the people of these islands, particularly for both communities in Northern Ireland. It would allow the process of economic and social co-operation on the island to realise its full potential for prosperity and mutual understanding. It would transform the prospects for building on the progress already made in the Talks process, involving the two Governments and the constitutional parties in Northern Ireland. The Taoiseach and the Prime Minister believe that these arrangements offer an opportunity to lay the foundations for a more peaceful and harmonious future devoid of the violence and bitter divisions which have scarred the past generation. They commit themselves and their Governments to continue to work together, unremittingly, towards that objective.

# Appendix B: Parsing the Paragraphs of the Declaration [1]

The drafters of the Jont Declaration for Peace, or the Downing Street Declaration, went to extravagant lengths to produce a document intended to reassure everybody. Each paragraph bears the marks of the necessary ambiguities in constructing such a declaration. It is an exquisite diplomatic patchwork, though it remains to be seen whether it is a stepping stone towards peace and conflict-resolution or merely another milestone in Northern Ireland's continuing political and military stalemate. Below we analyse the text of the Declaration.

1

The first paragraph suggests that 'the development of an agreed framework for peace' originated with the two prime ministers *last year*. This statement was designed to reassure unionists that the Declaration did not stem from the work of John Hume and Gerry Adams, who had been meeting regularly and who had declared that they had produced a basis for peace which Hume had transmitted to the two governments. It was also intended to reassure those people in the Republic and Britain who disliked any contact, however indirect, between the governments and Sinn Féin [although as it happens the British government had been communicating, if not negotiating, with Sinn Féin and the IRA for the best part of three years in the run-up to the Declaration].

2

The second paragraph tip-toed over numerous egg-shells. The key sentence is this:

[The two prime ministers] make a solemn commitment to promote co-operation at all levels on the basis of the fundamental principles, undertakings, obligations under international agreements, to which they have jointly committed themselves, and the guarantees which each Government has given and now reaffirms, including Northern Ireland's statutory constitutional guarantee.

Here the prime ministers avoided an explicit mention of the Anglo-Irish Agreement, so as not to antagonize unionists. However, the reference to 'obligations under international agreements, to which they have jointly committed themselves' implicitly reaffirmed the Anglo-Irish Agreement so the SDLP and constitutional nationalists could be assured that the Declaration had not undermined the 1985 Agreement.

The two prime ministers then seemingly made an explicit reaffirmation of 'Northern Ireland's *statutory* constitutional guarantee', obviously to reassure unionists. The relevant guarantee must refer to the Northern Ireland Constitution Acts of 1973, 1974 and 1982, which specify that the status of Northern Ireland is part of the United Kingdom, as long as a majority of its citizens so wish. However, the problem here is that the Taoiseach could not in constitutional law, or in fact, 'reaffirm' Northern Ireland's statutory constitutional guarantee. To recognize the relevant British statutes would be invalid under Ireland's Constitution, and to 'reaffirm' them would be impossible because no Irish government had previously given Northern Ireland the relevant guarantee, and none could do so given its Constitution.

We must therefore read the key sentence, which on a natural reading implies that both prime ministers reaffirm Northern Ireland's statutory constitutional guarantee, as one in which *only* the British government reaffirms this guarantee. There is a simple choice here: either the Taoiseach unintentionally recognized Northern Ireland's statutory constitutional guarantee, in which case his action is constitutionally void, or he did not, in which case there is no change in the status quo, and no net political benefit for unionists as regards the status of Northern Ireland. The latter is the right reading. The status quo is re-described in the Declaration to make it slightly more palatable to unionists.

There is one remaining ambiguity related to this sentence. Neither here, nor elsewhere in the document, is there an explicit exclusion of the idea of shared sovereignty or joint authority. The text refers, however, to the promotion 'of co-operation at all levels' by both governments. Northern Ireland's 'statutory constitutional guarantee' confirms its status as part of the United Kingdom as long as a majority of its citizens so wish, but, legally speaking, it does not rule out Northern Ireland becoming part of both the United Kingdom *and* the Republic of Ireland. Our reading of the text of the Declaration suggests that it excludes only two options for the future of Northern Ireland: its expulsion from the United Kingdom against the will of a local majority, and the imposition of a united Ireland against the will of a local majority in Northern Ireland. Neither the British nor Irish government can invoke anything in the Declaration which explicitly rules out from consideration in any subsequent constitutional dialogue any of the following options for Northern Ireland: agreed integration into the UK, an agreed power-sharing devolved government, an agreed power-sharing devolved government with strong Irish dimensions, or an agreed system for sharing sovereignty, or any other 'agreed' system.

3

The third paragraph was designed to appeal to the SDLP, the most Europhile party in Ireland. It was originally much longer and more 'Euroactive', but, according to our sources, was pared down at the insistence of the British government. It states that 'the development of Europe, will, *of itself*, require *new approaches* to serve interests common to both parts of the island of Ireland' (our italics). These phrases, which envisage cross-border institutions and functional co-operation within a European rather than within an explicitly Irish national framework, have long been commended by the SDLP. They are balanced by the suggestion that the 'new approaches' will also apply 'to Ireland and the United Kingdom as partners in the European Union'. However, no explicit reference is made to new institutions, so that Europhobic Tories and unionists cannot formally be disturbed.

4

The major paragraph is the fourth. It is a solemn commitment from the British prime minister. It opens with John Major apparently restating the British government's unionist guarantee *and* the principle permitting change in the status of Northern Ireland cherished by constitutional nationalists:

> The Prime Minister, on behalf of the British Government, reaffirms that they will uphold the democratic wish of *a greater number of the people* of Northern Ireland on the issue of whether they prefer to support the Union or a sovereign united Ireland.

One novel feature here was the deliberate use of the phrase in italics. James Molyneaux, the leader of the Ulster Unionist Party, prefers this wording to the normal expression 'a majority' – on the grounds that it shows that those in favour of the Union go beyond 'the majority', i.e. Northern Irish Protestants, and include Northern Irish Catholics. Symbolically John Major was being as courteous as he could to the leader of the Ulster Unionist Party. Whether the expression 'a greater number of people' is the same as a majority might seem a moot point, since it could be translated as 'a plurality'. However, because it is specified that the wish of the greater number will be upheld only with regard to a dichotomous choice between the Union and a united Ireland the phrase 'a greater number' can only be interpreted as the equivalent of a majority in a referendum conducted on that basis. Moreover, in subsequent clarification of the text with Sinn Féin the British government made it plain that there was no difference between 'a greater number' and 'a majority'.

Another noteworthy feature is that the British prime-ministerial 'reaffirmation' was confined to giving unionists a majority veto on being expelled from the Union or in consenting to a united Ireland. The unionists, by implication, have no majority veto on the nature of the Union, the manner in which it is to be governed, or the UK's relations with the Republic of Ireland – other than having a majority veto on coerced unification.

The next sentence 'reiterates' previous statements by Peter Brooke and Sir Patrick Mayhew that the British Government 'have no selfish strategic or economic interest in Northern Ireland', and adds that the British Government's primary interest is to see peace, stability and reconciliation established by agreement among all the people who inhabit the island, and they will work together with the Irish Government to achieve such an agreement, which will embrace the totality of relationships.

This wording had several objectives. It was designed to treat seriously, and politely reject, the classical republican thesis that British imperialism is the key cause of the conflict (see chapters 1 and 2). The message was, firstly, that the British state is not the cause of the conflict, and secondly, that the 'totality of relationships', a phrase first coined by Brian Lenihan of Fianna Fáil, was open to negotiation and agreement between the two governments and those who live in Ireland. The language is also close to 'the agreed Ireland' long advocated by the SDLP. These words were meant to soothe constitutional nationalists and constitutional republicans, north and south.

Indeed the British Government now offered a new definition of its role:

to encourage, facilitate and enable the achievement of such agreement over a period, through a process of dialogue and co-operation based on full respect for the rights and identities of both traditions in Ireland.

This role falls short of what many believe Gerry Adams, Martin McGuinness and Sinn Féin wanted, namely a commitment on the part of the British Government to become an active persuader, an advocate of Irish unity, but, together with the declaration that it has 'no selfish strategic . . . interest' it is clearly as close to neutrality as John Major's government felt it could go.

It is also worth observing that British Ministers are at pains to point out that it is significant that there is no comma separating selfish from strategic in the wording of the Declaration.[2] The meaning of the relevant phrase must therefore be that Britain has no 'selfish strategic interest' in Northern Ireland, but that it may have another selfish interest, such as self-identification with those who wish to remain part of the Union, although that selfish interest cannot be economic. Alternatively it may also be construed to mean that Britain has a non-selfish strategic interest in Northern Ireland – a possibility which is open to multiple interpretations, including a joint strategic interest with the Republic in stability.

Two vital sentences follow. The British Government

> accept that such agreement may, as of right, take the form of agreed structures for the island as a whole, including a united Ireland achieved by peaceful means on the following basis. *The British Government agree that it is for the people of Ireland alone,* by agreement between the two parts respectively, *to exercise their right of self-determination* on the basis of consent, freely and concurrently given, North and South, to bring about a united Ireland, if that is their wish.

The British government here confirmed that it rules out no agreed all-Ireland structures, including a united Ireland. More remarkably, however, as the italicized words demonstrate, it has recognized the right of the people of Ireland as a whole to self-determination, without explicitly mentioning any right of self-determination for Northern Ireland. This message is addressed directly to Sinn Féin and the IRA: the right to self-determination of the Irish people as a whole has been recognized by a British government. By implication, there is no need for their 'long war' to continue. This right of self-determination is, of course, qualified: a united Ireland can only come about 'by agreement' between North and South, respectively (meaning 'each separately'), on the basis of consent, freely and concurrently given.

The symbolic power of the formula is that Northern Ireland is not explicitly mentioned as having the right of self-determination, which makes us wonder whether this passage could conceivably have been agreed by James Molyneaux, the leader of the Ulster Unionist Party.[3] The practical import of the word 'concurrently' is that the mechanism through which an agreed united Ireland can occur, at some future juncture, is that advocated by the SDLP, namely two referendums, held in Northern Ireland and the Republic.

What is ambiguous is whether the mechanism of two referendums is to apply to any other form of agreed Ireland, other than a united Ireland. Our reading of the text is that the mechanism of two referendums is only required for consent to a united Ireland. It is not mandatory for any other form of 'agreed structures', but it is also not precluded. This reading, of course, implies that the two governments have not agreed precisely how to agree an agreed Ireland, merely on how to agree a united Ireland, at some future hypothetical juncture. Only the latter has a precise mechanism for implementation. However, John Major subsequently assured unionists that any negotiated settlement would be put to the population of Northern Ireland in a referendum.

The final section of paragraph 4 confirmed that the British will facilitate whatever agreement 'the people of Ireland' arrive at, presumably through inter-party negotiation, which is important because 'the people of Britain' are impliedly defined in a way which suggests that they are both geographically and politically different from 'the people of Ireland', including the people of Northern Ireland. In this respect the Declaration is symbolically significant: the people of Northern Ireland, irrespective of whether they support the Union, are explicitly not defined as British, but rather as Irish.

### 5 and 6

The Taoiseach confirms in a parallel statement that the Irish Government considers it would be wrong to attempt to impose a united Ireland 'in the absence of the freely given consent of a majority of the people of Northern Ireland'. He

> accepts, on behalf of the Irish Government, that the democratic right of self-determination by the people of Ireland as a whole must be achieved and exercised with and subject to the agreement and consent of a majority of the people of Northern Ireland.

He does so, in an appeal to both republicans and unionists, because he considers that

> the lessons of Irish history, and especially of Northern Ireland, show that stability and well-being will not be found under any political system which is refused allegiance or rejected on grounds of identity by a significant minority of those governed by it.

The Taoiseach plainly meant that a united Ireland achieved without consent would be no better than Northern Ireland is now, a political unit which lacks widespread allegiance.

This declaration by the Irish prime minister restates traditional nationalist and republican complaints about Northern Ireland, but in a balanced manner which recognizes that a second wrong – a united Ireland achieved without minority consent – would not correct the first wrong – the formation and maintenance of Northern Ireland without minority consent. It combines an appeal to unionists to remake Northern Ireland's political institutions in a manner acceptable to the northern nationalist minority with a promise from the Irish Government to protect national, religious, political, civil and socio-economic rights in its jurisdiction as part of 'any future political and constitutional arrangements emerging from a new and broadly based agreement'.

The only strange issue here is why the British Government failed to make a similarly explicit parallel declaration about entrenched rights which would accompany any new agreement. The British commitment to protect the 'rights and identities' of both traditions might have been considered sufficient, or the British government may have been reluctant to embrace either an individualist bill of rights or a bill protecting cultural rights. Alternatively the Irish emphasis on rights may flow from the Labour side of the coalition government. This interpretation is strengthened by paragraph 6, where it is stated that 'in recognition' of unionists' fears: 'The Taoiseach will examine *with his colleagues* any elements in the democratic life and organisation of the Irish State' which can be seen as 'not being fully consistent with a modern democratic and pluralist society'.

This sentence clearly suggests the influence of Dick Spring, and his Labour colleagues, and their agenda for altering the Irish Constitution and other public laws in the direction of moral liberalism. This interpretation probably explains why the above promise is immediately balanced by reassurances to Fianna Fáil, and Gaelic and Christian traditionalists that any such examination will have

> due regard to the desire to preserve those inherited values that are largely shared throughout the island or that belong to the cultural and historical roots of the people of this island in all their diversity.

There is, however, at least one other possible reading of paragraph 5. Confidential sources have suggested to us that the list of rights promised by the Irish government, beginning with 'the right of free political thought' and ending with 'the right to equal opportunity', is exactly what loyalist paramilitaries, through intermediaries, requested of the Irish government, and the wording of the rights is exactly what they requested. This explanation would account for why 'freedom of political thought' is specified in the Declaration rather than 'freedom of political expression'. 'Thought' is essentially private whereas expression is not, which is why it is strange to have 'political thought' protected in a carefully drafted international text. If the Irish government was seeking to reassure loyalist paramilitaries then this passage may explain why loyalist paramilitaries were initially quiet and restrained in the wake of the Declaration – they had been consulted, and had been assured of the good faith of the Irish government.

### 7 and 8

In paragraph 7 the two governments jointly accepted that Irish unity would be achieved only by persuasion and consent, and without coercion, and repeat, without explicitly saying so, the promises they both made in the Anglo-Irish Agreement. More importantly the Irish Government declares that 'in the event of an overall settlement' it will be willing to propose changes to Articles 2 and 3 of its Constitution which would 'fully reflect' the principle of consent.

This promise, which implicitly recognizes that Articles 2 and 3 are offensive to unionists because they do not 'fully reflect' principles of consent, is significantly qualified: any changes to the relevant Articles must be 'part of a balanced constitutional accommodation'. Fianna Fáil, the SDLP, and Sinn Féin are being reassured that constitutional republicanism, embedded in Articles 2 and 3, will only be modified if there are reciprocal but unspecified concessions forthcoming from unionists. This offer is obviously a key element in the 'open, frank and balanced approach' to constitutional dialogue encouraged by the Irish Government in paragraph 8.

### 9

The two Governments imply in paragraph 9 that, along with Northern Irish political parties, they will seek *through dialogue* 'to create institutions and structures' of a cross-border nature – across the land border in Ireland, and the sea border between Britain and Ireland. They also refer back to the mention of their joint membership of the European Union made in paragraph 3. No specific commitments are made here, but plainly both governments are accepting that cross-border bodies will form part of any wider settlement, or part of any interim settlement in the absence of broader agreement. Such bodies could be functional cross-border agencies, functional agencies with delegated executive powers, inter-ministerial conferences, inter-governmental conferences, a British and Irish equivalent to a Nordic Council, a British and Irish equivalent to the European Coal and Steel Community of the 1950s, and/or a British–Irish–Northern Irish inter-parliamentary body. In short, Irish dimensions are open to negotiation, as are British dimensions, and they can be put within European frameworks.

## 10, 11 and 12

The two Governments then confirmed the main purpose of the Declaration as regards the republican movement. 'Democratically mandated parties' will have a full place in democratic politics and dialogue provided they renounce violence and 'have shown that they abide by the democratic process'. This passage was particularly addressed to Sinn Féin, but also, by implication, to loyalist organizations which are, or might wish to become, political parties.

This offer was immediately followed by a declaration from the Irish Government that they 'would make their own arrangements within *their jurisdiction* to enable democratic parties to consult together and share in dialogue about the political future . . . [and] . . . make recommendations on ways in which agreement and trust between both traditions in Ireland can be promoted and established'. The Forum for Peace and Reconciliation, to be held within Ireland's 'jurisdiction', was obviously meant to entice Sinn Féin, and presumably was the Irish Government's response to what may have been contained in the proposals agreed by John Hume and Gerry Adams. The Forum opened in Dublin in October 1994.

# Notes

## Acknowledgements

1   John McGarry and Brendan O'Leary (eds), *The Future of Northern Ireland* (Oxford: Oxford University Press, 1990); Brendan O'Leary and John McGarry, *The Politics of Antagonism: Understanding Northern Ireland* (London and Atlantic Highlands, N.J.: Athlone Press, 1993); and Brendan O'Leary, Tom Lyne, Jim Marshall and Bob Rowthorn, *Northern Ireland: Sharing Authority* (London: Institute of Public Research, 1993).

## Introduction

1   John Pepper, *Ulster-English Dictionary* (Belfast: Appletree Press, 1981), 82.
2   Barrington Moore Junr, 'Thoughts on Violence and Democracy', *Proceedings of the Academy of Political Science*, 29, 1 (1968), 1.
3   Walker Connor, *Ethnonationalism: the Quest for Understanding* (Princeton: Princeton University Press, 1994), 178.
4   Otto Hintze, 'The Formation of States and Constitutional Development', in *The Historical Essays of Otto Hintze* (New York: Oxford University Press, 1975), 162.
5   Interview with Brendan O'Leary, conducted in the Northern Ireland Office (London), for *Analysis*, November 1992.
6   John Whyte, *Interpreting Northern Ireland* (Oxford: Clarendon Press, 1990).
7   Rupert Taylor, 'Social Scientific Research on the "Troubles" in Northern Ireland: the Problem of Objectivity', *Economic and Social Review*, 19, 2 (1988), 123–45.
8   Our analysis is distinguishable in three respects from John Whyte's masterly and posthumously published *Interpreting Northern Ireland* (Oxford: Clarendon Press, 1990), the only other substantive work that we know of with similar objectives to our own. First, we explore the explanations of the nature and patterns of violence in Northern Ireland; secondly, we are more critical of 'internal conflict' explanations; and finally, we endeavour to construct a clear synthesis to support proposals to resolve Northern Ireland's antagonisms, a step that Whyte, with characteristic modesty, declined to take explicitly.
9   A first version of this classification can be found in Brendan O'Leary, 'Explaining Northern Ireland: A Brief Study Guide', *Politics*, 5, 1 (1985), 35–41.
10   John Whyte, 'Interpretations of the Northern Ireland Problem: An Appraisal', *Economic and Social Review*, 9, 4 (1978), 257–82; and see also Whyte, *Interpreting Northern Ireland*, 194–206.
11   John Darby, *Conflict in Northern Ireland: The Development of a Polarised Community*

(Dublin: Gill and Macmillan, 1976), 196.

12  See chapter 1, pp. 20–1.

13  Paul Arthur, *The Government and Politics of Northern Ireland* (Harlow: Longman, 1984); Patrick Buckland, *A History of Northern Ireland* (New York: Holmes and Meier, 1981); Jonathan Bardon, *A History of Ulster* (Belfast: Blackstaff Press, 1992); Richard Rose, *Governing without Consensus: An Irish Perspective* (London: Faber and Faber, 1971); Michael Farrell, *The Orange State* (London: Pluto, 1980); Tom Wilson, *Ulster: Conflict and Consent* (Oxford: Basil Blackwell, 1989); Arthur Aughey, *Under Siege: Ulster Unionism and the Anglo-Irish Agreement* (London: Hurst, 1989); Kevin Boyle and Tom Hadden, *Ireland: A Positive Proposal* (Harmondsworth: Penguin, 1985); Padraig O'Malley, *Ireland: the Uncivil Wars* (Belfast: Blackstaff Press, 1984); *Northern Ireland: Questions of Nuance* (Belfast: Blackstaff Press, 1990); Dervla Murphy, *Northern Ireland: A Place Apart* (Harmondsworth: Penguin, 1978); David McKittrick, *Despatches from Belfast* (Belfast: Blackstaff Press, 1989); *Endgame* (Belfast: Blackstaff Press, 1994); Brendan O'Leary and John McGarry, *The Politics of Antagonism: Understanding Northern Ireland* (London and Atlantic Heights N.J.: Athlone, 1993); John McGarry and Brendan O'Leary (eds), *The Future of Northern Ireland* (Oxford: Clarendon Press, 1990); and Brendan O'Leary, Tom Lyne, Jim Marshall and Bob Rowthorn, *Northern Ireland: Sharing Authority* (London: Institute of Public Policy Research, 1993).

## Chapter 1  Nationalist Discourses: British Centrality or British Neutrality?

1  RTE broadcast, 11 April 1976.

2  'Introduction' in Sean Cronin and Richard Roche (eds), *Freedom the Wolfe Tone Way* (Tralee: Anvil Books, 1973), 59.

3  The Cardinal was replying to Winston Churchill's controversial attack on the neutrality of Eire in his victory speech of May 1945 – cited in Robert Fisk, *In Time of War: Ireland, Ulster and the Price of Neutrality 1939–45* (London: Paladin Books, 1985), 513, citing John W. Blake, *Northern Ireland in the Second World War* (Belfast: HMSO, 1956), 213.

4  Gerry Adams, *The Politics of Irish Freedom* (Dingle: Brandon Books, 1986), 89.

5  Our definition is more exacting than Ernest Gellner's: 'Nationalism is primarily a political principle, which holds that the political and the national unit should be congruent', *Nations and Nationalism* (Oxford: Basil Blackwell, 1983), 1.

6  'Particularistic nationalism bears the same relation to universal nationalism as selfishness does to individualism, selfishness being the pursuit of one's own interests without regard to the interests of others, and individualism being the doctrine that it is legitimate to pursue one's own interests on the same terms on which others are free to pursue theirs' – Brian Barry, 'Nationalism', in D. Miller, J. Coleman, W. Connolly, and A. Ryan (eds), *The Basil Blackwell Encyclopaedia of Political Thought* (Oxford: Basil Blackwell, 1987), 352–4.

7  The Irish people are those resident in Ireland. Irish nationalists regularly seek support from the Irish diaspora – in the USA, Great Britain, Canada, Australia and New Zealand – but, in the twentieth century, they have not vigorously sought to bring this diaspora 'home'. The Republic extends the right of citizenship to all those born in Ireland, and their immediate descendants, but it does not give Irish-born citizens living outside its borders the right to vote – with the exception of diplomats.

8    See, for example, Peter Alter, *Nationalism* (London: Edward Arnold, 1989), and Anthony Smith, *National Identity* (Harmondsworth: Penguin, 1991).

9    Gellner, *Nations and Nationalism*, 53–5.

10   John Hutchinson, *The Dynamics of Cultural Nationalism: the Gaelic Revival and the Creation of the Irish Nation-State* (London: Allen and Unwin, 1987). As Hutchinson observes, some cultural nationalists were unionists.

11   Particular Irish nationalists, past and present, embody different permutations of these mentalities which necessarily simplify the complexities of individual biographies.

12   See Appendices A and B.

13   The most extreme revisionist is one of Ireland's most famous intellectuals, Conor Cruise O'Brien. Once a radical socialist and civic Irish nationalist, and once the author of a perceptive and intelligent commentary on Northern Ireland *(States of Ireland,* London: Hutchinson, 1972), he now describes himself as a unionist, and has become more hard-line than liberal unionists. In 1976, as a Government minister considering repressive legislation, he described his task as to 'cleanse the culture' of nationalist influence. O'Brien has written an interminable apologia for Edmund Burke, whose career he has emulated – both began their adult lives as radicals and ended as reactionaries, while proclaiming their consistency, Conor Cruise O'Brien, *The Great Medley, A Thematic Biography and Commented Anthology of Edmund Burke* (London: Sinclair-Stevenson, 1992). O'Brien is right to think he is just like Burke – which he will take to be a compliment.

14   Brendan O'Leary 'Affairs, Partner-Swapping, and Spring Tides: The Irish General Election 1992', *West European Politics*, 16, 3 (1993), 401–16.

15   The Irish public is divided. A poll conducted by the *Sunday Independent* (24 July 1994) in the Republic showed that 42 per cent of its respondents were not willing to give unionists a veto over Irish unification, while 28 per cent were – the rest being 'don't knows'. Supporters of Fianna Fáil and the Irish Labour Party were much less willing to give unionists such a veto than supporters of Fine Gael and the Progressive Democrats.

16   Roy Foster, Professor of Irish History at the University of Oxford, and the author of *Modern Ireland, 1600–1972* (London: Allen Lane, 1988), is usually singled out in this regard. Neither colonialism nor imperialism figure in the index of Foster's influential book (though 'plantation and settlement' do), while the entry for 'republicanism' reads '*see* Anglophobia, Catholicism, nationalism and Irish Republican Brotherhood in Index of Names', 669. It is, however, worth noting that Foster's revisionism does not satisfy unionists such as David Trimble MP, see Maurna Crozier (ed.), *Cultural Traditions in Ireland* (Belfast: Institute for Irish Studies, Queen's University, 1989), 48–9.

     Claire O'Halloran's *Partition and the Limits of Irish Nationalism: An Ideology Under Stress* (Dublin: Gill and Macmillan, 1987) is the clearest specimen of the revisionist genre, and dovetails better with unionist writings. O'Halloran scores some effective hits against 'pragmatic partitionism' in independent Ireland and against southern stereotypes of Ulster unionism, but spoils her case with errors. Thus on her first page she manages to declare that 'the division of Ireland into separate administrations was not accompanied by violence or indeed by any significant public reaction', xii, while on the last page she finishes a dogmatic misreading of the New Ireland Forum Report by suggesting it had had no impact in the reassessment of nationalist ideology, 210.

     Brendan Bradshaw has provided the most vigorous condemnation of ideological revisionism in the work of historians, 'Nationalism and Historical

Scholarship in Modern Ireland', *Irish Historical Studies*, 104 (1989), and correctly observes that revisionism has a longer intellectual ancestry than is sometimes imagined: revisionism began in the Irish Free State amongst those opposed to what they deemed romantic and 'impossibilist republicanism'.

17  Desmond Fennell, *The Revision of Irish Nationalism* (Dublin: Open Air, 1989), 10. See also his essay 'Getting to Know Dublin 4', published in *Heresy: the Battle of Ideas in Modern Ireland* (Belfast: Blackstaff Press, 1993), 186–212. Contemporary revisionists, despite their own self-understanding as disinterested truth-peddlers, are best understood as an expression of the secular counter-culture in the Republic. Opposing the historical dominance of the Catholic Church they have come to see Irish Catholicism in the same way as do Ulster unionists, i.e. as indissolubly wedded to Irish nationalism. When of leftist disposition they frequently make an illiterate equation between fascism and nationalism, and when of liberal persuasion casually assume that European integration has transcended the idea of the nation-state.

18  The most inconsistent Irish nationalists are the establishment of the Irish Roman Catholic Church, who welcome the prospect of Irish national unification and imply that they are no obstacle to an inclusive civic nationalism. At the same time they defend Catholic 'fundamentalism' in the Republic – on contraception, divorce and abortion – on the grounds that it protects 'the' Irish national identity.

19  They think that the government of the Irish Free State 'in effect recognised the legitimacy of Northern Ireland' in 1925 and that the Republic should do the same, John Murphy, 'National Territory?' *Sunday Independent*, 22 April 1990, 10.

20  In 1885, when challenged as to whether his demand for home rule marked the limit of Irish aspirations, Charles Stewart Parnell replied in words now inscribed on his statue in Dublin that 'No man has the right to set a boundary to the onward march of a nation. No man has a right to say "Thus far shalt thou go and no further"'.

21  *Saorstát Éireann* is the Gaelic name for the Irish Free State.

22  *Bunreacht na hÉireann* (Constitution of Ireland) (Dublin: Stationery Office).

23  Ibid.

24  That is the viewpoint expressed in the speeches and writings of the SDLP leader, John Hume – see, for example, Barry White, *John Hume: Statesman of the Troubles* (Belfast: Blackstaff Press, 1984).

25  In these respects revisionists like Eamon Dunphy, Kevin Myers and Conor Cruise O'Brien endorse the demands of unionists.

26  Revisionist authors are not discussed because their arguments are indistinguishable from those of liberal unionists considered in chapter 3. Indeed Conor Cruise O'Brien has been heard by one of the authors describing Tom Wilson's *Ulster: Conflict and Consensus* (Oxford: Basil Blackwell, 1989) as the best book ever written about Northern Ireland.

27  The first elaboration of a nationalist interpretation of Northern Ireland dates to 1923 when the newly established Irish Free State was preparing to re-negotiate the partition of the island, see North-Eastern Boundary Bureau, *Handbook of the Ulster Question* (Dublin: Stationery Office, 1923). The *Handbook* maintained that 'Ireland is by natural design a complete geographical entity. This natural design enforced on the political life of Ireland at an early date the idea of national unity, and it is doing violence, not only to nature but to the whole trend of the political life of the island to divorce politically at this late date in her national existence a considerable section of the northern population

from the motherland', 91. Though it was designed to support the case for an extensive re-partition the *Handbook* was written to be consistent with the claim that any partition of Ireland was unjust and unworkable, and for this reason its arguments became widely used by northern nationalists and their supporters – see, for example, Geoffrey Bing, *John Bull's Other Island* (London: Tribune, 1951); C. Desmond Greaves, *The Irish Question and the British People* (London: Lawrence and Wishart, 1963); Cahir Healy, *The Mutilation of a Nation* (Derry: Derry Journal, 1945); Mansion House Anti-Partition Conference, *One Vote Equals Two; Ireland's Right to Unity*; and *Discrimination: A Study in Injustice* (Dublin: All-Party AntiPartition Conference, 1950); David O'Neill, *The Partition of Ireland: How and Why it was Accomplished* (Dublin: Gill and Macmillan, 1948); and 'Ultach', 'Orange Terror: The Partition of Ireland', *The Capuchin Annual* (1943).

28  In the subsequent local government elections, held in January and June 1920, Republican and Labour candidates who backed Irish independence won over 80 per cent of the seats in the island, majority-control in 28 of Ireland's 32 counties, and more seats than the Unionists in historic Ulster. This performance was remarkable because proportional representation (STV) had been introduced by the British government in 1920, arguably with the primary objective of preventing Sinn Féin from capturing control of local government. Frank Gallagher, *Indivisible Island: the Story of the Partition of Ireland* (London: Gollancz, 1957), 139. Ian Budge and Cornelius O'Leary claim that the objectives of British policy-makers were more balanced. They hoped to blunt the strength of Unionism in Ulster, and of Sinn Féin in the other three provinces of Ireland, *Belfast: Approach to Crisis* (London: Macmillan, 1973), 136–7.

29  The Government of Ireland Act, which partitioned Ireland, passed through Westminster without one vote in its favour from Irish representatives. No nationalist, *and* no Ulster or Irish Unionist MP, legitimated partition. Brendan O'Leary, Tom Lyne, Jim Marshall and Bob Rowthorn, *Northern Ireland: Sharing Authority* (London: Institute for Public Policy Research, 1993), 153. The republican expressions, the 'six counties' and 'twenty-six counties', emphasize the illegitimacy of the two entities created by partition.

30  New Ireland Forum, *Report* (Dublin: Stationery Office, 1984), 3.3.

31  Gallagher, *Indivisible Island*, 301, 306.

32  In the late 1950s and 1960s copies of *Indivisible Island* were made available by Irish embassies and consulates throughout the world. Its author, Frank Gallagher, was formerly the editor of the (Fianna-Fáil supporting) *Irish Press*, Deputy Director of Radio Éireann, and Director of the Irish Government's Information Bureau. Gallagher used the pseudonym David O'Neill in other anti-partitionist writings, see, for example, O'Neill, *The Partition of Ireland: How and Why it was Accomplished*.

33  'That 300 miles of artificial frontier separating the North from the rest of Eire is the deepest wound which keeps alive ancient antagonisms between the English (morally responsible for the existence of the division) and the overwhelming majority of the Irish race', cited in Dennis Gwynn, *The Partition of Ireland (1912–1925)* (Dublin: Browne and Nolan, 1950), 20.

34  New Ireland Forum, *Report of Proceedings* (Dublin: Stationery Office, 1983–4), no. 1, 8.

35  Martin McGuinness, interview with Brendan O'Leary, conducted in Sinn Féin offices in Belfast for *Analysis*, November 1992.

36  It even used to be a regular complaint against partition that it offended natural

law, as it was ironically put by an historian, and the father of the political adviser to the last two Irish prime ministers, 'Providence arranged the geography of Ireland' but Lloyd George 'changed it'. Nicholas Mansergh, *The Irish Question, 1840–1921* (Toronto: University of Toronto Press, 1965), 216–17.

37 See note 35 above.

38 When asked how British withdrawal might come about one senior republican replied that 'I think the British government has one simple role . . . : to convince the Irish people who at present subscribe to *some hazy idea of Britishness* that the British connection is going, and they have to come to some sort of accommodation with the other people with whom they share the island' (source: confidential interview, September 1990; our emphasis).

39 Tom Garvin, 'The Rising and Irish Democracy', in Máirín Ní Dhonnchadha and Theo Dorgan (eds), *Revising the Rising* (Derry: Field Day, 1991), 21–8.

40 See George Dangerfield, *The Damnable Question: A Study in Anglo-Irish Relations* (London: Quartet, 1979); and Ian Lustick, *Unsettled States, Disputed Lands: Britain and Ireland, France and Algeria and the West-Bank-Gaza* (New York: Cornell University Press, 1993) for a non-Irish historian and political scientist who follow the same theme.

41 Nationalist historians take special delight in highlighting the numerous twists and shifts in Lloyd George's views on partition between 1911 and 1921. No less than eight 'erratic and contradictory' shifts in his position have been documented. Gwynn, *The Partition of Ireland*, 237.

42 See Anthony Coughlan, 'A Unitary Irish State', in John McGarry and Brendan O'Leary (eds), *The Future of Northern Ireland* (Oxford: Clarendon Press, 1990), 48–68.

43 See Appendix B.

44 Martin McGuinness expresses the revised republican view that doesn't 'buy a lot of the [previous] notions' about British strategic interests: 'Personally, I believe they're here because they wish to uphold the right and support the position of unionism within the six counties, rather than any strategic or economic interests . . . the British government are so caught up in this idea of the "United" Kingdom, as they call it, that with increases in demands from people in Scotland, and . . . to a lesser extent in Wales, . . . they could possibly fear that the reunification of Ireland would be the beginning of the breaking up of what they call the "United" Kingdom', see note 35 above. McGuinness also referred to former Secretary of State Jim Prior's fears of an 'Irish Cuba' but without taking it seriously (see chapter 2, p. 67).

45 New Ireland Forum, *Report*, 3.5.

46 Ibid., 3.7.

47 Ibid., 3.9. See also, p. 447, n. 65.

48 Ibid., 3.14.

49 Ibid., 3.16.

50 Ibid., 3.20.

51 Ibid., 3.19.

52 Gerry Adams, *The Politics of Irish Freedom*, 62.

53 Ibid., 51, 69, 89.

54 Two legal authors, who are not republicans, show in considerable detail how Northern Ireland has always been governed under emergency laws, see Gerard Hogan and Clive Walker, *Political Violence and the Law in Ireland* (Manchester: Manchester University Press, 1990).

55 New Ireland Forum, *Report*, 3.18.

56 Adams, *The Politics of Irish Freedom*, 105–6; Anthony Coughlan, *Fooled Again: the*

*Anglo-Irish Agreement and After* (Cork: Mercier Press, 1986); and Kevin Boland, *Under Contract with the Enemy* (Cork: Mercier Press, 1987). For a full discussion of the Anglo-Irish Agreement and its aftermath see Brendan O'Leary and John McGarry, *The Politics of Antagonism: Understanding Northern Ireland* (London and Atlantic Heights, N.J.: Athlone, 1993), chs 6–7. The text of the Agreement is available as an appendix in McGarry and O'Leary (eds), *The Future of Northern Ireland*.

57 The Ulster Executive of Republican Sinn Féin, a small splinter-group which broke away from Provisional Sinn Féin in 1986, 'completely rejected' the Declaration, branding it a 'worse sell-out than the Treaty surrender in 1921' because 'Dublin now accepts that 18 per cent of the Irish people can dictate to the other 82 per cent', *News Letter*, 11 January 1994.

58 See chapter 10.

59 Elie Kedourie, *Nationalism* (London: Hutchinson, 1960), 140.

60 John Plamenatz, *On Alien Rule and Self-Government* (London: Longman, 1960).

61 Brian Barry, 'Self-Government Revisited', in David Miller and Larry Siedentop (eds), *The Nature of Political Theory* (Oxford: Clarendon Press, 1983), 143. Countering the conventional wisdom of English and American liberals (and Irish revisionists) Barry suggests 'that nationalism has been given a bum rap in recent political theory' and that 'the efforts . . . to conflate ethical individualism and anti-nationalism will not withstand scrutiny' – ibid., 154.

62 Barry, 'Self-Government Revisited', 127.

63 A British lawyer once remarked that on the surface the principle of self-determination seems reasonable as it means letting the people decide, but 'the people cannot decide until somebody decides who are the people', see Ivor Jennings, *The Approach to Self-Government* (Cambridge: Cambridge University Press, 1956), 56.

64 Brian Farrell, *Chairman or Chief? The Role of Taoiseach in Irish Government* (Dublin: Gill and Macmillan, 1971), 48.

65 One of them also observes that the 'Sinn Féin majority in votes in the South [i.e. the twenty-six counties] was roughly the same as that of the Unionists in the Six Counties'. Tom Wilson, *Ulster: Conflict and Consent* (Oxford: Basil Blackwell, 1989), 48.

66 Sinn Féin's electoral performance in Ulster was decidedly weaker than elsewhere in Ireland – it obtained an absolute majority of the votes cast in just two of the nine counties, Fermanagh and Monaghan, although its candidates were returned unopposed in Cavan. This weakness was partly because of a deal between Sinn Féin and the Irish Parliamentary Party, which divided the safe nationalist seats in Ulster, after arbitration by the Roman Catholic Church, see Michael McGrath, 'The Price of Faith: the Catholic Church and Catholic Schools in Northern Ireland since 1920', PhD thesis, London School of Economics and Political Science, University of London (1995).

67 Self-determination might have been implemented using local government wards as the plebiscite-areas, using the 1920 election results, but here the patchwork-quilt effect of the new map would have been more pronounced than under a plurality-rule parliamentary operationalization – and would have been strenuously rejected by British and Irish policy-makers.

68 Albert Reynolds, T.D., 'Self-Determination and Consent in the Joint Declaration for Peace in Northern Ireland', UCD Law Society's Cearbhaill Ó'Dálaigh Memorial Dinner, 20 January 1994.

69 The 1937 Constitution which declared the Republic's de jure sovereignty over Northern Ireland would probably not have won a majority in an all-Ireland

referendum, though there might have been sufficient support for Articles 2 and 3 taken on their own.

70    Harry Beran, 'A Liberal Theory of Secession', *Political Studies*, 32 (1984), 596–84.

71    One amendment to Beran's theory would require that each community should be given the right to name its area of plebiscite at the outset – otherwise those who 'go first' would obtain an advantage.

72    Even de Valera accepted this liberal theory of secession. In May 1972 a volume entitled *Private Sessions of Second Dáil* was released to deputies in Dublin. Its minutes of 22 August 1921 record de Valera arguing that the Dáil had not the power, and some deputies had not the inclination, to use force with Ulster, and that such a policy would not be successful. 'They would be making the same mistake with that section as England had made with Ireland . . . For his part, if the Republic were recognised, he would be in favour of giving each county power to vote itself out of the Republic if it so wished', cited in Conor Cruise O'Brien, *States of Ireland* (London: Panther Press, 1974), 276.

73    It does not follow, of course, that the injustice of the particular partition of Ireland implemented between 1920 and 1925 would have been rectified by the coerced incorporation of unionists into a united Ireland, 'Bitterly resenting an unfair border – itself the result of Ulster Unionist leverage – nationalists could easily ignore any merits in an Ulster unionist case for some border,' John Bowman, *De Valera and the Ulster Question* (Oxford: Oxford University Press, 1982), 11. Nor does it follow that a second partition of Ireland would be the best way of resolving conflict now, see chapter 9, pp. 369.

74    Michael Laffan, *The Partition of Ireland, 1911–1925* (Dundalk: Dundalgan Press, 1983), 123,

75    Gallagher, *Indivisible Island*, 65–88.

76    Laffan, *The Partition of Ireland*, 123.

77    Andrew Marr, *The Battle for Scotland* (Harmondsworth: Penguin, 1992).

78    See the 'Articles of Agreement for a Treaty between Great Britain and Ireland', in *Constitution of the Free State of Ireland* (Dublin: Stationery Office, 1922), 27–34. Article 7 was removed through negotiations between de Valera and Neville Chamberlain in 1938.

79    Initial republican opposition to the Treaty in what became the Irish Free State was not primarily based on partition and the formation of Northern Ireland. The debating positions taken by most of the anti-Treaty forces when Dáil Éireann considered the ratification of the Treaty in December 1921 demonstrate this. The text of the debate suggests that most nationalists did not regard partition as a major imperialist issue: a mere nine of the 338 pages of the Dáil Éireann debate concern partition. 'Critics of the treaty concentrated on the crown, the oath and the empire, for the most part, and several of those who did make a fleeting reference to the Northern Ireland question *were concerned not with the loss of the six counties, but rather with the fact that this part of Ireland could provide a bridgehead when Britain decided to re-establish her rule in Ireland*. Indeed document number 2 – the proposal put forward by Mr de Valera [as an alternative to the Treaty] – showed no alterations in the articles relating to Northern Ireland, and seems to indicate that President de Valera had been convinced by the delegates that the Boundary Commission would solve the problem of partition,' Maureen Wall, 'Partition: the Ulster Question (1916–1926)', in T. D. Williams (ed.), *The Irish Struggle, 1916–1926* (London: Routledge and Kegan Paul), 87. The italicized passage suggests that

nationalists feared British imperialism, and that Northern Ireland could be used for imperialist purposes; but the actual loss of the six counties – or slightly less after what was expected to be a favourable Boundary Commission – was not regarded as an imperialist action.

80 Adams, *The Politics of Irish Freedom*, 19.

81 O'Leary and McGarry, *The Politics of Antagonism*, chs 3–4.

82 Christopher McCrudden, 'Northern Ireland and the British Constitution', in J. Jowell and D. Oliver (eds), *The Changing Constitution* (Oxford: Clarendon Press, 1989), 297–342.

83 Negotiations to that end were managed by Neville Chamberlain and by Malcolm MacDonald, the man who had conducted the negotiations which had led to the return of the 'Treaty ports' in 1938 (see note 78 above). On 25 June 1940 the British War Cabinet approved a paper for presentation to de Valera: in return for Eire's joining the war with the Allies, the UK government would 'forthwith' issue a declaration accepting the principle of a united Ireland and establish a joint body, including delegations from the two Irish governments, to consider the constitutional and other practical details of the Union of Ireland, see Lord Longford and T. P. O'Neill, *Eamon De Valera* (Dublin: Gill and Macmillan, 1970), 365–6. MacDonald met de Valera, Lemass and Aiken on 27 June. Lemass was favourable, but Aiken was vigorous in demanding Irish unity and neutrality (as was de Valera, although less so). There was suspicion about the sincerity of the British offer, which MacDonald attempted to rebut. A revised British offer signed by Chamberlain was delivered on 28 June. The key new idea was that in addition to considering Irish unity the British agreed to drop the requirement that Eire enter the war, in return for an invitation to British forces to co-operate in securing Eire's security 'against the fate which has overcome neutral Norway, Holland, Belgium, Denmark and Luxembourg'. On 4 July de Valera replied that the Irish cabinet had rejected the plan because it envisaged 'the immediate abandonment' of neutrality, but gave 'no guarantee of unity', see Bowman, *De Valera and the Ulster Question*, 236. There is extensive debate about de Valera's (and his cabinet's) motives in rejecting the British offer. John Bowman (ibid., 205–66) and Joe Lee (*Ireland: Politics and Society, 1912–1985*, Cambridge: Cambridge University Press, 1989, 248) insist that de Valera and his colleagues doubted the British commitment to unity; had good grounds for doing so in the light of Churchill's position, which required Northern Ireland's consent to Irish unity; and had to consider Irish interests in continuing neutrality given Ireland's recent past, the widespread expectation that Germany would win the war, and the non-involvement of the USA in 1940. Others think that the British offer was sincere, and that the British government could have delivered the consent of the younger unionist leaders, see Cornelius O'Leary, 'Professor Lee's Ireland', paper presented to the Annual Meeting of the Irish Political Studies Association of Ireland, Cork (October 1990).

84 See Appendices A and B.

85 O'Leary and McGarry, *The Politics of Antagonism*, chs 5–7.

86 See Appendix A, esp. section 4.

87 Until 1990, when confronted with British willingness to consider Irish unification or reform Northern Ireland hard-line republicans typically unveiled the unfalsifiable argument that all British reforming or anti-unionist actions were merely expedient adjustments to nationalist protests or to the armed struggle of the IRA (non-attributable interviews with republicans in Belfast, Cork and Dublin 1989–90).

88 *Irish Times*, 11 October 1990. In late 1993 the release of secret discussions

between the British government and the IRA suggested that Brooke's speech was deliberately designed to encourage republicans to review their position.

89  See pp. 57–8.

90  Patricia Jalland, *The Liberals in Ireland: the Ulster Question in British Politics to 1914* (Brighton: Harvester Press, 1980); Robert Kee, *The Green Flag: the Story of Irish Nationalism* (London: Quartet, 1976); and F. S. L. Lyons, *Ireland since the Famine* (Glasgow: Collins, 1973), 348–52. This verdict on parts of Jalland's, Kee's and Lyons's research does not imply assent to all of their judgements.

91  Dennis Kennedy, *The Widening Gulf: Northern Attitudes to the Independent Irish State, 1919–49* (Belfast: Blackstaff Press, 1988); and see chapter 3.

92  Bernard Crick, *In Defence of Politics* (Harmondsworth: Penguin, 1964), 80.

93  Adams, *The Politics of Irish Freedom*, 89.

94  The official republican doctrine that Ulster Protestants are members of the Irish nation competed with a perception of unionists as colonial settlers. The North Eastern Boundary Bureau *Handbook* established the official view of Ulster unionists in independent Ireland. It classified them as 'a religious minority . . . which has been able through the use of assiduous outside forces to . . . insist on cutting off from the nation not only its own adherents but a large minority whose traditional allegiance was to the nation as a whole', North Eastern Boundary Review, *Handbook of the Ulster Question*, vi. This view has not been the only one. An Irish Senator observed in 1939 that 'We have had a habit, when it suited a particular case, of saying they were Irish, and when it did not suit a particular case, of saying they were British, or planters or the seed of planters', Claire O'Halloran, *Partition and the Limits of Irish Nationalism* (Dublin: Gill and Macmillan, 1987), 31. The latter mentality was present in the private musings of Éamon de Valera – at least as recorded by an American diplomat. De Valera is alleged to have considered what should have been unthinkable had he regarded Ulster Protestants as members of the Irish nation. As ethnic expulsions and mass population transfers were being executed by the victorious Allies throughout Europe in 1946, he privately discussed the idea of repatriating Ulster Unionists to Great Britain and re-settling the North with Irish emigrants living in British cities, see Bowman, *De Valera and the Ulster Question*, 260. The source of this story, David Gray, the American Minister to Ireland 1940–7, was extremely hostile to de Valera. However, he had recorded a similar conversation in 1943 – when de Valera apparently had in mind the population exchanges between Greece and Turkey implemented in the early 1920s – and de Valera had publicly ruminated upon a voluntary population exchange at a Fianna Fáil Ard Fheis in 1939, see ibid., 318. One possible consequence of regarding Ulster unionists as British settlers is to argue for their expulsion – which is how many Protestants decode the slogan 'Brits Out!' However, republicans are usually careful to insist that the demand extends only to the personnel of the British war machine.

95  Adams, *The Politics of Irish Freedom*, 26.

96  See note 35.

97  See Appendix A.

98  See note 35.

99  Sean Cronin, *Irish Nationalism: A History of its Roots and Ideology* (London: Pluto Press, 1983), 207.

100  O'Leary and McGarry, *The Politics of Antagonism*, ch. 1.

101  Ibid., 321.

102  O'Leary, 'Affairs, Partner-Swapping, and Spring Tides'.

103  One of the best discussions of just-war doctrines can be found in the work

of Michael Walzer, *Just and Unjust Wars: A Moral Argument with Historical Illustrations* (New York: Basic Books, 1977) – though certain passages appear to adjust the doctrines to justify Israeli wars.

104  These criteria were successively elaborated by, inter alia, St Augustine in the fifth century, Aquinas in the thirteenth century and Reinhold Niebuhr in the twentieth.

105  See M. L. R. Smith, 'The Role of the Military Instrument in Irish Republican Thinking: An Evolutionary Analysis', PhD thesis, King's College, University of London (1991).

106  The UDA's 'Doomsday Scenario', leaked to a Northern Irish newspaper, envisaged creating an 'ethnic Protestant homeland' if the British withdrew: expulsion, internment and 'nullification' of Catholics were considered legitimate tactics, *Sunday Life*, 16 January 1994.

107  D. Canning, B. Moore, and J. Rhodes, 'Economic Growth in Northern Ireland: Problems and Prospects', in Paul Teague (ed.), *Beyond the Rhetoric: Politics, the Economy and Social Policy in Northern Ireland* (London: Lawrence and Wishart, 1987); and Bob Rowthorn and Naomi Wayne, *Northern Ireland: the Political Economy of Conflict* (Oxford: Polity Press, 1988). These economists recognize that from the figures of jobs lost in manufacturing must be subtracted the jobs created which would not have been created without the conflict (e.g. in the police, prisons, security and health services). However, they rightly suggest that such jobs are less productive. Moreover, creating security jobs for Protestants is one of the oddest unintended consequences of the IRA's 'long war'.

108  See R. Davis, 'Irish Republicanism v. Roman Catholicism: The Perennial Debate in the Ulster Troubles', in Alan O'Day and Yonah Alexander (eds), *Ireland's Terrorist Trauma* (Hemel Hempstead: Harvester Wheatsheaf, 1989), 34–74. An especially lucid essay criticizing the IRA's belief that it is fighting a just war can be found in the work of the present Roman Catholic Primate of All Ireland, Cahal Daly, *The Price of Peace* (Belfast: Blackstaff Press, 1991), 49–72.

109  Whyte, *Interpreting Northern Ireland*, ch. 6.

110  W. Harvey Cox, 'Who Wants a United Ireland?' *Government and Opposition*, 1, 20 (1985), 29–47, and 'The Politics of Unification in the Irish Republic', *Parliamentary Affairs*, 38, 4 (1985), 437–54.

111  See Richard Sinnott, 'The North: Party Images and Party Approaches in the Republic', *Irish Political Studies*, 1: 15–32; and Paul Power, 'Revisionist "Consent", Hillsborough, and the Decline of Constitutional Republicanism', *Eire-Ireland*, 25 (1990), 20–39.

112  Peter Brooke MP, interview with Brendan O'Leary, conducted in the Northern Ireland Office, London, February 1991; and Sir Patrick Mayhew MP, interview with Brendan O'Leary, conducted in the Northern Ireland Office, London, for *Analysis*, November 1992.

113  See chapter 3, table 3.4.

114  John Hume MP, MEP, interview with Brendan O'Leary, conducted in the Westminster parliament, for *Analysis*, November 1992.

115  O'Leary and McGarry, *The Politics of Antagonism*, ch. 1.

116  Hume observed at the SDLP's 1989 party conference that 'If [the IRA] were to have the courage to shout "stop", there would also be an end to the military presence on our streets . . . Many of the things [republicans] complain about are a direct consequence of the campaign mounted by the IRA', *Irish Times*, 6 November 1989.

117  *Irish Press*, 17 January 1994. 'It is people who have rights not territory', John Hume, 'New ways of coming together in peace', *Irish Times*, 31 January 1994.

118 *Sunday Life*, 9 January 1994.
119 In his address to the SDLP conference in 1989 Hume declared that 'The fiction of total, undiluted sovereignty of the slogan Sinn Féin leads to isolation and powerlessness on the world scene – in its benign form to the cultivation of nostalgia or in its malign form to xenophobia and racism.' *Irish Times*, 6 November 1989.
120 See Appendices A and B.

### Chapter 2  Green Political Economy: British Imperialism as the Prime Mover

1 Liam O'Dowd, Bill Rolston and Mike Tomlinson, *Northern Ireland: Between Civil Rights and Civil War* (London: CSE Books, 1980), 208.
2 Marxists recognize these divisions themselves. Thus one Marxist refers to green, orange, and red species of socialism, identifying himself with the red variety, see Austen Morgan, 'Socialism in Ireland – Red, Green and Orange', in Austen Morgan and Bob Purdie (eds), *Ireland: Divided Nation – Divided Class* (London: Ink Links, 1980). Green Marxists prefer to divide Marxists into anti-imperialist and 'revisionist' camps, the latter being damned as objectively pro-unionist, see John Martin, 'The Conflict in Northern Ireland: Marxist Interpretations', *Capital and Class*, 18 (1982), 56–71.
3 See Bernadette Devlin, *The Price of my Soul* (London: Pan, 1969); Michael Farrell, *Northern Ireland: the Orange State* (London: Pluto Press, 1976, 1980); Eamonn McCann, *War and an Irish Town* (Harmondsworth: Penguin, 1974, 1980).
4 See, for example, Liam de Paor, *Divided Ulster* (Harmondsworth: Penguin, 1970, 1971); and the Sunday Times Insight Team, *Ulster* (Harmondsworth, Penguin, 1972).
5 Nine of the sixteen books listed by Gerry Adams as sources for his tract on *The Politics of Irish Freedom* (Dingle: Brandon Books, 1986), 170, are green Marxist. Four are texts of James Connolly; two were authored by Michael Farrell – *Northern Ireland* and *Arming the Protestants* (London: Pluto Press, 1983); two were written by Desmond Greaves – *Liam Mellows and the Irish Revolution* (London: Lawrence and Wishart, 1971) and *The Life and Times of James Connolly* (London: Lawrence and Wishart, 1961); and one was McCann's *War and an Irish Town*.
6 See, for example, James Anderson, 'Regions and Religions in Ireland: A Short Critique of the "Two Nations" Theory', *Antipode*, 12, 2 (1980), 44–52; James M. Blaut, *The National Question: Decolonizing the Theory of Nationalism* (London: Zed Press, 1987); and Diane Perrons, 'Ireland and the Break-up of Britain', *Antipode*, 12, 2 (1980), 53–65.
7 For Connolly's Ulster writings see the Cork Workers' Club, *Ireland upon the Dissecting Table: James Connolly on Ulster and Partition* (Cork: Cork Workers' Club, 1975); *The Connolly–Walker Controversy on Socialist Unity in Ireland* (Cork: Cork Workers' Club, 1969); and Peter Berresford Ellis (ed.), *James Connolly: Selected Writings* (Harmondsworth: Penguin, 1973), 261–84. There are several biographies of Connolly. Greaves's *The Life and Times of James Connolly* is eminently readable, but uncritical, while Austen Morgan's biography is very critical but almost unreadable – *James Connolly: A Political Biography* (Manchester: Manchester University Press, 1988).
8 Karl Marx and Friedrich Engels, *Ireland and the Irish Question* (London: Lawrence and Wishart, 1978).
9 See the writings of Desmond Greaves – *The Life and Times of James Connolly*;

Liam Mellows, *The Irish Question and the British People* (London: Lawrence and Wishart, 1963); and *The Irish Crisis* (London: Lawrence and Wishart, 1972) – and also the popular text of T. A. Jackson, *Ireland Her Own: An Outline History of the Irish Struggle*, edited and with an epilogue by C. D. Greaves (London: Lawrence and Wishart, 1947, reprinted 1971).

10    See, for example, Chris Bambery, *Ireland's Permanent Revolution* (London: Bookmarks, 1987); Geoffrey Bell, *The Protestants of Ulster* (London: Pluto Press, 1976); *The British in Ireland: A Suitable Case for Withdrawal* (London: Pluto Press, 1984); R. Dorn, *Irish Nationalism and British Imperialism* (Dublin: Plough Book Service); Paul Foot, *Ireland: A Rational Case for Withdrawal* (London: Chatto and Windus, 1989); Revolutionary Marxist Group, *British Strategy in Northern Ireland: From the White Paper to the Fall of Sunningdale* (Dublin: Plough Book Service, 1975); and the Socialist Workers' Party, *Why We Say 'Troops Out of Ireland!'* (London: Seven Sisters, 1980).

11    The key republican newspaper often displayed green Marxist traits in its writings in the 1970s and 1980s, and made use of the Algerian analogy – 'Broadly the Irish struggle is paralleled by Algeria's fight for freedom, one which was also hampered by a colonial enclave, one which, also, in its latter stages, was marked by the same collusion between fascist gangs and the French imperial armed forces, involving horror massacres similar to the recent cross-border outrages', *An Phoblacht*, 15 August 1975. For further discussion of the Algerian analogy see, pp. 161–2, and 333–5.

12    Bambery, *Ireland's Permanent Revolution*, 27.

13    Cork Workers' Club, *Ireland upon the Dissecting Table*, 38.

14    Ibid., 38–9.

15    Ibid., 60–2.

16    Farrell, *Northern Ireland*, 325ff.

17    See, for example, the Socialist Workers' Party, *Why We Say 'Troops Out of Ireland!'*, 8–9.

18    McCann, *War and an Irish Town*, 126. Given that capitalism is the root of all evil it would be interesting to learn McCann's explanations of wars in pre-capitalist societies, or between post-capitalist states.

19    Cited in Paul Arthur, 'Republican Violence in Northern Ireland: The Rationale', in J. Darby, N. Hodge, and A. C. Hepburn (eds), *Political Violence: Ireland in a Comparative Perspective* (Belfast: Appletree Press, 1990), 49.

20    See, for example, Sean MacStiofain, *Memoirs of a Revolutionary* (Farnborough: Gordon Cremonesi, 1975).

21    See Adams, *The Politics of Irish Freedom*, 128–36.

22    It also explains why many members of the Officials condemned members of the civil-rights movement who made socialist speeches and arguments: 'ultra-leftists' failed to appreciate that socialist arguments could only be successfully advanced after stage two!

23    Until 1982 the Workers' Party was known as Official Sinn Féin in the Republic, and as the Republican Clubs in Northern Ireland (and as Sinn Féin: the Workers' Party). It changed its name to reflect its (official) break from paramilitarism and its official espousal of Marxism. It developed as an orthodox European communist party, performing moderately well in urban areas of the Republic, winning 5 per cent of the first-preference vote in the elections to Dáil Éireann in 1989, see Brendan O'Leary and John Peterson, 'Further Europeanisation: The Irish General Election, July 1989', *West European Politics*, 13, 1 (1990), 124–36. In Northern Ireland it fared less well. Its membership contained a curious cocktail of former Official IRA personnel,

Stalinists, reformist communists, (originally Protestant) red Marxist intellectuals who favoured the Union, and secular enragés in the South who were dissatisfied with the Irish Labour Party. During 1991/2 the Workers' Party disintegrated. The bulk of the southern membership and the parliamentary deputies defected to form a new party, Democratic Left, after it was confirmed that the Official IRA had not been disbanded and that the party had been in receipt of Moscow gold. Democratic Left now berates paramilitarism and extols democracy with the zeal of the recent convert.

24  McCann, *War and an Irish Town*; Farrell, *Northern Ireland.*
25  McCann, *War and an Irish Town*, 243.
26  James Prior, *A Balance of Power* (London: Hamish Hamilton, 1986), 235.
27  See Marx and Engels, *Ireland and the Irish Question*, 404ff. Marx and Engels thought that anti-Irish sentiments amongst the English working class weakened proletarian solidarity. They reasoned that an Irish revolution – against the landed aristocracy – was an essential precondition of socialist revolution in England.
28  See Liam O'Dowd, Bill Rolston and Mike Tomlinson, *Northern Ireland*; and Bill Rolston, 'Reformism and Sectarianism: The State of the Union after Civil Rights', in John Darby (ed.), *Northern Ireland: the Background to the Conflict* (Belfast: Appletree Press, 1983), 197–224.
29  See D. Smith and G. Chambers, *Inequality in Northern Ireland* (Oxford: Clarendon Press, 1991); and see chapter 7.
30  O'Dowd et al., *Northern Ireland*, 24.
31  See Brendan O'Leary and John McGarry, *The Politics of Antagonism: Understanding Northern Ireland* (London: Athlone, 1993), ch. 2.
32  See, for example, Ian Lustick, *State-Building Failure in British Ireland and French Algeria* (Berkeley: Institute of International Studies, University of California, 1985); and *Unsettled States, Disputed Lands: Britain and Ireland, France and Algeria and the West-Bank-Gaza* (New York: Cornell University Press, 1993); Ronald Weitzer, *Transforming Settler States: Communal Conflict and Internal Security in Northern Ireland and Zimbabwe* (Berkeley and London, University of California Press, 1990); and Frank Wright, *Northern Ireland: A Comparative Analysis* (Dublin: Gill and Macmillan, 1987).
33  See chapter 3, pp. 100.
34  Leon Trotsky, *The Permanent Revolution and Results and Prospects* (New York: Pathfinder Press, 3rd edn, 1969).
35  One could challenge the premise of any simple-minded Marxist colonial analysis by arguing that in comparative terms the Irish economy, north and south, was highly developed in 1920, even if its economic performance since then has been one of the worst in western Europe, see J. J. Lee's *Ireland, 1912–85, Politics and Society* (Cambridge: Cambridge University Press, 1989), 511ff. In this perspective the colonial features of the Irish economy were largely wiped out by the repercussions of the Great Famine. In 1911 national product per capita in Ireland was higher than in Norway, Sweden, Italy and Finland, and not far behind that in Denmark and France, ibid., 513. Another evaluation of the state of the Irish economy before independence can be found in the work of Kieran Kennedy, Thomas Giblin and Deirdrie McHugh, *The Economic Development of Ireland in the Twentieth Century* (London: Routledge, 1988), 3–29. They emphasize the lack of industrialization in what became the Republic and present data suggesting stagnant levels of output and rates of growth in Ireland by comparison with a very large number of European countries. None the less, they maintain that Ireland had one of the highest per capita growth rates

in western Europe before the Great War, largely because of the impact of the Great Famine (and the consequent massive depopulation of the island, exacerbated by agrarian specialization in livestock production). 'Though the evidence is scanty, it points to the surprising conclusion that average incomes may not, in fact, have been significantly higher in [what became] Northern Ireland at about the time of the First World War', ibid., 20, 22.

36    One green Marxist, of Ulster Protestant background, simultaneously rejects the 'two nations' theory whilst describing Ulster Protestants as Britain's 'oldest settlers', Bell, *The British in Ireland*, 7–9, 104. In an earlier work, *The Protestants of Ulster*, he recounts numerous tales of unsavoury Protestant stereotyping of Catholics. Other researchers, by contrast, claim that Ulster Protestants recognize Catholics as human equals – albeit misguided and duped equals – rather than as racial inferiors – which is less typical of the colonialist mentality. For a nuanced anthropological study of stereotypes see Rosemary Harris, *Prejudice and Tolerance in Ulster: A Study of Neighbours and 'Strangers' in a Border Community* (Manchester: Manchester University Press, 1972), and for a survey-based examination of stereotypes see E. E. O'Donnell, *Northern Irish Stereotypes* (Dublin: College of Industrial Relations, 1977).

37    Farrell, *Northern Ireland*, 81.

38    John Whyte, *Interpreting Northern Ireland* (Oxford: Clarendon Press, 1990), 180–1.

39    Jon Elster, *Sour Grapes: Studies in the Subversion of Rationality* (Cambridge: Cambridge University Press, 1983), 141ff.

40    Jon Elster, *Making Sense of Marx* (Cambridge University Press, 1985).

41    The anachronism is palpable: Britain did not exist as a political entity in 1169, and Norman barons were not British.

42    D. R. O'Connor Lysaght, 'British Imperialism in Ireland', in Austen Morgan and Bob Purdie (eds), *Ireland: Divided Nation, Divided Class* (London: Ink Links, 1980), 12.

43    Some green Marxists realize that there are some problems with instrumentalist accounts of British imperialism, and therefore propound an absentee model of the workings of the British state in Ireland: 'The relationship between British imperialism and Ireland is reminiscent of the theologian Paley's metaphor for God's working of the universe – the Divine Watchmaker as first cause. Britain initiated its control over Ireland, and then left the conditions thereby established to work themselves out, intervening only when matters threatened to get out of hand. The metaphor might be extended further – as the watch ages the maker has had to resort to his repair services with increasing frequency', ibid., 14. This metaphor has a better purchase on historical realities, but it scarcely explains why the absentee British state should want to keep the watch going into the twenty-first century. Another school of green Marxists operates with a functionalist model of the (British) capitalist state, see, for example, Liam O'Dowd et al., *Northern Ireland*. In this world-view the function of the capitalist state is to reproduce the capitalist mode of production, including class-based relations of production. Given that sectarian and class relations are fused in Northern Ireland, the British state can only 'modernize' sectarianism, it cannot reform it. This teleological reasoning implies that socialism alone can perform the eradication of sectarianism, i.e. it is wishful thinking cloaked in dogma. It is also at odds with reality – if it means that no capitalist states can be free of institutionalized sectarianism.

44    Leslie Clarkson, 'The City and the Country', in J. C. Beckett et al., *Belfast: The Making of the City* (Belfast, Appletree Press, 1988), 153.

45 Liam Cullen, *An Economic History of Ireland since 1660* (London: Batsford Press, 1972), 156–70, *passim.*
46 Patrick Buckland, *Irish Unionism, 1885–1923, A Documentary History* (Belfast: HMSO, 1973), 2–11.
47 McCann, *War and an Irish Town*, 127, our emphasis.
48 The unionist representative on the Boundary Commission of 1923–5, J. R. Fisher, privately advocated that Northern Ireland should include Donegal, over 80 per cent Catholic in population, in order to reduce the border which would need to be defended. He spoke of Donegal as an Afghanistan. 'With North Monaghan *in* Ulster and South Armagh *out*, we should have a solid ethnographic and strategic frontier to the South, and a hostile "Afghanistan" on our north-west frontier would be placed in safe-keeping', Denis Gwynn, *The History of Partition (1912–1925)* (Dublin: Browne & Nolan, 1950), 215–16. These motivations were racist and imperialist, but they had nothing to do with economics, see Oliver MacDonagh, *States of Mind: Two Centuries of the Anglo-Irish Conflict, 1780–1980* (London: Pimlico, 1983), 23.
49 Bob Rowthorn and Naomi Wayne, *Northern Ireland: the Political Economy of Conflict* (Oxford: Polity Press, 1988), 83.
50 Frank Gaffikin and Mike Morrisey, *Northern Ireland: the Thatcher Years* (London: Zed Press, 1990), 49.
51 House of Commons, Hansard, 13 July 1994, Written Answer 100.
52 A considerable proportion of the subvention is explained by Northern Ireland's very high level of unemployment – and therefore its high level of social security expenditure. There are also 'small-country' effects in explaining the costs of public administration in Northern Ireland, i.e. there are economies of scale in delivering public services to a large urbanized population (like England's).
53 Bob Rowthorn, 'Northern Ireland: An Economy in Crisis', *Cambridge Journal of Economics*, 5, 1 (1981), 1–32; and Vanni Borooah, 'Northern Ireland – Typology of a Regional Economy', in Paul Teague (ed.), *The Economy of Northern Ireland: Perspectives for Structural Change* (London: Lawrence and Wishart, 1993), 2.
54 Rowthorn and Wayne, *Northern Ireland*, 82, 98. Rowthorn and Wayne's excellent economic analysis is detachable from the largely green Marxist politics of their book, and their endorsement of 'troops out'. Rowthorn has since abandoned these political perspectives, and now shares much of our analysis, see Brendan O'Leary, Tom Lyne, Jim Marshall, and Bob Rowthorn, *Northern Ireland: Sharing Authority* (London: Institute of Public Policy Research, 1993).
55 *The Economist*, 26 March 1988.
56 As late as 1976 it was being argued that the British state was in Northern Ireland to protect capitalist investment interests: the region was the locus of production for one-third of the total output of artificial fibres in the UK, see Farrell, *Northern Ireland*, 326. The artificial fibre industry was annihilated in Thatcher's 'monetarist' recession of 1979–81. As the British government has not withdrawn from Northern Ireland these investments cannot have been as important in determining British public policy as Farrell seems to have imagined.
57 McCann was a leading activist in the civil-rights movement, as was Michael Farrell. The latter's historical work is very detailed, well-written, and based upon original primary historical research. He has uncovered damning material on Northern Ireland government before 1972, which may explain why his efforts to gain access to public records have sometimes been denied through straightforward censorship. However, Farrell's former political prescriptions gave vulgar Marxism a bad name – see, for example, 'Northern Ireland – An

Anti-Imperialist Struggle', in Ralph Miliband and John Saville (eds), *Socialist Register* (London: Merlin Press, 1977), 71–80. He has since developed a more nuanced and thoughtful left-wing political stance.

58    McCann, *War and an Irish Town,* 121.

59    Ibid., 124.

60    Ibid., 128–9, 143–4. McCann's vigorous anti-clericalism might suggest to the naive reader that Roman Catholicism is as pivotal as capitalism or imperialism in a rounded explanation of 'the troubles'.

61    Ibid., 123–4.

62    See table 3.4. See also Richard Rose, Ian McAllister and Peter Mair, 'Is there a Concurring Majority about Northern Ireland?', *Studies in Public Policy,* 22 (Glasgow: University of Strathclyde, 1978), 27–9; Roger Jowell and Colin Airey (eds), *British Social Attitudes: the 1984 Report* (Aldershot: Gower, 1984) 33; and Harvey Cox, 'Public Opinion and the Anglo-Irish Agreement', *Government and Opposition,* 22, 3 (1987), 348–51.

63    *An Phoblacht/Republican News,* 5 August 1984.

64    See Paul Canning, *British Policy Towards Ireland, 1921–41* (Oxford: Clarendon Press, 1985); Robert Fisk, *In Time of War: Ireland, Ulster and the Price of Neutrality, 1939–45* (London: Granada, 1983); and Deirdrie McMahon, *Republicans and Imperialists, Anglo-Irish Relations in the 1930s* (London: Yale University Press, 1984).

65    See Bell, *The British in Ireland,* 96.

66    Ibid, 96.

67    Ian McGough, *International Affairs,* May (London: David Davies Institute of International Studies, 1982), cited in Bell, *The British in Ireland,* 97–8.

68    There is a frequent and less compelling addition to the argument that Britain has a strategic interest in Ireland, which is popular with the ultra-left: the British ruling class is alleged to keep 'its Army' well-exercised in Northern Ireland in preparation for future repressive counter-insurgency operations against the left and other Celtic nationalists in Great Britain. The Army may be better equipped for policing repression elsewhere because of its deployment in Northern Ireland, but these consequences are not the deliberate ambitions of British policy-makers, and British generals do not enjoy the 'theatre' of Northern Ireland – precisely because they are required to conduct liberal democratic policing rather than prepare for conventional war.

69    See J. K. Mitchell, 'Social Violence in Northern Ireland', *Geographical Review,* April (1979), 193–5; Russell Murray, 'Political Violence in Northern Ireland 1969–1977', in F. W. Boal and J. N. H. Douglas (eds), *Integration and Division: Geographical Perspectives on the Northern Ireland Problem* (London: Academic Press, 1982), 315ff; Michael Poole, 'The Geographical Location of Political Violence in Northern Ireland', in John Darby, N. Hodge, and A. C. Hepburn (eds), *Political Violence: Ireland in a Comparative Perspective* (Belfast: Appletree Press, 1990), 64–82; and O'Leary and McGarry, *The Politics of Antagonism,* 9–11.

70    Murray, 'Political Violence in Northern Ireland, 1969–77', 320ff.

71    Martin Dillon, *The Dirty War* (London: Hutchinson, 1990); Paul Foot, *Who Framed Colin Wallace?* (London: Macmillan, 1989).

72    SDLP councillors refer ruefully to 'ACWD' as the objective of loyalist paramilitary killers – 'Any Catholic Will Do'. Unionist politicians interpret the killing of police personnel and civilians by republican paramilitaries as attacks on Protestants.

73    These strategies may help explain why the conflict has been controlled and

prevented from escalating into full-scale genocidal war, John Darby, *Intimidation and the Control of Conflict in Northern Ireland* (Dublin, Gill and Macmillan, 1986). The IRA's attack on the former headquarters of the UDA in the Shankill Road in October 1993, which resulted in ten civilian deaths and numerous serious injuries to other civilian by-standers, and the UVF's killing at Loughinisland of seven Catholic civilians and the injury of numerous others watching the Ireland football team in the World Cup tournament in June 1994 are recent examples of 'communal deterrence'.

74   Incidentally, this campaign, designed to precipitate a British withdrawal, implied that Northern Ireland was costly for Britain, and was conducted on the assumption that Britain might be persuaded to withdraw for capitalist reasons.

75   See, for example, Roger Faligot, *Britain's Military Strategy in Ireland: the Kitson Experiment* (London: Zed Press, 1983).

76   Dillon, *The Dirty War*.

77   See, for example, John McGuffin, *Internment* (Tralee: Anvil Books, 1973); John McGuffin, *The Guineapigs* (Harmondsworth: Penguin, 1974); Peter Taylor, *Beating the Terrorists?* (Harmondsworth: Penguin, 1980); John Stalker, *Stalker* (London: Harrap, 1988); Paul Foot, *Who Framed Colin Wallace?*, and Fred Holroyd, *War Without Honour* (Hull: Medium, 1989).

78   O'Leary and McGarry, *The Politics of Antagonism*, ch. 1.

79   Data from O'Leary and McGarry, *The Politics of Antagonism*, ch. 1.

80   See chapter 4, table 4.3.

81   In times of crisis (1912, 1972, 1974, 1985-) the Protestant working class has been mobilized in large numbers into loyalist paramilitary organizations. The pathological and murderous activities of the 'Shankill Butchers' can fairly be described as the actions of lumpenproletarians, see Martin Dillon, *The Shankill Butchers: A Case Study of Mass Murder* (London: Arrow, 1990). However, these spectacular examples should not disguise the extent to which loyalist paramilitaries – and the local security forces – are supported and staffed by 'respectable' members of the Protestant working class.

82   The most complete statement of Soviet literature on Northern Ireland is contained in I. D. Birjukov's *Ol'ster: Krisis Britanskei Imperialistcheskov Politiki: 1968-84* (Moscow: Progress Publishers, 1985) ('Ulster: The Crisis of British Imperialist Policy: 1968-84').

83   The notable exception has been Libya, the solitary state to support the IRA's war against British imperialism. However, its motivation has been to retaliate against the British state in the interests of the green of radical Islam rather than green Marxism.

84   One reason why Irish green Marxists have been muted in such efforts has been strategic. Given that the sentiments of some Irish Americans were a valuable resource in the IRA's long war it would have been discourteous and impolitic to inform their American cousins that their money was funding a Marxist-supported war.

85   For example, Farrell, *Northern Ireland*; and O'Dowd et al., *Northern Ireland*.

86   O'Leary and McGarry, *The Politics of Antagonism*, chs 3-4.

87   Smith and Chambers, *Inequality in Northern Ireland*; O'Leary and McGarry, *The Politics of Antagonism*, ch. 5.

88   A doctoral thesis has been devoted to demonstrating that even in recent times the Queen's University, Belfast, far from being a haven of liberalism in a sectarian sea, has mirrored rather than transcended the society in which it lives – see Rupert Taylor, 'The Queen's University of Belfast and "the Troubles":

The Limits of Liberalism', PhD thesis, University of Kent at Canterbury, and see 'The Limits of Liberalism: The Case of Queen's Academics and the "Troubles"', *Politics*, 7, 2 (1987), 28–34.

89   See, for example, Bambery, *Ireland's Permanent Revolution*; and David Reed, *Ireland: the Key to the British Revolution* (London: Larkin Books, 1984).

90   See the recent appraisal of a unionist of Marxist persuasion, Henry Patterson, *The Politics of Illusion: Socialism and Republicanism in Modern Ireland* (Hutchinson: London, 1989); and 'Gerry Adams and the Modernisation of Republicanism', *Conflict Quarterly*, 10, 3 (1990), 5–23.

### Chapter 3   Unionist Discourses: Irish Irredentism and British Absenteeism

1   Hugh Roberts, *Northern Ireland and the Algerian Analogy: A Suitable Case for Gaullism?* (Belfast: Athol Books, 1986), 29.

2   Arthur Aughey, *Under Siege: Ulster Unionism and the Anglo-Irish Agreement* (London: Hurst, 1989), 58.

3   *Toronto Star*, 31 October 1993, F2.

4   Peter Utley's book *Lessons of Ulster* (London: Dent, 1975) is an exemplary statement of British unionism. It was sold with this accolade from Enoch Powell, 'I would like to make it a punishable offence for anyone to speak or write about Ulster until they had obtained a certificate that they had read these Lessons and digested them.' Utley later developed a more sophisticated understanding, and former Secretary of State for Northern Ireland James Prior claims he persuaded him to educate Margaret Thatcher in favour of an Irish dimension in the run-up to the Anglo-Irish Agreement, interview with Brendan O'Leary (GEC London, November 1990).

5   The Reverends Ian Paisley and William McCrea recently claimed that their forefathers carved civilization out of the Irish wilderness: according to Paisley, 'it was all bog land' before their arrival, Emmanuel Kehoe, 'Who Fears to Speak on '98?', *Sunday Press*, 23 January 1994. The northern nationalist ethnic memory is rather different: 'They got the land and we got the views; you can't farm a view', ibid. In 1836 Paisley's historical forerunner, the Reverend Henry Cooke, declared that 'Our Scottish forefathers were planted in the wildest and most barren portions of our lands . . . Scottish industry has drained its bogs and cultivated its barren wastes, has filled its ports with shipping, substituted towns and cities for its hovels and clachans and given peace and good order to a land of confusion and blood.' The liberal unionist who cites this passage, Robert McCartney, remarks that this 'was the theology of the children of Ham; a frontier christianity of Praise the Lord and Pass the Ammunition', R. L. McCartney, *Liberty and Authority in Ireland*, Field Day Pamphlet No. 9 (Derry: Field Day, 1985), 23.

6   Devolution is considered the road to perdition by hard-line unionists: Enoch Powell, former Conservative minister and former UUP MP, used to maintain that Britain's support for devolution was part of NATO's grand strategy to bring Ireland into the American defence system.

7   See the discussion in John McGarry and Charles Graham, 'Co-determination', in John McGarry and Brendan O'Leary (eds), *The Future of Northern Ireland* (Oxford: Oxford University Press, 1990), 162–81.

8   This idea echoes that of the 'Home Rule All Round' movement which developed in the early twentieth century as a response to Irish nationalism and 'colonial nationalism' in the British dominions.

9   This request was conceded by the Conservative government on 16 December 1993, the day after the Downing Street Declaration.
10  There is a sardonic English saying that 'The Irish often complain that they are misunderstood; this is so, and much to their advantage': Ulster unionists maintain they derive no such benefit.
11  Aughey, *Under Siege*, 1–2.
12  See, for example, Aughey, *Under Siege*; Brian Barton and Patrick Roche (eds), *Northern Ireland: Myth and Reality* (Aldershot: Avebury, 1991); Cadogan Group, *Northern Limits: Boundaries of the Attainable in Northern Ireland Politics* (Belfast: Cadogan Group, 1992); Roberts, *Northern Ireland and the Algerian Analogy*; and Tom Wilson, *Ulster: Conflict and Consensus* (Oxford: Basil Blackwell, 1989).
13  It is a stereotype that external observers make a better case for unionism than local unionists. John Whyte once suggested that the ablest statement of traditional unionism before the 1980s came from a Dutch geographer, M. W. Heslinga, 'Interpretations of the Northern Ireland Problem: An Appraisal', *Economic and Social Review*, 9, 4 (1978), 269. See M. W. Heslinga, *The Irish Border as a Cultural Divide* (Assen, Netherlands: Van Gorcum, 1979), and for a discussion of Heslinga's views see chapter 6.
14  See Ronald McNeill, *Ulster's Stand for Union* (London: J. H. Murray, 1922); St John Ervine, *Craigavon: Ulsterman* (London: Allen and Unwin, 1949); W. A. Carson, *Ulster and the Irish Republic* (Belfast: W. Cleland, 1957); W. Brian Maginnis, 'Why the Border Must Be', in Lord Brookeborough, W. B. Maginnis, and G. B. Hanna, *Why the Border Must Be: the Northern Ireland Case in Brief* (Belfast: Government of Northern Ireland Publications, 1956); Terence O'Neill, *Autobiography* (London: Rupert Hart Davies, 1972); A. T. Q. Stewart, *The Narrow Ground: Aspects of Ulster 1609–1969* (Belfast: Pretani Press, 1977/86); and Brian Faulkner, *Memoirs of a Statesman*, ed. J. Houston (London: Weidenfeld and Nicolson, 1978).
15  Other external agents held responsible for the crisis in the more paranoid unionist arguments have included the Papacy, Moscow, and, more sensibly, the British Foreign Office – see, for example, James Molyneaux's remarks cited in Padraig O'Malley, *Ireland: the Uncivil Wars* (Belfast: Blackstaff Press, 1983), 162–3. Since we are committed to presenting and criticizing the strongest arguments of each party to the conflict we do not examine these overly conspiratorial assumptions here – although we do treat seriously Protestant fears of Roman Catholicism.
16  The literary scholar Professor Edna Longley observes that Northern Irish students, Catholic and Protestant, see being 'British' as 'primarily a matter of allegiance: a constitutional and administrative rather than cultural designation', cited in Maurna Crozier (ed.), *Varieties of Britishness* (Belfast: Institute for Irish Studies, 1990), 23. However, she errs in maintaining that Britain lacks nationalist content, *From Cathleen to Anorexia: the Breakdown of Irelands* (Dublin: Attic Press, 1990), 6–7.
17  Articles 2 and 3 are fully cited above, see chapter 1, pp. 23–4.
18  All persons born in Northern Ireland are automatically entitled to Irish citizenship, and to travel on Irish passports.
19  *McGimpsey and McGimpsey* v. *Ireland*, High Court, 29 July 1988.
20  *McGimpsey and McGimpsey* v. *Ireland*, Supreme Court, 1 March 1990.
21  See also Ken Maginnis, 'Implications and Repercussions of Recent Irish Court Cases', *Ulster Unionist Information*, Summer 1990.
22  *Irish Times*, 29–30 October 1990.
23  Ibid.

24 Peter Robinson, MP, deputy leader of the DUP, interview with B. O'Leary (House of Commons, Westminster, for *Analysis*, November 1992).

25 They reject the argument that by legitimizing the national territorial claim in Ireland's Constitution, and thereby repudiating the Treaty, de Valera considerably assisted the ending of paramilitary republicanism in independent Ireland, bringing Sean MacBride and other IRA refuseniks in from the cold in the 1930s.

26 *Irish Times*, 29–30 October 1990. This passage is lifted, unacknowledged, from the Dutch geographer M. W. Heslinga, *The Irish Border as a Cultural Divide* (Assen: Van Gorcum, 1979), 202–3.

27 See, for example, Heslinga, *The Irish Border as a Cultural Divide*; D. G. Pringle, *One Island, Two Nations? A Political Geographical Analysis of the National Conflict in Ireland* (Letchworth: Research Studies Press, 1985); John Bowman, *De Valera and the Ulster Question* (Oxford: Oxford University Press, 1982), ch. 1; and Wilson, *Ulster*, ch. 1.

28 This is a typical ideological anachronism: 'Northern Ireland' did not exist until 1920.

29 *Irish Times*, 29–30 October 1990. An academic unionist puts the same case: 'there is no physical law of nature which prescribes that one island shall correspond to one nation, and no law of nature which prevents two islands from being a single nation . . . The partition of the British Isles caused by the establishment of the Irish Free State in 1921 was just as 'artificial' as the partition of Ireland', Wilson, *Ulster*, 7.

30 Brian Faulkner, *Memoirs of a Statesman* (London: Weidenfeld and Nicolson, 1978), 157.

31 Queen's University Belfast Ulster Unionist Association, pamphlet (Belfast: Ulster Unionist Association, 1989).

32 Ibid.

33 They generally attempt to refute the historicism of Irish nationalist myth-makers: pointing out, correctly, that in recorded history there was no united all-Ireland central Irish administration until that established by the English in the seventeenth century, see, for example, J. C. Beckett, *The Making of Modern Ireland, 1603–1923* (London: Faber, 1966), 13; and observing that far from being a pure and ancient race the Irish are, *inter alia*, a mongrel mixture of pre-Celtic, Celtic, Scandinavian, Anglo-Saxon and Norman peoples.

34 The Preamble to the Irish Constitution begins: 'In the Name of the Most Holy Trinity, from Whom is all authority and to Whom, as our final end, all actions both of men and States must be referred, We, the people of Éire, Humbly acknowledging all our obligations to our Divine Lord, Jesus Christ, Who sustained our fathers through centuries of trial . . . ', *Bunreacht na hÉireann* (Dublin, Stationery Office). However, the preamble is not a justiciable part of the constitution, and Article 6 is more pertinent and not theocratic 'All powers of government, legislative, executive and judicial, derive, under God, *from the people*, whose right it is to designate the rulers of the State and, in final appeal, to decide all questions of national policy, according to the requirements of the common good' (our italics).

35 James Molyneaux thinks that Northern Ireland should have the constitutional right to independence if the Westminster parliament decides to alter the terms of the Union, interview with B. O'Leary (House of Commons, Westminster, for *Analysis*, November 1992).

The UDA's doomsday scenario envisages an independent 'Ulster' being carved out of Northern Ireland if the British government withdraws, accompanied by ethnic cleansing and 'nullification' of Catholics, *Irish Independent*, 17 January 1994.

36  Thus one analysis of speeches made by Ulster's Unionist MPs during the Home Rule crisis of the 1880s suggests they regarded themselves as members of the British race and nation; and moreover, that this British identity outweighed in importance both their imperial identity and their purely instrumental attachments to the United Kingdom. J. Loughlin, *Gladstone, Home Rule and the Ulster Question 1882–1893* (Dublin: Gill and Macmillan, 1986).

37  Heslinga, *The Irish Border as a Cultural Divide.*

38  T. J. Pickvance, *Peace with Equity* (Birmingham: the author, 1975).

39  There is one Ulsterman, Dr Ian Adamson, attempting to forge an Ulster history and identity which incorporates both Ulster Catholics and Ulster Protestants in a new nation, see *The Identity of Ulster: The Land, the Language and the People* (Belfast: Pretani Press, 1982/7); and *The Ulster People: Ancient, Medieval and Modern* (Belfast: Pretani Press, 1991). He is self-consciously engaged in nation-building, working for the future existence of the Ulster nation rather than pretending it presently exists, and others argue that he is literally engaged in historical forgery.

40  Thomas Hennessy, 'Ulster Unionist Territorial and National Identities 1886–1893: Province, Island, Kingdom and Empire', *Irish Political Studies*, 8 (1993), 21–36.

41  The Irish political scientist John Coakley provides a lucid study of the treatment of Northern Ireland in the schools of independent Ireland, which shows that the teaching of history no longer follows a conventional nationalist canon, 'The Northern Conflict in Southern Irish School Textbooks', in Adrian Guelke (ed.), *New Perspectives on the Northern Ireland Conflict* (Aldershot: Avebury, 1994), 119–41.

42  At least one conservative political sociologist has advanced what he regards as persuasive evidence in favour of some of these arguments, see Christopher Hewitt, 'Catholic Grievances, Catholic Nationalism and Violence in Northern Ireland during the Civil Rights Period: a Reconsideration', *British Journal of Sociology*, 32, 3 (1981), 362–80. See also the ensuing debate: Denis O'Hearn, 'Catholic Grievances, Catholic Nationalism: A Comment', *British Journal of Sociology*, 34, 3 (1983), 438–46; 'Again on Discrimination in the North of Ireland: A Reply to the Rejoinder', *British Journal of Sociology*, 34, 3 (1983), 94–102; and 'Catholic Grievances: A Comment', *British Journal of Sociology*, 38, 1 (1987), 94–101; K. A. Kovacheck, 'Catholic Grievances in Northern Ireland – Appraisal and Judgement', *British Journal of Sociology*, 38, 1 (1987), 77–87; and Christopher Hewitt, 'Discrimination in Northern Ireland: a Comment', *British Journal of Sociology*, 34, 3 (1983), 446–52; 'Catholic Grievances and Violence in Northern Ireland', *British Journal of Sociology*, 36, 1 (1985), 102–6; and 'Explaining Violence in Northern Ireland', *British Journal of Sociology*, 38, 1 (1987), 88–94.

43  See, for example, Utley, *Lessons of Ulster*, 39, and the discussion in Bob Purdie, 'Was the Civil Rights Movement a Communist/Republican Conspiracy?', *Irish Political Studies*, 3 (1988), 33–42.

44  Even liberal unionists have argued for selective detention, i.e. judicial as opposed to executive internment, longer jail terms for convicted terrorists, the removal of the common-law right to silence for suspected terrorists, see Wilson, *Ulster*, 265–6. Several of these measures were introduced by the British government after 1988, see O'Leary and McGarry, *The Politics of Antagonism*,

270–3. Wilson's argument that the defeat of terrorism is the most urgent task – primarily a policing and military commitment – is typical of unionists. The security forces' lack of success is blamed on their inability to cross the border into the 'inadequately policed' Irish Republic; on the consequences of permitting 'no-go' areas to develop in Belfast and Derry/Londonderry in the early 1970s; and on constraints imposed by civil-liberties. The use of single-judge and no-jury courts since 1973 is considered entirely reasonable, and the Republic's request for three-judge courts is rejected as both unnecessary and impractical, Wilson, *passim*.

45  Utley, *Lessons of Ulster*, 147.
46  See John Oliver, 'Constitutional Uncertainty and the Ulster Tragedy', *Political Quarterly*, 59, 4 (1988), 427–36; and Wilson, *Ulster*, 271–3.
47  Utley, *Lessons of Ulster*, 146, 147.
48  Oliver MacDonagh has observed that 'What northern Unionists mean by "place" and "people" is Protestant Ulster. But in terms of the land area of even their state (sic!) this cannot account for much more than two-thirds of the whole. Yet – apart from anodyne "Northern Ireland" employable for official purposes – what alternative do they have to "Ulster"? One cannot very well write Protestant Supremacy upon a map', Oliver MacDonagh, *States of Mind: Two Centuries of Anglo-Irish Conflict* (London: Pimlico, 1992), 26–7.
49  See, for example, McNeill, *Ulster's Stand for Union*.
50  Jim Allister, the former Press officer of the DUP, once declared that 'If Britain decided tomorrow to expel us, she should remember what happened in 1912 when Britain sought to expel the whole of Ireland. *The people of Northern Ireland* not only said, "We don't wish to go" they said, "We won't go". And it paid off. So there's a message there: that the people of Northern Ireland have it within their power to say "We won't go"', O'Malley, *Ireland*, 187–8 (our italics). Note also Allister's misuse of history: the British were not seeking to expel any part of Ireland in 1912, but rather to create an autonomous (not an independent) parliament for Ireland. Tom Wilson also displays a majoritarian mentality, anachronistically talking of 'a Northern majority' before Northern Ireland came into existence in 1920, *Ulster*, 36.
51  See, for example, Gregory Campbell, *Discrimination: the Truth* (Belfast: Democratic Unionist Party, 1987).
52  Edward Moxon-Browne, *Nation, Class and Creed in Northern Ireland* (Aldershot: Gower, 1983), 119.
53  Stewart, *The Narrow Ground*.
54  Tom Wilson (ed.), *Ulster under Home Rule* (Oxford: Oxford University Press, 1955), 208–9 (his emphases).
55  Wilson, *Ulster*, 129.
56  O'Leary and McGarry, *The Politics of Antagonism*, ch. 3.
57  Wilson's liberalism is apparent in his firm support for integrated education. However, his is a Protestant rather than a Catholic liberalism. He holds Catholics mainly responsible for refusing integrated education, and is romantic about the nature of state (i.e. overwhelmingly Protestant) schools, as one of the authors of this book can testify from experience.
58  For a recent discussion of unionist denial of discrimination see John Doyle, 'Workers and Outlaws: Unionism and Fair Employment in Northern Ireland', *Irish Political Studies*, 9 (1994), 47–8.
59  See, for example, Cadogan Group, *Northern Limits*, and several contributions to Barton and Roche (eds), *Northern Ireland*. One neat explanation of the otherwise inexplicable simultaneous willingness of unionists to deny that discrimination

against Catholics exists *and* to justify such discrimination is provided by John Doyle: since republicans place themselves beyond the legitimate state it is not discrimination to treat them as 'outlaws', see Doyle, 'Workers and Outlaws: Unionism and Fair Employment in Northern Ireland'.

60   Our intuitive response to such arguments is similar to one professor's reaction to a lunch-time chat with the American economist Thomas Sowell: 'there is, surely, something clinically crazy about maintaining in the face of evidence that the market left to itself will eradicate racial discrimination', Brian Barry, *Does Society Exist? The Case for Socialism* (London: Fabian Tract 536, 1989), 22–3. There are remarkable parallels between the arguments employed by neo-conservatives in America to explain inequalities between blacks and whites and arguments employed by unionists to explain inequalities between Catholics and Protestants in Northern Ireland. There are equally remarkable parallels in the rebuttals of such arguments: compare Thomas Boston's work, *Race, Class and Conservatism* (London: Unwin Hyman, 1988) with the writings of David Smith and Gerald Chambers, *Inequality in Northern Ireland* (Oxford: Clarendon Press, 1991).

61   Wilson, *Ulster*, 119.

62   See especially SACHR, *Religious and Political Discrimination and Equality of Opportunity in Northern Ireland: Report on Fair Employment* (London: HMSO, Cmnd. 237, 1987); and Smith and Chambers, *Inequality in Northern Ireland*.

63   Wilson, *Ulster*, 107–23. The methodological quibbles made by Wilson and others have been ably replied to by Smith and Chambers, *Inequality in Northern Ireland*, and are discussed in chapter 7.

64   Wilson, *Ulster*, 119 (italics in original).

65   See, for example, the submission of the Cadogan Group, *Northern Limits*, to the Opsahl Commission. The Group quote the statement in the New Ireland Forum Report of 1984 that for fifty years nationalists had 'suffered systematic discrimination. They were deprived of the means of social and economic development', before commenting that 'There is *no factual evidence* for such an arbitrary and exaggerated generalisation, and it is hardly consistent with the population statistics of both parts of the island' (p. 7, our emphasis). To say that there is 'no factual evidence' for the Forum view is a more arbitrary and exaggerated statement than the one they are criticizing. For evidence on systematic discrimination in Northern Ireland see Smith and Chambers, *Inequality in Northern Ireland*, and O'Leary and McGarry, *The Politics of Antagonism*, ch. 3. The Cadogan Group declares that the absolute rise of the Catholic population in Northern Ireland between 1926 and 1981 (18 per cent) argues 'very strongly against *any idea* of the Catholics as a sorely oppressed minority in Northern Ireland' (ibid., our emphasis), especially when compared with the 3 per cent drop in the Catholic population and the 37 per cent drop in the Protestant population in the South in the same period. '*Any idea*'? We wonder whether the Cadogan group would suggest that the Albanians of Kosovo can not have been a sorely oppressed group in Yugoslavia because their population has been growing exponentially. The Cadogan goup's selective statistics ignore *inter alia* the fact that intermarriage and voluntary assimilation were more extensive in the Republic, and the fact that the higher Catholic birth-rate in Northern Ireland was offset by the higher Catholic emigration rate from Northern Ireland (encouraged by discrimination), which meant that between 1926 and 1951 the Catholic share of the population of Northern Ireland remained more or less constant. It was not until post-war British welfare state reforms, originally opposed by the UUP at Stormont, improved the lot

of Catholics that their absolute numbers and relative share of the population began to rise significantly. This improvement in their absolute position did not lead to any significant relative improvement in their position compared with Protestants, see Edmund Aunger, 'Religion and Occupational Class in Northern Ireland', *Economic and Social Review*, 7, 1 ( 1975), 1–17.

66   Wilson complains that 'When Catholics are bigoted, they usually manage to be so in a better tone of voice', *Ulster*, 211. If so, Wilson might benefit from more elocution lessons from Catholics. The scale of discrimination has been exaggerated in republican discourse, but that should not lead one to deny its significance. One appraisal of the scale and extent of discrimination before 1972 can be found in John Whyte's cautious study: 'How much discrimination was there under the unionist regime, 1921–68?', in T. Gallagher and J. O'Connell (eds), *Contemporary Irish Studies* (Manchester: Manchester University Press, 1983), 1–35. Whyte's review, though astringent with exaggerated republican propaganda, and unionist apologias, must be criticized for its inadequate treatment of inequalities in economic opportunity (structural discrimination), and his lack of attention to the intimidatory nature of Northern Ireland's political system, which disorganized the nationalist opposition.

67   Robert Miller, *Attitudes to Work in Northern Ireland* (Belfast: Fair Employment Agency, 1978), Research Paper No. 2, 15. The same survey, incidentally, refuted myths of a Protestant work ethic and a Catholic ethic of idleness, concluding that, with the major exception of perceptions of discrimination, 'one cannot conclude that major differences exist between Protestants and Catholics in their attitudes to work', ibid., 15–16.

68   David Smith, *Equality and Inequality in Northern Ireland. Part III: Perceptions and Views* (London: Policy Studies Institute, 1987), table 75.

69   O'Leary and McGarry, 1993, *The Politics of Antagonism*, ch. 7.

70   It is improper because the question-wording was different, in 1990 people could identify themselves as Northern Irish.

71   Jennifer Todd, 'Two Traditions in Unionist Political Culture', *Irish Political Studies*, 2 (1987), 11–20.

72   Ibid., 4.

73   David Miller, *Queen's Rebels: Ulster Loyalism in Historical Perspective* (Dublin: Gill and Macmillan, 1978).

74   Interview with Brendan O'Leary, House of Commons, 18 December 1990. When asked to confirm that he meant that 'British-Ireland, so to speak, is Belfast and the Lagan Valley, the rest of the island is Ireland?' Rees replied 'Yes'.

75   While the Labour government held referenda in Scotland and Wales in 1979 on a modest measure of devolved self-government, after an amendment in the legislature the referenda required support from (a) a majority, and (b) at least 40 per cent of the electorate; and (c) the outcomes were not binding on the government. Scotland and Wales, by contrast with Northern Ireland, have never been given the right to secede from the United Kingdom. For details of the referenda see John McGarry, 'The British Homogeneity Thesis and Nationalism in Scotland and Wales', London, Canada: PhD thesis, University of Western Ontario (1986).

76   Richard Rose, 'Is the United Kingdom a State?: Northern Ireland as a Test Case', in P. Madgwick and R. Rose (eds), *The Territorial Dimension in United Kingdom Politics* (London: Macmillan, 1982), esp. 106 and 128ff. The exclusion provisions in the Prevention of Terrorism Act, which allow citizens of the UK resident in Northern Ireland to be prevented from entering Great Britain (and

vice versa), indicate how the 'real British' do not regard Northern Ireland as an integral part of the UK, see, *inter alia*, Gerard Hogan and Clive Walker, *Political Violence and the Law in Ireland* (Manchester: Manchester University Press, 1990). The relevant 'Siberian exile' clauses confirm that Northern Ireland is regarded as a place apart, both legally and politically.

77  John Wilson Foster, 'Processed Peace?', *Fortnight*, 326 (1994), 35.
78  *Daily Telegraph*, 17 January 1994.
79  For similar polls reported in British newspapers see Bell, *The British in Ireland: A Suitable Case for Withdrawal* (London: Pluto Press, 1984), 90ff; Adrian Guelke, *Northern Ireland: the International Perspective* (Dublin: Gill and Macmillan, 1988), 100–1; Brendan O'Leary, 'Public Opinion and Northern Irish Futures', *Political Quarterly*, 63, 2 (1992), 143–70; and Frank Wright, *Northern Ireland: A Comparative Analysis* (Dublin: Gill and Macmillan, 1987), 307, n. 49.
80  Bell, *The British in Ireland*, 90.
81  New Ireland Forum, *Report* (Dublin: Stationery Office, 1984), 23.
82  Jennifer Todd, 'The Limits of Britishness', *The Irish Review*, 5 (1988), 11.
83  Ibid., 11–15.
84  Todd also mentions 'participation in wars', ibid., 12. Belfast was bombed by the Luftwaffe during World War II, and the Republic was neutral, differentiating the two parts of Ireland in their experience of world wars. However, participation in British wars scarcely distinguishes Northern Ireland's population from the rest of Ireland. More Irishmen from the twenty-six counties fought and died in British uniforms in world wars than men from the six counties – though the proportion from the latter was higher. The key differentiating feature was the ideological enthusiasm with which Ulster Protestants fought in British uniforms.
85  See Brendan O'Leary, Tom Lyne, Jim Marshall, and Bob Rowthorn, *Northern Ireland: Sharing Authority* (London: Institute of Public Policy Research, 1993), ch. 5.
86  Todd, 'The Limits of Britishness', 14. Todd cites Peregrine Worsthorne as exemplifying this last trait. After the SAS's executions of unarmed IRA personnel in Gibraltar he declared: 'IRA terrorists who have taken up arms against the British state and killed innocent people deserve to be shot down like dogs' (*Sunday Telegraph*, 8 May 1988). She also emphasizes that supremacist traits are not confined to Ulster unionists: they are widely dispersed in British political culture. Indeed, the extent to which the construction of British national identity was historically dependent upon popular pan-Protestant fear and loathing of Catholicism has been ably re-emphasized in work of Linda Colley, *Britons: Forging the Nation 1707–1837* (London and New Haven: Yale University Press, 1992). Irish cultural Catholics do not need reminding of this fact, unlike the secular British who have 'forgotten' the anti-Catholic roots of their national culture.
87  Todd, 'The Limits of Britishness', 16.
88  Considerable numbers of unionists go one step further than majoritarianism. They do not believe that any part of Northern Ireland, let alone Northern Ireland itself, should have the right to secede from the United Kingdom. This is an expression of integral British nationalism.
89  A similar logic applies to nationalists: if they reject the right of a majority in Northern Ireland to impose its will on the minority they must logically accept that the nationalist majority in Ireland as a whole has no right to impose its will on the unionist minority in Ireland as a whole.
90  The thesis advanced by Arthur Aughey that unionists are not British nationalists

is not persuasive. It is what many unionists say they are, and that is what they mean when they say 'Ulster is British', Aughey, *Under Siege*. It is possible to be a (political) British nationalist while insisting on an Irish cultural identity.

91 Etain Tannam, 'Trespassing on Borders? The European Community and the Relationships between Northern Ireland and the Republic of Ireland: A Test of Neo-Functionalism', London, England: PhD thesis, London School of Economics and Political Science (1994).

92 See chapter 1, pp. 35–44.

93 See chapter 1, p. 24.

94 Guelke, *Northern Ireland*.

95 See, for example, A. T. Q. Stewart, *The Ulster Crisis* (London, Faber, 1967).

96 Wilson, *Ulster*, 40.

97 See Brendan O'Duffy, 'Violent Politics: A Theoretical and Empirical Examination of Two Centuries of Political Violence in Ireland', London, England: PhD thesis, London School of Economics and Political Science (1995).

98 O'Leary and McGarry, *The Politics of Antagonism*, 268–9. The comparison was with civilians aged 16–65, i.e. those who were eligible to serve in the UDR.

99 Ibid., 267.

100 Sarah Nelson, *Ulster's Uncertain Defenders: Loyalists and the Northern Ireland Conflict* (Belfast: Appletree Press, 1984), esp. 117–27.

101 O'Leary and McGarry, *The Politics of Antagonism*, ch. 5.

102 In 1987 the UDA, concerned that complete unionist intransigence was bad politics, advocated a change of strategy – and agreed to share power but without an Irish dimension, see New Ulster Political Research Group, *Common Sense* (Belfast: NUPRG, 1987). Subsequently leading unionists from the UUP and the DUP (Harold McCusker, Frank Millar, and Peter Robinson) advocated that unionists should recommend 'proportionality' for a Northern Ireland assembly.

103 See, for example, Aughey, *Under Siege*; Roberts, *Northern Ireland and the Algerian Analogy*; and 'Sound Stupidity: The British Party System and the Northern Ireland Question', in John McGarry and Brendan O'Leary (eds), *The Future of Northern Ireland* (Oxford: Clarendon Press), 100–36; also in *Government and Opposition*, 22, 3 (1987), 315–35. Some revisionist unionists go further, and believe that British policy is doing what the IRA wants: in this perspective British policy, at least since the Anglo-Irish Agreement and the signing of the Downing Street Declaration, 'is to phase its withdrawal in such a way as to avoid destabilizing Ireland, and possibly parts of the mainland . . . [and] to use the national media, the educational curriculum, the economic seduction of the business and farming community, the intellectual manipulation of the liberal great and good, and the distribution of government opposition to turn Unionist opposition into acquiescence and to convert acquiescence into consent', Robert McCartney, 'Has IRA Hijacked Peace?', *Belfast Telegraph*, 3 February 1994.

104 Aughey, *Under Siege*, 27.

105 Roberts, *Northern Ireland and the Algerian Analogy*.

106 Aughey, *Under Siege*.

107 This is especially problematic. The British political tradition is widely regarded as pluralistic but it is also regarded as highly unusual because it has had no real concept of 'the state' – see, for example, K. Dyson, *The State Tradition in Western Europe* (Oxford: Martin Robertson, 1980). Aughey's argument is therefore especially unusual.

108 Ibid., 10.

109 Ibid., 25.

110  Ibid., 132–67; and see Davidson, *Electoral Integration* (Belfast: Athol Books, n.d.); and Roberts, 'Sound Stupidity'.
111  Aughey, *Under Siege*, 40. Aughey's 'civic integrationism' and 'anti-consociationalism' are not dissimilar to Schlesinger's impassioned criticism of multiculturalism in the USA, see Arthur Schlesinger Jr, *The Disuniting of America* (New York: W. W. Norton, 1992).
112  Ibid., 75, 55. Aughey claims that 'non-protestant unionists' were equally outraged by the Agreement, 65, but in fact the biggest political bloc of non-protestant unionists, i.e. the Alliance Party's Catholic members and voters, did not oppose the Agreement.
113  See Ian Lustick, *State-Building Failure in British Ireland and French Algeria* (Berkeley: Institute for International Studies, 1985); O'Leary and McGarry, *The Politics of Antagonism*, ch. 2.
114  Henry Patterson, 'Review of Alvin Jackson's "The Ulster Party: Irish Unionists in the House of Commons, 1884–1911"', *Irish Political Studies*, 5 (1990), 114; and see Alvin Jackson, *The Ulster Party: Irish Unionists in the House of Commons, 1884–1911* (Oxford: Clarendon Press, 1989).
115  Cited in Vernon Bogdanor, *Devolution* (Oxford: Oxford University Press, 1979), 46.
116  See, for example, Garret FitzGerald, *Towards a New Ireland* (London: Charles Knight, 1972) and the discussion in Jeffrey Prager, *Building Democracy in Ireland: Political Order and Cultural Integration in a Newly Independent Nation* (Cambridge: Cambridge University Press, 1986), 38–42.
117  The denizens of the 'white dominions' used to have automatic British citizenship because they were considered 'kith and kin', not because of an imperial commitment to an ideal of civic citizenship.
118  In a preliminary measure of political freedom carried out for the Centre for the Study of Global Governance, the Republic of Ireland scored 93.8 out of 100, whereas the United Kingdom scored 88.9 out of 100. The Republic was ranked 12th in the world whereas the UK was ranked 20th. The index measured political participation, the rule of law, freedom of expression and non-discrimination. Megnad Desai, *Measuring Political Freedom* (London: Centre for the Study of Global Governance, 1994), table 4.
119  Constitution of Ireland, Article 44, paragraph 2.1.2.
120  The relevant sub-articles of Article 44 declared that: 'The State recognises the special position of the Holy Catholic Apostolic and Roman Church as the guardian of the Faith professed by the great majority of the citizens. The State also recognises the Church of Ireland, the Presbyterian Church in Ireland, the Methodist Church in Ireland, the Religious Society of Friends in Ireland, as well as the Jewish Congregations and the other religious denominations existing in Ireland at the date of the coming into operation of this Constitution.'
121  S. McDonagh (ed.), *The Attorney General v. X and Others: Judgements of the High Court and Supreme Court, Legal Submissions made to the Court* (Dublin: Incorporated Council of Law Reporting for Ireland, 1992).
122  A programme for moral liberalism was part of the agreed programme of government of the Fianna Fáil–Labour coalition government established after the November 1992 election, see O'Leary, 'Affairs, Partner-Swapping, and Spring Tides: The Irish General Election, 1992', *West European Politics*, 16, 1 (1993), 401–16. Any new Irish coalition government is likely to pursue the same agenda.
123  Kurt Bowen, *Protestants in a Catholic State: Ireland's Privileged Minority* (Kingston: McGill–Queens, 1983).

124 Aughey's contention that nationalism is an archaic, non-modern notion is not only premature but led him into an embarrassing error: publishing in 1989 he wrote confidently of the German experience as an illustration of modern 'loyalty to the idea of the nation, while acknowledging the reality of two separate states', *Under Siege*, 45.

125 Aughey, *Under Siege*, 305. Aughey's more recent judgements on the Republic are far more nuanced, see 'What is Living and What is Dead in the Ideal of 1916?', in M. Ní Dhonnchadha, and T. Dorgan, T. (eds), *Revising the Rising* (Derry: Field Day, 1991), 71–90.

126 Cyril M. White, 'Social change in contemporary Irish society: the remaking and reshaping of modern Ireland' (Dublin: University College, mimeo, 1994) – we are grateful to Dr White for a copy of his paper.

127 See Brendan O'Leary, 'Towards Europeanization and Realignment? The Irish General Election, February 1987', *West European Politics*, 10, 3 (1987), 455–65; Brendan O'Leary and John Peterson, 'Further Europeanization: The Irish General Election, July 1989', *West European Politics*, 13, 1 (1990), 124–36; and O'Leary, 'Affairs, Partner-Swapping, and Spring Tides'.

128 *Daily Telegraph*, 14 July 1986.

129 *Belfast Telegraph*, 6 October 1988.

130 Recent work by Geoff Evans and Mary Duffy of Nuffield College, reviewing three years of surveys of British Social Attitudes, confirms our arguments – we thank the authors for letting us see drafts of their work in progress.

131 For further discussion see chapter 4, pp. 153–9.

132 One of us shared this naïveté when it appeared that advocates of British party integration were neither national nor religious partisans and before he had engaged in comparative analysis of the success of electoral integrationist parties – O'Leary, 'The Accord: Meanings, Explanations, Results, Prospects and a Defence', in Paul Teague (ed.), *Beyond the Rhetoric: Politics, Economics and Social Policy in Northern Ireland* (London: Lawrence and Wishart, 1987), 11–40.

133 Arend Lijphart, *The Politics of Accommodation* (Berkeley: University of California Press, 1968); and *Democracy in Plural Societies: A Comparative Perspective* (New Haven: Yale University Press, 1977).

134 See chapter 8, pp. 338–44.

135 See, *inter alia*, Sir Arthur Lewis, *Politics in West Africa* (Toronto: Oxford University Press, 1965); Lijphart, *Democracy in Plural Societies*; and O'Leary, Lyne, Marshall and Rowthorn, *Northern Ireland: Sharing Authority*, ch. 3.

**Chapter 4 Oranges and Reds: Revisionist Marxism**

1 Paul Bew, Peter Gibbon, and Henry Patterson, *The State in Northern Ireland 1921–1972: Political Forces and Social Classes* (Manchester: Manchester University Press, 1979), 221.

2 Ernest Gellner, *Nations and Nationalism* (Oxford: Basil Blackwell, 1983), 130.

3 The publisher of the BICO's pamphlets, Athol Books, produced much of the 1980s pamphlet literature advocating electoral integration – see, for example, Brendan Clifford, *Parliamentary Sovereignty and Northern Ireland: A Review of the Party System in the British Constitution, with Relation to the Anglo-Irish Agreement* (Belfast: Athol Books, 1985); *Parliamentary Despotism: John Hume's Aspiration* (Belfast: Athol Books, 1986); *Government without Opposition* (Belfast: Athol Books, 1986); *The Road to Nowhere: A Review of Unionist Politics from O'Neill to Molyneaux and Powell* (Belfast: Athol Books, 1987); Jim Davidson, *Integration: A*

*Word without Meaning* (Belfast: Athol Books, 1986); *Electoral Integration* (Belfast: Athol Books, n.d.); Hugh Roberts, *Northern Ireland and the Algerian Analogy: A Suitable Case for Gaullism?* (Belfast: Athol Books, 1986); and J. Keenan, *An Argument on behalf of the Catholics of Northern Ireland* (Belfast: Athol Books, 1988).

4  Red Marxism is especially associated with the writings of Paul Bew, Peter Gibbon, and Henry Patterson – *The State in Northern Ireland 1921–1972*; and 'Some Aspects of Nationalism and Socialism in Ireland: 1968–1978', in Austen Morgan and Bob Purdie (eds), *Ireland: Divided Nation, Divided Class* (London: Ink Links, 1980), 152–71; Bew and Patterson, *The British State and the Ulster Crisis: from Wilson to Thatcher* (London: Verso, 1985); Patterson, *Class Conflict and Sectarianism: the Protestant Working Class and the Belfast Labour Movement 1868–1920* (Belfast: Blackstaff Press, 1980); and *The Politics of Illusion: Socialism and Republicanism in Modern Ireland* (Hutchinson: London, 1989).

5  'Revisionist Marxism' is sometimes contrasted with Connollyite Marxism, once orthodox Marxism in Ireland. Irish revisionists are not uniformly revisionist Marxists in the international sense, i.e. disciples of Bernstein and Kautsky's revisions of Marx and Engels. Irish Marxist revisionists include both Stalinists and social democrats.

6  See, for example, B. Barton, *The Government of Northern Ireland* (Belfast: Athol Books, 1980); and A. Carr, *The Belfast Labour Movement 1885–1893* (Belfast: Athol Books, 1974).

7  For example, Conor Lynch, *Equal Citizenship and the End of Sectarian Politics* (Belfast: Athol Books, 1987).

8  Some of the BICO's authors came from Catholic backgrounds. They can be decoded as secular enragés, so hostile to their former Catholicism that they endorse all things anti-Catholic, and all things which prove their uncompromising modernity.

9  See Lynch, *Equal Citizenship and the End of Sectarian Politics*; and Roberts, *Northern Ireland and the Algerian Analogy*.

10  We regard the following authors as red Marxists: Austen Morgan, Bob Purdie, Henry Patterson, Peter Gibbon, Paul Bew, Belinda Probert, Anders Boserup, and Tom Nairn – see Anders Boserup, 'Contradictions and Struggles in Northern Ireland', in *Socialist Register* (1972), 157–92; Bew, Gibbon, and Patterson, *The State in Northern Ireland*; and 'Some Aspects of Nationalism and Socialism in Ireland: 1968–1978'; Bew and Patterson, *The British State and the Ulster Crisis*; 'Unionism and the Anglo-Irish Agreement', in Paul Teague (ed.), *Beyond the Rhetoric: Politics, the Economy and Social Policy in Northern Ireland* (London: Lawrence and Wishart, 1987), 41–57; and 'Scenarios for Progress in Northern Ireland', in John McGarry and Brendan O'Leary (eds), *The Future of Northern Ireland* (Oxford: Oxford University Press, 1990), 206–19; Peter Gibbon, *The Origins of Ulster Unionism: the Formation of Popular Protestant Politics in Nineteenth Century Ireland* (Manchester: Manchester University Press, 1975); and 'Some Basic Problems of the Contemporary Situation', *Socialist Register* (1977); Austen Morgan and Bob Purdie (eds), *Ireland*; Henry Patterson, *Class Conflict and Sectarianism*, and *The Politics of Illusion*; Belinda Probert, *Beyond Orange and Green: the Political Economy of the Northern Ireland Crisis* (London: Zed Press, 1978); and Tom Nairn, *The Break-up of Britain* (London: Verso, 1981).

11  See Morgan, 'Socialism in Ireland – Red, Green and Orange', in Morgan and Purdie (eds), *Ireland*, 198; Bew, Gibbon and Patterson, 'Some Aspects

of Nationalism and Socialism in Ireland: 1968–1978', 160; and Boserup, 'Contradictions and Struggles in Northern Ireland', in *Socialist Register* (1972), 187.

12  Bew and Patterson, *The British State and the Ulster Crisis*, 3.

13  Differential economic development, according to Gibbon, was a consequence of the differences between the English and Scottish colonizations of Ireland, and the different 'modes of production' they fostered (this conception of a mode of production is unorthodox). Southern landlords acquired huge estates, while northern *colons* were settled with smaller parcels of land and capital, and commercial textile production paved the way for the development of capitalism in Ulster in the eighteenth century, *The Origins of Ulster Unionism, passim.*

14  Boserup, 'Contradictions and Struggles in Northern Ireland'. Northern industrialization and southern backwardness is linked by some Marxists to a relatively benign land-tenure system, the 'Ulster custom', which facilitated investment in agriculture and later in cottage industries.

15  Nairn, *The Break-up of Britain.*

16  See, *inter alia*, Boserup, 'Contradictions and Struggles in Northern Ireland', 160; Patterson, *Class Conflict and Sectarianism*, 25; Probert, *Beyond Orange and Green*, 16; Morgan, 'Socialism in Ireland – Red, Green and Orange', 176; Nairn, *The Break-up of Britain*, 229, 234; and Bew and Patterson, *The British State and the Ulster Crisis*, 4.

17  Patterson, *Class Conflict and Sectarianism*, 29. Bew, Gibbon, and Patterson claim that uneven development across Ireland was more important for Protestants than their relatively superior position within Northern Ireland; that the Protestant labour aristocracy was not reactionary but progressive; and that while discrimination existed, Protestants earned their privileged positions through possession of superior skills, see Bew, Gibbon, and Patterson, *The State in Northern Ireland, 1921–72*, 218; 'Some Aspects of Nationalism and Socialism in Ireland: 1968–1978', 158; Gibbon, *The Origins of Ulster Unionism*, 93; Patterson, *Class Conflict and Sectarianism*, 28.

18  Bew and Patterson argue that the resistance to Home Rule was not simply an 'orange' affair but part of a much wider coalition of social forces, including a non-orange labour aristocracy and the explicitly anti-orange ideology of liberal unionism – Bew, Gibbon, and Patterson, *The State in Northern Ireland, 1921–72*, 132; and Bew and Patterson, *The British State and the Ulster Crisis*, 3.

19  Patterson, *Class Conflict and Sectarianism*, 84–5.

20  Ibid., 6. Protestant workers 'regularly attacked upper-class Unionist leaders for their tendency to compromise in defence of Protestant interests', ibid., 144.

21  Bew and Patterson, *The British State and the Ulster Crisis*, 143; Bew, Gibbon and Patterson, *The State in Northern Ireland, 1921–72*, 50–6, 208; and Morgan, 'Socialism in Ireland – Red, Green and Orange', 203.

22  Boserup, 'Contradictions and Struggles in Northern Ireland', 184–5; Morgan, 'Socialism in Ireland – Red, Green and Orange', 199; see also Michael MacDonald, *Children of Wrath: Political Violence in Northern Ireland* (Oxford: Polity Press, 1986), 3–32.

23  Probert, *Beyond Orange and Green*, 47; and Boserup, 'Contradictions and Struggles in Northern Ireland', 184.

24  Bew, Gibbon, and Patterson, *The State in Northern Ireland, 1921–72*, 75; and Boserup, 'Contradictions and Struggles in Northern Ireland', 180. See chapter 1, p. 45 and n. 83, p. 432.

25  Bew and Patterson, *The British State and the Ulster Crisis*, 8–9.

26  Ibid., 141–2.

27  Ibid., 186.

28  Probert, *Beyond Orange and Green*, 46.

29  'To British capital, Ireland provides a supply of labour, a protected environment for ailing companies and a not unimportant export market. None of these would be jeopardised by Irish unity and Irish independence' – Boserup, 'Contradictions and Struggles in Northern Ireland', 183–4. See also Probert, *Beyond Orange and Green*, 12–13; and Morgan, 'Socialism in Ireland – Red, Green and Orange', 199–200.

30  By the 1970s, the annual subvention to Northern Ireland 'easily exceeded the total amount of modern industrial capital there', Bew, Gibbon, and Patterson, *The State in Northern Ireland, 1921–72*, 175.

31  Ibid., 19–29; Morgan, 'Socialism in Ireland – Red, Green and Orange', 198–203.

32  Morgan, 'Socialism in Ireland – Red, Green and Orange', 199.

33  Boserup, 'Contradictions and Struggles in Northern Ireland', 180; Bew and Patterson, 'Unionism and the Anglo-Irish Agreement', 44.

34  Bew and Patterson, *The British State and the Ulster Crisis*, 142–3. Bew and Patterson apply the same reasoning to the impact of the Anglo-Irish Agreement, see 'Scenarios for Progress in Northern Ireland'.

35  Bew and Patterson, *The British State and the Ulster Crisis*, 48; Morgan, 'Socialism in Ireland – Red, Green and Orange', 207–8; Boserup, 'Contradictions and Struggles in Northern Ireland', 158–9, 188–9; and Nairn, *Break-up of Britain*, 246.

36  Bob Purdie, 'Is the Cause of Ireland the Cause of Labour?', *Fortnight* (November 1983).

37  Michael Farrell, *Northern Ireland: the Orange State* (London: Pluto Press, 1976), 335.

38  Bew and Patterson, *The British State and the Ulster Crisis*, 144.

39  Boserup, 'Contradictions and Struggles in Northern Ireland', 168; and Probert, *Beyond Orange and Green*, 52–8, 68. 'The "family firm" was the typical unit of production in the province, and the local economy remained largely unaffected by the rise of monopoly capitalism in the rest of the United Kingdom', ibid., 52.

40  Boserup, 'Contradictions and Struggles in Northern Ireland', 169.

41  Ibid., 173.

42  Probert, *Beyond Orange and Green*, 75–6, 116. This benign view of the multinationals was shared by the most prominent green Marxists – see Farrell, *Northern Ireland*; and Eamonn McCann, *War and an Irish Town* (Harmondsworth: Penguin, 1974).

43  Boserup, 'Contradictions and Struggles in Northern Ireland', 173.

44  Probert, *Beyond Orange and Green*, 146.

45  Paisley's opposition to internment was allegedly '*rooted in his defence of working-class interests*, in the knowledge that it could be used equally well against loyalists as against republicans', ibid., 130 (our italics).

46  Ibid., 149. Probert's view of the progressive potential of Protestant paramilitaries was shared by prominent members of the Labour government of 1974–9, see Merlyn Rees, *Northern Ireland: A Personal Perspective* (London: Methuen, 1985), 92.

47  'Far from being merely a continuation of that older colonising imperialism which had plagued Ireland ... [foreign-owned capitalist operations] spelt the ruin of the Orange Order and Southern clericalism alike. It was their quarrel

with hopeless social and political archaism which was the motor of the new troubles', Nairn, *The Break-up of Britain*, 243. Nairn provides no evidence for this assertion.

48   Ibid., 236.

49   Ibid., 242–3.

50   It is tempting to see Nairn's espousal of independence for 'Ulster' and his hostility to the Irish nationalist minority as a reflection of stereotypical Scottish Protestant prejudices about Irish Catholics – laced with the politically correct language of the *New Left Review*.

51   Ibid., 243.

52   Ibid., 240.

53   For a critical introduction to Marxist theories of the liberal democratic state see Patrick Dunleavy and Brendan O'Leary, *Theories of the State: the Politics of Liberal Democracy* (London: Macmillan, 1987), ch. 5.

54   Bew, Gibbon, and Patterson, *The State in Northern Ireland, 1921–72*, 38, 212, 86.

55   Ibid., 48–9, 198–9; Patterson, *Class Conflict and Sectarianism*, xii; Bew and Patterson, *The British State and the Ulster Crisis*, 4–5. According to Bew, Gibbon, and Patterson some fraction of the bourgeoisie always dominates the state apparatus. The hegemony of this fraction, however, is not a result of inter-bourgeois conflict over the spoils of office (as Boserup and Probert maintain). Instead, as the crucial role of the capitalist state is to divide the dominated classes, it is the bourgeois fraction associated with the most effective way of achieving this task which emerges victorious, *The State in Northern Ireland, 1921–72*, 39. The fraction which is dominant in every state 'is that whose leading role is most conducive to class peace', ibid., 87. The teleological and dogmatic characteristics of these formulations are self-evident, but the authors relied on them to argue that during 1919–20 the bourgeoisie had to 'concede a portion of class power to the Orange section of the working-class [in order to] re-establish a militant basis for resistance to republicanism which could operate independently of the British', ibid., 49.

56   Bew and Patterson, 'Unionism and the Anglo-Irish Agreement', 45. Henry Patterson claims that Protestant workers could be sectarian (Orange) and simultaneously display a 'limited' degree of class-consciousness, *Class Conflict and Sectarianism*, 6, 10, 147.

57   Bew, Gibbon, and Patterson, *The State in Northern Ireland, 1921–72*, 216–17.

58   Ibid., 131, 90, 120.

59   According to Bew, Gibbon, and Patterson the decline of the traditional bourgeoisie was exaggerated. They were not 'displaced' by new multinationals and, most importantly, the new capital didn't behave any differently from the old. By 1970, 60 per cent of the manufacturing and 86 per cent of the total workforce were still employed in old establishments. The new external firms did not advocate reforms to combat sectarianism, although they did raise complaints about physical planning. They continued to hire in the same traditional way, through word of mouth and personal contacts, rather than through impersonal labour exchanges. 'In 1965, when new industry provided about 60,000 of 190,000 manufacturing jobs, the first development plan complained that only 10 per cent of new vacancies were being filled through labour exchanges', *The State in Northern Ireland, 1921–72*, 189. New capital allegedly had as much of a political interest as the old in supporting Stormont, because they could influence it more easily than the Westminster parliament.

60  Ibid., 131–2, 151.
61  Ibid., 151.
62  Ibid., 130. Although Probert's book was published before that of Bew and his colleagues she clearly rejects their analysis: there was no 'labour-based' challenge to Unionist hegemony, only a threat from middle-class liberalism, *Beyond Orange and Green*, 78.
63  Bew, Gibbon, and Patterson, *The State in Northern Ireland, 1921–72*, 132.
64  Opposition to O'Neill from unionists was not initially caused by his (symbolic) anti-sectarian measures but rather by his centralizing measures – O'Neill's new policies happily co-existed with continuing discrimination, ibid., 153, 133, 156.
65  Ibid., 165–6.
66  Ibid., 170–1.
67  Ibid., 167.
68  The illusion that the NILP was capable of transcending sectarian politics was shared by James Callaghan, the British Home Secretary who urged the British Labour Party to give its enthusiastic support to the NILP in 1969–70. He believed that it was capable of taking the place of the imploding UUP, see James Callaghan, *A House Divided* (London: Collins, 1973), 152, 157, 161.
69  Bew and Patterson are not unqualified supporters of the Union, like the BICO. However, they claim that material aid from the British state limits support for reactionary forces in the Protestant population, and that progressive periods in Northern Irish politics are associated with radical surges in Britain, *The British State and the Ulster Crisis*, 144–6. They presumably exclude the Liberal governments of 1905–14 and the Labour government of 1974–9 from the ambit of 'progressive periods'.
70  Bew and Patterson, 'Scenarios for Progress in Northern Ireland', 216–17. This thesis follows from the argument that the Catholic mass-basis of the civil-rights movement was a result of their material deprivation under the Stormont state. Bew and Patterson argue that while their 'reformist agenda' would leave '"ultimate" constitutional aspirations untouched, it would provide for a more expansive and positive form of citizenship within Northern Ireland', ibid., 217. The nature of an expansive and positive form of citizenship is left inadequately defined.
71  Bew and Patterson, 'Unionism and the Anglo-Irish Agreement'; 'Scenarios for Progress in Northern Ireland'.
72  Bew and Patterson, *The British State and the Ulster Crisis*, 147–8; 'Scenarios for Progress in Northern Ireland'. 'The predominant concern of the Catholic masses has been for an end to the Unionist regime and its oppressive policies. Compared with this, the question of reunification is of little more than sentimental significance . . . Sympathy for the Catholics in the North amongst the masses in the south is sympathy for an oppressed group – it cannot be taken as support for reunification', Bew, Gibbon, and Patterson, *The State in Northern Ireland, 1921–72*, 160.
73  Ibid., 170, italics in original.
74  Bew and Patterson were better disposed to 'red' members of the SDLP, like Paddy Devlin and Gerry Fitt, and regretted their passing from the political scene. Their disagreements with the 'green' SDLP are undiluted: they think that the present problem is that John Hume's analysis of the conflict has been accepted by the British and Irish governments and has informed the Anglo-Irish Agreement, see Bew and Patterson, 'Unionism and the Anglo-Irish Agreement', 45–6.

75  Bew and Patterson argue that the British approach simultaneously encourages republicans, angers Protestants, and isolates moderates in both camps: an argument which fits well with our own perspective on the importance of exogenous forces in shaping the politics of antagonism within Northern Ireland, see O'Leary and McGarry, _The Politics of Antagonism: Understanding Northern Ireland_ (London: Athlone Press, 1993).

76  Other red Marxists offer non-sectarian prescriptions. Austen Morgan believes the erosion of working-class divisions should be sought through a serious trade union commitment to abolish discrimination, 'Socialism in Ireland – Red, Green and Orange', 219. Dennis Tourish called for an indigenous Labour Party to be launched by the Northern Ireland trade unions, which would 'very rapidly acquire a mass base and outstrip the other parties' – 'Towards a New Labour Party', _Fortnight_ ( March 1978). Two French-speaking Marxists have urged support for the Union on grounds of its economic benefits, see S. Van der Straeten and P. Daufouy, 'La Contre-révolution Irlandaise', _Les Temps Modernes_, 311 (1972), 2069–104.

77  BICO, _The Economics of Partition_ (Belfast: Athol Books, 1972).

78  BICO, _The Two Irish Nations_ (Belfast: Athol Books, 1975), _Against Ulster Nationalism_ (Belfast: Athol Books, 1977).

79  BICO, _The Economics of Partition_, 7, 47, 49.

80  BICO, _The Economics of Partition_; A. Carr, _The Belfast Labour Movement_ (Belfast: Athol Books, 1974).

81  BICO, _The Economics of Partition_, 19.

82  Ibid., 14. The last 'argument' is reminiscent of white trade unionists in the UK who condemn black migrant workers for undercutting their wage-bargaining power.

83  BICO, _The Economics of Partition_, 31–2. Curiously, for Marxists, the BICO argue that one of the failings of the southern culture was its labour militancy, which deterred investment, ibid., 27. Among the negative characteristics of the Catholic religion are its reliance on authority, its repression of individuality, and its 'shifting of . . . the moral centre of gravity to a future existence', ibid., 50. To us that sounds like a good description of the communism which BICO was supposed to be in existence to advance.

84  BICO, _The Economics of Partition_, 12.

85  Cromwell is portrayed as a bourgeois revolutionary (rather than a genocidal maniac) who got a bad press from Catholic reactionaries for his Irish exploits. Orangeman's Day is celebrated annually because of the 'far-reaching progressive social effects' of the Williamite settlement, BICO, _Against Ulster Nationalism_, 36. In one memorable passage, the BICO compare the closing of the gates at Londonderry in 1689 with the storming of the Winter Palace in 1917, and Lillibulero, the Orange marching song, is given equivalence with the Internationale, ibid., 35. Readers are left wondering why later revolutionaries chose red rather than orange as their colour, and why the 'Sash my father wore' is not the anthem of European socialist parties.

86  BICO, _Against Ulster Nationalism_, 26. See also Roberts, _Northern Ireland and the Algerian Analogy_, 60–6.

87  BICO, _Against Ulster Nationalism_, 33. As Hugh Roberts wrote: 'Westminster seemed resolved at last on a policy of progressive reform in Ireland, and was no longer engaged in propping up the corrupt Ascendancy in the South', _Northern Ireland and the Algerian Analogy_, 62.

88  BICO, _Against Ulster Nationalism_, 49. Roberts claims that 'Protestant Ulster . . . supported every demand for progressive democratic reform in

the Catholic interest from the 1770s to 1920', *Northern Ireland and the Algerian Analogy*, 64. It rejected O'Connell's repeal of the Union movement and subsequently Parnell's home-rule movement because 'the substance of these demands was Catholic-nationalist not democratic ... The entire spirit of Ulster Unionism was to acknowledge the right of the Catholic South to go its own way, while simply insisting on the right of Protestant Ulster similarly to decide for itself what its political future should be', ibid. Evidence of the existence of this spirit is insubstantial.

89   BICO, *Against Ulster Nationalism*, 81. See also Roberts, *Northern Ireland and the Algerian Analogy*, 65–6.

90   'The Catholic minority ... only ever accepted the regime in the sense of desisting from making war on it until a favourable opportunity presented itself ... The only de facto acceptance that we are aware of is a sheer military acceptance that the state won the war over its existence in 1921-2, and that it was necessary to resort to more devious ways of attacking it', BICO, *Against Ulster Nationalism*, 16–17.

91   Ibid., 81.

92   The BICO explain gerrymandering as follows: 'Local government areas with Catholic majorities raised the Tricolour and refused to function, *causing* the development of gerrymandering ... Better (to) have gerrymandered Unionist local government, discriminating against Catholics, and thus keeping the nation alive, than have democratic local government administered by Catholics within the Unionist state!', ibid., 16 (our italics). For related views see Barton, *The Government of Northern Ireland, 1920-1923* (Belfast: Athol Books, 1980), 1; and Roberts, *Northern Ireland and the Algerian Analogy*, 66–7.

93   BICO, *Against Ulster Nationalism*, 55–6.

94   Ibid., 17, underlining in original.

95   Ibid., 20–1.

96   Ibid., 59, 71, 72.

97   Ibid., 80.

98   Ibid.

99   Integrationists often imply that many Catholics are more unionist than the Unionists! While Catholics show in polls that they want to be in the UK, the Unionist parties refuse to disband or support the organization of the British parties in Northern Ireland, and so show themselves to be more interested in perpetuating sectarian divisions than in integrating with Britain, see Lynch, *Equal Citizenship and the end of Sectarian Politics*, 9.

100   BICO, *Against Ulster Nationalism*, 82. Even geography-as-destiny arguments were invoked by the BICO: 'There are parts of Ulster which actually look English, and which might be placed in Worcestershire without arousing comment', ibid., 92. Elsewhere the BICO humourlessly claim that 'It requires great ignorance of geography to be able to believe that Ulster is geographically detached from Britain' (sic!), ibid., 25.

101   Campaign for Labour Representation in Northern Ireland (CLRNI), *The Labour Party and Northern Ireland* (Belfast: CLRNI, 1986); Campaign for Democratic Rights in Northern Ireland (CDRNI), *The Fulham Manifesto* (London: CDRNI, 1986); Roberts, *Northern Ireland and the Algerian Analogy*; Lynch, *Equal Citizenship and the End of Sectarian Politics*. The links between the various organizations influenced by Orange Marxism are fairly clear. Hugh Roberts, for example, a former member of the Communist Party and the founder of the Campaign for Democratic Rights for Northern Ireland, may not have been a member of BICO, but his analysis is quite similar. However, it does not follow that

all those who support electoral integration supported or would support the BICO's analysis.

102  Hugh Roberts, 'Sound Stupidity: The British Party System and the Northern Ireland Question', in McGarry and O'Leary (eds), *The Future of Northern Ireland*, 100–36.

103  CLRNI, *Bulletin: 1986 Conference Issue* (Belfast: CLRNI, 1986), 4.

104  See, for example, Roberts, 'Sound Stupidity', 125.

105  Ibid., 126.

106  CLRNI, *The Labour Party and Northern Ireland*, 3.

107  Roberts, 'Sound Stupidity', 126.

108  See, for example, Brian Barton and Paddy Roche (eds), *The Northern Ireland Question: Myth and Reality* (Aldershot: Gower, 1991); Christopher Hewitt, 'Catholic Grievances, Catholic Nationalism and Violence in Northern Ireland during the Civil Rights Period: a Reconsideration', *British Journal of Sociology*, 32, 3 (1981), 362–80; T. Wilson, *Ulster: Conflict and Consent* (Oxford: Basil Blackwell, 1989); A. T. Q. Stewart, *The Narrow Ground: Aspects of Ulster, 1609–1969* (Belfast: Pretani Press, 1986); BICO, *Against Ulster Nationalism*; and Roberts, *Northern Ireland and the Algerian Analogy*.

109  See, for example, Frank Parkin, *Marxism and Class Theory: A Bourgeois Critique* (London: Tavistock, 1979). See also chapter 7 below, *passim*.

110  Ernest Gellner, *Nations and Nationalism* (Oxford: Basil Blackwell, 1983).

111  Ibid., 88–109; Donald Horowitz, *Ethnic Groups in Conflict* (Berkeley: University of California Press, 1985). Communist politicians had to come to grips with the strength of ethnicity, whether leading a struggle against colonialism in China, Vietnam, or Angola, or making federalist concessions in what were the USSR and Yugoslavia. Ethnic divisions were suppressed by coercive communist state apparatuses, and were not transcended through the creation of supra-ethnic classless societies – Walker Connor, *The National Question in Marxist–Leninist Theory and Strategy* (Princeton: Princeton University Press, 1984).

112  See chapter 5, pp. 174–5, and chapter 8, pp. 319–20.

113  Ian Budge and Cornelius O'Leary, *Belfast: Approach to Crisis. A Study of Belfast Politics, 1613–1970* (London: Macmillan, 1973), 224. By comparison, in Glasgow, one of the most religiously divided cities in Great Britain, class was then a better predictor of party support than religion. The relative weakness of religion (as opposed to class) in explaining political partisanship in Glasgow compared with Belfast does not, however, confirm the electoral integrationist argument that the key factor is British Labour Party organization in Glasgow and its absence in Belfast. Budge and O'Leary's data are based on work carried out in the 1960s, when the Ulster Unionist Party was an off-shore wing of the Conservative Party, and when the Northern Ireland Labour Party claimed kinship with the British Labour Party. More importantly, religious divisions in Scotland, though they have an ethnic base, and though they affect the distribution of support for political parties in Scotland, are not divisions between peoples who wish Scotland to remain within the Union and those who want Scotland to integrate with another state.

114  Richard Rose, *Governing without Consensus: An Irish Perspective* (London: Faber, 1971), 281.

115  See John Curtice and Tony Gallagher, 'The Northern Ireland Dimension', in R. Jowell, S. Witherspoon, and L. Brook (eds), *British Social Attitudes: 7th Report* (Aldershot: Gower, 1990), 194.

116  Ibid., 197–8.

117  O'Leary and McGarry, *The Politics of Antagonism*, 121–5.

118 Calculated from table 1.13 in S. Elliott, *Northern Ireland Parliamentary Election Results* (London: Chichester Publications, 1973), 96.
119 The NILP was also almost entirely a Belfast party: with the solitary exception of South Armagh in 1938, the party never won a Stormont seat outside Belfast.
120 Rose, *Governing without Consensus*, 284.
121 Callaghan, *A House Divided* , 162.
122 Patrick Buckland, *A History of Northern Ireland* (Dublin: Gill and Macmillan), 108. See also Erhard Rumpf, *Nationalism and Socialism in Twentieth Century Ireland*, English translation, edited by A. C. Hepburn (Liverpool: Liverpool University Press, 1977), 205. Moreover, some activists, eager to increase their support among Protestants, 'opportunistically dabble[d] in sectarianism', Morgan, 'Socialism in Ireland – Red, Green and Orange', 184.
123 Ibid.
124 Rose, *Governing without Consensus*, 235.
125 Ibid., 233.
126 Ibid., 283.
127 Eamonn McCann was forced to leave the NILP because of his support for Bernadette Devlin in the 1970 Westminster general election; Paddy Devlin, who joined the party to 'talk to Protestants', left to become a founding member of the SDLP; while Billy Hull went on to form the Loyalist Association of Workers (LAW).
128 Buckland, *A History of Northern Ireland*, 137.
129 See pp. 133–5.
130 Curtice and Gallagher, 'The Northern Irish Dimension'.
131 Rose, *Governing without Consensus*, 288.
132 Ibid., 282.
133 See Liam O'Dowd, Bill Rolston, and Mike Tomlinson, *Northern Ireland: Between Civil War and Civil Rights* (London: CSE Books, 1980); and Smith and Chambers, *Inequality in Northern Ireland*.
134 An attempt by the British TUC to lead the strikers back to work was 'an abject failure', Rees, *Northern Ireland*, 70. Other red Marxists sensibly rejected Probert's analysis. Morgan condemned 'leftists' who celebrated the strike for appropriating 'the language of socialism for an all too virulent loyalism', 'Socialism in Ireland – Red, Orange and Green', 210; Bew and Patterson accused those who saw a potential for working-class politics in the strike of 'fatuous optimism', *The British State and the Ulster Crisis*, 74; and Peter Gibbon saw the loyalist forces as 'reactionary', 'Some Basic Problems of the Contemporary Situation', *Socialist Register*, 83.
135 Probert, *Beyond Orange and Green*, 140. In December 1987, John McMichael, a prominent UDA leader who promoted thinking in a non-sectarian direction, was assassinated by the IRA, acting on information from a member of the UDA. According to Probert, the UVF also discovered class-consciousness in 1974, but here too the progressives were overthrown by those with 'right-wing populist tendencies', ibid., 140.
136 Figures calculated from Malcolm Sutton, *An Index of Deaths from the Conflict in Ireland, 1969–93* (Belfast: Beyond the Pale Publications, 1993), 201–3.
137 In claiming that Orangeism was not merely a functional instrument of the bourgeoisie to ensure class peace, but compatible with class-consciousness and class conflict (albeit of a 'limited' kind), Henry Patterson makes a similar if less obvious error to that of Probert, *Class Conflict and Sectarianism*, xi–xii, 10, 85, 143–4. Class unity and class conflict were much less important for Orange workers than ethnic unity and sectarian conflict. The relevant class

consciousness was as exclusionary towards Catholics as it was usurpationary towards employers, Parkin, *Marxism and Class Theory*, 93–4.

138 Edward Said and Christopher Hitchens (eds), *Blaming the Victims: Spurious Scholarship and the Palestinian Question* (London: Verso, 1988).

139 Roberts, *Northern Ireland and the Algerian Analogy*.

140 Bill Johnson, 'Ireland and the Runcible Men', *New Society*, 25 June 1981, 531–2, reprinted in R. W. Johnson, *The Politics of Recession* (London: Macmillan), 184–9.

141 Ian Lustick, *State-Building Failure in British Ireland and French Algeria* (Berkeley: Institute of International Studies, University of California, 1985); and *Unsettled States, Disputed Lands: Britain and Ireland, France and Algeria, Israel and the West-Bank-Gaza* (New York: Cornell University Press, 1993).

142 Hereward Senior, *Orangeism in Ireland and Britain 1795–1836* (London: Routledge and Kegan Paul, 1966).

143 See Kurt Bowen, *Protestants in a Catholic State: Ireland's Privileged Minority* (Kingston: McGill–Queen's, 1983); and Jack White, *The Protestant Community in the Republic of Ireland* (Dublin: Gill and Macmillan, 1975).

144 Walker Connor, 'Eco- or Ethno-nationalism?', *Ethnic and Racial Studies*, 7, 3 (1984), 349.

145 Walker Connor, 'Ethno-nationalism and Political Instability: An Overview', in H. Giliomee and J. Gagiano (eds), *The Elusive Search for Peace: South Africa, Israel and Northern Ireland* (Capetown: Oxford University Press, 1990), 10.

146 See, for example, Barbara Solow, *The Land Question and the Irish Economy, 1870–1913* (Cambridge, Mass.: Harvard University Press, 1973).

147 Both Boserup and Probert claimed that economic changes in the 1950s and 1960s had destroyed the basis of partition. If so, the Protestants of Northern Ireland did not notice.

148 The more sophisticated Marxists, like Bew and Patterson, try to by-pass this problem by ceding a 'relative autonomy' to culture, but since that is still determined 'in the last instance' by economic forces the concession is insignificant. These analysts, who emphasize the autonomy of unionism, fail to recognize the autonomy of nationalism from economic causes – which is why they are seen as biased in a unionist direction.

149 Consider Canada, where the most developed province is Ontario and the poorest Newfoundland, with the others ranked in between. Supporters of the uneven-development thesis would predict a separatist movement in Newfoundland, rather than Quebec.

150 Nairn, a Scottish nationalist as well as a Marxist, advocates for Northern Ireland what he does for Scotland – and for rather similar reasons. He thinks it will aid a modernizing break from the archaic UK state.

151 In opinion polls, support for independence in Northern Ireland hardly ever rises over 4 per cent. Loyalist parties advocating it have performed abysmally in the few elections they have contested. The group which Nairn alleged was leading the intellectual charge towards a unilateral declaration of independence, the BICO, was so incensed that they launched a long polemic against him, *Against Ulster Nationalism*.

152 P. Gibbon, 'Some Basic Problems of the Contemporary Situation', 82. All academics become 'bourgeois' in some sense, even Marxists with tenure. For the record: one of the authors (McGarry) has a working-class and the other (O'Leary) a middle-class background.

## Chapter 5 Warring Gods: Theological Tales

1  Conor Cruise O'Brien, *States of Ireland* (London: Panther Books, 1974), 149.
2  Richard Rose, *Governing without Consensus: An Irish Perspective* (London: Faber and Faber, 1971), 248.
3  Simon Lee, 'Unholy Wars need Holy Solutions', *Fortnight*, 292 (1991), 13.
4  Donald H. Akenson, *God's Peoples: Covenant and Land in South Africa, Israel and Ulster* (Ithaca, N.Y.: Cornell University Press, 1992), 9.
5  It could be argued, and it has been, that one or more religious factions are aided or provoked by external co-religionists, and that the relevant religions were originally cultural imports.
6  Unless otherwise stated we use Catholic to refer to an adherent of the Roman Catholic and Apostolic Church, and Protestant to refer to all other (non-Orthodox or Coptic) Christian believers.
7  Rose, *Governing without Consensus*, 248, 264, 427.
8  David Smith and Gerald Chambers, *Inequality in Northern Ireland* (Oxford: Clarendon Press, 1991), 35.
9  John Fulton, *The Tragedy of Belief* (Oxford: Clarendon Press, 1991), 9–12; Rose, *Governing without Consensus*, 264–5; Smith and Chambers, *Inequality in Northern Ireland*, 36; Peter Stringer and Gillian Robinson (eds), *Social Attitudes in Northern Ireland, 1990–91 Edition* (Belfast: Blackstaff, 1991); and *Social Attitudes in Northern Ireland, the Second Report, 1991–92* (Belfast: Blackstaff, 1991).
10  Ed Cairns, 'Is Northern Ireland a Conservative Society', in Stringer and Robinson (eds), *Social Attitudes in Northern Ireland, 1990–91 Edition*, 145. The survey was explicitly designed to elicit religiosity: 'Apart from special occasions such as weddings, funerals and baptisms, how often nowadays do you attend services or meetings connected with your religion?' Consequently the responses are not exactly comparable to the questions asked by Rose in *Governing without Consensus*, or by Edward Moxon-Browne in *Nation, Class and Creed in Northern Ireland* (Aldershot: Gower, 1983).
11  See, for instance, Padraig O'Malley, *Ireland: The Uncivil Wars* (Belfast: Blackstaff Press, 1983), 118; and Sabine Wichert, *Northern Ireland since 1945* (Harlow: Longman, 1991).
12  If every Protestant had voted Unionist and no Catholic had done so, the index of religious voting would be 100. If Catholics had voted for the Unionists in the same proportions as Protestants, the index would have been zero.
13  Arend Lijphart, 'Review Article: The Northern Ireland Problem: Cases, Theories and Solution', *British Journal of Political Science*, 5, 3 (1975), 87.
14  Anthony Heath, Bridget Taylor and Gabor Toka, 'Religion, Morality and Politics', in R. Jowell, L. Brook, and L. Dowds (eds), *International Social Attitudes: the 10th BSA Report* (Aldershot: Dartmouth, 1993), 49–80.
15  See, for example, S. W. Beach, 'Religion and Political Change in Northern Ireland', *Sociological Analysis*, 38 (1977), 37–48. The same shortcut would define the Lebanese and Serbo-Croat-Bosnian conflicts as religious.
16  Not the Catholic Archbishop of Canterbury, as stated by O'Malley in *Ireland*, 185.
17  Edward Pearce, 'One Long Piece of Perplexity', *Fortnight*, 296 (1991), 15. He explains that the English, by contrast, have had their 'religious passion' drained out of them 'like watered beer out of a staved-in barrel'. Pearce, like another British columnist, Alan Watkins, consistently interprets the conflict as religious – and consistently displays Cathophobic passions.
18  *Fortnight* (April 1991), 21.

19   Andrew Boyd, *Holy War in Belfast* (Tralee: Anvil Books, 1969).
20   B. Mawhinney and R. Wells, *Conflict and Christianity in Northern Ireland* (Grand Rapids, Michigan: Eerdman, 1975); Duncan Morrow, 'Pastors and Politics', *Fortnight*, 296 (1991), 'Special Supplement: Religion in Ireland', 3–4.
21   'In a world in which Protestant and Catholic leaders endorse ecumenical efforts to draw together Christians of all denominations, Northern Ireland remains a monument to an earlier age of faith and wars of faith', Rose, *Governing without Consensus*, 247. 'The peculiarity . . . is that the conflict which took place in the remainder of Europe and in the United States some centuries ago is taking place in the province *now*.' John Hickey, *Religion and the Northern Ireland Problem* (Dublin: Gill and Macmillan, 1984), 81.
22   Lee, 'Unholy Wars need Holy Solutions', 13.
23   Morrow, 'Pastors and Politics'.
24   David Rapoport, 'Some General Observations on Religion and Violence', *Terrorism and Political Violence*, 3, 3 (1991), 118–40.
25   Ibid., 119.
26   Ibid., 121.
27   Rapoport is sympathetic, if reserved, about René Girard's argument that religion originates in the attempt to manage violence in kin-based societies: the function of religious ritual is to keep violence outside the religious community and to control the otherwise destructive norm of vengeance, *Violence and the Sacred* (London: Athlone, 1981).
28   Cited in John Darby, *Conflict in Northern Ireland: the Development of a Polarised Community* (Dublin: Gill and Macmillan, 1976), 114.
29   Rose, *Governing without Consensus*, 401.
30   Fulton, *The Tragedy of Belief*, 125–31.
31   Lee, 'Unholy Wars need Holy Solutions', 13; Mawhinney and Wells, *Conflict and Christianity in Northern Ireland*.
32   Mawhinney and Wells, *Conflict and Christianity in Northern Ireland*, 7.
33   Ken Heskin, *Northern Ireland: A Psychological Analysis* (Dublin: Gill and Macmillan, 1980), 24.
34   Wilson, *Ulster: Conflict and Consensus* (Oxford: Basil Blackwell, 1989), 211.
35   Patrick Buckland, *A Short History of Northern Ireland* (New York: Holmes and Meier, 1981), 100.
36   Heskin, *Northern Ireland*, 47.
37   O'Malley, *Ireland*, 178.
38   O'Brien, *States of Ireland*, 168.
39   Rose, *Governing without Consensus*, 216–17.
40   Heskin, *Northern Ireland*, 42–4.
41   The shift in the religious balance between 1961 and 1991 was disguised by the imperfections of the 1971 and 1981 censuses, but must also be partly attributed to a change in the comparative communal rates of migration. Between 1921 and 1971 Catholics migrated absolutely and relatively more than Protestants. Over the last two decades this pattern *may* have been reduced – for example some claim that a Protestant 'brain-drain' is now under way; Protestants, who are more likely to go to British universities, are more likely to decide to stay in Great Britain. See also pp. 502–3, n. 24
42   O'Brien, *States of Ireland*, 168.
43   Ibid., 168; Wright, 'Protestant Ideology and Politics in Ulster', *European Journal of Sociology*, 14 (1972), 213–80.
44   Rose, *Governing without Consensus*, 216–17.
45   Steve Bruce, *God Save Ulster! The Religion and Politics of Paisleyism* (Oxford:

Oxford University Press, 1986); Roy Wallis, Steve Bruce, and David Taylor, 'Ethnicity and Evangelicalism: Ian Paisley and Protestant Politics in Ulster', *Comparative Studies in Society and History*, 29 (1987), 293–313.

46 Bruce, *God Save Ulster!*, 249.

47 Ibid., 263.

48 Ibid.

49 In a subsequent book Bruce emphasizes that the core of Paisley's church is anti-ecumenical, and sees the clash with Catholicism as a test of the elect status of Ulster Protestants, see *The Edge of the Union: the Ulster Loyalist Political Vision* (Oxford: Oxford University Press, 1994).

50 *God Save Ulster!*, 123; and Steve Bruce, 'Ulster Loyalism and Religiosity', *Political Studies*, 35, 4 (1987), 643; see also Heskin, *Northern Ireland*, 37.

51 Bruce's view is derived from Rose, who argues that the vast majority of Catholics regard themselves as Irish by national identity whereas Protestants, unsure of their nationality, fall back on their religion for symbols of identity, *Governing without Consensus*, 216–17.

52 Bruce, *God Save Ulster!*, 251.

53 Ibid., 253.

54 Ibid., 264.

55 Akenson, *God's Peoples*.

56 Ibid., 16, 23, 118, 137, 193.

57 Ibid., 258.

58 Nationalists differ about how to produce this happy state of affairs. For civic nationalists 'The Irish problem is quite simply the fruit of Northern Protestant reluctance to become part of what they regard as an authoritarian Southern Catholic State', Garret FitzGerald, *Towards a New Ireland* (London: Charles Knight, 1972), 88. Republicans argue that partition allowed clerical empire-builders to run amok in both parts of Ireland, exacerbating religious divisions. They support Wolfe Tone's prophesy that an independent and united Ireland would 'unite the whole people of Ireland . . . abolish the memory of all past dissensions and . . . substitute the common name of Irishman in place of the denominations of Protestant, Catholic and Dissenter' – see, for example, Hilda McThomas, 'Neutral Wins Few Converts', *Fortnight*, 292 (1991), 17.

59 See table 5.3 and O'Leary and McGarry, *The Politics of Antagonism*, 136–8.

60 This view is shared by FitzGerald, *Towards a New Ireland*, 35.

61 Fulton, *The Tragedy of Belief*, ch. 5.

62 Wilson, *Ulster*, 213–14.

63 Conor Cruise O'Brien, *God Land: Reflections on Religion and Nationalism* (Cambridge, Mass.: Harvard University Press, 1988). O'Brien does not specify to what type of holy nationalism, if any, unionist ideology belongs, and has apparently reversed his previous opinion, expressed in *States of Ireland*, that unionism is more impregnated by Protestantism than Irish nationalism is with Catholicism.

64 Hickey, *Religion and the Northern Ireland Problem*, 84–5.

65 The fact that many nationalist militants, including those in the INLA, IPLO and Official IRA, are more Marxist than Christian causes no problem *if* communism is also regarded as a Catholic conspiracy – just as it was regarded as a Jewish conspiracy in Nazi Germany (Heskin, *Northern Ireland*, 27). Fundamentalist Protestants regard both communism and Roman Catholicism as godless forms of paganism.

66 Ian Paisley, 'Submission by Dr. Paisley, M.P., M.E.P. at Plenary Session of Strand One Talks, Stormont, June 1991' (mimeo), 3.

67    One DUP spokesperson regarded the visit by Pope John Paul's special envoy to persuade the hunger-strikers to abandon their fast as a direct attempt to strengthen their resolve! – O'Malley, *Ireland*, 90.

68    Ibid., 189.

69    J. Allister, *Irish Unification Anathema: the Reasons why Northern Ireland Rejects Unification with the Republic of Ireland* (Belfast: Crown Publications, n.d), 20–1.

70    See Arthur Aughey, *Under Siege: Ulster Unionism and the Anglo-Irish Agreement* (London: Hurst, 1989); and Hugh Roberts, *Northern Ireland and the Algerian Analogy: A Suitable Case for Gaullism?* (Belfast: Athol Books, 1986).

71    Hugh Roberts turns the tables in the debate over which community is more religious by arguing that Protestant persecution of Catholics in Ireland, *in so far as it existed*, was directed at destroying their political power not their religion. He claims that, by contrast, Catholics have been preoccupied with extirpating Protestant religious heresy. 'To come under the Republic is to come under the hegemony of the Roman Catholic church . . . There can be no doubt that the ideological core of anti-British nationalism in Ireland was furnished by Roman Catholicism', *Northern Ireland and the Algerian Analogy*, 41, 35 and 38.

72    Bruce maintains that the British do not understand Northern Ireland because they are unaware of the central importance of the Protestant religion for unionists ('Ulster Loyalism and Religiosity', 643). His project is to educate them. He is preaching to the converted – as Arthur Aughey has pointed out.

73    Aughey approvingly cites Robert McCartney's view that the Unionist tradition has as much in common with the ideas of Paine, Mill and the framers of the US Constitution as it has with Calvin, Luther, or Paisley, see *Under Siege*, 10.

74    Ibid., 8.

75    Ibid., 28, and see chapter 3, pp. 126–8, above.

76    Aughey, *Under Siege*, 7, 12. Similarly Henry Patterson writes that 'for many republicans, nationality and Catholicism were integrally linked . . . "secular" republicanism was very much a minority creed', *The Politics of Illusion: Socialism and Republicanism in Modern Ireland* (London: Hutchinson, 1989), 64. The British and Irish Communist Organizations also attempted to discredit the claim that republicanism had solid secular foundations – see chapter 4, *passim*.

77    Aughey, *Under Siege*, 11.

78    An exemplary early anthropological study, set in rural 'Ballybeg', is Rosemary Harris's *Prejudice and Tolerance in Ulster* (Manchester: Manchester University Press, 1972).

79    Some activities organized by the Catholic church, such as bingo, attract mass followings from both sides of the ethnic boundary.

80    Fulton, *The Tragedy of Belief*, 131; also see Richard Jenkins, 'Northern Ireland: In what sense "Religions" in Conflict?', in R. Jenkins, H. Donnan, and G. McFarlane, *The Sectarian Divide in Northern Ireland Today* (London: Royal Anthropological Institute of Great Britain and Ireland, Occasional Paper No. 41, 1986), 6–7.

81    Rose, *Governing without Consensus*, 329; also see John Whyte, *Interpreting Northern Ireland* (Oxford: Clarendon Press, 1990), 40.

82    Fulton, *The Tragedy of Belief*, 199.

83    Whyte, *Interpreting Northern Ireland*, 42.

84    Fulton, *The Tragedy of Belief*, 223.

85    Rupert Taylor, 'The Queen's University of Belfast and "the Troubles": the Limits of Liberalism', PhD thesis, University of Kent at Canterbury; and see 'The Limits of Liberalism: the Case of Queen's Academics and the "Troubles"', *Politics*, 7, 2 (1987), 28–34.

86 Darby, *Conflict in Northern Ireland*, 130.
87 Cardinal William Conway, *Catholic Schools* (Dublin: Catholic Communications Institute, 1970).
88 Fulton, *The Tragedy of Belief*, 185.
89 Rose provides an example of this misperception: 'Protestants often complain that the existence of separate schools causes or helps maintain political conflict in Northern Ireland. Many Catholics reject this argument', *Governing without Consensus*, 335.
90 Darby, *Conflict in Northern Ireland*, 126–7; Arthur, *The Government and Politics of Northern Ireland* (London: Longman, 1984), 38; E. Gallagher and S. Worrall, *Christians in Ulster, 1968–1980* (Oxford: Oxford University Press, 1982), 154; Dominic Murray, *Worlds Apart: Segregated Schools in Northern Ireland* (Belfast: Appletree Press, 1983), 141–2; and Michael McGrath, 'The Price of Faith: the Catholic Church and Catholic Schools in Northern Ireland since 1920', London: PhD thesis, London School of Economics and Political Science (1995).
91 John Sugden and Alan Bairner, *Sport, Sectarianism and Society in a Divided Ireland* (Leicester: Leicester University Press, 1993).
92 R. J. Cormack and R. D. Osborne (eds), *Religion, Education and Employment in Northern Ireland* (Belfast: Appletree Press, 1983).
93 Murray, *Worlds Apart*, 149.
94 Darby, *Conflict in Northern Ireland*, 130–1.
95 International media frequently assume that segregated education is the cause of conflict, and argue that if only integration could be adopted, then Northern Ireland's troubles would be over. In October 1993, after the IRA killed ten people in the Shankill Road, a BBC film was widely shown around the world in which the explanatory theme was that Catholic and Protestant children went to separate schools. The faith which hard-boiled journalists display in educational solutions is often touching.
96 Heskin, *Northern Ireland*, 155.
97 Terence O'Neill, *The Autobiography of Terence O'Neill* (London: Hart Davies, 1972), 79.
98 Robert G. Crawford, *Loyal to King Billy: A Portrait of the Ulster Protestants* (London: Hurst, 1987), 32, 121; Morris Fraser, *Children in Conflict* (Harmondsworth: Penguin, 1973); Fulton, *The Tragedy of Belief*; Jenkins, 'Northern Ireland: In what sense "religions in conflict"?'; C. Irwin, *Education and the Development of Social Integration in Divided Societies* (Belfast: Queen's University Press, 1991).
99 'Ulster – The Need for a New Outlook', *The Tablet*, 13 September 1975.
100 Gallagher and Worrall, *Christians in Ulster*, 166; Crawford, *Loyal to King Billy*, 66.
101 Gerald McElroy, *The Catholic Church and the Northern Ireland Crisis* (Dublin: Gill and Macmillan, 1991), 86.
102 Rose, *Governing without Consensus*, 336.
103 Moxon-Browne, *Nation, Class and Creed in Northern Ireland*, 134.
104 A. M. Gallagher and S. Dunn, 'Community Relations in Northern Ireland: Attitudes to Contact and Integration', in Peter Stringer and Gillian Robinson (eds), *Social Attitudes in Northern Ireland*, 1990–91 edition (Belfast: Blackstaff Press, 1991), 16.
105 Gallagher and Worrall, *Christians in Ulster*, 193; Heath, Taylor and Toka, 'Religion, Morality and Politics'.
106 Smith and Chambers, *Inequality in Northern Ireland*, 36–7.
107 Gallagher and Worrall, *Christians in Ulster*, 193.
108 See Whyte, *Interpreting Northern Ireland*, 27.

109 Wilson, *Ulster*, 204.
110 Sarah Nelson, *Ulster's Uncertain Defenders: Loyalists and the Northern Ireland Conflict* (Belfast: Appletree Press, 1984).
111 Bruce, *God Save Ulster!*, 263.
112 O'Leary and McGarry, *The Politics of Antagonism*, figure 1.
113 Gallagher and Worrall, *Christians in Ulster*.
114 Roy Foster, 'Varieties of Irishness', in Maurna Crozier (ed.), *Cultural Traditions in Northern Ireland* (Belfast: Institute of Irish Studies, 1989), 13–14.
115 'Analytically, one of the most surprising findings is the very limited relationship between *individual* regime outlooks and *individual* religious influences. Within each community, exposure to religious influences does not greatly differentiate one Protestant from another, or one Catholic from another. People who are more regular in church attendance, or stronger in their faith, or more fundamentalist in their faith are not much more likely to be ultras, disaffected, or fully allegiant citizens', Rose, *Governing without Consensus*, 274. The result is only surprising if one supposes the primacy of religious explanations. Rose is a very good political scientist so he reports data at odds with his preconceptions. See also the work of his colleague, Ian McAllister, 'The Devil, Miracles and the Afterlife: The Political Sociology of Religion in Northern Ireland', *British Journal of Sociology*, 33, 3 (1982), 340–7.
116 There is a story, probably apocryphal, about an English journalist who enquired of a Catholic farmer why he had voted for Bernadette Devlin, given that she was known to be an atheist. 'Sure', the farmer replied, 'she is a Catholic atheist.'
117 Rose, *Governing without Consensus*, 252.
118 Fulton, *The Tragedy of Belief*, 130.
119 Gallagher and Worrall, *Christians in Ulster*, 59; Wilson, *Ulster*, 215.
120 Anglican Archbishop and Nobel peace-prize winner, Desmond Tutu, has argued that violence against an oppressive state is justified under certain conditions, and would be surprised to hear he was enunciating 'Roman Catholic' doctrine.
121 Frantz Fanon, *The Wretched of the Earth*, with an introduction by Jean-Paul Sartre (Harmondsworth: Penguin, 1963).
122 Rose correctly observed that 'Physical assaults, when they occur, are usually directed at lay Catholics and their property', *Governing without Consensus*, 250. One priest, Father Hugh Murphy, was kidnapped by loyalists and held as a hostage for the safe return of an RUC officer, William Turbitt, held by the IRA. The priest was released unharmed, the officer was found dead – *Fortnight*, 170 (1978), 9.
123 O'Malley, *Ireland*, 198. In an incisive analysis, usually ignored by sociologists of religion and partisans of religious interpretations of the Northern Ireland conflict, Ian McAllister uses data gathered in a 1973 survey to test whether having more or less religious commitment is related to people's political attitudes. He finds little relationship between the political attitudes of Catholics and Protestants and their religious commitment, see Ian McAllister, 'The Devil, Miracles and the Afterlife: The Political Sociology of Religion in Northern Ireland', 330–47.
124 Opinion poll data are imperfect, especially in deeply divided territories. Apart from the problem of loaded questions, for which the assiduous interpreter can control, respondents may be unwilling to reveal what they really think, either because they judge their views deviant or because these views might put them at risk. Opinion polls in Northern Ireland therefore tend to

over-emphasize moderation and downplay extremism, which accounts for the facts that (i) opinion poll support for the moderate Alliance Party is roughly twice what it receives in elections, (ii) power-sharing receives high support in polls while politicians advocating it flounder at elections, and (iii) huge numbers of Protestants vote for Ian Paisley while hesitating to admit it.

125 This evidence supports that of the Commission which reported on the immediate causes of the present conflict, Cameron, *Disturbances in Northern Ireland: Report of the Cameron Commission* (Belfast: HMSO, 1969).

126 See chapter 6.

127 Denis Kennedy, *The Widening Gulf: Northern Attitudes to the Independent Irish State, 1919–49* (Belfast: Blackstaff Press, 1988).

128 Bruce, *God Save Ulster!*, 123.

129 Bruce, 'Ulster Loyalism and Religiosity', 643.

130 'If the 1937 constitution of the Republic was scrapped and if it came to be even that the Catholic hierarchy no longer exercised the power, influence, and control over the government of Dublin, then Protestants in Northern Ireland would look upon the Republic in a different light and there would be good neighbourliness in the highest possible sense', cited in O'Malley, *Ireland*, 192; see also FitzGerald, *Towards a New Ireland*, 89–90.

131 Rose, *Governing without Consensus*, 247.

132 Ibid., 257; Moxon-Browne, *Nation, Class and Creed in Northern Ireland*, 38–9.

133 Smith and Chambers, *Inequality in Northern Ireland*, 35.

134 Rose, *Governing without Consensus*, 485; and see chapter 3, table 3.3, p. 110.

135 Wallis, Bruce, and Taylor', 'Ethnicity and Evangelicalism: Ian Paisley and Protestant Politics in Ulster', 301.

136 Bruce, *God Save Ulster!*, 260–1.

137 Aughey, *Under Siege*, 7.

138 See, for example, the text of the UDA's think-tank, New Ulster Political Research Group, *Common Sense* (Belfast, 1987).

139 Historically the underfunding of Catholic schools by the state has been denied by unionists, and historically loyalists demanded an end to any public funding of Catholic schools which were accused of encouraging disloyalty to the state, see J. F. Galliher and J. L. DeGregory, *Violence in Northern Ireland: Understanding Protestant Perspectives* (Dublin: Gill and Macmillan, 1985), 75.

140 Bruce, *God Save Ulster!*, 249.

141 Ibid., 1–2, 118.

142 Ibid., 267–8.

143 Bruce, 'Ulster Loyalism and Religiosity', 643.

144 See Brendan O'Leary 'Appendix 4. Party Support in Northern Ireland, 1969–1989', in John McGarry and Brendan O'Leary (eds), *The Future of Northern Ireland* (Oxford: Oxford University Press, 1990), 342–57.

145 Ibid. Bruce's judgement may have arisen from the fact that his research was conducted in the early 1980s when the DUP was doing well.

146 Bruce acknowledges that the 'vast majority' of the DUP's supporters are not evangelical Protestants, 'Ulster Loyalism and Religiosity', 645.

147 Bruce presents data inconsistent with his own thesis – *God Save Ulster!*, 136.

148 Probert, *Beyond Orange and Green*, 123.

149 Nelson, *Ulster's Uncertain Defenders*.

150 Some of those active in the DUP are 'so committed to the Union' that they are 'prepared to go some way towards moving some of their evangelical principles into the area of private life and personal choice, rather than alienate

non-evangelical unionists', *God Save Ulster!*, 148. Bruce is right about this, but errs in not spelling out its significance.

151 Bruce, 'Ulster Loyalism and Religiosity', 647.

152 The primary source for Bruce's work was interviews with leading Free Presbyterians, not with secular DUP voters, see *God Save Ulster!*, viii. Others who have researched the loyalist working class in Belfast arrive at significantly different conclusions, see Sarah Nelson, 'Protestant Ideology Reconsidered', *British Sociology Yearbook*, 11 (1975). Hickey's book has similar methodological imperfections. His arguments are constructed from long and tedious quotations from *The Protestant Telegraph* and *The Junior Orangeman's Catechism*. After citing these 'representative' works, he claims that 'enough evidence should have been quoted . . . to show that Paisley's attitude towards the Roman Catholic Church is not untypical of Protestant views in Northern Ireland', Hickey, *Religion and the Northern Ireland Problem*, 78.

153 Akenson, *God's Peoples*.

154 One liberal unionist suggests that the Republic's government 'felt impelled to consult the Papacy before any important decision was taken'!, Wilson, *Ulster*, 208. For an objective assessment of the Roman Catholic church's influence in the Irish Republic, see John Whyte, *Church and State in Modern Ireland, 1923–1979* (Dublin: Gill and Macmillan, 1980), especially 362ff.

155 Tom Inglis, *Moral Monopoly: the Catholic Church in Modern Irish Society* (Dublin: Gill and Macmillan, 1987).

156 O'Leary and McGarry, *The Politics of Antagonism*, ch. 3.

157 Farrell, *The Orange State*, 101.

158 McGrath demonstrates that debates over funding for schools and hospitals figured prominently in the nationalist press during elections and by-elections, especially when rival nationalists were competing, *The Price of Faith*.

159 Few English observers realize that in Scotland Catholic schools were granted full funding as early as 1918.

160 O'Leary and McGarry, *The Politics of Antagonism*, chs 3–4.

161 See Wilson, *Ulster*, 108, and chapter 7 below, pp. 283–5.

162 See chapter 7, pp. 283–5.

163 Darby, *Northern Ireland*, 117–18.

164 See *Fortnight*, 320 (1993), 7.

165 Patrick Bishop and Eamonn Mallie, *The Provisional IRA* (London: Hutchinson, 1987), 344; Gallagher and Worrall, *Christians in Ulster*, 121ff.

166 By 15 February 1971 the Catholic Cardinal claimed to have made statements denouncing violence 23 times, Gallagher and Worrall, *Christians in Ulster*, 60; and see McElroy, *The Catholic Church and the Northern Ireland Crisis*. The DUP's claim that Father John Magee visited the hunger-strikers in 1981 to strengthen their resolve ignores the fact that the envoy's task was to talk the prisoners out of the hunger strike, and that he was unsuccessful.

167 Michael MacDonald, *Children of Wrath*, 12.

168 Whyte, 1986; *Interpreting Northern Ireland*, 33–9.

169 While attaching primary blame to Catholic policy for endogamy, one sociologist acknowledges that Catholics might have other reasons for not marrying Protestants: they may consider them to be 'bigots, or oppressors or ethnic aliens', Fulton, *The Tragedy of Belief*, 226.

170 One mixed marriage required a police escort to protect the 'happy couple' from their families! Whyte, *Interpreting Northern Ireland*, 41.

171 Darby, *Northern Ireland*, 138–9.

172 Murray, *Worlds Apart*, 139.

173 Ibid., 143.
174 Gallagher and Worrall, *Christians in Ulster*, 164–5; Rose, *Governing without Consensus*, 334–5.
175 D. H. Akenson, *Education and Enmity: the Control of Schooling in Northern Ireland* (Newton Abbott: David and Charles, 1973); Darby, *Northern Ireland*, 133.
176 Arend Lijphart, *Democracy in Plural Societies: A Comparative Exploration* (New Haven: Yale University Press, 1977), 39–44. The Canadian Constitution Act of 1867 gives the Protestant minority in Quebec and the Catholic minority outside Quebec the right to have their own educational systems. In Ontario, Catholic schools enjoy full funding from the provincial government.
177 Edmund Aunger, 'Religion and Occupational Class in Northern Ireland', *Economic and Social Review*, 7, 1 (1975), 1–17.
178 Rose, *Governing without Consensus*, 336.
179 Darby, *Northern Ireland*, 139; Gallagher and Worrall, *Christians in Ulster*, 154.
180 Gallagher and Worrall, *Christians in Ulster*, 160–1.
181 Fulton, *The Tragedy of Belief*, 181; Gallagher and Worrall, *Christians in Ulster*, 162–3. The 1978 Act provided machinery to convert segregated into integrated schools managed by a joint committee, on which Catholics and Protestants would be represented in equal numbers.
182 Those who support the state (Protestant) sector in Northern Ireland have not raised the issue of the duplication of resources and high costs involved in a segregated system. On the contrary, Rose's Loyalty Survey indicated that 64 per cent of Protestants would have approved funding Catholic schools on an equal basis to Protestant schools – a fact which Rose curiously interpreted as meaning that Protestants were against segregated education, *Governing without Consensus*, 336.
183 Rose, *Governing without Consensus*, 336–7.
184 J, Darby, D. Murray, D. Batts, S. Dunn, S. Farren, and J. Harris, *Education and Community in Northern Ireland: Schools Apart?* (Coleraine: New University of Ulster, 1977); see also Gallagher and Worrall, *Christians in Ulster*, ch. 10.
185 Heskin, *Northern Ireland: A Psychological Analysis*, 145.
186 Irwin, *Education and the Development of Social Integration in Divided Societies*.
187 Rose, *Governing without Consensus*, 337.
188 Census of Northern Ireland (London: HMSO, 1992).
189 *Irish Times*, 6 November 1992.
190 SACHR (Standing Advisory Commission on Human Rights) (1991).
191 For an unconvincing argument in this vein, see Conor Cruise O'Brien's *God Land*. For him, nationalism as a collective emotional force 'makes its first appearance, with explosive impact, in the Hebrew Bible', in which a land and power are promised to a chosen people, *God Land*, 2. He also believes that once deities and kings are de-sacralized it is nations which inherit their religious charisma. He differentiates three scales of 'holy nationalism' in ascending order of arrogance and exclusivity: the 'chosen people', the 'holy nation' (the chosen people with tenure), and the 'deified nation'. Logical and factual errors in O'Brien's discussion of religion and nationalism are pointed out by Ernest Gellner, 'The Sacred and the National', *LSE Quarterly*, 3, 4 (1989), 357–69; and Brendan O'Leary, 'Review', *Ethnic and Racial Studies*, 12, 4 (1990), 586–8.
192 The Norwegian philosopher Jon Elster has argued that 'willing what cannot be willed', i.e. willing what can only come about as an unintended by-product of other processes, is a paradigm form of irrationality, *Sour Grapes: Studies in the Subversion of Rationality* (Cambridge: Cambridge University Press, 1983), 44–52.

## Chapter 6 Fiery Values: Cultural Interpretations

1  This declaration is usually attributed to Herman Goering although a British newspaper 'credits' it to Hanns Johst, *Observer*, 10 June 1934.

2  Said at the Princeton Institute, in March 1969, according to Louis Dumont, *Essays on Individualism: Modern Anthropology in Ideological Perspective* (Chicago: Chicago University Press), 158.

3  'Ventures into the Belly of the Beast', *Independent on Sunday*, 6 March 1994. Banville cites as 'obvious examples', the poetry of Michael Longley, Seamus Heaney, Paul Muldoon, and Ciaran Carson, and the fiction of Brian Moore and John McGahern.

4  Seamus Heaney, 'Whatever You Say Say Nothing', in *North* (London: Faber, 1975).

5  Thomas Hobbes, *Elements of Law*, Part One, ch. 16, 11.

6  I. Kant, *Zum Ewigen Frieden* (1795).

7  Very unusually Richard Rose makes the silly statement that 'the political history of Northern Ireland is a record of centuries of violence', *Governing without Consensus: An Irish Perspective* (London: Faber and Faber, 1971), 18. Northern Ireland has not yet existed for a century, and it was quiescent, if not peaceful, between 1922 and 1969.

8  After giving a lecture at the University of Uppsala in March 1991 O'Leary was thanked, sincerely, by one of the staff for having broadcast live from the seventeenth century.

9  A snobbish know-it-allism is nicely illustrated by the literary critic George Steiner who sucks up to his English audience by telling them (wrongly) that they cannot understand Irish history because their country has never experienced continental European religious fanaticism: 'There is hardly a European city which does not bear traces of scission and apartheid as between doctrinal communities. The present ugliness in Northern Ireland, with which English sentiment is finding it so difficult to cope, represents an atavistic but also routine aspect of Continental history. So much of Europe is a consequence of exhaustion after generations of religious civil warfare. Dogmatic fury has played a minor, sporadic role in the English scene', George Steiner, 'Ringing in the Old', *The Listener*, 4 January 1973, 2.

10  Pierre van den Berghe, *The Ethnic Phenomenon* (New York: Elsevier, 1981).

11  Rose, *Governing without Consensus*, 48.

12  Robert Ardrey, *The Territorial Imperative: A Personal Inquiry into the Animal Origins of Property and Nations* (London: Collins, 1969).

13  Anthropological investigations have frequently suggested that there are few differences in cultural heritage and practice between Catholics and Protestants – and have often emphasized the low impact of the conflict upon such communities – however, these researches have been carried out disproportionately in rural areas, John Darby, *Intimidation and the Control of Conflict in Northern Ireland* (Dublin: Gill and Macmillan, 1986), 6.

14  Gabriel Almond, 'Communism and Political Culture Theory', in his *A Discipline Divided: Schools and Sects in Political Science* (London: Sage, 1990), 157.

15  The school we attended at Garron Tower annually hosts the John Hewitt summer school to facilitate cross-community dialogue in the region, and we can testify that one could, if one wanted, spend the entire year in Northern Ireland at such conferences.

16  See, *inter alia, Tribalism and Christianity in Ireland* (New Ulster Movement Publications, 1973); The Two Traditions Group, *Northern Ireland and the Two*

*Traditions in Ireland* (Belfast: Two Traditions Group, 1983); Maurna Crozier (ed.), *Varieties of Irishness* (Belfast: Institute of Irish Studies, Queen's University, 1989); and *Varieties of Britishness* (Belfast: Institute of Irish Studies, Queen's University, 1990).

17 'The Ethnic Sources of Nationalism', in Michael E. Brown (ed.), *Ethnic Conflict and International Security* (Princeton: Princeton University Press, 1993), 27–41.

18 M. W. Heslinga, *The Irish Border as a Cultural Divide* (Assen: Van Gorcum, 1979), 3rd edition.

19 T. J. Pickvance, *Peace through Equity: Proposals for a Permanent Settlement of the Northern Ireland Conflict* (Birmingham: the author, 1975).

20 His chapter which discusses 'some differences between Ireland and Great Britain' is headed 'The Unity of the British Isles', Heslinga, *The Irish Border as a Cultural Divide*, 84ff.

21 Ibid., 78.

22 Ibid., 204.

23 Ibid., 78.

24 Edna Longley, *Fortnight*, 256 (November 1987).

25 John Whyte, 'How is the Boundary Maintained between the Two Communities in Northern Ireland?', *Ethnic and Racial Studies*, 9, 2 (1986), 219–34.

26 For discussions of the attempt to Gaelicize independent Ireland, see, *inter alia*, Oliver MacDonagh, 'The Politics of Gaelic', in *States of Mind: Two Centuries of Anglo-Irish Conflict* (London: Pimlico, 1992), 104–25; John Hutchinson, *The Dynamics of Cultural Nationalism: the Gaelic Revival and the Creation of the Irish Nation State* (London: Allen and Unwin, 1987), 304ff; Desmond Fennell, *The State of the Nation: Ireland since the Sixties* (Dublin: Ward River Press, 1983), 118ff; and Terence Brown, *Ireland: A Social and Cultural History* (London: Fontana Press, 1985), 45–78.

27 The 'liberal' Terence O'Neill began his parliamentary political career with this gambit: 'Is it not a fact that for sheer waste of time there is little worse than learning *Erse*?', HC (Stormont), vol. 30, col. 4750, 13 March 1947, cited in Michael McGrath, 'The Price of Faith: the Catholic Church and Catholic Schools in Northern Ireland', PhD thesis, London School of Economics and Political Science, University of London (1995), ch. 6.

28 Ibid.

29 On arrival in Garron Tower, a Catholic grammar school, in September 1969, O'Leary's mother had a welcoming conversation with the school's President. It included, as O'Leary recalls, the following gambit, 'All boys learn French and Latin here Mrs O'Leary, but as for the second modern language we have a policy in this school: the bright boys, they learn German; the other boys, well they learn Irish ... Which second language would you like your son to learn Mrs O'Leary?' The mother in question, a fluent and originally working-class Irish-speaker from the Republic, looked at her eleven-year-old son with pride, and decided – with his equally proud assent – that German would be best.

30 SACHR, *Religious and Political Discrimination and Equality of Opportunity in Northern Ireland, Second Report* (London: HMSO, 1990), 8.42, and 8.47.

31 Peter Brooke, 'Religious and Political Discrimination and Equality of Opportunity in Northern Ireland Second Report, Response by the Secretary of State for Northern Ireland', in SACHR, *Report for 1991–92* (London: HMSO, 1992), 293–320.

32 Source: Northern Ireland Readership Survey 1993, Macmillan Media.

33 The Northern Irish Sunday newspaper market is dominated by papers from Britain and the Republic, although British Sundays take care to run 'Irish

editions' with sufficient 'local content' to guarantee their market-share. The pro-unionist and tabloid *Sunday Life* is the exceptional local Sunday, with a circulation of over 80,000 and an estimated readership of 220,000.

34    The most extensive treatment is provided by John Sugden and Alan Bairner, *Sport, Sectarianism and Society in a Divided Ireland* (Leicester: Leicester University Press, 1993).

35    It may be significant that the USA and the Republic of Ireland were less receptive to cricket than either the 'white' or 'black' dominions'.

36    The survey was carried out by N. P. McGivern as part of a BA dissertation at the University of Ulster in 1991 and is cited by Sugden and Bairner, *Sport, Sectarianism and Society in a Divided Ireland*, 79.

37    Some other historians are more obviously imbued with their own cultural biases. Consider this: 'It is doubtful whether any party to the Northern Ireland conflict has shown such a desire as the British government to reach a settlement consonant with generally accepted principles of political equity, or pursued so rocky a penitential path, strewn with the debris of successive political initiatives, towards it.' Charles Townshend, *Political Violence in Ireland: Government and Resistance since 1848* (Oxford: Clarendon Press, 1983), 396. This prejudice is the antithesis of Oliver MacDonagh's treatment of British governments as irresponsible amnesiacs, in *States of Mind*, especially ch. 8.

38    F. S. L. Lyons, *Culture and Anarchy in Ireland 1890–1939* (Oxford: Oxford University Press, 1979), 1–2, 177.

39    Ibid., 117.

40    Ibid., 144. Lyons continues 'These ways of life are founded on religion because this is a region where religion is still considered as a vital determinant of everything important in the human condition.'

41    David Miller, *Queen's Rebels: Ulster Loyalism in Historical Perspective* (Dublin, Gill and Macmillan, 1978).

42    Ibid., 4.

43    Ibid., 5.

44    Louis Hartz, *The Founding of New Societies: Studies in the History of the United States, Latin America, South Africa, Canada and Australia* (New York: Harcourt, Brace & World, 1955). Miller's arguments about the contractarian nature of unionism are widely endorsed, see, for example, Padraig O'Malley, *Uncivil Wars: Ireland Today* (Belfast: Blackstaff Press, 1983), 150, 187; and J. J. Lee, *Ireland: Politics and Society, 1912–85* (Cambridge: Cambridge University Press, 1985), 14.

45    Charles Townshend appears to hold much the same opinion as Miller. He writes, of the decision to drive Catholic and known socialist workers from the Belfast shipyards in 1920, that 'Its perversity (sic!) was an expression of the idiosyncratic Ulster-Protestant sense of community – a sense which may convincingly be seen as an arrested development towards modern nationalism', *Political Violence in Ireland*, 342.

46    This theme is not confined to Miller: the Scottish Marxist Tom Nairn has complained that Ulster Protestants have been unable to develop a proper nationalism (see chapter 4, pp. 144–5), while the sociologist Liam O'Dowd observes that Ulster unionism has been a political movement in which modern intellectuals have traditionally been marginalized, see Liam O'Dowd, 'Intellectuals and Political Culture: a Unionist–Nationalist Comparison', in Eamonn Hughes (ed.), *Culture and Politics in Northern Ireland, 1969–1990* (Buckingham: Open University Press, 1991), 151–73. O'Dowd observes that no professional or intellectual has led the Unionist Party since partition,

ibid., 158 [this must mean that former JP James Molyneaux is not counted as a professional]. One result, allegedly, is that unionists and nationalists lack 'a common political discourse' which might inform a political accommodation, ibid., 169.

47   Roy F. Foster, *Modern Ireland: 1600–1972* (London: Allen Lane, 1988).
48   Ruth Dudley Edwards, *Patrick Pearse: The Triumph of Failure* (London: Gollancz, 1977).
49   Marianne Elliott, *Wolfe Tone: Prophet of Irish Independence* (New Haven: Yale University Press, 1989). Elliott manages to imply that even as late as 1796 Tone did not really have national independence as his primary political objective because his previous political activity had not been separatist but rather reformist and devoted to bringing the different denominations of Ireland together behind reform. This is very odd history. Tone, after all, helped organize a separatist insurrection modelled on the French Jacobins, and was on a boat doing just that in 1796. The author's reading of Tone seems best understood as that of a reformist Northern Irish cultural Catholic who thinks that unifying the Irish before pursuing independence would have been a good idea. Perhaps it would, but it is not a sensible way to treat Tone. See also Elliott's much less ideological and more impressive text, *Partners in Revolution: the United Irishmen and France* (New Haven: Yale University Press, 1982).
50   Foster is detached and even-handed, and certainly not inclined to treat Ulster unionism as any more rational than its republican opposition. Of political philosophy and discourse throughout the island he writes that 'political aspirations and social thought, for Protestants as well as Catholics, often derive from ethics, theology and emotion rather than from economics or politics', which suggests a symbiotic cultural backwardness in both Irish Catholics and Protestants, Roy Foster, 'Varieties of Irishness', in Maurna Crozier (ed.), *Cultural Traditions in Northern Ireland* (Belfast: Institute of Irish Studies, Queen's University, 1989), 17.
51   A. T. Q. Stewart, *The Narrow Ground: Patterns of Ulster History* (Belfast: Pretani Press, 1986), 48.
52   Ibid., 53. He reports, tellingly, the verdict of nineteenth-century commissioners reporting on a riot in Derry which followed annual Protestant celebrations. Unlike Ulster Protestants few others had 'committed the imprudence of continuing to celebrate a victory in a civil war: in ancient times both the Greeks and Romans had been careful never to tolerate it', ibid., 71.
53   Ibid., 56–7.
54   Ibid., 113ff.
55   Ibid., 113.
56   MacDonagh, *States of Mind*.
57   Ibid., 25.
58   Ibid., 7.
59   Ibid., 9.
60   Ibid., 32.
61   Ibid., 13.
62   Ibid., 14.
63   Ibid., 143.
64   See John Darby, *Intimidation and the Control of Conflict in Northern Ireland* (Dublin: Gill and Macmillan, 1986); and Frank Wright, *Northern Ireland: A Comparative Analysis* (Dublin: Gill and Macmillan, 1987).
65   It is well known that Catholics and Protestants display a high level of stereotyping of the other community. One psychologist reviewing the evidence

sums up: 'both groups see themselves as decent, fine, ordinary people, but each other as bitter or brainwashed', E. E. O'Donnell, *Northern Irish Stereotypes* (Dublin: College of Industrial Relations, 1977).

66  Anthropologists have noted variations in Catholic–Protestant relations within Northern Ireland, and indeed persuaded the late John Whyte that different political solutions/institutions might be appropriate for different areas of the region, *Interpreting Northern Ireland* (Oxford: Clarendon Press, 1990), 242–3.

67  In a perfect illustration of how ethnic abuse can become a badge of ethnic pride, the expression 'The Fighting Irish' has been adopted by the American football team of the heavily Catholic Irish University of Notre Dame. Its T-shirts proudly advertise an ape-like caricature of a nineteenth-century Irish faction-fighter, complete with pipe and shillelagh.

68  This fact explains the title of Fionnula O'Connor's insightful book, *In Search of a State, the Catholics of Northern Ireland* (Belfast: Blackstaff Press, 1993).

69  Stewart, *The Narrow Ground*, 115.

70  Townshend, *Political Violence in Ireland*.

71  Ibid., ix.

72  Ibid., 394.

73  Wright, *Northern Ireland*, 112,ff.

74  For this reason, amongst others, Steve Bruce's classification of loyalist paramilitary violence as 'pro-state' is problematic. However, he is not wrong to suggest that 'collusion in violence' is much more widespread in both communities than generous liberals wish to suggest, *The Edge of the Union*, 127.

75  Martin Gilbert, *Winston Churchill, 1916–1922* (London: Heinemann, 1975), 703.

76  See Brendan O'Leary and John McGarry, *The Politics of Antagonism: Understanding Northern Ireland* (London: Athlone, 1993), ch. 3.

77  See M. Thompson, R. Ellis, and A. Wildavsky, *Cultural Theory* (Boulder: Westview Press, 1990).

78  *The Edge of the Union: the Ulster Loyalist Political Vision* (Oxford: Oxford University Press, 1994). This work, in which empathy sometimes veers towards sympathy, is based on limited and unspecified interviews, and as with Bruce's writings on evangelical Protestantism, seems to take a small and extreme 'sample' to be representative of mainstream Unionism.

79  Paisley was commenting on O'Neill's efforts 'to build bridges' between the two communities in the 1960s.

80  Stewart, *The Narrow Ground*.

81  Darby, *Intimidation and the Control of Violence in Northern Ireland*, 52–3.

82  Stewart, *The Narrow Ground*, 116.

83  *Irish News*, 11 April 1994.

84  Paul Wilkinson, *Terrorism and the Liberal State* (Basingstoke: Macmillan, 1986), 2nd edition, revised, extended and updated, 67. Any terrorist who performs tasks in a state of sacrificial ecstasy is likely to be very incompetent. For the defects in Wilkinson's writings see Brendan O'Leary, 'Review Article', *British Journal of Criminology*, 28, 1 (1988), 97–107.

85  MacDonagh, *States of Mind*, 89.

86  Padraig O'Malley, *Biting at the Grave: the Irish Hunger Strikes and the Politics of Despair* (Belfast: Blackstaff Press, 1990).

87  For a discussion of fasting as a mechanism of judicial conflict-resolution in Gaelic Brehon law, see Roy Foster's *Modern Ireland: 1600–1972* (Harmondsworth: Penguin, 1988), 13.

88  Ibid., 117 (our italics).

89   As Stewart observes, many enjoy quoting with malice a contemporary's description of the seventeenth-century English and Scots settlers of Ulster as 'the scum of both nations', *The Narrow Ground*, 81.

90   J. J. Lee, *Ireland: Politics and Society, 1912–85* (Cambridge: Cambridge University Press, 1985), 3, 4, 79; Bruce, *At the Edge of the Union*, 37–71.

91   See chapter 4.

92   A. Pollak (ed.), *A Citizens' Inquiry: the Opsahl Report on Northern Ireland* (Dublin: Lilliput Press, 1993), 113.

93   See, for example, Arend Lijphart, 'Consociation: The Model and its Application in Divided Societies', in Desmond Rea (ed.), *Political Co-operation in Divided Societies: A Series of Papers Relevant to the Conflict in Northern Ireland* (Dublin: Gill and Macmillan, 1982), 166–86.

94   Harold Jackson, *The Two Irelands: A Dual Study in Inter-Group Tensions* (London: Minority Rights Group, 1971).

95   For an exceptional study of British federalism – albeit of the largely WASP variety – see J. Kendle, *The Round Table Movement and Imperial Union* (Toronto: University of Toronto Press, 1975).

96   E. J. Hobsbawm and T. Ranger (eds), *The Invention of Tradition* (Cambridge: Cambridge University Press, 1983).

97   Jon Elster, *The Cement of Society: A Study of Social Order* (Cambridge: Cambridge University Press, 1989), 97.

98   This is not to say that we believe that all cultures are efficient adaptations to their environments. Our preference is methodological: make the assumption that cultures are efficient until it is clear that it is useless, then, and only then, consider whether the relevant cultures are sub-optimally adapted to their environments.

99   See, for example, M. L. R. Smith, 'The Role of the Military Instrument in Irish Republican Strategic Thinking', PhD thesis, King's College, University of London (1991); and Brendan O'Duffy, 'Violent Politics: A Theoretical and Empirical Examination of Two Centuries of Political Violence in Ireland', PhD thesis, London School of Economics and Political Science, University of London (1995).

100  What follows draws heavily on Brendan O'Leary's review of Padraig O'Malley's work in *Irish Political Studies* , 6 (1991), 118–22.

101  See Ken Binmore, *Fun and Games* (Lexington, Mass.: D. C. Heath, 1992), 7.1.3.

102  The fact that certain Irish Catholic priests tried to argue that the hunger-strikers were not threatening suicide is irrelevant. In so far as their reasonings condoned the strikers' actions they were not Catholic. The fact that some English Catholic priests thought the hunger-strikers were suicidal may have been motivated by their English nationality, but the theological arguments were on their side.

103  See David Beresford, *Ten Men Dead* (London: Grafton, 1987).

104  The anthropologist Begona Aretxaga seems to share our verdict: 'The mythology of sacrifice as the alleged cause of the current political violence in Northern Ireland seems to me to be a new origin myth that conviently allows one to ignore the field of power relations at play in the use of political violence, both by the state and the IRA . . . Further, this mythology reinforces the too common view of Irish people as irrational myth followers. This is not to deny the existence of a mythology of sacrifice in the Nationalist community, especially in the Republican section; rather, it is to deny that the sacrificial narrative constitutes the etiology of the IRA violence', 'Striking with Hunger: Cultural Meanings of Political Violence in Northern Ireland', in Kay B. Warren (ed.),

*The Violence Within: Cultural and Political Opposition in Divided Nations* (Oxford: Westview Press, 1993), 238.

105  In 1973 an advertisement appeared in *Republican News* for Irish classes: 'The British Army speak English. What do you speak?', Darby, *Intimidation and the Control of Conflict in Northern Ireland*, 153.

106  See Arthur Aughey, *Under Siege: Ulster Unionism and the Anglo-Irish Agreement* (London: Hurst, 1989), 23; and 'Recent Interpretations of Unionism', *Political Quarterly*, 61, 2: 188–99. In any case unconditional loyalty is only demanded by despotic rulers who can never be sure that their subjects are sincere when they profess it – a theme brilliantly explored in Xenophon's *Hiero* – see Leo Strauss, *On Tyranny* (London: Free Press, 1991). Thanks to R. Wintrobe.

107  See, for example, the Northern Ireland Constitutional Convention (1975); and the Democratic Unionist Party, *Ulster: The Future Assured* (Belfast: DUP, 1984). Sir James Craig used similar spurious arguments to reject a proportional electoral system in the 1920s, O'Leary and McGarry, *The Politics of Antagonism*, 121.

108  Bill Craig suggested a temporary power-sharing deal with the SDLP at the Constitutional Convention of 1976. He justified it as compatible with the Westminster model of government, which had allowed temporary coalitions during the depression and two world wars.

109  Some of the 'principled' unionist supporters of majority-rule in Northern Ireland supported 'minority-rule' in South Africa. When unionists invited the South African Ambassador, Dennis Worrall, to speak to them they were disappointed when he announced he was in favour of power-sharing, Adrian Guelke, 'The Political Impasse in South Africa and Northern Ireland: A Comparative Perspective', paper presented at IPSA World Congress, Washington, DC, 28 August – 1 September 1988. The Convention report which outlined unionists' 'democratic arguments' against power-sharing managed to contain a plea for a federal United Kingdom – to protect Northern Ireland's Protestant 'minority' from the Westminster government – an argument which rests on an unacknowledged criticism of majority-rule.

110  Paul Arthur and Keith Jeffrey, *Northern Ireland since 1968* (Oxford: Basil Blackwell, 1988), 52. The instrumental approach to voting rules which all unionists display is evident in their advocacy of the d'Hondt rule for allocating committee chairships and seats in any future Northern Ireland Assembly. Unlike other proportionality rules, such as the Sainte-Laguë rule, d'Hondt is biased towards larger parties, see Brendan O'Leary et al., *Northern Ireland: Sharing Authority* (London: IPPR, 1993), Appendix B. See also chapter 10, below.

111  See, for example, Brian Barry, *Sociologists, Economists and Democracy* (Chicago: Chicago University Press, 1978). Culturalists, of course, reply that institutions are condensations of cultures; they are codified norms rather than rationalist rules.

112  Barrington Moore, Jr, *The Social Origins of Dictatorship and Democracy: Lord and Peasant in the Making of the Modern World* (Boston: Beacon Press, 1966), 486.

113  Rene Lemarchand, 'Burundi in Comparative Perspective', in John McGarry and Brendan O'Leary (eds), *The Politics of Ethnic Conflict Regulation: Case Studies of Protracted Ethnic Conflicts* (London: Routledge, 1993), 151–71.

114  Some anthropologists maintain that the clans of Somalia are like this. Thanks to Peter Loizos

115  Richard Rose, *Governing without Consensus*, 324. Protestants and Catholics

had much the same likes and dislikes about Northern Ireland, similar views on emigration, trade unions, big business, authority and class. They even displayed similar degrees of difference from or closeness to the English and the southern Irish.

116 'Our "authentic" and well-manicured cultural traditions frequently seem indistinguishable or cross-bred to "outsiders"', Keith Robbins, 'Varieties of Britishness', in Maurna Crozier (ed.), *Cultural Traditions in Northern Ireland: Varieties of Britishness* (Belfast: Institute of Irish Studies, Queen's University, 1990), 5.

117 'In many respects the peoples of the different parts of the United Kingdom are very similar in their social characteristics . . . Even in Northern Ireland, similarities between Protestants and Catholics greatly outnumber differences', Richard Rose, 'The Constitution; Are We Studying Devolution or Break-Up?', in Denis Kavanagh and Richard Rose (eds), *New Trends in British Politics: Issues for Research* (London: Sage, 1977), 34.

118 Michael Ignatieff, *Blood and Belonging: Journeys into the New Nationalism* (London: Chatto and Windus, 1993), 14ff.

119 'One of the classic complaints about Irish politics . . . is that men who have at one time espoused idealistic causes have been only too ready to turn to the machinations of machine politicians, and adopt policies showing too much regard to their personal and private fortunes', Rose, *Governing without Consensus*, 454.

120 Adrian Guelke, 'Loyalist and Republican Perceptions of the Northern Ireland Conflict: the UDA and the Provisional IRA', in Peter Merkl (ed.), *Political Violence and Terror: Motifs and Motivations* (Berkeley: University of California Press, 1986); and *Northern Ireland: the International Perspective* (Dublin: Gill and Macmillan, 1988), ch. 2.

121 Declan Kiberd, 'The Elephant of Revolutionary Forgetfulness', in M. N. Dhonnchadha and T. Dorgan (eds), *Revising the Rising* (Derry: Field Day, 1991), 13.

122 D. J. Hickey and J. E. Doherty, *A Dictionary of Irish History* (Dublin: Gill and Macmillan, 1980), 73.

123 F. S. L. Lyons, *Ireland since the Famine* (Glasgow: Fontana, 1973), 467–8. Lyons's figure is the more credible of the two.

124 Brendan O'Leary and John McGarry, *The Politics of Antagonism: Understanding Northern Ireland* (London: Athlone, 1993), chs 3 and 4.

125 '[I]t is not always when things are going from bad to worse that revolutions break out. On the contrary, it oftener happens that when a people which has put up with oppressive rule over a long period without protest suddenly finds the government relaxing its pressure, it takes up arms against it . . . [T]he most perilous moment for a bad government is one when it seeks to mend its ways . . . [Oppressive rule] patiently endured so long as it seemed beyond redress . . . comes to seem intolerable once the possibility of removing it crosses men's minds', Alexis de Tocqueville, *The Ancien Régime and the French Revolution*, trans. Stuart Gilbert (London: Collins/Fontana, 1966), 196.

126 Rose, *Governing without Consensus*.

127 C. Tilly, *From Mobilisation to Revolution* (Reading, Mass.: Addison-Wesley, 1978). Other names for the same body of ideas include 'resource-mobilization' theory, political process theory, political contention theory and strategic interaction theory. This approach also rejects relative deprivation theory, and avoids the difficulties with the narrowly individualist rational-choice approach to explaining political violence, see chapter 7.

128 James B. Rule, *Theories of Civil Violence* (London: University of California Press, 1988), 184ff. We have added an additional assumption, the last one, which we believe is consistent with the realism of this school of thought.

129 See the researches of Robert White on republican paramilitaries: 'Commitment, Efficacy and Personal Sacrifice among Irish Republicans', *Journal of Political and Military Sociology*, 16 (1988), 77–90; 'From Peaceful Protest to Guerrilla War – Micromobilization of the Provisional Irish Republican Army', *American Journal of Sociology*, 94, 6: 1277–1302; and Terry Falkenberg White, 'Revolution in the City: On the Resources of Urban Guerrillas', *Terrorism and Political Violence*, 3, 4 (1991), 100–32. Analysts also maintain that loyalist paramilitaries are representative of their working-class constituencies; with a few exceptions such as the Shankill butchers, they are not psychopathic deviants, see Sarah Nelson, *Ulster's Uncertain Defenders: Loyalists in the Northern Ireland Conflict* (Belfast: Appletree Press, 1984); and Steve Bruce, *The Red Hand: Protestant Paramilitaries in Northern Ireland* (Oxford: Oxford University Press, 1992). Given that able working-class Protestants have the chance to fight for their cause legally, through joining the RUC or the RIR, one might, however, anticipate that loyalist paramilitary organizations have had, at the margins, a less talented pool of potential recruits than their republican counterparts.

130 The liberal Chairman of the Alliance Party, Dr Philip McGarry, who, given his moderate political beliefs, might be expected to endorse the thesis of the atypicality of extremists, in fact maintains that most paramilitaries are normal, representative of their working-class communities. They see themselves as soldiers in their respective national causes. (Discussion with B. O'Leary, September 1994.)

131 Schellenberg found that population-density and the proportion of Catholics within his chosen 34 sub-districts of Northern Ireland were significantly positively correlated with deaths – in short, urbanity and Catholicism were good predictors of high levels of political violence; while Mitchell found that the death-rate in areas with Catholic majorities is six times as high as in areas which are over 80 per cent Protestant, and is twice as high as in areas with large Catholic minorities (although his unit of analysis was not precisely specified). Murray, by contrast, found that the sub-districts with the highest death-rates have a Catholic majority within a set of adjacent territories with Catholic majorities – such as sub-districts contiguous to the border with the Republic of Ireland. However, Belfast clearly does not fit this story. Poole established that in the 27 towns with a population of over 5,000 in 1971 the total number of Catholics was the best single predictor of the level of the death-rate. In short, the ethnic demography of a town is the key factor in explaining inter-urban variations in violence, whereas in rural areas proximity to the border is an important explanation of variations in death-rates, see J. A. Schellenberg, 'Area Variations in Violence in Northern Ireland', *Sociological Focus*, 10 (1977), 69–78; J. K. Mitchell, 'Social Violence in Northern Ireland', *Geographical Review* (1979), 179–200; Russell Murray, 'Political Violence in Northern Ireland 1969–1977', in F. W. Boal and J. N. H. Douglas (eds), *Integration and Division: Geographical Perspectives on the Northern Ireland Problem* (London: Academic Press, 1982); Michael Poole, 'The Demography of Violence', in John Darby (ed.), *Northern Ireland: the Background to the Conflict* (Belfast: Appletree Press, 1983), table 7.3; and also 'The Geographical Location of Political Violence in Northern Ireland', in J. Darby, N. Hodge and A. C. Hepburn (eds), *Political Violence: Ireland in a Comparative Perspective* (Belfast: Appletree Press, 1990), 64–82.

132 Needless to say we are not seeking to deny that emotions, including fear and

loathing, play a role in accounting for political violence. Our point is that the timing and use of premeditated violence has instrumental functions.

133 Brendan O'Leary and John McGarry, *The Politics of Antagonism: Understanding Northern Ireland* (London: Athlone, 1993), chs 3 and 4.

134 See chapter 10.

135 MacDonagh, *States of Mind*, 66.

136 We embrace what has been called the 'inherent' rather than the 'contingent' approach to explaining collective political violence, see 'Explaining Collective Political Violence', in Harry Eckstein, *Regarding Politics: Essays on Political Theory, Stability and Change* (Berkeley: University of California Press, 1992), 304–42.

137 Leo Kuper maintains that Northern Ireland is non-genocidal because paramilitaries are obliged to respond to the cultural values of the societies from which they emanate, *Genocide: Its Political Use in the Twentieth Century* (Harmondsworth: Penguin, 1981).

138 Readers who want 'what it's really like' accounts of local prejudices, hatreds and fears should read psychologist Geoffrey Beattie's *We are the People: Journeys through the Heart of Protestant Ulster* (London: Mandarin, 1993). The supremacism of local Ulster Protestant culture comes through strongly in this text, though its anecdotal nature is problematic. For British soldiers' prejudices see Max Arthur, *Soldiers Talking* (London: Sidgwick and Jackson, 1988).

139 See Seamus Deane's astringent review of British perceptions of Ireland, *Civilians and Barbarians* (Derry: Field Day, 1983).

### Chapter 7 Mammon and Utility: Liberal Economic Reasoning

1 *Belfast Telegraph*, 5 May 1969.

2 *Fortnight*, 276 (1989).

3 'Making a Killing: The High Cost of Peace in Northern Ireland', *Harpers Magazine*, 288, 1725 (February 1994), 46; see also Peter Hitchens, *International Express*, 9–15 February 1994, 7; and Paul Clare, 'Subcultural Obstacles to the Control of Racketeering in Northern Ireland', *Conflict Quarterly*, X, 4 (1990), 30.

4 Garret FitzGerald, *Towards a New Ireland* (London: Charles Knight, 1972), 112–13.

5 Rationality is conceived of by most economists, as well as by most liberals, as the maximization of individual utility. This conception does not tell us what the individual is interested in, or what s/he gets utility from. Individuals' interests are conceived of as individualistic, in liberal political theory, rather than formed in society through identification with particular values, beliefs and communities – see, for example, Margaret Moore, *Foundations of Liberalism* (Oxford: Clarendon Press, 1993). This strictly individualist liberalism generally assumes that self-interest is material rather than cultural or communitarian.

6 Daniel Moynihan, *Pandaemonium: Ethnicity in International Relations* (Oxford: Oxford University Press, 1993), 55. Moynihan was referring to an earlier criticism he made with Nathan Glazer about the tendencies of liberals and socialists to wish ethnicity away – 'Introduction', in Nathan Glazer and Daniel Moynihan (eds), *Ethnicity: Theory and Experience* (Cambridge, Mass.: Harvard University Press, 1975), 16.

7 Seymour Martin Lipset, 'The Changing Class Structure and Contemporary European Politics', *Daedalus*, 93 (1964), 271–303.

8 Among the more fashionable of the liberal explanations of current ethnic conflict is 'long-wave' theory, which suggests that we are at the trough of

a 45–60 year economic cycle. As one leading advocate puts it, during this trough, 'politically, society enters the parochial phase. People are now out for themselves. Many believe the only way to improve their own stations or that of their social, ethnic or religious group is at the expense of others. "If the pie is shrinking, I must get a bigger slice for myself just to stay even."' John Sterman, 'Caught by the Long Wave', *Globe and Mail*, 20 February 1993, B4.

9    See, *inter alia*, Nathan Glazer, *Ethnic Dilemmas, 1964–1982* (Cambridge, Mass.: Harvard University Press, 1983); and *Affirmative Discrimination: Ethnic Inequality and Public Policy* (Cambridge, Mass.: Harvard University Press, 1987).

10   Around one-quarter of SDLP supporters believe the conflict is caused by unemployment and discrimination, see Cynthia Irvin and Edward Moxon-Browne, 'Not many Floating Voters Here', *Fortnight*, 273 (1989), 7–9.

11   *Fortnight*, 274 (June 1989), 8.

12   Derek Birrell, 'Relative Deprivation as a Factor in conflict in Northern Ireland', *Sociological Review*, 20, 3 (1972), 317–44.

13   David Smith and Gerald Chambers, *Inequality in Northern Ireland* (Oxford: Clarendon Press, 1991).

14   Ibid., 1–3, 368.

15   Ibid., 161–2, 212.

16   See table 3.2, pp. 110, above.

17   Smith and Chambers, *Inequality in Northern Ireland*, 12.

18   Ibid., 75–7.

19   Ibid., 56.

20   'This type of thinking is probably important in explaining the rise of Paisleyism during 1964–68 and the reaction against O'Neill. The aim was to combat the threat to their marginal advantages over working-class Catholics', Birrell, 'Relative Deprivation as a Factor in Conflict in Northern Ireland', 331. Compare Birrell's explanation of Paisleyism with Bruce's suggestion that Paisleyism was a religious phenomenon, not a materialist one.

21   Geoffrey Bell, *The Protestants of Ulster* (London: Pluto, 1976); David Boulton, *The UVF 1966–73: An Anatomy of Loyalist Rebellion* (Dublin: Gill and Macmillan, 1973); Michael MacDonald, *Children of Wrath: Political Violence in Northern Ireland* (Cambridge: Polity, 1986).

22   *Fortnight*, 316 (1993), 29–30.

23   For details on the disparities between Northern Ireland and the rest of the United Kingdom, see Smith and Chambers, *Inequality in Northern Ireland*, 51–2.

24   Marxists also claim that deprivation can cause instability, but prescribe revolution rather than economic growth as the solvent.

25   Bob Rowthorn and Naomi Wayne, *Northern Ireland: the Political Economy of Conflict* (Cambridge: Polity, 1988), 124.

26   In the summer of 1993, former Northern Ireland Office minister Michael Mates urged cuts in public expenditure in Northern Ireland so that 'people would be pressing for a settlement', *Fortnight*, 320 (1993), 33.

27   According to Robin Wilson, IRA violence was the result of failures to reform the state's security apparatus 'and the pursuit to theoretical destruction of neo-liberal social and economic policies that sustain[ed] the IRA campaign in the face of palpable war-weariness', *Fortnight*, 314 (1993), 5.

28   John Whyte, *Interpreting Northern Ireland* (Oxford: Oxford University Press, 1990), 53. See also Jonathan Bardon, *A History of Ulster* (Belfast: Blackstaff Press, 1992); Paul Clare, 'Subcultural Obstacles to the Control of Racketeering in Northern Ireland', 34; and John Simpson, 'Economic Development: Cause or

Effect in the Northern Ireland Conflict', in John Darby (ed.), *Northern Ireland: the Background to the Conflict* (Belfast: Appletree Press, 1983), 109.

29  Padraig O'Malley, *The Uncivil Wars: Ireland Today* (Belfast: Blackstaff Press, 1983), 246.

30  Andy Pollak (ed.), *A Citizen's Inquiry: the Opsahl Report on Northern Ireland* (Dublin: Lilliput Press, 1993), 80.

31  See, for example, Birrell, 'Relative Deprivation as a Factor in Conflict in Northern Ireland'.

32  James B. Rule, *Theories of Civil Violence* (London: University of California Press, 1988), ch. 7.

33  Ibid., 202.

34  Ibid., 206-7.

35  Mancur Olson, *The Logic of Collective Action* (Cambridge, Mass.: Harvard University Press, 1965).

36  Rational-choice explanations of social phenomena have become increasingly fashionable amongst political scientists, legal scholars and sociologists – though they have always been popular amongst economists. For a critical review see Patrick Dunleavy, *Democracy, Bureaucracy and Public Choice* (Brighton: Wheatsheaf, 1991).

37  *Fortnight*, 316 (April 1993), 30.

38  Brendan O'Duffy, 'Containment or Regulation? The British Approach to Ethnic Conflict in Northern Ireland', in John McGarry and Brendan O'Leary (eds), *The Politics of Ethnic Conflict Regulation* (London: Routledge, 1993), 132.

39  See B. O'Leary, T. Lyne, J. Marshall, and B. Rowthorn, *Northern Ireland: Sharing Authority* (London: Institute for Public Policy Research, 1993), 82.

40  Chris Ryder, *The RUC: A Force under Fire* (London: Mandarin, 1990), 126, 140; and Martin Dillon, *The Dirty War* (London: Arrow Books, 1991), 419.

41  Ryder, *The RUC: A Force under Fire*, 147.

42  See Clare, 'Subcultural Obstacles to the Control of Racketeering in Northern Ireland', 30.

43  Ibid., and see also Ryder, *The RUC: A Force Under Fire*, 215; Fintan Cronin, 'Extortion Rackets line UDA Coffers', *Irish Independent*, 11 November 1986; and 'Swindlers bankroll Workers' Party: the Official IRA is Alive, Armed, and on the Fiddle', *Irish Independent*, 20 August 1987; Fergal Keane, 'Mafia IRA', *Sunday Tribune*, 28 December 1985; Scott Anderson, 'Making a Killing: the High Cost of Peace in Northern Ireland', *Harpers Magazine*, 288, 1725 (February 1994), 46; and Peter Hitchens, *International Express*, 9–15 February 1994, 7.

44  Paddy Devlin, cited in Dillon, *The Dirty War*, 420.

45  Clare, 'Subcultural Obstacles to the Control of Racketeering in Northern Ireland', 29-30.

46  Irvin and Moxon-Browne, 'Not many Floating Voters Here', 7-9.

47  FitzGerald, *Towards a New Ireland*, 6.

48  Ibid., 161.

49  Ibid., 54.

50  DKM Economic Consultants, *The Economic Impact of the Northern Ireland Conflict* (Dublin: DKM, 1994), 13.

51  Keith Kyle, 'The Panorama Survey of Irish Opinion', *Political Quarterly*, 50, 1 (1979), 24-35.

52  Tom Wilson, *Ulster: Conflict and Consent* (Oxford: Blackwell, 1989), 283.

53  FitzGerald, *Towards a New Ireland*, 165; see also Fine Gael, *Ireland: Our Future Together* (Dublin: Fine Gael, 1979), 33.

54  Rowthorn and Wayne, *Northern Ireland: the Political Economy of Conflict*, 151.

55  Bob Rowthorn has since repudiated this analysis: the implosion in the Balkans persuaded him that when the chips are down national communities place national survival and collective values ahead of any narrow economic calculus (personal communication with the authors).

56  Tom Lyne, 'Ireland, Northern Ireland and 1992: the Barriers to Technocratic Anti-Partitionism', *Public Administration*, 68, 4 (1990), 417–33.

57  Ibid.

58  Fine Gael, *Ireland: Our Future Together*, 31–4; Rowthorn and Wayne, *Northern Ireland: the Political Economy of Conflict*, 157–8.

59  Wilson, *Ulster: Conflict and Consent*, 77. Unionists counter these arguments in two ways. On the one hand, they like to draw attention to the non-monetary debt Britain owes Northern Ireland. Ulster's sacrifice at the Somme and the number of Field-Marshals it has contributed to Britain's wars, when Irish Catholics were stabbing Britain in the back, form recurrent themes in unionist speeches. On the other hand, they argue that as nationals of a deprived part of a modern welfare state, the subvention is theirs by right, that its current size in part flows from past neglect, and that it is in any case probably exaggerated because it ignores the flow of investment funds from Northern Ireland to the United Kingdom – see ibid., 79–86.

60  See, for example, Wilson, *Ulster: Conflict and Consent*, 227; and O'Malley, *The Uncivil Wars: Ireland Today*, 90.

61  See, for example, the Cadogan Group, *Northern Limits: Boundaries of the Attainable in Northern Ireland Politics* (Belfast: Cadogan Group, 1992), especially the Appendix.

62  DKM Economic Consultants, 'The Economic Impact of the Northern Ireland Conflict', 13.

63  Lyne, 'Ireland, Northern Ireland and 1992'.

64  FitzGerald, *Towards a New Ireland*, 104–5.

65  See Etain Tannam, 'Trespassing on Borders? The Effect of the European Community on the Relationships between Northern Ireland and the Republic of Ireland: A Test of Neo-Functionalism', PhD thesis, London School of Economics and Political Science, University of London (1994).

66  FitzGerald, *Towards a New Ireland*, 110–11.

67  Ibid., 111–12.

68  Ibid., 108–09.

69  Greece has a land link, although this goes through the former Yugoslavia.

70  *Fortnight*, 284 (May 1990).

71  James Anderson and Ian Shuttleworth, 'Currency of Co-operation', *Fortnight*, 312 (December 1992), 18.

72  *Fortnight*, 307 (June 1992), 17–23.

73  Adrian Guelke, *Northern Ireland: the International Perspective* (Dublin: Gill and Macmillan, 1988).

74  *Fortnight*, 288 (October 1990), 11–12.

75  Cadogan Group, *Northern Limits* (Belfast: Cadogan Group, 1992); see also Denis Kennedy, 'Agreeable Aspiration?', *Fortnight*, 314 (February 1993), 24–5.

76  See Tom Hadden and Kevin Boyle, 'Fourth Dimension', *Fortnight*, 307 (June 1992), 25; Elizabeth Meehan, 'Citizens are Plural', *Fortnight*, 311 (November 1992), 13–14; David Martin, 'Cutting the Democratic Deficit', *Fortnight*, 284 (May 1990), 10–11.

77  See, *inter alia*, Ernest Wistrich, *After 1992: the United States of Europe* (London: Routledge, 1991), new and revised edition. In his futuristic Epilogue, Wistrich has Gabriella Bosconi re-elected as the President of the United States of

Europe in 2014, with 'Patrick Antrim', the first Protestant Taoiseach of the Irish Federation, elected as one of her running mates. In this scenario 'Antrim' has just successfully negotiated 'the re-unification of Ireland', while allowing Ulster to retain a constitutional link with Britain, 151. Political scientist Brian Walker maintains, by contrast, that European integration has exhausted the project of Irish nationalism and that of Ulster unionism, and will by-pass them, observing that 'one era is ending and another is beginning. Looking back, we will see that neither side achieved its ultimate objective [Irish unification or the restoration of majority rule at Stormont] but at least each had the satisfaction of seeing its opponents fail to achieve their goal', 'No More Dreary Steeples', *Fortnight*, 291 (1991), 13–14.

78  Walker Connor, 'The Seductive Lure of Economic Explanations ("Eco- or Ethno-Nationalism?")', in Walker Connor, *Ethnonationalism: the Quest for Understanding* (Princeton: Princeton University Press, 1994), 146.

79  Ibid., 153.

80  See Brendan O'Leary and John McGarry, *The Politics of Antagonism: Understanding Northern Ireland* (London: Athlone Press, 1993), 262, where we summarize the arguments of Smith and Chambers, *Inequality in Northern Ireland.*

81  Ibid., 263–5, where we initially presented some of the following points.

82  Paul Compton, 'The demographic background', in David Watt (ed.), *The Constitution of Northern Ireland* (London: Heinemann, 1981), 74–92. The suppositions in Compton's arguments have been refuted in many places – see, for example, Anthony Murphy and David Armstrong, *A Picture of the Catholic and Protestant Male Unemployed, Employment Equality Review, Research Report No. 2* (Belfast: Central Community Relations Unit, 1994), 83–4.

83  Smith and Chambers, *Inequality in Northern Ireland*, 156–60.

84  Ibid., table 5.6.

85  Ibid., 170.

86  Ibid., 171–5.

87  Ibid., 183–4.

88  A subsequent report commissioned by the Central Community Relations Unit of the Northern Ireland Office found that religion accounted for about half the male unemployment differential between the two communities. It maintained that these findings 'are robust and are consistent with the results of Smith and Chambers', see Murphy and Armstrong, *A Picture of the Catholic and Protestant Male Unemployed, Employment Equality Review, Research Report No. 2*, 65. By contrast, an unpublished paper presented at the same seminar used to launch Murphy and Armstrong's paper, attempted to maintain (on the basis of dynamic simulations) that one could account for all the variations between Protestant and Catholic male unemployment without invoking either direct or indirect discrimination, see Graham Gudgin and Richard Breen, 'Evaluation of the Ratio of Unemployment Rates as an Indicator of Fair Employment' (Belfast: unpublished paper, the authors). This absurd argument was dealt a double blow by the discussants: Professor Bob Rowthorn of Cambridge University pointed out that if correct, the paper presupposed a massive difference between Protestants and Catholics in emigration-rates – in which case it provided further evidence of very extensive indirect discrimination; whereas Professor Stephen Nichol of Oxford University observed that the paper relied upon an entirely unwarranted assumption about migration-rates, and if a more reasonable assumption was made then Gudgin and Breen's results became compatible with Murphy and Armstrong's – and those of Smith and Chambers. The lengths to which some economists and sociologists will

go to deny the obvious – the existence of direct and indirect discrimination – beggars unbelief (until one recalls that 'research' is often the servant of a political agenda).

89  O'Leary and McGarry, *The Politics of Antagonism: Understanding Northern Ireland*, 266–7.

90  Chris McCrudden, 'The Northern Ireland Fair Employment White Paper: a Critical Assessment', *Industrial Law Journal*, 17, 3 (1988), 162–81; and 'The Evolution of the Fair Employment (Northern Ireland) Act in Parliament', in John Hayes and Paul O'Higgins (eds), *Lessons from Northern Ireland* (Belfast: SLS, 1990), 57–79.

91  For a sensitive essay on the subject of recognition see Charles Taylor, 'The Politics of Recognition', in A. Gutmann (ed.), *Multiculturalism and 'The Politics of Recognition'* (Princeton: Princeton University Press), 25–74.

92  It may be that Smith and Chambers' arguments were circumscribed by the fact that they were policy advocates for reforming Northern Ireland, commissioned by a reformist body, the Standing Advisory Commission on Human Rights, and concerned to make their case effectively to a Conservative government then swimming in the high-tide of Thatcherite economics. See also note 96 below.

93  This is something unionist politicians appreciate. They constantly point out that republican and constitutional nationalist campaigns continue despite the settlement of [most of] the grievances of the Civil Rights Association. Where unionists get it wrong, on the other hand, is when they argue that the nationalist desire for recognition must be repressed rather than accommodated.

94  Smith and Chambers, *Inequality in Northern Ireland*, 44, 13, 11, 77.

95  Ibid., 89.

96  David Smith agrees that both collective recognition of northern nationalism and individual equality of opportunity are necessary for conflict-resolution in Northern Ireland (personal communication, June 1994). The work of Robert White, based on a careful set of interviews with republican paramilitaries, suggests that experience of repression at the hands of state officials, rather than unemployment or economic deprivation, best explains who gets mobilized into the IRA – Robert White, 'From Peaceful Protest to Guerilla War: The Micro-Mobilisation of the Provisional IRA, *American Journal of Sociology*, 94, 6 (1988), 1277–1302.

97  See, *inter alia*, Michael Poole, 'The Geographical Location of Political Violence in Northern Ireland', in John Darby, N. Hodge and A. C. Hepburn (eds), *Political Violence: Ireland in Comparative Perspective* (Belfast: Appletree Press, 1990), 64–82; and O'Leary and McGarry, *The Politics of Antagonism*, figure 1.

98  Work soon to be published by Geoffrey Evans and Mary Duffy of Nuffield College, Oxford University, demonstrates this beyond all reasonable doubt.

99  See Brendan O'Duffy, 'Violent Politics: A Theoretical and Empirical Examination of Two Centuries of Political Violence in Ireland', PhD thesis, London School of Economics and Political Science, University of London (1995).

100  This data is very crude, and simply tests whether the regional level of unemployment is correlated with the regional level of violence. More sophisticated tests would examine whether the spatial distribution of violence is linked to the spatial distribution of male unemployment or the spatial distribution of the growth in male unemployment. Our argument is, however, entirely consistent with Ian Budge and Cornelius O'Leary's pioneering historical investigation of Belfast's politics, in which they maintain that the nineteenth-century pattern of Protestant and Catholic rioting was politically rather than economically

determined, *Belfast: Approach to Crisis. A Study of Belfast Politics, 1613-1970* (London: Macmillan, 1973), 91-2.

101 Higher levels of employment might have reduced violence between Mondays and Fridays, according to Steve Bruce, who attributes part of the recent increases in loyalist paramilitary violence to high unemployment – when loyalists had jobs, they had to restrict their paramilitary activities to the weekends!, Steve Bruce, 'Alienation Once Again', *Fortnight*, 317 (May 1993), 18-19.

102 Christopher Hewitt, 'Catholic Grievances, Catholic Nationalism and Violence in Northern Ireland during the Civil Rights Period: a Reconsideration', *British Journal of Sociology*, 32, 3 (1981), 362-80.

103 See chapter 6, p. 257.

104 See, *inter alia*, Kevin Boyle, Tom Hadden, and Paddy Hillyard, *Ten Years On in Northern Ireland* (Nottingham: Coben Trust, 1980), 22-3, 199; and Robert White and Terry Falkenberg White, 'Revolution in the City: On the Resources of Urban Guerillas', *Terrorism and Political Violence*, 3, 4 (1991), 111.

105 Boyle, Hadden, and Hillyard, *Ten Years On in Northern Ireland*.

106 Robert White, 'From Peaceful Protest to Guerilla War'.

107 Ibid.

108 Ted Gurr, *Why Men Rebel* (Princeton: Princeton University Press, 1970).

109 Marc I. Lichbach, 'Deterrence or Escalation? The Puzzle of Aggregate Studies of Repression and Dissent', *Journal of Conflict Resolution*, 31, 2 (1987), 266-97.

110 Ibid.

111 For republicans, see *inter alia*, White and White, 'Revolution in the City: On the Resources of Urban Guerillas', 100-32; Robert White, 'Commitment, Efficacy and Personal Sacrifice among Irish Republicans', *Journal of Political and Military Sociology*, 16 (1988), 77-90; 'From Peaceful Protest to Guerilla War – Micromobilization of the Provisional Irish Republican Army'.

112 Patrick Bishop and Eamonn Mallie, *The Provisional IRA* (London: Heinemann, 1987), ch. 1.

113 Geoffrey Beattie, *We are the People: Journeys through the Heart of Protestant Ulster* (London: Mandarin, 1993), 31ff.

114 'The police also suspect that redundant terrorists will retrain as ordinary criminals', see 'No More Ordinary Decent Criminals', *The Economist*, 22 October 1994.

115 Anderson acknowledges that 'even its most bitter enemies concede that the Provisional IRA funnelled most of its money back into the war machine', by comparison with other paramilitary organizations, 'Making a Killing', 51. One acute observer of Ulster Protestants also maintains that it is a myth that the UDA and UVF are 'rich gangster organisations'. The rewards from protection money are meagre and have to be widely distributed: 'the professional criminals I've met in England wouldn't even entertain the risks for those returns', Beattie, *We are the People*, 29.

116 Anderson argues that collusion between republicans and loyalists over protection rackets is widespread and pervasive. He spoils his case by claiming that 'Belfast, I quickly discovered, is a very small and incestuous place, where the killers of one side often have links – *school, marriage, prison* – with the other', *Making a Killing*, 48 (our emphasis). Only sloppy research would 'reveal' that republican and loyalist paramilitaries have 'often' gone to school together, or that they are related by marriage. In prison they are segregated as long as they retain affiliations with their respective organizations.

117 See Ken Heskin, 'Societal Disintegration in Northern Ireland: A Five Year Update', *Economic and Social Review*, 16, 3 (1985), 187–99; and J. Van Dijk, P. Mayhew, and M. Killias, *Experience of Crime across the World: Key Findings of the 1989 International Crime Survey* (Cambridge, Massachusetts).

118 Bob Rowthorn has outlined how formulae for aid to Northern Ireland could work with appropriate incentives to economize on security under a system of shared authority, see O'Leary, Lyne, Marshall, and Rowthorn, *Northern Ireland: Sharing Authority*, Appendix D, and see also 71–82. However, such a 'security tax' could operate with other constitutional settlements.

119 Donald Horowitz, *Ethnic Groups in Conflict* (Berkeley: University of California Press, 1985), 131.

120 Nicholas Mansergh, *The Irish Question, 1840–1921* (Toronto: University of Toronto Press, 1965), 103.

121 Tom Garvin, *Nationalist Revolutionaries in Ireland 1858–1928* (Oxford: Clarendon Press, 1987).

122 Richard Rose, *Governing without Consensus* (London: Faber and Faber, 1971), 213, 299.

123 Wilson, *Ulster: Conflict and Consent*, 79.

124 Edward Moxon-Browne, *Nation, Class and Creed in Northern Ireland* (Aldershot: Gower, 1983), 38; and see the discussion in chapter 5, pp. 197–8, 199ff, above.

125 Rose, *Governing without Consensus*, 299.

126 In any case why should the British want to impose sanctions to force Protestants into a united Ireland?

127 See chapter 1, n. 83, p. 432.

128 W. Harvey Cox, 'Who wants a United Ireland?', *Government and Opposition*, 20, 1 (1985), 36.

129 Tom Wilson, *Ulster: Conflict and Consent*, 260; also see Cadogan Group, *Northern Limits: Boundaries of the Attainable in Northern Ireland Politics*, 17.

130 See the discussion in Tannam, 'Trespassing on Borders?'

131 See Edward Moxon-Browne, 'The Impact of the European Community', in B. Hadfield (ed.), *Northern Ireland: Politics and the Constitution* (Buckingham: Open University Press, 1992), 50–1.

132 Anderson and Shuttleworth, 'Currency of Co-operation', 19.

133 Interview with B. O'Leary, Derry/Londonderry, August 1990.

134 In March 1993, former DUP assembly-member Dr Clifford Smyth argued that after the fall of communism, the Vatican was poised to take over the world via the Maastricht Treaty, *Fortnight*, 316 (April 1993), 31.

135 In 1981 UDA leader John McMichael described the Anglo-Irish agenda to Padraig O'Malley: 'Instead of having political institutions like a Council of Ireland, they are trying to by-pass the Ulster people and make Northern Ireland more economically dependent on southern Ireland . . . Eventually, if things go the way they expect them to, the people of Northern Ireland will depend on the South for their natural gas supply and will be hooked up to the European electricity grid through the south . . . The next steps would be political frameworks emerging on an all-Ireland rather than on a UK basis', O'Malley, *The Uncivil Wars: Ireland Today*, 335.

136 Richard Cameron, *Self-Determination: the Question Ulster must Answer* (London: Ameron, n.d. but *circa* 1992).

137 See Peter Lynch, 'From Versailles to Maastricht: Nationalist and Regionalist Parties and European Integration', PhD thesis, London School of Economics and Political Science, University of London (1994).

138  Adrian Guelke, *Northern Ireland: the International Perspective* (Dublin: Gill and Macmillan, 1988).

### Chapter 8  No Place Apart: Comparative Political Analysis

1  Hugh Trevor Roper, 'The Lost Moments of History', *New York Review of Books*, 27 October 1988.
2  Richard Rose, *Governing without Consensus: An Irish Perspective* (London: Faber, 1971), 19.
3  John Hewitt, *Out of my Time* (Belfast, 1974), cited in Tom Nairn, *The Break-up of Britain* (London: Verso, 1981), 224.
4  Adrian Guelke, *Northern Ireland: the International Perspective* (Dublin: Gill and Macmillan, 1988).
5  See Richard Rose, 'Is the United Kingdom a State? Northern Ireland as a Test Case', in P. Madgwick and R. Rose (eds), *The Territorial Dimension in United Kingdom Politics* (London: Macmillan, 1982), 100–36.
6  Reginald Maudling, *Memoirs* (London: Sidgwick and Jackson, 1978), 185.
7  Ronald Weitzer, *Transforming Settler States* (Berkeley: University of California Press, 1990), 132. Weitzer claims that the Labour government hesitated to get involved in Northern Ireland because it did not want to provoke a unilateral declaration of independence as in Rhodesia, and that subsequent British governments hesitated to get involved in Rhodesia in the 1970s because they did not want another Northern Irish quagmire, 133, 104, 115.
8  Maria McGuire, *To Take Arms* (London: Macmillan, 1973), 103–4.
9  See Gerry Adams, *The Politics of Irish Freedom* (Dingle: Brandon Books, 1986), 5, 27, 28, 113, 118.
10  See Bill Rolston, *Drawing Support: Murals in the North of Ireland* (Belfast: Beyond the Pale Publications, 1992), plate 109, 58.
11  Richard Rose's otherwise fascinating comparison of Northern Ireland and the Deep South overlooks this difference, 'On the Priorities of Citizenship in the Deep South and Northern Ireland', *Journal of Politics*, 38, 2 (1976), 247–91.
12  See chapter 3, p. 98. It is interesting that Hitler's claim on the Sudetenland, recognized by Britain in 1938, is so often used to reject all irredentism. However, using any reasonable principle of self-determination it is clear that the Sudetenland should not have been incorporated as part of Czechoslovakia in 1919. The placement of the Sudetenland in Czechoslovakia, like the borders of Northern Ireland, is a good example of how power politics amongst the Allies at Versailles had more impact than the principle of self-determination.
13  Anthony Alcock, 'Northern Ireland: Some European Comparisons', in B. Hadfied (ed.), *Northern Ireland Politics and the Constitution* (Buckingham: Open University Press, 1992), 150, 160. These comparisons are, needless to say, contentious. Thus the Aland islands do not, and by law cannot, have any Finns resident on them, so no conflict can arise between Finns and Swedes on the islands themselves; the conflict in and over the Basque region of Spain and France has not been resolved, even though the French and Spanish states recognize each other's boundaries; and limited autonomy was granted to Corsica after large-scale settlement of the island by non-Corsicans, especially former *pieds noirs*, prompted separatist nationalism amongst native Corsicans.
14  Ibid., 151.
15  In the course of comparing Northern Ireland with Nagorno-Karabakh, Frank

Wright made apposite comments on Northern Irish readings of the fall of the Berlin Wall, 'Walls Aren't Easy to Do Without', *Fortnight*, 280, 16–17.

16  'Pluralist societies', i.e. entities in which there are many interests and democratic institutions, should not be confused with 'plural societies', i.e. divided (or parallel or segmented) societies. The latter are characterized by reinforcing rather than cross-cutting cleavages, see Patrick Dunleavy and Brendan O'Leary, *Theories of the State: the Politics of Liberal Democracy* (London: Macmillan, 1987), 71, 59–63.

17  Edmund Aunger, *In Search of Political Stability: A Comparative Study of New Brunswick and Northern Ireland* (Montreal: McGill–Queen's, 1981); Ian Budge and Cornelius O'Leary, *Belfast: Approach to Crisis* (London: Macmillan, 1973); Arend Lijphart, 'The Northern Ireland Problem: Cases, Theories, and Solutions', *British Journal of Political Science*, 5, 3 (1975), 83–106; *Democracy in Plural Societies* (New Haven: Yale University Press, 1977); and 'Consociation', in Desmond Rea (ed.), *Political Co-operation in Divided Societies: A Series of Papers Relevant to the Conflict in Northern Ireland* (Dublin: Gill and Macmillan, 1982); John McGarry, 'A Consociational Settlement for Northern Ireland', *Plural Societies*, xx, 1 (1990), 1–21; Brendan O'Leary, 'The Limits to Coercive Consociationalism in Northern Ireland', *Political Studies*, 37, 4 (1989), 562–88; Claire Sterling, *The Terror Network: the Secret War of International Terrorism* (New York: Holt, Rinehart and Winston, 1981); Dervla Murphy, *Changing the Problem: Post-Forum Reflections* (Gigginstown: Lilliput Press, 1984); Jack Holland, *The American Connection: US Guns, Money and Influence in Northern Ireland* (Swords: Poolbeg Press, 1987); Adrian Guelke, *Northern Ireland*; Ian Lustick, *State-Building Failure in British Ireland and French Algeria* (Berkeley: Institute of International Studies, 1985); Joseph Ruane and Jennifer Todd, '"Why Can't You Get Along with Each Other?" Culture, Structure and the Northern Ireland Conflict', in Eamonn Hughes (ed.), *Culture and Politics in Northern Ireland* (Buckingham: Open University Press, 1991), 27–44; Kevin Boyle and Tom Hadden, *Ireland: A Positive Proposal* (Harmondsworth: Penguin, 1985); Michael MacDonald, *Children of Wrath: Political Violence in Northern Ireland* (Oxford: Polity Press, 1986); and 'The Dominant Communities and the Costs of Legitimacy', in Hermann Giliomee and Jannie Gagiano (eds), *The Elusive Search for Peace: South Africa, Israel, Northern Ireland* (Cape Town: Oxford University Press, 1990), 33–53; Ronald Weitzer, *Transforming Settler States: Communal Conflict and Internal Security in Northern Ireland and Zimbabwe* (London: University of California Press, 1990); Barry Schutz and Douglas Scott, *Natives and Settlers: A Comparative Analysis of the Politics of Opposition and Mobilisation in Northern Ireland and Rhodesia* (Denver, Colorado: University of Denver, 1974); and Donald Akenson, *God's Peoples: Covenant and Land in South Africa, Israel and Ulster* (Ithaca, NY: Cornell University Press, 1992). We have discussed Akenson's analysis in chapter 5, pp. 181–2, 204–5.

18  'Multiple and politically inconsistent affiliations, loyalties, and stimuli reduce the emotion and aggressiveness involved in political choice. Where a man belongs to a variety of groups that all predispose him toward the same political choice, he is ... much less likely to be tolerant of other opinions ... The available evidence suggests that the chances for stable democracy are enhanced to the extent that groups and individuals have a number of crosscutting, politically relevant affiliations. To the degree that a significant proportion of the population is pulled among conflicting forces, its members have an interest in reducing the intensity of political conflict', Seymour Martin Lipset, *Political Man* (London: Hutchinson, 1960), 77–8.

19  Eric Nordlinger, *Conflict Regulation in Divided Societies* (Cambridge, Mass.: Harvard University Press, 1972), 93.
20  Rose, *Governing without Consensus*, 28.
21  Ibid., 41.
22  Aunger, *In Search of Political Stability*, 3.
23  Ibid., 184.
24  Ibid., 185.
25  Ibid., 14.
26  Ibid., i.
27  Budge and O'Leary, *Belfast*.
28  Lipset, *Political Man*, 12–13.
29  Budge and O'Leary, *Belfast*, 365.
30  Arend Lijphart, *Democracy in Plural Societies*.
31  Proportionality applies to both public employment and public expenditure – and may also apply to private-sector employment.
32  Brendan O'Leary and John McGarry, *The Politics of Antagonism: Understanding Northern Ireland* (London and Atlantic Heights, NJ: Athlone, 1993), chs 5–7.
33  Arend Lijphart, 'The Northern Ireland Problem: Cases, Theories, and Solutions'.
34  Lijphart, *Democracy and Plural Societies*, ch. 3; and 'Consociation', 183.
35  Here Lijphart follows Hans Daalder, 'The Consociational Democracy Theme', *World Politics*, 26 (1974), 604–21.
36  Lijphart, 'The Northern Ireland Problem; Cases, Theories and Solutions'; and *Democracy in Plural Societies*, 134–41.
37  Lijphart, 'The Northern Ireland Problem: Cases, Theories and Solutions', 99–100.
38  'By contrast [with the Netherlands], the division of Northern Ireland's people into two groups, with one permanently in the majority, removes the need or possibility of coalition groups with an alternation of groups in power', Rose, *Governing without Consensus*, 449. 'It seems clear that the division of Northern Ireland into two relatively distinct groups, one with permanent majority status and the other with permanent minority status, prevented the kind of coalition and compromise that would have been possible in a multi-communal political structure', David Schmitt, 'Bicommunalism in Northern Ireland', *Publius*, 18, 2 (1988), 40. These views support the old joke that the way to bring Protestants and Catholics together in Northern Ireland (or in Ireland) is to settle it with a large colony of black Muslims. Schmitt also suggests that unionist fears about a united Ireland are related to the imbalance of power that would develop in a united Ireland: these fears would be reduced 'were the Republic of Ireland socially divided into numerous groups in such a way that Unionists did not have to fear being a permanent minority', ibid.
39  Lijphart, 'The Northern Ireland Problem: Theories, Cases and Solutions', 100.
40  See Brendan O'Leary, Tom Lyne, Jim Marshal, and Bob Rowthorn, *Northern Ireland: Sharing Authority* (London: Institute of Public Policy Research, 1993).
41  See Brendan O'Leary, 'The Limits to Coercive Consociationalism in Northern Ireland', *Political Studies*, 37, 4 (1989), 562–88; and Paul Mitchell, 'Conflict Regulation and Party Competition in Northern Ireland', *European Journal of Political Research*, 20, 1 (1991), 67–92.
42  If the Northern Ireland Conservatives are included within the unionist bloc then unionists still have an electoral majority, and if the Alliance Party is included then unionists have a 60 per cent majority.

43   Lijphart calculates that the angle and index of cross-cutting between the religious and party cleavage systems in 1968 were both very low: 2° and 0.21 respectively, *Democracy in Plural Societies*, 135.
44   Lijphart, 'The Northern Ireland Problem: Theories, Cases and Solutions', 100.
45   Lijphart calculates that the angle of cross-cutting between religion and social class is 68° and that the index of cross-cutting equals 0.50, *Democracy in Plural Societies*, 138. These measures, based on 1960s data, indicate considerable, but not extreme, inequalities. See also chapter 7, pp. 269–70.
46   See chapter 7, pp. 269–70.
47   Adriano Pappalardo, 'The Conditions for Consociational Democracy: a Logical and Empirical Critique', *European Journal of Political Research*, 9 (1981), 379.
48   See, *inter alia*, Robert Fisk, *The Point of No Return: the Strike which Broke the British in Ulster* (London: André Deutsch, 1975), Richard Rose, *Northern Ireland: A Time of Choice* (London: Macmillan, 1976); Paul Bew and Henry Patterson, *The British State and the Ulster Crisis* (London: Verso, 1985); Cornelius O'Leary, Sidney Elliott, and Rick Wilford, *The Northern Ireland Assembly, 1982–1986: A Constitutional Experiment* (London: Hurst, 1988); and O'Leary and McGarry, *The Politics of Antagonism*, chs 6–7.
49   There is some evidence that the proportion of Catholics voting for nationalists is increasing, Brendan O'Leary, 'More Green, Fewer Orange', *Fortnight*, 282 (1990), 13; and there is also evidence of growth in the Catholic population, see chapter 10, n. 24, pp. 502–3.
50   See chapter 9.
51   Consociation is not extensively discussed in a deservedly influential book written by Kevin Boyle and Tom Hadden. They dismiss power-sharing as requiring 'a highly unrealistic degree of consensus', requiring politicians 'to agree on everything all of the time'; and as incapable of providing 'any mechanism for resolving the differences of opinion that are bound to arise within a cabinet or executive', *Ireland*, 49, 73, 84. These are rather Anglocentric legalistic judgements: if they were true, much of western Europe would have been ungovernable in the post-war period. Power-sharing may not be capable of working in Northern Ireland, but its fragile prospects are more deeply-rooted than these obstacles.
52   Arend Lijphart, *Power-Sharing in South Africa* (Berkeley: University of California Press, 1985).
53   Stephen Ryan overstates the case when he declares that consociational theory 'ignore[s] the international setting within which attitudes of elites and nonelites are formed', *Ethnic Conflict and International Relations* (Aldershot: Dartmouth, 1990), 21, 26. Consociational theory does allow some importance to the international environment. Common external threats are said to facilitate consociation, and Lijphart recognizes that the Lebanese consociational experiment fell apart partly because of an 'unfavourable international environment', *Democracy in Plural Societies*, 154. None the less, Ryan correctly implies that consociational theory tends to treat individual states as closed entities, stressing endogenous factors and putting relatively little weight on exogenous influences. For example, in the Lebanon, perhaps the clearest case of an internal arrangement being wrecked by international interference, Lijphart maintains that the 'main' problem was the inflexible institutionalization of consociational principles, ibid., 149.
54   J. Whyte, *Interpreting Northern Ireland* (Oxford: Clarendon Press, 1990), 203.
55   See, for example, J. Rosenau (ed.), *Linkage Politics: Essays on the Convergence*

*of National and International Systems* (New York: Free Press, 1969); A. Suhrke and L. Garner Noble (eds), *Ethnic Conflict in International Relations* (New York: Praeger, 1977); and Stephen Ryan, *Ethnic Conflict and International Relations*.

56    Sterling, *The Terror Network*, 1; Holland, *The American Connection, passim*.

57    Guelke, *Northern Ireland*; see also Ryan, *Ethnic Conflict and International Relations*, 28-9. Whyte discussed Guelke's text in his chapter on 'internal-conflict' interpretations, *Interpreting Northern Ireland*, 200-1 – even though Guelke's argument focuses on the exogenous causes of the conflict.

58    See, for example, Boyle and Hadden, *Ireland*; Murphy, *Changing the Problem*; O'Leary and McGarry, *The Politics of Antagonism*; O'Leary, Lyne, Marshall and Rowthorn, *Northern Ireland*; Joe Ruane and Jennifer Todd, '"Why Can't You Get Along with Each Other?" Culture, Structure and the Northern Ireland Conflict'.

59    'Through crisis after crisis, through rebellion and defeat, through a century and a half marked by famine and war, Ireland's exiled generations in America have provided the protesters, often the passion, and usually the material to enable Irish rebels to continue their quest for the imagined republic', Holland, *The American Connection*, 1. Holland's position is tempered by comparison with other versions of the influence of the USA on violence in Northern Ireland. One of the authors remembers a Protestant shopper expressing her fears to a TV news journalist that Ronald Reagan's election in 1980 could only provide a boost to the IRA, given his 'Republican' affiliations. One American has been cited saying that 'All the money that keeps the violence in Northern Ireland going comes from the United States. It is the Kennedys who finance the IRA and Bob Jones University gives money to the Protestants'!, *Fortnight*, 312 (1992), 54.

60    *The Terror Network*, 156.

61    Ibid., 156.

62    M. Tugwell, 'Politics and Propaganda of the Provisional IRA', in P. Wilkinson (ed.), *British Perspectives on Terrorism* (London: Allen and Unwin, 1981), 24.

63    Guelke, *Northern Ireland*, 13.

64    M. McKinley, 'The International Dimensions of Terrorism in Ireland', in Yonah Alexander and Alan O'Day (eds), *Terrorism in Ireland* (London: Croom Helm, 1984), 6.

65    See, for example, 'The South African Link', *Sunday News*, 24 July 1983, cited in Guelke, *Northern Ireland*, 211.

66    C. Johnson, 'The National Front and the Ulster Connection', *Fortnight*, 242 (1986), 7-8.

67    See, for instance, Tugwell, 'Politics and Propaganda of the Provisional IRA', 23; Alexander, 'Terror International: the PLO-IRA Connection', in *American Professors for Peace in the Middle East: Bulletin* (1979), 3; Sterling, *The Terror Network*.

68    Guelke, *Northern Ireland*, 17. For a review, see Brendan O'Leary, 'Northern Ireland through the Telescope', *Irish Times*, 3 February 1989.

69    The international consensus on the determination of self-determination defines the 'self' as the territorial majority at the time of decolonization. The partition of decolonized entities, as happened in Ireland in 1921, is, therefore, frowned upon; see also Stephen Ryan, *Ethnic Conflict and International Relations*, 28.

70    Guelke, *Northern Ireland*, 3.

71    Ibid., 17-20.

72    Murphy, *Changing the Problem*, 9.

73    Ibid.

74  Boyle and Hadden also draw attention to the willingness of southern political elites to put separation from Britain ahead of Irish unity, as indicated by their rejection of the Government of Ireland Act, withdrawal from the Commonwealth, and declaration of a Republic.

75  Boyle and Hadden, *Ireland*, 63.

76  See Kevin Boyle, 'Northern Ireland: Allegiances and Identities', in Bernard Crick (ed.), *National Identities: the Constitution of the United Kingdom* (Oxford: Basil Blackwell), 69, 78. Boyle and Hadden have since tempered their Euro-enthusiasm, see Kevin Boyle and Tom Hadden, *Northern Ireland: the Choice* (Harmondsworth: Penguin, 1994).

77  Ruane and Todd, '"Why Can't You Get Along with Each Other?" Culture, Structure and the Northern Ireland Conflict', 39; Boyle and Hadden, *Ireland*, 17–18.

78  Frank Wright, *Northern Ireland: A Comparative Analysis* (Dublin: Gill and Macmillan), 276–7, 282–3 and 285.

79  Ibid., 219–20. 'Switzerland's recognised eternal neutrality and Belgium's sovereignty guaranteed by Great Power Treaty in 1830 may have made it much easier to avoid getting caught up in the external dependency syndrome, which once created generates endless reasons for itself', 219. Wright also believes that intra-Canadian relations might have been severely damaged by de Gaulle's 'Vive le Québec libre!' speech in 1967, had it not been for the distance, in all senses, between Quebec and France, 276.

80  Wright cites, approvingly, Raymond Pearson's judgement that 'The principal lesson to be drawn from continental experience, steadily reinforced as the century progressed, was that nationalist successes depended less on who you were than *where* you were', Raymond Pearson, *National Minorities in Eastern Europe 1848–1945* (London: Macmillan, 1983), 91.

81  Wright, *Northern Ireland*, xiv–xv. Joint authority 'would be the only way in which both internal communities could relate to the state power in symmetrical ways', ibid., 220. See also Frank Wright, 'Northern Ireland and the British–Irish Relationship', *Studies*, 78 (1989), 151–62.

82  See, for example, Karl Deutsch, *Nationalism and Social Communications* (New York: Technology Press of MIT, 1953); Karl Marx and Friedrich Engels, *The Communist Manifesto* (Harmondsworth: Penguin, 1967); Charles Tilly (ed.), *The Formation of National States in Western Europe* (Princeton: Princeton University Press, 1975); Seymour Martin Lipset and Stein Rokkan, 'Cleavage Structures, Party Systems, and Voter Alignments: An Introduction', in S. M. Lipset and S. Rokkan (eds), *Party Systems and Voter Alignments: Cross-National Perspectives* (New York: Free Press, 1967), 1–64.

83  We elaborate this argument in O'Leary and McGarry, *The Politics of Antagonism*.

84  Lustick, *State-Building Failure in British Ireland and French Algeria*. Michael MacDonald also emphasizes settler colonialism in explaining the historic origins of the contemporary conflict, and, like Lustick, also stresses the differences between administrative and settler colonialism, and the complex dialectic between settler insecurity, native insurgence, and metropolitan failures to generate legitimate structures of government, *Children of Wrath*.

85  Lustick, *State-Building Failure in British Ireland and French Algeria*, 5.

86  Ibid., 37.

87  Ibid., i.

88  His argument can be seen as an attack on the nationalist and green Marxist premise that Britain is the obstacle to a national reconciliation in Ireland, a

view once summed up by Liam de Paor: '"Planters and natives" can undoubtedly come to an agreement in Ireland . . . What keeps the sterile quarrel of Orange and Green alive is the constant pressure of the third party, Great Britain', *Divided Ulster* (Harmondsworth: Penguin, 1970), xix–xx.

89   His approach is, however, also incompatible with unionist accounts – especially those which deny any similarities between Ireland and Algeria; see, for example, Hugh Roberts, *Northern Ireland and the Algerian Analogy: A Suitable Case for Gaullism?* (Belfast: Athol Books, 1986).

90   The stark differences between Lustick and Roberts can be seen in their contrasting accounts of the settlers' attitudes towards Catholic emancipation and the Act of Union. Here is Lustick, 'As soon as the Union was established, the Protestant opponents of the scheme joined with those leaders of the ascendancy who had favoured it to reorganise the defence of their dominant position in Ireland. Now, under the banner of a Union, sacred and eternal, whose integrity Catholic emancipation would threaten, Irish peers and the Orange Order lobbied hard in England to mobilise "no-popery" opinion, stiffen opposition to the measure by the king, and encourage high-ranking sympathetic peers to act on their behalf against Emancipation . . . Pitt and his associates succumbed to pressure from Irish Protestants and the anti-Catholic inclinations of the king', *State-Building Failure in British Ireland and French Algeria*, 37. Roberts argues, on the other hand, that it was Britain's decision to improve the lot of Catholics that swung Protestant opinion behind the Act of Union, 'since Westminster seemed resolved at last on a policy of progressive reform in Ireland, and was no longer engaged in propping up the corrupt Ascendancy in the South, the Protestants of Ulster decided that their own democratic objectives would be best served by the union', *Northern Ireland and the Algerian Analogy*, 62. After 1800, Ulster Protestants continued to support 'the Emancipation movement, because their own democratic principles would not allow them not to do so', 63. Readers must wonder if the two authors are writing about the same lands.

91   Lustick, *State-Building Failure in British Ireland and French Algeria*, 84.

92   Lustick's aim was to demonstrate that Israel's settlement of the West Bank with Jews will create tremendous obstacles to a peaceful settlement in this region. Although the settlers number only around 125,000 people, their ability to disrupt the Israeli–Palestinian peace process is already evident.

93   See Schutz and Scott, *Natives and Settlers*; MacDonald, *Children of Wrath*; Weitzer, *Transforming Settler States*; 'The Harsh Fact is that Ulster is a "Settler" Problem', *Sunday Times*, 10 April 1988.

94   Weitzer, *Transforming Settler States*, 30 (our emphasis). This does not mean that settler–native conflicts are the only intense type of ethnic conflict. Other competitive ethnic groups, which do not 'enjoy' native–settler relationships, past or present, are also capable of developing profound antagonisms, based on a range of historic and present differences.

95   Robert A. Williams Jnr, in a lucid and powerful work of historical jurisprudence, shows the extent to which the Elizabethan colonial projects for Ireland drew upon Spanish colonial doctrine and practices in the Americas, and also that the English genocidal, exclusionary and enserfing management of the 'savage Irish' in turn influenced the elimination and control of North American Indians, Robert A. Williams Jnr, *The American Indian in Western Legal Thought: The Discourses of Conquest* (New York: Oxford University Press, 1990).

96   MacDonald maintains that settlers must practise dominance for existential reasons – it is vital for their survival that they maintain solidaristic dominance, 'The Dominant Communities and the Costs of Legitimacy', 38–9.

97 Policy-makers are still trying to deal with the effects of the seventeenth-century colonial conquest and settlement. Unionist apologists never link Catholics' relatively impoverished background to the plantation, the English conquests of the seventeenth century or the various pieces of punitive legislation that resulted from it. Instead, they maintain that inequality results from the fecklessness of the natives, their willingness to have large families and their inferior educational qualifications. Similar arguments are used by whites in North America to explain why they are better off than native Indians.

98 MacDonald, *Children of Wrath*.

99 Weitzer, *Transforming Settler States*; Schutz and Scott, *Natives and Settlers*.

100 Ian Lustick, *Unsettled States, Disputed Lands: Britain and Ireland, France and Algeria and the West-Bank-Gaza* (New York: Cornell University Press, 1993).

101 'In settler societies, however, class interests are often neutralised by caste interests', Weitzer, *Transforming Settler States*, 50; and see also MacDonald, *Children of Wrath*, 15–16.

102 Weitzer, *Transforming Settler States*, 10–11, 92; MacDonald, *Children of Wrath*, ch. 1, *passim*.

103 Ibid.

104 Louis Hartz, *The Founding of New Societies: Studies in the History of the United States, Latin America, South Africa, Canada and Australia* (New York: Harcourt, Brace and World, 1955).

105 Rose, *Governing without Consensus*, 74.

106 Walker Connor comments on the cross-pressure thesis: 'such a prognostication ignores the evidence offered by several ethnonational separatist movements, that the well-springs of national identity are more profound than are those associated with religion, class and the like, and may, therefore, not be susceptible to sufficient amelioration, because of other shared interests, to preserve the state', 'A Nation is a Nation, is a State, is an Ethnic Group, is a . . . ', *Ethnic and Racial Studies*, 1, 4 (1978), 392. See also Nordlinger, *Conflict Regulation in Divided Societies*, 97; and Donald Horowitz, *Ethnic Groups in Conflict* (Berkeley: University of California Press, 1985), 334.

107 See chapter 5. The weakening of religious divisions between Canadian Francophones and Anglophones as a result of secularization has not reduced ethnic conflict in Quebec. On the contrary, secularization, by removing an important cultural barrier against 'Anglicization', heightened the insecurity of the Quebecois and intensified their quarrel with 'les Anglos'. The Quebec separatist movement dates from the time, the 1960s, when, according to cross-pressure theory, there should have been increasing integration and stability.

108 Aunger, for example, argues that cross-cutting cleavages are a pre-requisite for political stability.

109 On Canada, Fiji, and Malaysia, see the contributions by Sid Noel, Ralph Premdas and Dianne Mauzy to John McGarry and Brendan O'Leary (eds), *The Politics of Ethnic Conflict Regulation: Case Studies of Protracted Ethnic Conflicts* (London: Routledge, 1993).

110 Lijphart, *Democracy in Plural Societies*; Nordlinger, *Conflict Regulation in Divided Societies*.

111 Francophones constitute around 26 per cent of the Canadian population, yet they are proportionately represented in the federal cabinet, supreme court and public services. Most Francophones also enjoy cultural autonomy – through their control of the provincial government of Quebec – and until 1982 they possessed an informal veto over constitutional change. In addition, the offices of Chief Justice and Governor-General, as well as the leadership of the Liberal

Party, have normally been alternated between members of the two language groups.

112 See O'Leary and McGarry, *The Politics of Antagonism*, ch. 6.

113 Another reason given by Lijphart to explain why unionists reject power-sharing, namely their cultural commitment to majority rule on grounds of democratic principle, should be treated sceptically, as we have argued in chapter 6, see pp. 248-9 above.

114 Debate over the merits and defects of consociational theory has been extensive amongst political scientists. See, *inter alia*, Brian Barry, 'Political Accommodation and Consociational Democracy', *British Journal of Political Science*, 5 (1975), 477–505; and 'The Consociational Model and Its Dangers', *European Journal of Political Research*, 3 (1975), 393–412; Hans Daalder, 'The Consociational Democracy Theme'; Sue Halpern, 'The Disorderly Universe of Consociational Democracy', *West European Politics*, 9, 2 (1986) 181–97; Kenneth McRae (ed.), *Consociational Democracy: Political Accommodation in Segmented Societies* (Toronto: McLellan and Stewart, 1974); Eric Nordlinger, *Conflict Regulation in Divided Societies*; Adriano Pappalardo, 'The Conditions for Consociational Democracy: a Logical and Empirical Critique', *European Journal of Political Research*, 9 (1981), 365–90; and M. van Schendelen, 'The Views of Arend Lijphart and Collected Criticism', *Acta Politica*, 19, 1 (1984), 19–55. Debate centres on three issues. First, are consociational democracy and its cognate terms (grand coalition, segmental autonomy, proportionality, minority veto, stability) well-defined? Secondly, does Lijphart provide an explanation of consociational democracy, i.e. a set of well-specified necessary and sufficient conditions for the creation of consociational systems? Finally, is consociation a strategy which elites can pursue in any circumstances?

115 E. Nordlinger, *The Autonomy of the Democratic State* (London: Harvard University Press, 1981), 225.

116 This is the central theme of Nordlinger's *Conflict-Regulation in Divided Societies*. See also Pappalardo, 'The Conditions for Consociational Democracy', 387; and Barry, 'The Consociational Model and Its Dangers', 396.

117 Pappalardo, 'The Conditions for Consociational Democracy', 387.

118 See chapter 7. For recent descriptions of the Northern Ireland economy, see the essays by Rowthorn and by Canning, Moore and Rhodes, in Paul Teague (ed.), *Beyond the Rhetoric: Politics, the Economy and Social Policy in Northern Ireland* (London: Lawrence and Wishart, 1987); and another collection edited by Paul Teague, *The Economy of Northern Ireland: Perspectives for Structural Change* (London: Lawrence and Wishart, 1993).

119 Ed Moloney and Andy Pollak, *Paisley* (Dublin: Poolbeg Press, 1986), 338.

120 See chapter 3, pp. 93-5.

121 Consociationalism has been called 'government by elite cartel': communal leaders make the key decisions 'from above' so as to avoid democracy 'down below' producing civil war. The naïveté of the Opsahl commissioners on the subject of political leadership in Northern Ireland is palpable. They believe that Northern Irish politicians require training – which demonstrates a simple failure to realize that the local politicians are representative: if they were not they would not be so regularly re-elected, see A. Pollak (ed.), *A Citizen's Inquiry* (Dublin: Lilliput Press, 1993), 113.

122 Nordlinger, *Conflict Regulation in Divided Societies*, 79–82.

123 There is perhaps one exception. The DUP seems to enjoy 'structured elite predominance achieved through an hierarchical and disciplined party organisation, as well as a considerable degree of deference towards party elites largely

fostered by its ancillary organisations', Paul Mitchell, 'Conflict Regulation in Divided Societies: Northern Ireland, A Consideration', London, MSc thesis, London School of Economics and Political Science (1986), 13. However, it might also be argued that far from being a modern mass party whose bureaucratic structures generate autonomy for its leadership, the DUP is in fact a charismatic organization built around an individual and his church. It certainly displays some structured elite predominance, but does so because it is a charismatic organization rather than a modern bureaucratic political party.

124 Even the leadership of Sinn Féin and the IRA may be constrained by the internal egalitarianism of its constituency. The leaders of Sinn Féin and the IRA, when edging towards a cessation of violence, were not prepared to accept the Downing Street Declaration, partly because their followers were clearly not so minded – and therefore the leadership had to avoid the possibility of a damaging split.

125 See O'Leary and McGarry, *The Politics of Antagonism*, ch. 1.

126 Lijphart and his critics debate the relevance of consociation as a method of conflict-regulation for deeply divided societies. Lijphart emphasizes voluntarism – that clever elites can overcome any amount of social or historical division. His critics are more sceptical, thinking that consociation may only be practical in moderately as opposed to deeply divided societies.

127 Lijphart refers elsewhere to a 'tradition of accommodation' as a factor facilitating consociation, see *Democracy in Plural Societies*, 99–103. However, he appears to think that the absence of 'traditions of accommodation' in Northern Ireland is unimportant, or much less important than the other obstacles to which he draws attention.

128 Brian Barry, 'Political Accommodation and Consociational Democracy', in *Democracy and Power: Essays in Political Theory, 1* (Oxford: Oxford University Press), 131.

129 See Horowitz, *Ethnic Groups in Conflict*, 57–64; and Anthony Smith, *The Ethnic Origins of Nations* (Oxford: Basil Blackwell, 1986), ch. 2.

130 Our own proposals for the future of Northern Ireland, outlined in the next chapter, contain consociational elements, albeit within a framework of shared sovereignty or its functional equivalent.

131 We doubt the validity of Schmitt's claim that unionists' fear of a united Ireland would be reduced if there were to be a multiple balance of power in the Republic. Would it make sense to argue that Polish reluctance to unite with Germany or Portuguese reluctance to unite with Spain would be reduced if only the newly enlarged state had no majority community?

132 See, for example, the New Ulster Political Research Group, *Common Sense* (Belfast: 1987).

133 See Terrance Carroll, 'Northern Ireland', in A. Suhrke and L. Garner Noble (eds), *Ethnic Conflict in International Relations* (New York: Praeger, 1977), 21–42; and M. McKinley, 'The International Dimensions of Terrorism in Ireland', in Yonah Alexander and Alan O'Day (eds), *Terrorism in Ireland* (London: Croom Helm, 1984), 10–11.

134 In the course of the most recent US presidential elections one newspaper reported that the British government feared a pro-IRA bias in a Clinton White House, *Fortnight* (December 1991), 9. This fear was absurd. The American government's decision to grant Gerry Adams a visa to travel to the USA in 1994, despite British objections, did not flow from pro-IRA sympathies, but rather from the belief that this decision would assist the peace process outlined in the Downing Street Declaration (confidential sources).

135 Anyone who televisually witnessed the beating and shooting of the two British soldiers who accidentally drove into an IRA funeral cortege in November 1988, or has read of the activities of the Shankill butchers, appreciates that sophisticated weaponry is a dispensable luxury in ethnic conflict.

136 Tugwell, 'Politics and Propaganda of the Provisional IRA'. As a serving officer in the British parachute regiment which killed thirteen civilians on Bloody Sunday, 30 January 1972, and as someone present in Derry/Londonderry on the day in question, Tugwell may have understandable reasons for attributing the blame to an external agent. He also has problems with the name of the day, which he describes as 'the event in Londonderry that has been called "Bloody Sunday"', 24.

137 This is a common phenomenon in ethnic conflict. Dominant ethnic groups often hold external provocateurs responsible for the unrest of the dominated group(s).

138 Guelke, *Northern Ireland*, 12–14.

139 Interestingly a poll reported in the *Observer* (31 December 1989) found that far more people in Britain (53 per cent of respondents) supported keeping the Falkland Islands than supported keeping Northern Ireland (36 per cent).

140 International opinion clearly favours a united Cyprus, but it would be surprising if Greek Cypriots simply gave up their claims if and when international opinion changed.

141 See Frank Wright, *Northern Ireland: A Comparative Analysis* (Dublin: Gill and Macmillan, 1987), 219–22.

142 John McGarry and Brendan O'Leary (eds), *The Future of Northern Ireland* (Oxford: Clarendon Press, 1990), 293–4; O'Leary and McGarry, *The Politics of Antagonism*, 286–7; and O'Leary, Lyne, Marshall and Rowthorn, *Northern Ireland*, 102–4.

143 O'Leary and McGarry, *The Politics of Antagonism*.

144 In the Irish case the Constitution of the Irish Free State was much better regarded by the unionist minority than the one which succeeded it in 1937.

145 Tom Garvin, the witty Professor of Politics at University College, Dublin, perhaps expressed the revisionist viewpoint more vigorously than he intended when he wrote that if Britain were to make the offer of a united Ireland to the Republic 'it would have devastating, and possibly destabilising effects on the Republic . . . The structure of the Dublin state is predicated on the unspoken assumption of indefinite continuance of partition, as is its party system. Furthermore, the Republic has developed a corporate identity of its own that sudden reunification would threaten; an analogy would be requiring the United States to absorb Mexico', 'The North and the Rest: The Politics of the Republic of Ireland', in Charles Townshend (ed.), *Consensus in Ireland: Approaches and Recessions* (Oxford: Clarendon Press, 1988), 109. The analogy, unwittingly, indicates extraordinary distancing by Professor Garvin.

146 See Linda Colley, *Britons: Forging the Nation 1707–1837* (New Haven: Yale University Press, 1992).

147 For example, see Paul Bew, Peter Gibbon and Henry Patterson, *The State in Northern Ireland, 1921–1972: Political Forces and Social Classes* (Manchester: Manchester University Press, 1979), 156.

148 Kevin Boyle and Tom Hadden, 'Restoring the Momentum of the Anglo-Irish Agreement', in McGarry and O'Leary (eds), *The Future of Northern Ireland*, 194.

Chapter 9 Pain-killers, Panaceas and Solvents:
Explanations and Prescriptions

1   Richard Rose, *Governing without Consensus: An Irish Perspective* (London: Faber
    & Faber, 1971), 21. See also Oliver MacDonagh, 'The Politics of Gaelic', in
    *States of Mind: Two Centuries of Anglo-Irish Conflict* (London: Pimlico, 1992),
    cited in chapter 6, p. 232.
2   *Irish Times*, 14 June 1974.
3   Adrian Guelke, 'Limits to Conflict and Accommodation', in Adrian Guelke
    (ed.), *New Perspectives on the Northern Ireland Conflict* (Aldershot: Avebury,
    1994), 205.
4   John McGarry and Brendan O'Leary, 'Preface', in John McGarry and Brendan
    O'Leary (eds), *The Future of Northern Ireland* (Oxford: Clarendon Press, 1990),
    ix.
5   Donald Horowitz, *Ethnic Groups in Conflict* (Berkeley: University of California
    Press, 1985); Anthony Smith, *The Ethnic Origins of Nations* (Oxford: Blackwell,
    1986); and *National Identity* (Harmondsworth: Penguin, 1991).
6   Michael Ignatieff, *Of Blood and Belonging: Journeys into the New Nationalism*
    (London: Chatto and Windus, 1983); Horowitz, *Ethnic Groups in Conflict*, 74.
7   'The meaningfulness of ethnic identity derives from its birth connection . . . or
    from acceptance by an ethnic group as if born into it. In this key respect (the
    primacy of birth), ethnicity and kinship are alike', Horowitz, *Ethnic Groups in
    Conflict*, 57.
8   Afro-Caribbean and African Francophones who emigrate to Quebec from
    outside Canada are having some difficulty assimilating into the Quebecois
    and being accepted by them. The reason is that the newcomers only share
    the cultural marker and not the other features which make up the group.
    This may change in time, but the existence of colour differences will obstruct
    it. Similarly, while Northern Ireland does not have many immigrants, we believe
    that adherence to Catholicism or Protestantism alone would not be enough to
    ensure group membership for an immigrant.
9   Walker Connor, *Ethnonationalism: The Quest for Understanding* (Princeton:
    Princeton University Press, 1994), 69.
10  John Whyte, *Interpreting Northern Ireland* (Oxford: Clarendon Press, 1990).
11  See chapter 10, pp. 385–6.
12  Lest we be accused of caricaturing the positions of civic integrationists, it should
    be made clear that many of them are aware of the national dimension of the
    conflict, and that many of them want their prescriptions to be implemented in
    tandem with some constitutional change which addresses the national question.
    Equally there are those, such as ourselves, who stress the national dimensions
    of the conflict but who acknowledge the virtue in many of the proposals put
    forward by liberals.
13  Tom Hadden and Kevin Boyle, *Northern Ireland: the Choice* (Harmondsworth:
    Penguin, 1994).
14  Brendan O'Leary, Tom Lyne, Jim Marshall, and Bob Rowthorn, *Northern Ireland:
    Shared Authority* (London: Institute for Public Policy Research, 1993).
15  See note 14 above.
16  See chapter 10.
17  Both governments will have to ensure that northern nationalists believe that
    they too have exercised their right to national self-determination, and the
    Irish Government will have to ensure that constitutional change does not

affect the Irish citizenship rights of people born in Northern Ireland, which under the Republic's 1956 citizenship law is dependent upon Article 2 of the Constitution, which defines the entire island of Ireland and its territorial waters as the national territory.

18  Provided the district magnitude is 5 or more, STV produces very proportional outcomes – in relation to the first-preference votes cast for candidates representing political parties. Moreover, because it allows voters to transfer their preferences it creates incentives for parties to attract second or third-preference support from other parties, it therefore provides some incentives for some parties to appeal to both nationalists and unionists, or Catholics and Protestants – though its effects in ethnic-conflict zones should not be exaggerated.

19  It would also be helpful if Northern Ireland's representation at Westminster were to be based upon proportional-representation rules. Presently plurality rule gives the UUP 9 seats out of 17 (53 per cent) on the basis of about 34 per cent of the popular vote.

20  Alternatively, the settlement could provide for cantonization, the creation of homogeneous jurisdictions at the local level. In this scenario, special devices to ensure power-sharing would not be needed. However, this pattern would be too centrifugal in its consequences.

### Afterword: The Sound of Breaking Ice

1   Cited by Thomas Moore in *Memoirs of Captain Rock* (London, 1824), 368.

2   Manuscript of the late Professor Whyte's – posthumously published in revised form as 'Dynamics of Social and Political Change in Northern Ireland', in Dermot Keogh and Michael Haltzel (eds), *Northern Ireland and the Politics of Reconciliation* (Cambridge: Cambridge University Press, 1993), 103–16.

3   *Independent*, 1 September 1994.

4   *Sunday Times*, 3, 4 December 1994.

5   *Irish Times*, 2 January 1995.

6   The text of the Declaration and our interpretation of it are contained in the Appendices.

7   Routine paramilitary punishments of those accused of anti-social behaviour in both loyalist and republican districts continue, but without the use of guns.

8   The second meeting between Sinn Féin and NIO officials provoked acrimony because the NIO officials asked Sinn Féin to take a letter to the IRA requesting the return of the money stolen in Newry and reassurances about the decommissioning of arms. The Sinn Féin delegation refused to take the letter, or to address the decommissioning of weapons, on the grounds that its party is separate from the IRA (confidential sources).

9   The departures of 'the Iron Lady', Margaret Thatcher, and 'the Boss', Charles Haughey, widely, but inaccurately, seen as the incarnations of unreconstructed British and Irish nationalism, and their replacements by the more pliable and flexible finance ministers John Major and Albert Reynolds, may also have facilitated the peace process – but that is a subject for historians.

10  See chapter 1, pp. 47–8.

11  For a discussion of the 1991–2 talks see Brendan O'Leary and John McGarry, *The Politics of Antagonism* (London: Athlone, 1993), ch. 9.

12  The idea that 'a hurting stalemate' makes a conflict 'ripe for resolution' is associated with the work of William Zartman, *Ripe for Resolution: Conflict and Intervention in Africa* (New York: Oxford University Press, 1985).

13   Hume's most ferocious critics were 'revisionist' journalists writing in the Dublin press.
14   See Appendices.
15   A group of Irish-Americans known as the Morrison peace delegation, with the unofficial support of the American administration, acted as third-parties during 1993–4. Consisting of politicians, businessmen, trade unionists and journalists, they made the case that more effective political support and economic investment to support constitutional Irish nationalist objectives could be forthcoming, provided there was a cessation of republican violence (confidential sources). They also ensured that unionists were subsequently invited to make their case in America. They became, in effect, the peace envoy that President Clinton promised to send to Northern Ireland. They were not the only third-party mediators – clergymen, notably the Catholic priest Alec Reid and the Presbyterian minister Roy Magee were effective go-betweens for governments and paramilitaries in the run-up to the cessations of violence.
16   This assumption remains widespread. Hard-line republicans, such as Bernadette McAliskey, believe that 'The war is over, and the good guys [i.e. the IRA] have lost'; while hard-line loyalists in the DUP believe that the IRA's cessation of violence means that the British government is about to sell them out. There have, in fact, been 'no surrenders'.
17   The exemplar of this simple-mindedness has been Conor Cruise O'Brien, for example, 'The idea of a "political solution" to terrorism is an illusion . . . the quest for a non-existent political solution distracts attention from the harsh necessity to meet increasing terrorism with more stringent security measures', 'Appeasement is the Real Terror', *Independent*, 29 July 1994.
18   Aaron Wildavsky, *Speaking Truth to Power: The Art and Craft of Policy Analysis* (New Jersey: Transaction Books, 1987).
19   Harold Nicolson, *Peace-making, 1919* (London, 1943), vii.
20   'Common to [ethnic frontier societies is] the absence of anything metropolitan societies call peace. At best they [enjoy] a tranquillity of communal deterrence', Frank Wright, *Northern Ireland: A Comparative Analysis* (Dublin: Gill and Macmillan, 1987), Preface.
21   The latter assumption governed O'Brien's first reaction, 'This is not peace; it is simply a prelude to a different war', *Independent*, 1 September 1994.
22   The strange planting of a bomb in Enniskillen on 19 December 1994, and leaks to British newspapers from 'security sources', have led some to suggest that sections of the British intelligence services are not altogether happy with unfolding developments.
23   Donald Horowitz, *Towards a Democratic South Africa? Constitutional Engineering in a Divided Society* (Berkeley: University of California Press, 1991), 153–5.
24   There remains some controversy about the size of the cultural Catholic population in the 1991 census. The minimum size is 38.4 per cent, the figure recorded for declared Catholics. The Catholic share of declared Christians, by contrast, is 43.4 per cent (see the table).

| | All respondents | | All Christians |
|---|---|---|---|
| *Religion* | *per cent* | *Religion* | *per cent* |
| Catholics | 38.4 | Catholics | 43.35 |
| All Protestants | 50.2 | Protestants | 56.65 |
| Non-Christians | .2 | | |
| Not stated | 7.3 | | |
| None | 4 | | |
| Total | 100.1 | Total | 100 |

The difficult question is 'what is the size of the "cradle Catholic" or "cultural Catholic" population?' Any answer requires us to allocate the categories 'Not stated' and 'None' to the total numbers of Catholics and Protestants. The 'Not stated' category is best distributed proportionately between Catholics and Protestants because there is no compelling reason to do otherwise – for example, the proportions in eastern Northern Ireland where Protestants are concentrated (e.g. 8.2 per cent in Belfast and 9 per cent in North Down) are close to the figure in the entire census (7.3 per cent). By contrast, it is reasonable to assume that a higher absolute number and relative proportion of cradle Protestants are more likely to answer 'None' than cradle Catholics. Throughout the world, and in Ireland, Protestants are less likely than Catholics to retain their childhood religious beliefs. For instance, North Down, which is highly Protestant, has over twice the proportion declaring no religion as the proportion in the census as a whole. One should therefore distribute the 'Nones' disproportionately to the cultural Protestant category. On these assumptions we estimate the 1991 cultural Catholic population to comprise 42.9 per cent of the Northern Irish population, and cultural Protestants to comprise 56.9 per cent – figures which exclude the minute part, 0.2 per cent, of the population which is not culturally Christian.

25  'Where the relationship between competing parties is primarily *stratificational*, the dominant ethnic community controls the bulk of power, wealth, and prestige and allocates them to their collective advantage, relegating others to subordinate positions. The contrasting relationship is *segmental*, where each of the competing parties contains a full range of class actors – owners, managers, professionals as well as workers and peasants – maintains parallel sets of institutions, and participates in the operation of the economy and the polity on equitable terms', Milton J. Esman, *Ethnic Politics* (Ithaca and London: Cornell University Press, 1994), 21 (our emphases). This distinction is similar to Donald Horowitz's contrast between 'ranked' and 'unranked' groups, *Ethnic Groups in Conflict* (Berkeley: University of California Press, 1985), 21–36.

26  Brendan O'Leary, 'More Green, Fewer Orange', *Fortnight*, 282 (February 1990), 13.

27  If Sinn Féin nurtures good candidates and engages in detailed constituency work it could also make an electoral breakthrough in the Republic. All previous republican insurrectionaries have benefited from going into politics after abandoning violence (e.g. Fianna Fáil, Clann na Phoblacht and the Workers' Party), and the same might occur with Sinn Féin – especially if it takes advantage of the presence of Labour and Democratic Left in the present Irish coalition government and becomes the party of left-wing protest.

28  Electoral deals between the UUP and the DUP might still apply in Westminster elections – as long as the system of plurality rule is preserved for UK elections.

29  Esman, *Ethnic Politics*, 23.

30  John M. Richardson Jr and Jianxin Wang, 'Peace Accords: Seeking Conflict-resolution in Deeply Divided Societies', in K. M. de Silva and S. W. R. de A. Samarasinghe (eds), *Peace Accords and Ethnic Conflicts* (London: Frances Pinter, 1993), 185.

## Appendix B  Parsing the Paragraphs of the Declaration

1   These notes draw heavily on an article written by Brendan O'Leary for the *Sunday Press*.
2   Discussion with Northern Ireland Office Minister Michael Ancram, MP, March 1994.
3   Confidential sources have suggested to us that Molyneaux, despite protestations to the contrary, did not see paragraph 4 until the evening before it was published.

# Additional References

This bibliography includes other items consulted in the composition of this book, but excludes those cited in the notes.

Arthur, P. (1974) *The People's Democracy* (Belfast: Blackstaff).

Arthur, P. (1985) 'Anglo-Irish Relations and the Northern Ireland Problem', *Irish Studies in International Affairs*, 2: 37–50.

Barritt, D. P. and Carter, C. F. (1972) *The Northern Ireland Problem: A Study in Group Relations* (Oxford: Oxford University Press).

BICO (1972) *Connolly and Partition* (Belfast: Athol Books).

BICO (1975) *Imperialism* (Belfast: Athol Books).

Birrell, D. and Murie, A. (1980) *Policy and Government in Northern Ireland: Lessons of Devolution* (Dublin: Gill and Macmillan).

Boal, F. W. and Douglas, J. N. H. (eds) (1982) *Integration and Division: Geographical Perspectives on the Northern Ireland Problem* (London: Academic Press).

Boyce, D. G. (1988) *The Irish Question and British Politics 1868–1986* (London: Macmillan).

Boyce, D. G. (1991) *Nationalism in Ireland* (London: Routledge), 2nd edition.

Chambers, G. (1987) *Equality and Inequality in Northern Ireland. Part II: The Workplace* (London: Policy Studies Institute).

Cochrane, F. (1994) 'Any Takers? The Isolation of Northern Ireland', *Political Studies*, 42, 3: 378–95.

Committee on the Government of Northern Ireland of the Northern Ireland Assembly (1986) *First Report* (Belfast: HMSO).

Compton Report (1971) *Report of the Enquiry into Allegations against the Security Forces of Physical Brutality in Northern Ireland Arising out of Events of 9th August 1971* (London: HMSO, Cmnd. 4823).

*Constitution of Ireland* (Dublin: Stationery Office).

*Constitution of the Free State of Ireland* (Dublin: Stationery Office).

*Dáil Éireann* Debates (1918–) (Dublin: Stationery Office).

Darby, J. (1983) *Dressed to Kill: Cartoonists and the Northern Irish Conflict* (Belfast: Appletree Press).

Darby, J. (ed.) (1983) *Northern Ireland: the Background to the Conflict* (Belfast: Appletree Press).

Diplock Report (1973) *Report of the Commission to Consider Legal Procedures to deal with Terrorist Activities in Northern Ireland* (HMSO: London, Cmnd. 5185).

Eversley, D. (1989) *Religion and Unemployment in Northern Ireland* (London: Sage).

Fanning, R. (1983) *Independent Ireland* (Dublin: Helicon).

Flackes, W. D. and Elliott, S. (1989) *Northern Ireland: A Political Directory, 1968–1988* (Belfast: Blackstaff Press).

Gallagher, M. (1990) 'How Many Nations Are There in Ireland?', paper presented to the Political Studies Association of Ireland Conference, Cork, October.

Gardiner Report (1975) *Report of the Committee to Consider in the Context of Civil Liberties and Human Rights Measures to Deal with Terrorism in Northern Ireland* (London: HMSO, Cmnd. 5847).

Hadfield, B. (1989) *The Constitution of Northern Ireland* (Belfast: SLS Legal Publications).

Harbinson, J. F. (1973) *The Ulster Unionist Party 1882–1973* (Belfast: Blackstaff Press).

House of Commons (Westminster) Debates (1964–) (London: Hansard).

House of Commons Debates (Northern Ireland) (1920–72) (Belfast: Hansard).

Hunt Report (1969) *Report of the Advisory Committee on Police in Northern Ireland* (Belfast: Cmnd. 535).

Kenny, A. (1986) *The Road to Hillsborough* (Oxford: Pergamon Press).

Kilbrandon Commission (1973) *Report of the Royal Commission on the Constitution 1969–1973* (London: HMSO, Cmnd. 5460), vol. 1.

Kilbrandon Committee (1984) *Report of an Independent Inquiry 'To Consider the Report of the New Ireland Forum, Examine the Practicality of any Proposals Made in the Report by Any Other Sources, and Make Recommendations* (Oxford: British–Irish Association).

McGarry, J. (1986) 'The British Homogeneity Thesis and Nationalism in Scotland and Wales', PhD thesis, University of Western Ontario.

McNamara, K., Marshall, J. and Mowlam, M. (1988) *Towards a United Ireland. Reform and Harmonisation: A Dual Strategy for Irish Unification* (London: published by the authors).

New Ireland Forum (1983–4) *Report of Proceedings*, Nos 1–13 (Dublin: Stationery Office).

New Ireland Forum (1984) *Report* (Dublin: Stationery Office).

New Ireland Forum (1984) *The Cost of Violence arising from the Northern Ireland Crisis since 1969* (Dublin: Stationery Office).

New Ireland Forum (1984) *The Legal Systems, North and South* (Dublin: Stationery Office).

New Ireland Forum (1984) *Sectoral Studies: An Analysis of Agricultural Developments in the North and South of Ireland and of the Effects of Integrated Policy and Planning* (Dublin: Stationery Office).

New Ireland Forum (1984) *Sectoral Studies: Integrated Policy and Planning for Transport in a New Ireland* (Dublin: Stationery Office).

New Ireland Forum (1984) *Sectoral Studies: Opportunities for North/South Co-operation and Integration in Energy* (Dublin: Stationery Office).

New Ireland Forum (1984) *The Macroeconomic Consequences of Integrated Economic Policy, Planning and Co-ordination in Ireland* (Dublin: Stationery Office).

*Northern Ireland Constitution Act* (1974) (Belfast and London: HMSO, Cmnd. 5675).

O'Neill, S. (1994) 'Pluralist Justice and its Limits: the Case of Northern Ireland', *Political Studies*, 42, 3: 363–77.

Rabushka, A. and Shepsle, K. (1972) *Politics in Plural Societies: A Theory of Democratic Instability* (Columbus, Ohio: Merrill).

Rea, D. (ed.) (1982) *Political Co-operation in Divided Societies: A Series of Papers Relevant to the Conflict in Northern Ireland* (Dublin: Gill and Macmillan).

Rose, R. (1975/6) *Northern Ireland: A Time of Choice* (London: Macmillan).

Rose, R. (1989) 'Northern Ireland: the Irreducible Conflict', in J. V. Montville (ed.),

*Conflict and Peacemaking in Multiethnic Societies* (Lexington, Mass.: Lexington Books).

SACHR (1977) *The Protection of Human Rights in Northern Ireland* (London: HMSO, Cmnd. 7009).

Scarman Report (1969) *Violence and Civil Disturbances in Northern Ireland* (Belfast: Cmnd. 566).

Seanad Éireann (1937–) *Debates* (Dublin: Stationery Office).

Senate Debates (1920–72) Senate Debates: Northern Ireland (Belfast: Hansard).

Smith, A. (1981) *The Ethnic Revival* (Cambridge: Cambridge University Press).

Smith, A. (1983) *Theories of Nationalism* (London: Duckworth).

Smith, D. (1987) *Equality and Inequality in Northern Ireland: Part I: Employment and Unemployment* (London: Policy Studies Institute).

Smith, D. (1987) *Equality and Inequality in Northern Ireland. Part III: Perceptions and Views* (London: Policy Studies Institute).

Standing Advisory Commission on Human Rights (SACHR) (1991) *The Financing of Schools in Northern Ireland* (Belfast: HMSO).

*The Northern Ireland Constitutional Convention: Reports and Proceedings* (1975) (Belfast: HMSO).

Walker, B. (1989) *Ulster Politics: the Formative Years, 1868–86* (Belfast: Ulster Historical Foundation and Institute of Irish Studies).

Walsh, D. P. J. (1983) *The Use and Abuse of Emergency Legislation in Northern Ireland* (London: Cobden Trust).

Watt, D. (ed.) (1981) *The Constitution of Northern Ireland: Problems and Prospects* (London: Heinemann).

# Glossary and Terminology

Political charges accompany the words employed in writing on Northern Ireland, so we are explicit in our conventions. Below we list the most controversial proper names and the less well-known concepts used in this book.

*Catholic* is a short-hand expression for a believer in the doctrines of the Holy Roman Catholic and Apostolic Church; it is not a synonym for an Irish nationalist. The expression 'cultural Catholics' refers to practising Catholics as well as persons born into the Roman Catholic religion who no longer believe or practise its tenets.

*Consociation* is the name of a political system used in some culturally divided societies to share and divide governmental power and authority. Political power is shared by the rival cultures on a proportional basis – in the executive, the legislature and public employment. Each cultural community enjoys rights of veto and autonomy.

*Dáil Éireann* is the lower house of the parliament of the Republic of Ireland.

*Derry/Londonderry* is the second city of Northern Ireland. Irish nationalists call it Derry, most unionists who live outside the city call it Londonderry, and in official designations both names have been used.

*Eire* is the official constitutional name for Ireland in the Irish language. It was given this name in *Bunreacht na hÉireann* (Ireland's 1937 Constitution). We use Eire to refer to independent Ireland between the years 1937 and 1949.

*Great Britain* is that part of the United Kingdom which excludes Northern Ireland: it is more accurate than the partisan term 'the British mainland'. Northern Ireland is part of the United Kingdom, but it is not part of Great Britain, and to describe it as British, either geographically or administratively, is to beg political questions. There are British people in Northern Ireland but that does not make it British, although it helps explain why it is part of the United Kingdom.

*Integration* is the attempt to organize a territory and its peoples under one unified set of political norms. Two main types of integration are advocated for Northern Ireland: into Britain and into Ireland.

(i)    Integration into Britain. *Administrative integration* would ensure that Northern Ireland is administered like Great Britain (or like England, or like Scotland, or like Wales); *electoral integration* would mean that all Great British political parties would compete for support in Northern Ireland; while *educational integration* would ensure that Protestants and Catholics attended the same schooling institutions.

(ii)   Integration into Ireland: *Administrative integration* would mean that Northern Ireland was incorporated into the unitary Republic of Ireland; *electoral integration* would mean that the Republic's political parties competed for support in Northern Ireland; and *educational integration* would ensure that Protestants and Catholics attended the same schooling institutions.

*Integrationists* support at least one type of integration (administrative, electoral or educational) and (with the exception of educational integrationists) are hostile to confederation, consociation (q.v.) or federation.

*Ireland.* We use 'Ireland' to refer to the geographical entity, or the unit of administration before 1920. Ireland is the official constitutional name of the Republic of Ireland in the English language (Constitution of Ireland, Article 4).

*Irish Free State* is the name of the independent Irish state established in 1922, which acquired full sovereignty in 1937, and was declared a Republic in 1949. We use the expression to refer to independent Ireland between 1922 and 1937.

*Joint authority or joint sovereignty* is the sharing of ultimate governmental authority over a territory by two or more states (see shared authority).

*Nationalist* with a capital 'N' means a member of the Nationalist party, whereas a lower case 'n' refers to an Irish nationalist, usually a cultural Catholic. Although most unionists are British nationalists for clarity we do not call them nationalists.

*Northern Ireland* is the name of the formal political unit created by the Government of Ireland Act, not the 'Six Counties' or 'Ulster' as nationalists and unionists respectively prefer to describe it.

*Paramilitaries*, meaning members of illegal or semi-legal armies, is a more precise and less emotive expression than 'terrorists'. Terrorism can be practised by both state officials and insurgents.

*Protestant* is a short-hand expression for somebody who is a believer in the doctrines of one of the many Protestant (including Presbyterian) churches in Northern Ireland; it is not a synonym for a unionist, although most Protestants are unionists; cultural Protestants are those who have Protestant religious backgrounds.

The *Republic of Ireland* is the formal political unit established in 1949. We use 'the Republic' as short-hand, and avoid the derogatory use of the terms the 'Free State' or the 'twenty-six counties'.

*Shared authority (or sovereignty)* is the sharing of constitutional and governmental authority by peoples and states – as opposed to joint authority, (q.v.) in which authority is solely possessed by states. It is compatible with consociation (q.v.).

*Ulster* properly speaking is 'historic Ulster', i.e. the province which encompassed nine counties of pre-1920 Ireland; we do not use it as a synonym for Northern Ireland, although Ulster unionists do exactly that. However, we use the expression Ulster Protestants rather than Northern Irish Protestants since that is how one ethnic community generally describes itself.

*Unionist* with a capital 'U' refers to a member of one of the parties which bears this name, whereas with a lower case 'u' it refers to anybody who believes in preserving the United Kingdom of Great Britain and Northern Ireland.

*Unitary state* is an entity in which sub-central governments enjoy no autonomous constitutional power; their authority is revocable at the discretion of the central government. Both the Republic of Ireland and the United Kingdom are unitary states.

*Westminster model* is any system of liberal representative government modelled on the British original: a unitary state, with no codified or entrenched constitution, with parliamentary sovereignty, plurality rule in single-member constituencies as the electoral law, and single-party government and simple majority rule as the norms in the executive and legislature.

# Abbreviations

AIA       Anglo-Irish Agreement.

AOH       Ancient Order of Hibernians.

APNI      Alliance Party of Northern Ireland, supports power-sharing devolved government within the Union as well as an Irish dimension.

BIA       British Irish Association.

BIIC      British-Irish Intergovernmental Council.

CEC       Campaign for Equal Citizenship.

CDRNI     Campaign for Democratic Rights in Northern Ireland.

CLRNI     Campaign for Labour Representation in Northern Ireland.

CSJ       Campaign for Social Justice, formed in 1960s and became part of NICRA.

CnG       Cumann na nGaedheal, political party formed by the pro-Treaty faction in Sinn Féin which formed the first government of the Irish Free State (1922–32), and merged into Fine Gael in 1933.

DL        Democratic Left, political party formed from the collapse of the WP, a 'post-communist' party.

DUP       Democratic Unionist Party, hard-line loyalist political party, formed by Reverend Ian Paisley in 1971.

EOC       Equal Opportunities Commission.

EMU       Education for Mutual Understanding, educational programme for schools in Northern Ireland.

EPA       Emergency Provisions Act.

FEA       Fair Employment Agency.

FEC       Fair Employment Commission.

FET       Fair Employment Tribunal.

FF        Fianna Fáil, 'Warriors of Destiny', party with the English title 'The Republican Party', formed by de Valera from the anti-abstentionist wing in Sinn Féin, and now the most frequent party in government-formation in the Republic.

FG        Fine Gael, party formed in 1933 from the merger of Cumann na nGaedheal with the National Guard (Blueshirts) and the National Centre.

| | |
|---|---|
| GAA | Gaelic Athletic Association. |
| IGC | Inter-governmental conference of the Anglo-Irish Agreement. |
| ILP | Irish Labour Party. |
| INLA | Irish National Liberation Army, Marxist and republican paramilitary organization. |
| IRA | Irish Republican Army (see PIRA and OIRA), name given to Irish Volunteers in the Irish war of independence (1919–21), then used by anti-Treaty forces in the Irish civil war, now used by paramilitary organization which has sought to unify Ireland through insurrection. |
| IRB | Irish Republican Brotherhood, one of the predecessors of the IRA. |
| NICRA | Northern Ireland Civil Rights Association. |
| NILP | Northern Ireland Labour Party. |
| NIO | Northern Ireland Office. |
| NUPRG | New Ulster Political Research Group. |
| OIRA | Official IRA. |
| OO | Orange Order, anti-Catholic and pan-Protestant organization, integrally linked to the UUP. |
| OSF | Official Sinn Féin, political faction which supported the OIRA. |
| OUP | Official Unionist Party (see UUP). |
| PD | Progressive Democrats, 'New Right' liberal party formed in the Republic in 1986. |
| PIRA | Provisional IRA, illegal republican paramilitary organization, formed in 1969. |
| PR | Proportional Representation. |
| PSI | Policy Studies Institute (London). |
| PSF | Provisional Sinn Féin, republican political party which supported the PIRA, now known as Sinn Féin. |
| PUP | Progressive Unionist Party. |
| RSF | Republican Sinn Féin, break-away faction from PSF, formed in 1986. |
| RUC | Royal Ulster Constabulary. |
| SACHR | Standing Advisory Commission on Human Rights. |
| SDLP | Social Democratic and Labour Party of Northern Ireland, formed in 1970 from the merger of civil-rights activists, labour activists and former members of the Nationalist Party and the National Democratic Party. |
| SF | Sinn Féin (Ourselves), political party formed in 1905, reformed in 1917, and split between pro-Treaty and anti-Treaty factions in 1921/2. The pro-Treaty faction formed CnG, the remainder opposed the Treaty. Subsequently FF broke away to form a constitutional republican party. The rump of militant republicans supported the IRA until a new split occurred between Provisional and Official Sinn Féin in 1970. Since Official Sinn Féin disappeared Provisional Sinn Féin is known as Sinn Féin. |
| STV | Single Transferable Vote. |
| TD | Teachta Dála, deputy elected to Dáil Éireann. |

UDA     Ulster Defence Association, illegal loyalist paramilitary organization, formed in 1972.

UDP     Ulster Democratic Party.

UDR     Ulster Defence Regiment, former regiment of the British Army recruited in Northern Ireland, with an almost exclusively Protestant composition.

UFF     Ulster Freedom Fighters, loyalist paramilitary organization and component of the UDA.

UUP     Ulster Unionist Party (also known as the Official Unionist Party (OUP), governed Northern Ireland from 1920 until 1972, presently the most conservative of the unionist parties.

UUUC    United Ulster Unionist Council, temporary coalition of the UUP, DUP and VUP which fought to end the Sunningdale agreement.

UVF     Ulster Volunteer Force, illegal loyalist paramilitary organization which takes its name from the body recruited to oppose Irish Home Rule in the early twentieth century and was 're-formed' in 1966.

VUP     Vanguard Unionist Party, hard-line loyalist political party formed and led by William Craig in the 1970s.

WP      Workers' Party, Marxist–Leninist party formed from Sinn Féin the Workers' Party – previously OSF.

# Name Index

Note: Only the text has been indexed; names in the notes are not included.

# Subject Index

Note: Only the text has been indexed; subject matter in the notes is not included.